BRITAIN

1688–1815

[handwritten] 12,1

[signature] Paul Cooke

BRITAIN
1688-1815

Derek Jarrett

SENIOR LECTURER IN HISTORY AT GOLDSMITHS' COLLEGE;
FORMERLY SENIOR HISTORY MASTER, SHERBORNE SCHOOL

LONGMAN

LONGMAN GROUP LIMITED
London

*Associated companies, branches and representatives
throughout the world*

© *J. D. Jarrett 1965*

First published 1965
Seventh impression 1977

ISBN 0 582 31351 1

*Printed in Hong Kong by
Sheck Wah Tong Printing Press Ltd*

Preface

This book sets out to tell in a few hundred pages the story of several million people over a period of more than five generations. This is in itself a sufficiently presumptuous enterprise: to preface it with an attempt to sum up in a few sentences the 'main trends' of the period would be even more presumptuous. I will content myself, therefore, with recording my gratitude to all those scholars whose researches have illuminated the complexities of eighteenth-century life and politics. I hope that they will feel I have treated their work with due respect and not turned simplification into distortion.

I am especially grateful to Professor J. S. Bromley and Professor A. Goodwin, who first introduced me to eighteenth-century history; to the Master and Fellows of Corpus Christi College, Cambridge, who elected me to a Schoolmaster Fellow Commonership which made the completion of this book possible; to Mr Charles Blount, who made valuable suggestions; to Mrs P. M. McDougal who compiled the Index; and to all those colleagues and pupils, both at Sherborne and at Goldsmiths', who helped me to formulate my ideas. Above all, I am indebted to the men and women of the eighteenth century: without their tenacity and enterprise, their vigour and their sheer common sense, this book could never have been written.

London 1964   J. D. J.

Contents

CONTENTS

PART IV

THE RISE OF A NEW TORYISM, 1770–1789

PART V

THE YEARS OF WAR AND TORYISM, 1789–1815

BRITAIN, 1688–1815

Appendices

x

Maps

Acknowledgements

We are indebted to the following for permission to include copyright material on which certain tables in this book have been based:

The Cambridge University Press for material from *Abstract of British Historical Statistics* by B. R. Mitchell and Phyllis Dean; The Clarendon Press for material from the appendices to *The Oxford History of England*, Vols. 9, 10 and 11, and The Clarendon Press, Macmillan & Co. Ltd, The Macmillan Company of Canada Ltd and St. Martin's Press Inc. for material from Appendix A to *King and Commons, 1660–1832* by Betty Kemp.

PART I

The Legacy of Revolution
1688–1714

I

The Bloodless Revolution
1688–1689

1 The choice of a King

For a large part of the seventeenth century England, Scotland and
Ireland were involved in a series of complex political crises and
civil wars. Sometimes they were about religion, sometimes about
taxation, sometimes about foreign policy. At one point they might
seem to resolve themselves into a struggle between localism and
centralism, at another into a clash between the propertied classes and
the labouring classes. But, whatever they might feel about these
subsidiary issues, men had to ask themselves in the years of crisis
one simple question: dare they overthrow the King? If he would not
guarantee the sort of religious, economic, social or constitutional
pattern that they wanted, should they obey him or coerce him?
Were kings made to serve their subjects, or were subjects made to
serve their kings?

A few centuries earlier, the answer would have been relatively
simple: either the King obeyed the laws of God, in which case he
must himself be obeyed, or he did not, in which case he must be
overthrown. But those days were over. The Church had lost her
unity and different religious leaders gave very different accounts of
the laws of God and the duties of kings. It had never been easy for
churchmen to establish, or for laymen to accept, the distinction
between a true Christian prince and a tyrant; now, in a Christendom
divided against itself, it was impossible. And if the Church could no
longer provide either a yardstick against which to measure kings or
a clear definition of the greater Power to which they were subordinate,
then the lawyers and philosophers must do so instead. If the King
could not be called to account before God, then he could at least be
called to account before the Common Law of the land or before some
abstract definition of the rights of the subject. Kings might be by

3

God appointed, but since men no longer agreed about the terms on which He had appointed them their appointments must be dependent on good behaviour. And some general statement of what constituted good behaviour could be and must be drawn up.

Men who argued along these lines usually called themselves Whigs. Their reasons for being Whigs differed widely: they might be consciously and callously defending their own particular local privileges or they might be inspired with a genuine vision of the ideal state. But they all agreed that limits must be set on the powers of the King in order to safeguard something which was in the end more important than the King. As to what that something was, they disagreed profoundly: for some it was the Protestant Succession, for some it was the rights of chartered companies and local authorities, for some it was economic and commercial freedom. But men will unite to defend a house even though they may differ as to the relative value of its contents.

To the Tories, on the other hand, arguments of this kind seemed not only impious but self-destroying. To coerce the King because he was not doing what you happened to want him to do was like trying to shoot down the sun from the sky because it was not shining on your particular fields. It was not just a necessary adjustment of the political machine: it was an interference in the very nature of things. Whig lawyers and theorists might imagine that the monarchy was something which men had constructed for their own convenience, but to the Tories it was much more than that: it was the indispensable framework within which men lived and moved and had their being. Men who tried to do without kings would very soon find their new won liberty turning to chaos and emptiness in their hands. The Whigs saw the presence of kings as potential tyranny, but the Tories were sure that the absence of kings was potential anarchy. If the King fell, the whole social hierarchy would fall with him. Jack would be as good as his master and Whig gentlemen and Tory gentlemen alike would be swallowed up in the excesses of 'the lower sort of people', that many-headed monster which they both detested and feared.

By the 1670s the Tories found themselves facing a new difficulty, in that their heir to the throne, James, Duke of York, was a Roman Catholic and seemed prepared to overthrow the Church of England, the cornerstone of the whole Tory position. When they had waxed enthusiastic about the religious nature of monarchy and denounced

4

the Whig claims to make and unmake kings, it had not occurred to them that the Almighty might present them with a legitimate King who was not an Anglican. In the face of this dilemma, Tory policies became confused and uncertain; but by the late 1670s and early 1680s a situation had emerged in which the Whigs wished to exclude James from the succession and replace him with the Duke of Monmouth, Charles II's illegitimate son—thus asserting the right of subjects to make and unmake kings—while the Tories were determined that James should succeed, in order that the principle of Legitimism, the divinely ordained succession of kings by hereditary right, should be maintained. If the worst came to the worst, they were prepared to limit his powers and even to establish a regency. It is significant that the Regent whom they proposed was William of Orange, ruler of the protestant United Provinces and the acknowledged champion of European protestantism against the Catholic Louis XIV of France. It was the Tory minister Danby[1] who had in 1677 negotiated the marriage of William of Orange to Mary, eldest daughter of James by his first wife Anne Hyde. If these two, William and Mary, could produce a son and if James's second marriage to the Catholic Mary of Modena continued childless, then the Catholic threat would pass away with James's death and the Tory principles of Legitimism and Anglicanism would be reconciled. Over against Monmouth, the Whig symbol of king-making, the Tories set the figure of William of Orange, who was to save the long-term situation by producing a Protestant heir, and might yet be called in to save the immediate situation by restraining James if he looked like endangering the Anglican establishment.

James's short reign changed this situation in three very important respects: it eliminated Monmouth, who was executed in 1685 after an abortive attempt to seize the throne; it produced a Catholic heir in the person of James, Prince of Wales, born to Mary of Modena on 10 June 1688; and it made abundantly clear James's determination to bring Britain back to the Catholic faith. The first consideration made the Whigs as well as the Tories turn to William of Orange, while the second and third made both parties realize that it was idle

---

[1] Danby's career presents a good example of the confusion caused in history books by the same man taking different titles. Born Thomas Osborne, he became successively Viscount Osborne of Dunblane, Baron Osborne of Kiveton, Viscount Latimer of Danby, Earl of Danby, Marquis of Carmarthen and Duke of Leeds. In this book I have tried to reduce this confusion by calling men by the titles by which they are best known: Danby remains Danby throughout.

to pin their hopes on a Protestant Succession. They must turn from William's long-term function of producing an heir (which, in any case, he had so far failed to do) to his immediate function of restraining the Catholic James before it was too late. Thus William was now the hope both of Whigs and of Tories. But whereas the Whigs were ready to unmake King James and make King William, the Tories saw his intervention as a means of restraining James, whom they had no intention of deposing.

For his part, William was quite happy to contemplate the prospect of becoming King of England, in order to use her resources against his traditional enemy the King of France. But he had no intention of being used as a mere figurehead by the Whigs, whom he regarded as little better than republicans, nor did he intend to do the Tories' dirty work for them, only to be pushed aside later when they came to contort and twist the succession in order to preserve their precious principle of Legitimism. When, at the end of June 1688, he sent Count Zuylestein to England to negotiate with the malcontents under cover of congratulating James on the birth of the Prince of Wales, he knew perfectly well that the two parties expected different things from him. The outcome of Zuylestein's efforts was a document signed by seven of the most important men of the realm, including both Whigs and Tories, inviting William to land in England 'in a condition to give assistance this year sufficient for a relief under these circumstances'. This might mean almost anything. William decided that even if it meant only a British alliance and not a British throne the adventure would be worth while. He set off for England with a force of 15,000 men.

Once he had landed, at the beginning of November 1688, and had been joined by both Whig and Tory magnates, the underlying division between Whig and Tory attitudes that had been glossed over in the invitation began to show itself. It was all very well for William to say on his banners that he stood for 'the Liberties of England and the Protestant Religion', but it was difficult to see how such slogans could reconcile Whig and Tory attitudes to kingship. Free elections might be held, Catholics might be excluded from office, but sooner or later, if James stood his ground, the old dilemma would present itself and men would take sides again along the old familiar lines.

James, however, did not stand his ground. He fled to France and by so doing brought to an end the civil wars of the seventeenth

6

century. For two generations men had fought and argued about their loyalty to the King: now there was no King to be loyal to. Halifax, who had been more successful than most in bridging the gulf between Whiggery and Toryism and had been dubbed a turncoat for his pains, saw the truth of the situation when he wrote: 'A people may let a King fall, yet still remain a people; but if a King let his people slip from him, he is no longer King.' The King had left his people, but the skies had not fallen. The realm without a king remained a reality, but the King without a realm, carried ashore by fishermen at Ambleteuse and trundled off to the palace prepared for him by the King of France, was only a ghost.

There remained the problem of filling the throne which he had vacated so precipitately. The peers of the kingless realm, meeting as a provisional government under the presidency of Halifax, called together a body of Lords and Commons which could not be called a Parliament, since it had not been summoned by a king, and was therefore known as the Convention. The majority of the members of the lower house of this assembly, the Commons, accepted the Whig view of the situation and on 28 January 1689 they passed and submitted to the Lords a resolution in which they said quite categorically that James had broken the original contract between King and People and that the throne was thereby vacant. The Tory majority in the Lords jibbed at this and by fifty-five to forty-one the Lords voted to leave out the phrase 'the throne is thereby vacant'. This was more than mere chop-logic. Whatever the Whigs might say about the conduct of James, it was essential for the preservation of the Tory principle of Legitimism that they should not be allowed to say that the throne had ever been vacant. The Whigs saw the Convention as a reality greater than kings, which could and would make a new king; but the Tories insisted that its task was merely to recognize and do homage to the existing King, the representative of a monarchy whose divine continuity had not been broken.

But which King was this? For the extremists, the High Tories (led by Sancroft, that same Archbishop of Canterbury who had led the Church of England in its defiance of James II in 1688), it was James himself. His perversity in accepting the Catholic faith justified them in treating him as insane and in appointing William as Regent for him. At first Danby himself was attracted by this plan, but as he realized its implications—it would, for instance, result in Regent William making war in King James's name on the King of France

7

whom James supported—he and his followers in the Lords voted against it, with the result that it was defeated by the narrow margin of fifty-one to forty-nine. Having declared against a Regency, the Tories must now accept the fact that James had abdicated (they were able to avoid any official declaration that he had been deposed) and that the next legitimate heir was King of England. It was here that they were helped by the absurd legend, which was still widely believed, that the Prince of Wales was an impostor who had been smuggled into his mother's bed in a warming pan. There had been over sixty witnesses in the Queen's bedchamber at the birth, many of them Privy Councillors peering in at the foot of the bed, and the warming pan story had been closely examined and utterly exploded at a subsequent public inquiry. But men will believe what they want to believe. As long as Whigs were anxious to blacken James still further, as long as Tories were anxious to save their Legitimist consciences and as long as both were anxious to deny the possibility of a Catholic succession, the warming pan story would be accepted. If it were accepted, then the Princess Mary, as James's eldest daughter, was the legitimate Queen of England. She was still in the United Provinces and Danby wrote to her, with a view to persuading her to be Queen in her own right and thus give relief to tender Tory consciences.

Mary, however, was a dutiful wife. She replied that she would only occupy the throne with her husband as King by her side; and she sent Danby's letter, with a copy of her reply, to William in England. He told the Convention roundly that the government must be put in his own person for life: 'If they did think it fit to settle it otherwise, he would not oppose them in it, but he would go back to Holland and meddle no more in their affairs.'

Faced with this ultimatum, the two sides in the Convention had to come to a compromise. The Whigs agreed to drop the phrase about the breaking of the original contract, while the Tories accepted that the throne was vacant and should be offered to William and Mary jointly. Such an offer was accordingly made and accepted on 13 February 1689. With its acceptance the Revolution was over and the reign of William and Mary had begun. On the face of it, it was a Whig victory. But the Tories could argue that the principle of Legitimism had been preserved, however tenuously. For them the reign was really the reign of Mary, and it had begun as soon as her father had fled to France and thus abdicated his crown. True, she chose to rule in company with her husband, which was unfortunate; but he was twelve years older than she was, an ailing man and a soldier exposed to all the hazards of the battlefield. Once he was dead the Stuart dynasty could go on its way undisturbed in the persons of Mary and any children she might have, followed if necessary by her younger sister Anne and her children. In fact, the Tories were in for two rude shocks—the first when Mary died childless in 1694, more than seven years before her husband, and the second in 1700, when Anne's only surviving child died at the age of eleven. But these troubles were in the future. In 1689 the Tories could congratulate themselves on having saved as much as could possibly be expected from this latest shipwreck of Stuart monarchy. James had thrown away the crown of England: the Tories had picked it up and rescued it from Whig attempts to treat it as something dependent on a contract of good behaviour. They had saved the monarchy in spite of the monarch.

2 The Revolution Settlement

As well as deciding who was the appointed monarch and whether the appointment had been made by God or man, the Convention had to decide on the terms of the appointment. Even the Tories were no longer prepared to regard the unfettered will of the King as the only law of the land; but, whereas they were concerned merely to define the existing constitution and to prevent breaches of it in the future, many of the Whigs wanted to go much further and introduce changes which would reduce the royal power still more.

In late January the Commons set up a Committee to decide on this question of constitutional guarantees. The Committee's report, which was submitted to the Commons on 2 February and subsequently debated by both Houses, started off with a forthright assertion of the Whig doctrine of the 'Original Contract' between King and People and went on to recommend several important changes in the constitution. These included proposals which would have prevented the King from removing judges and from pardoning those of his ministers who were impeached by Parliament—concrete applications of the doctrine of the Crown's subordination to the Law and of the responsibility of the King's ministers to Parliament. Both clauses were dropped during the debates on the report, as were others for regulating the courts of justice, prohibiting the sale of offices and changing the procedure in treason trials. Further suggestions, made by individual Whig members but not included in the report, included guarantees for the regular summoning of Parliament and for the inviolability of the chartered rights of corporations and companies. These also failed to find their way into the final Declaration of Rights which was read to William and Mary before they accepted the crown, and to which they gave their royal assent as the Bill of Rights on 16 December 1689.

The Declaration of Rights is not only the central document of the Revolution Settlement: it *is* the Revolution Settlement. Other provisions which are sometimes regarded as part of the settlement are contained in Acts of Parliament, passed after William and Mary had accepted the crown and therefore subject not only to the royal assent but also to the more subtle pressures which the King could apply to ensure that Parliament complied with his wishes. But the Declaration of Rights is unique in that it was published *before* the assumption of the crown and was therefore generally regarded, in spite of the lack of any formal promise on the part of the King and Queen, as a statement of the terms on which the crown of England was offered and accepted. Later enactments sprang from usual constitutional forms, from the King in Parliament legislating for his realm; but the Declaration of Rights was the product of the realm in Parliament legislating for its King.

It is therefore important to understand clearly just what the Declaration did and did not say. It began by stating that James had tried to destroy the Protestant religion and the laws and liberties of the kingdom, but it carefully refrained from any mention of an Original Contract on which those liberties depended and which might be invoked in the future. It then recited the things which the King might not do without breaking the law. He was not to exercise the suspending power (that is, the power to suspend the operation of Acts of Parliament) or the dispensing power (the power to dispense with the operation of Acts in specific cases, as when James had allowed Catholics to hold offices from which the Test Act excluded them) without the consent of Parliament.[1] He was not to use his royal prerogative (that is, the power vested in him to act without Parliament in certain spheres) to set up new law courts.

[1] The use of the dispensing power was declared illegal 'as it hath been exercised of late'; but, as a subsequent clause forbade its use unless the Act in question specifically allowed it, it was in practice made subject to the consent of Parliament.

Finally, he could neither levy money nor keep a standing army in time of peace without Parliament's consent. These provisions, taken in conjunction with the new Coronation Oath whereby William and Mary swore to govern according to 'the statutes in Parliament agreed upon, and the laws and customs of the same', ensured that the enactments of past Parliaments should be respected and the wishes of future Parliaments consulted by the King's ministers. They ensured, in short, the supremacy of Statute, the absolute and unchallenged authority of an Act of Parliament.

But this was nothing new. It had been the basic principle of the English constitution since the days of Henry VIII, if not before. The point was that Parliament was not just the Lords and Commons: it was also the King, whose assent was needed before any Bill could become law and whose ministers exercised considerable pressure both at elections and during the sitting of Parliament to make sure that the King's measures were accepted by both Lords and Commons. It was for this reason that the second part of the Declaration of Rights, that dealing with the acknowledged liberties of the subject rather than with the acknowledged limitations of the sovereign, laid such emphasis on the liberties of Parliament. Having claimed for all Englishmen the right to petition the King, to be free from excessive bail and to be tried by a jury of freeholders if they were accused of treason, it went on to insist that elections to Parliament should be free, that there should be freedom of speech in Parliament and that Parliament should be summoned frequently for the redress of grievances.

But these were vague and insufficient guarantees, especially when compared with the sweeping demands made by Whigs earlier in the century. Parliaments were to be 'frequent', but there was no statutory obligation on the King to call them at given intervals. Elections were to be 'free', but there was nothing to stop the King using the promise of office and other rewards in order to influence them. Although there was to be freedom of speech in Parliament, the King might still deprive men of their place in the public service or of their commissions in the armed forces if he did not like what they said in Parliament. It would be less easy for him to influence the House of Lords in this way, but he could still swamp a hostile House by creating new peers whenever he pleased. The Declaration of Rights made it clear to the King that he must rule through Parliament, but it also left intact the means of his doing so. He still had his prerogative of making war and peace, choosing his own ministers, pardoning criminals, creating peers, summoning, proroguing and dissolving Parliament, and minting coin. It could not be pretended that this last was of great constitutional significance; but the others, skilfully used, might well make the King something much more formidable than the chained and hobbled figurehead that the extreme Whigs of the seventeenth century had envisaged.

Meanwhile there was another problem to be tackled, one which seemed to most men of the time to be more important even than the constitutional settlement. This was the religious settlement. Here, it seemed, there was less danger of disagreement. The original resolution of 29 January 1689, 'that it hath been found by experience to be inconsistent with the safety and welfare of this Protestant kingdom to be governed by a Popish Prince', passed through both Houses without any of the difficulties that the constitutional resolutions encounted. It was duly turned into statutory form in the Bill of Rights, which laid it down that no Roman Catholic nor anyone marrying a Roman Catholic should be capable of succeeding to the throne. Whatever they might think about the relations of King and Parliament, most Englishmen were determined to establish a Protestant Succession and to defend it, by force if necessary, against any Catholic monarch who might seek to overthrow it. The age of genuine religious conviction was passing, but even the most free-thinking and sceptical Englishman regarded Roman Catholicism as the ultimate horror, the mark of a society based on tyranny and obscurantism. Just as men in the twentieth century who have ceased to believe in the infallibility of capitalist free enterprise may still be dominated by an overriding fear of communism, so men in the seventeenth century whose own faith was wearing very thin were still obsessed by a blind and unreasoning fear of Catholicism and especially of Catholic France. William III's English subjects may not have seen the war which he declared against the French King on 7 May 1689 as a theological crusade, but they did see it as a struggle for a way of life which stood or fell with the Protestant faith.

But what was the Protestant faith? Was it the Calvinism of William himself and of his Dutch subjects, or was it the Anglican faith professed by the majority of his English subjects? Or was it to be found in the Presbyterian Kirk in Scotland? Or was it one of the creeds of the dissenting sects—Baptists, Unitarians, Quakers, Congregationalists? It was difficult to see how the gulf between Calvinism and Anglicanism was to be bridged, while the religious settlement of Scotland was a separate problem.[1] But something might be done to persuade the Church of England to open her doors a little wider and admit some of the Dissenters. Between 1,000 and 2,000 ministers, or between 10 and 20 per cent of the country's clergy, had been ejected from their livings in 1662 for refusing to subscribe to the Thirty-Nine Articles of the Church of England. Some, like the Wesleys, returned to the Church of England after a generation or so,[2] but the majority of them, with their congregations, continued as separate communities outside the Church. In March 1689 the Earl of Nottingham, a Tory and a High Churchman, introduced into the Convention Parliament a Comprehension Bill, aimed at making the Church sufficiently comprehensive to embrace most of these Dissenters. It would have relaxed requirements about kneeling at the communion and wearing surplices, and it would have enabled any dissenting minister to render himself eligible for a living in the Church of England by taking an oath against transubstantiation and by expressing general approval of the doctrine, worship and government of the Church. Strong opposition from the High Church party, especially in the Commons, led to the Bill being dropped in the following month and hopes of bringing the Dissenters into the Church had to be abandoned. The alternative, once again supported by Nottingham, was to give them some measure of toleration. He brought in a Bill to legalize Dissenters' meeting houses and to exempt from the penal laws all those dissenting laymen who would take an oath of loyalty to William and Mary and an oath against transubstantiation. Dissenting ministers were to be allowed to preach and teach if they would take these oaths and also subscribe to a certain number of the articles of the Church. Except for the Unitarians, who could not accept the article about the Trinity, the dissenting ministers were ready to meet these requirements. The Bill was passed and a settlement was thus reached which gave toleration to all but Unitarians and Roman Catholics.

This did not mean, however, that the Revolution stood for the principle of toleration. Nottingham's measure, which has come to be called the Toleration Act, was known at the time as the Bill of

---

[1] See below, p. 72.

[2] Bartholomew Wesley was ejected from the living of Charmouth in Dorset in 1662; but his son Samuel, though educated for the dissenting ministry, became Anglican rector of Epworth in 1695. For a fuller account of the Dissenters see below, p. 68.

Indulgence; and there is a great difference between granting a temporary indulgence and asserting once and for all the doctrine of religious toleration. Over a century earlier, Elizabeth I had declared that, though she did not want to make 'windows into men's souls', she must enforce external observance of a definite religious settlement, however wide and comprehensive that settlement might be. The men of 1689 were nearer to Elizabeth, both in time and in spirit, than to modern liberals who think that society need not enforce any observance since men's devotions are their private affairs and have no political significance. The religious settlement of 1689 was conceived in fear, fear of Catholic French domination, and men's chief concern was not that Protestantism should be liberal but that it should be strong. There were undoubtedly a few men in 1689 who looked forward to a secular society in which religion and politics would be separated and in which governments would not concern themselves with men's beliefs; but to the great majority the Bill of Indulgence seemed necessary because of the relevance, not the irrelevance, of religion to politics. Had they felt that it was to point the way to a world in which it did not matter what a man believed they would have been more disturbed than uplifted.

By the early summer of 1689 the Convention Parliament had thus laid down the main lines of the constitutional and religious settlement, but it had not dealt with the most important and most difficult problem of all: how was the country to be governed? There was no longer any doubt that the King in Parliament was the sovereign power of the realm and that the King out of Parliament, the King ruling through his prerogative powers, had only a very limited authority. But if the King in Parliament was to govern effectively—indeed, if he was to govern at all—certain delicate and complex problems concerning the relation of King and Parliament, of the executive and legislative aspects of the sovereign power, had to be solved.

The Convention Parliament left them unsolved. The key question of the length and frequency of Parliaments was not resolved until 1694, when William gave his reluctant assent to a Triennial Act limiting the duration of any parliament to three years. But even this did not guarantee regular parliaments. It is sometimes suggested that the Mutiny Act of March 1689 served this purpose, since it authorized military law for six months only and thus ensured that the King's soldiers would all mutiny if Parliament remained unsummoned for more than six months. But in fact the next few years saw several periods when there was no Mutiny Act in force. Parliament's control over finance was still uncertain, since the greater part of the King's revenue came from the Customs and Excise, which Parliament could not withhold at will as it could the Land Tax. In the event William's wars were to place him at the mercy of Parliament because they could only be financed with the help of direct taxes and government loans, both of which needed Parliament's approval; but it was still possible in 1689 to envisage a King managing his affairs in peace-time without recourse to supplies voted by Parliament. More than seven years were to pass before Parliament was given the chance to review and approve the government's 'budget' or proposed expenditure; and it was still longer before the 'Civil List' was established, to distinguish the revenue used to maintain the ordinary government of the country and granted on a permanent basis from that used to keep up the armed forces and voted by Parliament as and when the military situation demanded it.

Measures such as these, together with certain unwritten conventions which grew up in the course of the reign, did a lot to ease relations between William and his Parliaments and make government by King in Parliament a practical possibility. But it is important here to distinguish between cause and effect. These enactments and conventions were in no sense part of the Revolution Settlement. Still less did they determine the parliamentary history of the reign. On the contrary, they were determined by it. William was able to arrive at these solutions to his problems because, and only because, he managed to rule through ministers who had followings in Parliament. The Revolution Settlement, having set up the two sovereign powers, King and Parliament, made no attempt to bridge the gulf between them. That was a task left to the politicians, to ordinary men forming themselves into parties and factions in order to seek and wield political power.

3 'A Revolution not made but prevented'

The Revolution Settlement soon became the object not merely of admiration but of veneration. By the middle of the eighteenth century it was being acclaimed, especially by the Whigs, as something much more than a skilful piece of political compromise. To them it was more like a divine revelation: the men of 1689 had gone up into the Holy Mountain and had come down with the Tables of the Law from which their children would deviate at their peril. Above all, it was the conservative nature of the Revolution which was emphasized: it was a Revolution not made but prevented. James II had been the real revolutionary, trying to destroy the balance between the executive power of the King and the legislative power of Parliament. If he had had his way there would have been one power only, the power of the King, comprehending and superseding all other powers. Laws, religion and the rights of the subject would have been defined by the personal whims of the monarch and by nothing else. This was the revolution which had been prevented in 1689.

But James II's revolution was not the only one which had been prevented. If he had been trying to swallow up the power of Parliament within that of the King, it was equally true that the seventeenth-century Whigs had been trying to swallow up the power of the King within that of Parliament. During the Civil Wars the danger of the executive taking over the legislative had been matched by the danger of the legislative taking over the executive. Men had had cause to complain of the tyrannies of a King ruling without Parliament but they had also felt the heavy hand of a Parliament ruling without a King. The eighteenth-century Whigs were right to look back on the Revolution as having preserved the balance of the constitution, but they were wrong in assuming that the only threat to that balance had come from kings denying, in the name of Divine Right and Legitimism, the right of Parliaments to limit their power. It had also been threatened by Parliaments which denied, in the name of the Consent theory of government, the King's right to limit the powers of Parliament.

When John Locke wrote his *Two Treatises of Government*[1] he stressed once again the need for this balance: 'Governments are dissolved', he wrote, 'when the Legislative, or the Prince, either of them act contrary to their trust.' For him, monarchy was not a divinely ordained institution but something which men had made for their own convenience and for the protection of their goods. 'The Reason why Men enter into Society, is the preservation of their Property; and the end why they chuse and authorize a Legislative,

---

[1] The work did not appear until 1689 but was probably composed between 1679 and 1683. The edition by P. Laslett (Cambridge, 1960) has an excellent introduction which helps to correct some of the traditional misconceptions about the book and its influence.

is, that there may be Laws made, and Rules set as Guards and Fences to the Properties of all the Members of the Society.' Since government was based ultimately on the consent of the governed, who could call it to account when it broke the law, it was necessary that there should be a distinction between the government itself and the law-making body: '. . . thus the Legislative and Executive come often to be separated.'

The Revolution certainly did not bring a general acceptance of Locke's ideas on government: whatever he might say about men entering into societies for their own selfish ends, many of his country-men continued to think in terms of a divinely established monarchy. His distinction between the Legislative and the Executive was, however, taken up with enthusiasm by men of all parties and pushed even farther than he had intended. It was not long before 'the Separation of Powers', the insistence on a complete split between executive and legislative, became a slogan and even a dogma among politicians. Sir Thomas Hanmer, a staunch Tory, put it forcefully when he remarked: 'Distrust of the Executive is the principle on which the whole of our Constitution is grounded.'

In practice there was only one body which could put this distrust into practice, and that was Parliament. Parliament must be the watch-dog of the constitution, an assembly of sturdy independent men who who could not be bribed, intimidated or in any way influenced by the King and his ministers. The House of Commons viewed the Executive in very much the same way that the heroes of the traditional school story view their masters. They saw a great gulf fixed between the authorities and themselves and despised as a careerist and a toady anybody who sought to bridge it. Like the schoolboy heroes, they considered that they were there to hamper the establishment, not to help it. Parliament was not part of the government, but part of the machinery set up to check the government. And how could it per-form that function if any of its members had an interest in the government themselves, or stooped so low as to accept office at the hands of the King? Throughout William III's reign the independent members pressed for the exclusion of such men and finally, in the Act of Settlement of 1701, they forced upon the King a clause providing that anyone holding an office of profit under the Crown should be ineligible for membership of the House of Commons.

But the House of Commons was only one part of Parliament. How was the executive to be prevented from controlling the House of Lords? It was unthinkable that peers should be expected to renounce their peerages if they became the servants of the King; and it was equally unthinkable that the King should be prevented from appointing peers as his ministers or household officials. It seemed, therefore, that complete separation between the executive and this part of the legislative was impossible. But at least the King might be prevented from ruling through a small group of peers and using them to control the Lords as a whole. With this aim in view a further clause in the Act of Settlement laid it down that all matters 'relating to the well governing of this kingdom which are properly cognizable in the Privy Council by the Laws and Customs of the Realm shall be transacted there and all Resolutions taken there shall be signed by such of the Privy Council as shall advise and consent to the same'. A large number of peers were members of the Privy Council—in William III's reign the House of Lords stood at about 150 and the Privy Council at about fifty—and Privy Councillors were normally appointed for life. Thus the clause sought to ensure that the King should rule through a large body of permanent hereditary advisers rather than an inner group of temporary favourites. Furthermore, the responsibility of ministers to Parliament would be underlined once each act of policy had a definite author or authors who had put their names to it and could be called to account if it went wrong. Rule through the Privy Council would enable Parliament to check and control the executive power more effectively.

These attempts to assert the doctrine of the Separation of Powers proved abortive. By the time the Act of Settlement came into effect on the accession of George I both the clause excluding office-holders from the Commons and the clause insisting on government through the Privy Council had been repealed. The first was replaced by a clause allowing members to accept office as long as they gave up their seats and stood for re-election. The second was dropped altogether, 'since it was visible that no man would be a privy councillor on those terms'. The re-election requirement did not do much to reduce the number of placemen (i.e. those holding 'places' under the Crown) in the Commons, since over three-quarters of those appointed were duly re-elected by their constituents. Many of these constituents were themselves anxious to secure places in the Church, the armed forces, the revenue service or some other department of central or local government, either for themselves or for their friends and relations. They needed spokesmen at Westminster who were in favour with the ministers of the day, not men who did nothing but boast of their independence.

Meanwhile the decline of the Privy Council and the King's increasing reliance on a small group of ministers whom he called into his inner audience chamber or 'cabinet' was becoming more and more marked. Only by entering the charmed circle of the 'Cabinet Council', or by securing the backing of one of the magnates who had entered it, could anyone hope to win any sort of power or office. The House of Lords was full of men who thought that they should be ministers of the Crown and the House of Commons was full of their followers, waiting for some sort of reward once their respective patrons came into power. However loudly the members of both Houses might proclaim their independence and their incorruptibility, few of them could afford to despise the fruits of royal favour or resign themselves to being deprived of it. They preached the doctrine of the Separation of Powers to one another with undiminished fervour but they practised, when they got the chance, an undignified scramble for offices and places and pensions and sinecures which made nonsense of it.

This domination of the political scene by the power of royal patronage was not just an unfortunate accident, a regrettable by-product of human greed which distorted the glorious achievements of 1689. It was, on the contrary, a necessary and inevitable result of the Revolution Settlement since it provided the only possible answer to the question which that Settlement left unanswered: How was the country to be governed? In confirming the balance of the constitution and maintaining the two powers of King and Parliament the Revolution made good government dependent on the forging of a link between them, rather than on their complete separation for doctrinaire reasons. It is, on the face of things, uplifting to applaud the sturdy independents of William's reign, just as it is to applaud the unflagging courage and ingenuity of the fictitious schoolboys who plague the lives of fictitious headmasters. But if all schoolboys took such an attitude there could be no schools. If all the politicians of William III's reign had taken it there would soon have been no powers left to separate.

4 The Party System

It would seem, then, that the politicians of William's reign were faced with an agonizing dilemma. If they set their faces against any sort of link between executive and legislative there would be no government; if they did not there would be no escaping the insidious and pervasive influence of the King's patronage. They must either face the possibility that the Revolution Settlement might prove unworkable in practice or they must help to make it work at the risk of delivering themselves over into the hands of the King. After all their efforts they found themselves presented with the old seventeenth-century choice, anarchy or enslavement, in a new form.

But the King's power did not really stem from his right to *appoint* men to his service but from his ability to *choose* them. If he had no choice he would have no power. As long as there were two or more groups of men vying with one another for his favour and for the rewards of office, he would be like a man in the middle of a seesaw, able with the slightest movement to bring up one group and plunge the other down. But if all men in politics, whether great lords seeking appointment as ministers or humbler men in line for the lesser places, refused to allow themselves to be divided by their petty rivalries, then the King's weapons would break in his hands. For the King must be served: he needed the politicians as urgently as they needed him. It was faction, the unnecessary division of men into different groupings, which turned the King's right to appoint his servants into a weapon by which he might bend Parliament to his will. The old division must be healed and men must stand together, serving the King and checking him when necessary, but without rancour and without party hatred. The King must not be allowed to think that if one man would not serve his purposes he could improve his position by dismissing him and bringing in his rival.

Thus a second slogan took its place alongside the Separation of Powers in the political language of the period after the Revolution. This was the Evil of Party. Party divisions were relics of the bad old days of civil war. Then, perhaps, there was some excuse for them, but now there was none. The settlement of 1689 had not only established a compromise between the positions of the Whigs and the Tories but had also rendered both positions obsolete. Tories could no longer preach obedience to the King at all costs, since this implied that James and not William was King; while Whigs could hardly go on with their policy of weakening the King now that to do so was to strengthen the King in exile whom they feared more than William. As rival political philosophies Whiggery and Toryism were outdated and meaningless: the sooner they ceased to be rival party labels the better. Only men inspired by 'the spirit of faction' would continue to allow themselves to join rival political groupings along these or any other lines.

Unfortunately three generations of civil strife could not be expunged thus easily. By 1689 the gulf between Whigs and Tories was something much more than a theoretical difference of opinion over the nature of kingship: it was a division which ran right through the country and was mirrored at every social level. Wherever there was a great Whig landed family its local rival was Tory; wherever there was a Tory chartered company its commercial competitors attached themselves to the Whigs; wherever there was a Whig corporation its civic rivals called themselves Tories. To hope for a country freed from the division between Whig and Tory was to hope for a country where there was no rivalry between great families and no competition between men for social prestige, profitable jobs or commercial advantages. Pamphleteers and political speakers might cry 'A plague on both your Houses!' but they were powerless to break down a division which was as rigid and as all-pervading as that between the Montagues and the Capulets had ever been. Whiggery and Toryism might be dead but Whigs and Tories were very much alive. As long as they remained alive and continued to oppose each other the King's power to choose his ministers would be the controlling pivot of the political seesaw.

Indeed the King gained rather than lost power by the fact that both parties had had their essential doctrines rendered paradoxical by the Revolution. Previous Kings had had a choice of ministers, but they had had very little scope to exercise it. They were faced with one party which was favourable to the monarchy, the Court Party, and another, the Country Party, which was anxious to oppose and reduce the powers of the King. In such a situation it would have been a very brave or a very foolish King who threw over a loyal and monarchist Tory minister in order'to replace him with a Whig who was little better than a republican and was dedicated to the weakening of the monarchy. Charles II had been forced to do this in 1679, but he would hardly have done it of his own free will. His prerogative to choose ministers had been worth more in theory than practice.

William's, on the other hand, was much more real. He had a choice between two parties, either of which might reasonably be expected to form a satisfactory administration. The Whigs were traditional enemies of the monarchy, but they had pressing reasons to be loyal to William personally since he could be said to represent their theory of kingship as against Tory ideas of Divine Right and Legitimism. The Tories might be more tempted to look to the King in exile, who symbolized their legitimist ideas, but they had a stronger tradition of loyalty to kings than the Whigs had. The Whigs were suspicious of kings in general, but were loyal to William in particular; the Tories were suspicious of William but loyal to kings in general. William could thus choose between being served by Whigs, being served by Tories, being served by a combination of the two, or being served alternately by Whigs and by Tories. He was inclined to the third course and he tried to create ministries which included members of both parties. But gradually, in the course of his and succeeding reigns, the fourth choice, the principle of alternation, crept in. It was to be a very long time before it was accepted that ministries ought to be made up entirely of men from one party, but the idea of the swing of the pendulum, of one party governing while the other waited in the wings hoping to take over, began to appear.

Of all the results of the Revolution, this was to prove in the long run the most important for the future of parliamentary democracy. Very few men in 1689 had any vision of government by 'the people'. Even the radical deist John Toland wrote in 1701 that 'Constant Experience and the Reason of the Thing itself, have induc'd all Legislators not only to pronounce Men of Property to be the truest Lovers of that LIBERTY which begets, inlarges and preserves it, but they have also decreed 'em a natural Right to share in the Government'. 1689 established not representative government but government by men of property for men of property. It also established, almost by accident, the principle which is the real guarantee of liberty in a modern democracy: the agreement to disagree. For totalitarian government is based on the proposition that there is a right way and a wrong way of doing things, while democracy is based on the admission that there may well be several ways, each of which may be expedient. Translated into terms of government this means that whatever government is in power there should be another potential government waiting with alternative policies. If the one falls and the other takes its place this does not mean that the one has been proved wrong and should be punished: it merely means that another course is being tried.

William's new subjects were certainly not prepared to agree to disagree in this way. They had been used to thinking in absolute terms: either the King's ministers were good and their enemies were traitors or the opposition leaders were good and the King's ministers were tyrants. In either case there was only one thing which could resolve the situation: the axe. Ministers did not go in and out like the figures in a weatherhouse. They rose and fell. And when they fell they did not rise again.

All this was changed by the fact that William was himself neither a Whig nor a Tory and could not regard one party as his friends and the other as his enemies. He steadily resisted all demands for a general purge of James II's supporters, and in May 1690 he induced Parliament to pass instead an Act of Grace. Thirty-one persons were excluded from the pardon proclaimed by this Act but none of them was executed and one, Sunderland, lived to be a member of William's Cabinet Council in 1697. The old idea that men were divided into King's Friends and King's Enemies was coming to be replaced with something much more like the modern concepts of Her Majesty's Government and Her Majesty's Opposition. It was a long time before opposition politicians ceased to clamour for impeachments and executions, but men gradually became accustomed to seeing fallen ministers walking around with their heads still on their shoulders. As well as providing an outward and visible sign of the end of the civil wars, their presence gave one of the earliest indications of a principle which was to become vital in modern democratic thought—the principle that in politics no man is absolutely right or absolutely wrong.

It would indeed have been hard for a politician of the 1690s to claim that his point of view was absolutely right and his rival's absolutely wrong, considering that neither party had any clearly defined principles at all. The paradox of the late seventeenth-century party system and the thing which makes it so hard to understand is the fact that party conflict was so fierce at a time when party labels apparently meant so little. Swift's satirical picture of the Lilliputian politicians arguing about the way to crack an egg or the height to wear their heels was a fair comment on the age he had lived through. Never, it seemed, had so many quarrelled so violently about so little.

But what gave the struggle its real meaning and its real force was not its subject but its object: it was a struggle for power. The old divisions of the seventeenth century led to the Revolution Settlement being worked out in terms of a contest for power and that contest in its turn hardened and deepened the divisions. It might also confuse and complicate them, but it would always prevent them being resolved or reconciled. However much men might shift their positions, so that it was hard to tell the Whigs from the Tories, they would still need such terms to give definition and dignity to the political scene. Everybody had a bad conscience about 'the spirit of faction', so that it was always the other fellow who was the party man: many of the politicians whom history calls Tories would have described themselves as non-party men who had been forced into the field to combat the sinister machinations of the Whigs. 'Whig' and 'Tory' were not so much rallying cries as terms of abuse, serving much the same purpose as 'red' and 'reactionary' in our own day. Such labels, though few men wear them willingly as badges of their political allegiance, do at least serve to define the extremes of the political spectrum.

Political life under William III and Anne is sometimes described as a kind of football match between two teams, the Whigs and the Tories, in which a lamentably large number of players crossed from one side to the other and showed a distressing lack of team spirit. Such a picture is peculiarly unhelpful and misleading. If politics was a sport, it was much more like sailing than football. The great magnates, as they jostled for position in the race for power, were sometimes able to run before the wind of royal favour; but for long periods they had to beat up to windward, sometimes on the Whig tack and sometimes on the Tory. Some members of their crew might prefer one tack to the other, even to the extent of sitting out on the wrong side of the boat and capsizing it, but nobody seriously expected a politician to keep to one tack all the time. One does not talk of port helmsmen and starboard helmsmen, but the fact remains that every helmsman must be one or the other at any given moment. The boat that lies with her head into the wind gets nowhere. To study the politics of the seventeenth and eighteenth centuries without using the terms 'Whig' and 'Tory' is like studying a sailing race without using the terms 'port' and 'starboard'.

Important though such terms are, the really essential thing for most contemporaries was to know whether a man was sailing with the wind or against it, whether he was 'in' or 'out', whether he could

THE BLOODLESS REVOLUTION, 1688–1689

be relied upon to champion the cause of the government or that of the governed. In a country which still lacked any effective bureaucracy or civil service, where central and local authorities were rivals rather than partners, this tension between the government and the governed dominated the political scene. Men of the time spoke of it in terms of the pull between 'the Court' and 'the Country'; and only by understanding the realities that lay behind these words is it possible to comprehend the political life of the time.

2

The Court

1 The men: courtiers and councillors

The government of England was the King's government, based on the King's Court. In early medieval times this body had undertaken all the functions of government: when the King held court he might find himself hearing petitions, dispensing justice, receiving revenues, consulting with his great lords, or simply ordering the affairs of his own household. The increasing volume and complexity of the King's business had long since made this all-embracing system obsolete and the King's various functions were now exercised in different courts, often through deputies. It was in his High Court of Parliament that the King heard the petitions of his subjects and turned them, by his royal assent, into Acts of Parliament, solemn statements of the law of the land; but it was his deputies, the Lord Chancellor in the House of Lords and the Speaker in the House of Commons, who presided over the debates. The King's justice was dispensed by his judges in the Courts of Law, headed by the Court of King's Bench for criminal cases and the Court of Common Pleas for civil suits between subject and subject. The Court of the Exchequer saw to the collection of revenue, although it was rapidly being swallowed up in the larger organization known as the Treasury, which dealt with the wider ramifications of financial policy. Formal consultation with the great lords of the realm took place in the Privy Council. It seemed as though those in immediate attendance upon the King, his courtiers, had little left to do but order the affairs of his household.

But in fact the Court had enhanced rather than diminished its importance by thus increasing and multiplying. One writer in 1692 described it as 'a monarchy within a monarchy, consisting of ecclesiastical, civil and military persons and government'. His view may have been exaggerated, but it was nearer the truth than that which saw the Court as an unimportant collection of personal retainers. Government by the courts rather than by the Court did

26

not mean that those in attendance on the King were no longer important; on the contrary, it meant that they formed an indispensable inner ring, a means whereby he could control the multiplicity of courts, councils, committees and boards which went to make up the government of England. The great Officers of State who took precedence at Court immediately after the King and the Princes of the Blood were also the men who held responsibility for the principal organs of government. The Lord High Chancellor, as well as being the King's deputy in the House of Lords, was also the keeper of the Great Seal and the effective head of the judiciary. The Lord High Treasurer was president of the Court of the Exchequer and was also responsible for appointing the officers who collected the King's revenues. Until fairly recently the Customs and Excise had been farmed—that is, their collection had been undertaken by private individuals in return for a certain percentage of what they gathered —but the end of the farming of the Customs in 1671 and of the Excise in 1683 had created something like 8,000 posts in revenue services. By 1797 the number of revenue offices had risen to 12,584, as against 3,683 in all the other branches of government put together. With such a fund of patronages at his disposal the Lord High Treasurer could and did organize the distribution of places in such a way as to build up a following for the King in the House of Commons. Through him the Court could control the men who voted taxes as well as the men who collected them. After the Revolution it became customary to appoint a board of commissioners, known as 'the Lords of the Treasury', to carry out the Lord High Treasurer's duties,[1] but this did not diminish the Court's hold on the Treasury. The First Lord of the Treasury soon became Lord High Treasurer in all but name; and it is significant that in 1691 Sir Charles Sedley included the commissioners of the Treasury in his list of 'crafty old courtiers' who surrounded the King.

Of the other great Officers of State, the Lord High Steward, Lord Great Chamberlain, Lord High Constable and Earl Marshal were more concerned with the ceremonial of the Court than with the government of the country. But the Lord President of the Council, the link between the Court and the Privy Council, had an important part to play, as had the Lord Privy Seal, through whose hands passed

---

[1] Godolphin was Lord High Treasurer from 1702 to 1710, Oxford from 1711 to 1714 and Shrewsbury for a few months in 1714. For the rest of the period the Treasury was in commission.

all royal letters, charters and grants. The Lord High Admiral,[1] quite apart from his responsibilities in time of war, was in the position to dispose of many profitable offices and contracts in the royal dock-yards and could thus do his bit towards building up a following for the King in Parliament.

Alongside these great dignitaries were the King's more personal retainers, the members of his Household, headed by his Lord Steward and Lord Chamberlain and including such colourful figures as the Master of the Revels, the Master of the Buck Hounds and the Keeper of the Lions, Lionesses and Leopards in the Tower.[2] But there was no question of a clear-cut division between men who ministered to the King's personal needs and men who helped him rule the country. For most of the eighteenth century the Lord Chamberlain, a Household officer, could attend the Cabinet Council while his counterpart among the Officers of State, the Lord Great Chamberlain, could not; and during Anne's reign it was not unusual for the Groom of the Stole (the particular title given to the first Gentleman of the Bedchamber) and even the Master of the Horse to attend Cabinet meetings. Thus courtiers were frequently councillors and councillors had often to practise the arts of the courtiers. Wherever the King was, there power and influence were to be won. Whether they were won by flattering and amusing him or by carrying on the business of his government depended largely on the King's own character and inclinations.

William III was not particularly interested in flattery or amuse-ments: his chief concern was to use the resources of England in his struggle against France and he was therefore prepared to give his confidence only to those men who could offer practical political skill and sound military, naval or financial knowledge. Much of his time was spent abroad, and even when he was in England he found that the fog and stench of London brought on his asthma, so that he moved his Court from Whitehall Palace to Hampton Court Palace. Most of the government departments had their offices in Whitehall or Westminister, so that officials had to ride backwards and forwards along roads often frequented by highwaymen in order to get state documents signed. This produced a separation between Court and

[1] In fact, there was a Lord High Admiral only for à short period between 1702 and 1708: for the rest of the period the Admiralty, like the Treasury, was in commission. But the First Lord of the Admiralty was Lord High Admiral in all but name.

[2] When Cesar de Saussure visited the King's menagerie in the Tower in 1725 he found it 'a small and rather dirty place containing ten lions, a panther, two tigers and four leopards'. There was also a large striped monkey from Sumatra, dubbed 'Tiger-man' by his keeper.

government which was only partially healed when the King agreed to settle for Kensington Palace and when the Palace of Whitehall was almost totally destroyed by fire in 1698. The Secretaries of State and other important working members of the government continued to have their offices in what was left of Whitehall Palace. By Anne's reign it had become customary for the chief ministers to meet informally in the Secretary's rooms at Whitehall once or twice a week in order to hear reports from the battle fronts and from officials at home and to sketch out rough ideas on policy; but it was only when they met at Kensington in the presence of the Queen that decisions could be taken and policies made or unmade. In Whitehall they were merely 'the Lords of Committee', but in Kensington they formed the Cabinet Council, the innermost organ of government. It was there, in the midst of all the intrigues and pressures of the Court and sitting cheek by jowl with courtiers, that they had to guide the Queen in the management of her realm.

This picture of ministers working out the details of administration in Whitehall and then coming to Court to get the monarch's approval for their policies seems to suggest that the Cabinet was the means whereby the big world of practical affairs imposed itself on the narrow and artificial world of the Court. But men of the time saw things the other way round: whereas the Privy Council enabled the country to control the Court, the Cabinet did quite the reverse. In 1691 one member of the Commons complained that in the past 'Kings consulted with their Privy Councils; formerly they went not into Cabals'; and in the following year another member insisted that Cabinet Councils were 'not to be found in our Law books'. 'You cannot punish them,' he said, 'because you have no light on their actions.' As late as 1770 the Cabinet was described as 'a midnight assembly'. In the Privy Council the country, in the persons of the great men of the realm, advised and assisted the King in public and in a way that enabled Parliament to call them to account if necessary, but in Cabinet the King's personal favourites plotted illegally and in secret. Consequently men continued to clamour for government through the Privy Council, even after the attempt to enforce it in the Act of Settlement had broken down. But it was a forlorn hope: the task of government had grown too big for the Privy Council and the Privy Council had grown too big for the task of government. In 1685 there had been 45 Privy Councillors; in 1712 there were 82; by the end of the eighteenth century there were 131. Even the Cabinet soon became too big—in 1720 it was referred to as 'the Mob of the Cabinet' and by 1761 Horace Walpole said that the rank of cabinet councillor would soon be 'indistinct from Privy Councillor by growing as numerous'—so that business had to be carried on by an inner ring, sometimes known as the 'effective' cabinet as opposed to the 'nominal' cabinet. This, of course, led to all the old suspicions being revived: Burke was saying and thinking the same things about the 'Court Cabal' in the 1760s that men had said and thought about the Cabinet in the 1690s. In both cases it was feared that an inner ring of courtiers was usurping the influence that ought to be wielded by councillors.

What was clear, in spite of all this argument and confusion, was that government could only be carried on properly by a small group of men who possessed the confidence of the King, practical experience of affairs and the necessary influence to push their measures through Parliament. Whether they were courtiers or councillors, whether they worked from the inside outwards or from the outside inwards, was really immaterial. What mattered was that they should be efficient. Government by a small inner group might lead to suspicions, but government without it would certainly lead to chaos. For better or worse the Cabinet had come to stay.

As well as a selection of the great Officers of State and of the Household, the Cabinet always included the King's two Secretaries of State, one for the Southern Department and one for the Northern. It is important to realize that these two officials, in spite of their titles, were not regarded as heads of government departments in the modern sense of the term. Originally they had been the King's private secretaries and the division between them meant not that one governed the southern half of the country and the other the northern, but simply that one dealt with correspondence with countries in Southern Europe while the other was concerned with the powers of the North—Holland, Germany and the Baltic. For this reason the Secretary for the North, previously regarded as the junior of the two, became the more important after the coming of the Hanoverian Kings in 1714. William III tended to appoint non-entities as Secretaries of State and to work through his personal secretary, William Blathwayt; but under Anne the Secretaries grew in importance until by the end of the reign Bolingbroke, as Secretary for the South, stood second only to the Lord High Treasurer. After 1714 one of the Secretaries—usually a peer, in order that he might negotiate on equal terms with foreign magnates—tended to specialize in foreign affairs and to accompany the King on his frequent visits to Hanover, while the other concerned himself with domestic affairs. But it was not until 1782 that the old division was swept away and the two men renamed Secretary of State for Foreign Affairs and Secretary of State for Home Affairs respectively. Even then they did not stand at the head of great establishments like the modern Foreign Office and Home Office: the appointment of the King's ambassadors, envoys and consuls abroad and of his deputies and dignitaries at home was still controlled from the Court, while the two Secretaries of State between them employed fewer clerks than did the Hackney Coach, Hawkers and Pedlars Office. Nobody else in the Cabinet had a greater share in the Crown's business, or a smaller share in the Crown's patronage. When the wits said in 1757 that the Duke of Newcastle (First Lord of the Treasury) gave everything while Pitt (Secretary of State for the South) did everything, they were describing not just the ministry of 1757 but eighteenth-century government as a whole. If you want to see an eighteenth-century ministry in action, running the affairs of the country, look in the papers of the Secretaries of State; but if you want to see it in repose and judge its real strength as it works to extend its influence down through every office-holder and office-seeker in the realm, look in the papers of the First Lord of the Treasury. Without vigorous and efficient Secretaries a ministry could not move; but without a firm hand at the Treasury it could not stand.

William III dominated his ministers so effectively that none of them was ever able to stand out as a 'prime' minister, but under Anne the Treasury, in the hands of Godolphin from 1702 to 1710 and of Harley from 1711 to 1714, came to be regarded as the most important office at Court and in the Cabinet. When it was put into commission it soon became obvious that the First Lord of the Treasury had an added advantage over the Lord High Treasurers of the past in that he could sit in the House of Commons himself[1] and exercise his powers of management and patronage directly instead of by remote control. All the really stable ministries of the eighteenth century—Walpole's from 1721 to 1742, Pelham's from 1743 to 1754, North's[2] from 1770 to 1782 and the younger Pitt's from 1783 to 1801

[1] In spite of the habitual title 'First Lord', he was in fact merely First Commissioner and could be a commoner.

[2] Frederick North, son of the Earl of Guildford, had the courtesy title of Lord North but was eligible to sit in the Commons until his father's death in 1790.

—were led by First Lords who were in the Commons. Only occasionally could an able and active Secretary of State dominate the scene to the point where men saw him rather than the First Lord as the King's chief minister. Stanhope did it between 1718 and 1721, and the elder Pitt did it from 1757 to 1761; but both these were periods when the First Lord did not sit in the Commons. More significant, they were also periods when policy, in the shape of diplomacy or war, was particularly important. Normally the King's ministers were not concerned to plan great enterprises, carry through programmes of legislation or undertake extensive administrative action. Such things were only done from time to time when the need arose: ministers might have to legislate in order to hold office, but they did not hold office in order to legislate. As late as the 1780s Shelburne, a relatively forward-looking politician, remarked that 'providence has so organized the world that very little government is necessary'. His words summed up the whole tradition of the last hundred years, a tradition of management rather than government, of 'holding the ring' rather than of positive action. Brought up in such a tradition, ministers naturally looked for leadership not to the makers of policy but to the managers of patronage. If the government had been an administrative machine dedicated to running the country's affairs the Secretaries of State would have been found in control of it. But it was nothing of the sort: it was just a group of men managing the King's business for him and manipulating his influence and patronage in such a way as to ensure that his measures were accepted by Parliament and his peace maintained throughout the country. The business of government, such as it was, was carried out not by a corps of professional administrators but by ordinary men who regarded their places under the crown either as sources of profit or as marks of their social status. It was by appealing to men's greed and to their sense of their own importance, rather than by utilizing their talents and their industry, that the King's courtiers and councillors managed the affairs of his realm.

2 The setting: London and Westminster

When the realm was left kingless by the flight of James II in December 1688 one of the first concerns of the peers was to preserve 'the peace and security of these great and populous cities of London and Westminster'; and the assembly which was summoned to advise William later in the month included the Mayor and Aldermen of the City of London, with fifty members of the Common Council. It was clear to William, as it was to be to later Kings, that no government could hope to maintain itself unless it could manage London.

By 1688 there were more than 100,000 people in the City of London, about 12,000 of them freemen of the City. In each of the twenty-six wards the freemen were responsible for preserving law and order, looking after the poor and electing an alderman (who served for life)—and a number of Common Councillors (who served for a year at a time). The twenty-six aldermen formed the Court of Aldermen, one of their number being chosen each year to be Lord Mayor. Since they included or represented the great merchants and bankers and the powerful privileged companies, they were usually in conflict with the Court of Common Council, most of whose two hundred members were in a smaller way of business. Governments did their best to keep on terms with the Court of Common Council—in the last year of his life George I entertained them at St James's Palace—but on the whole they sided with the Aldermen, chiefly because they included some of the most important government creditors.

When it became obvious, in the early 1690s, that the war with France could not be financed out of current taxation, governments began to borrow more and more heavily from the great goldsmiths and bankers of the City. At the same time the war, by making foreign trade increasingly difficult for the small man, brought considerable prosperity to the great companies and there was a boom in the shares of the East India Company, the Royal Africa Company and the Hudson's Bay Company—a boom from which mainly the big men profited. In 1675 only just over 30 per cent of East India stock was held by men who had over £2,000 worth, but by 1693 the proportion had risen to well over 70 per cent and two men, Sir Josiah Child and Sir Thomas Cooke, held between them £92,000 worth— more than an eighth of the total stock. When the Bank of England was founded in 1694 as a finance company empowered to deal in bills of exchange and to issue notes, in return for a loan to the government at 8 per cent, nearly half its stock was in the hands of those with more than £2,000 worth; and as the national debt rose inexorably, from just over £3,000,000 in 1691 to £54,000,000 in 1720, so the government's dependence on the monied men of the City became more and more pronounced. By the middle of the eighteenth century the government's financial advisers were insisting on the absolute necessity of 'securing the five companies'—the Bank of England, the East India Company, the South Sea Company, the Royal Exchange Assurance Company, and the London Exchange Corporation.

The management of these interests depended on manipulating financial and commercial privileges, just as the management of Parliament depended on manipulating places and pensions. Lending to the government involved a certain risk, but it was profitable; and in the eighteenth century, as men like Robert Walpole and Henry Pelham steadily strengthened government credit and eliminated the risk, it became a valuable privilege. Instead of being thrown open to public subscription, government loans were raised privately in the City and the creditors, like the placemen and the contractors, found themselves in a privileged position which they would be foolish to jeopardize by ill-considered opposition to the government of the day. It became increasingly clear that Defoe was right when he said that 'they that have the Management will have the Money'. As long as the country gentlemen thundered against their excessive interest rates in the House of Commons and the small businessmen attacked their commercial privileges in the Court of Common Council, the monied men could be trusted not to withhold funds from the government upon whose needs they depended.

Alongside London and intimately connected with it was Westminster. Strictly speaking, it was limited to the parish of St Margaret's, Westminster—in 1724 it was called 'the only city of one parish in England'—but the parishes of St Martin-in-the-Fields, St James's, Piccadilly and St George's, Hanover Square were normally considered as coming within its orbit. The courts of justice and the exchequer, as well as both Houses of Parliament,[1] met in the Palace of Westminster and much of the business of government was carried on from the offices of the Secretaries of State at the Cockpit in Whitehall. After the experiments of William III and Anne with Hampton Court and Kensington, the Hanoverians settled down at St James's Palace, so that Westminster became the home of the Court as well as of Parliament. More and more of the nobility,

---

[1] The Lords had the White Chamber and Westminster Hall at their disposal, but the Commons had to make do with St Stephen's Chapel. In 1691 they complained of the 'ruinous and dangerous' condition of the place and appealed to the King for a new home; but it continued to house them—with some structural alterations made to accommodate the forty-five Scottish members added in 1707 and the hundred Irish members added in 1800—until 1834.

especially those with ambitions at Court, built great town houses like the Duke of Bedford's in Bloomsbury and for most of the eighteenth century Leicester House, on the site of the present Leicester Square, housed the Court of the Prince of Wales, which vied with that of the King at St James's. Amusements and diversions of all kinds grew up around the fashionable world of the town. In 1705 Her Majesty's Theatre in the Haymarket became the first opera house in England and from 1711 onwards many of Handel's operas had their first performances there. Handel had a rival in Giovanni Bononcini, who was patronized by the Prince of Wales, and after Bononcini was caught out in plagiarism in 1732 and forced to leave the country another rival, Niccolo Porpora, established a new opera house in Lincoln's Inn Fields in 1733 under the patronage of a powerful section of the nobility. Jonathan Tyers, who had leased the New Spring Gardens at Vauxhall in 1728 for £250 a year, opened them to the public in 1732 at a shilling a time, with season tickets in silver and permanent tickets in gold, designed by Hogarth. Ten years later rival pleasure gardens were opened at Ranelagh. Painters, also, found plenty of patronage—Godfrey Kneller and James Thornhill, although working in very different genres, both made considerable fortunes—but it was not until 1768 that a Royal Academy of Arts was first established at Somerset House. George III disliked its first president, Sir Joshua Reynolds, and vastly preferred the painting of Benjamin West to whom he gave over £34,000 in the course of thirty-three years for some sixty-four paintings; but he consented to subsidize the Academy all the same.

The capital abounded, too, in men of letters of all kinds. At Court poetry was taken care of by the Poet Laureate, who produced odes at regular intervals—one particularly pleasing one describes the virtues of George II which, it says, 'shine peculiarly nice, un-gloomed with a confinity to vice'—while the Master of the Revels saw to the production of plays and masques. Some of the plays of Shakespeare presented difficulties for him, especially in the light of the events of 1688, and *King Lear* had to be banned altogether. More important than these decorative figures were the more prosaic writers whom the government employed from time to time to popularize its policies or satirize those of its opponents. Defoe, Swift, Addison and Steele were all commissioned to write pamphlets in this way during the reigns of William III and Anne, and the practice continued under the Hanoverians, although by the end of the eighteenth century it was usual to pay editors rather than authors. One secret service account in 1784 reads: 'Mr Harris, for Mr Longman, to be divided between the editors of the *Ledger, Saint-James's* and *London Evening*— £300.' From the establishment in 1702 of the *Daily Courant*, the first daily newspaper in the world, the regular journal steadily ousted the occasional pamphlet as a vehicle for propaganda. In 1694 Parliament refused to renew the Act for licensing printing presses, so that anyone could set up a press; and the need for reliable financial, commercial and political information and for an advertising medium helped the growth of the newspapers, in spite of a tax on them which rose from 1d a sheet and 1s for every advertisement in 1712 to 4d a sheet and 3s 6d for an advertisement in 1815.

Because it was the home of the fashionable world and of all the arts, amusements and other activities that were dependent on it, the capital came to devote itself more and more to the task of providing for that world. Not only London and Westminster but the districts around and between them—Southwark, Soho, Covent Garden, Marylebone, St Giles, parts of Middlesex and Surrey—were filled with drapers, caterers, provision merchants and a host of other traders who ministered directly or indirectly to the needs of the Court and those who frequented it. 'Between the Court and the City', wrote Defoe in 1724, 'there is a constant communication of business to that degree, that nothing in the world can come up to it.' London was becoming less concerned with industry, more concerned with distributive and administrative activities. To contemporary critics it seemed that it was no longer a place that increased the nation's wealth by turning raw materials into manufactured goods or trading them on advantageous terms for foreign produce, but a place that decreased it by taking in vast quantities of goods of every description and giving nothing in return. Long before Cobbett, in the early nineteenth century, called it 'the great wen', London was being described in similar terms, as a malignant growth which sucked at the vitals of the nation. Even human beings were swallowed up by it. Most countrymen would have agreed with Arthur Young who complained angrily in 1771 that labourers were tempted to 'quit their healthy clean fields for a region of stink, dirt and noise'. Once there, the honest fellows would be gulled by the tricksters who thronged the London streets, endangered by the badly built houses (in 1738 Samuel Johnson said that in London 'falling houses thunder on your head'), fleeced by ruthless property racketeers like Mrs

Farrel of St Giles, who was reputed to have made £6,000 by letting out lodgings at twopence a time, and finally killed by disease, gin-drinking or in some murderous brawl.

There was some truth in all this. London's population[1] could only grow by drawing on healthier stock from the country, since like most towns of the time it had a death-rate which exceeded its birth-rate. In the first half of the eighteenth century most London parishes buried three people for every two that they baptized. Typhus, small-pox, influenza and other diseases ran continually through the squalid and insanitary tenements into which the London poor crowded. Great quantities of gin were consumed, much of it distilled from rotten grain that was unfit for anything else; and it was not until 1751 that effective steps were taken to check the gin trade. Although one foreign visitor said that he met with fewer disturbances and affrays in a fortnight in London than in one morning in Paris, crimes of violence were unpleasantly common. When the Duke of Bedford's tenants in Bloomsbury petitioned him to block up a certain un-savoury alley they said that they were 'continually disturbed by the dismal cry of Murder and other disagreeable noises'. In the absence of any proper police force, the authorities relied in increasingly ferocious punishments to check crime: the number of offences punishable by death, which was fifty in 1688, had risen to 223 by the early nineteenth century. As late as 1777 a fourteen-year-old girl was condemned to be burnt alive for hiding whitewashed farthings and was only saved by a last minute intervention by the Secretary of State.

To most country gentlemen and provincial traders the capital was a place where courtiers and placemen, fops and scoundrels, pastry-cooks and periwig makers, jobbers and speculators, all united together to drain the nation's resources. Even the riotous apprentices and artisans who formed the 'London mob' and broke heads and windows from time to time were part of the conspiracy, stirred up and possibly paid by unscrupulous politicians for their own nefarious ends. By destroying proper subordination and encouraging the 'inferior sort of people' to get above themselves, London squandered the country's manpower as well as its wealth. 'The debauched life of its inhabitants', wrote Arthur Young, 'occasions them to be more idle

[1] Gregory King calculated that the population of the whole London area, as distinct from just the City, was 500,000 in 1688. By the end of the eighteenth century it was probably about 1,000,000.

than in the country . . . the very maxims and principles upon which life is founded in great cities are the most powerful of all enemies to common industry.' The antipathy between government and governed, between Court and Country, was reflected in that between London and the rest of the country.

3 The means: patronage and management

Lady Sundon, who was woman of the Bedchamber to Queen Caroline in the 1730s and had great influence at Court, once caused a stir by wearing in public a pair of diamond ear-rings given her by the Earl of Pomfret in return for getting him the post of Master of the Horse. When the aged Duchess of Marlborough complained of her effrontery Lady Mary Wortley Montagu replied, realistically enough: 'Madam, how can people know where wine is to be sold unless there is a sign hung out?' Few of the courtiers hung their signs out as flagrantly as Lady Sundon, but they were in business all the same. Pomfret had made a good bargain: his Mastership of the Horse was worth £1,266 13s 4d a year and he probably intended to augment that figure by taking a 'consideration' from the cornchandlers and others with whom he dealt, just as Lady Sundon took considerations for the influence she exerted. At Court and in the country all offices and places, high or low, were seen as investments which must be made to yield a proper return. When some revenue officers were suspended for corruption in 1728 one newspaper was quite indignant that they should have been punished 'only for taking care of their families and making the most of their places'. Places were expensive things, whether they were bought openly for cash, secretly by bribes, or indirectly by years of service to a patron: it was natural, therefore, that their holders should seek to 'make the most of them'.

Normally the greater part of the profit from a place came in the form of fees. Every bishop, on translation from one diocese to another, had to pay fees ranging from £10 to the Lord Chamberlain and £5 to the Groom of the Stole down to £1 to the Gentleman of the Ewery; every town through which the King and his Court passed paid a total of £37 6s in fees to various court officers; new Knights of the Garter had to pay fees totalling £440 13s 7d. Even the King himself was not exempt: George I was horrified to find that he was expected to pay a man five guineas for bringing him his own carp out of his own pond at St James's. The system of fees ran right down from the most dignified Court official to the humblest clerk. In between there were men like the Paymaster of the Forces, who expected a consideration from foreign rulers on all money paid out in subsidies, or the Auditors of Imprest, who did very little and collected such huge sums in return that when their posts were abolished in 1785 they had to be given £7,000 a year each for life in compensation for loss of fees.

Alongside the thousands of office-holders who sought to increase the yield (and therefore the market value) of their places were thousands more whose dependence on the government was less obvious but no less real. The Court, the councils and committees and boards, the Customs and Excise, the Army and the Navy,[1] all needed goods and services of one sort or another; and the men who supplied them, the 'contractors', were as concerned to exploit their contracts as the placemen were to exploit their places. Whether they were supplying crepe for Court mourning, pens and ink for the Victualling Office, hired cutters for the revenue services or dockyard facilities for the Navy, they had made an investment and they expected guaranteed dividends. Even further down the line were the tradesmen in those boroughs where the Post Office, the Customs and Excise, the Board of Ordnance or the Admiralty spent a great deal of money. All told there were tens of thousands of families throughout the country whose prestige, advancement or livelihood depended ultimately on the government. Properly organized and skilfully handled, they could be welded into a 'Court interest' which would give the King's ministers the support and stability that they needed. The creation and management of such an interest, both in Parliament and in the country as a whole, was a complex and difficult task, calling for constant care and attention. But without it no ministry could hope to survive for long.

The first necessity was to ensure a strong ministerial following in the House of Commons, so that the King's revenues could be voted and his measures carried. For this purpose the ministers relied mainly on the boroughs. Originally the King's High Court of Parliament had been a court of petitions: anyone who desired some privilege or had some grievance would go himself, or send a representative, to petition the King. If the King decided to grant the petition he would

---

[1] The Navy of 1688 has been described by one historian as 'the most comprehensive and in some respects the largest industry in the country'. (J. Ehrman: *The Navy in the War of William III, 1689-1697*, 1953, p. 174.)

do so with the words 'Le Roi le veult', and the document would then become an enactment of the Court of Parliament, to be observed by all men. Gradually it had become more and more advisable for all the shires and boroughs of the realm to have their representatives in Parliament in order to plead for their own petitions or—what was just as important—against those of others which might harm their own interests. In the counties it was usually easy to find a gentleman who could afford the time and money to go to Westminister and sit as 'knight of the shire' to represent his county; but for the boroughs it was not always so easy. In many cases the burgesses were only too grateful when some great landowner offered to put forward his own nominee to represent them in Parliament, thus saving them the expense of paying or compensating one of their own number to do so. In this way the great lords of the country had become 'patrons' of many of the borough seats and filled them with clients and followers of their own—sometimes burgesses, but more often members of their own families or neighbouring gentry. By 1689 the 513 members of the House of Commons were made up of 92 knights of the shire, 50 members for London and the other cities, 369 borough members and one member each for the Universities of Oxford and Cambridge.[1] In theory, therefore, the middle-class burgesses and merchants should have outnumbered the landed gentlemen by about four to one. But in fact it was the other way about: at no time between 1689 and 1815 were there more than a hundred men in the Commons who were not members of the gentry or nobility. Moreover the balance was not only tilted in favour of the landed classes, but also in favour of a small group within thoses classes: it has been estimated that over 60 per cent of the members of the House of Commons between 1734 and 1832 were drawn from only 922 families, while over 17 per cent were sons of peers.[2] There was some truth in the elder Pitt's description of the House of Commons as 'a parcel of younger brothers': the great majority of M.P.s, and especially those who sat for the boroughs, were either related to the members of the House of Lords or dependent on them. If the 'Court interest', the interest of all the placemen and contractors and other hangers-on,

[1] The 40 English counties each sent two members, the 12 Welsh counties one, London four, the 23 other cities two, the 8 Cinque Ports two, the 167 boroughs two, the 5 lesser boroughs one, the 12 Welsh boroughs one and the Universities one. The Union with Scotland in 1707 added 45 members and that with Ireland in 1800 added 100, so that by the end of the period the House of Commons stood at 658.

[2] G. P. Judd: *Members of Parliament, 1734–1832*, 1955, pp. 31, 33.

was to have its full effect in the Commons, it must be exerted through the boroughs and in collaboration with the great men who controlled them.

During the reigns of William III and Anne the great men steadily tightened their grip on the boroughs. In most of them there were very few electors—sometimes only the mayor and corporation, sometimes only the holders of certain properties, sometimes only the freemen of the borough—and in these cases it was merely a matter of getting the right man into the right office or buying up the right piece of property. Even in the sixty or so boroughs where all the ratepayers or all the householders had the vote, pressure might be applied in all sorts of ways. Donations might be made to local charities, public buildings might be erected or repaired, tenants might be offered or refused the renewal of their leases, entertainments might be given. If the patron were known to be in favour with the Court further inducements in the form of places or contracts could be offered. Lesser men found it increasingly difficult to challenge the great patrons, especially in the boroughs with a restricted franchise: whereas seventy such boroughs were contested in the 1690 election only fifteen were still being contested by the middle of the eighteenth century. In the rest the patron's nominee was regularly returned unopposed. Meanwhile the increasing cost of fighting elections and election petitions[1] was driving all but the richest men out of electioneering altogether. One borough which cost £70 to fight in 1690 cost £719 by 1717. Not only the patron but the elector as well was concerned to make things as expensive as possible for the interloper. The elector regarded his vote as the placeman his place or the contractor his contract: it was a piece of property which must be made to return a dividend, either in the form of favours from his patron or a cash equivalent. The Septennial Act of 1716, by extending the maximum life of a Parliament from three years to seven, contributed to the general raising of costs: candidates were prepared to pay more for a seven-year investment than for a three-year one and electors expected higher dividends now that they could collect them less often. By the early eighteenth century borough-mongering was becoming a very expensive game indeed and those who played it had to have

[1] It was normal practice for defeated candidates to petition the Commons to annul the election on the grounds of some real or imagined irregularity. This involved considerable expense in transporting witnesses to and from Westminster. Since petitions were usually regarded as trials of party strength the scales were heavily weighted against a candidate who did not have the backing of a great patron.

extensive resources and a reasonable expectation that they would see a fair return on their outlay. Thus the magnates needed the Court as much as the Court needed the magnates: without the resources of the borough patrons the Court could not bring its influence to bear on the House of Commons, but without the rewards of office for themselves and their clients the patrons could not maintain their own influence. It was a common saying of the time that 'whoever is out of the House is out of the way to be provided for'. The great patrons were prepared to bring men into the House, but only if there was a fair chance that they would be provided for.

Providing for them was by no means a simple task, in spite of the vast extent of government patronage. The number of places falling vacant at any one time was limited and careless disposal of them might produce more enemies than friends: the continual stream of requests from members for places, pensions and reversions (rights to succeed to places when they should fall vacant) had to be dealt with in such a way as to satisfy as many as possible and offend as few as possible. Moreover it was necessary to provide for the patron as well as for the client: a discontented patron might bring his men out against the ministers, even if the men themselves had been given places. One member of the House of Lords excluded from the Cabinet might mean a dozen votes lost in the House of Commons. The place-men brought in by previous ministries—and they were always in the majority—had to be won over to the present one by further 'grati-fications'. Dependents and relatives of members, as well as the members themselves, had to be provided with places in the Church or the Army or the Customs and Excise. Sometimes downright bribery might be used, but it was fairly limited: the amount of secret service money spent in this way was seldom more than thirty or forty thousand pounds a year. Occasionally a crack of the whip might be necessary, as when Walpole dismissed some of those who voted against his Excise Bill in 1733. Only by skilful use of all these weapons could the two hundred or so placemen in the Commons be dragooned into providing regular support for the government. With the electors themselves the government had little contact— there were never more than two or three dozen boroughs controlled directly by the government of the day, and these were mainly used to provide seats for the 'men of business', the experienced adminis-trators which every ministry needed. But the knowledge that government patronage would only reach them through M.P.s who were themselves in favour worked wonders with the electors. Any government that could manage the patrons and the candidates could afford to let the management of the electors take care of itself. Ministries were often endangered by quarrels between the great lords who formed them or by desertions of their supporters in the Commons; but no eighteenth-century ministry ever lost a general election.

However successful a ministry might be in moulding and managing it, the House of Commons was never an entirely subservient body, a mere organ of government. It was, rather, the frontier between government and the governed, and it never completely forgot its historic role as a court of petitions. Although it spent an increasing amount of time on the King's business, debating measures brought in by his ministers and providing him with his revenues, it also concerned itself with the petitions of his subjects. Many of its measures, such as the numerous Private Acts authorizing enclosures, were strictly in the medieval tradition of petitions turned into enactments by the King's assent; and even Public Acts often originated in the same way. From 1717 onwards members concerned with the weaving industries supported a series of petitions against the 'associations' that journeymen weavers were forming in order to press for higher rates, and in 1725 these were turned into an Act prohibiting such associations. Not all the borough members were career politicians brought in by patrons and even among those who were there was always a large number associated with patrons who opposed the government of the day. Finally, even if all the borough members had become corrupted, there would still have been the ninety-two knights of the shire to contend with. County elections were on the whole more open than those in the boroughs, and they returned sturdy independents who distrusted the professional politicians and regarded themselves as a sort of Grand Jury of the realm, ready to call ministers to account and to insist on the old principle that 'redress of grievance should precede supply'. They bitterly resented the placemen and brought in a series of Place Bills to exclude them—between 1707 and 1715 there were five such bills, all killed in the House of Lords. They resented also the borough-mongering of the great patrons and pressed continually for safeguards against it, such as shorter parliaments or stricter property qualifications for M.P.s. Properly handled they could be useful allies for an opposition leader —Harley used them in Anne's reign and Walpole used them when he was in opposition in 1719 to defeat the government's Peerage Bill, a measure which would have made the House of Lords a closed shop and robbed the country gentlemen of their hopes of becoming peers themselves.

The spectacle of the Lords throwing out Place Bills and the Commons throwing out the Peerage Bill seemed to confirm the theory, widely held at the time, that the British Constitution was based on a triple balance between King, Lords and Commons. De Lolme said in 1775 that the Lords and Commons 'have by turn effectually defeated the attacks of each other upon the King's prerogative'. Nevertheless a wise government thought not in terms of playing Lords and Commons off against one another but of driving them both together in double harness. Management of the Lords was intimately connected with management of the Commons and depended on much the same devices—Court or Cabinet posts for the peers themselves, pensions and places for their followers in the Commons. Only a minority of the two hundred or so members of the Upper House[1] had political followings or political ambitions at the national level, but all were jealous of their position and dignity in their own areas. The careful distributions of honours like the Garter and of the lord-lieutenancies of the counties was important, as was the manipulation of the bishoprics. In 1689 six bishops who refused to take the oath to William and Mary were replaced by men acceptable to the new régime, and by 1692 fifteen new bishops had been consecrated, all of them politically reliable and loyal to the Court. Anne sometimes allowed religious considerations to influence her choice of bishops, but from 1714 onwards appointments were normally made on political grounds and a bishop who was reluctant to support the government, either in the Lords or in his diocese, was unlikely to get further preferment. Lay and spiritual peers alike had to be bound as closely as possible to the government, not only for the sake of their votes in the House of Lords but also because of the power they wielded in the localities. Like the House of Commons, the House of Lords was a frontier, but it was not so much a frontier between the government and the governed as between the central government and the great magnates through whom it sought to manage the country.

[1] The number of lay peers rose from 145 in 1685 to 176 in 1719, after which it remained fairly constant until the 1780s. The archbishops of Canterbury and York and the twenty-four other bishops also sat in the Lords; and from 1707 onwards there were also sixteen representative Scottish peers.

4 The limitations: independent magistrates and local self-government

One of the shrewdest observers of the struggle between King and Parliament earlier in the seventeenth century had been John Selden; and in 1689, as if to remind men of the issues that were still at stake, a posthumous collection of his table talk was published. It included a bitter comment on the early part of Charles I's reign: 'Now the judges they interpret the law—and what judges can be made to do we all know.' The Stuarts, like the Tudors before them, regarded the judges as an integral part of the government, to be controlled through the Privy Council. It was not for nothing that the celebrant at the Holy Communion prayed for the King's 'whole Council, and all that are put in authority under him, that they may truly and indifferently minister justice to the punishment of wickedness and vice'. The original Whig draft of the Declaration of Rights had included a proposal for making the judges' commission *quamdiu se bene gesserint* ('as long as they behave themselves'), but it had been turned down and William, like his predecessors, could still remove judges at will. In 1692, when Parliament presented him with a Bill embodying the same proposal linked with another giving the judges definite salaries instead of letting them collect fees, William vetoed it; and it was not until 1701, by the Act of Settlement, that provision was made to pay judges fixed salaries and allow them to hold their commissions *quamdiu se bene gesserint*. Even then the changes were not to come into force immediately but only at the accession of the House of Hanover. Meanwhile the Lord Chancellor, the head of the whole judicial hierarchy, sat in the Cabinet Council and some of the judges were themselves Privy Councillors. The separation of the judiciary from the executive was important not only in Whig theory but also in practical affairs, since without it there was no guarantee that the 'laws and liberties of the kingdom' would be impartially defined and upheld. But it was far from being an established fact in the reigns of William III and Anne.

In this uncertain situation the character and behaviour of the judges themselves was to be the crucial factor, and the Chief Justice of the King's Bench, as the man mainly responsible for the definition and interpretation of the criminal law, was to be the key figure. In April 1689 this office was given to Sir John Holt, a man who had already shown considerable courage and independence. When the House of

Commons wanted to impeach the Tory Lord Danby in 1679, Holt
was ready to defend him; in 1683 he appeared for the Whig Lord
Russell when the Crown prosecuted him for treason; in 1687 he was
dismissed from his office of Recorder of London for refusing to find
that the King could give army commissions to Roman Catholics. As
Lord Chief Justice he defended the independence of the judges both
against the Lords and against the Commons. In 1698 the Lords
summoned him before them to answer for a judgment he had given
in the Court of King's Bench, only to be told: 'I am not to be
arraigned for what I do judicially.' When the Commons proceeded
against Ashby and his counsel[1] in 1704 it was Holt, alone among the
judges, who defied them and insisted that they were seeking to
arrogate to themselves matters which were properly the concern of
the common law. On one occasion he challenged the Crown itself
and got a judgment against it, though the matter at stake (his right
to give his brother a lucrative sinecure in the Court of King's Bench)
was not particularly creditable. Many of his actions, such as his
refusals to take the office of Lord Chancellor and his scrupulous fair-
ness to Lord Preston at his trial for treason in 1690, may have been
the result of political caution rather than of a lofty respect for the
independence of the Bench or the liberties of the subject; but his
career as a whole added up to a vindication of those two principles.
In other ways, too, he brought a new spirit of tolerance and common
sense to the ministering of justice: he refused to have prisoners
brought before him in irons, he would not punish Dissenters for not
attending Anglican services, he dismissed cases of witchcraft and
treated prosecutors in such cases as common impostors. If the years
after 1689 saw a new respect for the law as something which stood
above both King and Parliament, much of the credit must go to
Holt. The tradition which he established ensured that the government
would never be able to manage the judges with the same assurance
with which it managed Parliament. By the middle of the eighteenth
century the independence of the judges had come to be seen as an
essential principle of the constitution, and it was finally secured in
1760 when George III brought in an Act providing that their commissions should no longer lapse on the King's death. By depriving
future Kings of their right to remove judges at their accession he
gave a further demonstration of the maxim that the King is beneath
the Law.

[1] See below, p. 131.

The independence of the judges was a comparatively new thing, but the independence of the magistracy as a whole, of the men responsible for the day to day maintenance of law and order, had a much more ancient origin. At the root of it lay the medieval principle of local obligation: it was not the King's business to govern the country but merely to see that the country governed itself in accordance with his laws. He therefore issued for each county and for a number of cities and towns his 'Commission of the Peace', naming certain people whom he would hold responsible for seeing that their neighbours kept the King's Peace. By 1688 there were about 3,000 of these 'justices of the peace'. Although answerable to the King's judges, they were not subordinate to them. When the judges came round the country three times a year on their circuits to try cases presented to them they represented the central government, albeit a part of it independent of ministers of state; but the justices of the peace represented the governed. James II had not scrupled to remove justices known to be against his policies, and after the Revolution there was a further purge, so that by 1691 it was said that 'none were left that did not go with the humour of the Court'. But they were certainly not placemen, to be manipulated and managed by the government of the day. While other men—members of the Commons, revenue men, army officers, even parsons—might owe their local influence and authority to the position they held, the justices were men of substance, sturdy independents who owed their position to the local influence and authority they exercised. The lord-lieutenants of the counties, on whose recommendations the Commissions were based, would normally only put forward the names of men known to them as leaders of local society. Nevertheless the Commons always suspected the government of putting in landless upstarts and in 1732 they carried a measure raising the property qualification from £20 to £100 a year in land. In 1744 a further Act required justices to swear that they had the requisite income and even to give details of it; and it was in that same year that the Lord Chancellor felt himself obliged to reject a man who had been put forward as a justice for Westminster, because he was an organist by profession. But the suspicions and accusations continued: Smollett spoke of the justices of Westminster and Middlesex as 'needy, mean, ignorant and rapacious', and Burke called them 'the scum of the earth'.

Even at their Petty Sessions, when two or three of them met in the local tavern or in their own houses, the justices had very wide powers to punish vagrants, poachers and other offenders; and at their Quarter Sessions the justices of the county assembled to form its supreme judicial tribunal, empowered to deal with all crimes except treason.[1] Moreover, they were concerned to punish their neighbours not only for what they had done but also for what they had left undone. The principle of local obligation extended down through the county to the parish and each of the 9,000 or so parishes throughout the land was answerable to the justices for the proper running of its own affairs. The parishioners had to provide from among their own number churchwardens to see to the needs of the church, a constable to keep law and order, a surveyor of highways to look after the roads in the parish and an overseer of the poor to provide relief for the destitute. The office of churchwarden was usually sought after, being dignified and not too burdensome, but the other jobs were very unpopular. The surveyor of highways had to fight a losing battle against the mud and against the reluctance of his neighbours to perform their statutory duty of labouring six days a year on the roads, while the overseer of the poor was caught between two fires: if he looked after his paupers too well people complained that he was squandering the poor rates, while if he neglected them and one of them died of starvation he was liable to be indicted for manslaughter. As for the constable, he had the unpleasant and sometimes dangerous task of arresting criminals and was also responsible for the parish as a whole. One can almost hear Thomas Dale's sigh of relief as he presents his account of the proper discharge of his duties as parish constable of Little Gransden in 1750: 'We have no Popish recusants; no common drunkards; our Hues and Cries have been pursued; watch and ward kept; we have not been remiss in apprehending vagrants; we have no unlicensed ale-houses or inns; we have no unlawful weights or measures; we have no new erected cottages or inmates; we have no young persons idle out of service; we have no ingrossers of corn, no forestallers of markets; our town stock is employed for the relief of the poor; we have no profane swearers or cursers; we have no riots, routs or unlawful assemblies.' Although the eighteenth century was the great age of sinecures, the office of parish constables was certainly not one of them.

A parish which had neglected any of these duties might find itself

[1] Cases which involved the death penalty were normally referred to the judges on circuit.

or its officers presented for trial at Quarter Sessions; and it was at Quarter Sessions also that disputes between parishes over settlement questions were thrashed out. Until 1697 the laws of settlement forbade any poor person to leave his own parish, but an Act of that year allowed him to do so if he had a settlement certificate, signed by a justice, by which his parish agreed to take him back if he became a charge on the poor rates of another parish. This led to frequent difficulties and disputes, as harassed overseers and constables sought to get rid of stray paupers and fix responsibility for them on to some other parish. An increasing portion of the poor rate was spent in shuttling paupers across the country and fighting law cases to establish their parish of origin. In May and June of 1709 Mrs Hood, a poor widow with two small children, was deported six times over, starting in London and finishing up in Nottingham; but it still proved impossible to find where she really belonged. Some paupers found these indignities too much for their self-respect: when John Chapman was told that his settlement on the parish of Eltringham in Northumberland was not valid he solidly refused to seek poor relief anywhere else. Some time later he was found dead of starvation on the high road.

All this meant that Quarter Sessions were much more than judicial tribunals. In that they punished the neglectful and decided doubtful cases the justices still filled their old role as magistrates; but since these duties led them more and more to undertake the general supervision of such things as poor relief and highway maintenance they became administrators as well. As such they represented not just a system of local obligation for the keeping of the King's Peace, but a thorough-going system of local self-government. Quarter Sessions supervised contracts of employment and indentures of apprenticeship, regulated wages and prices, licensed various kinds of traders, fixed the rates for poor relief and other purposes, saw to the inspection of roads, bridges and gaols[1] and generally ran the affairs of the county. By the early nineteenth century they were spending more than £1,000,000 a year (in 1739 an Act had been passed allowing them to levy a general County Rate, instead of a series of separate rates for different purposes) and employing an increasing number of salaried clerks, treasurers and surveyors. In reality they were not just County

[1] This last duty does not seem to have been very conscientiously performed, largely owing to the fear of gaol fever. 'These gentlemen think that if ever they come into my gaol they shall soon be in their graves', said one gaoler.

Courts but County Councils, governments in miniature. Beside them, the other and older dignitaries of the county looked very insignificant. The lord-lieutenant, although in theory he was the King's deputy and the representative of the central government, had very little to do. From time to time, as in 1690, 1692 and 1745, he might have to call out the county militia, but this body was becoming less and less important. The general dislike of a standing army led to the polite fiction that the militia was an effective substitute and could defend the country in time of need; but in fact it was not until its re-organization in 1757 that it began to be at all formidable. Lord-lieutenancies were highly valued as marks of local prestige and in 1700, when the old Duke of Bedford died, Lady Russell lost no time in writing to William III to get her son, the new Duke, appointed to his lord-lieutenancies of Bedfordshire, Cambridgeshire and Middle-sex; but they could hardly be said to be a means whereby the government could control the counties. The other officer of the county, the high sheriff, was usually of inferior status—the lord-lieutenant was normally a peer, the sheriff a commoner—and had equally limited powers. The writs for parliamentary elections were addressed to him and he had the duty of calling out the *posse comitatus* to round up particularly desperate criminals. This still had to be done occasionally: in 1735 Henry Rogers, a pewterer of Skervis in Corn-wall, barricaded himself in his house and shot two of the *posse* when they came to take him. But for the most part the office of sheriff had only a negative importance in that it debarred its holder from being elected to the Commons. In the game of management and patronage it was sometimes as important to see that your rivals were made sheriffs as it was to ensure that your friends were made lord-lieutenants.

This pattern of local self-government at both parish and county level meant that the central government had no network of officials through which it could govern the country as a whole. Most other European countries had some kind of bureaucracy or civil service; and even in those which did not the police force or the army or the tax collectors acted as agents of the central authority. But in England the government had none of these things. As crime increased English-men adopted all kinds of devices to deal with it: stiffer penalties, increased rewards for informers,[1] voluntary associations for the

1 The inducements offered included the 'Tyburn Ticket', which exempted its holder for life from all parish offices. One was once sold by auction in Manchester for £300.

detection and apprehension of criminals, even connivance in the activities of men like Jonathan Wild, who acted as agent between thieves and their victims, arranging the restitution of stolen property in return for a commission. But they were determined not to submit to the establishment of a police force, which seemed to them a symbol of continental tyranny. The army, too, was seen as a tyrannical device, 'A standing army in England whether in time of Peace or of War', said Swift, 'is a direct absurdity, for it is no part of our business to be a warlike nation, otherwise than by our fleets.' William III found it so difficult to raise troops in England that by the 1690s his guards regiments were advertising rewards in the London papers for the recapture of a deserter 'having one leg smaller than the other', and for another who was blind in one eye. In 1696 insolvent debtors were made liable to compulsory enlistment and in 1702 convicted felons were offered a free pardon if they joined the colours. Meanwhile there was steady opposition to the building of barracks (in spite of the resentment of the innkeepers, who were liable to have soldiers billeted on them at the rate of only fourpence per man per day) and to the use of troops in putting down riots. Chief Justice Holt is said to have threatened a guards officer with an indictment for murder if he ordered his men to fire on the crowd. As for the revenue officers, they were even more unpopular than the army and when Walpole proposed to increase their number by his Excise Scheme of 1733 he was accused of trying to bring in a system of continental tyranny. In the ten years from 1723 to 1733 no less than 250 revenue men were beaten up and six were murdered; since justices and juries were notoriously reluctant to present members of the smuggling gangs for trial, a system of collective fines had to be introduced. A dead revenue officer cost the county a fine of £100 and a wounded one £40. At best, the ordinary man regarded himself as a spectator in the struggle between the smugglers and the authorities. One traveller who rode in 1752 from an inn full of smugglers to one full of excisemen remarked, 'As we were neutral powers we have passed safely through both armies.' No government could hope to govern the country through the army or the revenue service.

A more promising means of controlling the localities was the Church. Here was a hierarchy that stretched from the King himself, who was 'Supreme Governor of this realm . . . as well in all spiritual or ecclesiastical things or causes as temporal', right down to the remotest parish, where the parson read out the King's proclamations in church, exhorted his parishioners to do their duty in that state of life unto which it had pleased God to call them, and was responsible for their morals. Anybody who wished to leave his employment or embark on some new enterprise, such as opening an alehouse or a slaughterhouse, needed a certificate of good character signed by the parson; and one observer remarked that 'it might be discerned whether or not there was a clergyman resident in a parish by the civil or savage manner of the people'. Meanwhile at the top of the hierarchy the bishops and archbishops were associated with the government and there was no clear-cut distinction between churchmen and statesmen: the Archbishop of Canterbury sat in the Cabinet Council and as late as 1713 a bishop was employed on a diplomatic mission, as one of the plenipotentiaries at the Peace of Utrecht.

Unfortunately, however, the Church of England was divided against itself in a way that made it reflect, rather than bridge, the gulf between government and the governed. For those with influence and connection there were rich prizes: the epitaph of one Mrs Bates records gratefully that 'by means of her alliance with the illustrious family of Stanhope she had the merit to obtain for her husband and children twelve several appointments in Church and State'. But for men without powerful patrons there was little hope of rich bishoprics, deaneries held *in commendam*, or prebendaries that brought in £300 or £400 a year for preaching two sermons. There were too many great men jostling for too few places in order to distribute them among their relatives and clients; the ordinary cleric had to be content with livings that were seldom worth more than £30 or £40 a year, even after 1704, when Queen Anne gave the Crown's income from first fruits and tenths[1] to augment poor livings. The country clergy were by no means the uneducated and bigoted oafs painted by Macaulay;[2] some of them, such as Stephen Hales and Gilbert White, were distinguished scholars in a variety of fields, but few were in a position to challenge the authority of the local gentry. They had to farm their own glebe land and they depended on neighbouring farmers for their tithes. Economically and socially their interests were those of the governed and not of the government. The split between the Upper and Lower Houses of Convocation, which got steadily

---

1 First fruits and tenths were taxes paid originally to the papacy and annexed to the Crown in 1534. By the 1660s they brought in about £14,000 a year, which Charles II used to maintain his mistresses.

2 See the third chapter of Macaulay's *History of England*.

worse from 1689 onwards and resulted in its final prorogation in 1717, was not just a quarrel between Latitudinarian Whig bishops and High Church Tory clergymen: it was also a reflection of an economic, social and political division between the upper and lower clergy which was made worse by the patronage system of the eighteenth century. By using it as a means of management, ministers reduced the Church's potential as an instrument of government.

3

The Country

1 The Countryside

In order to govern, it is useful to know something of the people you
are to govern—to know, for instance, how many of them there are.
Eighteenth-century governments, concerned only with management,
did not trouble to collect information of this kind and the first census
was not taken until 1801; but private individuals had for a long time
been interested in what they called 'political arithmetic' and had tried
to assemble reliable statistics. The hearth tax, although it was no
longer levied after 1689, provided a series of returns which were some
guide to the number of households in the kingdom, while parish
registers gave information about births, marriages and deaths, and
thus made it possible to get some idea of the average size of families.
Using such sources Gregory King calculated that in 1688 the
population of England and Wales was 5,500,520, of which 4,034,000
lived in villages or hamlets. His methods and his data both had their
faults, but his estimate was probably not very far out. At the time of
the Revolution the country contained something between five and
six million people, well over three-quarters of them living in the
countryside. English life was predominantly village life.

As well as dividing people into countrymen and townsmen, King
made another and more revealing distinction—revealing, that is, in
that it made clear his basic assumptions about the nature of society.
He reckoned that there were 2,675,520 people—landowners, merchants and other men of substance, with their families—who were
'increasing the wealth of the country', while the other 2,825,000 were
labouring people, out-servants, cottagers, paupers, common seamen
and common soldiers, who were decreasing it. Behind this calculation
stood a view of society based on ownership rather than duty. The old
ideal of a Christian Commonwealth had given way to the Freeholders'
Society. In the past, society had been seen in terms of functions—
each man, however humble, had his part to play. The old fable of

the Stomach and the Members, in which the latter rebel against the idleness and greed of the former, only to find that they cannot do without him, could also be applied in reverse: men of property could not do without labourers.[1] But King and his contemporaries had no time for old fables. In their eyes the wealth of the nation was a solid and tangible thing and those who held it and manipulated it and increased it—magnates, farmers, merchants, professional men, skilled artisans and craftsmen—were the only ones who could be said to have something positive to offer society. Their position entitled them to the freedom of the country, just as the members of a guild or corporation were entitled to the Freedom of their City. Freedom was not an abstract thing, floating about in the air for all men to breathe, but an attribute, something which certain men possessed for definite reasons. If a man was free, it was not just because he was a man but because he was a freeman, a freeholder, or the equivalent.

As for the poor, the 2,825,000 whose incomes were less than their expenditure and who had no stake in the country, they were by definition more of a liability than an asset and might become an unmitigated liability unless they were firmly handled. Not all of them were landless—the term 'cottager' implied a small holding to go with the cottage—but none of them held their land in freehold and few of them held enough to make them self-supporting. If they were fortunate and diligent they might get fairly regular work (although it was very unusual to employ labourers on a permanent basis) and thus maintain themselves and their families for a time. But they were always liable to lose what source of income they had and become a charge on the poor rates. If they avoided this during their working lives, they would almost certainly become paupers when they were old and infirm, so that the freeholders of the parish, having provided them with employment all their lives, would have to provide them with relief for their old age as well. They were often idle—one writer remarked that 'the poor do not labour, upon an average, above four days a week, unless provisions happen to be very dear'— and they had an unhealthy hankering after luxuries: '. . . the lower ranks of the people', said Dr Price in 1773, 'are altered in every respect for the worse, while tea, wheaten bread and other delicacies are necessaries which were formerly unknown to them.' Worst of all, they multiplied, in spite of vigorous attempts to discourage them

---

[1] It is worth pointing out that in its original form it provided an answer to those who complained about London consuming the country's resources.

from marrying young. Cogan's charity in Hull, set up to educate poor children in a useful trade, offered its girls marriage portions of £6 each as long as they didn't marry until they had been at least six years in 'respectable servitude'. But in spite of all the deterrents, and in spite of the appallingly high rate of infant mortality, freemen found that the poor were always with them, and with them in increasing numbers.

The children born in the cottages of the poor had an expectation of life of about twenty-five or thirty years. Their homes were damp, draughty and overcrowded, but the lack of sanitation mattered less than it did in the towns and it was possible (though at the risk of being caught and punished) to collect firewood to keep the cold at bay. Outbreaks of typhus, smallpox and other infectious diseases were less common than among town children but they were still dangerous, while wasting diseases associated with malnutrition and tuberculosis were widespread. One child in every three died before the age of six. For those that survived there might be some sort of occasional work such as minding the beasts that were put out to graze on the village commons or stubbles, scaring birds off the crops or even snaring them—one parish paid eighteen shillings a gross for sparrows' heads. But regular work for children was hard to come by, at any rate in those villages where the sole occupation was farming, and even the poorest children were sometimes able to pick up a smattering of education at charity schools or dame schools. Bewick remarked that in Northumberland in the middle of the eighteenth century the 'poor labouring men' were often better read than the farmers. However, in areas where there was regular work that they could do the children were kept fully occupied. In the quarrying village of Eyam in Derbyshire labourers had their daily wage of 8d augmented to 10d if they had a couple of children to help them carry away the dirt in baskets, while in the weaving areas of Somerset and the West Riding it was said that children of four and five could earn enough to keep themselves.

Some of the more fortunate children might secure fairly regular jobs as indoor or outdoor servants and some might even be apprenticed to a trade, although the latter was often only a cover for the former: of 178 children apprenticed in one parish, 157 were bound to 'husbandry' or 'housewifery'. For those who became agricultural labourers things were less secure. At harvest time there was plenty of work, but only the strongest and the most diligent could expect to be hired regularly for the whole year. When they were in work they usually worked from dawn to dusk, with Sundays and a few other days such as Good Friday, May Day, the Parish Feast Day and Christmas as holidays. Wages varied from 9*d* a day in the north to 1*s* 4*d* a day in the home counties. In Devonshire in 1691 a man and a horse cost 1*s* 6*d* a day, but most of this was for the horse—the army at this time allowed 9*d* a day for the upkeep of a horse, but only 4*d* for a man. Occasionally special factors put up wages, as in Suffolk in the 1730s when the smugglers forced them up to 1*s* 6*d* by offering men 2*s* 6*d* a day retainer themselves. But on the whole rates changed very little and by the 1770s men were still only getting 10*d* or 1*s* in the south and west, although in the areas around London they got as much as 1*s* 9*d*.

Most overseers of the poor seem to have regarded 4*s* or 5*s* a week as the minimum required to keep a pauper alive, so that it is difficult to see how a labourer with a wife and two or three children could manage, even though his own food and drink during working hours were normally provided by his employer. Certainly he could not hope to live in the style of the pensioners at Greenwich hospital, who in 1705 were allowed per week 7 pounds of bread, 3 of beef, 2 of mutton, and 1¾ of cheese, as well as a pint of peas, 2 ounces of butter, 14 quarts of beer and a shilling for tobacco. With bread at 1¼*d* the pound, meat at 3*d* and cheese at 2½*d* (this was Cheshire—Cheddar cost 8*d*) these items alone would run away with his wages, leaving nothing for such other necessities as rent, fuel, boots and clothing, rushlights, pots and pans and beer.[1] He and his family would have to live mostly on bread and beer, with an occasional piece of bacon or salted meat. When he was out of work he would have to apply for poor relief and the overseer would try to find him some sort of employment, such as breaking stones or ditching, and provide him in return with the necessaries of life. The 1697 Act tried to draw a line between paupers and the rest of the poor, requiring the former to wear on their right shoulders a large 'P' with the first letter of the parish, but this practice of 'badging the poor' was abandoned in many parishes. Most overseers, recognizing that even the most diligent might sometimes find themselves destitute, were not unduly harsh in the administration of relief. In 1738 the poor children of one Bedfordshire

---

[1] Since water supplies were often inadequate and impure, beer was an essential and not a luxury or indulgence. It did not occur to even the most puritanical to condemn people for drinking it—tea, rather than beer, was seen as the insidious and corrupting drink.

parish were given twelve pounds of cherries and six years later they got 2s 8d with which to enjoy themselves at the local fair. As long as labouring men and their wives and children showed themselves willing to take work when it came, and as long as the total cost of poor relief was not too great, the system worked quite well. In Sheffield in 1721 poor relief cost £70 9s 1d, which represented only about a shilling a year each from the 1,320 people who were assessed. It was only in the late eighteenth century, when poor rates started to soar (they increased by five times between 1785 and 1817), that overseers became harsh and niggardly.

The poor were certainly better off in England than in most other countries. They lived at subsistence level but they rarely starved as peasants abroad sometimes did. Their diet, though very far from being 'the roast beef of old England' was better than it was on the Continent—foreign visitors complained that it was impossible to get decent soup in England because the servants refused to eat the remainder of the meat after it had had its goodness extracted. Apart from the poll tax levied between 1690 and 1698 there was no direct taxation of the poor (partly because it was feared that it might put up the cost of labour) whereas in France the peasantry bore the largest share of the tax burden. Nor were they entirely without rights: they were entitled to graze their beasts on the village commons and Acts of Parliament authorizing the enclosure of these commons usually required that land should be set aside to provide for the poor. Defoe remarked that the poor regarded the rights of commonage 'to be as much their property as a rich man's land is his own'.

The men of substance in the village, who paid its rates and ran its affairs, included the parson, the miller, the inkeeper and perhaps a few craftsmen and tradesmen, but principally they were farmers, either freeholders or tenants. Gregory King reckoned their number at 1,730,000 and their total income at £16,960,000 a year—nearly half of the whole national income. In the midlands, the eastern counties and parts of the south, they carried on communal arable farming on the old open field system and a man could ride for miles without seeing a hedge. The enormous village fields were divided into strips, some rented out to tenants and others farmed by their owners, but all cultivated according to a common agreed pattern. As soon as the harvest was in, the village cattle were turned out to graze on the stubble, so that any enterprising farmer who had sown any of the new grasses which were coming in from the Continent, such as St Foin or 'Holy Hay', instead of the standard agreed arable crop, would find his neighbours' beasts eating it up. In Suffolk a new type of farming based on the growing of turnips as cattle fodder had been practised since the 1640s, but the open field system militated against this also. As well as making it difficult for arable farming to help cattle farming, the system worked the other way round: the systematic folding of sheep, so that their dung could enrich the land, was only coming in very gradually. Defoe, who was one of its great advocates, was delighted to find it in use in the 1720s on the Wiltshire Downs, where the arable farmers paid ten shillings a night per thousand sheep. Whether it was a question of getting the most out of the land or putting the most into it, there had to be fences and hedges. One of the most influential manuals of farming was John Mortimer's *The Whole Art of Husbandry; or The Way of Managing and Improving of Land*, published in 1707; and it started with a detailed description of fences, ditches, walls and hedges and the means of constructing them. 'Enclosure' and 'improvement' seemed almost synonymous.

In the north and west and in Kent enclosure had already made some progress, but in different ways and for different reasons. In some areas great sheep farmers had bought out their neighbours and refused to renew tenants' leases, so as to build up huge grazing grounds for their flocks, while in others hop fields, fruit orchards and small farms, sometimes run on the new 'improved' methods, had been carved out of the village fields by enterprising farmers or by the squire himself. But even where the open field system had gone altogether, the communal nature of village life remained. Whatever the pattern of their landholding and cultivation might be, most villages were self-contained and almost self-sufficient units. Travel was difficult and expensive, so that few villagers had ever been farther than the nearest market town. Their only effective contact with the big world outside was through the local lord of the manor, who stood at the head of village society and was its acknowledged spokesman in county and national affairs.

Some villages had a nobleman as lord of the manor and might find themselves ruled by his agent or bailiff, but for most of them the squire was either a knight or a gentleman and took a personal interest in their affairs. The word 'gentleman' was already changing its meaning and in 1710 Steele wrote that 'the Appellation of Gentleman is never to be affixed to a Man's Circumstances, but to his behaviour in them'. But to most people it was still a description of status rather than of behaviour. It meant a man who had a coat of arms recognized by the College of Heralds and an estate large enough to enable him to live at leisure on its profits without actually having to cultivate it himself. Tradesmen could and did become gentlemen, and Defoe listed an iron merchant and a wholesale grocer among the country squires of Essex in 1723, although he was rather shocked to find the landlord of a Doncaster inn 'living like a gentleman' and even keeping a pack of hounds. By an Act of 1671 the killing of game was restricted to gentlemen owning land to the value of £100 a year or leasing it to the value of £150. Stockbrokers, attorneys, surgeons 'or other inferior persons' might help as beaters, but they were not allowed to take part in the killing. The Act specifically mentioned hares and thus covered hunting as well as shooting— it was only in the 1750s, when Mr Meynell of Quorndon Hall started to breed faster hounds, that fox-hunting became popular. Hunting and shooting, and the leisure in which to enjoy them, were among the most important distinguishing marks of the gentry. Foreign visitors found that the life of the English country house centred on these pursuits. After a very informal breakfast their hosts would disappear to the hunting field and would not be seen again until dinner, which was served at three or four o'clock in the afternoon. They would then satisfy the considerable hunger and thirst they had acquired in the field: the meal would be long and stately and one traveller said that an English dinner was like eternity—it had no beginning and no end.

There was in fact an end, but it was often lost to sight in the haze of drinking that followed the meal, after the ladies had left the table. Although many gentlemen still drank beer, wine was becoming more and more usual and the choice of it came soon to be a political gesture. The Tories, who were opposed to the war against France, drank French claret while the Whigs drank port, which came into the country at a lower rate of duty as a result of our alliance with Portugal against France in 1703. Since port was not at this time fortified with brandy, the Whig drink was no stronger than that of their rivals. As for the food, it was plentiful and fairly varied: fish, meat, game of all kinds, tarts and pies and cheese. Near the sea fish could be bought cheaply—mackerel were sold for as little as a hundred a penny, lobsters at 6d or 8d each—but inland it was much more expensive and seldom fresh. River fish such as tench, pike, perch and eels were highly prized and salmon could be bought for about 1½d a pound in the areas where it was caught. But once again there was the problem of transport: experiments were made in Norfolk with waggons constructed to carry fish alive to London in great butts of water, but they were not successful. Until the improved feeding methods became widespread, which was not until the end of the eighteenth century, cattle had to be killed off in the autumn so that the only meat available in the winter was salted. It was perhaps the shortage of really fresh meat and fish that led the very rich to import French cooks to dress their dishes—by the 1730s the Duke of Bedford was paying his French cook the enormous wage of £60 a year, twice what he gave his English cook. A great deal of game and wildfowl was eaten, including such birds as ruffs, reeves, cygnets and wheatears. These last were described as 'the English ortolans, the most delicious taste that can be imagined'. Finally, although there was a considerable difference between the diet of the gentry and that of the poor, they had one thing in common—an almost complete lack of vegetables. As a result rich and poor alike suffered constantly from scurvy.

The squires were by no means mere bucolic sots, for all their interest in hunting, shooting, eating and drinking. When young they had had some learning beaten into them by a tutor or at the local grammar school (Westminster and Eton were beginning to be fashionable, but the other public schools were not popular among the landed classes) and it had not all evaporated in drinking bouts at Oxford or Cambridge. For generations fathers had insisted on their sons having a thorough grounding in law, so that they should be equipped to hold on to and manage the estate; and their increasing reliance on mortgages to tide them over difficult periods forced them to be efficient men of affairs. Profitable marriages had to be arranged for their sons and daughters and younger sons had to be found places or professions, now that estates were normally settled on the eldest son to keep them intact from generation to generation. All this meant moving in the fashionable world, making contacts, seeking patronage. The Cornish gentry were famous for their refusal to do this: they resisted the influence of the great patrons and they married among themselves, so that it was said that 'all the Cornish gentlemen are cousins'. But most country gentlemen were men of the world. They moved in it with ease and with assurance, for they regarded themselves and were regarded by others as the outward and visible symbols not only of a million and a half farmers, with the labourers who were dependent on them, but of the land itself.

2 Commerce and industry

There was no clear-cut distinction between the landed interest and the monied interest, between agriculture and industry, between the country and the towns. As long ago as 1632 Sir John Oglander had written: 'It is impossible for a mere country gentleman ever to grow rich or raise his house. He must have some other vocation with his inheritance, as to be a courtier, lawyer, merchant or some other vocation. If he hath no other vocation, let him get a ship and judiciously manage her . . .' Few country gentlemen were in the position to manage ships and it was in any case a risky business—Mrs Elizabeth Howland, the mother-in-law of the Duke of Bedford, made £400 profit on the £2,000 she put into the East India Company's ship the *Tavistock* in 1700, but on the other hand she had to write off as a dead loss the £1,250 she had put into another ship which was captured by the French. But they could and did invest in trading and industrial enterprises, as well as buttressing their family fortunes with the proceeds of political patronage. Sir Thomas Lyttelton, lord of the manor of Halesowen in Worcestershire, was the chief partner in an iron furnace which brought in at least 10 per cent on his money even in bad years and as much as 20 per cent in the profitable war years of the 1740s. Landed families no longer apprenticed their sons to a craft —earlier in the seventeenth century Yorkshire families like the Foljambes and the Wortleys had bound their younger sons to Sheffield cutlers—but they were prepared to send them into trade, as long as it was wholesale or overseas trade. And for every family that participated directly in trade or industry there were a good many more that did so indirectly by holding stock in the great trading companies. Rates of interest were limited by law to 6 per cent (5 per cent after 1714) but even this was a better return than most gentlemen could look for on the money they had sunk in land. Rents of more than 5 per cent of the market value of the land were unusual and the general level was nearer 3½ per cent. Squires who were in the position to farm their own land by the new methods might make it yield good returns, but those who had let it out on long leases and had to rely on their rent rolls found that trade and industry offered them tempting prospects.

Many farmers and country labourers were concerned with other things than agriculture. In the country around Newcastle they dug coal out of holes in the ground, letting men down on ropes, and by

1770 it was said that in parts of Cheshire only one farmer in ten got his living solely from agriculture. Many industries, such as the iron-smelting of the Forest of Dean and the tin and copper mining of Cornwall, were rural rather than urban. One firm of ironmasters supplying the Birmingham market at the beginning of the eighteenth century had furnaces scattered all over the midlands and as far afield as Bodfari in North Wales and Tredegar in South Wales. Riding in the remote Peak district of Derbyshire, Defoe was surprised to see a man, lean and pallid and clothed entirely in leather, wriggling out of a hole just wide enough to take him and his load of a hundredweight of ore. It was a lead miner. The hole was over 300 feet deep and it had to be kept narrow so that he could climb up and down without ladders or ropes, by wedging his body in it. Living in a cave nearby were his wife and five children, with a few pigs and a lean cow grazing outside. He earned 5d a day and his wife was sometimes able to make a further 3d a day washing the ore. They were not agricultural labourers, but their life was very far from urban.

Even those tradesmen and manufacturers who did live in towns were often dependent on the country around. Defoe said of Bury St Edmunds: 'Here is no manufacturing in this town, or but very little, except spinning; the chief trade of the place depending upon the gentry who live there, or near it, and who cannot fail to cause trade enough by the expense of their families and equippages among the people of a country town.' As well as supplying the needs of the countrymen they provided a centre for the sale of their produce, by virtue of their ancient privileges and chartered rights of holding markets and fairs. Occasionally the country gentry even took it upon themselves to invade these rights and regulate the fairs: in 1771 the justices of Surrey told Mrs Phipps that if she set up her roundabout at Mitcham Fair she would do so 'at her peril'. But they were forced to recognize that they were exceeding the limits of their jurisdiction and the prohibition was quietly dropped. Most market towns preserved good relations with the surrounding countryside and their friendly aspect contrasted strongly with that of towns on the Continent, where strong walls frowned down on the countryman and town officials exacted tolls on all his goods. Englishmen had come to take for granted their freedom from internal customs barriers and also the security which enabled them to let their town walls fall into ruin. But foreign travellers marvelled at these things and realized how much they did to stimulate trade.

Less of a stimulus was the state of the roads, which were among the worst in Europe. Things were particularly bad where there was clay, as in large areas of the midlands and in Sussex. The roads around Lewes were so bad that the judges were often unable to get through in the winter and the assizes had to be held at Horsham or Guildford. One lady of high estate in Sussex had to be dragged to the local church by a team of oxen; and even around London geese could not be driven along the roads later than October without sinking in the mud. In 1663 the first turnpike trust had been set up by Act of Parliament and by 1688 there were several of them, each maintaining a stretch of road and collecting tolls in return. They were regarded with suspicion and became a target for rioting in times of high prices, but in many cases they produced an overall reduction in transport costs, sometimes as much as sixpence or a shilling per hundredweight. However, it was a slow and piecemeal business: it took a hundred years for the Great North Road to be fully turnpiked. The period since the Civil Wars had also seen other improvements in communications. A Post Office had been set up and regular stage coach services had been started, although their timetables reflected only too clearly the conditions of the roads they had to use. It took a fortnight to get from London to Exeter. Most important of all, the systematic construction of weirs and locks had made many important rivers navigable for the greater part of their length. By using the Don, the Trent, the Ouse, the Thames, the Severn, the Mersey or their tributaries it was possible to send goods to the coast from almost any part of England.

The inadequacy of inland communications underlined the importance of the sea. Gregory King estimated that the sea 'constantly employing about 40,000, precipitates the Death of about 2,500 per annum'. Certainly seafaring was a very dangerous occupation. In one storm off Yarmouth in the 1690s two whole fleets of colliers, 200 vessels in all, were wrecked; and in the great storms of 1703 sixteen warships were lost, some of them while they were in harbour, as well as a great deal of merchant shipping. Some of those who went to sea were fishermen, but transport difficulties hampered trade in fresh fish and it only became a really important commodity when it could be preserved: by the early eighteenth century Yarmouth was curing up to 40,000,000 herrings a year. The majority of seamen were engaged either in overseas trade or in the coastwise traffic, as little ships plied from port to port up and down the coast with the goods that it was so much more expensive to send by land. Most of London's coal supply came by sea, either from Newcastle or from Swansea, and of the seven largest towns in the kingdom five were ports—London, Bristol, Newcastle, Liverpool and Hull.

Although it was one of the world's greatest shipbuilding centres and also excelled in clock-making, glass-blowing and other skilled crafts, London was above all a trading centre and an entrepot of world importance. By the end of the seventeenth century the country was importing goods to the value of over £3,000,000 and exporting or re-exporting a similar amount; and the greater part of this trade went through the port of London. As well as providing unrivalled facilities for the ships themselves—between Southwark and Blackwall there were over twenty docks and more than thirty repair yards—London also offered other services essential for trade. Mr Edward Lloyd's coffee house was already being frequented in 1688 by men interested in underwriting ships and their cargoes, and by the time he died in 1713 it was the recognized centre of marine insurance. London financiers accepted and discounted bills of exchange[1] as well as providing straightforward credit facilities. Countrymen might grumble about London being an all-consuming stomach, but it was also the heart that kept the country's circulation going and the brain that directed its business affairs.

Of the other ports, Bristol was by far the greatest, acting as a centre for the iron and coal and metal products of South Wales and the midlands, which came down the Severn or the rivers that drained into its estuary, as well as for the cloth industry of the west country and for much agricultural produce. It also had thriving china and glass industries of its own. Above all, it had the rich 'triangular' trade of the Atlantic: merchants sent their ships to the West African coast to buy slaves, sold these in the Caribbean and brought back tobacco, sugar and other American products. Liverpool, which was said to have doubled its population between 1690 and 1724, was also well placed for this trade and by the middle of the eighteenth century it handled as much American merchandise as Bristol, as well as possessing a slaving fleet of some fifty vessels. Newcastle was the greatest of the east coast ports, 'a spacious, extended, infinitely populous

[1] A bill of exchange was an order by a creditor to his debtor to pay the holder a certain sum by a certain date. To 'accept' a bill was to guarantee payment if the debtor defaulted and to 'discount' it was to buy it in for a reduced sum before it was due—i.e. if interest was 5 per cent a bill for £100 due for payment in a year's time would be discounted at £95.

place', which traded extensively with the Baltic and Northern Europe and also shipped the produce of the north (chiefly coal, but including such delicacies as smoked salmon) down the coast to London. Hull, too, had a thriving trade with Northern Europe, importing iron, copper, canvas, linen and yarn, and carried on trade with Spain and the West Indies by way of London.

Although most towns depended on trade in one form or another, there were some that were primarily manufacturing centres. Birmingham, famous since Tudor times for its metal wares, was the greatest of these. Strictly speaking it was not a town at all but a collection of villages; and its freedom from the control of guilds and corporations had played a significant part in its development. Metals of all kinds came there to be wrought: iron from Wales and the midlands, steel and zinc from abroad, copper and tin from Cornwall. It produced everyday things like nails and skewers and pots and pans as well as ingenious mechanisms and elaborately decorated snuff boxes. Sheffield was a much smaller town—about 2,000 inhabitants as compared with Birmingham's 10,000—with an equally well-established reputation for metal goods and especially for cutlery. Both towns were assured of a steady and expanding market, for even the poorest needed their wares—one poor widow in Bedfordshire who had been living on poor relief died possessed of 'one pair of hooks, one pair of tongs, one pair of bellows, one middling brass kettle, one small brass porrage pot, one little kettle, one brass skillet and two pewter dishes'—and they could not easily be made locally or at home, as wooden articles normally were. Sheffield cutlers were already installing mills to drive their grindstones and in one workshop on the Thames near Marlowe brass kettles and pans were made with the help of great hammers driven by water power; but for the most part work in the metal industries was done by hand and was therefore exhausting and dangerous. Towards the end of the eighteenth century, when iron and steel had come to be forged by power instead of by hand, people noticed that the number of maimed and deformed men in the Sheffield area was falling dramatically. However, there was good money to be made and a skilled man could earn 12s or more a week, although the ordinary labourer, like his counterpart in the trading towns, only made about 6s. Except for the higher cost of housing (even the meanest lodgings cost 2s or 2s 6d a week) and the fact that there was no free fuel to be had, the life of the poor was much the same in the town as in the country, although by the

1770s Arthur Young found that in the south and west 'manufacturers' were earning up to 5s a week more than 'labourers'.

It is significant that Young saw no need to specify what these 'manufacturers' were manufacturing. Everyone knew that he was speaking of the workers in the woollen cloth industry, which had been for centuries the most important of all the country's commercial and industrial activities. Its main centres were in Norfolk, the south-western counties and the West Riding of Yorkshire, but its influence and importance spread all over the country and it was second only to agriculture as a producer of wealth and a provider of employment. Wherever there was suitable pasture there were farmers ready to put sheep on it; wherever a poor man's wife needed to earn extra money or an overseer had to provide employment for a female pauper, spinning provided the most obvious answer; wherever a cottager had managed to put some money by, his thoughts might well turn to buying a loom and setting up as a weaver. And among all these people the woolmen and the clothiers moved, dealing in raw wool, combed wool, yarn and cloth, and making a profit at every stage. It was said that by the time the wool had completed its journey from the sheep's back to the cloth merchant's shelves it had increased its value ten times over, a fact which delighted the economists of the time, who measured the value of an occupation purely in terms of the difference between the cost of raw materials and the value of finished product. By the 1690s our woollen exports were worth £1,600,000 a year, four times as much as the coal, iron, steel, hardware, cotton, linen and silk goods exports, all put together. And almost everybody shared in this wealth, from the landlords whose rents were kept up by it to the merchants who shipped the cloth to the great fairs and markets of Europe. It was hardly surprising that Parliament was always ready to protect the wool trade, even to the extent of enacting in 1678 that everyone in the land should be buried in a woollen shroud. The wool trade towered over the world of commerce and industry and linked it firmly with the landed interest and with the countryside.

Weaving was largely an urban occupation, at any rate in the south. Norwich, centre of Norfolk cloth manufacturing, was the third largest city in the kingdom and Defoe reckoned that the Somerset cloth town of Frome was bigger than either Bath or York. But a certain amount of the weaving, as well as most of the combing and spinning, extended far into the countryside: the cloth trade of

Somerset, Wiltshire, Dorset and Gloucestershire was said to cover 780 parishes and employ 374,000 people. In the West Riding a great deal of the weaving was done by farmers who each employed a few men in a workshop attached to the farm; and this pattern of employer and employed was beginning to appear in the south as well, as merchant clothiers used their capital to buy out domestic weavers and group them together in workshops. But it was to be a long time before the workshops turned into factories. The 1690s saw a great deal of inventive ingenuity (sixty-four patents were sealed in three years from 1691 to 1693, a higher rate than at any time before the 1760s) but it was not as yet applied to the mechanization of the textile industries.

3 The Dissenters

Since few people were brave enough or misguided enough to reject Christianity altogether, the only people outside the Anglican fold were the Roman Catholics, usually called 'papists' or 'recusants', and the Protestant Dissenters. The former were a very small minority and it was not until the nineteenth century that they came to play any positive part in national life. In the eighteenth century they had only a negative importance, in that the hysterical fear and hatred which they aroused was a potent political force. The Dissenters on the other hand constituted one of the great formative influences of eighteenth-century England. In 1676 the bishops had put the number of Dissenters at 108,676, compared with 2,477,254 Anglicans; but they admitted that many of those whom they counted as Anglicans never took the sacraments (a possible indication of secret dissenting sympathies) and in any case their figures covered only freeholders. There must have been many members of dissenting congregations who were outside this category. By 1688 there were probably at least 200,000 people who had sympathies or connections with dissent and their numbers continued to grow. Between 1689 and 1709 there were nearly 1,000 chapels and meeting houses built and in 1710 a parliamentary committee reckoned that there were 101,500 Dissenters in the London area alone.

As well as French, Dutch and German Calvinist refugees, they included Presbyterians, Congregationalists, Baptists, Quakers, Unitarians and other minor sects. Their main quarrel with the Church was over authority, which they insisted must come upwards from the congregations and not downwards from the bishops. Above all, they condemned the control of the Church by the State. Even the Presbyterians, whose church was established by law in Scotland, saw church government as a means whereby the Church could influence the State and not the other way about; and they asserted firmly the right of congregations to reject ministers imposed on them from above. The Baptists, although sometimes accused of sharing the extremist views of the sixteenth-century Anabaptists, were really descended, like the Congregationalists, from the puritans of the earlier seventeenth century. George Fox, who had founded the Society of Friends and who was still alive in 1688, had called on them to 'tremble at the word of the Lord' and they had therefore been nicknamed Quakers. Their dress and way of speaking drew upon them a certain amount of ridicule, but they were respected for the strict honesty of their business dealings. Their refusal to take oaths sometimes led them to be prosecuted for contempt of court, until in 1696 an Act was passed allowing them to make instead a 'solemn affirmation or declaration'. This concession was extended and confirmed by further Acts in 1722 and 1749. Unitarianism had few avowed supporters, since it had been excluded from the toleration offered by the Bill of Indulgence; but if it was inconsiderable as a sect it was enormously influential as an idea. Its belief in the essential goodness of man and its hostility to the doctrines of original sin and eternal punishment did much to soften the harshness of seventeenth-century puritanism. Under its influence Dissenters came to think more of man's potentialities and less of man's sin, to concern themselves with hopes for this world rather than with fears of the next.

The puritans of the 1640s and 1650s had included such revolutionary groups as the Levellers and the Diggers, but the Dissenters of 1688 had little enthusiasm for the militant radicalism of the past. A few still thundered against the landowners—Richard Baxter, author of *The Poor Husbandman's Advocate to Rich Racking Landlords*, did not die until 1691—but most were beginning to prosper in business or in industry and did not want to overthrow society, even though they might disapprove of those who were running it. However, the Anglicans, and especially the High Church Tories, had long memories. 'The heads and preachers of the several factions', said the bishops in 1676, 'are such as had a great share in the late rebellion.' Even by the beginning of the eighteenth century there were many who believed or pretended to believe that dissent stood for social revolution.

William III, as the ruler of Dutch Calvinists as well as Anglicans, was concerned to defend protestantism in its widest sense and it was not until the accession of Anne that the Tories had a chance to attack the Dissenters. In 1702 they brought in an Occasional Conformity Bill, providing that anyone who attended a Dissenters' meeting house after he had once taken Anglican sacraments and qualified for public office should be fined and dismissed from his office. In spite of strong support from the Queen the Bill was thrown out by the Lords. After further defeats in 1703 and 1704 it was finally passed in 1711, but it seems to have had little effect. Dissenters wishing to take offices or places on corporations still made their token communion in an Anglican church and then continued their own forms of worship in private. The Schism Act, passed in 1714, was a more serious blow since it attacked their right to teach: nobody could keep a school or act as a tutor unless he made a declaration agreeing to conform to the liturgy of the Church of England. But even here there were loopholes, since the Act did not extend to those who only taught reading, writing, mathematics, navigation or mechanics and who carried on their teaching in English. The assumption was that real learning, the sort that needed to be guarded from the sinister influence of the Dissenters, was based upon Latin; but by pushing them towards more practical subjects and towards the use of English in their teaching the Act probably did them more good than harm. Nevertheless, they saw Anne's sympathy with the Tories as a real menace. When the minister of Fetter Lane Chapel got the news of the Queen's death he interrupted his service to announce: 'My friends, I have to call upon you to thank God for a Great Deliverance. The Queen is dead. Long live King George.'

King George, like King William, was a Protestant before he was an Anglican; and as soon as he came to the throne he promised to take the protestant Dissenters under his special protection. In 1719 the Occasional Conformity and Schism Acts were repealed and from 1723 a half-yearly grant was made from the royal purse to the widows of poor dissenting ministers. By the end of his reign the Presbyterians, Congregationalists and Baptists had formed an association for joint political action, and from 1732 a committee of 'Dissenting Deputies' sat regularly to protect and advance the interests of dissent. When local authorities refused to licence a meeting house or tried to prosecute or victimize a Dissenter, the Deputies took up the case and usually won it. In 1767 they got a very important decision from the House of Lords in the case of the dissenting sheriffs of the City of London. Having passed a by-law in 1748 saying that anyone who refused nomination as sheriff would be heavily fined, the City nominated conscientious Dissenters to the office in order to fine them. This ingenious and iniquitous device, by which the City made over £15,000, was declared illegal by the decision of 1767. The eighteenth-century Dissenters had to put up with infuriating restrictions and a great deal of stupid prejudice, but they can hardly be said to have been persecuted.

This ambiguous position halfway between acceptance and rejection meant that their energies were turned into certain specific and limited channels. Since it was impossible for them to make their way in the law, in politics, in the armed services, in the corporations of great cities or as landed gentlemen, they tended to congregate in the new and expanding towns of the north and midlands, where corporations were weak or non-existent, or in those parts of London where the City itself could not check them. Both Manchester and Birmingham had been puritan in the Civil War and the Dissenters continued to dominate both towns. Cross Street Chapel in Manchester numbered among its congregation great merchant families like the Hibberts, the Touchets and the Bayleys; and later in the century the Octagon Chapel in Liverpool came to have the same sort of wealth and influence. John Wilkinson, father of the Staffordshire iron industry, and Jedediah Strutt, the greatest of the Derbyshire cotton magnates, were both Dissenters. They were strong in Birmingham and the Lunar Society founded there in the 1760s brought together the speculative science of the dissenting academies and the practical experience of men like Matthew Boulton and Josiah Wedgwood who were applying it to the engineering and pottery industries. As if to provide a symbol of this union, Joseph Priestley the dissenting teacher and scientist married the daughter of ironmaster John Wilkinson. The great landed families might dominate the politics of the present, but the industrial dynasties built up by the Dissenters were to forge the economic and political life of the future.

The dissenting academies, about seventy of which can be traced in the period between 1688 and 1815, were not just concerned with the training of dissenting ministers. About half of them were open to ordinary pupils as well and they taught practical subjects like mathematics and mechanics as well as the classics. The traditional education of a gentleman at a grammar school and at Oxford or Cambridge might fit him to ruminate on the past and observe the present, but the dissenting academies and the Scottish universities equipped a man to build the future. Some of the academies might be said to represent the puritan tradition of the past (Richard Frankland, who had been offered a post in Cromwell's projected University of Durham in 1657, lived to found an academy at Rathmell which eventually became Manchester College), but they were nevertheless broad-minded and forward-looking, respected even by the Anglican establishment. Both the Tory leaders of Anne's reign, Harley and St John, were at dissenting academies, as were Archbishop Secker of Canterbury, Bishop Butler of Durham and Lord Hardwicke, one of the greatest Whig statesmen of the eighteenth century. At a time when there was still no proper degree examination at Oxford or Cambridge, the Dissenters educated their own children and other people's efficiently and intelligently, turning them out not as puritanical radicals but as potential reformers.

4 Scotland, Ireland and the Plantations

For centuries Scotsmen had seen the English as tyrannical aggressors while Englishmen had dismissed the Scots as barbaric cattle thieves. In 1603, when King James VI of Scotland became King James I of England and tried to bring about the union of his two kingdoms, his plans met with such violent opposition that they had to be dropped; and the political and religious upheavals of the seventeenth century had complicated the tensions between the kingdoms without lessening them. The Scottish Convention which met in Edinburgh in March 1689 and in the following month offered the Crown of Scotland to William and Mary was not making a gesture of solidarity with England, but merely registering the triumph of one party in Scotland over the other. By the autumn, after a brief civil war between the parties, William could call himself King of Scotland as well as King of England; but he was far from being the ruler of a United Kingdom of Great Britain.

The main divisions within Scotland were between Presbyterians and Episcopalians and between Lowlanders and Highlanders. The Episcopalian Church, restored in Scotland in 1661, had never really taken roots and its adherents, hovering unhappily between diluted Presbyterianism and an unconvincing Scottish brand of Anglicanism, were unable to offer any effective opposition to the re-establishment

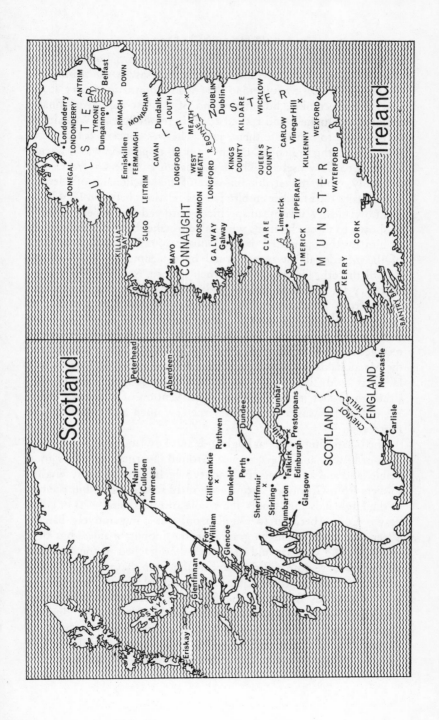

of the Presbyterian Kirk in 1689. The Highland clans, however, were determined to resist a revolution which they saw as the triumph of the Lowlands. On 27 July 1689 they won a dramatic victory at the pass of Killiecrankie, but at the end of August they were finally defeated at Dunkeld and retired to their remote glens. William III was anxious to conciliate them, just as he was concerned to extend toleration to the Episcopalians; but in both respects he was thwarted by the Scots themselves. The Episcopalian ministers were ejected ruthlessly, while the terrible massacre of the Macdonalds of Glencoe in February 1692 further embittered the relations between Highlands and Lowlands. William had specifically ordered that leniency should be shown to those chieftains who failed to take the oath of allegiance to him by the appointed day, 1 January 1692; but when the chief of the Macdonalds was prevented by a technicality from taking it until the 6th, his enemies saw their chance. Sir John Dalrymple, Secretary for Scotland and an old enemy of the Highland clans, wrote from London rejoicing that they would now be able to 'extirpate that set of thieves'; and Campbell of Glenlyon, who went to Glencoe with 100 men at the beginning of February, received a letter on the 13th ordering him to 'fall upon the rebels, the Macdonalds of Glencoe, and put all to the sword under seventy'. He was told that this was 'by the King's special command', although in fact it was in direct contravention of William's order. He did as he was told and forty men, women and children were murdered.

The bad feeling between Highlands and Lowlands was the product both of history and of geography. Around Inverness there was good arable land and a farming community which included many English soldiers from Cromwell's armies who had settled there; but the rest of the Highlands and Islands, the whole area north and west of a line drawn from Aberdeen to Dumbarton, was comparatively barren. Sheep and cattle could be grazed on the mountain sides, but they never became very fat and the prices they fetched in the Lowland markets were seldom sufficient to buy the grain that the Highlanders lacked. Venison and other game was plentiful, as was fish, but the great coniferous forests of the far north were still virtually undeveloped and the Lowlands imported their timber from Scandinavia. Unable to get what they needed from the Lowlands by trading, the Highlanders had been used to taking it by force. The almost impassable mountains which separated their glens one from another had helped to perpetuate the old tribal pattern of society, so that each clan owed complete allegiance to its chief and was equally effective as a war band or as a raiding party.

The great majority of Scotland's million or so inhabitants lived in the Lowlands, the funnel-shaped area with its mouth facing out to the North Sea and its sides resting against the Highlands to the north and the Cheviots to the south. Here there were no clans, but the feudal powers of the nobility were still very extensive and most of the arable farming was done by peasants on the old open field system. Agricultural improvement came slowly in Scotland, even though the landlords were able to ride rough-shod over their tenants' rights and enclose the land without parliamentary authority. Industries included mining, distilling, sugar-refining and cloth-making, but these were all on a relatively small scale and the iron and coal deposits of the area were almost completely unworked except in the immediate neighbourhood of Edinburgh. In the eighteenth century the manufacture of linen cloth was developed extensively and by the 1750s it was Scotland's most valuable export. Glasgow was already beginning to carry on an illicit trade with the English colonies and plantations in America, for which it was very well placed—it was said that the Glasgow ships could 'be at the capes of Virginia before the London ships get clear of the Channel'—and in 1695 an attempt was made to extend Scotland's share in colonial trade. An Act was passed in the Scottish Parliament setting up a company to trade in Asia, Africa and America, with a capital of £600,000, half of it provided by English merchants anxious to contest the monopoly of the East India Company and the Royal Africa Company. Powerful lobbying at Westminster by those whose interests were threatened produced an outcry in England against the company, so that the English capital was withdrawn. The Scottish directors managed to raise £400,000, although not more than half of it seems to have been paid up, and in July 1698 an expedition of five ships sailed from Leith to establish a settlement at Darien, on the Panama Isthmus. Partly because of the pressure from English commercial interests and partly because of the need to avoid war with Spain, whose sphere of influence the company was invading, William III refused it all support and even forbade the British West Indian colonists to send it supplies. Ravaged by disease, harassed by Spanish attacks and unsuccessful in its commerce (it had brought cargoes of periwigs and Bibles and the natives, not unnaturally, were reluctant to buy these) the venture finally collapsed in 1700, having cost about £200,000 and 2,000 lives.

The failure of the Darien Company produced a ferocious outburst of anti-English feeling in Scotland and it also confirmed the English in their contemptuous attitude to the Scots, whom they regarded as a primitive and backward people incapable of grasping the mysteries of commerce and finance. But behind all the hysteria and prejudice there remained one inescapable conclusion to be drawn from the affairs: a country of a million people with hardly any naval, commercial or financial resources could not hope to enter the fiercely competitive field of overseas trade unless it did so under the aegis of a country already established in that field. However detestable the English might be, union with them was the only feasible way for Scotland to obtain a position in world trade. The English, for their part, feared that such a union would condemn the prosperity of England to carry and subsidize the poverty of Scotland. It was only when the separation of the kingdoms came to threaten the security of both that they began to move towards the union of 1707.

Considerations of security were even more important in our relations with Ireland. For more than a hundred years Englishmen had feared the establishment of a Catholic Ireland under the control of either Spain or France and they had sought to safeguard themselves against this threat by settling more and more Protestant English landowners in Ireland. From the time of Queen Elizabeth to that of Lord Protector Cromwell, Irish land had been used as a cheap way of rewarding favourites, paying off soldiers or satisfying creditors; and as each grant of land meant the dispossession of the present owner, there were many more people with claims to land in Ireland than there was land to satisfy them. Some of the dispossessed were Irishmen, dreaming of throwing off the English yoke altogether, but the majority were the Catholic Anglo-Irish who had been invading the country, settling there and marrying there, ever since the twelfth century. They were not opposed to the existing constitutional position (whereby the kingdom of Ireland had its own Parliament, but could be bound by the Acts of the English Parliament and was subject to the English Privy Council), but merely wished that it should be manipulated in their own interests. They had been disappointed in 1660, when Charles II had failed to oust the Cromwellian settlers, and they were determined not to be disappointed again in 1689.

Whereas Presbyterian Scots in 1689 could only rid themselves of the English-supported Episcopalian minority by accepting King William, Catholics in Ireland could only get rid of the English-supported Protestant minority by supporting King James. When he landed in Ireland on 12 March 1689 with a French force of 8,000 men the Catholics rallied to him, while some of the more militant Protestants retired to the towns of Londonderry and Enniskillen in the north. In May William sent over a small force under Colonel Kirke to save Londonderry, which had been besieged since 19 April. Kirke spent several weeks doing nothing, but he at last managed to relieve Londonderry on 30 July, while one of his officers organized the Protestants in Enniskillen into an efficient force which defeated a Catholic detachment at Newton Butler on the same day. By August, the end of the campaigning season, William had managed to scrape together an army of 10,000, mostly untrained and untried men, which he sent to Ireland under the Huguenot General Schomberg. Heavy rain made movement difficult and Schomberg, who had been joined by 4,000 Irish Protestant volunteers, settled down at Dundalk. With no proper clothing and no proper shelter his men died quickly in the cold and the wet; and as they died the survivors piled up their bodies to keep out the wind. By the time Schomberg retreated to Belfast in November he had about 7,000 men left. It was not until 1690, when William went over himself with an army of 35,000, that James's hold on Ireland was broken. After his army had been defeated by William at the battle of the Boyne on 1 July 1690 he fled back to France, and by the end of the year his supporters only held the western areas around Limerick and Galway. William returned to England in September 1690 and it was the Dutch General Ginkel who took the last Catholic stronghold of Limerick in October 1691. The Treaty of Limerick, signed later that month, ended the Irish war.

It did not end Irish grievances. As far as it went, it was a generous treaty: it promised the Irish Catholics all the privileges they had enjoyed under Charles II and it allowed Irish soldiers to take service with the French. It served very well its main purpose of demonstrating to the world, and especially to William's Catholic allies, his moderation and his desire to conciliate the Irish. But it was rendered almost valueless by Ireland's legislative dependence on England. In 1691 the English Parliament passed an Act barring Catholics from sitting in either House of the Irish Parliament,[1] so that the Parliament which met at Dublin in 1692 was dominated by the Protestants. During the next five years both Parliaments passed a series of Acts against the Catholics which made nonsense of the Treaty; and by 1697, when it was at last confirmed by the English Parliament, the Irish Catholics had been shorn of all the privileges it had promised them. They were excluded from all offices and from the learned professions, they were forbidden to carry arms and their right to purchase or manage land was severely curtailed. The established Church in Ireland, headed by archbishops and bishops and deans who had revenues running into hundreds of thousands of pounds a year, was a rootless and synthetic structure modelled on Anglican lines, ministering to little more than a tenth of the population. Probably about 500,000 of Ireland's 2,000,000 inhabitants were Protestant, but most of them were not Anglicans but Presbyterians; and many Anglican bishops were even more hostile to them than they were to Catholics. Some bishops tried to insist that Presbyterian marriages were invalid, so that Anglican gratitude to the men of Londonderry (all of whose children had died in the siege) took the form of declaring their subsequent children illegitimate.

The economic grievances of Ireland also sprang from her dependence on the English Parliament, which in 1660 had initiated a series of anti-Irish measures with one putting heavy duties on the import of Irish woollens into England. Further Acts followed preventing the Irish from exporting sheep, cattle, butter, cheese or meat; and in 1699 the series culminated in an Act forbidding them to export woollen goods or goods made partly from wool to foreign countries or to the English plantations overseas. As well as protecting their home markets from the competition of Irish agriculture, the English were determined to protect their foreign markets from the competition of Irish industry. The ports of southern Ireland sold butter and cheese and meat to ships victualling for the Atlantic crossing, while from the east coast linen, hides, timber and other commodities were sent to England in small quantities—just enough to pay for the English goods that were imported. But for the most part Irish agriculture and Irish industry languished for lack of markets. Protection for the English

[1] The Irish House of Lords numbered twenty-eight Catholic peers and seventy-two Protestant peers. The former were barred in 1691 and the attendance of the latter was so poor that they were often outnumbered by the bishops. The House of Commons was made up of sixty-four knights for the thirty-two counties and 234 burgesses for the boroughs and for Trinity College, Dublin.

meant stagnation for the Irish. Potentially, the country was very fertile and earlier in the seventeenth century travellers had been amazed by the copious supplies of cheap provisions. But now agriculture decayed and the peasantry with it. Absentee English landlords took money out of their estates but had very little inclination or incentive to put any back in. In the absence of any profitable outlet for the produce of the land there was little prospect of profits going up, and rents could only be collected by dint of constant bullying by unscrupulous middlemen. The very cheapness of food in normal years made it hard for tenants to produce enough to pay their rent, and few of them could afford to consume the best of what they produced: the pig was 'the gentleman who paid the rent' and he was seldom eaten by his owners. They lived on oatmeal, sour milk and a few vegetables—by the middle of the eighteenth century the potato had become their staple food—and in bad years they starved or emigrated to the plantations. Archbishop Boulter of Armagh reckoned that during the famine years from 1726 to 1729 thousands of peasants had died of starvation and thousands more had gone to the West Indies. In order to pay the cost of their transportation, they had to submit to a period of indentured servitude which was little better than slavery. In England, though paupers and convicts were transported and people were kidnapped in order to be shipped off, hardly anyone went willingly. It is significant that peasants in Ireland, and also to a lesser extent in Scotland, were prepared to do voluntarily what even the poorest in England would only do under compulsion.

Though the plantations were regarded with horror by the poor in England, they were a source of considerable satisfaction to the rich and especially to the rich merchants. During the last two hundred years Europe had vastly extended her trade with the world around her and there was a great deal of money to be made by bringing the world's produce to Europe. The object of plantations, trading stations and other settlements was to cultivate or collect this produce, so that it could be brought home in English ships. Some of it would be consumed in England, but the rest would either be re-exported or used as the raw material for manufactured goods which would be exported in their turn. In this way a network of overseas possessions enabled England to supply her own needs, maintain a powerful and lucrative shipping fleet, obtain raw materials for her industries on favourable terms and sell on equally favourable terms to those

European countries that lacked overseas possessions of their own.

The East India Company, which had once operated trading stations from the Persian Gulf to New Guinea, now relied mainly on its settlements along the India coast at Surat, Bombay and Madras, which collected coffee from Arabia, silk from Persia, cotton, indigo and saltpetre from India itself, tea from China and spices from the East Indies. In Africa there were the Royal Africa Company's forts in Gambia and the Gold Coast, where gold, ivory and dyestuffs were brought for shipment to England, but the climate made it very difficult to maintain and staff them. The slave trade, carried on by hit-and-run raiders rather than by settlers, was the more profitable side of the Company's business.

In America the settlements were more populous, although the total number of Englishmen living in the whole of that continent was still less than half the number living in London. Some of them were visitors rather than settlers, like the fishermen who spent a couple of months each year in hutments along the Newfoundland coast or the traders and trappers of the Hudson's Bay Company who collected furs in the north of Canada. Further south, the plantations of Maryland and Virginia yielded valuable crops of tobacco, while the newly arrived settlers in the Carolinas had failed in their attempts to cultivate vines, silkworms and indigo, and were turning instead to rice and tobacco. Cotton was not yet an important crop, though a little was grown in the Caribbean Islands, which also produced essential dyestuffs for the textile industries in England. The planting of sugar had been started in Barbados around 1640 and had spread to Jamaica and the rest of the Caribbean possessions, although Bermuda was still largely concerned with tobacco. Beyond the Panama Isthmus the Pacific or South Sea lay virtually unexplored and unexploited. William Dampier's *New Voyage Round the World*, published in 1697, stimulated interest in it, but the South Sea Company founded in 1711 never got as far as sending a single ship into the South Sea.

Strung out along the American seaboard from the coasts of Maine to the Delaware estuary was another and very different group of settlements which the merchants in London viewed with far less satisfaction. The New England colonies of Massachusetts, Connecticut, Rhode Island and New Hampshire were dominated by the harshly puritanical church-state of Massachusetts, where the elders ruled society with a narrowness and a self-righteousness long since outgrown by the English Dissenters. New York and New Jersey,

THE COUNTRY

conquered from the Dutch, and Pennsylvania and Delaware, founded by the Quaker William Penn, were much more cosmopolitan and much more tolerant. But all these colonies were independent in their attitude to the home government as well as in their religion, and in 1691, when William III restored the Massachusetts charter annulled by James II, he insisted that the governor of the colony should in future be appointed by him and not elected locally as before. Whereas other settlements were outposts of English trade, the New England group and their neighbours to the south represented attempts to create new societies. Whether the Pilgrim Fathers left England because English society would not tolerate them or because they would not tolerate English society is an open question, but they certainly did not leave in order to act as the agents of some London merchant and grow or buy the exotic commodities in which he wished to trade. The climate of the regions in which they settled was similar to that of England and as they increased and multiplied their economies came to duplicate, rather than complement, that of the home country. Instead of providing England with things she could not produce herself they grew and made precisely the things that were made and grown at home.

The establishment of a Board of Trade and Plantations in 1696 indicated the determination of both King and Parliament to rule all the overseas possessions from England and in the interests of England. Already it was feared that their woollen industries might compete with that of England and the Act of 1699 forbidding the export of woollens from Ireland also applied to the colonies and plantations. At one time the London merchants thought that the New England colonies might make themselves useful by producing timber and lessening England's dependence on the Baltic countries for her shipbuilding needs. They did produce timber, but they proceeded to use it to build ships of their own which competed with English ships. Altogether the New England colonies and the Central colonies were unwelcome growths in the carefully planted pattern of English commerce. The most that could be hoped was that their large and growing populations would provide useful markets for English goods. The Acts forbidding them to export were therefore accompanied by others forbidding them to import from foreign countries. If they would not supply England's needs they could at least consume her surplus. Even so, their usefulness to England and England's usefulness to them were to become increasingly open to question.

81

4

The Revolution defended
1689–1702

1 King William and the war against France

On 23 December 1688, as soon as he knew that James II had fled, William ordered the French ambassador to leave the country. Even at this early stage, with the outcome of the Revolution still uncertain, the Prince of Orange wanted to make it clear to all Europe that his expedition to England was an integral part of his preparations for the coming struggle with Louis XIV of France. Quite apart from his own resolve to carry on that struggle with every means at his disposal, he had to reassure his Dutch subjects as to the usefulness of his English adventure. If he was to exploit to the full his dual position as ruler of the United Provinces[1] and King of England, he had to convince each partner in this alliance of Maritime Powers that the partnership was to its advantage. Dutchmen must be shown that the resources of William's newly acquired realm could help to defend them against France, while Englishmen must be made to see that the security of the United Provinces was vital to the security of England.

The Dutch did not need much convincing. For over thirty years they had been worried by French expansion towards their frontiers, either through the Spanish Netherlands or by way of the Rhine and the Duchy of Cleves. Their attempts to conciliate France had broken down in 1672, when they had had to turn to William of Orange to save them from a French invasion. Whereas many of the merchants of Holland and Zeeland believed that it was possible to come to terms with France in order to carry on trading wars against the English,

[1] The seven northern provinces of the Netherlands—Holland, Zeeland, Utrecht, Guelderland, Overyssel, Friesland, Groningen—had gained their independence from Spain in 1648. They were known as the United Provinces, while the ten southern provinces still under Spanish rule were called the Spanish Netherlands. William had been Captain-General of the United Provinces since 1672 and also *stadtholder* of each individual province.

William himself was a living symbol of the alternative policy of hostility to France and alliance with England. In the eyes of most Dutchmen, the anti-English policy of the merchants had been tried and found wanting, so that they were prepared to recognize that a firm alliance with England was the best way of checking French expansion.

William's new subjects in England were more sceptical about the value of the Maritime Alliance. During the critical years between 1689 and 1692, when it looked as though Louis XIV might successfully dispute William's title to Ireland, to Scotland, and even to England itself, the alliance with the United Provinces was generally accepted as a useful and necessary means of defending the Revolution and of waging what was in effect the War of the British Succession. But as the danger of a Stuart restoration receded after 1692 William's expensive campaigns in the Netherlands became more and more unpopular. In effect the English objection to the Maritime Alliance was that it was not merely maritime. English merchants and seamen were happy to cooperate with the Dutch for the purpose of despoiling French trade and extending their own, but they did not want to maintain large standing armies to defend the land frontiers of the United Provinces. They could see that France might be dangerous if she supported the exiled James II or if she threatened their trade and their colonial ventures, but few of them saw her preponderance on the continent of Europe as dangerous in itself. To them the war in the Netherlands was King William's war. It took them a long time to learn that it was also their war, that the balance of power in Europe was of vital importance for the security of the British Isles.

In 1689 the balance of power in Europe hinged upon the contest between Louis XIV of France and the House of Habsburg. This remarkable dynasty, as well as monopolizing the office of Holy Roman Emperor[1] for the past four hundred years, had also come to control Spain and all her overseas possessions, including the Spanish Netherlands, parts of Italy and the greater part of America. Since 1556 the Habsburg dominions had been divided, one branch of the family ruling the Empire while the other ruled Spain; and the French,

---

[1] As its name implied, the Holy Roman Empire had originally been an attempt to revive in Christian form the universal empire of ancient Rome; but by 1689 it was little more than a loose confederation of German princes. Eight of these princes (the Elector Palatine, the Electors of Bavaria, Saxony and Brandenburg, the Archbishop-Electors of Cologne, Mayence and Treves and the King of Bohemia) had the right to elect the Emperor.

who had been encircled and almost engulfed by Habsburg power in the days when it had been at its height, were determined to prevent the two halves joining up again. At first they had drawn to their side many of the smaller countries of Europe, who were as frightened of the Habsburgs as they were. German princes, Italian dukes and merchant republics, Dutch burghers, even the insular English—all had been glad to welcome France as their protector against the Habsburgs. But by 1689 they were beginning to think that the protector might prove more dangerous than the original assailant. Once rescued, the damsels in distress wondered whether the dragon was not after all preferable to the knight.

The reason for this change of attitude was simple: the French were no longer concerned simply to weaken Habsburg power, but to take it over themselves. In 1659 Louis XIV had married a Spanish princess and for a time it had looked as though his son by her, Louis the Dauphin, might inherit the Spanish throne. This possibility had receded and Louis had contented himself with biting pieces off the Spanish Empire instead of swallowing it whole. But Carlos II of Spain, the degenerate and childless product of years of Habsburg intermarriage, could not live long; and it was clear that when he died Louis would seek to assert the Dauphin's claim to Spain. Meanwhile it was noticeable that when the King of France signed treaties with those German princes who were also Electors he made a point of getting them to promise to vote for him at an Imperial election. Those who had been frightened of Habsburg power did not relish the King of France taking it over in this way. Whether or not he would ever succeed in making the Habsburg lands into his lands, Louis XIV had certainly succeeded in making the enemies of the Habsburgs into his enemies.

In the summer of 1688 Louis was told by his agents in Madrid that Carlos II was dying. Accordingly, he prepared to assert the Dauphin's right to the Spanish empire and to defy the alliance between the Habsburgs and their ex-enemies—the German princes, the Maritime Powers and the Italian states—which such an assertion would undoubtedly provoke. He massed his fleets in the Mediterranean and sent his armies over the Rhine to attack the Elector Palatine, his chief enemy in Western Germany. He was taking a calculated risk, since this concentration on Germany and the Mediterranean stopped him from menacing the Dutch with his armies or the English with his navies. It thus gave William of Orange the opportunity to embark on his English adventure. To Louis, however, the risk seemed well worth taking. The struggle between James II and William of Orange would probably be lengthy and would incapacitate the United Provinces long enough for him to take over Spain. Then, if it was still necessary, he would be able to intervene in England at his leisure.

His calculations were upset by the behaviour of the two monarchs chiefly concerned in them. Carlos II of Spain failed to die and James II of England failed to stay and fight for his throne. As a result, Louis was confronted in the summer of 1689 with the Grand Alliance, which included Spain, the Emperor, Great Britain, the United Provinces and many of the princes of Germany and Italy. Even the Pope gave it his secret support. Instead of being able to seize Spain, dominate the Mediterranean, terrorize Germany and profit from civil war and disunity in Britain and the United Provinces, the King of France would have to fight every inch of the way against a coalition which united most of Europe against him. The only monarch who could be said to be fighting for him was the Sultan of Turkey—not an ally he could acknowledge openly, but one who nevertheless helped him considerably by attacking the eastern frontiers of the Holy Roman Empire.

Impressive though it was, the Grand Alliance was by no means in a position to overwhelm France. With a population which equalled that of Spain, the Empire and the Maritime Powers all put together, France could field armies which were as numerous as those of her enemies and a good deal more efficient. Her navy, too, was powerful and well organized: she had over two hundred warships, as well as fleets of privateers which could do very considerable damage to enemy trade. Above all, she possessed the two great advantages always enjoyed by a single power fighting against a coalition: interior lines of communication and the prospect of disagreements among her enemies. To some extent these two factors were connected: the fact that the French could move troops quickly from one theatre of war to another while the Allies had considerable difficulty in sending one another reinforcements made it relatively easy for French diplomacy to open up rifts in the Alliance. As well as disagreements which arose in this way there was the underlying distrust between the Habsburgs themselves and those who had joined them temporarily against France. The Catholic King of Spain and the Catholic Emperor had reservations about fighting with Protestant heretics against the Catholic King of France. The Protestant Powers, for their part, never forgot that the old threat of Habsburg domination of Europe might at any moment reappear and eclipse the threat of French domination.

In these circumstances, the only man who could hold the Alliance together was William III and the only way he could do it was by using the English and Dutch fleets. If its members were effectively linked by seapower, the Grand Alliance might be forged into a steel ring which could throttle the French war effort; but without seapower it would be no more dangerous to her than a necklace with a sagging thread. This need to put a ring of seapower around France was recognized in the treaties which made up the Grand Alliance; the English and the Dutch agreed to maintain three naval squadrons, the largest in the Mediterranean and the other two in the English Channel and the Irish Sea. The English contribution to this force was fixed at fifty ships, but in the event our naval resources proved unequal to the tasks imposed on them. Not all the ships were seaworthy and the victualling was in the hands of inefficient and sometimes corrupt contractors. In one squadron over five hundred men were killed by food poisoning and even the dogs—those of them that could be induced to eat the food provided for the men—fell ill and died. The idea of sending the main fleet to the Mediterranean had to be dropped, so that the French were able to bring their own Mediterranean fleet round from Toulon to Brest and concentrate all their ships for action in the Channel.

If they had used their seapower properly at this point, the French might have prevented William from getting any troops into Ireland at all; but instead they contented themselves with attacking Allied merchant shipping. By November 1689 London merchants were complaining of losses in the Channel totalling £600,000 and an increasing number of warships had to be used to escort convoys of merchantmen and to patrol the coasts in search of French privateers. This reduced the amount of naval support available for the English campaigns in Ireland, but it did not prevent William from bringing them to a successful conclusion in the autumn of 1690.[1]

Meanwhile the French admiral Tourville had come out of Brest in June 1690 with a fleet of more than seventy warships, as well as frigates and fireships. One English squadron under Killigrew was on its way back from the Mediterranean with a convoy of two hundred merchant ships, another led by Sir Cloudesley Shovell was in Irish waters and only Lord Torrington, with a combined English and

[1] See p. 77 for an account of the war in Ireland.

Dutch fleet of fifty-six ships, was left to dispute with Tourville the control of the English Channel. Queen Mary and the Cabinet Council in London sent him strict instructions to engage the French at all costs and he did so off Beachy Head on 30 June, against his own better judgment. He decided to send only the rear of his fleet to engage the French rear, while his centre and van stood off and avoided action. But the Dutch ships in the van, spoiling for a fight and unfamiliar with his signals, bore down on the French van. Some of the leading French ships were able to turn up ahead of them, so that they were attacked from both sides. The Allied line was broken[1] and a murderous confusion ensued, in which the French would have been able to destroy the English and Dutch ships at will if Torrington had not made all his ships anchor, so that the French drifted downwind away from them. Tourville was so frightened of having his own line broken that he failed to order a general chase; but even so Torrington lost a large part of his fleet—eight according to his own estimates and sixteen according to the claims made by the French.

The battle of Beachy Head was the greatest naval victory France has gained over the English. For the first and only time in modern history she was mistress of the Channel and could have launched an invasion of England without any serious interference from the crippled and divided English fleets. In England the authorities prepared to repel the expected invasion and the militia was called out, even though it was harvest time and the men were badly needed in the fields. But Louis XIV was in no position to muster an army of invasion. His forces were heavily engaged in the Netherlands, where they won a victory over the Allies at Fleurus in July, and in Italy, where they defeated the Duke of Savoy at Staffarda in August. Large numbers of French troops were tied down in Ireland and it was necessary to keep an army on the Rhine, where there was still some desultory fighting. French control of the Channel might be used to blockade the Thames, as the French privateering captain Jean Bart suggested, or to attack Killigrew's Mediterranean convoy, which had taken refuge in Plymouth; but there was little prospect of its being used to mount an invasion of England.

[1] 'The line' was the formation in which each ship followed closely on the one ahead, so that the fleet formed one long line. The advantage of 'keeping the line' lay in the fact that an approaching enemy was exposed to the combined broadsides of the whole fleet, whereas once an enemy ship 'broke the line', by sailing between the bows of one ship and the stern of the next ahead, she was able to use her broadsides while remaining herself invulnerable.

In the event it was used for none of these things. In August Tourville took his fleet back into Brest after making a token attack on the small fishing village of Teignmouth. James II, when he returned to France from his defeat in Ireland, tried to interest Louis in an invasion of England; but he received little encouragement and in 1691 the main theatre of war moved from the Channel to the Netherlands. Parliament had agreed to the English armies there being increased to 70,000 men—the original figure agreed upon in the treaties of 1689 had been 8,000—so that William was able to return to the United Provinces in January 1691 as the accepted ruler of Great Britain and the leader of a powerful British expeditionary force. After two years of danger and uncertainty, it seemed to his Dutch subjects that his English adventure was about to pay dividends.

The dividends proved depressingly meagre. An ambitious scheme for a joint attack on France from both north and east, put forward by William at a conference at The Hague, failed to materialize and when the campaigning season opened it was the French who took the initiative. They seized the important fortress of Mons in April 1691, and allied attempts to recapture it later in the year yielded nothing but frustration and humiliation. Meanwhile the failure of the Allies to put a ring of seapower around France enabled her to use her fleets effectively both against Spain and against the Duke of Savoy, the Alliance's chief supporter among the princes of Italy. In the Mediterranean in 1691 Louis XIV profited, if only indirectly, from the victory off Beachy Head.

When in 1692 he decided to profit from it directly by undertaking an invasion of England it was too late. Tourville's fleet in Brest had dwindled to forty-four ships and it proved impossible to bring the Toulon squadron round in time to join them. The English meanwhile had been working strenuously to increase their naval efficiency: in December 1690 Parliament voted £570,000 for the building of twenty-seven new warships and at the same time work had begun on a new naval base at Plymouth, to supplement the existing ones at Chatham and Portsmouth. When Tourville sailed out of Brest in May 1692 with his fleet of forty-four ships of the line and thirty-eight fireships he found a vast allied fleet of sixty-three English and thirty-six Dutch warships, together with thirty-eight fireships, waiting for him off Barfleur. All his flag officers agreed that it would be madness to risk a combat but Louis, who believed that the English admiral Russell was secretly in sympathy with James II had sent strict orders that the French fleet was to engage at all costs. The action, fought off Barfleur on 19 May, was inconclusive: partly owing to Tourville's own skill and partly owing to a sudden drop in the wind, Russell was unable to encircle the French as he had intended and not a single French ship was sunk. However, during the next few days the French fleet became divided and the English were able to chase part of it into the bay of La Hogue, where fifteen French ships of the line and several transports were destroyed. James II watched from the shore as the ships which were to have taken him and his supporters back to England were sent instead to the bottom of the sea.

The English failure to follow up the battles of Barfleur and La Hogue was even more marked than the French failure to follow up Beachy Head two years earlier. Queen Mary did her best to get Russell to take an expeditionary force to France, but he seemed determined to block her plans. Even when the force did join the fleet at the end of July it failed to make a landing on the French coast. Meanwhile, the attacks made by Jean Bart and the other French privateers on allied shipping were becoming more and more damaging and the English merchants were clamouring for warships to be used to escort commercial convoys rather than invasion attempts. English taxpayers saw La Hogue not as the signal to take the offensive but as a chance to resume the defensive. Now that French naval power in the Channel was broken and the War of the British Succession as good as won, they could see little point in straining the resources of England in order to influence events on the Continent. Instead they could safely return to their instinctive policies of insularity and 'business as usual'. And if William insisted on continuing the war against France, then at least he ought to see that English merchantmen were properly protected against the licensed piracy to which not only the French privateers but even the French battle fleets devoted themselves from 1692 onwards. In granting the land tax of 1693 Parliament took the opportunity of laying down the exact number of warships which were to be used for the protection of commerce. But heavy losses continued. In June 1693 a convoy of four hundred ships bound for Smyrna was attacked by Tourville off Lagos and nearly a quarter of the convoy was lost, as well as four out of the small squadron of warships which was its only escort. This disaster caused violent criticism, not only of the Admiralty but of the war itself. To the taxpayers it seemed that shipping losses running into millions[1] of pounds formed a poor return for the princely sums they had given for the armies in the Netherlands. If the war was to mean money lost at sea, as well as money squandered on soldiers, why not have done with it altogether?

William's costly campaigns in the Netherlands certainly seemed to be achieving remarkably little. Early in 1692 the French laid siege to the great fortress of Namur and William's attempts to relieve it were foiled by a heavy rainstorm which flooded the countryside and bogged down his army. After the fortress had fallen in June, his efforts to recapture it ended only in the defeat of Steenkirk on 24 July. In 1693 the pattern was repeated, but instead of taking one fortress the French took two—Huy and Charleroi—and instead of snatching a marginal victory, as at Steenkirk, they inflicted a really shattering defeat on William at Neerwinden on 19 July 1693. In the appalling carnage of this battle he lost over a third of his army.

Since the capture of Mons, Namur and Charleroi had given the French an almost impregnable position in the eastern Netherlands, William decided in 1694 to turn west towards the Channel ports. Although the French managed to move their army from one end of the front to the other in time to block his advance, he succeeded in forcing them on to the defensive; and in the following year he was able to achieve his only real success of the war, the recapture of Namur. But the fortress did not surrender until 22 August 1695, by which time the campaigning season was almost over and he was unable to follow up his victory. By 1696 both sides were running into financial difficulties and the opposing armies contented themselves with marching and countermarching. One officer reported in August 1696 that 'there was not one bloody nose among 400,000 men'. This military stalemate in the Netherlands continued until the war was brought to an end in September 1697.

Meanwhile William remained convinced that the grand strategy of the war depended not on armies but on navies. In the summer of 1693, after the attack on the Smyrna convoy, the thread of seapower which linked the members of the Alliance together came near to breaking altogether. An enormous French fleet of over ninety warships ranged through the Mediterranean and might well have knocked Spain and Savoy out of the war for good if it had not been more interested in

---

[1] In November 1693 a member of the House of Commons reckoned the loss from privateering at £3 million. The attack on the Smyrna convoy accounted for £1 million of this.

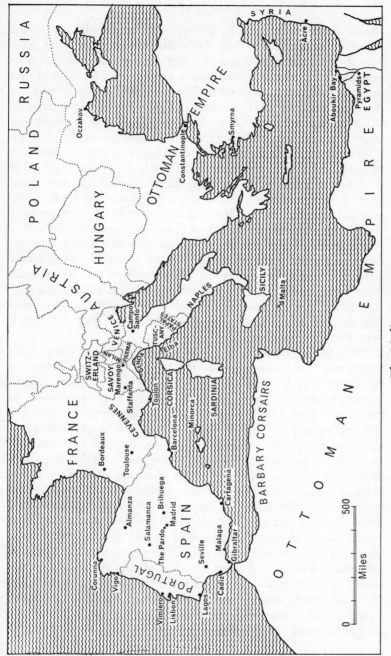

The Mediterranean

attacking allied commerce. By the end of the year English and Dutch shipping had been driven from the Mediterranean, so that even those who thought of the navy as a protector of commerce rather than an instrument of strategy agreed on the need to send a powerful fleet through the Straits of Gibraltar. The main fleet under Russell was therefore ordered to sea in the spring of 1694. First it was to cover an allied landing at Camaret Bay, near Brest; then it was to pursue and attack Tourville's fleet if he succeeded in escaping from Brest; finally it was to sail to the Mediterranean and give every possible assistance to Spain and Savoy. Owing to inexplicable delays and leakages of information the first two enterprises failed: Tourville got away from Brest five weeks before Russell left England and the landing was repulsed with heavy losses. But once he arrived in the Mediterranean the advantages of Russell's presence there were enormous. As well as relieving the siege of Barcelona and bringing to a halt the French campaigns in Spain and in Italy, he was able to keep the Toulon fleet bottled up and prevent it from joining the Brest fleet. Quite apart from any considerations of maintaining a continental alliance or supporting military action in southern Europe, it was clear that British naval forces in the Mediterranean could keep the French fleet divided and weakened.

But how was the British fleet to be kept there long enough to make its presence felt? Seventeenth-century admirals thought it dangerous to take their ships out of harbour before the middle of March or to keep them out after the middle of September; and as the voyage to the Mediterranean took several weeks this left very little time for effective operations. William III saw the obvious and inescapable answer to this problem and he decided that Russell should spend the winter at Cadiz instead of returning to England. This decision, made in the face of considerable opposition from ministers and admirals alike, was one of the most important in the history of British naval strategy. Once the policy of keeping a fleet in the Mediterranean throughout the year had been adopted it was clear that a naval base would have to be acquired there. Cadiz could only be used if Spain was our ally and in any case it was fifty miles outside the Straits of Gibraltar. William's decision pointed ahead, therefore, to the seizure of Gibraltar in 1704 and of Minorca four years later. He did not make Britain into a Mediterranean power, but he did show her why she must be one and how she might become one.

In January 1696 the Mediterranean fleet had to be recalled to deal with a new threat of invasion. Louis hoped that his fleets would be able to keep the English navy divided and diverted long enough for him to land a force in Kent; but in April, after the English squadron from the Mediterranean had managed to avoid the Toulon and Brest fleets and join the home fleet in the Downs, he had to give up the attempt. In the Mediterranean itself, however, he benefited enormously from the withdrawal of the English ships: Savoy made peace with him in August 1696, the Emperor agreed to withdraw all his troops from Italy two months later and in August 1697 the French campaign in Spain was brought to a triumphant conclusion with the capture of Barcelona.

In spite of these dramatic developments there was still no real prospect of final victory for either side. The stalemate at sea was less obvious than the stalemate on land in the Netherlands, but it was no less real: William could not tighten the naval noose around France, but Louis could not break out of it altogether. Both Kings saw the need for peace, especially since Carlos II of Spain was now very ill indeed and might die at any moment. Peace negotiations began in May 1697 and two months later William authorized private talks between the Earl of Portland and the French general Boufflers. The result was the Peace of Ryswick, signed on 10 September 1697. There was a general restoration of conquests and Louis agreed 'not to trouble or disturb in any way whatsoever the King of Great Britain in the possession of his kingdoms, countries, states, lands or governments'. It was an inconclusive and unsatisfactory peace, but it would have to do. Both sides knew that they must shelve the War of the British Succession if they were to avoid the War of the Spanish Succession.

2 Danby and the Court Party

When William III settled down to the business of ruling England in the spring of 1689 neither he nor his subjects thought in terms of a new kind of kingship. It was generally accepted that he would rule as previous kings had ruled, by calling the lords of his realm to his Court and distributing among them' the great offices of State. Nobody thought of him as 'forming a ministry' or 'bringing a party into power' to the exclusion of its rivals. It was true—though regrettable —that Englishmen were divided into Whigs and Tories and that this division was especially marked in Parliament; but this did not mean that the King should allow party divisions to influence his choice of ministers or that he should necessarily appoint men who had followings in Parliament. It was felt that Parliament ought in future to be summoned at regular intervals, but not that it ought to dominate the day-to-day business of running the country. The King's role was to stand above the party squabbles in Parliament, not to allow himself to be identified with any one party.

Most of the men whom William appointed to high office in 1689 shared this view. Halifax, who became Lord Privy Seal, was already well known for his dislike of party, which he described as 'a kind of conspiracy against the rest of the nation'. Shrewsbury, the Secretary of State for the South, was equally disdainful in his attitude to party politics, although he was generally labelled a Whig. The other Secretary, Nottingham, was a Tory, but his sponsoring of the Bill of Indulgence showed that he did not share the narrow prejudices of the rank and file Tories. The offices of Lord Treasurer and Lord Chancellor were put into commission and the commissioners were for the most part moderate and efficient men of business rather than party fanatics. It was the kind of administration that a nineteenth-century politician would have described as 'an all-party coalition'; but to William III and to the men who served him it was an assertion of the irrelevance of party to the business of managing the King's affairs.

There was, however, one man in the ministry who had learnt from experience that kings need parties. This was Danby. He had been Charles II's Lord High Treasurer from 1674 to 1678 and his greatest achievement during that time had been the creation of a Court party, an obedient following for the King and his ministers, in the House of Commons. He was convinced that what had been done then could be and must be done again. If the King did not give his attention to building up the sort of party he needed, the parties would soon be in the position to force upon him the sort of ministry tney wanted. So far from being something which would drag the King down into the mud-slinging of party politics, the existence of a Court Party was the one thing which would enable him to remain aloof from it.

It was for this reason that Danby hoped to be appointed to his old office of Lord High Treasurer. Instead, he was given the relatively unimportant post of Lord President of the Council and had to stand by and watch while increasingly turbulent debates in the House of Commons made clear the need for those techniques of parliamentary management which he understood so well and which William had chosen to neglect. Without a firm hand at the Treasury there was little hope of either party giving regular or effective support to the Crown. The Tories were suspicious of William's sympathies for the Dissenters and they were furious with him for giving his assent, in February 1689, to an Act turning the Convention into a Parliament. They saw it as an illegal body, brought together in circumstances which had enabled the Whigs to pack it, and they wanted fresh elections. The Whigs, on the other hand, tried to behave as though the Revolution had been all their own work and they seemed to expect William to dismiss all his Tory ministers and allow Parliament to take vengeance on those who had served James II. 'Nothing washes away blood but blood', said one member ominously in June 1689.

Even more serious was the reluctance of both parties to grant William and Mary an adequate revenue. There was nothing in the Declaration of Rights to suggest that the traditional grant of the Customs and Excise to the sovereign for life should be discontinued, but at the end of 1689 it had still not been made. The Commons had got as far as fixing the annual costs of government in peace-time at the impossibly low figure of £1,318,680, but they had not indicated how they proposed to raise even this limited sum. If the King was to be properly provided for the Court must take the initiative in the Commons. The longer it delayed doing so, the more the Commons would be encouraged to use their power of granting taxes as a bargaining weapon. Already the idea of granting Customs and Excise for a limited period only was gaining ground. 'It is our security', said Sir William Pulteney, 'to have the revenue in our disposition.'

Early in 1690 it became clear that William's attempt to rule without party had failed and that he was beginning to think in terms of a Tory administration. The resignations of Halifax and Shrewsbury left Danby and Nottingham supreme in the ministry, while a reshuffle at the Treasury brought in Sir John Lowther, a close associate of Danby, as First Lord. At last Danby was in a position to take up again his old task of party management.

Rank and file Tories in the Commons, as well as those in more lofty circles, had reason to feel that the King was coming down on their side. He showed increasing impatience with the vengeful and partisan behaviour of the Whigs and on 27 January he prorogued the Convention Parliament. The delighted Tories held a meeting to affirm their loyalty to the King and a few days later he ordered a dissolution and a general election. The new Parliament, which met on 20

March 1690 and lasted until 3 May 1695, soon became notorious for the large number of placemen in it—it was for this reason, and not merely because of those who held military and naval commissions, that it was called the Officers' (i.e. office-holders') Parliament. Conversely, there were comparatively few members who had been strenuous opponents of the monarchy, either under William or under his predecessors. The election of 1690 was not so much a victory for the Tories as a victory for the Court. Now that it was clear which way the wind of royal favour was blowing both electors and elected took care to trim their sails accordingly.

Even before Parliament met Danby was at work regaining for the Court the initiative it had lost in 1689. He drew up lists of his potential supporters—at this stage he reckoned on about fifty in each House—and began to dispose of offices in a way calculated to buttress and extend this following. One troublesome voice was muffled when Sir William Pulteney was made a Commissioner of the Privy Seal; and it was made clear to him and to other office-holders that in future their contributions to debates were to be helpful and not obstructive. 'The King will please to speak to the Commissioners of the Treasury', Danby wrote, 'to desire all such members as have employments in the Customs, Excise, or that are officers of the revenue, or that have pensions or have advantages under the Crown, to forward the King's supply.'

While Sir John Lowther and other 'managers of the King's directions' carried out his instructions in the Commons, Danby himself undertook to manage the Lords. With unerring skill he fastened on the points at which peers might be vulnerable: one was 'not willing to lose his patent for lands not yet perfected', while another 'would not lose his lieutenancy which supports his popularity'. By playing on these fears and on others of a more obvious kind—of the Earl of Manchester he wrote simply that he was 'not willing to lose his place' —he was able to ensure impressive majorities for the Court in the House of Lords.

The effectiveness of Danby's methods was seen as soon as Parliament met. Within a week it had granted William and Mary the Excise for life and the Customs for a period of four years, thus ensuring them a regular income of some £2,000,000 a year. It was a compromise—Danby's managers had demanded that both Customs and Excise should be granted for life—but it was a better one than had seemed possible at the end of the previous year. By the time William brought the session to a close late in May he had also obtained Parliament's approval for an Act of Grace pardoning all but a handful of those who had opposed him in 1688. The vindictiveness of the Whigs, as well as their reluctance to provide for the Crown, had been frustrated by the efforts of Danby and his Court Party.

William's departure for Ireland in June helped to confirm Danby's leadership of the ministry. Mary dreaded the prospect of ruling England and she despised most of the councillors who were appointed to advise her: the Great·Council, she said, was 'of a strange composition' while the Cabinet Council was 'not much better'. Danby, however, proved more reliable and helpful than his colleagues and she came to depend on him, though she said that she could never bring herself to like him. As well as enabling the Tory leader to win the confidence of the Queen, William's absence gave an opportunity for the Queen to win the confidence of the Tories. They had always regarded her as the protector of the Church of England against the Calvinist tendencies of William and now, in the critical weeks that followed the battle of Beachy Head, she provided a centre for that personal loyalty to the monarch which was such an important element in Toryism. Her popularity extended beyond the ranks of the Tories to the country as a whole: 'Though I cannot hit on the right way of pleasing England,' said William on one occasion, 'I am confident that she will.' She did. By October 1690, when Parliament presented her with an enthusiastic vote of thanks, it seemed as though Danby had found the right answer to William's problems by exploiting the Tory tradition of loyalty to the monarchy in general and to Mary in particular.

But Danby soon began to run into trouble, largely as a result of his own success. By 1692 he could count on the votes of over a hundred office-holders in the House of Commons and this formidable body of placemen was giving rise to anxiety not only among the Whigs but also among the Tories themselves. They might be traditional supporters of the Crown, but they were also independent country gentlemen who resented this invasion of the legislative by the servants of the executive. Fears of the growing influence of the Crown were intensified in February 1692, when William vetoed a Bill which would have prevented him from removing judges at will. The next parliamentary session, from November 1692 until March 1693, was very stormy and the Court had considerable difficulty in obtaining the money necessary for carrying on the war in the

Netherlands. Now that the immediate danger of a French invasion was past, many Tory gentlemen found that their concern for their pockets and their dislike of continental entanglements outweighed their traditional loyalty to the Crown.

Attacks on the war were coupled with attacks on those who managed it. A motion to limit the King's appointments to the Admiralty was only lost by a narrow margin, while one to exclude all placemen from the House of Commons was carried in the Lower House and defeated in the Lords by a mere three votes. Meanwhile, the Lords debated the idea of appointing a standing committee of both Houses to act as a Council of State. This proposal, which would have countered the executive's control over the legislative by extending the legislative's control over the executive, was dropped; but William was faced at the end of the session with a Triennial Bill, which would have limited the life of the existing Parliament and all future ones to three years. Rather than face the weakening of the Court Party which this would have entailed he once again used his veto.

Ministerial changes in 1692 and 1693 reflected the King's dissatisfaction with the existing system and his search for a more broadly based one. Somers, generally accounted a Whig, was made Attorney-General and later Lord Keeper while Montagu, another Whig, came in as a commissioner of the Treasury. Sunderland, a Whig under Charles II and a Catholic under James II, was being taken more and more into William's confidence, in spite of the fact that he had been specifically excluded from the pardon granted under the Act of Grace. By June 1693 he was advising the Court on the management of its party in Parliament. Finally, in November 1693, Nottingham was replaced as Secretary of State by Sir John Trenchard, who had had considerable experience of organizing the Whig party during Charles II's reign. William was clearly ceasing to rely exclusively on Danby and the Tories for the management of his affairs.

At first Danby was not unduly worried: he was quite glad to be rid of High Tories like Nottingham and to build instead on a broader and more moderate basis. After weathering another difficult session from November 1693 to April 1694—the Commons attacked army and navy appointments, revived the Triennial Bill, carried a Place Bill and finished up by protesting, when William vetoed it, that he had done so by 'the secret advices of particular persons who have private interests of their own'—the new and extended Court Party began to get Parliament under control again. William opened the new session in November 1694 with a confident speech and received grants calculated to bring in £5,000,000 a year. He agreed to give his consent to a Triennial Bill and in return the Commons voted down a Place Bill they had been debating. It seemed that relations between Court and Parliament were better than they had been for the last three years.

But William was not satisfied. His acceptance of the Triennial Bill, so far from being a desperate attempt to conciliate Parliament at all costs, was a deliberate move in his campaign to rid himself of the Tories altogether. He had decided that the Whigs could be of more use to him than their rivals and he therefore wanted to leave himself free to summon a new Parliament, so that the electors might have the chance to endorse his change of heart. The death of Mary at the end of 1694 loosened the ties that bound the legitimist and High Church Tories to the monarchy and by the spring of 1695 even the existing Parliament had been sufficiently emboldened by the new drift in affairs to turn on Danby and his managers. The Speaker of the House of Commons and the Secretary of the Treasury, two key men in his system, were both convicted of corruption; and he himself was impeached on the grounds that he had taken bribes from the East India Company. When William returned to England in the autumn, fresh from the victory of Namur, he decided that the time had come for an election. As in 1690, the electors were anxious to return men who were in favour at Court and would be able to pass down to their constituents the benefits of that favour. This time it was the Whigs who were most likely to be able to do this; and William's third Parliament, which lasted from November 1695 until July 1698, was as Whig as its predecessor had been Tory. Only the Whigs, with their connections with the great monied men of the City of London, could do William's business for him now. William had had enough of ministers who knew only how to manage men. Henceforth he would rely on those who knew also how to manage money.

3 Montagu and the Monied Men

The nature of William's new reliance on the Whigs can be expressed far more effectively in figures than in words. In 1694, the last year of Tory rule, he had received £4,004,000 in revenue and had spent

£5,602,000. Three years later he was receiving £3,298,000 and spending £7,915,000. The volume of government borrowing had jumped from just over 20 per cent to nearly 60 per cent of total expenditure. Whereas his Tory ministers had striven to persuade the landed gentlemen of England to pay for the war by taxation, his Whig ministers were more concerned to get the financiers of London to pay for it by loans. The National Debt, which in the last year of Tory rule had stood at just over £6,000,000, totalled well over £17,000,000 by the time William dissolved his Whig Parliament in July 1698. The King continued to value the techniques of parliamentary management, but he had come to value even more highly the financial skill which could create and maintain government credit.

Charles Montagu, a commissioner of the Treasury since 1692 and Chancellor of the Exchequer since April 1694, had already shown that he possessed this skill. In January 1693 he raised a loan of £1,000,000 by offering interest in the form of 14 per cent annuities, which were paid out of the proceeds of a special additional excise duty. Some of the annuities were on the 'tontine' principle, by which those who lived longest received most—one child on whose behalf £100 was subscribed was drawing £1,000 a year by the time he died in 1783. In 1694 the 'Million Adventure' took the gambling principle a stage further: £140,000 a year, raised by means of taxes on salt and beer, was set aside for sixteen years as the interest on a new £1,000,000 loan, but only £100,000 of it was paid out in the form of regular annuities at 10 per cent. The remaining £40,000 went into a prize fund and lots were drawn for the prizes which ranged from £10 to £1,000.

From offering prizes Montagu moved to offering privileges. Earlier in the century kings had turned their courtiers into rich men by granting them exclusive commercial rights, but plenty of other men had nevertheless contrived to grow very rich indeed without such rights. The time had now come for William to bind these new men to his cause by offering them new privileges. It might be possible to wind up existing privileged companies, most of which were associated with the Tories, and transfer their rights wholesale to the great Whig financiers who had been inveighing against them for so long; but it would be a drastic and difficult business. It would be far better if a new field of commercial activity could be found in which privileges could be given to those who were prepared to lend to the King.

The field which Montagu chose was that of banking. Goldsmiths had for many years past acted as bankers, accepting cash deposits and offering the depositor facilities for settling debts by means of written orders drawn on his account. Orders of this kind, together with bills of exchange[1] and other promissory notes, had come to circulate more and more freely, so that the paper promise to pay money, as long as it was backed by a reputable banker, was regarded as an acceptable alternative to the money itself. Montagu's Tonnage Act of April 1694 offered to all those who would subscribe to a new loan of £1,200,000 a chance to enter this highly profitable business of banking on privileged terms, with the security of the State itself behind them. In return for accepting an interest rate of only 8 per cent on their money—the Act imposed tonnage duties calculated to raise £100,000 for this purpose—they were to be incorporated as 'The Governor and Company of the Bank of England', the first joint stock bank in the country. The offer proved so attractive that the whole £1,200,000 was subscribed within twelve days. By August the Treasury was already making arrangements for spending the money.

As well as providing the King with a dependable source of future loans, the foundation of the Bank of England also extended and confirmed his control over Parliament. Members of both Houses took advantage of the clause in the Act which specifically allowed them to be 'concerned in the Corporation' and their shares in the Bank helped to bind them to the Court. Great Whig monied men like Thomas Papillon, who had been trying for years to break the Tory monopoly of the East India Company, turned eagerly to the new corporation and very soon William's Whig ministers had a more powerful following in the City of London than the Tories had ever had. Court and City joined hands in the financial management of the war and also in the political management of the House of Commons.

There was violent Tory opposition to the Bank, not only among the small group of monopolists connected with the old privileged companies but also among the backbench Tory squires. From their point of view there was little to choose between office-holders at Court and financiers in the City: both were growing rich on the proceeds of the taxes which the gentry paid so grudgingly and both were undermining the independence of Parliament which the gentry cherished so jealously. Just as the dislike of office-holders had led

[1] See p. 65, note 1.

backbench Tories to vote with the Whigs against their own leaders a few years earlier, so now the dislike of privileged government creditors led backbench Whigs to vote with the Tories. In the spring of 1696 a Bill to create a rival Land Bank, providing the same sort of services and opportunities for landed men as the Bank of England provided for monied men, was passed through Parliament and sent up to the King.

William was particularly anxious to conciliate the country gentlemen by whom and for whom the Land Bank scheme had been devised. A couple of months earlier, in February, he had revealed to Parliament the details of a plot to assassinate him and this had produced a wave of loyalty throughout the country. Many Tory squires had been converted, at any rate temporarily, from secret Jacobitism to wholehearted devotion to King William. Quite apart from his determination to raise money from whatever source he could find, it seemed the right moment for a gesture which would show that he was above mere party allegiances. He gave his assent to the Bill and promised to subscribe £5,000 himself.

Nevertheless, the scheme failed dismally. Only £7,000 was subscribed out of the proposed total of £2,000,000 and the Bank of England, which had previously had its offer of a loan spurned, had to step into the breach and raise the required sum. Since its own position had been shaken by the Land Bank episode, to such an extent that there had been a serious run on its notes, it now took the chance to exploit the government's renewed dependence on it. In April 1697 an Act was passed incorporating it as a body politic, with power to buy and sell land and with an assured monopoly of joint stock banking until the year 1710. At the same time it was allowed to enlarge its stock by a further £1,000,000. The same Act set up a general fund from which deficiencies in particular branches of the revenue were to be made good. Previously those who had lent to the government had had to accept as their security the yield of a particular tax: if the yield fell below expectations they might stand to lose money, just as a pawnbroker stands to lose money if the article on which he has advanced a pound turns out to be worth only ten shillings. The Act of 1697 introduced the modern idea of a consolidated National Debt and gave government creditors the whole of the national revenue as their security.

Winning the confidence of the monied classes was not just a matter of persuading them to lend their money to the government: Montagu had also to create and maintain conditions in which they could be sure of making more money. By popularizing the joint stock principle he gave a great impetus to commerce and industry: by 1695 there were about 150 joint stock companies in the country, possessing between them a capital of some £4,000,000 and devoted to such varied pursuits as 'improving Native Manufactures to keep out the Wet' and developing 'the Sucking Worm Engines of Mr John Loftingh'. Land was losing some of its attractions as a form of investment—since 1693 a run of bad harvests had forced many landowners to sell up—and foreign trade was in an uncertain state because of the depredations of the French privateers. In these circumstances more and more people put their money into commercial ventures which aimed to produce goods for the home market.

The increased circulation of money and goods throughout the country put a severe strain on the currency, which was already in a very poor condition. Clipping of coin was so widespread that in 1695 a sample of 500 bags of old coins was found to weigh little more than half of what it should have done. Quite apart from the loss to the Crown and to the country's bullion reserves which it entailed, the depreciation of the coinage destroyed business confidence and hampered the natural development of the economy. After exhaustive preliminary inquiries, in which he had the assistance of John Locke and Isaac Newton, Montagu steered through Parliament at the end of 1695 a scheme for a complete recoinage. Up to 1 February 1697 anyone bringing old coin to the Treasury was to receive its face value in new milled coined; but after that date it would only be taken by weight. The Royal Mint, assisted by special mints set up in Exeter, Bristol, Chester, York and Norwich, worked flat out for the next three years and produced nearly £7,000,000 worth of new coins. The old coins, which were melted down in special furnaces in the gardens of the Treasury, turned out to be worth little more than £4,000,000 and the deficit had to be made up by imposing a special window tax for the next seven years.

The growing importance of commerce and industry led inevitably to demands that the commercial classes should have more control over the country's economic affairs. One writer in 1695 suggested that there should be a special assembly for this purpose, chosen from shipowners, manufacturers and the trading companies; and in the spring of 1696 the House of Commons discussed the idea of setting up a parliamentary committee with power to control trade. William was so alarmed by this threatened invasion of the executive by the legislative that he took the initiative himself and appointed sixteen commissioners 'for promoting the trade of this our kingdom and for inspecting and improving our plantations in America and elsewhere'. This body, which came to be known as the Board of Trade, was an offshoot of the Council rather than of Parliament; but it provided, nevertheless, a link between the Court and those members of Parliament who represented the commercial interest. Like the account which Montagu rendered to the Commons in December 1696 of the government's financial position—an account which has been seen as the first Budget—it was a recognition of the need to maintain proper businesslike relations with those upon whom the government relied for its financial support.

By this time the Whig financiers were sure enough of their hold on Court and Commons to launch an attack on the last great stronghold of the Tory monopolists, the East India Company. From January 1696, when they instigated a parliamentary inquiry into its affairs, they worked steadily to undermine the Company's position. At the beginning of 1698 a group of them offered to lend the government £2,000,000 at 8 per cent if it would allow them to set up a new East India Company of their own. Montagu accepted the proposal and with his support a Bill giving effect to it was passed through Parliament. The new Company was granted a charter giving it exclusive control of the East India trade until 1711 and the old Company was given three years in which to wind up its affairs. In fact, the old Company continued in existence until 1708, when both companies were amalgamated as 'The United Company of Merchants of England trading to the East Indies'.

Their victory over the old East India Company was the last that the Whigs were to taste for some time, for they were already losing the confidence of the King. Ever since the conclusion of the Peace of Ryswick in September 1697, William had been faced with insistent demands in Parliament for the disbandment of his armies and for a reduction in taxation; and his Whig ministers seemed quite unable to control the situation. They stood by helplessly, not even daring to press for a renewal of the Mutiny Act, while the Commons resolved that the army in England should be reduced to 8,000 men and that the King should be granted a Civil List of only £700,000. Parliament's determination to put the country's finances back on to a peace-time footing made the privileged government creditors even more vulnerable to attack from the 'County Party' than the placemen had been back in 1693. A ministry which depended on the City could not hope to manage Parliament if the enormous loans of the last few years were to be rendered unnecessary.

William's dissatisfaction with the Whigs was based on something more than their evident failure to manage his affairs in the Commons. He had always suspected that they were little better than republicans, out to make the King dance to their own tune, and their behaviour since they had been in power had confirmed his worst suspicions. Danby, though he had been too much of a party man for William's taste, had at least created his party in order to serve his King. The Whigs seemed to think that their King had been created to serve their party. Their leaders—Somers the Lord Chancellor, Russell the First Lord of the Admiralty and Montagu, new First Lord of the Treasury—met regularly at Winchendon, the home of the great Whig magnate Lord Wharton, in order to concert among themselves schemes which they then tried to foist on the King. One such scheme, put before him in April 1698, involved making Wharton himself Secretary of State. Coming on top of the resignation of Sunderland, who had been forced out of office by parliamentary attacks from which his colleagues had made no attempt to shield him, this new demand suggested that the Whig leaders were deliberately using what little influence they still had in Parliament against the King rather than for him. He employed them to get votes for the maintenance of his armies and instead they had produced votes for the dismissal of his favourite minister, the one man who had challenged their monopoly of office. Now they were adding insult to injury by suggesting the appointment to high office of a man whom he despised and whose only virtue lay in his control over some two dozen seats in the House of Commons. He refused to countenance the idea and two months later he gave public proof of his readiness to be rescued from the Whigs: he appointed Marlborough, one of their most steadfast opponents, to the important post of Governor to the young Duke of Gloucester, Princess Anne's only surviving son. He then dissolved Parliament in July 1698 and set out for the United Provinces, where he was to spend the next five months. Burgesses and freeholders throughout the country were left to draw what conclusions they pleased and to elect to the new Parliament, due to meet as soon as the King returned, the men who would best serve their interest there.

4 Harley and the Country Party

It was not easy for the electors to know what William expected of them. Instead of inviting them to support the men he had decided to favour, as in 1690 and 1695, he had merely encouraged them to turn on the men he had come to dislike. They could only conclude that he was as sick as they were of the party manipulators and was inviting them to elect a Parliament which would represent neither Whig nor Tory, neither Court nor City, but the country as a whole. Now that the war was over it was time for both King and country to teach the corrupt placemen and greedy financiers a lesson. All over the country men who had grown rich by office-holding or by financing the war found themselves rejected by the electors. Even Whig magnates as powerful as Wharton lost control of boroughs which they had come to regard as their private property. When William returned to England in December 1698 he was faced with a Parliament which waited eagerly for him to redeem the promise he had made to its predecessor a year earlier, when he had said: 'I esteem it one of the greatest advantages of the Peace that I shall now have leisure to rectify such corruptions and abuses as may have crept into the administration.' Assisted by the independent country gentlemen who dominated his new Parliament, the King could go forward and guide the country into the ways of peace and purity.

However attractive this idea may have been to the country gentlemen, it was not practical politics; and no one was more keenly aware of its impracticabilities than William himself. He was indeed sick of the party manipulators and their insatiable retinues of office-seekers and financiers, but he knew very well that he could not do without them. It was quite unrealistic to imagine that the King could entrust the management of his affairs in Parliament to a turbulent and undisciplined body of backbenchers. Robert Harley, the acknowledged leader of this body, certainly had the makings of a great parliamentary manager, as great as Danby or Montagu; but he would inevitably lose a great part of his following if he went to the Treasury himself and had to manipulate those same levers of patronage and preferment which he had denounced so roundly. The popularity he had acquired as the spokesman of the 'country interest' would very soon evaporate once he became the manager of a fully-fledged 'Country Party' dedicated to the King's service.

Even if Harley could succeed in this supremely difficult task, there would still be the problem of finding enough men of real political stature to fill the other great offices of State. After eight years of party rule there were not many genuinely independent men left in politics. Sunderland was certainly a non-party man but he was distrusted by his fellow politicians and by the backbenchers themselves. Shrewsbury, who had done his best to keep William on speaking terms with his Whig ministers, had now retired in disgust and it would not be easy to tempt him back into office. Marlborough and Godolphin, the two men were generally regarded as the most likely leaders of a possible Country Party, had always been closely associated with the Princess Anne and were thus more concerned with the future than the present. They were not likely to prejudice their chances in the next reign by taking office in this one. In short, the idea of the Country Party as an effective government was unrealistic and unworkable.

Quite apart from all these considerations, there was one fatal and fundamental flaw in the country gentlemen's view of things: they assumed that the Peace of Ryswick would prove permanent. William knew that it almost certainly would not. Throughout the summer, while the gentlemen of England had been working themselves into an electioneering frenzy over the evils of war finance, their King had been trying desperately to prevent the one thing which threatened to sweep away all that the war had achieved: the succession of Louis the Dauphin, son of Louis XIV, to the Spanish Empire. If this took place, all the assurances that the French King had given at Ryswick would prove valueless. Whatever the insular English might think, William knew that the things which were so precious to them—the maintenance of the Protestant succession and the maintenance of English trade—depended on the maintenance of the balance of power. This balance would be gravely endangered, both in Europe itself and in the world beyond Europe, if the vast dominions of Spain were to be united either with the kingdom of France or with the Holy Roman Empire.

To a superficial observer it might seem that the struggle over the Spanish succession was one between Louis XIV and the Emperor Leopold, the two rulers whose sons had claims to the inheritance. But William saw deeper than this. He saw that the real question was not who was to have the Spanish empire, but whether that empire was to remain intact. The Spaniards themselves and their Habsburg cousins in Vienna were determined that it should; the smaller states of Europe, who had spent two centuries fighting the power of the

Habsburgs, were equally determined that it should not. Everything hinged on the attitude of France. This was the moment of truth in her relations with the smaller states. For years she had posed as their ally in the fight against Habsburg supremacy and had exhibited pained surprise when they joined the Habsburgs in war against her. If she really was their friend she would set aside her desire to seize the whole of the Spanish empire and join them in their efforts to get it divided up. It was William III's task as the acknowledged spokesman of the smaller states to convert Louis XIV to the idea of partitioning the Spanish empire.

By the autumn of 1698 he had some reason to think he had succeeded. After long and difficult negotiations the King of France had agreed that in the event of Carlos II's death the Spanish empire should be divided up. The lion's share—Spain itself, the Indies, the Spanish Netherlands and the island of Sardinia—was to go to a neutral claimant, the Electoral Prince of Bavaria. Louis XIV's candidate, Louis the Dauphin, was to have Naples and Sicily and other Spanish possessions in southern and central Italy. The Emperor's candidate, his younger son the Archduke Charles, would have to be content with the Duchy of Milan. Since Carlos II might die at any moment and since he would do all he could to obstruct the partition treaty if he knew about it, there was need for both speed and secrecy. As soon as the terms were agreed, William ordered his Secretary of State to draw up a blank commission and his Lord Chancellor to affix the Great Seal of England to it. Armed with this instrument he signed the Partition Treaty with France in September and it was confirmed in the following month by representatives of the United Provinces.

William was well aware how precarious this diplomatic victory was. Some of his Dutch advisers were convinced all along that Louis had no intention of keeping his word. At the very beginning of his reign the French King had denied the validity of a treaty on the grounds that it had not been ratified by the Spanish Cortes and he might well use the same excuse again, for there was no prospect of Parliament ratifying the Partition Treaty. In this critical situation, when it was essential for William to be able to negotiate from strength, the Country Party in Parliament insisted on the army being reduced to a mere 7,000 men, all of whom were to be natural-born Englishmen. Since it entailed the loss of his Dutch generals and his Dutch guards, the proposal was a personal affront to the King as well as a blow to national security; but there was nothing he could do about it now that he had left himself with a disparate collection of ministers whom he was known to distrust and who were therefore rendered incapable of managing Parliament. He thought about returning to the United Provinces and leaving the English to their fate, but in the end he swallowed his pride and gave his assent to the Act disbanding the forces at the beginning of 1699.

On the Continent events were moving quickly. Carlos II got wind of the Partition Treaty, secret though it was, and countered it with a will leaving all his dominions to the Electoral Prince of Bavaria. Then both treaty and will were nullified in January 1699 by the death of the Electoral Prince, and William had to begin his work all over again. He managed to keep Louis XIV loyal to the idea of partition and in February 1700 a second Partition Treaty was signed by the two monarchs. Apart from adding the Duchy of Milan to the Dauphin's share and arranging for it to be exchanged for the Duchy of Lorraine, it did no more for France than the first treaty. The greater part of the inheritance, the share allotted to the Electoral Prince by the first treaty, was to go the the Archduke Charles. In spite of this the Emperor refused to agree to the treaty. He was convinced that when it came to the test the understanding between William and Louis would break down and he would be able to profit by their dissensions and acquire the whole of the Spanish empire.

More important than the effect of the Second Partition Treaty on the Emperor was its effect on Carlos II of Spain. He was a sad figure, racked by inherited disease and prematurely senile at the age of thirty-nine, but he was not just a feeble-minded nonentity to be manipulated by the diplomats of other countries. He was a proud and tenacious man who was determined that the Spanish empire should not be parcelled out in lots simply in order to preserve the European balance of power. His envoys had been instructed to do what they could to wreck the negotiations between France and the Maritime Powers; and the Spanish ambassador in London had even threatened to reveal the whole story of the Partition Treaties to Parliament, where-upon he had been unceremoniously bundled out of the country. Now, with the signing of the Second Partition Treaty, it seemed that France had once again given her support to the idea of partition. She must be won from it at all costs. In order to achieve this end Carlos was prepared to do what he had refused to do all his life: he was prepared to recognize the French claim to the throne of Spain. He was not, however, prepared to contemplate Spain becoming merely a possession of the French Crown. He therefore made a will bequeathing all his dominions, not to the Dauphin, but to Louis XIV's younger grandson Philip of Anjou, on condition that the crowns of France and Spain should never be united. If the French refused this offer and stood by their Partition Treaty with William, the inheritance was to pass to the Archduke Charles. The will was signed at the end of September 1700 and a month later Carlos II was dead. Louis was left to decide between a treaty which gave Italy to the French crown and a will which gave the whole Spanish empire to a younger branch of the French royal family.

While the King of France was debating whether to accept a will that would bring him to the pinnacle of his greatness, the King of England was debating whether to dissolve a Parliament that had brought him to the depths of humiliation. Not satisfied with the army reductions which they had forced upon him at the beginning of 1699, the Country Party had gone on to accuse him of breaking promises he had made back in 1688 and also of allowing corruption and inefficiency in the Admiralty. They had then raised the question of the Irish lands he had granted to his Dutch favourites. A Bill appointing commissioners to inquire into these grants had been 'tacked' on to the Bill granting a Land Tax, so that William had been forced either to reject both or accept both. He had done the latter, only to be faced in the 1699-1700 session with a further Bill—again tacked to a Land Tax Bill—which revoked the grants. Attempts made by the House of Lords to amend the Bill had provoked a bitter quarrel between the two Houses, which William had cut short by proroguing Parliament in April 1700. Conscious that they had lost both the confidence of the King and the confidence of Parliament, his ministers resigned in quick succession: by the spring of 1700 Russell, Montagu and Somers had all gone, as well as the aged Danby who had been hanging on to office without power for the last five years. While Louis XIV held all Europe in the palm of his hand, William III could not even hold together a ministry to manage his affairs in Parliament. The offices which the Whig leaders had vacated were filled with ineffective nonentities and even the King's innermost circle of Dutch advisers was torn by a quarrel between the old favourite, William Bentinck, Earl of Portland, and the new favourite, Arnold van Keppel, Earl of Albemarle.

Early in November 1700 the French King informed William of his decision: he had accepted the will and his grandson had been proclaimed as Philip V of Spain. William can hardly have been surprised. If Louis had intended the Partition Treaties merely as levers to force the Spaniards into recognizing the French claim it was only natural that he should abandon them now that they had served their purpose; while even if he had meant them seriously there was little chance of enforcing them now. If he refused the will, and thus allowed the crown of Spain to pass to the Archduke Charles, he could hardly expect the latter to give up Italy to the Dauphin without a fight. Louis XIV and William III would have to go to war against the Emperor in order to enforce the Treaty. Was it likely that the English would support such a war, when they disapproved of the Treaty and feared French commercial supremacy in the Mediterranean? The conflict between William and his Parliament, which had already thrown doubts upon the validity of the treaty, now made its enforcement almost impossible. Carlos II had seen all this and had produced a will which killed the idea of partition stone dead. All that Louis had to do was to read the funeral oration.

William had learnt his lesson. It was clear that he could not hope to influence the course of events in Europe as long as he was at odds with Parliament. There was little chance of his present Parliament supporting him in his fight against French preponderance, so at the beginning of December he dissolved it without even deigning to call it together again for an autumn session. Elections for the new Parliament occupied the next few weeks and as soon as it met, in February 1701, it was clear that relations between king and Commons had taken a turn for the better. When the Country Party, which was once again in the majority, put up its leader Harley for the office of Speaker, the King himself ensured his election by asking the Speaker of the previous Parliament not to stand against him. Secret conversations between Harley and the King had been taking place ever since the previous summer and now they were about to bear fruit. The Country Party's touchiness over its 'independence' made it difficult for ministers to manage it in the way that Danby had managed the Court Party or Montagu the monied men, but it might well be possible to manage it by winning over its leader and placing him in a position from which he could direct proceedings in the Commons. The appointment of Godolphin as a commissioner of the Treasury at the end of 1700 and of Marlborough as Commander-in-Chief of the army in May 1701 indicated the King's readiness to.

work with men who had the confidence of the Country Party, but this was less important than the understanding with Harley. It was the Speaker, not the men at the Treasury, who must do the King's business for him now.

William's speech to the new Parliament linked the death of the King of Spain with that of the Duke of Gloucester, Princess Anne's last surviving child, at the end of the previous July. It was unlikely that either Anne or William himself would be able to provide further heirs and there was a very real danger of a Jacobite restoration. If this was to be averted and the Protestant succession secured, Parliament must do two things: it must settle the crown on a Protestant prince and it must take steps to see that Louis XIV was not in a position to meddle in British affairs and put a Catholic prince back on the thrones of England, Scotland and Ireland. This meant challenging the newly won French supremacy in Europe. If the British did not interfere in the Spanish succession, it was highly likely that the French would interfere in the British succession. To give substance to his warning William produced evidence which suggested that the French were already planning another invasion of Britain. Louis himself played into his hands by making a series of provocative gestures: he got the French law courts to recognize Philip V's claim to the French throne in the event of his elder brother's death and he repudiated Spanish treaty obligations to the Dutch, turning them unceremoniously out of the fortresses which the Spaniards had agreed they should occupy in the Netherlands. On 12 June, the day on which William gave his assent to the Act regulating the succession, the Commons agreed to support whatever alliances he saw fit to make. Ten days later Harley announced that the Commons had granted him a larger revenue than ever before in time of peace, in order that he should be able 'to support his allies to procure either a lasting peace or to preserve the liberties of Europe by a necessary war'. The significant phrase was 'the liberties of Europe': at long last William III, with the assistance of Robert Harley, had made the country gentlemen realize that the balance of power on the continent of Europe was their concern. The point was driven home for them in September, when James II died and the French recognized his son as the rightful King of England, Scotland and Ireland.

By this time the second Grand Alliance between Britain, the United Provinces and the Emperor, the nucleus of the coalition which was to fight the War of the Spanish Succession, was already in being.

It had been negotiated by William and by Marlborough—who had been appointed Ambassador Extraordinary to the United Provinces as well as Commander-in-Chief—and signed late in August. Now that he was definitely committed to war, William's thoughts began to turn to the monied men who would have to pay for it. The commercial classes had already shown more determination than the country gentlemen in opposing French control of Spain, particularly French control of the Spanish possessions in the Mediterranean and of the lucrative slave trade with the Spanish colonies. While the City of London led the way with loyal addresses and offers of loans, the Country Party still dragged its feet. It had taken an angry petition from the freeholders of Kent, as well as the astute management of Harley, to make the Commons express their support for war in June; and they had exacted a price for their support for war by writing into the Act of Settlement a series of clauses designed to reduce the King's control over Parliament[1] and to stop him from involving England in continental wars without Parliament's consent. William was not unduly worried by these clauses, because they were not due to come into effect until the accession of the Electress Sophia of Hanover, upon whom the Act settled the succession after the deaths of William and Anne;[2] but he must have wondered whether the spirit that prompted them was really the spirit needed to fight a major European war. In spite of the Country Party's attempts to whip up popular feeling by impeaching the Whig leaders for their share in the Partition Treaties, it was clear from the Kentish petition and other manifestations that the country as a whole was more patriotic than the present Parliament. Somers urged the King to dissolve Parliament and leave the electors to produce a new one more committed to the war. 'Let the majority fall as it will,' he said, 'the present temper will force them to do what the King desires.' William took the advice, which proved to be sound. At the elections of November and December 1701 the Country Party suffered a severe setback: independent gentlemen who had posed for so long as the sturdy champions of the country against the Court and the City now found themselves accused of disloyalty and even of corruption. It was rumoured, and widely believed, that some of them had been bribed with French gold to put obstacles in William's way. In the new Parliament, which was opened on 31 December, the Whigs and the monied men had a majority of about thirty over the Country Party and the Tories.

[1] For details see above, pp. 17–18.　　　　[2] See genealogical table, p. 458.

The King's speech to his Parliament, written for him by Somers, was both challenging and flattering. 'The eyes of all Europe are upon this Parliament;' he said, 'all matters are at a stand till your resolutions are known . . . If you do in good earnest desire to see England hold the balance of Europe and to be indeed at the head of the Protestant interest, it will appear by your right improving the present opportunity.' Even the most distrustful of country gentlemen found it hard to resist such an appeal. They showed their readiness to 'improve the present opportunity' by voting 40,000 soldiers and an equal number of seamen for the coming war against France; and it was the Tory Sir Edward Seymour who moved that a clause be inserted into the Grand Alliance pledging the allies to continue the war until Louis XIV recognized the Protestant succession in Britain. His motion was carried and the necessary clause was added to the treaty in April 1702. On 4 May the allies formally declared war on the King of France.

William III did not live to see the opening of the war for which he had prepared so diligently. He had a fall from his horse at the end of February and was laid up with a broken collar bone. For a time it looked as though he might recover, but complications set in and he died on 8 March. After thirteen weary and often heart-breaking years he had turned the Maritime Alliance of Britain and the United Provinces from a desperate gamble into an accepted part of the pattern of Europe. It was a great achievement and it established him as a grand master in the game of European war and diplomacy. But in the new and hazardous game of British politics he was only a beginner. So, indeed, was everyone else: the rules of the game were only just emerging from the uncertainties and anomalies of the Revolution Settlement. William and his ministers had learnt the values of some of the cards and above all of the four suits—the office holders, the great borough-mongers, the monied men and the country gentlemen. But they had yet to learn how to hold them all in one hand and how to play them to the best advantage.

5

The Revolution Confirmed
1702–1714

1 *The War of the Spanish Succession*

King William's war had been fought to defend the Revolution Settlement and the Protestant succession in England, Scotland and Ireland against the threat of intervention from France. Louis XIV's attempts to reverse the verdict of 1689 and put a Catholic king on the thrones of the three kingdoms had been frustrated. The alliance of the two greatest protestant and maritime nations of Europe—Britain and the United Provinces—had been preserved. Now in 1702 this alliance was ready to go over to the offensive. It was no longer a question of defending the Revolution but of confirming and consolidating its place in the European scheme of things. Louis XIV, who in the previous war had sought to prevent the union of Britain and the United Provinces, now found that these same two countries were determined to prevent him from uniting France and Spain. The Maritime Alliance was pledged to carry out the policy laid down by its founder William III: 'to hold the balance of Europe and to be indeed at the head of the Protestant interest.'

It was an aggressive policy, a policy which asserted the right of the Maritime Alliance to be the arbiter of Europe and to decide the outcome of the struggle between France and the Empire for the Spanish inheritance. Paris and Vienna and Madrid might propose, but London and The Hague intended to dispose. Nevertheless, the foundations of this apparently offensive and overweening policy were essentially defensive. If France held the Spanish Netherlands, she threatened the security both of the United Provinces and of Britain. If she held the Spanish possessions in Italy she threatened Anglo-Dutch commerce in the Mediterranean. If she controlled the Spanish overseas empire she threatened Anglo-Dutch colonial trade, and especially the profitable trade in slaves for the Spanish colonies.[1] The second Grand Alliance, signed on 27 August 1701 between the Emperor, Great Britain and the United Provinces, was therefore concerned to counter these three threats. The Spanish Netherlands were to be recovered so that they might be 'a fence and rampart, commonly called a barrier, separating and distancing France from the United Provinces'. The French were to be ejected from Milan, Naples, Sicily and the other Spanish territories in Italy. Finally, the crowns of France and Spain were to be permanently separated, so that Spanish colonial trade should not be run from Paris in the interests of French merchants.

These aims committed the Allies to an offensive war, since France was already in possession of the things they intended to wrest from her. Two courses were open to them. Their offensive could either take the form of a concerted invasion of France, with the aim of dictating peace terms in Paris itself, or it could be a haphazard and piecemeal affair, with each of the allies tackling the objective which concerned him most immediately. The British Commander-in-Chief, the Earl of Marlborough, was convinced that a joint Allied invasion of France was the best way of winning the war. Antoine Heinsius, Grand Pensionary of the United Provinces, and Prince Eugene, the ablest of the Emperor's generals, were inclined to agree with him; but all three men had the greatest difficulty in carrying their fellow countrymen with them. In England, both the Country Party and the merchants wanted a limited war waged at sea against French trade rather than an all-out effort on land against France herself. The Dutch were reluctant to let their armies be used for anything other than the conquest of the Spanish Netherlands and the Emperor, harassed by a Hungarian rebellion and by fears of attack from Poland and Turkey, was not prepared to do much more than contest the French occupation of Milan. Those of his princes who had joined the Alliance—they included the Electors of Hanover,[2] Brandenburg, Mayence, Treves and the Palatinate, as well as the Margrave of Baden—were ready to carry the war across the Rhine into France, but it was difficult to see how their various armies could be moulded into an effective striking force. The Elector of Hanover, who would probably lose

[1] One of the first results of Philip V's accession to the Spanish throne had been the transference of the Asiento, the contract to supply slaves, from a Portuguese syndicate friendly to English slave traders, to the French Guinea Company.
[2] In 1692 the Duke of Brunswick-Luneburg had been created Elector of Hanover, bringing the number of Electors to nine.

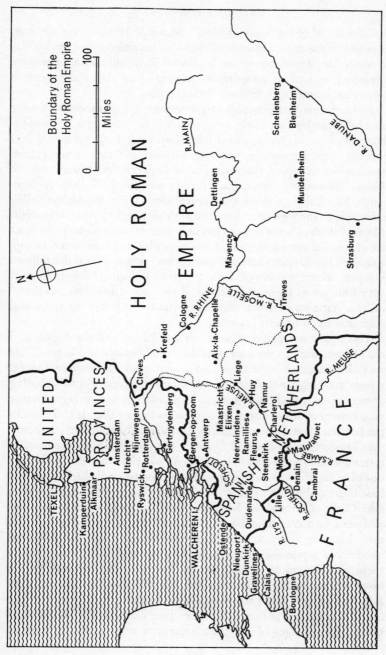

The North Eastern Frontiers of France

his chance of being King of Great Britain if France won the war, was one of the most vigorous of them but his claim to leadership was contested by Brandenburg and by Baden. It would take a superlative diplomat, as well as a superlative strategist, to plan and execute a joint attack on France in these circumstances.

Nevertheless Marlborough was determined that it should be done and he spent his first campaign preparing for it. Joseph of Wittelsbach, Bishop of Liége and Archbishop-Elector of Cologne, had joined Louis during the previous autumn and as a result French armies had occupied the crucial area between the Rhine and the Meuse. By making a feint attack further west, in the Spanish Netherlands, Marlborough drew the French away from the Meuse valley and took all the fortresses there, from Venloo right up to Liége itself. Meanwhile the Dutch and the German princes made a successful joint attack on Kaiserswerth, one of the two places at which the French straddled the Rhine. The other one, Bonn, held out until the following year; but it was cut off from the main French armies and was of very little use to them. By the end of 1702 the Allies were in control of the waterways which would enable their forces to unite and converge upon eastern France.

This attack on eastern France via the Rhine and the Meuse and the Moselle was not the only plan that Marlborough had in mind. He was also attracted by the idea of an invasion of southern France, where the Huguenot rebels in the Cevennes were already pinning down appreciable French forces. The situation in southern Europe was, however, much more favourable to France than it had been in the last war: Spain was on her side and so was Savoy, with the result that Prince Eugene and the Emperor's armies had been hard put to it to maintain their position in Milan. It was clear that England could not play an effective part in the Mediterranean until she had a naval base there and in the summer of 1702 Sir George Rooke was sent to take Cadiz. Although he had fifty warships, nearly 150 other ships and some 14,000 men he failed to attack the town. Instead he spent his time harrying the nearby villages and winning for the Allies an unenviable reputation for cruelty and looting which was to do them great harm in Spain later in the war. On his way home, however, he managed to seize the Spanish treasure fleet in Vigo Bay and capture ten French warships. In the eyes of some of the cautious taxpayers at home this more than made up for his failure at Cadiz. The ravages of the French privateers were already making themselves felt—by the autumn of 1702 the price of coal in London had risen to unprecedented heights because the colliers were afraid to sail from Newcastle without a naval escort—and men were reluctant to see the navy tied down in Marlborough's ambitious schemes in southern Europe. They preferred to see it used for the protection of commerce and for attacks on French and Spanish trade and colonies.

In spite of these criticisms of his European strategy, Marlborough's reputation stood very high in England at the beginning of 1703. He had been raised from an earl to a duke and the Commons had congratulated him not only on his victories but also on his diplomacy, which, they said, 'vindicated the Gentlemen of England, who had, by the vile practices of designing men, been traduced, and industriously represented as false to Your Majesty's Allies'. For all their protestations, the gentlemen of England were still very suspicious of the Allies. In January 1703 they complained bitterly about Dutch trade with the enemy and made the supply of soldiers for the Netherlands campaign dependent on this trade being broken off. Nor did the campaign of 1703 do much to allay Anglo-Dutch distrust: Marlborough wanted to strike a decisive blow either on the Moselle or against Antwerp, but the Dutch refused to give effective support to either plan and in the end little was achieved. Bonn was captured, but farther south, in the area between the upper Rhine and the upper Danube, an ugly situation was developing. The Elector of Bavaria had come into the war on the French side in September 1702 and his armies had now established contact with those of France. They defeated the German princes in September 1703 and it looked as though they would make a joint attack on Vienna itself in the following year. It seemed that Germany was to be the scene not of an allied convergence on France but of a French dismemberment of the Alliance.

Count Wratislaw, the Emperor's ambassador in London, implored Marlborough to send an army to defend Vienna, but it was difficult to see how this could be done without creating still more tensions within the Alliance. Neither the gentlemen of England nor the merchants of the United Provinces were keen to see British forces drawn away from the Netherlands to southern Germany in support of an ally who had so far done little to help the common cause. But the fact remained that the loss of Vienna would be disastrous to the Allies and might well result in the deposition of the Emperor and the

setting up of the Elector of Bavaria as a French-supported Holy
Roman Emperor. By the spring of 1704 Marlborough had decided
to march to the relief of Vienna, but he kept his intentions to himself
and told the Dutch that he was only going as far as the Moselle, to
attempt yet again a converging attack on France. At the end of May
he met Prince Eugene at Mundelsheim, halfway between the Rhine
and the Danube, and three weeks later he took the fortress of the
Schellenberg, a key point on the Danube separating the advancing
French from Vienna and from the greater part of Bavaria itself. The
allied forces carried out a systematic devastation of Bavarian territory
in an attempt to force the Elector to change sides, but he left his
electorate to its fate and joined forces with the French. By the beginning of August the French and Bavarian armies, numbering nearly
60,000 men, were drawn up in an extremely strong position near
the village of Blenheim, on the north bank of the Danube a few miles
up river from the Schellenberg. On 2 August 1704 Marlborough and
Eugene, with something like 52,000 men, attacked them and shattered
them. Over 30,000 Frenchmen were killed, captured or wounded.
At one blow Louis had lost one of his finest armies and his whole
position in Germany.

Marlborough himself regarded the battle of Blenheim not as an
end but as a beginning. Two months later he was back in the valley
of the Moselle, clearing it of French forces in readiness for his long-
awaited invasion of France. Now that he had scotched once and for
all the French attempt to drive a wedge into the Alliance, he could
lead its members forward into the final and decisive phase of the war,
a concerted attack upon France herself. But the Allies had no wish to
be led into any such enterprise. Now that the danger in Germany was
past the Emperor wished to turn back to the Hungarian rebellion and
the campaigns in Italy, while the Dutch were concerned only with
the Netherlands. When Marlborough arrived back on the Moselle
front in the spring of 1705 he found that neither the Dutch nor the
German princes were prepared to support him wholeheartedly, and
after some inconclusive manœuvring he was forced to drop the whole
idea in June 1705 and hurry back to the Netherlands, where the Dutch
were falling back before a new French offensive on the Meuse. He
was never to return and Germany, which might have been the
springboard for a united allied offensive against eastern France, was
to become instead an inert and neglected zone separating the war in
the Netherlands from the war in southern Europe. Instead of using

Blenheim as a chance to tighten their grip on France, the Allies insisted on seeing it as an excuse to loosen it.

Marlborough arrived on the Meuse in time to push the French back and penetrate their main lines of defence at Elixem, some twenty miles north of Namur, but he was not able to follow up his success. Even so the French King was sufficiently alarmed to put out peace feelers in the autumn of 1705. He suggested that the Archduke Charles might have Naples and Sicily, though not Milan, and that the Spanish Netherlands might be made into an independent state. The proposals were rather vague, but they did go some way towards ensuring a partition of the Spanish empire and might have provided a basis for negotiations if the aims of the Allies had been the same as those laid down at the beginning of the war. Unfortunately this was not the case. Ever since 5 May 1703, when they had signed the Methuen Treaties with the King of Portugal, the Allies had been committed to a new and much more sweeping war aim: the establishment of the Archduke Charles as King of the whole Spanish empire. 'You know as well as I do,' wrote Marlborough to Heinsius in August 1705, 'that England can like no peace, but such as puts King Charles in the possession of the monarchy of Spain.' Louis's overtures were accordingly rejected and the war which had been conceived by William III as a struggle for the partition of the Spanish empire was carried on in an attempt to give the whole of that empire to a Habsburg prince. It was a short-sighted and impracticable attempt and was to become even more absurd in 1711, when Archduke Charles became Emperor. The failure to follow up Blenheim threw away a chance to win the war; the insistence on 'no peace without Spain' was to throw away repeated chances of winning the peace.

Strangely enough, this transformation of the war for partition into a war for Spain was the work of Nottingham, an inveterate Tory enemy of all continental entanglements. During his period as Secretary of State, from 1702 to 1704, he had deliberately opened up the Spanish theatre of war as an alternative to the Netherlands. In the Netherlands, he argued, England was fighting for Dutch interests with hired armies; but in Spain and the Mediterranean she could fight for her own trading interests with her own navy. And in order to wage this trading war against Spain, either in the Mediterranean or the Atlantic, she needed to ally with Portugal. The Portuguese refused to come into the war unless the Allies sent armies into Spain to put Archduke Charles on the throne; and so the treaties of May

1703 provided for this to be done. They also provided for mutual commercial concessions—the English lowered duties on Portuguese wines and the Portuguese reduced those on English cloth—and for the use of Lisbon by the English navy. As a result an English fleet was able to undertake an extended cruise in the Mediterranean in 1703, which helped to bring Savoy over from the French side to that of the Allies in October 1703.

The allied attack on Spain began in May 1704, with an invasion from Portugal and a seaborne attack on Barcelona. Both these enterprises failed, but in July Sir George Rooke captured Gibraltar. For the Spaniards the loss of this tiny peninsula was only a humiliation, but for the French it was a disaster. Gibraltar was not yet a naval base—it had no dockyards and no proper harbour—but it was a fortress of supreme strategic importance, the possession of which would allow the English to separate the Brest and Toulon fleets at will. The Toulon fleet made an immediate attempt to recapture it, but was held off by Rooke in the indecisive battle of Malaga on 13 August 1704, the only major naval engagement of the war. The Spaniards laid siege to Gibraltar throughout the ensuing winter and on three occasions it was saved in the nick of time by a small squadron under Admiral Leake, based on Lisbon. After April 1705 attempts at recapture were given up and the fortress remained in the hands of the Allies for the rest of the war, providing them with an essential link between their Atlantic invasion of Spain via Portugal and their Mediterranean invasion aimed at Barcelona. The former was once again unsuccessful in 1705, but Barcelona was taken in October and the Archduke Charles was established in eastern Spain. In the following spring a powerful French assault on Barcelona almost drove him out again, but the town was relieved from the sea by Leake's fleet at the end of April. Meanwhile the Allies swept into Spain from Portugal and occupied Madrid itself in June 1706; but by the time the Archduke had made up his mind to join them they had been pushed out of the capital and forced to fall back to the Mediterranean coast. When they tried to move inland again in the spring of 1707 they were disastrously defeated at Almanza on 14 April. Although the area around Barcelona remained loyal to the Archduke, it was clear by this time that the chances of getting him accepted as King of the whole of Spain were very slender.

Meanwhile the original war aims of the Grand Alliance had already been achieved. Early in 1706 Louis had sent his finest army to attack the Allies north of Namur, only to have it pulverized by Marlborough at the battle of Ramillies on 12 May 1706. Within a few weeks the Allies had overrun the whole of the Spanish Netherlands except for a handful of fortresses which held out until October. France herself was threatened and Louis had to pull troops out of Italy to defend his northern frontiers. As a result his whole position in Italy collapsed during the autumn of 1706. By the time the news from Almanza arrived the Allies held, or could easily take, everything for which they had gone to war in 1702. It was clear, however, that if they diverted their forces from the Netherlands and Italy in order to conquer Spain they might well lose all that they had gained. Nottingham's policy of 1703 had produced a grimly amusing paradox, a war that could not be won because it was won.

Marlborough's perennial scheme for a joint invasion of France seemed to offer the best answer to this dilemma. If the Allies could converge on Paris they could there dictate to Louis whatever terms they wished, including the deposition of his own grandson. The old idea of a rendezvous with the German princes on the Moselle had to be abandoned because the princes were frightened by the appearance of the King of Sweden in eastern Germany and would not commit themselves to full-scale operations in the west. But this hardly seemed to matter now that the Allies were in full control of the Netherlands and Italy. Combined attacks from these two bridgeheads would surely bring France to her knees.

They failed to do so. In 1707 Marlborough's campaigns on the borders of France and the Netherlands were completely inconclusive, while Prince Eugene's march from Italy into southern France was halted at Toulon in August of that year. Sir Cloudesley Shovell, the English admiral who was helping Eugene, succeeded in crippling a large part of the French Toulon fleet, but only at the cost of keeping his own ships out far too late in the season. At the end of October, on his way back to England, part of his fleet was wrecked off the Isles of Scilly and he himself was killed. This disaster helped to convince the Admiralty that the navy must have a proper base in the Mediterranean, so that it could winter there; and the Allied efforts in the Mediterranean in 1708 were therefore concentrated on the capture of the Spanish island of Minorca, with its fine naval base of Port Mahon, rather than with attacks on southern France. The conquest of the island, which was completed by the end of September 1708, led to increased friction between the Allies, since the English had no intention of giving it up to the Archduke Charles. 'England ought never to part with this Island, which will give the law to the Mediterranean in time of war and peace', wrote General Stanhope, the man who captured it. As well as offending the Archduke, Stanhope's attitude offended the Dutch, who had always suspected the English of wanting to take over for themselves the commercial power of Spain, both in the Mediterranean and in the Atlantic.[1] In spite of Marlborough's great victory at Oudenarde in the Netherlands, the year 1708 was a bad one for the Allies because of the divisions which it opened up between them. If he could exploit those divisions effectively, Louis might still retrieve much of what he had lost. Meanwhile he demonstrated his continued ability to hit back at his enemies by launching a Jacobite invasion of Scotland in March 1708. It failed, but it helped to remind Englishmen that their continued preoccupation with the Spanish succession was keeping the British succession in jeopardy.

The summer of 1708 was cold and wet and harvests were bad all over Europe. The Allies used their seapower to stop France importing food and by the beginning of 1709 she was in a desperate state, her sufferings increased by one of the coldest and longest winters that anyone could remember. Faced with widespread famine and possible economic collapse, Louis was ready to do everything in his power to secure peace. But this was not enough for the Allies, who insisted that he must also do what was not in his power. When the French foreign minister arrived at The Hague early in May to sue for peace, he was told that the French would have to give up all Bourbon claims to the Spanish empire, make over their rights in Newfoundland to the English, demolish the fortifications of Dunkirk and surrender to the Allies the fortresses of Lille and Strasbourg, which guarded the approaches to France from the north and from the east respectively. To all this he agreed. He was then told that Louis must 'so manage it that the duke [i.e. Philip V, whom the Allies recognized only as Duke of Anjou] shall depart from the limits of the kingdom of Spain'. If he failed to persuade his grandson to give up his throne, the war would be renewed after two months. Louis could not and would not agree to this preposterous condition and so the war went on. Marlborough led the allied armies into northern France and won

[1] These suspicions were justified. In January 1708 Archduke Charles had signed a secret treaty giving Britain exclusive rights to trade with Spanish America when the war was over.

another great victory at Malplaquet on 31 August, though at the cost of the most appalling slaughter: the Allies lost well over 20,000 men and the French nearly 15,000. Throughout Europe men had been shocked by the breakdown of the peace negotiations and they were even more shocked by the carnage of Malplaquet. Marlborough himself told Godolphin: 'It is melancholy to see so many brave men killed, with whom I have lived these last eight years, when we thought ourselves sure of a peace.'

By this time the Dutch were convinced that the British were only prolonging the war for their own selfish ends, in order to corner the Spanish American trade. Their suspicions had to be lulled, and their support for the continuance of the war bought, by the Barrier Treaty of December 1709. This gave them a chain of barrier fortresses across the Spanish Netherlands and a guaranteed share in the Spanish American trade. It also provided for England to give up Minorca to the Archduke Charles. Thus reunited, the Allies met the French again at Gertruydenberg in the spring of 1710 and again demanded that Louis should get his grandson out of Spain. He had already withdrawn his troops from the country and he now offered to subsidize allied armies to dethrone Philip. It was not enough: he was told that he must send French troops against his own grandson. He refused and the Allies made one more attempt to get Philip out of Spain themselves. They failed dismally and at Brihuega in November 1710 the British army in Spain was caught in a trap and forced to surrender. Meanwhile Marlborough's campaign in northern France was inconclusive and resulted only in the capture of a few fortresses.

At last, in 1711, the thing that the French had been waiting for happened: the Grand Alliance broke apart. In London the ministers who had been the keenest supporters of the war had been dismissed in the autumn of 1710 and replaced by men who had made secret approaches to France for a peace 'without Spain'. Then, in April 1711, the sudden death of the Emperor and the election of the Archduke Charles as his successor made it necessary to reconsider, even in public, the future of the Spanish crown. The Archduke, now the Emperor Charles VI, still expected it for himself, but his Allies were reluctant to give the Spanish empire to the man who now ruled the Holy Roman Empire. They were reminded of what William III had taught them and they had forgotten in 1703: that it was their business to 'hold the balance of Europe' and not allow it to be upset either by France or by the Habsburgs. But if the Spanish empire was, after all, to be partitioned, the Dutch wanted it done in a way which would honour the promises made to them in the Barrier Treaty of 1709. The British, on the other hand, were prepared to let the Dutch have the barrier itself, but were determined to seize for themselves the Spanish American trade and the control of the Mediterranean. They therefore worked out a settlement with France along these lines and when their Allies refused to accept it they made a separate armistice, withdrew their troops from the front and left the Dutch and Prince Eugene to be defeated by the French at Denain in July 1712. Although the Emperor went on fighting until 1714, the Dutch saw that this was the end of the road. At Utrecht on 31 March 1713 they gave their grudging consent to the arrangements which Britain and France had made for Europe and for the world.

The basis of the Peace of Utrecht was the partition of the Spanish empire. Spain and Spanish America went to Philip V, on the under-standing that the crowns of France and Spain should never be united. The Netherlands, Milan, Naples and Sardinia went to the Emperor, Sicily to Savoy, Minorca and Gibraltar to Britain. Britain also acquired extensive trading concessions in Spanish America, as well as Newfoundland, Nova Scotia, the Hudson Bay territories and the West Indian island of St Kitt's from France. Louis XIV also agreed to recognize the Protestant succession in Britain and demolish the fortifications of Dunkirk.[1]

It was to take Britain eight more years to persuade the European Powers to accept the Peace of Utrecht as a final settlement. In the meantime her friends and her enemies alike were appalled by her lack of good faith and her cynical disregard of treaty obligations, for she had broken promises made in 1701 as well as those made in 1703 and 1709. To the British ministers this seemed justifiable, since the promises had been made by their political opponents. Party politics had shaped the war, so party politics must shape the peace: the men of 1713 must make a dishonourable peace because the men of 1703 and the men of 1709 had made an absurd war. Foreign rulers, how-ever, were not interested in the peculiar nature of British political

[1] During the War of the Spanish Succession, and especially after 1708, the French had concentrated on privateering to an even greater extent than in the previous war. Dunkirk had been the most dangerous centre for these activities, accounting for nearly a quarter of the total losses inflicted on Allied shipping. It was for this reason that British merchants insisted on the destruction of its fortifications and the filling up of its harbour. See J. S. Bromley: 'The French Privateering War, 1702-1713' in *Historical Essays presented to David Ogg*, London, 1963.

life. All they knew was that Britain was not to be trusted. This realization, and the widespread anti-British feeling which it produced, was to bedevil Britain's foreign policy for the next hundred years.

2 The rule of the Triumvirate

When Anne became Queen in March 1702 she naturally wanted those who had been her friends while she was heir to the throne to be her ministers now that she occupied it. The 'reversionary interest', that group of politicians who had preferred to support the person to whom the crown would revert rather than the person who was actually wearing it, were now to have their reward. Chief among them were Marlborough and Godolphin. Marlborough was already Commander-in-Chief of the armies in the Netherlands and he was now made Captain-General of all the Queen's land forces, while his wife Sarah, a close personal friend of the new Queen, was made Groom of the Stole, Mistress of the Robes and Comptroller of the Privy Purse. Within forty-eight hours of Anne's accession Marlborough's influence was so powerful and so widely recognized that he was being referred to as 'the Grand Vizier'. Godolphin, an old friend of the Marlboroughs and connected to them by the marriage of his son to their eldest daughter, became Lord High Treasurer. These two men were well equipped to manage the war to which the new Queen was committed—Marlborough was a great diplomat as well as a great soldier and Godolphin was an extremely able financier —but they were not in a position to manage the men who must pay for it. Their personal following of about a dozen members of the House of Commons would be supplemented, now that they were firmly established in power, by a hundred or more office-holders and other supporters of the Court; but this was still not enough to ensure the proper management of the Queen's affairs in Parliament. If she was to govern effectively and raise the taxes and loans necessary for her wars she would have to look farther afield than Marlborough and Godolphin for her ministers.

It was generally assumed that she would look to the Tories, and most of her early appointments seemed to justify this view. The key post of Comptroller of the Household, which had come to carry with it a great part of the management of the Court interest in Parliament, was taken from Wharton and given to the Tory High Churchman Sir Edward Seymour, who had very considerable electoral influence among the Tory squires of the western countries. The Earl of Rochester, the Queen's uncle and a prominent High Tory, was made Lord-Lieutenant of Ireland, and the Earl of Nottingham, another Tory, became Secretary of State for the South. Both men were known not only for their staunch devotion to the Anglican Church but also for their hostility to William III and his continental wars. Rochester, in particular, had taken little trouble to disguise the fact that he did not regard William as his rightful King at all but merely as Queen Mary's widower. Whig leaders like Somers, Montagu and Russell, who had been identified with the late King's policies, were not only stripped of their offices but excluded from the Privy Council. As ever, the electors were anxious to underwrite the new arrangements and put into Parliament men who could transmit royal favour down the line to them. In the old Parliament which the Queen dissolved at the end of May there were ninety members of the House of Commons who could be considered as followers of Marlborough, Godolphin, Seymour, Rochester or Nottingham. In the new one which she opened in October there were 129. The Whig lords, on the other hand, found their following reduced from sixty-four to forty-nine.

All this did not mean, however, that Anne intended to put herself into the hands of great Tory borough-mongers like Seymour, Rochester or Nottingham. For all her devotion to the Anglican Church and for all her hatred of William III's Whig financiers and favourites, she saw clearly enough that the dignity of her crown depended on keeping both parties firmly in their places. Time and time again she insisted that her ministers must keep her out of the hands of 'the merciless men of both parties' and in 1706 she was to tell Godolphin to employ 'all those that concur faithfully in my service, whether they are called Whigs or Tories, not to be tied to one or the other'. If there was any party with which she felt in sympathy it was neither the Tories nor the Whigs but the Country Party. The ordinary country gentlemen, with their distrust of factious party magnates, their loyalty to Church and Queen and their belated realization that war against France was necessary to safeguard the Protestant succession, were the people in Parliament whose political attitude came nearest to her own. If she was to have the sort of ministry she wanted, the third element in it, to stand alongside Marlborough and Godolphin, must be not a group of High Tory lords but a man who could rally the country gentlemen to her side.

The obvious man for the job was Robert Harley, who was still the acknowledged leader and manipulator of the Country Party in the Commons. He was taken into the Queen's confidence as soon as she succeeded and he helped Marlborough and Godolphin to draft her first speech to Parliament. When the new Parliament met in the autumn of 1702 he was once again elected Speaker and entrusted with the task of looking after the Queen's interests in the Commons. This was not easy, for the Tories were concerned to use their ascendancy to crush their enemies rather than to further the Queen's business. They voted supplies for the war, but they showed their distrust of Marlborough's continental preoccupations by allotting twice as much to the navy as to the army. They pursued their vendetta against the Whigs by trying to revive the impeachments which had been dropped in 1701 and by seeking to revoke all grants of land made by William III. These proposals were scotched, as was their attempt to purge the Treasury of Whig officials. Godolphin, who was more interested in administrative efficiency than party vengeance, persuaded the Queen not to give in to this demand; but he was not able to prevent Nottingham from getting a large number of Whig lord-lieutenants, sheriffs and justices of the peace dismissed in the spring of 1703. Faced with this factious and vengeful spirit in the Commons, there was little that Harley could do except give the Tories enough rope and hope that they would hang themselves. He was, however, able to discipline the country gentlemen effectively and dramatically in the matter of placemen. Two days before Christmas 1702, in a rapidly thinning House, they voted by 135 to 80 that all placemen should be excluded from the Commons; but later the same evening they were persuaded to reverse their decision by 138 to 77.

By the beginning of 1703 Anne was already beginning to resent the way in which the Tories were trying to run away with her. In February 1703 she forced her uncle Rochester to resign his post as Lord-Lieutenant of Ireland and in the same month she stood firm against requests that she should swamp the House of Lords by a wholesale creation of Tory peers. But it was the behaviour of the Tories over the Occasional Conformity Bill that really turned her against them and determined her to rely on the Triumvirate of Marlborough, Godolphin and Harley rather than on any coalition with the Tories.

Ever since 1689 High Churchmen had resented the growing power and influence of the Dissenters, and especially the way in which some of them made a token annual communion in an Anglican church in order to qualify themselves for municipal office. The accession of Anne, who was known to be a devout Anglican, was hailed as a chance to do something about this practice and in December 1702 a Bill was passed through the Commons making it illegal. The Whig majority in the Lords, supported by the Archbishop of Canterbury himself, killed the Bill by hostile amendments and precipitated a violent quarrel between the two Houses. As passions mounted on both sides Anne became increasingly disgusted with the whole business and she was particularly shocked by the vindictiveness with which the Tories hounded down Daniel Defoe for his satirical pamphlet *The Shortest Way with the Dissenters*. When Defoe was made to stand in the pillory in July 1703 the London mob turned his punishment into a triumph and before long Harley himself was employing him to collect information for him on the state of public opinion. By October Marlborough was writing to Harley deploring 'the heats that continue between the two parties', and a month later Godolphin told Harley that 'it is necessary above all that you and I should meet regularly, at least twice a week if not oftener, to advise upon everything that shall occur'. The Triumvirate were drawing closer and closer together in their determination to unite Queen and Country against the parties and the borough-mongers. It was a policy which was summed up admirably by Harley in a letter which he wrote to Godolphin in September 1705: 'If the gentlemen of England are made sensible that the Queen is the head and not a Party, everything will be easy and the Queen will be courted and not a party.'

When Parliament met again in the autumn of 1703 the Occasional Conformity Bill was again passed through the Commons amid ferocious controversy. On the night of the 26 November, while the crisis was at its height, a terrible storm swept across the country causing appalling damage and loss of life. Among the casualties was Richard Kidder, Bishop of Bath and Wells, who was killed in his bed by a falling chimney stack. High Churchmen had regarded him as a Whig time-server and a secret ally of the Dissenters and, while resisting the temptation to see his death as an instance of divine retribution, they certainly wanted to see him replaced by someone more to their own taste. Anne seemed quite ready to oblige them and even offered to give the bishopric back to Thomas Ken, the High

Churchman who had been deprived of the see in 1691 because he would not take the oath of allegiance to William and Mary. When Ken refused to be reinstated she appointed his friend George Hooper, another eminent High Church divine whose views were said to have so annoyed William III that he had told him angrily: 'Well, Dr Hooper, you will never be a bishop.' His appointment suggested that Anne's devotion to High Church principles remained unshaken and that she could still be relied upon to support the Occasional Conformity Bill. Accordingly, when it was thrown out by the Lords in December 1703, the Tories began to talk about tacking it on to a Money Bill, so that the Lords should not be able to reject it again. By the time Marlborough left for his German campaign in April 1704 he was seriously worried by the evident determination of Nottingham and the other Tories in the ministry to support the 'tack' and drag the Queen into another crisis. The remark made by one Whig lord that 'if they passed this Bill they had as good tack the pretended Prince of Wales to it', showed how high feeling was running. It would be a tragedy if, in the middle of a war against the Pretender and his French supporters, the Queen allowed herself to be dominated by ministers whom the country was coming to regard as secret Jacobites.

Marlborough need not have worried. Anne's High Church views were indeed unshaken, but she saw that the Occasional Conformity Bill was not just a matter of religious principles but of party politics as well. Many Tory borough-mongers were less interested in purifying the Church than in seizing control of those boroughs where Whig patrons were working through dissenting burgesses and corporations. As if to underline the all-pervading preoccupation with party advantage, the two Houses of Parliament fell to quarrelling afresh in the spring of 1704 over the case of Matthew Ashby, a Whig burgess of Aylesbury who had been prevented from voting by a Tory returning officer, William White. Encouraged by Lord Wharton, who was assiduously building up a Whig interest in Aylesbury, Ashby brought a case against White. The Tory majority in the Commons denied his right to do so, whereupon the Whig majority in the Lords denied their right to deny his right. Although important constitutional and legal issues were involved, the squalid struggle between party magnates which lay at the root of the matter was not a pretty sight. By the end of the session in April 1704 Anne was sick of party politics and party politicians, including those within her ministry. Seymour was dismissed later that month and at the beginning of May Harley replaced Nottingham as Secretary of State.[1] Undeterred, the Tories brought in their motion to tack the Occasional Conformity Bill to the Land Tax at the beginning of the next session, only to be defeated by 251 votes to 134. Even Rochester and Nottingham found that they had lost control of their followers, less than half of whom voted for the motion. It was a signal victory for Harley, who was still Speaker even though he was Secretary of State, and it was to him that Daniel Williams, a dissenting minister with important connections among the monied men, addressed his letter of congratulation on 29 November, the day after the crucial debate. Earlier that month Defoe had reported to Harley that people in the street 'call the Duke of Marlborough, the Lord Treasurer and yourself *the Triumvirate* who manage the State'. The Triumvirate, which had been at work behind the scenes ever since its members had come together to write the Queen's first speech to Parliament, had now come out into the open and taught the party magnates a sharp lesson, showing them that the Queen could do without parties better than the parties could do without the Queen.

For a time it seemed as though its success might prove permanent. Blenheim renewed men's confidence in Marlborough's ability to win the war, while Godolphin was giving clear proof of his ability to finance it. In 1704 he raised no less than £7,000,000 in loans at 6 per cent, as well as a further £878,000 in annuities secured on the Excise. Harley played his part by getting the Commons to vote over £4,600,000 for the war and by securing the defeat of yet another Place Bill. To keep both parties at arm's length and yet prevent them combining against the Court interest in Parliament was a considerable achievement. Once the tacking of the Occasional Conformity Bill had been scotched, the main cause of friction between the parties was the Ashby and White case, in which five more burgesses of Aylesbury had now become involved. Both Houses got themselves into positions from which they could not retreat, the Lords arguing that the Commons could not override the Common Law and the Commons arguing that the Lords could not interfere with their privileges, so that there was general relief when Anne cut short the quarrel by dissolving Parliament in April 1705.

If they had stood strictly by their principles, the members of the Triumvirate would have made no attempt to influence the general

[1]The other Secretary, Sir Charles Hedges, moved from the Northern department to the Southern and Harley took over the Northern.

election of June 1705 one way or the other: they would have waited
for the electors to reject the party magnates and produce a Parliament
in which Court and country could unite against faction. But they
remembered only too well what had happened to William III
when he had done this in 1698 and they did not want it to happen
again. Whether they liked it or not—and Harley liked it a good deal
less than his colleagues—they would have to balance their rejection of
the Tories with a little discreet wooing of the Whigs. Accordingly,
several Tory lord-lieutenants were replaced by Whigs just before the
election, while the Duke of Newcastle, an influential Whig borough-
monger, became Lord Privy Seal in April. The electors took the hint.
Newcastle's following was increased from sixteen to twenty-four,
while that grouped around Wharton, Somers, Montagu, Russell and
Sunderland jumped from forty-nine to sixty-four. Rochester and
Nottingham, on the other hand, found their group in the Commons
reduced from 111 to 79; and of the 134 men who had voted for the
'tack' only eighty were re-elected. Although Godolphin and Harley
consoled themselves with the thought that there were a hundred or so
'Queen's servants' who would hold the balance between the parties,
it was pretty clear that in escaping from the Tories they had run
into the arms of the Whigs. When Parliament met in October they
decided to give government support to the Whig candidate for the
office of Speaker and they dismissed one of the office-holders who
failed to vote for him. At the same time another gesture was made
towards the Whigs by the appointment of William Cowper as
Lord Keeper of the Great Seal. He was later raised to the peerage and
made Lord Chancellor.

Meanwhile the violence of the Tories was pushing the Queen
steadily towards the Whigs. In December 1705 Rochester brought
forward a motion in the Lords asserting that she had endangered the
Church of England itself by entrusting her affairs to her present
ministers. Both the Queen and Parliament were infuriated by this
suggestion and a large majority in both Houses passed a resolution
stating that 'whoever goes about to suggest and insinuate that the
Church is in danger under Her Majesty's administration is an enemy
to the Queen, the Church and the Kingdom'. The Tories' next move
was more ingenious and even more offensive to Anne: they suggested
that the Electress Sophia should be invited to come and live in
England, in order to prevent any possibility of a Jacobite restoration
if Anne should die suddenly. It was well known that Anne resented

bitterly this reminder of her own expected death, but the Tories hoped that the Whigs would not dare to save her from it for fear of being branded as secret Jacobites or, even worse, secret republicans. As it was the Whigs rallied to the Queen's side and the Whig Lord Somers, even though he was still excluded from office, drafted a Regency Bill providing for a regency of lords justice to run the country between the Queen's death and the arrival of her successor. It was this Bill, passed into law in its final form in 1707 after the Union with Scotland, which repealed the clause in the Act of Settlement excluding office-holders from the Commons and replaced it with one allowing them to seek re-election.

Anne was still suspicious of the Whigs, but she could not help being impressed by their loyalty and efficiency in saving her from having to have Sophia in her country, waiting for her to die. Harley was still afraid that a closer alliance with the Whigs would mean the alienation of the Country Party: 'the embodying of gentlemen (country gentlemen, I mean) against the Queen's service is what is to be avoided' he told Godolphin. But Godolphin and Marlborough were now convinced of the need to work with the Whigs, since without them the war could neither be won nor paid for. Admitting moderate Whigs like Newcastle and Cowper into the ministry was not enough: Anne would have to accept a member of the great Wharton –Somers–Montagu–Russell–Sunderland connection, the central core of the Whig party. Sunderland, the youngest and least Whiggish of the group, seemed the most eligible. He was the son of the Sunderland who had served both James II and William III and he was married to one of Marlborough's daughters; and it was he who hinted to his mother-in-law in September 1706 that if he was not given office the Whigs would not support the government in the coming session of Parliament. Backed by Godolphin and by her husband, the Duchess of Marlborough exerted all her influence to get him accepted. She lost a good deal of it in the process, but she finally succeeded. On the day Parliament met, 3 December 1706, Sunderland became Secretary of State for the South and the Whigs in the Commons were given their orders. Within three weeks they had voted supplies to the tune of £5,500,000 for the prosecution of the war.

Meanwhile, the Triumvirate were engaged on an enterprise that made the need for Whig support even more vital: the knitting together of England and Scotland into one United Kingdom.

3 *The Union with Scotland*

Ever since the Stuart Kings of Scotland had inherited the English throne in 1603 they had found it difficult to rule their two kingdoms in double harness. William III, preoccupied with the threat from France and mindful of the traditional alliance between the French and the Scots, was particularly concerned to forge the countries into one; and at the very end of his life he urged his Parliament to give the matter its serious attention. Commissioners from both kingdoms met accordingly in London in November 1702, but their work was brought to a standstill at the beginning of the following year because the English Parliament would not allow its commissioners to concede the two things upon which the Scots were particularly insistent— freedom of trade with England and guarantees for the maintenance of the Presbyterian religion in Scotland. These two issues reflected the tangled and contradictory nature of the problem. While High Churchmen disliked the Scots because they were Presbyterians, dissenting merchants disliked them because they sought to invade English trading privileges. The former were indifferent on the question of trade but adamant over religion, while the latter were sympathetic about religion but unyielding over trade. The Tory concern for the Church of England and the Whig concern for the monied interest would make it difficult for the party magnates to accept a union with Scotland, while the backbench country gentlemen upon whom Harley placed such reliance were known to view it with distaste.

Scottish attitudes to England were even more varied and even more hostile than English attitudes to Scotland. To the Jacobite chieftains in the Highlands the matter was simple enough: the hated Lowlanders had sold the country to the even more hated English and there was nothing to be done but await an opportunity to put King James VIII on the throne. To the more moderate Highlanders and to the Episcopalians the link with England, which under William III had been a symbol of the triumph of their enemies the Presbyterians, was now a means by which they might get back to power themselves. If Anne was determined to crush the Dissenters in England, she could surely be persuaded to crush the Presbyterians in Scotland. For their part, the Presbyterians were alive to this alarming possibility but they did not want to end the connection with England if it meant throwing themselves into the arms of the Catholic James

Stuart, the man whom they thought of as 'the Pretender' but who was called King James VIII by the Jacobites.

Quite apart from these particular considerations, all Scotsmen resented rule from London and they were especially resentful of the way in which they had been bundled into the War of the Spanish Succession. If the English wanted to wage a trading war against France and Spain they were welcome to do so; but why should they expect the Scots, whom they excluded from all their trading activities, to support them? Whatever their religion, Scotsmen in 1702 felt that the time had come either to mend or end their association with England. The English must be made to realize that if they wanted the security which a friendly Scotland could give them, they must pay for it. In the new Scottish Parliament elected in the spring of 1703 the anti-English Country Party had an overwhelming majority and was able to push through a series of Acts designed to bring pressure to bear on the government in London. An Act Anent Peace and War prevented future kings of England and Scotland from involving Scotland in war without the consent of the Scottish Parliament, while a Wine Act legalized for Scotsmen the trade in French wine which was illegal for Englishmen. Finally, the Act of Security provided that on Anne's death the Scottish Parliament should choose a successor different from the person who succeeded in England, unless in the meantime the English agreed to 'such conditions of government . . . as may secure the honour and sovereignty of this crown and kingdom, the freedom, frequency and power of Palriaments, the religion, liberty and trade of the nation from English or any foreign influence'.

Like most people in England, Anne was infuriated by this political blackmail. She refused to give her assent to the Act of Security and dismissed her ministers in Edinburgh, replacing them with men who claimed to be able to manage the Scottish Parliament into accepting the Hanoverian succession. But the new ministers were as helpless as the old, and the Parliament in Edinburgh passed the Act of Security again in the 1704 session, refusing to grant supplies until it had received the royal assent. On 5 August 1704 the Queen gave in and signed the Act.

When the English Parliament met in the autumn of 1704 the Tories attacked Godolphin vehemently for allowing the Queen to surrender to the Scots in this way. He pointed out that when he had advised acceptance of the Act the news of Blenheim had not yet arrived and the situation in Europe had appeared far too critical to risk a civil war with Scotland. The Tories brushed this argument aside and it became increasingly clear that they were more interested in humbling the Scots than in beating the King of France. The Whigs, on the other hand, were coming to see that the only way of winning the war and preserving the Hanoverian succession was to come to terms with the Scots. Whatever reservations their monied friends might have about admitting Scotsmen to English trade, they could not afford to risk an open clash between the two nations, which could only benefit the French and the Jacobites. After some initial doubts the Whigs came down on the side of the government and supported a policy of further negotiation with the Scots. This was to be accompanied by an Act providing that if they did not either accept the Hanoverian succession or agree to a Treaty of Union by the end of 1705 they were to be treated as aliens in England and their goods prohibited from entering the country. The English as well as the Scots could back up their negotiations with threats.

For a time it looked as though the two countries might be on the brink of war. The Scottish militia was called out in force and trained regularly, while in the English House of Commons it was suggested that the northern counties of England should be organized to repel a possible Scottish invasion. This did not prove to be necessary, but it was certainly true that anti-English feeling was running very high in Scotland. In April 1705 Anne's ministers in Edinburgh were forced by popular clamour to execute three English seamen on charges of piracy, although they had received from London evidence to suggest that the men were innocent. This miserable surrender to the demands of the mob so shocked the authorities in England that they secured the dismissal of the Scottish ministers, replacing them with a ministry centred on the Duke of Argyle, the Duke of Queensberry and the Earl of Seafield, three of the most prominent advocates in Scotland of a closer union with England. In September the Duke of Hamilton, who was a possible candidate for the throne of Scotland and had been up to that time a critic of the union, changed his tactics and supported the ministers in the Scottish Parliament. As a result they were able to push through an Act appointing Commissioners to treat for a union. The English Parliament helped to smooth the path to settlement by repealing the Aliens Act in December 1705, a few weeks before it was due to come into effect. In April 1706 the Commissioners for the two countries met in London and three months later they signed the

Treaty of Union. All that remained was for it to be accepted by the Parliaments of the two kingdoms.

The treaty's passage through the Scottish Parliament between October 1706 and January 1707 was stormy, but it was clear from the beginning that the supporters of union were in a majority. The treaty conceded the vital point of freedom of trade, so that the real issue was, as one Scotsman pointed out, 'whether Scotland should be subject to an English Ministry without trade, or be subject to an English Parliament with trade'. The other important point, the safety of the Scottish Kirk, was secured when an 'Act for securing the Protestant Religion and Presbyterian Church Government within the Kingdom of Scotland' was incorporated into the treaty in November; and from that time on, although there was a good deal of noisy rioting and vehement petitioning, serious opposition to the treaty dwindled and it received Anne's assent as Queen of Scotland on 16 January 1707. As Queen of England she then recommended it to her English Parliament at the end of February and within a week it had passed through both Houses, in spite of violent protests by the High Tories against the toleration of Presbyterianism which it involved. It came into effect on 1 May 1707 and was received with acclamation in both countries, although some of the more super-stitious of the Scots were worried by the sudden appearance of thirty-one large whales on the sands of Kirkcaldy, a disturbing omen for the beginning of English rule in Scotland.

The Act of Union provided that the succession to the throne of the United Kingdom of Great Britain should be as laid down in the Act of Settlement and that there should be one Parliament for the whole realm. In this body Scotland was to be represented by sixteen members of the House of Lords, chosen by the Scottish peers them-selves, and by forty-five members of the House of Commons elected by the Scottish shires and burghs. It was reckoned that Scotland's contribution to taxation would entitle her to only twelve members and her population to eighty-five, so that forty-five was a reasonable compromise. She was to pay the same taxes as England and her share of the Land Tax was fixed at one-fortieth of the English assessment. She was, however, to be exempted from certain temporary taxes im-posed to pay for the war, such as those on legal documents, windows, malt and home-consumed coals. Scotsmen were to have complete freedom to trade 'within the said united kingdom and the dominions and plantations thereunto belonging' and they were to receive from the English an immediate payment of £398,000, most of which was to go to compensate investors in the Darien Company. Some of it, however, was used to settle debts owed by the Scottish government to individual Scottish noblemen; and this gave the Jacobites a chance to assert that the Union was pushed through by means of bribery.

Most Scotsmen were satisfied with these arrangements and hoped that they could trust the English to abide by them. Unfortunately they could not: within a very short time the English were eagerly using their overwhelming majority in the Parliament at Westminster to make adjustments to the Act of Union. The abolition of the Scottish Privy Council in 1708 did not cause much resentment, but the introduction of the English law of treason into Scotland in the same year was more disturbing, since the Act of Union had promised that Scottish Law should remain unaltered. In 1711 the House of Lords refused to let Scottish peers who were given British titles take their seats, and in the following year Parliament passed an Act reintroducing lay patronage into the Scottish Church. Both these steps violated the spirit, if not the letter, of the Act of Union, as did the imposition of the Malt Tax on Scotland in 1713. By this time the Scots were furious at the bad faith of the English and even the Duke of Argyle was anxious to repeal the Union. A motion for its repeal introduced into the Lords in May 1713 was only defeated by four votes; and discontent continued to smoulder in Scotland for generations to come.

Whatever the Union's future in Scotland might be, its immediate effect in England was to drive the Queen and the Triumvirate still further into the arms of the Whigs. It was Wharton who had made the Union possible by saving Godolphin from the Tory onslaught of 1704 and it was Somers who had been largely responsible for the drafting of the treaty itself. The Duchess of Marlborough urged Anne to admit these and other Whig leaders to office, while Godolphin thought that only a firm alliance with the Whigs would enable the government to face Parliament. Marlborough himself had no love for the Whigs, but he was coming to think that the war could not be won without them. Only Harley continued to cling to the ideal of government without party by which the Triumvirate had originally been inspired. To him, at least, Anne could still look for protection against 'the merciless men of both parties'. Her affection for Abigail Hill, a Lady of the Bedchamber who was in Harley's confidence, drew her closer to him and embittered her relations with the Duchess of Marlborough. In the summer of 1707 the Duchess quarrelled violently with the Queen when she found out that Abigail had been secretly married to a courtier called Masham in the Queen's presence. By the time Parliament met, reinforced by the representatives of Scotland, in December 1707, the Triumvirate was hopelessly divided and its two wings were engaged in a vicious struggle for the Queen's favour.

The outcome of that struggle was decided by events in Parliament, where the Tories attacked the ministry vigorously for its management of the war and in particular for its failure to provide proper protection for merchant shipping. Unless the Whig magnates could be persuaded to rally their followers to the government's side, there would be nobody to defend it: both monied men and country gentlemen were joining in the attack and the Low Churchmen who might otherwise have stood by the Queen against the Tories were furious with her for appointing High Churchmen to the bishoprics of Chester and Exeter. In the middle of the session Harley's position was undermined when one of the clerks in his office was caught spying for the French. By February 1708 Marlborough and Godolphin had decided that Anne must drop Harley and turn to a closer alliance with the Whigs; and when she still refused to do so they resigned. She tried to carry on without them but some of the most moderate and least Whiggish of her councillors refused to support her and even Harley himself saw that the end had come. On 10 February he persuaded the Queen to accept his resignation.

4   The swing of the pendulum

Harley's resignation did not produce a new administration, but a reshuffle of the old one. Henry Boyle, the Chancellor of the Exchequer, became the new Secretary of State. Harley's supporter St John was replaced as Secretary at War by Robert Walpole, who had held a minor post at the Admiralty since 1705. John Smith, the Speaker of the House of Commons, took over from Boyle as Chancellor of the Exchequer. None of these men could be said to be committed to the Wharton–Somers group, which the Queen was still determined to keep at arm's length. When Newcastle asked her at the end of April to admit Somers to the Cabinet she refused peremptorily. Marlborough was dismayed by this refusal which, he told Anne, 'will be a demonstration . . . to everybody, that Lord Treasurer and

I have no credit with your Majesty, but that you are guided by the insinuation of Mr Harley'. He was particularly worried about its effect on the ministry's standing in the new Parliament which, he predicted, would be dominated by the Whigs.

His forecast proved correct. When they went to the polls in May the electors had no clear indication of the Queen's intentions, since she had refrained from making any of the usual pre-election changes among the lord-lieutenants and the justices of the peace. But the Whig magnates shamelessly used her name in their own interests,[1] while the attempted invasion of Scotland in March had, like all Jacobite scares, told against the Tories. When the results came in, Sunderland was convinced that he and his friends had secured 'the most Whig Parliament . . . since the Revolution'. But they were still far from securing a Whig ministry. All through the summer they pressed for a greater share of the spoils of office and by October they were demanding that Anne should dismiss her husband, Prince George of Denmark, from his post as Lord High Admiral and give it to the Earl of Pembroke. Pembroke's present posts, of Lord President of the Council and Lord-Lieutenant of Ireland, were then to be given to Somers and Wharton respectively. Prince George was seriously ill and quite incapable of carrying out his duties, so that from an administrative point of view the suggestion was sensible enough; but to the Queen personally it was highly offensive. At the end of October Prince George died and Anne was too overcome by grief to stand out any longer: Pembroke took over the Admiralty, Somers the Lord Presidency and Wharton the Lord-Lieutenancy of Ireland. At last the Whig lords were in. But in getting in they had humiliated the Queen, soured her friendship with the Duchess of Marlborough and darkened the last weeks of her husband's life. For these things she never forgave them.

In spite of these concessions to the Whigs, the new Parliament proved difficult to manage,[2] largely owing to the skill with which Harley stirred up the Country Party against his former colleagues. The ministers were harried by attacks on the Allies, by accusations

[1] Sunderland told one of his electoral contacts in Scotland: 'I would not have you be bullied by the Court Party [i.e. those ministers who were not Whigs] for the Queen herself cannot support that faction long.' Anne was so annoyed by his electioneering that she came very near to dismissing him.

[2] See J. H. Plumb: *Sir Robert Walpole*, vol. i, pp. 142–3. Those who think that Anne's reign saw the beginnings of 'parliamentary government' make much of the Whigs' ability to control this session of Parliament; but Professor Plumb shows that the evidence does not support their view.

of muddle and mismanagement in Spain and by a campaign against the new proposals for compulsory recruiting. All these were themes dear to the hearts of the country gentlemen, who were already in a peevish mood after the bad harvests of 1708 and the ruinously cold winter that followed them. The cold weather lasted into the following July and by Michaelmas 1709 wheat stood at over 70s a quarter, a price which it had never reached before and was never to reach again until the 1790s. There was widespread distress and the country gentlemen were not pleased when the government made things worse by encouraging a large-scale influx of destitute German refugees. The failure of the peace negotiations had already revived the old cry that the monied men were prolonging the war for their own ends; and in the autumn, when it became known that Marlborough had asked to be made Captain-General for life, he too was accused of using the war to gratify his own inordinate ambition. All the traditional prejudices of the gentry against Whig financiers and military despots and factious politicians were well and truly aroused.

It was Sir Samuel Garrard, Lord Mayor of London, who put a match to all this combustible material by asking one of the most notorious High Church extremists in the country, Dr Henry Sacheverell, to preach before him on Guy Fawkes Day. Instead of condemning popery, as was usual on these occasions, Sacheverell preached against the Dissenters and the government which tolerated them. His sermon included a thinly disguised attack on Godolphin and it ended by attributing all the present ills of the Church to the pernicious doctrine of 'resistance' which had been behind the Revolution of 1688. When he had finished his diatribe the Lord Mayor invited him to share his coach, thus indicating publicly his approval of what had been said.

This was a challenge which could not be ignored. Godolphin and his new Whig allies, already unsure of the Queen and of the Country, were now under fire from the City as well. Moreover, the City had chosen as its spokesmen a man who peddled Jacobitism under the guise of devout Anglicanism. Few people could take the warming-pan story seriously any longer, and Sacheverell's condemnation of the Revolution therefore led straight to the conclusion that 'James III', and not Anne, was the rightful ruler of Great Britain. The ministers decided to impeach him before the House of Lords, on the grounds that he had tried 'with a wicked, malicious and seditious intention to undermine and subvert her Majesty's government and

142

the Protestant succession as by law established'. The country must be made to realize, before it was too late, that its fondness for cheering on the churchmen and hounding down the Dissenters would lead it eventually into the arms of the papists and the Jacobites.

The country refused to be convinced. When the Lords, after finding Sacheverell guilty by sixty-nine votes to fifty-two, imposed upon him the lightest possible sentence—he was merely ordered to abstain from preaching for three years—their verdict was greeted as a victory for Sacheverell and for the Church. Dissenters' meeting-houses were attacked by rioters and Sacheverell's journey across England to his new parish on the borders of Wales was turned into a triumphal progress. Harley, who had been keeping in close touch with the Queen via Mrs Masham ever since his resignation, decided that the time had come to encourage her to strike a blow against the Whigs. Once again Court and Country could act together to oust the party magnates from power.

Anne was only too ready to rid herself of those who had taken her captive. In April 1710 she asserted her independence by making the Duke of Shrewsbury Lord Chamberlain without consulting Godolphin. Shrewsbury, who had played little part in politics since his vain attempts to reconcile William III and the Whigs at the end of the previous reign, was still dedicated to the ideal of moderate all-party government and was working closely with Harley to achieve it. He wanted to bend the Whigs, not to break them. The Queen, however, was out for revenge and not for moderation. She dismissed Sunderland in June and Godolphin at the beginning of August. By the end of the year Somers, Wharton and even the moderate Henry Boyle had all gone. In January 1711 the Queen put the finishing touch to her work by dismissing the Duchess of Marlborough from all her offices. Only Marlborough himself remained, to fight a war which the Queen's new ministers were determined to end and to keep together the Alliance which they were determined to destroy.

By this time Harley was becoming frightened by his own success. He had always feared that the Sacheverell affair would drive the Country Party into the arms of the High Tories and he had been desperately anxious to retain the support of moderate Whigs like Cowper and Newcastle. He succeeded with Newcastle, but failed with Cowper. Meanwhile the Duke of Somerset, another moderate who had worked with Harley in the early stages of the business, broke with him after Godolphin's fall and prepared to use his electoral influence on behalf of the Whigs. The Tories, for their part, were anxious for an early election and Harley was forced to advise the Queen to dissolve Parliament in September 1710, although he would have preferred to wait until the excitement caused by the Sacheverell affair had died down. He did his best to reassure the Dissenters and the moderate Whigs, but the electors were convinced that the Queen wanted them to drive out all the enemies of the Church, together with the whole tribe of war-mongering financiers. Sir Gilbert Heathcote, the Governor of the Bank of England who had tried to save the Whigs by threatening the Queen with a credit crisis, was spat on in the street outside Guildhall; and all over the country moderates and Whigs alike were ousted by Tories. Instead of bringing the pendulum of party politics to rest, Harley had only succeeded in pushing it from one extreme to the other.

Henry St John, who had succeeded Boyle as Secretary of State, was ready to push it still further. Unlike Harley, who saw the country gentlemen as independent of both parties, he regarded them as the natural allies of the Tories. For years past he had talked of the need to 'reunite the Tory party' and now that this was achieved he was anxious 'to break the body of the Whigs, to render their supports useless to them, to fill the employments of the Kingdom down to the meanest with Tories'. The Tories must be secured firmly in power and the Whigs, with their friends the monied men and the Dissenters, smashed for ever.

The attack on the monied men began with an Act imposing property qualifications for membership of the Commons— £600 a year in land in the case of county members and £300 for borough members. St John insisted that unless it was passed 'we might see a time when the monied men might bid fair to keep out of that house all the landed men'. Meanwhile Harley was defying the Whig control of the City by raising £3,500,000 from lotteries and by promoting a new company to rival the Bank of England and the East India Company. He proposed that the holders of £9,000,000 of unsecured National Debt should be incorporated to trade with Spanish America and in September 1711 the new company, known as the South Sea Company, was given its charter and Harley himself was made its first Governor. While the future of the Whig financial monopoly was threatened by the South Sea Company, its past was investigated by a parliamentary committee. This committee, which was entirely composed of Tories, reported that £35,000,000 of public money remained unaccounted for. Robert Walpole, the late Secretary at War, successfully challenged its findings, but in the next session he was himself sent to the Tower on charges of corruption.

The more the new ministers attacked those who had financed the war, the more essential it became for them to make an advantageous peace. The Asiento, in particular, must be secured for the new South Sea Company. By the autumn of 1711 journalists in government pay were busy forecasting the great benefits which Britain would derive from the peace. When a hostile newspaper, the *Daily Courant*, got hold of the proposed terms and published them, showing how unsatisfactory they really were, the ministry was forced to justify itself by turning on its Allies. Swift was commissioned to write *The Conduct of the Allies*, a scathing attack on the Dutch, on the Emperor, and above all on Marlborough, as the general who had waged for their sakes and his own a war entirely opposed to Britain's true interests. Its impact was tremendous, but it did not save the government from a defeat in the House of Lords when Parliament met in December. Nottingham, infuriated by the abandonment of the policy he had initiated in 1703, united with the Whig lords to carry a motion declaring that 'no peace could be safe or honourable to Great Britain or Europe if Spain and the West Indies were alloted to any branch of the House of Bourbon'. The Queen was forced to come to the aid of her ministers by creating enough new peers to give them a majority in the Lords. Meanwhile Marlborough was stripped of his offices and resolutions accusing him of corruption were pushed through the Commons. By the beginning of 1712 St John had won his campaign against the Whig war.

But the cost had been heavy, much too heavy for Harley's liking. The High Churchmen had brought in the Occasional Conformity Bill again and this time it had been passed, the Whig lords accepting it in return for Nottingham's support against the peace proposals. Thus Harley's efforts to protect the Dissenters, with whom he was closely connected, were swept aside as St John pushed the ministry towards the Tories. Harley was now in the Lords—he had been made Earl of Oxford and Lord High Treasurer in May 1711—and St John, left to manage the Commons, showed himself more interested in courting the Tory magnates and their followers than the independent gentlemen. Harley, who in 1705 had feared that Godolphin's overtures to the Whigs might lead to 'the embodying of gentlemen (country gentlemen, I mean) against the Queen's service', now saw that St John's reliance on the Tories might well have the same result. But there was little he could do about it and in any case he was in poor health: he had been stabbed in the chest by a French spy in March 1711 and the wound continued to trouble him. St John, who also came up to the Lords in July 1712 as Viscount Bolingbroke, worked assiduously to discredit Oxford's policy of moderation, both at Court and in Parliament. In the autumn of 1713, just before the general election, he tried to get the Queen to dismiss all the Whig lord-lieutenants and replace them with Tories. He failed to get his way, but he did succeed in getting the High Tory leader William Bromley appointed as his fellow Secretary of State. In the new Parliament the Tories were stronger than ever and pushed through another measure against the dissenters, the Schism Act of June 1714.[1]

Meanwhile, at the end of 1713, Anne became seriously ill. Bolingbroke, who had been one of the chief sponsors of the Act of Settlement back in 1701, now began to reconsider it. The Electress Sophia was eighty-four and her son, the Elector of Hanover, looked like being the next effective King of Great Britain. As a keen supporter of the War of the Spanish Succession he had been angered by Bolingbroke's betrayal of the Allies and had made it clear that his sympathies lay with the Whigs. Moreover, he was a German and a Lutheran. Having rescued the Tories and the Church of England from foreigners, financiers, standing armies, war-mongers and Dissenters, Bolingbroke could hardly deliver them over to a King who stood for all these things. But what was the alternative? The Tories and the country gentlemen disliked the idea of a German King but they disliked even more the idea of a Catholic King: there could be no question of repealing the Act of Settlement unless James Stuart was prepared to become an Anglican. Both Bolingbroke and Oxford, convinced that they would be disgraced if the Hanoverians came in, worked hard to achieve this end. In February 1714 Oxford told James that Anne would name him as her heir and Parliament would repeal the Act of Settlement, if only he would renounce Catholicism. James refused, but negotiations between him and his sister's ministers continued. The Jacobites distrusted Oxford and supported Bolingbroke's efforts to get him dismissed; but to moderate opinion in England it seemed that both ministers were endangering the Protestant succession. By the time Anne's illness became critical at the end of July 1714,

[1] For an account of the Schism Act and its effects see p. 70.

Oxford's attempt to steer a middle course had completely broken down. The very people who had looked to him in 1710 to save them from the extremists were now convinced that he was in the hands of the worst extremists of all, the Jacobites. When Bolingbroke finally persuaded the Queen to dismiss Oxford on 27 July, nobody wasted much sympathy on the fallen minister; but the situation that he had left behind him, of a dying Queen in the hands of men who were too deeply committed to the Stuart cause to turn back, looked extremely threatening.

On 30 July the Dukes of Argyle and Somerset, two moderate non-party men whose names were still on the Privy Council list but who had not been summoned to attend, saw the Hanoverian agent in London and told him that they were going to the Privy Council in order to ensure the Protestant succession. When they appeared at the Council they persuaded Anne to appoint the Duke of Shrewsbury, the constant advocate of government without party, as Oxford's successor. Back in 1710, a Yorkshire squire had written to Harley: 'I cannot be persuaded that you and the Duke of Shrewsbury, after having rescued the nation from the tyranny of one set of men, can be for subjecting it to another of priests.' He may have been wrong about Harley, but he was right about Shrewsbury. As Lord High Treasurer, Lord Chamberlain and Lord-Lieutenant of Ireland, he was now the most powerful man in the kingdom and he used his power to ensure the peaceful accession of the Elector of Hanover. For two days he worked at top speed, issuing the necessary orders to the army and the navy and the lord-lieutenants; and on 1 August 1714, at half-past seven in the morning, Queen Anne died.

PART II

The Years of Peace and Whiggery
1714–1742

6

The Triumph of Management
1714–1727

1 *King George I and the Politicians*

In accordance with the Regency Act of 1707, George I had already appointed eighteen Lords Justices to help the great Officers of State run the country until his arrival. When their names were announced, shortly after Anne's death, it was found that they included four Tories, as well as Shrewsbury, Argyle and Somerset, the three moderate men who had controlled the events of the past few days. Some of the remaining eleven could be classed as Whigs, but few of them were extremists. Great Whig lords like Somers, Wharton and Sunderland were left out. Like William III and Anne, George was determined not to be taken captive by either of the parties. He would rule only through those men who were prepared to carry out his policies.

Since he was already fifty-four years old and had been Elector of Hanover for the past sixteen years, it was only to be expected that his policies should be fundamentally Hanoverian. He had taken Hanover into the War of the Spanish Succession, hoping for great things from it, only to have the spoils of victory snatched from him by Bolingbroke's betrayal of the Allies in 1712. He was not foolish enough to imagine that the Peace of Utrecht could be torn up and the war reopened, but he could at any rate make sure that the same thing did not happen again. There was another war going on in Europe, the Great Northern War between Sweden and her Baltic neighbours, and this too might be made to benefit Hanover. Whatever he might feel about British politicians and the parties they belonged to, he needed men who could combat the insularity and isolationism of the British. He distrusted the Whigs as 'king-killers', men who wanted to make the King serve their own ends; but he had to face the fact that they were more likely to do his Hanoverian business for him than were their opponents. Neither the Country Party nor the High Tories would be likely to forward the continental entanglements of a German King.

When he landed in England late in September 1714 he found that Bothmer, his agent in London, had come to the same conclusion. The Whigs might be unpleasant, but they were indispensable. Moreover, Bothmer was in a position to know that they were less dangerous than they seemed, because they were disunited. For months past they had been vying for his favour and he was able to assure his master that it would be reasonably easy to play them off against each other. The Act of Settlement forbade the King to make his Hanoverian advisers members of his Privy Council, but it could not stop him consulting them whenever he pleased; and they would thus form an inner ring around him, a ring which each of his ministers would have to conciliate if he wished to be sure of royal favour. By making use of their undoubted ascendancy at Court, the Hanoverians could reduce the Council to a subordinate position and ensure that it was divided against itself. The Whigs might come in as a party, intent on bending the King to their will, but they would soon find that their intrigues at Court turned them from colleagues into rivals.

The ministry which George I built up in the autumn of 1714 was thus more Whiggish than his selection of Lords Justices had been. Lord Halifax, the same Charles Montagu who had managed the Whig financiers for William III, came back to the Treasury, but only as First Lord and not as Lord High Treasurer. The latter office had come to be equated with that of 'prime' minister and George therefore put the Treasury into commission to show that he was determined to be his own chief minister. Wharton was made Lord Privy Seal and Sunderland Lord-Lieutenant of Ireland, while the moderate Whig Lord Cowper became Lord Chancellor. Shrewsbury remained as Lord Chamberlain and Nottingham, a Tory but an opponent of the Peace of Utrecht, became Lord President of the Council. Stanhope, Secretary of State for the South, was known as a soldier and a diplomat rather than as a party politician. The other Secretary, Lord Townshend, was a member of the Newcastle connection, which had supported Harley in the crisis of 1710 but had subsequently become identified with the Whigs. Townshend's brother-in-law, Robert Walpole, was made Paymaster of the Forces, an office which enabled him to build up his own fortune and distribute lucrative posts to his political followers.

At the beginning of 1715 the old Parliament was dissolved and the new King's ministers set about the task of modelling a new one. Tory lord-lieutenants and justices of the peace were systematically removed and the King issued a special proclamation in which he advised the electors to favour 'such as showed a firmness to the Protestant succession when it was in danger'. The country gentlemen were not too pleased with this gesture and many of them agreed with Sir William Wyndham's assertion that it was an unwarrantable interference with the freedom of elections; but it had the desired effect. The Parliament which met in March 1715 and was to sit until March 1722 was dominated by the followers of those who had secured office under the new régime. Even so the ministers were not satisfied and at the end of May they resolved to follow up their purge of local office-holders with a similar purge in the army. At the same time they embarked on the impeachment of the principal Tory leaders— Oxford, Bolingbroke and Ormonde[1]—for their part in the Peace of Utrecht and their intrigues with James Stuart. Oxford stayed to face his accusers and the charges against him were eventually dismissed; but Bolingbroke and Ormonde fled to France and offered their services to James. Their flight helped to give point to the Whig charge that all Tories were secret Jacobites and traitors, especially since Ormonde had been actively planning a Jacobite rising in the west country. After his escape the direction of this attempt was taken over by Lord Lansdowne and Sir William Wyndham, but they were both arrested in September. At the end of October, when Ormonde's ship anchored in Torbay and fired three guns as a signal to the Jacobites on shore, there was no reply. The western rebellion had failed.

In Scotland and in the north of England things looked more dangerous. The Earl of Mar raised James Stuart's standard in the Highlands early in September and within a week he had gathered an army of some 5,000 men at Perth. His advance into the Lowlands was blocked by the Duke of Argyle's army at Stirling, but this was only 1,500 strong and was threatened from both sides: the Jacobites of Northumberland, having failed in an attempt to capture Newcastle, had turned north and joined up with James's supporters in the

---

[1] It was Ormonde who had succeeded Marlborough as Commander-in-Chief at the beginning of 1712 and who had, under orders from Bolingbroke, refrained from cooperating with the Allies in the campaigns of that year. He had also been deeply involved in the negotiations with James Stuart at the beginning of 1714.

Scottish Lowlands. Instead of mounting a joint attack on Stirling the rebels divided their forces, Mar remaining at Perth while the Lowlanders and their allies from Northumberland marched south into England. Not until November, when his army had grown to over 10,000, did Mar try to push past Argyle and join the invasion of England. He was, however, halted at the inconclusive battle of Sheriffmuir on 13 November and forced back into Perth. On the same day the Jacobites in England, who had got as far as Lancashire, were surrounded at Preston and forced to surrender. Once the invasion of England had collapsed, the Jacobites in Scotland began to lose heart also. When James Stuart landed at Peterhead at the end of December he found that Mar's army had dwindled to little more than 3,000. After six weeks spent in rather aimless journeys around the Highlands he went back to France again at the beginning of February 1716. Within two months of his departure the rebellion was at an end and both England and Scotland recognized George I as King.

In the eyes of the Whig politicians the rebellion had demonstrated once and for all the unreliability of the Tories. The King and his Hanoverian advisers must now accept the fact that they could not play one party off against the other and they must be prepared to work only through the Whigs. When Nottingham came out publicly in the House of Lords in favour of clemency towards the leaders of the rebellion, his colleagues insisted on his dismissal. He and his relatives left office at the end of February 1716 and the Duke of Devonshire, an undistinguished Whig, took over the Lord Presidency. More important were the changes necessitated by the deaths of Halifax and Wharton in the previous year: Walpole became First Lord of the Treasury and Sunderland Lord Privy Seal. Both men were connected with the great Whig borough-mongers and together with the two Secretaries of State, Stanhope and Townshend, they formed the core of the ministry. To consolidate their position they pushed through Parliament in May 1716 a Septennial Act extending the life of Parliaments from three years to seven. Since the elections of 1715 had undoubtedly helped to bring discontent and Jacobitism to the surface, there was something to be said for the measure; but to the independent members it looked like a deliberate attempt by the borough-mongers to perpetuate and extend their power. As always, ministers who worked through the party magnates incurred the hostility of the Country Party. Meanwhile, their position at Court and their ability to force their will upon the King still depended on their readiness to trust one another. A Whig ministry in which each man suspected his colleagues of intriguing with the Hanoverians behind his back would be no stronger than a mixed ministry of Whigs and Tories.

In the spring of 1716 George I decided that his position in Britain was sufficiently assured to allow him to visit Hanover. The obnoxious clause in the Act of Settlement which required him to get Parliament's permission before leaving the country was repealed by a unanimous vote: not even the most truculent of the squires dared to oppose the King in this matter. The Prince of Wales, whom the King disliked and distrusted profoundly, was made Regent but with very limited powers—he could not fill any office or place, even a lieutenancy in the Guards, without his father's consent. While the majority of the ministers remained in England to run the country and advise the Prince, Stanhope was to accompany the King in order to help him with the diplomatic business which was the main purpose of the journey. These arrangements made, the King left England at the end of July 1716.

This situation was almost bound to produce a split in the ministry. If the ministers at home won the favour of their immediate master the Prince they would lose the favour of their ultimate master the King; while if the ministers abroad lent themselves too readily to the King's European policies they would be reviled at home for sacrificing Britain to Hanover. When Sunderland left England in the autumn of 1716 and made his way to Hanover, the scene was finally set for the shattering of Whig unity. The Whig politicians and their followers in Parliament would have to choose between father and son, between Court and country, between Hanover and Britain. The crisis could only be averted if the King's Hanoverian policies could be shown to be in the interests of Britain and if the ministers, both at home and abroad, cooperated in presenting them to Parliament in the best possible light.

Neither of these things happened, because George and Stanhope very soon found themselves drawn into an alliance with France, the traditional enemy of Britain. Only Britain and France, the two chief architects of the Peace of Utrecht, were really satisfied with it; and if the settlement was to be made permanent the two powers must draw together to defend it. The resentment which the Emperor and the Dutch felt towards the British for letting them down was matched

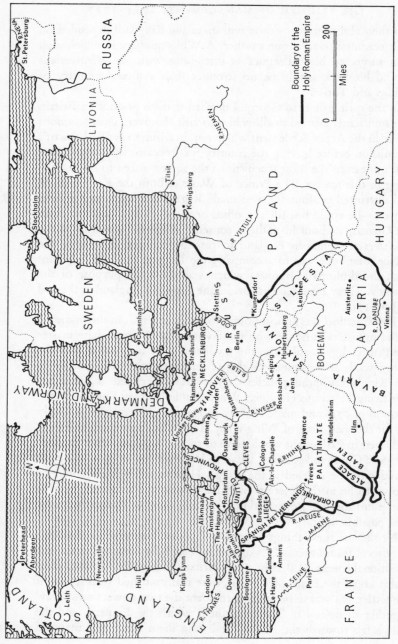

Northern Europe

Boundary of the
Holy Roman Empire

0   200
    Miles

by Spanish dislike of France. To Philip V it seemed that Louis XIV had bought peace for France in 1713 at the cost of concessions by Spain. French attempts to restore good relations with Spain had not had much success and in the autumn of 1715, on the death of Louis XIV, they had broken down altogether. His successor Louis XV was a delicate and ailing child of five and his cousin the Regent feared, with some justification, that Philip V of Spain might assert his claim to the French throne if an opportunity arose. It looked as though Europe, having wrestled with the problems of the British succession and the Spanish succession, might now be faced with the problem of the French succession. To guard against this danger and to rescue France from the perilous isolation into which she had been drifting since 1713, the Regent sent his minister Dubois to The Hague in the summer of 1716. Stanhope was there on his way to Hanover and Dubois approached him secretly with proposals for a Franco-British alliance based on reciprocal guarantees for the Hanoverian succession in Britain and for the claims of the Regent himself, as against Philip V of Spain, in the event of the death of the young Louis XV of France.

At first Stanhope and George I were suspicious of the idea. They had already made some progress in conciliating the Emperor and the Dutch and in rebuilding the Grand Alliance that Bolingbroke had shattered, while a trade treaty with Spain signed in May 1716 suggested that she might be brought into their system. A weak and isolated France, hemmed in by a network of alliances directed from London, seemed the best guarantee of the Hanoverian succession and of British trading rights. Nevertheless the resentment of the countries that had been disappointed at Utrecht was still smouldering and if it flared up again it would undoubtedly be necessary for Britain and France to defend the settlement they had imposed on Europe. Meanwhile, there was trouble brewing in the Baltic: both Sweden and Russia, though at war with one another, were threatening Hanover and seemed ready to make common cause with the discontented countries of Europe against her. Sweden had already declared war on her in October 1715 and now, in the autumn of 1716, Russian troops started moving into the Duchy of Mecklenburg, which bordered on the Electorate of Hanover. On 14 September 1716 Stanhope wrote from Hanover to Townshend in London: 'The King now wishes, and so doth your humble servant, very heartily that we had secured France. . . . I was, you know, very averse at first to this treaty, but I think truly as things now stand we ought not to lose a minute in finishing it.' Whatever the ministers at home might think about allying with Britain's traditional enemy for the sake of Hanover's security, the ministers abroad were convinced that it was essential. It was arranged that the alliance should be signed in The Hague, to give the Dutch a chance of joining, and George ordered Townshend to give the British envoys there the necessary powers.

Townshend played for time. He saw that the proposed treaty would be unpopular and on 16 October he wrote to Stanhope saying that 'if the Northern affairs were brought into Parliament by His Majesty's order upon the foot they now stand, His Majesty would be so far from obtaining any assistance on that head, that there would be great danger from such a step of ruining his credit and influence in both Houses'. Encouraged by Stanhope and Sunderland, George persisted in interpreting this as deliberate disloyalty rather than political caution. He became convinced that Townshend was plotting with the Prince of Wales to undermine the King's authority in Britain and frustrate his policies. In the middle of December he dismissed him from his Secretaryship and made him Lord-Lieutenant of Ireland instead. Although the full extent of the crisis was not revealed until the King returned to England in January 1717, everyone in politics realized that the dismissal of Townshend was an epoch-making event. Under the strain of dealing with Hanoverian advisers and Hanoverian policies, the Whig ministry and the Whig party had split apart. The nature of that split was to determine the shape of political life for a generation to come.

Meanwhile the alliance with France had finally been signed in November 1716 and in the following January it was turned into a Triple Alliance by the accession of the Dutch. Its immediate effect was to drive Spain into challenging the Peace of Utrecht openly: in August 1717 she attacked and conquered the island of Sardinia, which had been taken from her in 1713 and given to the Emperor. She also stirred up George I's Baltic enemies against him. Sweden had been plotting with the Jacobites for some time and now she began negotiations for peace with Russia, so that the two great powers of the Baltic might unite against Hanover. For a time it looked as though all the enemies of George I and of the Regent in France might band together in a concerted attack on the Peace of Utrecht and the Hanoverian succession. But the danger soon passed and the Triple Alliance in the end became, in spite of Townshend's fears, a basis for a general European settlement. The Emperor, much as he disliked the Peace of Utrecht and the Franco-British combination which had made it, could not stand up to the Spanish offensive in Italy and the Mediterranean unless he had the support of the British navy. For five years he had been nursing a grievance against the British for giving him too small a share of the Spanish possessions in the Mediterranean, but he now saw that without their help he might lose even what he had got. In the summer of 1718 he joined the Triple Alliance, making it into the Quadruple Alliance, and the British navy sought out the main Spanish fleet off the coast of Sicily and destroyed it. The British ships spent the winter of 1718–19 in the ports of southern Italy and their presence put an end to Spain's hopes of reconquering her Mediterranean empire. She was now standing alone against the Quadruple Alliance. The war between Austria and Turkey, which she had been counting on to weaken the Emperor, had been brought to an end in July 1718 as a result of British mediation; and the reconciliation between Sweden and Russia, which she had been counting on to act as a threat to Hanover, failed to materialize. Her last hope lay in a Jacobite invasion of Britain which was launched from Spanish ports in the spring of 1719 but proved to be a miserable fiasco. In February 1720 Philip V of Spain gave in, ended the war and joined the Quadruple Alliance. Although the final settlement between Spain and the Emperor had to be left over until the conference of Cambrai, which did not meet until the beginning of 1724, a general pacification had in fact been achieved by the end of 1721. Even the Baltic powers agreed to bring their wars to an end: Sweden made peace with Hanover in November 1719 and ceded to her the important territories of Bremen and Verden, lying between the mouths of the rivers Weser and Elbe. This was something which helped British trade as well as Hanoverian prestige, so that the merchants of London became slightly less suspicious of George I's Baltic policies. By the end of 1720 all the Baltic countries except Russia had made peace on terms favourable to British commerce and Hanoverian security; and in August 1721, after mediation by Britain and France and a visit of the British fleet to the Baltic, Russia joined in the settlement. The chain of events set in motion by the Franco-British alliance of 1716 had led to the pacification of Europe.

Meanwhile, the events springing from Townshend's dismissal had led to dramatic changes in the British political situation.

2 *Robert Walpole and the Country Party*

When George I returned to London in January 1717 and opened Parliament he found the country gentlemen in an ugly mood. They resented the long delay in the summoning of Parliament—the King had forbidden his son to call it in his absence—and they resented their Hanoverian King's attempt to drag them into war with Sweden. The revelation that the Swedish ambassador in London had been plotting with the Jacobites helped to bring them round, but even so their traditional prejudices were well and truly aroused and the ministry's motion to take steps against Sweden was passed by only four votes in the Commons.

While the country gentlemen fulminated against Hanoverian policies, the party magnates tried to sort out their confused relations with the Hanoverian Court. The Prince of Wales had already defied his father openly, ordering his followers in the Commons to withdraw their support from the ministry, and by the autumn of 1717 there were two Courts, one centred on the King at St James's Palace and the other centred on the Prince at his house in Leicester Square. The King made it known that those who dared to frequent his son's Court would not be welcome at his own, so that politicians had to decide whether to seek the favour of the present King or the future King, of the person who was actually wearing the crown or the person who would wear it in the years to come. The influence and patronage of the Crown, which could so easily dominate the political scene when it was properly managed, was now divided against itself. Instead of the King being able to choose between two parties, the parties could choose between two Kings.

In such a situation Townshend and his friends could do the remaining ministers a great deal of harm if they chose to go into open opposition, join forces with the Prince's followers and stir up the country gentlemen against the King's policies. George I therefore went out of his way to be gracious to Townshend, who was persuaded to accept his new post as Lord-Lieutenant of Ireland. For a few months, from January to April of 1717, the ministry preserved an outward appearance of unity, but it could not last. Townshend was already opposing the King's measures in the Lords and Walpole's followers were voting against the ministry in the Commons. In April Townshend was dismissed from his Lord-Lieutenancy and Walpole resigned as First Lord of the Treasury. They were followed by William Cavendish, Duke of Devonshire and Lord President of the Council, by Paul Methuen, Secretary of State for the South, by William Pulteney, Secretary at War and by the veteran Whig Edward Russell, Earl of Orford and First Lord of the Admiralty. Methuen and Pulteney, though they both came of Whig families, were not great borough-mongers; but the rest were among the most influential of the Whig party magnates. When George had first come to England he had congratulated himself on the fact that the Whigs, the 'king-killers', were on his side; but now it seemed that the Whig habit of opposition to the Crown might be taken up again. Wharton's son had already turned Jacobite, arguing that it · was his duty to carry on by the most effective means possible his father's lifelong task of opposing kings. Few Whigs were likely to go as far as this, but they might well think that an alliance with the Country Party, made respectable by the support of the Prince of Wales, was preferable to unquestioning obedience to a Hanoverian King.

Stanhope and Sunderland did their best to plug the gaps, but the result was not very convincing. Stanhope himself became First Lord of the Treasury, while his old office of Secretary of State for the North was taken by Sunderland, who also succeeded Devonshire as Lord President of the Council. The other offices were filled by rather unimpressive figures. Joseph Addison, the new Secretary of State for the South, was a man of some note, but as a journalist rather than a politician. Few ministries since the Revolution had been built on such narrow foundations: Stanhope and Sunderland had the support of the office-holders, but their following among the party magnates, among the monied men and among the Country Party was very limited. They possessed, however, the greatest of all political assets, the favour of the King. As long as they retained that and the King himself retained his health, they were in no real danger. The party politicians and the London merchants and the country gentlemen might speak against them and even vote against them, but in the end they would come to heel and make their peace with the Court, the source of all profit and all advancement.

In the meantime the discontented Whigs were determined to show just how awkward they could be, in order to push up their price when the time came to seek office again. Townshend's activities in the Lords, where he opposed and obstructed the ministry on issue after issue, were matched by Walpole's success in taking over the leadership of the Country Party in the Commons. It was little more than a year since he had been denouncing the Tories and many of their allies among the country gentlemen as secret Jacobites; but now he was only too ready to take up their traditional cries and use them as sticks with which to beat his former colleagues. Whenever the country gentlemen denounced standing armies or demanded shorter parliaments, whenever they spoke against placemen in the Commons or Dissenters in town corporations, they found Walpole at their head urging them on. By June 1717 his campaign against the ministry was so virulent that Pope said that 'the parties of Walpole and Stanhope are as violent as Whig and Tory'. Under Walpole's leadership the Country Party harried the government with charges of corruption and even managed to get a High Churchman appointed to preach before the Commons, in spite of the fact that the Court opposed his appointment.

Walpole's new accord with the Country Party was strained by the impeachment of the Earl of Oxford, which was at last taken up by the Commons in June 1717 after a delay of two years. In 1715 Walpole, then a vigorous supporter of the impeachment, had been made Chairman of the committee set up to manage it; but now this position was a source of embarrassment to him. He could hardly woo the Country Party and at the same time hound down the greatest of all its leaders. He resolved his dilemma by studiously neglecting his duties as Chairman and in the end the impeachment broke down. Its failure discredited Stanhope and Sunderland, but it also showed them how wedges might be driven between Walpole and his new allies.

In December 1718 the ministers came up with another and more effective wedge, in the shape of a proposal to repeal the Occasional Conformity Act and the Schism Act. Walpole, who had always been opposed to both Acts, now joined the Country Party and the Tories in defending them against the ministerial threat. Although he tied himself into some ingenious knots in order to explain this desertion of Whig principles, it did him little good. Stanhope and Sunderland were victorious: the Commons voted for the repeal by a majority of forty-one. The unity of the opposition, which had been bolstered up by the successes of the past year, began to crack under this defeat. By the beginning of 1719 the discontented Whigs were beginning to think that they must make what terms they could with the Court. Already the Duke of Argyle, whose disgrace in the summer of 1716 had formed the prologue to the split in the Whig ranks, had found his way back to office as Steward of the Household. He had been a prominent figure at the Prince's Court and his defection left the other rebel Whigs there wondering who would be the next to go. Meanwhile the unsuccessful Jacobite invasion of 1719 helped to rally the country gentlemen to the government. By the summer of 1719 Stanhope and the King felt sufficiently sure of themselves to set off once again for Hanover.[1]

When they returned in the autumn they brought with them plans to crush the opposition once and for all. These plans were unfolded in the King's speech at the opening of Parliament on 23 November 1719. After forecasting that Spain would soon be forced to acknowledge British leadership of the concert of Europe, he went on to outline a sweeping programme of domestic reform designed primarily to perpetuate the existing régime. The royal prerogative of creating peers was to be limited, so that no future King would be able to shake the supremacy of the Whig lords. The Septennial Act was to be swept away and the life of the present House of Commons prolonged indefinitely. The High Church parsons, who were the mouthpieces of Toryism and the oracles of the Country Party, were to be muzzled by tightening ministerial control over the universities which bred them. Finally, the City and the Court were to collaborate in a great scheme to mobilize the country's credit resources. The Scottish financier John Law had undertaken such a scheme for the French government, with such success that Paris was fast becoming the financial capital of the world and was attracting funds from London on a large scale. Already the British ambassador in Paris had written home to say that unless something was done quickly Law would 'raise the trade of France on the ruins of our trade'. Stanhope was determined to float a similar scheme in London, in order to gain the support of the monied men and establish his ministry on an unshakeable financial foundation. Meanwhile his proposals for the two Houses of Parliament would perpetuate the power of the existing party magnates and his proposals for the universities would draw the teeth of the Tories and of the Country Party. Above all, the proposed restrictions on the creation of peers would stop the Prince bringing in new men when he became King. It was this consideration

[1] In March 1718 Stanhope and Sunderland had exchanged offices, the latter going to the Treasury while the former became once again Secretary of State for the North, with special responsibility for foreign policy and relations with Hanover.

that led George I to limit his own right to make new peers. He was prepared to accept a rigid and self-perpetuating oligarchy if it would hamper the actions of the son he loathed.

A Peerage Bill, preventing the King from creating new peerages except for members of his own family or when old peerages became extinct, had already been introduced into the Lords in the spring of 1719. Brought in by the Duke of Somerset, the very epitome of aristocratic disdain and pomposity,[1] it had provoked a public outcry and Stanhope had dropped it before it got to the Commons. Now, however, he tried to rush it through both Houses in the first few days of the autumn session, while some of the county members were still lingering on their estates. At first, it seemed that he might succeed: Townshend, Devonshire and Orford failed to oppose the Bill in the Lords and they seemed reluctant to let their followers oppose it in the Commons. But Walpole saw his chance and he was determined to seize it. However unconvincing his alliance with the country gentlemen might have been in the past, this was an issue on which he felt sure of carrying them with him. He persuaded the other discontented Whigs to oppose the Bill in force, thus frustrating Stanhope's attempt to hustle it through quickly and quietly. By the time it came up for its second reading on 8 December the country gentlemen had arrived in strength and they spoke passionately against it. Sir John Pakington, a fiery Tory from Worcestershire, summed up their feelings when he said: 'For my part, I never desire to be a lord, but I have a son who one day may have that ambition.' Walpole's own speech made a great impression. He dwelt on the evils of a narrow aristocratic caste and he pictured the ministers as tyrannical oligarchs seeking to shut out the country gentlemen for ever from all honour and advancement and power. Other speakers followed his lead and at the end of the debate the Bill was rejected by 269 votes to 177.

Stanhope and Sunderland, who had been confident that they could get the Bill through, were severely shaken by this defeat. They had already decided to drop their plans for repealing the Septennial Act and now they dropped their proposals for the universities as well. All that was left of their ambitious programme was the scheme to mobilize credit resources; and they pushed ahead with this

---

[1] Somerset's sense of his own importance took many ludicrous forms, including the habit of sending outriders on in front of his carriage to clear the roads, so that the vulgar herd should not look upon him. One infuriated farmer is said to have defied the Duke's servants and thrust his pig in at the carriage window, shouting: 'I woull zee him, and my pig shall zee him too.'

as vigorously as possible. The scheme was based on the proposal that the South Sea Company (which had become closely associated with the Court in 1718 when the King had become its Governor) should take over the National Debt. This now stood at £31,000,000, £16,000,000 of it in the form of straight loans which could be repaid if only the money could be found and £15,000,000 in annuities which were irredeemable—that is, the annuitants could not be forced to forgo their right to an annual payment. The annual cost of the Debt, in interest payments and annuity payments, was about £1,500,000. The directors of the South Sea Company had always been more interested in finance than in trade and now the war with Spain, which cut off all legitimate trade with the South Seas, led them to concentrate entirely on the manipulation of money instead of on the management of ships. They proposed to create £31,000,000 worth of new South Sea shares and offer them to government creditors in exchange for their government stock. Thus a man who had lent £1,000 to the government at 6 per cent, or who had bought for £1,000 an annuity of £60 a year, would surrender to the South Sea Company his claims on the government and receive in exchange £1,000 worth of South Sea shares. Instead of his regular interest payment or annuity from the government he would receive from the Company such dividends as it cared to pay him. Having thus become the sole government creditor, the Company would accept lower rates of interest—after seven years they were to level down to a flat 4 per cent—and let the government redeem any part of the Debt, whether loan stock or annuity stock, at any time. Finally, it was to pay the government £3,000,000 towards the redemption of the Debt. This sum was later raised to £7,000,000 to outbid rival offers from the Bank of England.

The one thing about which the Company did not commit itself was the thing on which the success of the whole scheme depended: the rate at which the conversion of government stock into South Sea stock was to take place. If it was done at par, when the market price of £100 of South Sea stock was only £100, the Company would gain nothing from the deal and would be unable to find the £7,000,000 it had promised to the government. But if it was done at current prices on a rising market, when the price of South Sea shares was going steadily up, it could yield an enormous profit. If, for instance, its shares stood at 200, the Company could buy in the whole Debt for £15,500,000 worth of the newly created shares and then sell the other £15,500,000 worth for £31,000,000. Furthermore, the prospect of these vast gains would serve to push up the price of South Sea shares still more, as everyone rushed to share in this huge financial concern. It would outdo Law's achievements in France and enable the Company, together with its associates at Court and in the ministry, to dominate the political scene. 'A body of men with a stock of forty-three millions and credit for as much more, acting by united counsels, must fill the House of Commons and rule this little world', wrote Erasmus Lewis in February 1720. 'What occasion will there be for Parliaments hereafter?' Once the Court and the City had between them spawned this financial leviathan they could smother all their enemies. The opposition of the Prince of Wales, the activities of the discontented party magnates, the triumph of the Country Party over the Peerage Bill, the strength of the High Churchmen in the universities—all these things would count for nothing if the ministry's South Sea scheme was a success.

For a time it was indeed a success. The plan was put before Parliament in January 1720 and by the beginning of February, when it had been accepted in principle and the Bank's rival offer rejected, South Sea stock had risen from 129 to 160. Later in February came news of a fall in the price of shares in Law's company in Paris; but instead of seeing this as a warning investors took it as a sign that the South Sea Company was carrying all before it. By 7 April, when the Bill embodying the scheme received the royal assent, South Sea stock stood at 335. The Prince of Wales and the rebel Whigs, overawed by the ministry's success, decided to make their peace with the King. On 23 April George I and his undutiful son were officially reconciled; and the next day Townshend and Walpole, with their friends and followers, were once again received at Court. They returned not as conquerors but as penitents: it was not until June, after Walpole had worked his passage by getting the Commons to take over £600,000 worth of the King's debts, that they were given office again. Townshend became Lord President of the Council, Walpole Paymaster, and Methuen Comptroller of the Household. The rest got nothing. During their period of opposition the Whig rebels had achieved great things: they had used their strength as party magnates and their alliance with the Country Party to defeat the ministry in the House of Commons on several occasions. More than any other group in politics, they could claim to represent the Commons as against the Court. But this did not of itself entitle them to office or oblige the King to employ them. The most that they could hope for was to be allowed to use their influence in Parliament on the King's behalf and on the King's terms.

Meanwhile the South Sea boom continued. By the end of May most of the holders of government loans and annuities had exchanged them for South Sea stock at rates which ensured a handsome profit for the Company and thus encouraged even more eager buying of South Sea shares. At the beginning of June they stood at 610 and two days later they had risen to 870. The Court, determined that its Company should have as few rivals as possible, passed an Act restraining the numerous 'Bubble' companies which had sprung up to take advantage of the fever of speculation. By the end of June South Sea stock had risen to 1,050 and John Blunt, the South Sea director who had evolved the scheme, had been made a baronet by a grateful King, 'for his extraordinary services in raising public credit to a height not known before'. Having made this gesture, George left for Hanover secure in the knowledge that his Court and his Company dominated the political scene.

Things looked very different when he returned in November. The price of South Sea shares had started to drop in August, as those who had bought earlier in the year began to sell out at a profit. As the volume of selling increased prices fell steadily and the same people who had previously rushed to get into South Sea before it rose any higher now rushed to get out of it before it went any lower. By early September it was down to 575 and the Company had to turn to its hated rival the Bank of England for help. The Bank agreed to take over some of the Company's shares, but insisted that it should abandon its connection with the Sword Blade Company, a rather shady finance company which had acted as its banker and which had always been regarded by the Bank of England as an illicit interloper. 'If the South Sea Company is to be wedded to the Bank,' said the veteran Sir Gilbert Heathcote, 'it cannot be allowed to keep a mistress.' The Sword Blade Company went bankrupt and this resulted, as Sir Gilbert had probably foreseen, in a further fall in South Sea stock. By the end of September it was down to 180. Not only the South Sea Company but the whole credit system was shaken by the panic, as everyone struggled to exchange stocks and shares and bonds and bills for gold. The Mint struck fresh supplies of coin, but even so the dangerous drain on the country's gold reserves threatened to undermine the whole monetary system, until it was halted by the arrival of 100,000 guineas in gold from Rotterdam in the middle of October. Just as confidence was beginning to be restored the Bank announced that it could not after all undertake to shore up the Company. South Sea stock slumped again and by the time the King returned it stood at 135, its lowest point since January.

When Parliament met on 8 December the King announced that his ministers were busy with plans to restore public credit. This was true, but it was not the whole truth. Their real concern was not so much to clear things up as to hush things up. Many important people at Court and in the ministry had been bribed by the Company with blocks of shares held under false names; and they had played a rather disreputable part in the squalid business of market-rigging and share manipulation. Sunderland himself was involved, as were the Chancellor of the Exchequer and at least two of the King's mistresses. Many people believed that the Prince of Wales and even the King himself were mixed up in the affair; and it is possible that they were right. Robert Knight, the South Sea Company's cashier, said later: 'If I should disclose all I know, it would open such a scene as the world would be surprised at.' These dark hints from a ruined and disgraced man may not have meant very much, but it is significant that even Thomas Brodrick, the Chairman of the parliamentary committee set up to investigate the scandal, saw the danger of probing too deeply. 'I shall not join with those whose losses have so far exasperated them,' he wrote, 'as to be desirous, out of revenge, to run to extremes, which may endanger the nation.' However much outraged investors might clamour for all to be uncovered, hard-headed politicians knew that revelations which discredited the Court might shake the dynasty. Things were in a bad enough way already without opening the door to the Jacobites.

One such politician was Robert Walpole. In January he had opposed the South Sea scheme, partly because he was then in opposition and partly because he preferred the Bank's rival offers, but once it was accepted he had made no further criticisms of it and settled down to make money out of the boom. He did not succeed very well and late in June, when prices were at their highest, he was still anxious to buy. He certainly did not see through the scheme or anticipate its disastrous consequences, but he happened to be out of London, and thus dissociated from the rest of the ministry, when the crash came in September. Combined with his reputation as a financier and his following among the country gentlemen in Parliament, this helped to create the impression that he was the man to save the Country from this latest extravaganza of the Court. 'They all cry out for you to help them,' his banker wrote to him on 1 November, '. . . you will be prodigiously importuned by all the sufferers to do more than any man can do; and more than you in your judgement would think ought to be done, if it could be done.' It was a shrewd comment. There were indeed things which in Walpole's judgement ought not to be done: one of them was the uncovering of the full extent of the scandal. He was much more concerned to save the Court from the Country than to save the Country from the Court.

For most of December he managed to keep the Commons occupied with a scheme, worked out for him by his banker, to transfer £18,000,000 of South Sea stock in equal portions to the Bank and the East India Company. The plan had to be dropped in the end, but discussion of it did something to restore confidence. South Sea stock rose a little. By the beginning of 1721, however, it was clear that even Walpole could not deflect Parliament any longer from its intention to 'punish the authors of our present misfortunes'. He had to agree to an Act confiscating the estates of the South Sea directors and forbidding them to leave the country, and also to the setting up of a committee of inquiry. The committee produced a report full of damaging revelations, but Walpole managed to persuade the Commons not to have it printed. Charges of corruption were brought against Charles Stanhope, Secretary of the Treasury and cousin of the Secretary of State, and against Sunderland himself. The evidence was pretty convincing, but Walpole used his mastery of the Commons to secure the acquittal of both men. John Aislabie, the Chancellor of the Exchequer, was too deeply involved to be saved and had to spend some time in the Tower. Two other ministers, the Secretary of State for the South and his father the Postmaster-General, died before the Commons could bring them to trial. Meanwhile, in the Lords, Stanhope was so infuriated by the attacks made on him that he lost control of himself and collapsed. Three days later he died of a cerebral haemorrhage. By the beginning of April the King's situation was desperate: death had removed both his Secretaries of State, his Chancellor of the Exchequer had been disgraced and imprisoned, and Sunderland, his First Lord of the Treasury and favourite minister, was too tarnished by the South Sea affair to remain at the Treasury. Only Walpole's skill and determination had saved the ministry from complete collapse and the Court from embarrassing disclosures. At the cost of violent unpopularity—he was reviled throughout the country as 'the Skreen Master General', the man who had screened and shielded the Court from popular retribution—he had salvaged all that could be salvaged from the wreck of the ministry.

The King felt no gratitude and Walpole expected none. He knew that George hated him and admired Sunderland; and he had not saved the latter in order to win his love but in order to demonstrate his own power. The King was undisputed master of the political situation, but he must be shown that it was expedient to have ministers who could manage his affairs in the Commons. Just as Walpole had checked the Country Party when it threatened to bring down the Court, so he would bring the Court to heel if it sought to ignore the Country. He was determined to run King and Country in double harness, even if both hated him for it.

3 For King and Country

Early in April the King reorganized his ministry. Walpole replaced Sunderland as First Lord of the Treasury and he also took over Aislabie's post of Chancellor of the Exchequer. Townshend, who had been acting as Secretary of State for the North since Stanhope's death, was now transferred permanently to this office, his place as Lord President of the Council being filled by Lord Carleton. But nobody, least of all Walpole and Townshend, imagined that this meant the end of Sunderland. He was still Groom of the Stole, a key position at Court, and he refused to hand over to Walpole the control of the secret service funds, a vital factor in the management of Crown patronage. His friend and supporter Lord Carteret was made Secretary of State for the South, while the Duke of Newcastle, Lord Chamberlain and one of the most powerful borough-mongers in the country, continued to support him loyally. Walpole's supporters among the monied men and the country gentlemen were still angry with him because of his 'Skreen Master' activities, but Sunderland's position at Court and with the party magnates remained unimpaired. Walpole might be First Lord of the Treasury, but he would never be chief minister if the King, the Court and the Whig factions of Sunderland and Newcastle could prevent it. It was said that the King was grimly amused by a remark of Lord Oxford's, to the effect that removing Sunderland to take in Walpole was like taking off one dirty shirt to put on another. George knew very well that both shirts were dirty, but he only intended to wear the second until the first could be made fit to be seen in public once more.

Walpole, however, proved difficult to dislodge. All through the summer he fought patiently and tirelessly with the malcontents in the Commons and by August he had wound up the South Sea affair reasonably satisfactorily. He had still not succeeded in making himself popular, either with King or Country, but he had shown them both that he was useful. On 22 August 1721 Carteret told Newcastle that 'the King was resolved that the First Lord should not govern, but it was hard to prevent it'.

The best way of preventing it seemed to be the dissolution of Parliament and the election of a new one before Walpole had had time to build up his influence at the Treasury. He saw his danger and tried to persuade the King that the Septennial Act should be repealed and the present Parliament kept in being; but George brushed the proposal aside and began instead to prepare for an election. 'No one seems to doubt', wrote Dr Stratford to Edward Harley on 6 December 1721, 'but that the new Parliament, if there be one, will be to the Court's mind. The counties are most of them compounded already.' It was said that the Court was even prepared to abandon the Quarantine Bill and the Bill to build a bridge at Westminster, two measures which had been bitterly opposed by the City of London, if the City would return men approved by the Court to the new Parliament. The deal did not come off and three out of the four City members were hostile to the Court. At Westminster, too, a candidate known to be favoured by the King was defeated by Archibald Hutcheson, a popular hero of the Country Party who had just brought in a Bill 'for the better securing freedom of elections'. But these were minor setbacks: on the whole the elections of March 1722 resulted in a Parliament ready to support whatever ministers the King might choose. If he intended to reinstate Sunderland, now was the time to do it.

Sunderland, however, was not destined to be reinstated. He was taken ill with pleurisy and on 19 April 1722 he died. Two days later, while George was still recovering from the blow, news came of a fresh Jacobite conspiracy and it became clear that the whole question of a ministerial reshuffle would have to be shelved until the emergency had been dealt with. The King cancelled his proposed visit to Hanover and a regiment of the Guards was stationed in

Hyde Park, where it remained for the rest of the summer. When Parliament met in October, Walpole persuaded it to suspend the Habeas Corpus Act and impose a fine of £100,000 on the Roman Catholics of the Country.

The plot which had occasioned all this feverish ministerial activity was a feeble and unimpressive affair. A lawyer from the Middle Temple, Christopher Layer, had planned to collect together a force to seize the Tower and other vital points, in the hope that the King's absence and the Court's unpopularity after the South Sea affair would lead London and Westminster to support him. The Bishop of Rochester, Francis Atterbury, was involved in the affair, as were two other peers of the realm. In the end Layer was executed and Atterbury banished for life.

Having shown the King and the Country that his presence was necessary for their security, Walpole sought to prove that it was also necessary for their prosperity. His scheme to pay off the National Debt by means of a Sinking Fund, first worked out in 1716 and continued during Stanhope's ministry, had enjoyed considerable success, as had his plans to deal with the South Sea crisis. They had had to be drastically pruned and revised, but they had done something to restore business confidence and offset his unsavoury reputation as the 'Skreen Master'. Now Townshend, himself immersed in the complexities of foreign policy and Court intrigue, urged Walpole to exploit his reputation as a financier. In this way, he insisted, they would be able to defeat the remains of the Sunderland faction. On 28 July 1723 he wrote suggesting that his brother-in-law should find 'some new expedient for the ease of the nation and the benefit of trade, which points his majesty has so much at heart that the succeeding in them will inevitably rivet us in his esteem'. He also pressed for a reduction of the Land Tax from 3s to 2s in the pound. If the firm of Townshend and Walpole could thus consolidate their following among the monied men and the country gentlemen, by promising the first more trade and the second lower taxes, they would be well on the way to winning over the two other essential elements in political management, the Court and the party magnates.

Walpole produced the required 'new expedient', in the form of the system of bonded warehouses. Dutiable goods coming into the country were stored in these warehouses and charged with duty only when they were withdrawn for sale on the home market. Thus goods intended for re-export did not have to pay duty. As well as encouraging foreign merchants to send their cargoes via British ports, the scheme increased the revenue by making smuggling more difficult. In 1723 it was applied to tea, coffee and cocoa beans, and within seven years the tax yield on these commodities had risen by £120,000 a year, even though the rates of duty had been reduced. The Land Tax was brought down to 2s in the pound in 1723 and kept there for the next four years; and Walpole also impressed the City and pleased the Country Party by his handling of the National Debt. He was unable to reduce the capital by very much, but the interest charges fell steadily, from a total of £2,919,000 in 1723 to £2,335,000 in 1728. As early as August 1723 Walpole was able to tell Townshend that the government could borrow money at little more than 3½ per cent; and lower rates of interest meant that capital was more easily available for commercial and industrial expansion. The building industry, in particular, enjoyed a boom that lasted throughout the 1720s. The new prosperity, and the increased employment which it brought with it, helped to reduce political tension: 'We are in a state of tranquillity and satisfaction', wrote Walpole to Townshend, 'beyond what I have ever known.' Whatever their position at Court, the two brothers-in-law could certainly congratulate themselves on their standing with the Country and with the City.

Their struggle at Court was primarily against Lord Carteret, Secretary of State for the South and the last surviving disciple of Stanhope and Sunderland. While Walpole had been ingratiating himself with the monied men and the country gentlemen, Carteret had been building up for himself a strong position at Court among the King's closest advisers. He spoke fluent German and was ready, like Stanhope before him, to forward George's European schemes even if they met with opposition at home. For him, politics was not the management of men or the manipulation of patronage but the prosecution of great designs in foreign policy. 'What is it to me,' he said many years later, 'who is a judge or a bishop? It is my business to make kings and emperors, to maintain the balance of Europe.'

Carteret's contempt for patronage politics, his belief that he could maintain himself in power by clever diplomacy and Court intrigues, irritated his ally the Duke of Newcastle. Newcastle was a brilliant exponent of those subtle arts of management which Carteret despised and so far he had exercised his skill on behalf of the Stanhope-Sunderland group. He had been quick to take action, for instance, when the Whig journalist Richard Steele attacked the Peerage Bill.

Steele had lost his patent as supervisor of the Theatre Royal, Drury Lane, worth £1,000 a year, and would have lost his seat in the Commons as well if he had not made his peace with the ministry. Newcastle was a suspicious man, quick to take offence, and he resented Carteret's bland indifference to his efforts. By the spring of 1723 he had deserted Carteret and given his support to Townshend and Walpole. A few months later the brothers-in-law received another and more dangerous offer of alliance: Bolingbroke returned to England and suggested that he might bring the Tories over to their side if he was given office. He had been granted a pardon in May 1723 and at the end of June he appeared at his father's house at Battersea, where a liberal distribution of strong beer and a 'stately bonfire' encouraged the people to demonstrate on his behalf. When it became clear, however, that Townshend and Walpole were not prepared to have any dealings with him he left for France again early in August.

Meanwhile Townshend had found a far more powerful ally than either Newcastle or Bolingbroke. Now in her fifty-seventh year, Ehrengard von der Schulenburg was at once the most venerable and the most influential of the King's mistresses. Although she had already been made Duchess of Kendal and given a pension of £7,500 a year from the British exchequer, she was avid for further rewards and honours; and her pursuit of them had led her to quarrel with the other Hanoverian favourites and strike out on her own. During the quarrel between the King and the Prince of Wales she had been one of the few people to bridge the gulf between them, with the result that she became even more powerful and even richer than before. In 1720 Walpole had declared that she was 'as much Queen of England as any ever was'. Townshend was now able to secure her support against Carteret and the rest of the Hanoverians: 'She reposes a more entire confidence in me at present than in any other person about the King', he wrote triumphantly to Walpole in October 1723.

Carteret tried to win the favour of another of the King's mistresses by arranging an advantageous marriage for her daughter, but his scheme fell apart in his hands and succeeded only in arousing the King's resentment. Undeterred, he carried on his campaign against the Duchess of Kendal by stirring up trouble for her in Ireland. In return for political services rendered, she had been given by Sunderland a patent to manufacture copper farthings and halfpennies for use in Ireland, where there was a desperate shortage of small change.[1] She had sold her rights to a certain William Wood of Wolverhampton, who began striking coins and shipping them to Ireland in 1723. There was nothing wrong with the coins, but the ministry's opponents in Ireland took the chance to raise an outcry against this latest exploitation of Ireland for the profit of English and Hanoverian courtiers. Swift's savage *Drapier's Letters* helped to fan the flames and by 1724 popular discontent and a boycott of the coins had produced a grave crisis in Ireland. The King was furious that his prerogative of striking coin, and of authorizing others to strike it, should be challenged in this way and he was particularly angry with Carteret, who was known to have supported the campaign against the coins. In April 1724 he dismissed him from his office of Secretary of State and appointed him Lord-Lieutenant of Ireland instead. It was a repetition of the humiliation which the Sunderland faction had inflicted upon Townshend seven years earlier, with the added piquancy that this time the new Lord-Lieutenant would have to deal with a crisis which he had helped to create. Carteret carried out his unpleasant task with a reasonably good grace, but by 1725 it was clear even to Walpole that the ministry would have to give way to the clamour in Ireland. Wood's patent was withdrawn and he was given instead a pension of £3,000 a year for eight years, to be paid out of the Irish funds.

Although they yielded over the actual issue of the patent, the ministers did not accept defeat in Ireland. Those Irish office-holders who had helped to stir up the trouble were dismissed from their places and replaced by docile supporters of Walpole. In Scotland, too, the ministry strengthened its position. There had been ugly riots in Glasgow and other towns over the extension of the malt tax to Scotland and the Duke of Roxburgh, Secretary of State for Scotland, had shown some sympathy for the rioters. He was dismissed from his post and no successor was appointed. For the next few years the affairs of Scotland and the election of Scottish members of Parliament were managed by the Duke of Argyle and his younger brother the Earl of Islay, both of them political allies of Townshend and Walpole. 'We have once more got Scotland and Ireland quiet,' wrote Walpole to his brother-in-law on 3 September 1725, 'if we take care to keep them so.'

[1] Shortages of copper coin were not unusual in the eighteenth century, nor were they confined to Ireland. The Mint concerned itself mainly with gold and silver and for long periods—e.g. between 1755 and 1762 and between 1763 and 1771—no copper at all was minted.

At the same time ministerial management was extending and strengthening its hold on England. No less than five bishops had died in 1723 and care was taken that their successors should be loyal supporters of the government. Bishop Gibson of London was particularly insistent on the need for proper management of church patronage, in order that 'the clergy will take all proper methods to recommend themselves to such of the nobility and gentry as are in the interest of the government'. He himself had earned his promotion from Lincoln to London a few years earlier by writing hack political pamphlets for the ministry. Army patronage, too, was brought more effectively under ministerial control with the appointment of the Duke of Argyle as Master General of the Ordnance in 1725. In the same year the ministers tightened their grip on the City of London by passing an Act giving more power to the Court of Aldermen.

Never before had the resources of the Crown been so efficiently deployed. Previous ministers had relied on the office-holders or the party magnates, on monied men from the City or independent gentlemen from the Country, but Walpole relied on them all and made them all move as one. His following in the Country strengthened his position at Court, while his position at Court increased his following in the Country. George I forgot his earlier distrust and showered honours on the man who had taught him how to manage his kingdom. In 1725 Walpole was made a Knight of the recently revived Order of the Bath and in the following year he became a Knight of the Garter as well. By the autumn of 1726 he was on such intimate terms with the King that they dined together in private on more than one occasion.[1]

Walpole did not forget that his favour with the King depended ultimately on his ability to manage the House of Commons. Although he accepted a peerage for his eldest son he refused to go to the Lords himself. In his attack on the Peerage Bill he had already exploited the ordinary country gentleman's instinctive distrust of the great party magnates in the House of Lords and he was determined to go on exploiting it. He was in fact closely allied with the greatest of all

[1] If George I and Walpole had had to converse in schoolboy Latin, as is sometimes asserted, they could hardly have got through these evenings together. In fact, Walpole had a good command of French, the language usually spoken at Court. In the Cabinet, however, the King had to rely on the Prince of Wales as his interpreter; and this so infuriated him that he gave up attending Cabinet meetings after 1718. This effectively excluded the Prince from the Cabinet, but it did little to reduce the King's own power: he could still exert his influence over his ministers in the Closet.

party magnates, the Duke of Newcastle, who succeeded Carteret as Secretary of State for the South in 1724; but the image he wished to create of himself was that of an ordinary country gentleman defending other country gentlemen against the wiles of the party politicians. All the members of the Commons, whether career politicians or independent backbenchers, must be made to look to him as their best friend. To the management of patronage and the management of money he added a still more important technique, the management of men.

7

Management in Difficulties
1727–1742

1 The forces of opposition

The triumph of management under Sir Robert Walpole soon began
to put forth the seeds of its own decay. The more successfully he
gathered into his own hands every scrap of patronage, the more
surely he swelled the ranks of the excluded and the discontented.
However skilfully he and his colleagues distributed their favours,
they could never satisfy everyone. An office might be given to one
man and its reversion, the right to take it over on the holder's death,
granted to another. Other claimants might be soothed with vague
promises and assurances of good will. Newcastle in particular was a
past master at pleasing as many people as possible with the places at
his disposal; but even he could not persuade all those who had been
turned away to live on hope. Many of them lived instead on resentment and the desire for revenge. If they were poor and unimportant
this did not matter, but if they were wealthy and influential it might
matter a great deal. Like other politicians before and after him,
Walpole was to find that the rich could not with safety be sent empty
away.

The opposition to Walpole's engrossing of patronage was not
based on mere envy, but on a genuine sense of injustice. Eighteenth-
century gentlemen regarded the holding of offices under the Crown,
and the exploitation of those offices for personal gain, as their undoubted right and freehold. Like land, office was bought and sold.
Like land, it gave the purchaser a regular return on his capital and a
recognized position in society. Like land, it was a means whereby
a man could provide for his children and establish the fortunes of
his family. A monopoly of the market in offices could be made to
appear as intolerable and outrageous as a monopoly of the land
market. If Walpole's enemies could organize an effective campaign

178

against his cornering of the patronage market, they might well be able to shake his position both in the country and at Court.

Such a campaign was well under way by the beginning of 1727. At its head, rallying the cohorts of the discontented, stood Walpole's old enemy Bolingbroke. The King had made Walpole push through Parliament in 1725 a Bill restoring Bolingbroke to his estates, though not to his seat in the House of Lords. Full of hopes of high office, Bolingbroke had come back to live in England; but his hopes had been disappointed and he had turned to opposition. His chief ally was William Pulteney, also a disappointed and embittered man, who had hoped to succeed Carteret in 1724. When Newcastle had been promoted instead of him, Pulteney had become more and more estranged from Walpole until in 1725 he had attacked him openly in the Commons and had been dismissed from his office of Cofferer of the Household as a result. Between 1725 and 1727 these two men had done their best to lead a campaign against the ministry's foreign policy, but without much success. The Treaty of Vienna, signed in April 1725 between the King of Spain and the Emperor, had been resented in Britain, and when Townshend countered it with the Treaty of Hanover between Britain, France and Prussia, he got a good deal of popular support. Opposition attempts to damn the treaty as a sacrifice of Britain's interests to those of Hanover made little headway. The commercial classes were anxious for a trading war against Spain and even the country gentlemen, worried though they were by the prospect of an increased Land Tax, were indignant at Spanish threats against Gibraltar. By 1727 feeling against the Spaniards and against the Emperor was running so high that the Commons voted £3,000,000 for war and agreed to a Land Tax of 4s in the pound. Bolingbroke and Pulteney had to drop their criticisms of the ministry and join in the jingoistic chorus. Having failed to brand the ministers as Hanoverian warmongers, they turned eagerly to the task of representing them as bloated monopolists, engrossers of patronage and corrupters of public morals.

There was little point in making such attacks in the House of Commons. Even the most naïve and simple-minded of the country squires had been long enough at Westminster to know that the opposition was concerned not to destroy the corner in patronage but to get it into its own control. They might be amused by Pulteney's onslaughts on Walpole's methods, but they shrewdly suspected that he would use the same methods himself if he were in office. What was needed was a campaign directed at the country as a whole, conducted from a point outside Parliament and reaching into every corner of the land by means of the printed word. Bolingbroke, excluded from both Houses of Parliament, was the ideal spokesman and *The Craftsman*, a periodical started in December 1726, was his chosen mouthpiece. It contained ferocious satires on Walpole and his engrossing of patronage, but it also published dignified homilies on the need for a 'reformation of government'. It spoke with two voices. One, possibly Pulteney's, was the angry screech of the defeated politician, working off his spleen in crude lampoons. The other, possibly Bolingbroke's, was the solemn cadence of the philosopher, of the distinguished elder statesman commenting sadly and sternly on the ways of his degenerate successors. The mixture proved very effective, although Bolingbroke was uneasily aware that his high-sounding appeals for purity in government did not square very well with the naked ambition shown by some of his allies. 'Whilst the minister was not hard pushed,' he wrote some years later, 'they appeared to have but one end, the reformation of government. The destruction of the minister was pursued only as a preliminary, but of essential and indispensable necessity to that end. But when his destruction seemed to approach, the object of his succession interposed to the sight of many, and the reformation of government was no longer their point of view.'

One thing seemed certain: the moment of success would be the moment of truth. Once Walpole fell, those members of the opposition who were office-hunters in disguise would be revealed in their true colours. The genuine reformers, the men of the Country Party who hoped for an end of 'management' and the restoration of a free market in offices, would see their allies as they really were.

In June 1727 it seemed that the moment of success had arrived. The King, who had left London at the beginning of the month for Hanover, was taken ill in his coach on his way across Germany. He insisted on going on as far as Osnabrück, but he was unconscious by the time he arrived there. He died there on 11 June and three days later the news was brought to Sir Robert Walpole as he sat at dinner in his house at Chelsea. He went immediately to the Prince of Wales and told him that he was now King George II.

Since his reconciliation with his father the Prince had avoided any overt alliance with the forces of opposition, so that there was no alternative group of politicians waiting to take over, as there would have been if his reign had begun at any time between 1717 and 1720. But he was known to dislike most of his father's ministers and it was generally assumed that there would be sweeping changes now that he was King. Politicians out of office quickly forgot their professions of sturdy independence, their alliance with the Country Party, and became courtiers again. Office-holders and office-seekers alike crowded to Leicester House to pay their respects to the new King and Queen. Few of them can have imagined that Walpole's carefully built structure of management was going to be demolished in the interests of political purity; but they all expected that it would be put into the hands of a new manager.

The new manager was to be Sir Spencer Compton, the Treasurer of the Prince's household. When Walpole asked the new King for instructions he was told curtly: 'Go to Chiswick and take your directions from Sir Spencer Compton.' George II was determined that the man who had been his principal servant while he was Prince should continue to occupy that position now that he was King. Compton, who was also Paymaster-General and Speaker of the House of Commons, was well placed for his new task. As Speaker he had an intimate knowledge of the Commons and as Paymaster he had an insight into the workings of the patronage structure. Above all, he was known to have the confidence of the new King. His was a strong hand. Played by a Harley or a Walpole it might well have been a winning hand.

Spencer Compton was not, however, a Harley or a Walpole. He failed to appreciate the true nature of his own strength and he did not realize that royal favour, like other political assets, was apt to waste away if it was not properly used. George II's accession had released a great flood of loyalty, so powerful that it would strengthen and deepen whatever channel it flowed through. Office-holders and officers-seekers, party magnates and City financiers, were all falling over one another to pay court to the new King. Even independent country gentlemen devoid of any political ambitions were anxious to demonstrate their loyalty, to prove that their previous opposition had been to particular ministers and not to the monarchy itself. If all this goodwill flowed in through Compton himself he would soon be accepted, both by the country and by the King, as its natural and permanent channel; but if he allowed anyone else to divert the flow he would find himself left high and dry, disused and disregarded. Eighteenth-century political conditions, both at Court and in the Commons, helped only those who helped themselves.

Instead of helping himself, Compton invited his rival to help him. Walpole, who was so desperate that he was ready to plead for a minor office such as the Comptroller of the Household, was prevailed upon to write the King's first speech to Parliament. The King was pleased with the speech and when Parliament met at the end of June it was Walpole who persuaded it to grant George II an augmented Civil List of £800,000 a year, including £100,000 each for the Queen and the Prince of Wales. George was already beginning to have his doubts about dismissing a minister who could manage his affairs in Parliament so efficiently and Queen Caroline, who had admired Walpole ever since they had intrigued together at Leicester House eight years earlier, did her best to increase her husband's doubts. Compton's complacent assumption that his favour with the King would of itself bring him into power had allowed Walpole to retain the initiative. The political world, which had almost unanimously prophesied his fall, now found that he was still the channel between it and the King. The King for his part found that Walpole had his uses after all. He may only have intended to use him temporarily, but the fact that he used him at all put up his political stock and thus made him more useful still. Favour at Court, however precarious it might be, meant a following in the Commons; and this in its turn made a man's foothold at Court less precarious. In the end the King contented himself with making his friend Lord Scarborough Master of the Horse and bringing in Lord Chesterfield, another personal favourite, as a Lord of the Bedchamber. Compton kept his Paymastership and was raised to the peerage as Lord Wilmington. For the rest, things continued as before. Walpole's position at the new King's Court was still uncertain and men like Scarborough and Chesterfield might well prove dangerous; but in the Commons and in the country it was generally assumed that he controlled the approaches to George II as surely as he had controlled those to George I.

A new reign meant a new Parliament and as soon as their continuation in office was assured Walpole and Newcastle settled down to make one. The Septennial Act had had the effect of consolidating local interests both in the boroughs and in the counties, so that relatively few constituencies went to the polls. Twelve counties and sixty-five boroughs actually held elections, as against fifteen counties and eighty-eight boroughs in 1722. In the counties, the absence of an election usually meant that the local landowners had agreed among themselves as to who should represent them at Westminster; but in the boroughs it was a sign of the tightening grip of the patronage manipulator, the great party magnate. Since Walpole and Newcastle between them controlled the majority of these men, they were able to secure a House of Commons which was largely to their liking. When it met, at the end of January 1728, it voted unanimously for Walpole's candidate, Arthur Onslow, as its Speaker.

Onslow's reign as Speaker of the House of Commons was destined to be as long as George II's reign as King of Great Britain: he was re-elected in 1735, 1741, 1747 and 1754 and he finally resigned owing to ill-health at the beginning of 1761. In some ways he represented the traditions of the past, when the Speaker had been closely associated with the ministry of the day as its manager in the Commons. He was made a Privy Councillor in July 1728 and he later became chancellor to Queen Caroline and Treasurer of the Navy. On several occasions he used his position to help the ministry. But his repeated re-election gave the office of Speaker a continuity which placed it above and beyond party politics. When he was first elected he was simply the King's spokesman in the Commons, but by the time he retired he had made his office into something far more than this. In practice, if not in constitutional theory, he had become the representative of the Commons itself, defending its privileges against all comers and presiding impartially over its debates with the King's ministers on his right hand and their opponents on his left. During George II's reign the Commons came to be seen more and more as the arena for a clear-cut contest between 'the Ministry' and 'the Opposition'. Apart from Pulteney, who continued to sit near Walpole on the Treasury Bench, the leaders of 'the Opposition' tended to congregate on the benches on the Speaker's left. In theory concerted opposition to the King's ministers was still thought to be disloyal and seditious; but in practice things were moving towards the two party system, towards the idea that any government must always be faced with an organized opposition which is itself capable of forming a government. Onslow's part in all this was a vital one: he provided an essential element of stability and continuity, a point from which the pendulum of the two party system could swing.[1]

There did not seem to be much chance of it swinging in 1728. The disappointments of the previous summer, coming after the high hopes of early June, had produced disunity as well as dejection in the

[1] J. Steven Watson, in 'Arthur Onslow and Party Politics' (*Essays in British History presented to Sir Keith Feiling*, 1964, pp. 139-71) argues that Onslow's connection with the administration was too close to enable him to transcend party politics.

ranks of the opposition. The moment of apparent victory had indeed been the moment of truth, when independent country gentlemen had seen their allies turn from lofty reformers into squalid place-hunters overnight. Even the place-hunters and professional politicians themselves were disunited. Those who were young enough and patient enough attached themselves to Frederick Louis, the new Prince of Wales, who arrived in England in December 1728 and took up residence at Leicester House. There was as yet no open breach between the new King and the new Prince, but there was a great deal of mutual suspicion. It was noted that when George went off to Hanover in May 1729 he refused to give his son any share in the running of the country while he was away. Very soon Leicester House had become once again a shelter for the discontented, a centre for those who were disappointed in the present and hoped for great things in the future. In the meantime it provided them with a useful, if limited, source of income: offices in the Prince's Household were worth less than their equivalents in the King's Household, but they were not entirely to be despised.

Whatever the younger men might do, Bolingbroke and Pulteney could not afford to think in terms of the next reign. George II was five years younger than Bolingbroke and only a few months older than Pulteney, so that neither of them could reckon on a long and vigorous political career under his successor. Nor could they expect to come to terms with Walpole after a decent interval spent in the shadow of Leicester House: the very violence of their past opposition made a future accommodation unlikely. They had nothing to gain from patience of from moderation. Only an all-out attack, designed to overthrow him completely, would serve their turn.

One of the lines of this attack was the old familiar assault on corruption and on the engrossing of patronage. Awkward questions were asked about the expenditure of the secret service money and the leaders of the Country Party were encouraged to bring forward measures for the reform of the electoral system, measures intended to embarrass the ministry. One of these, a Bill requiring electors to swear on oath that they had not received 'any sum or sums of money, office, place or employment, gift or reward', became law in 1729, but it does not seem to have had much effect. In the following year Samuel Sandys, the member for Worcester, brought in a Bill to exclude from the Commons all those who received government pensions. The ministry allowed it to pass through the Commons and then killed it in the Lords. Sandys refused to accept defeat and re-introduced his Bill year after year so that it became, like the opposition to the Mutiny Act, a regular feature of the Country Party's campaign.

Bolingbroke and Pulteney were shrewd enough to realize that the country gentry's dislike of placemen and soldiers would not of itself bring down Walpole. For all their denunciations of ministerial corruption and military tyranny, the country members were basically loyal to the King and deeply suspicious of the discontented career politicians who courted them. More promising material, from the opposition's point of view, was to be found in the City of London. At the end of the previous reign, when it had become clear that attacks on the ministers as Hanoverian war-mongers were not going to be profitable, the opposition had changed its tune and accused Townshend and Walpole of having too little, rather than too much, enthusiasm for war. These accusations had found ready support in the City of London, where men were keen to carry on the trading war against Spain as vigorously as possible, and two out of the four London members elected in 1727, Sir John Barnard and Humphrey Parsons, were vigorous opponents of the ministry. A third, Micajah Perry, joined forces with them in 1728. Sir John Barnard, in particular, was a formidable critic of Walpole. He was a successful and much respected Quaker merchant, who was regarded by the lesser men in the City as their champion against the great privileged Companies, the unscrupulous financiers and all the other forces by means of which the Court sought to control the City. He constantly attacked the East India Company and the Royal Africa Company, and in 1734 he pushed through Parliament an Act against stock-jobbing, and especially against the practice of offering for sale stock which the seller did not actually hold at the time, which revived bitter memories of 1720 and Walpole's 'Skreen Master' activities. Meanwhile he hammered away at Walpole's management of the National Debt and against his policy of subsidizing the export of corn. As long as they had Barnard to help them, the opposition could always be sure that the City would be made to see the ministry's policies in the worst possible light.

This was especially true of foreign policy. The desultory war with Spain which George II had inherited from his father was brought to an end in March 1728 and in November 1729 the Treaty of Seville was signed between Britain, France, Spain and the United Provinces.

Since one of its chief aims was to force the Emperor to abandon the Ostend Company, which he had founded in 1722 to trade between the Austrian Netherlands and the East Indies, the treaty could be said to be a blow for British trade as well as a triumph for British diplomacy. The opposition, however, denounced it as a national disaster and the culmination of the ministry's craven policy of conciliating France and Spain. Exports had fallen from £5,667,000 in 1725 to £4,605,000 in 1727 and there was still no sign of a recovery at the end of 1729; and the ministry's critics attributed this trade depression —which was in fact produced by the hostilities against Spain—to the ministry's failure to take a sufficiently strong line against the two Bourbon powers. As for the proposed destruction of the Ostend Company, it was pointed out that this would help the ministry's friends in the East India Company rather than the ordinary merchants. The real beneficiaries of the Treaty of Seville would be men like Edward Harrison, the rich East India Company magnate who had been made Postmaster-General by Walpole in 1727 and had married his daughter to Townshend's son.

This new attack from the City made use of the old Country Party line about ministerial corruption, but it gave it a new twist. Ministers were not only accused of engrossing patronage, but of using their privileged position to pursue policies which ran counter to the nation's real interests. In order to line the pockets of Walpole's creatures in the East India Company, the country was to be forced into an unnatural alliance with the Bourbon powers of France and Spain, its traditional enemies, and into a war against the Emperor, its traditional ally. In February 1730 the opposition brought forward evidence to show that the French were once again fortifying Dunkirk. This was a point on which British merchants were particularly sensitive[1] and it helped to discredit the ministers by suggesting that they either did not know or did not care about the treachery of their new allies. Excitement ran very high and many people expected that the ministry would be defeated in the Commons; but Walpole used his mastery of parliamentary procedure and his alliance with Speaker Onslow to get the debate postponed until he had obtained soothing assurances from the French. He then defeated the opposition by 270 votes to 149.

Even though the attacks on the Treaty of Seville had failed to bring down the ministry, they had helped to worsen relations between

[1] See above, p. 126.

Walpole and Townshend. For some time past Townshend had become increasingly resentful of his brother-in-law's domination of the ministry and he particularly resented his influence over Queen Caroline. While George II and Townshend were in Hanover during the summer of 1729 Walpole and the Queen had worked very closely together; and on his return Townshend realized that his own influence over the King was far less important politically than Walpole's over the Queen. The conflict between the brothers-in-law was brought to a head when Townshend sought to use the Treaty of Seville, which Walpole intended as the first stage in a general settlement of Europe, as an opportunity for a new war. Relying on the fact that the treaty bound Spain to support us over the Ostend Company, he planned to drive the Emperor into war and seize the Austrian Netherlands from him. Walpole thought that this would be to play France's game for her and he wanted to reach an understanding with the Emperor. Townshend stood out for an uncompromising attitude to the Emperor but in May 1730 even the King came round to Walpole's way of thinking and Townshend therefore resigned. Walpole took the opportunity for a general reshuffle: Carteret was dismissed from his Lord Lieutenancy of Ireland and Henry Pelham, Newcastle's very able younger brother, was promoted from Secretary at War to Paymaster of the Forces. Spencer Compton, now Lord Wilmington, became Lord Privy Seal instead of Paymaster, and Lord Taylor was promoted from Lord Privy Seal to Lord President of the Council. Lord Harrington, a dull but subservient man, took Townshend's place as Secretary of State for the North.

The resignation of Townshend, coupled with the long-delayed exit of Carteret, marked the final triumph of the managers over the courtiers. Townshend's policy had made Parliament difficult to manage and Walpole was therefore determined to change it. He was not prepared to go to war with Spain in order to please the City, since this would mean increased taxes which would displease the Country; but he was prepared to exchange the alliance with France for an alliance with the Emperor, even though this meant dropping some of George II's ambitions in Germany as Elector of Hanover. In March 1731 Britain and the United Provinces signed the second Treaty of Vienna with the Emperor, by which they agreed to recognize his daughter as his successor in return for the abandonment of the Ostend Company and the recognition of Spanish claims to

Imperial territories in Italy. This last provision made possible Spain's accession to the Treaty and the complete isolation of France. By the autumn, when a British fleet escorted the Spanish princes to their Italian possessions, Walpole could claim a notable diplomatic victory. He had reconstructed the anti-French coalition of William III's reign and he had broken apart the Franco-Spanish alliance which had been so threatening to British trade. He had already shown his ability to manage the Commons, aided by Newcastle's electoral influence and Pelham's financial skill; now he had shown that he could also manage the King into accepting a policy which put the interests of the City and the country before those of Hanover.

Unfortunately for Walpole, not all of his problems could be solved by management. Some of them implied a need for something more positive, for government rather than management. His attempts to provide it were to give the opposition their next and greatest chance.

2 The problems of government

While the professional politicians argued over Walpole's monopoly of honourable and reputable offices, offices which could enhance a gentleman's prestige and social standing, humbler men contented themselves with less dignified posts. In August 1728 Thomas Bambridge bought the office of Warden of the Fleet Prison from John Huggins for £5,000. It was a fair price, but he soon found that he had to use drastic methods if he was to get a proper return on his money. Prisoners who would not or could not pay him the fees to which he considered himself entitled were put in irons in a special cell above the sewers, sometimes with dead bodies to keep them company. Robert Castell, who had committed no offence but was in prison for debt, was unable to pay the fees Bambridge demanded and was therefore shut in a cell with another prisoner who had the smallpox. When he caught the disease and died his case aroused sufficient public interest to provoke a parliamentary inquiry and to get Bambridge tried at the Old Bailey for murder. He was, however, acquitted. An Act was passed to clear the debtors' prisons and thousands of prisoners were released—97,248 according to one contemporary pamphlet. But this provided only a temporary remedy and very soon the prisons filled up again and the jailers returned to their customary methods of extracting fees. No proper reform of the prison system could be expected as long as places in it were seen as investments rather than as jobs. Payment of officials by means of salaries instead of fees was a necessary first step, but it could not be taken if the country was determined to be managed rather than governed and regarded every extension of government activity and government expenditure with passionate hostility.

There were profits to be made out of catching criminals as well as out of lodging them. To a society anxious to reduce government to a minimum, the idea of a salaried police force was even more unpalatable than that of a proper prison service. Reluctant parish constables were not particularly zealous in hunting down offenders and the task was usually left to paid informers, who made sure that the sums they received from the courts for giving information about criminals were supplemented by the sums they received from the criminals for withholding it. Such payments could hardly be described as fees, but the private empires built up by some informers were as profitable and as closely guarded as those of many public officials. Jonathan Wild, who ran one such empire in Cripplegate from about 1712 until his execution in 1725, was not content with blackmailing criminals and then accepting payment from the courts when he finally betrayed them; he also conducted a lucrative trade in stolen property, which he bought from thieves at a very low price and restored to its owners in return for a handsome reward. Two Acts of Parliament, one in 1717 and the other in 1719, were needed in order to make this traffic illegal; and even then it was another six years before a charge against Wild could be proved. There was great excitement when he was hanged at Tyburn, but few people grasped the true significance of his case. Thomas de Veil, who became a justice of the peace for Middlesex and Westminster in 1729, was one of them: he saw that the business of preventing crime must eventually be taken out of the hands of private individuals and put into those of paid government officials. But it was a long time before he was able to do anything about it.

Few informers were interested in crimes of violence, which were seldom punished by fines and were in any case usually committed by people who were too poor to pay either fines or 'protection money'. A successful information about a comparatively trivial offence could mean that the informer's share of the fine was anything up to £200; but an information about a murder would probably yield nothing but a time-wasting attendance at court. It might also prove highly dangerous, especially if it concerned the exploits of the

Mohocks. These gangs of young noblemen and gentlemen, who roamed the streets of London and amused themselves by slashing the passers-by with their swords, were less common than they had been in Queen Anne's time; but they still sallied forth occasionally to beat up a watchman or assault some harmless citizen. Crimes of violence committed by the lower orders of society were less likely to go unreported, particularly when they took the form of rioting. Many justices who would not go out of their way to seek out a foot-pad or a murderer were provoked into drastic action by the least sign of an organized demonstration. The depression of the late 1720s resulted in many such demonstrations, especially among the cloth-workers of the West Country. In 1726 several towns in Devon and Somerset were terrorized by bands of workmen demanding higher wages and threatening violence unless they got them. At Crediton the ringleaders were arrested, only to be rescued again by an angry crowd, while at Taunton rioters attacked the Constable and a justice of the peace. When the Town Clerk read the Riot Act they pulled off his hat and wig and put dirt on his head. Both employers and workers petitioned the House of Commons and the result was an Act prohibiting all combinations of clothworkers formed for the purpose of securing higher wages. Workmen who threatened their employers were to be transported to the plantations for seven years and those who entered workshops with the intention of damaging machines or cloth were to be put to death. Ten years later the provisions of this Act were extended to workers in other industries.

There was a strong upward movement of trade in the 1730s and industrial disturbances became less common, but crimes of violence continued in spite of an increasingly ferocious penal code. In April 1731 Mr Newcomen of Chester, who had received several threaten-ing letters, was found at the end of Fishmongers' Lane with his head battered in. Two months later a shopkeeper at Windsor quarrelled with a customer over his bill and killed him by throwing him over a table. Later in the summer a baker got into an argument with a blacksmith in a skittle-alley at Highgate and killed him with a blow on the ear. Meanwhile a schoolboy at Eton had been convicted of manslaughter for stabbing another boy to death with his penknife. These incidents, along with many others of the same sort, were sufficiently lurid to secure a brief mention in Edward Cave's new journal, *The Gentleman's Magazine*; but countless other crimes passed without mention and often without detection. Savage punishments failed to deter potential criminals because the chances of being found out were so slender. Parliament passed an Act in 1731 providing that in future all proceedings in the law courts should be in English, but this was the limit of its concern with crime. For the rest of the session it concerned itself with Acts about the manufacture of sailcloth, the price of coal in London, the making of conveyances by lunatics, and other miscellaneous matters.

Nevertheless, some of the Acts passed during this session pointed the way ahead from management to government. They were concerned to tighten up the system of bonded warehouses, which had come to be known as 'the Excise'. Walpole himself tried to avoid the use of this word, knowing that it had unfortunate overtones. Like standing armies, excise had first been introduced during the civil wars of the previous century; and in the eyes of the Country Party it stood for foreign tyranny. Whereas customs officers were paid by means of fees, excise inspectors were salaried officials. They did not just concern themselves with preventing smuggling, but had power to enter premises where excisable goods were on sale in order to check that the goods had been through the bonded warehouses and had paid the excise duties. Customs duties were relatively easy to evade: once the goods had been successfully smuggled into the country, no one asked any further questions. But the excise was inexorable and ubiquitous. Above all, it was efficient. This, more than anything else, was its greatest crime as far as the country was concerned. Any extension of the excise would mean an extension of government.

The Acts of 1731 were merely concerned with preventing certain abuses of the existing regulations and they did not portend any general extension of the excise. Nevertheless, the opposition did its best to suggest that such an extension was imminent. In March 1731 *The Craftsman* asserted that a General Excise was already under consideration and printed some lines by Andrew Marvell which were to be constantly quoted, with various embellishments, during the next few years:

> Excise, a Monster, worse than e'er before
> Frighted the Midwife, and the Mother tore.
> A thousand Hands she hath, a thousand Eyes;
> Breaks into Shops, and into Cellars pries;
> With hundred Rows of Teeth the Shark exceeds;
> And on all Trades, like Casawar, she feeds.

It was not true that Walpole was planning a General Excise, but it was true that he was contemplating the extension of the bonded warehouse system to wines and tobacco. The smuggling of these commodities was particularly widespread and particularly audacious. Early in 1731 a sloop put into Marazion in Cornwall loaded with brandy, tobacco and soap. The customs men stopped her and put three officers on board, only to have them overwhelmed by a force of some fifty men who cut open the hatches, took away the brandy and rode off. No less than 192,515 gallons of brandy and 1,061,268 pounds of tobacco were seized by the customs between 1723 and 1733, but this was reckoned to be only a tenth part of the total amount smuggled into the country. In many areas tobacco was openly offered for sale at prices which would have been impossible if it had paid duty. Those retailers who refused to deal in smuggled goods found themselves undercut by their less scupulous competitors. Like the state of the prisons and the prevalence of crime, the nationwide addiction to smuggling presented a problem in government. Eighteenth-century gentlemen, who equated management with freedom and government with tyranny, refused to face this fact and tried to solve the problem by means of savage punishments. An act of 1726 made even the blackening of the face, the normal precaution taken by smugglers who operated at night, into a capital offence. It was ruthlessly enforced, but only had the effect of making smugglers more desperate, more efficient and therefore harder to catch with the existing machinery of the revenue service. The real answer to the problem lay with the executive rather than with the judiciary: more government, rather than more punishments, was needed.

Walpole was too deeply rooted in his own time to see the excise as an instrument of government. Like most country gentlemen, he had dealt in smuggled goods himself. He had a great respect for efficient administration and he could see the advantages of replacing the comparatively powerless customs officers with salaried excise men who could survey contraband at every stage in its journey from importer to consumer. Furthermore, he noted with satisfaction that the creation of more excise men meant the creation of more patronage. For him it was a matter of managing existing forces, not of creating new ones. By increasing the number of offices at his disposal the excise extension would help him to manage the party magnates and the professional politicians. By improving the yield of the indirect taxes it would enable him to lower the Land Tax and please the country gentlemen. By eliminating the payment of duties on goods intended for re-export it would increase London's prosperity as an entrepôt for world trade and thus make the merchants more amenable. Court, Country, City—all three should be easier to manage once the excise extension had come into force.

He was particularly anxious to win the support of the Country Party and he therefore proposed, in February 1732, to reduce the Land Tax to a shilling in the pound. In order to make this possible he revived the Salt Tax, which had been abolished two years before. Since salt was one of the necessities of life for all classes, the opposition was able to accuse him of taxing the poor to relieve the rich. He got his proposals through the Commons, but only by a majority of thirty-nine; and outside Parliament the outcry against the salt duties was linked with suggestions that a General Excise was once again being contemplated. 'One Reason for opposing the Revival of the Salt Tax', wrote *The Craftsman* in June 1732, 'was the making of a dangerous Precedent, which might prove a Step to the greatest of all Evils, a General Excise; which upon mentioning a year and a half ago, it was strenuously denied, and represented as a Fiction of Malcontents to stir up Sedition and Disaffection, but now is publicly avowed and justified.' Other opposition propagandists set themselves to arouse all the prejudices of the Country Party. Prints and pamphlets linking the excise with the hated standing army circulated widely. One picture showed the figure of Excise, drawn to look like Sir Robert, riding in triumph on a hogshead of tobacco and pulled by the British lion wearing wooden shoes, the symbol of continental tyranny. He was escorted by a troop of soldiers and the verses underneath proclaimed:

> Dejected Trade hangs down its drooping Head,
> While Standing Armies daring Colours spread;
> By these encouraged, on the Barrel strides
> Excise in Triumph, and like Bacchus rides:
> Still to enslave and make us more distrest
> They clap French Shoes upon the British Beast.

By the end of 1732 both the country gentlemen, whose burden of taxes would have been lightened by an extension of the excise, and the city merchants, whose trade would almost certainly have benefited from it, had been persuaded to view it as an intolerable invasion of the liberties of the subject. Walpole still disclaimed any intention of imposing a General Excise, but his plans for a wine and tobacco excise were well advanced. Early in 1733 he admitted to the Commons that the revived salt duties had not yielded as much as he had hoped; and he proposed that the deficit should be made up not by raising the Land Tax again but by taking £500,000 out of the Sinking Fund.[1] He justified this device by saying that it would not have to be repeated, since he was preparing a new scheme of taxation which would do away with the deficit for good without necessitating any increase in the Land Tax. He gave no details and many members must have feared that the threatened General Excise was, after all imminent. Nevertheless, he won the day with a majority of 110. The opposition stepped up their campaign against the General Excise to fever pitch and they were somewhat deflated when Walpole's proposals turned out to be limited to wine and tobacco only. Pulteney raged against them and Sir William Wyndham did his best to rally the country gentlemen to the opposition's cause. Sir John Barnard spoke for the City merchants, who had already announced publicly their intention of opposing 'any extension of the excise laws, under whatever name or pretence it may be attempted'. But in spite of all their efforts the debate ended with a victory for the ministry by a majority of sixty-one. All four members for the City of London voted against the proposals, as did members for other great trading towns like Bristol and Liverpool. But only just over half of the country members voted with the opposition, in spite of all that had been done to raise the Country Party against the excise. The ministry's following among the borough-mongers stood it in good stead. Newcastle's influence, in particular, was invaluable: borough members from areas like Yorkshire and Sussex, where he had great estates, voted obediently for the ministry. Although Walpole had lost the City he had not yet lost the Country; and his hold on the party magnates had hardly been shaken at all.

His real danger came from the discontented elements at Court. His overwhelming success over the last eleven years had had the same effect on reluctant colleagues as on open enemies: it had driven them to desperation. After each crisis he had emerged stronger than ever, determined to be *the* minister rather than *a* minister. Those who had hoped to be his equals found themselves his subordinates. Men like

[1] The Sinking Fund was a fund set aside for the gradual paying off of the National Debt. It had been devised by Walpole in 1716, established by Stanhope in the following year and carried on by Walpole when he returned to office in 1721.

Chesterfield and Scarborough, who had come into office in 1727 with the intention of sharing his power, found that after six years they were still doing no more than support it. They decided that they would support it no longer: they would use the excise crisis to break Walpole once and for all. They would show the King that he must trust them and not his precious Sir Robert, who was leading him to ruin. Early in April, when Parliament reassembled after the Easter recess, they made it clear that they would vote against the Excise Bill when it came up to the Lords. Other noblemen at Court followed their example and Walpole was faced with the possibility of a defeat in the House of Lords. Meanwhile, waverers in the House of Commons had started to follow the lead given by the discontented courtiers: an opposition motion to withdraw the Bill was defeated by 232 to 176 on 4 April, but the ministry's majority fell to thirty-six (236 to 200) when the second reading was carried in the early hours of the following morning. Next day it dropped to sixteen, but this was in a very thin House and was not really representative. More serious was the drop to seventeen (214 to 197) on 10 April, on a ministerial motion refusing to hear counsel on behalf of London's petition against the Bill.

By this time Walpole had already decided to retreat, but he was determined to do so with dignity. Having got the Commons to shelve the City's petition he moved the adjournment of the Excise Bill until 12 June. Since Parliament would no longer be sitting by then, this was tantamount to abandoning the Bill. Pulteney and Wyndham were infuriated by this device, but most backbenchers were ready to accept it. Charles Caesar, member for Hertfordshire, told Walpole privately that 'he thought a father should have the burying of his own child'. That night London celebrated the Bill's withdrawal with an unprecedented outburst of rioting and violence; and the next day Walpole was able to assert his authority by getting the Commons to send a unanimous condemnation of this outburst to the Lord Mayor. No one should say that he had bowed to popular clamour, whether in the Country or in the City.

Meanwhile, he was making up at Court for the ground he had yielded in the Commons. So far from undermining his position, the rebels had established him even more firmly in the King's favour. George had been an ardent supporter of the excise proposals and he was furious with those courtiers who had tried to force his hand and make him dismiss a minister as faithful and as useful as Sir

Robert. He decided to make an example of the ringleaders and he dismissed Chesterfield from his post as Lord Steward. Lord Clinton, who had played a prominent part in the rebellion, was deprived of his place as a Lord of the Bedchamber. The rebels, however, refused to admit defeat and carried the fight into the House of Lords. At the beginning of May they carried a motion for an inquiry into the affairs of the South Sea Company and three weeks later they defeated the ministry again in a crowded House. In fact, numbers were equal—seventy-five peers voted for the ministry and seventy-five against—but by the custom of the House of Lords the motion was negatived. Walpole and Newcastle, supported enthusiastically by the King, exerted all their arts of management. They coaxed and persuaded, promised and threatened, until by the beginning of June they had won back their control of the House of Lords. Then came the day of reckoning: one after another the courtiers who had voted against the ministry were stripped of their offices. Some, like Viscount Cobham of Stowe and the Duke of Bolton, lost their regiments as well. The King was determined that both his Court and his army should be purged of those who had dared to challenge his favourite minister. When it came to Lord Scarborough, his oldest and closest friend, he hesitated; but Scarborough rescued him from his dilemma by resigning of his own accord.

The crisis had demonstrated both the strength and the limitations of management. By trying to go beyond those limits Walpole had endangered his position; by retreating within them again he had saved it. He had successfully defended the citadel of power which he had inhabited for so long; but outside it, on the ground he had failed to capture, the problems continued to multiply.

3 The fall of Walpole

The excise on wine and tobacco was not the only new tax Walpole proposed in 1733. He also asked the Commons to approve a duty of sixpence a gallon on molasses brought into the North American colonies from the foreign sugar islands in the Caribbean. The colonists needed cheap molasses for their profitable rum distilling industry, but the British West Indian sugar planters were determined to protect themselves against foreign competition. Since the planters were more influential and articulate than the colonists, both with the ministry and in the House of Commons, the proposals were passed without a division. Sir John Barnard, however, spoke against them and pointed out that such a heavy duty would more than double the price of molasses in the colonies and would lead to extensive smuggling. Even if it had a whole army of excisemen, he said, the government would be unable to put it down. His fears turned out to be fully justified: the duties were widely evaded and the attempt to enforce them was soon given up. Over the Excise Bill itself he and his fellow merchants made the same point: Walpole might be able to pass it, but he would never be able to enforce it if the justices of the peace were against him. No administration could fly in the face of the local potentates who really ran the country.

Even when the ministry and the justices were working together it was not always possible to put new laws into effect. This was made painfully clear in 1736, when Walpole tried to curb the evils of gin drinking. In the past governments had welcomed the distilling of cheap gin as a way of disposing of surplus grain or grain which had been spoiled. 'What would become of our corn injured by bad harvests,' asked one pamphleteer, 'were it not for the Distillers?' But by the 1730s the effects of gin on the health and habits of the labouring classes had begun to cause their employers some anxiety and Walpole's Gin Act of 1736 imposed a duty of 20s a gallon and fixed the cost of a licence to sell spirits at £50. Special troops had to be drafted into London to deal with the riots which the Act provoked and after a few months the attempt to enforce it had to be given up. Informers, still the indispensable instruments of law enforcement, were frightened of being beaten up by angry crowds if they laid informations against offenders under the Act. 'There never was certainly an Act executed with such difficulty as this against gin', wrote one journalist in September 1737. Meanwhile the popular sympathy for law-breakers and the constant danger from the mob had been demonstrated in Edinburgh, where a crowd rioted after the hanging of a smuggler. Captain Porteous, the English commander of the troops on duty at the time, ordered his men to fire on the crowd and six people were killed. Porteous was condemned to death and when his execution was put off for six weeks on orders from London, the mob broke into the prison and lynched him. Walpole imposed a fine of £2,000 on the city of Edinburgh, only to find that the Scottish members were roused from their usual subservience into grumbling opposition. Once again an attempt at government had led to difficulties of management.

The rapid growth of the theatre in London presented Walpole with problems of both management and government. From his own personal point of view the political satires which had been staged during the past few years were, like the activities of opposition journalists, both offensive and dangerous. Management of the House of Commons was not made any easier when members were still chuckling over the thinly veiled references to Walpole in *The Beggar's Opera*, written by John Gay and produced by John Rich at Lincoln's Inn Fields in January 1728. Its sequel, *Polly*, was banned by the Lord Chamberlain because of its political overtones; but the Chamberlain could only exercise his control over the threatres which were licensed by royal patent. In unlicensed theatres and in portable booths set up in the streets, political satires continued to thrive and become more ferocious. Whereas newspaper attacks could be countered by maintaining government newspapers,[1] the ministry could hardly stoop to running its own theatres for political purposes. Walpole therefore decided to muzzle stage satire by means of an Act of Parliament. On 24 May 1737, when many members had already left London, he introduced into a thinning House a Licensing Bill in the form of an amendment to the Vagrant Act of 1731. New plays, as well as alterations to old ones, were to be submitted to the Lord Chamberlain at least a fortnight before they were performed. Licensed theatres were to be restricted to the City of Westminster and the performance of plays for money in unlicensed premises was to be heavily punished. The Bill passed through all its stages within a month and it was successful in its principal aim of halting the spate of political satires presented on the London stage. It did not, however, succeed in checking the growth of the theatre in the country as a whole. Travelling companies of players evaded its provisions by charging for music or refreshments rather than for the play itself and many justices of the peace turned a blind eye to these devices. As an aid to political management, the Licensing Act proved very useful; but as an instrument of government it was much less effective.

The ferocity of the attacks on Walpole sprang from a sense of failure, even of despair. Early in 1734 the opposition in the House of Lords brought in a Bill to prevent officers being summarily dis-

---

1 The *Daily Courant*, the *Free Briton* and the *London Journal* were the principal ministerial papers. They were distributed free by the Post Office and issued free to coffee houses. William Arnall, editor of the *Free Briton*, received £11,000 over four years and at one point nearly £1,000 was spent on the *Daily Courant* within four months. In June 1735 all three were amalgamated in the *Daily Gazetteer*.

missed from their regiments—an outright attack on the dismissals of the previous year. It failed by 100 votes to 62 and a similar Bill in the Commons was rejected without a division. The independent country gentlemen were outraged at what they regarded as an impertinent attack on the King's prerogative; and the only result of the affair was to widen the gulf between the professional politicians of the opposition and their uncertain allies among the Country Party. Bolingbroke was bitterly critical of Pulteney and his followers and insisted that they only wanted to use the Country Party 'as scaffolding to raise themselves to power'. Pulteney was even more outspoken about Bolingbroke and said that 'his very name and presence in England did hurt'. Weakened and discredited by these divisions, the opposition made relatively little headway at the 1734 elections. There were some 250 members of the new House of Commons who could be considered as potential opponents of the ministry, but there was little prospect of their acting together effectively and consistently. Even if they did so do, Walpole would still have a majority of between forty and fifty. After the intoxicating excitement of the excise crisis it was a disappointing result for the opposition leaders, who complained loudly of the unfairness of the elections. 'Nothing can be more ridiculous', said a ministerial writer in the *Free Briton*, 'than when a vanquished Party bullies in its ill success; and after having lost its cause by the Votes of the People, boasts of a Triumph in the Sense of the People.'

The idea that the votes of the people and the sense of the people were two different things might appear ridiculous in 1734, but the time would come when it would appear less so. In the end the opposition's appeal from the electoral system to the people it was supposed to represent was to prove their most powerful weapon; but it was to be a long time before they dared to use it to the full. In the meantime, whatever their journalists might proclaim, their politicians concerned themselves with the Court rather than the Country, with the politics of patronage rather than the politics of the people.

By the mid 1730s the politics of patronage had come to be centred once again on a quarrel between the King and the Prince of Wales. In April 1736, when he was married to Princess Augusta of Saxe-Gotha, the Prince asked that his allowance of £24,000 a year should be increased to £100,000. This was what George II himself had had when he was Prince of Wales and it was the sum provided for in the Civil List arrangements of 1727. The King refused to give him more than £50,000 and the Prince turned to the opposition politicians in a desperate attempt to get a majority in the House of Commons for the proposal to increase his allowance. In spite of his extravagant promises of future rewards for those who supported him, he was defeated by 234 votes to 204. Relations between father and son were further embittered in July 1737, when Frederick hustled his pregnant wife off to St James's Palace in the middle of the night rather than have his first child born under his father's roof at Hampton Court. The King announced that 'whoever goes to pay their court to their Royal Highnesses the Prince and Princess of Wales will not be admitted to His Majesty's presence', and once again, as in the previous reign, there were two rival courts. The Prince's court, held variously at Kew, Norfolk House and Leicester House, became the recognized and established centre of the 'Reversionary Interest'; and politicians who looked for advancement in the future rather than the present accepted places in the Prince's household. William Pitt, a young follower of Lord Cobham's who had been turned out of his commission in the Dragoon Guards for an offensive speech on the occasion of the Prince's marriage, now became a Groom of the Bedchamber to the Prince at a salary of £400 a year. George Lyttelton, another member of the Cobham group, became the Prince's Private Secretary.

Lord Hardwicke, a shrewd supporter of Walpole and the Pelhams who had been Attorney-General and Lord Chief Justice and was now Lord Chancellor, saw how useful the new situation was for the opposition. 'They will now find a head in the Prince,' he wrote. 'and he being the immediate successor in the Protestant line will be an irrefragible answer to the reproach of Jacobitism.' On the other hand, the emergence of Leicester House as the chief rallying point of the opposition was not entirely welcome to men like Pulteney and Carteret. They still had hopes of gaining office under George II and they could not afford to prejudice these hopes by committing themselves too deeply to the Prince whom the King hated so cordially. The death of Queen Caroline in November 1737 helped to make relations between father and son even worse. George had been out of the country from May to October of 1735 and again from May 1736 until January 1737; and during these protracted absences Caroline had acted as sole regent. Inevitably she had drawn even closer to Walpole and his friends at the very moment when her son was allying himself with the opposition. The King was deeply devoted to her in spite of his constant infidelities and he found it difficult to forgive Frederick for harrying her during the last months of her life. The young men of the opposition might dream—or pretend to dream—of the new dawn which would come with Frederick's accession to the throne; but their elders could not afford to wait that long and must therefore exercise more discretion. They must make it clear that they were merely the enemies of Sir Robert Walpole and not of the King himself.

Support of Prince Federick was not the only sure way of displeasing the King. An equally certain method of earning his undying hatred was to disparage his precious Electorate of Hanover. The Country Party had always distrusted the King's German connections, just as it had distrusted William III's Dutch connections at the end of the previous century; and this distrust was particularly marked in the field of foreign policy. In the summer of 1734, when Parliament had been called upon to provide supplies in case it became necessary to intervene in the War of the Polish Succession, Sir John Hynde Cotton was quick to remind the Commons that they had no business to provide for the security of the King's German dominions. Since the war had arisen out of a dispute between France and the Emperor as to who should be King of Poland, it certainly seemed as though Hanover was more directly effected than Britain. Walpole had no wish to provoke Cotton and the other country gentlemen into open opposition: he persuaded the King not to take an active part in the war, which ground to an indecisive halt late in 1735. The peace terms, which were not finally accepted by all the combatants until 1739, established French influence in Lorraine and Spanish influence in Italy. Thus Britain's two most dangerous commercial rivals, separated by Walpole's diplomacy in 1731, had been brought together again by the war and had been enabled to redraw the map of Europe to their own advantage and to the disadvantage of Britain. Walpole's policy of non-intervention, which he had pressed upon his colleagues and upon the King in an attempt to please the country gentlemen, had resulted in the isolation of Britain and a dangerous Franco-Spanish alignment both in the Mediterranean and in the Atlantic. In his anxiety to prove that he was not preoccupied with the interests of Hanover, he had laid himself open to the charge of neglecting the interests of Britain as well. Whichever way he turned he was caught in a hopeless dilemma: if he intervened in Europe he faced the anger of the Country Party and if he stayed out of Europe he risked not only the King's displeasure but also the possibility of Franco-Spanish supremacy at sea and in the colonies.

The younger members of the opposition believed, or pretended to believe, that the dilemma did not exist. They laid all past and present failures in foreign policy at the door of Hanover and proclaimed that an honest and patriotic minister could easily challenge the commercial power of France and Spain without involving Britain in unnecessary continental entanglements. To Walpole's idea of continental war, fought in Germany with expensive standing armies, they opposed the idea of a 'Patriot War', fought on the high seas and in the colonies with navies and with small detachments of troops. Instead of obtaining colonial concessions indirectly, by means of long and expensive European wars, Britain should seize them directly, without formality and without worrying about the need for allies in Europe.

Bolingbroke had been trying for many years to popularize the word 'Patriot' as a label under which all the elements of the opposition could unite. For him, a Patriot was a man who rose above party strife and served his country disinterestedly; but this vision of the Patriot Party as a kind of extended Country Party, fearlessly slaying the dragon of corruption with the lance of independence, never really caught on, and in 1735 he retired to France in disgust. Then, in his absence and in a context quite different from that he had envisaged, a Patriot Party was at last born. Its leaders included William Pitt and the other young men associated with Lord Cobham, and they claimed to speak for the whole trading community of Britain. In fact, their connections were mostly with the West India interest and their aim was to secure the revision of that same Treaty of Utrecht which Bolingbroke himself had negotiated a generation earlier. It had made possible an increasingly valuable Anglo-Spanish trade which was very profitable to both sides. Quite apart from the concessions obtained by the South Sea Company in Spanish America, British merchants supplied Spain herself with manufactured goods and took in return dyestuffs and soap, as well as essential supplies of gold and silver. By the late 1730s more than £1 million worth of goods a year were being sold to Spain and about £550,000 worth were being bought from her. Good trading relations with Spain also opened up rich markets in the Mediterranean. Many British merchants had good reason to bless the Treaty of Utrecht.

The British West Indian colonists, on the other hand, cursed it roundly. As soon as it was signed they complained that it had cut off

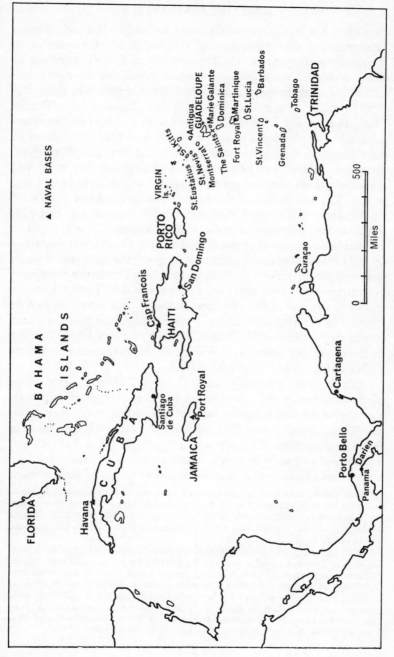

The Caribbean

▲ NAVAL BASES

FLORIDA

Havana

BAHAMA
ISLANDS

CUBA

Santiago
de Cuba

JAMAICA   Port Royal

Cap Francois

HAITI

San Domingo

PORTO
RICO

VIRGIN
Is.

St. Eustatius
St. Kitts
St. Nevis
Montserrat

Antigua
GUADELOUPE
Marie Galante
Dominica

The Saints

Fort Royal Martinique
St. Lucia

St. Vincent

Grenada

Barbados

Tobago

TRINIDAD

Curaçao

Cartagena

Porto Bello

Darien

Panama

0   500

Miles

their illicit but highly remunerative trade with the Spanish colonies. They resented the appearance of the South Sea Company as a privileged participant in Caribbean trade and they persisted in their contraband trade with the Spanish possessions. Spanish coast-guards frequently boarded and searched British ships and by the spring of 1738, when they decided to launch their demand for a 'Patriot War', the opposition could list no less than fifty-two merchant ships 'taken or plundered by the Spaniards since May 1728'. Some of the coastguards were little more than licensed privateers themselves: they took little account of orders from Madrid and they employed the most ruthless means to get their captives to confess to smuggling. In 1731 Captain Jenkins of the *Rebecca* was tortured and mutilated[1] and the crew of the *Robert* were tortured for three days on end with thumbscrews, lighted matches and other devices. These events had aroused little comment at the time, but now the Patriots dug them up and used them to raise a great outcry against the Spaniards. Spanish claims on Georgia, the most recently established of British colonies in North America,[2] were also used to fan the flames. The 1738 session was a stormy one in both Houses: in the Lords Carteret carried an Address to the King asking him to resist the Spanish claim to search British ships. 'No search', he said, 'is a cry that runs from the sailor to the merchant, from the merchant to the parliament, and from parliament it ought to reach the throne.'

Walpole was profoundly irritated by this clamour. His policy of dividing France and Spain, which had been temporarily upset by the War of the Polish Succession, was just getting under way again: the Spaniards had quarrelled with the French and were seeking Britain's friendship. The opposition's demand for a Patriot War jeopardized not only Britain's valuable trade with Spain but also her chances of establishing herself once more as one of the dominant

1 It has been suggested that Jenkins was lying when he told a committee of the House of Commons, in March 1738, that the Spaniards had cut off his ear seven years earlier; but there seems to be no real reason to doubt his story. It was fully reported in the press in June 1731 and three months later a British commander in the West Indies mentioned it in an official letter.

2 James Oglethorpe, the instigator of the 1729 parliamentary inquiry into the debtors' prisons, later launched a fund to start a new colony for the settlement of poor debtors. Parliament contributed £10,000, the King granted a charter and in November 1732 Oglethorpe set out with 120 settlers to found Georgia. He was its Governor for many years and ruled in an enlightened fashion, prohibiting slavery and cultivating good relations with local Indians. In August 1734 he presented King Tomo Chachi of the Cherokees to George II at Kensington Palace, having first dissuaded his retinue from appearing before the Court dressed only in loin cloths and warpaint.

powers in Europe. The desire of the Patriots to legalize the smuggling activities of their West Indian friends must be held in check, or it would undermine Walpole's whole position—his foreign policy, his financial policy, his carefully built structure of management. He got Parliament adjourned until the spring of the following year and turned to negotiate with Spain. By the time Parliament reassembled in February 1739 he had reached agreement with Spain by the Convention of the Pardo: the Spaniards agreed to pay £95,000 in compensation to the merchants whose ships had been seized, providing the South Sea Company paid its outstanding debts of £68,000 to the Spanish Crown. The debates on the Convention took place at the beginning of March, against a background of violent popular agitation. 'The Opposition has stirred up all the trading towns of England', reported the Spanish minister in London to his government, 'London, Bristol, Liverpool and the Directors of the Colony of Georgia memorialized Parliament ostentatiously. . . . Every day pamphlets are published by the opposition to inflame the people as though to rebellion.' Nevertheless, Walpole's management of Parliament triumphed again: the Convention was approved by 262 votes to 234 in the Commons and 95 to 74 in the Lords. The increase in the opposition's strength in the Commons was alarming but not disastrous. Walpole's own county of Norfolk was not as solid in his support as it had been over the excise crisis, but Newcastle's influence in Yorkshire and Sussex was as reliable as ever.

During the course of the summer the ministry's victory in Parliament was nullified by the South Sea Company's refusal to pay the sum demanded by the Spaniards; and by the time Parliament met again in November the two countries had drifted into war. The King, the City, the Country, even some of the great party magnates like Newcastle—all were for war and for the rejection of the Spanish claim to search British ships. Reluctantly, Walpole gave in. But when the opposition proposed an Address to the King asking him not to make peace unless the Spaniards abandoned the right to search, Walpole made a magnificent defence of his policy of peace. 'I have lived, Sir, long enough in the world', he said, 'to see the effects of war on this nation; I have seen how destructive the effects, even of a successful war, have been; and shall I, who have seen this, when I am admitted to the honour to bear a share in his majesty's councils, advise him to enter upon a war while peace may be had? No, Sir, I am proud to own it, that I always have been, and always shall be, an advocate for peace.' Nevertheless, the Address was carried and presented to a delighted King. The Patriot War, which in the end was to destroy not only Walpole but the system by which he had managed the King's affairs, had begun.

For two more years Walpole maintained himself in power, ill and embittered and overwhelmed by the complexities of a war which he had not wanted and could not control. The first winter of the war was bitterly cold and the newspapers contained stories of birds falling to the ground like stones, frozen in flight. The relentless frost lasted well into the spring and the harvests were pitifully inadequate. The price of wheat went soaring up and there was widespread discontent. Walpole presided gloomily over a Cabinet which had lost all unity of purpose. 'I oppose nothing,' he wrote to Newcastle, 'I give in to everything; am said to do everything; am to answer for everything, and yet, God knows, I dare not do what I think right.' At the end of 1740, when France gave her support to a coalition of princes formed to despoil the new Archduchess of Austria of her inheritance, Walpole begged the King not to involve himself in this new war. He still clung to his policy of playing off France against Spain and he was horrified at the prospect of a war against both these powers. The Patriots, however, were all for extending the war. 'Great Britain has it in her power to make a prosperous war against Spain, spite of the opposition that possibly can be made, even though France should meddle in the quarrel', wrote the Earl of Stair, an experienced and respected soldier and a staunch opponent of Walpole. 'By means of our colonies in America', he went on, 'Britain should get the better of any nation in a war in America.' The King was equally bellicose, though he was more interested in the war in Europe than in the war in America. In April 1741 he demanded and received £300,000 from Parliament to subsidize Austria. He then dissolved Parliament and went off to Germany to organize his war against France.

When the new Parliament met in December it soon became clear that the elections had dangerously reduced Walpole's majority in the Commons. Newcastle and the other great borough-mongers had remained loyal to him, in spite of growing differences of opinion within the cabinet, but the electoral influence of the Prince of Wales in Cornwall and of the Duke of Argyle in Scotland had brought in at least twenty new opposition members. Ministerial gains in some of the boroughs controlled by the party magnates helped to counterbalance these losses; but it was clear, nevertheless, that Walpole's control of the new House of Commons hung by a thread.

It was the King himself who helped to snap that thread. Having stirred up Parliament and the country to support him in a war against France, he took fright when he found that his Electorate was in danger of being invaded by the French. The troops which had been intended for the support of Austria were kept for the defence of Hanover, while the Archduchess was advised to make peace with her enemies. Finally, George signed a treaty with France agreeing to abandon his support of Austria in return for a guarantee of Hanover's neutrality. In doing so he sealed the fate of the minister who had served him for so long. Walpole's patient efforts to prove that the interests of Britain could be reconciled with those of Hanover were swept aside and the opposition demanded to know who had advised the King to make so dishonourable a treaty. The instinctive loyalty of the independent backbenchers and their reluctance to invade the royal prerogative enabled Walpole to defeat, by 237 votes to 227, a motion to have the King's correspondence laid before the House. He saved the King from the fury of the Patriots; himself he could not save. The two halves of British foreign policy, the West Indian policy of the Patriots and the Hanoverian policy of the King, lay shattered and broken apart and Walpole, who had approved of neither, had to take responsibility for both. Now that the gap between King and Country had grown too wide to straddle, the man who had devoted his life to straddling it must fall. Both his friends and his enemies naïvely believed that once he had gone the problem with which he had grappled for so long would, by some miracle, become soluble. Even Newcastle wrote petulantly to Hardwicke of 'the fatal obstinacy of one single man, resolved to ruin, or to rule, the State'. In debates on election petitions, the traditional test of strength at the beginning of a new Parliament, ministerial majorities fell ominously. By the end of January 1742 Walpole had suffered several defeats in the Commons and he decided to resign. On 2 February, after he had been defeated by 241 votes to 225 over the Chippenham election petition, he announced his resignation. The King adjourned Parliament for a fortnight while he constructed a new ministry. In fact it was to be four years before he found a solution to the problem posed by Walpole's fall.

PART III

War and Party Confusion
1742–1770

8

Pelhams and Patriots
1742–1754

1 The supremacy of the Whigs

February 1742 saw the fall of a minister, not the fall of a ministry. Nobody, not even the most uncompromising of the opposition politicians, seriously expected the King to dismiss all his servants and take in new ones just because a personal attack on his First Lord of the Treasury had succeeded. The whole burden of the charges against Walpole, and of the complaints made about him by his colleagues, was that he had taken too much upon himself. He had made what ought to have been a team into a one man band; and now it was time for the team to reassert itself. Walpole had made it appear as though the management—or mismanagement—of the King's affairs in Parliament had been his own doing; but in fact it had been achieved by the concerted efforts of some two hundred men. These men, with their dependents and followers, had served the King faithfully for many years and most people took it for granted that he would continue to rely upon their support. To dismiss them would be to admit defeat, to concede that kings could be bullied by parliaments. Worse still, it would mean that George would have to deliver himself over to those who had insulted the Electorate he loved and served the son he hated. He had been forced to drop the pilot, but he would not consent to change the crew.

The crew who had served under Walpole were known by a variety of names. To their enemies they were ministerial lackeys, courtiers, placemen, the corrupt creatures of Sir Robert. To the King they were, quite simply, 'my friends'.[1] For their own part, they insisted that they were more than mere courtiers, 'King's Friends'. They saw themselves

---

[1] 'I will part with no more of my friends', George told Pulteney angrily in the summer of 1742, when the latter asked him to sanction the dismissal of a customs official who had supported Walpole.

as the natural rulers of the land, men of substance and ability who had banded together to defend the Revolution Settlement and the Hanoverian dynasty against Jacobites and malcontents and giddy young men. After more than twenty years in power they were bound one to another by countless ties of family relationship and mutual obligation. Great men had given their daughters in marriage to those who were associated with them politically and had used their patronage to 'oblige' their ministerial colleagues. They had created something which was much greater than a mere Court Party, much more permanent than a loose association of borough-mongers. They controlled a network of political influence which penetrated every level of national life. They were more than a faction, more than a following, more than a party: they were *the* Party. And for such a party there was only one possible name: the Whig Party. A young Scottish philosopher called David Hume wrote an essay in 1742 on *The Parties of Great Britain* and admitted ruefully that 'to determine the nature of these parties is, perhaps, one of the most difficult problems that can be met with'. Since he was trying to define the parties by defining their beliefs, his bewilderment was not surprising. To the great Whig magnates, however, it was irrelevant. A Whig, in their eyes, was not a man who held this or that political doctrine. He was simply a man who was prepared to serve the King when asked to do so, a man who would join with other men to form an administration. Men who refused to do these things were Tories: if they showed an open aversion to all things Hanoverian they could be dubbed Jacobites. If not, then they were independent Tories, Country Party Tories. In either case they represented a threat to good order and government, a threat which could only be countered if all good men rallied to the Whig Party and the King whom it served.

Basically the Whig Party was, as its enemies asserted, a party of office-holders. The 124 placemen who sat in the House of Commons —courtiers, administrators, sinecurists, government contractors, army and navy officers—formed its hard core. But by themselves they could not give the administration the support it needed in the Commons. To be safe, a ministry needed a following in the House of between 250 and 300; and this could only be achieved by the concerted efforts of all the friends and followers of those in the ministry. Walpole's own personal following had been relatively small—two members for the borough of Callington, one for Great Yarmouth and one for Castle Rising—but some of his ministerial colleagues had more formidable retinues. At least nine members of the Commons owed their election directly to Newcastle and many more were connected with him in one way or another. More than any other man in the country, he epitomized the power of patronage and influence. If the Whig Party was to be an association of great men, rather than a well-drilled squadron of office-holders, then Newcastle was the man around whom it must form itself. Walpole had fallen because he had stood for autocracy, the monopolizing of power by one Great Man; Newcastle would survive because he stood for collective leadership. Whatever his faults, he had a great talent for bringing men together in the business of government.

He started to put these talents to work in the middle of January 1742, when it became clear that Walpole's days at the Treasury were numbered. He consulted with the King and together they decided that it would be necessary to bring some of the opposition leaders into the ministry. They chose to deal with Pulteney and Carteret, rather than with men like Argyle, Chesterfield and Cobham. Pulteney and Carteret had been unrelenting in their opposition, but it had at least been directed against Walpole rather than against the King himself. They had both held office before and they were both Whigs at heart. While Cobham and Argyle and their young friends talked of new principles and new ideals, of Patriotism and an end to corruption, Pulteney and Carteret had one simple aim: to get Walpole out and themselves in. Some time later, George II himself told Pulteney: 'I saw that I had two shops to deal with, and I rather chose to come to you, because I knew your aim was only directed against my minister, but I did not know but the Duke of Argyle wanted to be King himself.' Newcastle's overtures to Pulteney resulted in a meeting at Pulteney's house on 2 February, the day Walpole's resignation was announced. Newcastle was accompanied by the Lord Chancellor, Lord Hardwicke, and Carteret was also present. Newcastle said that he was authorized to offer Pulteney the Treasury and to ask what places he wanted for his followers. Pulteney was in a difficult position. He knew that many of his associates were hungry for office, but he also knew that his reputation with the Patriots and the Country Party depended on his disinterestedness, his refusal to associate himself with the remnants of Sir Robert's ministry. He could only hold together the disparate elements of the opposition—Patriots, Leicester House men, independent country gentlemen, West India merchants and so on—if he insisted on a clean sweep. Walpole's friends,

Walpole's system, Walpole's methods—all must be renounced. There must be a new ministry, new men, new measures. Then, and then only, would the Patriots be satisfied. But he knew full well that there was no chance of this happening. George II had no intention of giving up his right to choose his own ministers and there was no way of forcing him to do so. Even if extremists like Argyle stood out for a Patriot ministry and a general purge of all Walpole's supporters, they would never be able to carry the independent members of the Commons with them. There would be a reaction in the King's favour and the opposition might well find themselves condemned to another long period in the wilderness. Those who insisted on 'all or nothing' would probably be left with nothing.

Nevertheless Pulteney decided to emphasize his own integrity and impress his Patriot and Country Party allies by refusing the Treasury. He agreed that it should be given instead to the Earl of Wilmington, that same Spencer Compton who had hoped to displace Walpole in 1727. Wilmington was a personal favourite of the King, but he was also connected with Argyle and Cobham. Most important of all, he was a nonentity, a person who would be recognized by everybody as a mere figurehead. His appointment would provide a means whereby Pulteney could have power without office. While Wilmington acted as a useful lightning conductor for all the on-slaughts of the Patriots, Pulteney, cleared of all imputations of am-bition and office-seeking, could exercise the real power. Accordingly he asked nothing for himself except a seat in the Cabinet. Lord Harrington replaced Wilmington as Lord President of the Council and Carteret took over Harrington's office of Secretary of State for the North. Places were found on the boards of the Treasury and the Admiralty for several of the less important office-seekers in the opposition; and Samuel Sandys, one of Walpole's most dogged opponents, became Chancellor of the Exchequer. Those members of the opposition who had expected a clean sweep and a triumphant entry of their own forces were disappointed by these very limited changes; but at a meeting at the Strand Tavern on 12 February Pulteney and Sandys talked them round and assured them that this was only the first instalment. A few days later Pulteney persuaded the Prince of Wales to make his peace with his father and support the new administration. Even notoriously touchy figures like Argyle and Cobham agreed to accept the situation, at any rate for the time being, and come to Court again. It seemed that Pulteney had done what Walpole had done over twenty years before: he had reconciled King and Country and he had secured for himself a place in the inner circles of power without sacrificing his alliances with the independents and the enemies of the Court. Now, he hoped, he would be able to destroy the supremacy of the old Whig confederacy at his leisure, from within.

In fact it was his own career that he had destroyed. The gap between King and Country, which had been too wide for Walpole to bridge, was not to be narrowed thus easily. Within a few weeks the opposition had carried a motion setting up an inquiry into Walpole's management of affairs during the past ten years. The old Whigs, who had served with Walpole for so long, drew together to protect their chief; and Pulteney was once again placed in a quandary. If he supported the inquiry he would lose all favour with the King, while if he failed to do so he would be attacked as a renegade by the Patriots and the Country Party. In the end he pursued a middle course of half-hearted support which infuriated both the King and the opposition. By the time the parliamentary session ended in July the inquiry had ground to a halt, having unearthed nothing really serious. While the King blamed Pulteney for allowing the inquiry to take place at all, the opposition blamed him for its failure. Argyle and Cobham and their associates broke away from the ministry again, thus weakening Pulteney's position both in the House of Lords and in the House of Commons. Further ministerial changes in the summer of 1742, intended to conciliate the Prince of Wales and other elements in the opposition,[1] served only to emphasize the weakness of the administration and of Pulteney's position in it. Some of his followers were given office in the new reshuffle, but only on condition that he himself retired to the House of Lords as Earl of Bath. He did so, though with a very bad grace, and thus ended his political influence for ever. The future might lie with the Patriots, ostentatiously uncorrupted and the darlings of the City and the Country; it might lie with Carteret, the King's new favourite and an expert in European diplomacy; it might lie with Newcastle and his brother Henry Pelham, the acknowledged leaders of the old Whig confederacy and Walpole's heirs as managers of the Commons. But it certainly did not lie with Pulteney, who had lost both the confidence of the Commons and the favour of the King by trying to gather them both into his

[1] Even the Tories were brought in. Lord Gower, who came of an old established Tory family, was made Lord Privy Seal.

hands at once. He had already earned the epitaph which the satirist Hanbury Williams bestowed on him a year later:

> Tho' you have lost the people's hearts,
> You have not gain'd the King.

The man who had 'gain'd the King' was Carteret. In April 1743 he accompanied George to Germany, to plan and execute that European war which aroused such enthusiasm in the King and such suspicion among the Patriots. While they were away Wilmington died and the gap which his appointment had sought to conceal was revealed once again, wider and more dangerous than ever. It was 1716 all over again: one Secretary of State in London, trying to manage Parliament, and the other in Hanover, trying to manage the King. Each suspected the other of using his position for his own advancement, though Carteret was less suspicious of Newcastle than Stanhope had been of Townshend in 1716. He resented Newcastle's querulous criticisms of the war in Europe, but he did not resent his control of Parliament. Pulteney, who saw only too clearly that if Carteret fell he would fall too, tried to get him to take the problems of parliamentary management more seriously. He wrote to him in Germany, warning him that the Pelhams and their friends, 'would certainly get him out, if he relied solely on the favour of the King, and did not take care to secure himself by forming proper connections and dependencies'. Carteret did not pay much attention to the warning, nor did he feel very strongly the need to combat the influence of the Pelhams. Pulteney and Henry Pelham both wrote to the King asking for Wilmington's post and Carteret, out of loyalty to his friend, advised the King to appoint Pulteney. George, however, decided to give the position to Henry Pelham and Carteret was not unduly disturbed by his decision. '. . . as the affair is decided, in your favour, by His Majesty, I wish you joy of it;' he wrote to Pelham, 'and I will endeavour to support you, as much as I can.' Having thus disposed of a matter which he regarded as comparatively unimportant, he turned back with relief to the business of running the King's war in Germany.

Carteret was wrong in thinking that the appointment of Henry Pelham as First Lord of the Treasury was a comparatively trivial matter. It was, in fact, the first step in the long and painful business of reconstructing Walpole's system. For the first time since Sir Robert's fall the Treasury, the nerve centre of the patronage structure, was in the hands of a man who understood the arts of management and was in close touch with the leaders of the old Whig confederacy. Like his brother Newcastle, he stood for the principle of collective leadership. Walpole at the Treasury had meant the supremacy of Walpole; Pelham at the Treasury would mean the supremacy of the Whigs as a whole. In the 1720s Walpole had brought together borough-mongers and office-seekers, courtiers and contractors, and welded them into a political party. Now, in the 1740s, that party was ready to take on a life of its own and build a permanent bridge between King and Country. Walpole had straddled the gap himself, a spectacular but essentially temporary solution. The Whig solution would be more humdrum but more enduring.

When Carteret came back from Germany in November 1743 it soon became clear that he had little interest in this Whig idea of collective leadership. He did not think of an administration as a carefully composed structure of interlocking parts, each piece dovetailed into the next so that the whole could stand firm both at Court and in the Commons. All he knew was that he was the King's minister and that it was the business of his subordinates to push through Parliament the measures which he considered necessary for the King's service. He was furious when the Cabinet rejected, by nine votes to four, the convention he had signed with Austria giving her a subsidy for the duration of the war. Even with this convention omitted, the arrangements which Carteret had made for the prosecution of the war in Europe were frighteningly unpopular. Lord Sandwich, one of the opposition peers, wrote gleefully to the Duke of Bedford: 'The clamour and general discontent of all ranks of people, on account of our late Hanoverian measures, is greater than I could have imagined it could possibly have been, and, if rightly pursued by a vigorous attack at the beginning of the sessions, may be productive of very good ends.'

Sandwich was over-optimistic. The Patriot attacks on the ministry in December 1743 and January 1744, ferocious though they were, were defeated by Pelham's skilful management of the Commons. The nearest the opposition came to success was on 18 January, when they reduced the ministry's majority to forty-five (271 to 226) in a debate on the subsidizing of Hanoverian troops. It was significant that in this debate William Pitt, the most formidable of the Patriot speakers, made it clear that he regarded Carteret and Carteret alone as the author of the hated Hanoverian policies. He referred to the

Pelhams and their Whig friends as 'the amiable part of the administration' and hinted that they should make common cause with the Patriots against Carteret. Behind the scenes Walpole, now Earl of Orford, was thinking along similar lines. The Patriots must be won over if possible, as long as they would agree to moderate their attacks on Hanover. In this way the Whigs would broaden the basis of their party sufficiently to be able to convince the King that they were indispensable to the management of his affairs in the Commons. Having spent most of his life bridging the gap between the King and the Commons, Walpole saw that in the present circumstances it could only be bridged by the broad policies of the Whigs and not by the narrow individualism of Carteret. 'Upon this ground, you will be able to contend with Carteret', he told Pelham. 'He gains the King, by giving in to all his foreign views; and you show the King, that what is reasonable and practicable, can only be obtained from the Whigs.'

The prospects for an understanding between the Pelhams and the Patriots grew slightly brighter during the spring of 1744. Although they rose up in wrath to defeat a proposal to increase the duties on West Indian sugar, Pitt and his friends moderated their attacks on Hanover and the European war. This was partly due to the invasion scare of February 1744, when a French fleet sailed up the Channel to cover an invasion from Dunkirk. It was scattered by a storm, but the atmosphere of crisis which its appearance had generated served to lower the temperature of Parliament. The session ended in comparative calm on 12 May; but Carteret and the King gave little credit to the Pelhams. They merely argued that the docility of Parliament showed how unnecessary and obstructive the attitude of Newcastle and his brother had been. Things got steadily worse throughout the summer. The King yielded to the Pelhams' demand that he should not go off to Germany again, but he did so with a very bad grace and his behaviour towards his ministers showed very clearly where his affections lay. Newcastle, in particular, was driven nearly to despair by the way in which the King snubbed him in front of Carteret. 'No man can bear long', he wrote to his brother on 26 August, 'what I go through every day in our joint audiences in the Closet.'

He did not propose to bear it much longer. Careful soundings taken by Walpole, Hardwicke and the Pelhams themselves made it clear that the Patriots would in no circumstances support Carteret

against them. Having made sure that their rival was completely isolated, they proceeded to move against him. On 1 November Newcastle delivered a memorial to the King demanding that he should
abandon Carteret's foreign policy and adopt that of the Pelhams.
In particular, it insisted that the United Provinces should be required
to enter the war. The King struggled desperately to save Carteret:
he tried to detach Harrington from the Pelhams and he even approached the Patriots to see if they would serve with Carteret and
Pulteney. Even the Prince of Wales joined in these efforts to keep
Carteret and to dispense with the Pelhams. But it was all in vain: the
Pelhams had succeeded in broadening their party to such an extent
that they were now indispensable. No proper government, no bridge
between King and Commons, could be achieved without them. On
24 November, three days before Parliament was due to meet,
Carteret resigned and was replaced by Harrington. The first few
weeks of the parliamentary session went well for the administration,
since most the elements in the opposition were holding their fire in
the hope that they would be offered office. By Christmas the Pelhams had completed their reconstruction of the ministry, which they
achieved with considerable skill. The King was persuaded to
make Lord Chesterfield Lord-Lieutenant of Ireland[1] and minor
offices were found for George Lyttelton and George Grenville, two
of the most prominent Patriots in the House of Commons. Some of
the independent Tories were brought in, including Sir John Hynde
Cotton. The Pelhams were anxious not to offend their traditional
Whig allies and so it was the followers of Carteret and Pulteney,
rather than the old Whigs, who were dismissed to make room for
these new recruits.

The Whigs were very proud of this broadly based administration
which they had built up with such care, but the King took little
pleasure in it. He maintained a sullen silence when Hardwicke pointed
out to him that there was now 'no man of business or even of weight
left capable of heading or conducting an opposition'. For him the new
arrangements were not a guarantee of stability but a symbol of his
own defeat; and as long as he felt this the promised stability could not
be achieved. It was useless for the Pelhams to control the Commons if
they lost control of the Closet. By the beginning of April they had

[1] This was a considerable achievement, because George hated Chesterfield for his
attacks on Hanover. When his appointment was first suggested the King exclaimed:
'I command you to trouble me no more with such nonsense.'

been reduced once again to despair: Newcastle insisted that the King's obvious lack of confidence in them made it impossible for them to go on. He had better send for Carteret. George did not reinstate Carteret but it was clear that he was consulting with him in private. In May, as soon as Parliament was prorogued, he left for Hanover to take up the threads of a foreign policy which was Carteret's rather than the Pelhams'.

Charles Stuart's landing in Scotland at the end of July 1745 made it difficult for the Pelhams to carry out their threats of resignation: they could hardly precipitate yet another political crisis just when the dynasty itself was in peril. George, however, had no such scruples. He hurried back to London and within a few days of his arrival he was intriguing to divide the Pelhams from their friends and form an alternative ministry. When Parliament met in October, with Scotland in Stuart hands and England itself threatened with a Stuart invasion, it was common knowledge that the King was at odds with the men who were supposed to be in charge of his affairs. William Pitt, the one prominent Patriot leader who had been left out of the last reshuffle, now erupted into violent opposition. In the previous session he had been quite docile, as though he hoped to get office by a show of moderation. But now he lashed out against the King, against the ministers, even against his own patron Lord Cobham. As well as demanding the recall of all British troops in Europe he opposed the use of German mercenaries in England, in spite of the urgency of the situation. Whatever his motives may have been—genuine patriotism, fear of a Jacobite victory, determination to storm his way into office— he provided the Pelhams with just the lever they needed. In February 1746, once the danger of a Stuart restoration was past, they asked the King to bring Pitt into the ministry. In view of Pitt's recent outburst and his long record of rudeness to the King, it was a foregone conclusion that George would refuse. When he did so, the Pelham ministry resigned *en bloc*. For two days the King struggled to build a ministry round Carteret and Pulteney. Even Carteret himself 'saw it would not do and was amazed at it'. He refused to send letters abroad announcing his appointment, saying that he would be out of office again before the couriers arrived. He was right. On 13 February the King was forced to take the Whigs back on their own terms. They returned, as they had resigned, not as individuals but as a party. Joint action, which had already won the Pelhams the control of the Commons, now enabled them to control the King. What Walpole had once done by himself, they had now done as a party. For the supremacy of Walpole they had substituted the supremacy of the Whigs.

Meanwhile the wars against Spain and France were raising problems which were to disturb and eventually to destroy the delicate balance created by the Pelhams.

2 The defence of the dynasty

When the opposition pushed Walpole into war with Spain in 1739 they had no desire to involve the country in a European war. Like the independent gentlemen of William III's reign, the Patriots believed that it was possible to fight a naval war in the colonies without fighting a land war on the Continent; and they were firmly supported both by the Country and by the City. Most independent members would have agreed with the Lincolnshire squire who later described 'the balance of power' and 'the liberties of Europe' as a couple of cant phrases. So far as they were concerned Europe could take care of itself. They voted a Land Tax of four shillings in the pound, but they expected it to be spent on the navy rather than on the army. Although the British army was pathetically small—17,000 men on the home establishment and another 12,000 in Ireland—they had no desire to increase it. Soldiers were instruments of despotism and of Hanoverian ambition; it was the sailors who must defend Britain's trade and colonies against the Spaniards.

The Patriots were encouraged in this rather naïve view of the war by a resounding initial success. At the end of November 1739 Admiral Vernon, himself a supporter of the Patriots and an opponent of Walpole, captured the great Spanish American port of Porto Bello with a force of only six ships. It seemed as though the British had only to deploy their fleets effectively in the Caribbean and they would enjoy unlimited plunder. Vernon wrote to Newcastle telling him that once British seapower dominated the Caribbean, 'let who will possess the country, our Royal Master may command the wealth of it'. But difficulties soon began to appear. Although Britain had more ships than Spain, she could not always find the men to sail them. In February 1740 Walpole's aged First Lord of the Admiralty, Sir Charles Wager, brought in a Bill to set up a register of all seafaring men; but the Patriots defeated it on the grounds that it invaded the liberties of the subject. They tolerated the more violent and haphazard invasions of liberty carried out by the Press Gang, but this method of recruitment was not very satisfactory. It could just about provide enough men to sail the ships, but it certainly could not provide forces large enough to attack and reduce Spanish bases in America. Whatever Vernon and the Patriots might say, it was necessary to give the navy some sort of military support; and this raised further complications. No one in Britain had given much thought to the problems of amphibious warfare and the attacks on Cartagena, Santiago de Cuba and Panama in 1741 and 1742 were disastrous failures. Wentworth, the commander of the land forces, quarrelled violently with Vernon and in the end, after more than 5,000 men had died of disease, nothing whatsoever was achieved. The same sorry story continued for the next few years and in March 1744 Horace Walpole wrote bitterly: 'We have already lost seven millions of money and thirty thousand men in the Spanish war, and all the fruit of all this blood and treasure is the glory of having Admiral Vernon's head on alehouse signs.' A few months later he had reason to be more cheerful. Commodore Anson, who had originally set out in September 1740 to sail round Cape Horn and attack Spanish America from the Pacific side, arrived back in England in June 1744, having sailed round the world and captured a Spanish treasure ship valued at £1,250,000.

Anson's voyage underlined one essential fact about the Spanish war: it was a worldwide affair, which could not be thought of in purely Caribbean terms. If Britain had only been fighting the Spaniards, she might possibily have been able to concentrate all her forces in the West Indies without undue risk to her other vital interests. But from the very beginning of the war the hostile attitude of France made it obvious that Britain's position in the Mediterranean and in the Baltic might be threatened at any moment. Even her security and the future of the Hanoverian dynasty were in danger. In the spring and summer of 1740 the British fleets in the Channel had to be hastily reinforced after information had been received that the Spanish and French fleets intended to cooperate in landing a Jacobite force in England. This proved to be a false alarm, but it served to remind the Patriots that they had started something much bigger than a mere plundering campaign in the Caribbean. Their war might have begun as a defence of trade, but it would end as a defence of the dynasty.

The death of the Emperor Charles VI in October 1740 took away the last chance that the British might be left undisturbed to carry on a self-contained war in Spanish America. Charles's only heir was a daughter, Maria Theresa, and he had spent the last twenty years of his life trying to ensure that her succession to his dominions would be accepted by the powers of Europe. He had persuaded France, the German Princes, the United Provinces, Britain and Russia to agree to the Pragmatic Sanction. This document guaranteed the unity of the Habsburg possessions and recognized Maria Theresa's succession as Archduchess of Austria, Queen of Hungary and Queen of Bohemia. Her sex debarred her from becoming Emperor, but it was hoped to get round this difficulty by electing her husband, Francis of Tuscany, as Emperor. Within a few weeks of Charles's death it was clear that all his carefully contrived arrangements were going to be swept aside. The King of Prussia laid claim to Silesia, part of the kingdom of Bohemia, while the Elector of Saxony wanted another part of it, Moravia. Spain and Savoy claimed part of the Habsburg possessions in Italy and the Elector of Bavaria contested Francis of Tuscany's election as Emperor. Behind this predatory association stood France, the greatest power in Europe, ready to use her army of 160,000 men and her navy of eighty ships of the line against anyone who dared to come to the aid of Maria Theresa.

Walpole found this prospect very daunting and he felt that the only chance of rescuing anything from the fiasco of the Spanish war lay in preventing it from being swallowed up in a major European conflict. His gestures on behalf of Maria Theresa were not very convincing. A British fleet under Admiral Haddock tried to prevent the landing of Spanish troops in Italy in 1741, but it gave up the attempt when the French Toulon fleet appeared. George II promised to help Maria Theresa to defend her German possessions, but he thought better of it when the French threatened to invade Hanover. The King and his ministers did not see eye to eye about the war, but they all agreed that it would be inadvisable to challenge outright the combined might of Spain, France and the German and Italian princes. They turned instead to the task of persuading the princes to change sides. William III had once taught the smaller states of Europe that France was not their friend but their enemy; George II and his ministers would teach them the same lesson over again. This policy, which was launched by Walpole and continued by Carteret, had achieved a considerable degree of success by the end of 1742. Saxony and Prussia had both broken with France and made their peace with Austria, while the defection of Savoy from the French to the Austrian side had changed the balance of power in Italy and the Mediterranean. A British fleet under Admiral Mathews was able to keep the French and Spanish Mediterranean fleets bottled up in Toulon, and in August 1742 a detachment of five ships under Commodore Martin sailed into the Bay of Naples and threatened to bombard the city. The King of Naples was so alarmed by this threat that he agreed to withdraw his troops from the Spanish armies in north Italy.

While potential French and Spanish allies in the Mediterranean could be overawed by the British navy, the princes of Germany had to be won over by promises of money and soldiers. Carteret's effort to provide these aroused the fury of the opposition in Parliament, who would not believe that the best way of fighting France was to subsidize the princes who might otherwise have allied with her. In December 1742 the Commons were called on to approve the expenditure of British money in order to pay 16,000 Hanoverian troops which George II, as Elector of Hanover, had decided he could no longer afford. Carteret saw that Britain's chances of winning over the German princes would be reduced if the troops were disbanded altogether, so he proposed that they should be kept on foot and paid out of British funds. The ministry managed to get the proposal through the Commons by 260 votes to 193, but the Patriots launched a ferocious attack on Hanover and the malign influence which it appeared to exercise on British policy. 'It is now too apparent', thundered Pitt, 'that this great, this powerful, this formidable kingdom, is considered only as a province to a despicable Electorate.' The hired Hanoverian troops continued to give a handle to Carteret's critics for the rest of his period in office and to earn for him the name of 'the Hanoverian troop minister'. After his fall they were finally discharged by Britain and taken on by Maria Theresa; but it was the British Treasury that paid her an extra subsidy of £200,000 a year so that she could hire them.

The business of the Hanoverian troops was unfortunate, because it popularized and perpetuated the idea that the Patriot War and the German War were incompatible. In fact, France's determination to support Spain and the other claimants to the Habsburg dominions had already linked together inextricably the two aspects of the war. If British merchants and colonists wanted to seize more trade and more territory in America they were bound to clash with France and Spain, the two great colonial powers of western Europe. This being so there were only two ways of dealing with this Franco-Spanish alliance: to gain complete mastery of the sea, so that France and Spain could not get men and money to their colonies, or to ensure

224

that their resources were tied down in Europe. Since the British navy was not yet effective enough to do the first, British diplomacy must achieve the second. And British diplomats, because they spoke for a country that would not tolerate a large standing army of its own, must speak in terms of subsidies and hired troops. The Hanoverian troop minister, hateful as he might seem, was an essential.adjunct to the ambitions of the Patriots.

By the middle of 1743 he had succeeded in pushing the French and the Spaniards on to the defensive. The Spaniards were defeated at Campo Santo in Italy in February and later in the year the Pragmatic Army, made up of contingents from the German states and the United Provinces, entered Germany. It inflicted a fortuitous and rather inconclusive defeat on the French at Dettingen in June, George II in person leading his troops into battle. Meanwhile the Austrian army conquered Bavaria. The Elector of Bavaria, who had succeeded in getting himself elected as Holy Roman Emperor in January 1742, was now an Emperor with neither an Empire nor an Electorate to call his own. Maria Theresa, flushed with victory, talked in terms of a great allied advance into France from all fronts; but Carteret wanted a permanent settlement in Germany which should reconcile Austria with the rest of the princes and exclude French influence. His efforts to achieve it were unsuccessful and by the beginning of 1744 it was clear that France and Spain faced attack from Austria and her allies, even though those allies were divided in their aims. The French rightly saw the British as the authors of all their troubles in Europe, and of their Spanish ally's troubles in America; and they determined to knock the British out of the war by mounting a Jacobite invasion of Britain. While Charles Stuart made his way in secret to the Channel port of Gravelines, an army of more than 15,000 men was assembled under Marshal de Saxe at Dunkirk. The Brest fleet sailed up the Channel to cover the invasion, but it was scattered by a great storm at the end of February 1744. Admiral Sir John Norris, the eighty-four-year-old commander-in-chief of the Channel fleet, had sailed out to destroy the enemy's troop transport ships, but this proved unnecessary: like the Brest fleet, the Dunkirk invasion flotilla was scattered and wrecked by the storm.

In the Mediterranean the British navy was less fortunate. In February 1744 the Spanish and French fleets at last emerged from Toulon, and Admiral Mathews pursued them and brought them to battle. Although he had twenty-nine ships to their twenty-seven,

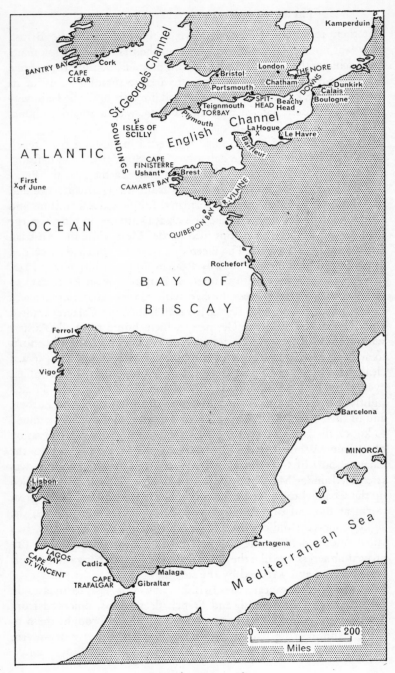

Western Approaches

the only result of the engagement was the capture of one Spanish ship, taken by Captain Hawke of the *Berwick*. This failure to destroy the enemy fleet when the opportunity offered was caused largely by the inadequacies of the signalling system and by the cautious and restricting provisions of the Fighting Instructions. These Instructions had originally been drawn up by Russell in 1691 and they were therefore dominated by the fear of 'breaking the line' and of the disastrous consequences which had followed this at the battle of Beachy Head.[1] Any captain who left the line without permission was threatened with suspension. In accordance with this provision, the majority of Mathews' captains failed to follow him when he bore down upon the enemy and their conduct was vindicated at the subsequent courts martial. Lestock, the commander of the rear division who had thrown away the chance of victory by refusing to join in the battle, was acquitted because he argued that the signal to keep the line was flying and he dared not disobey it. Mathews himself was cashiered because he had broken the line. Thus the supremacy of the Fighting Instructions, coupled with the fact that the signalling system made it impossible to issue any orders that were not part of the Instructions, discouraged captains from showing initiative and admirals from adopting offensive tactics.

The deadening rule of the Fighting Instructions was to last for another forty years. Vernon introduced supplementary signals, making it possible for an admiral to convey to his captains intentions that were not part of the Instructions, but it was a long time before anyone dared to use them effectively. The navy grew stronger, but its tactics remained essentially defensive. Not until 1782 did a British fleet inflict a really crippling defeat on an enemy fleet on the high seas. In the meantime, as long as commanders had to think more about 'keeping the line' than about destroying enemy ships, the task of defending Britain's ever widening interests grew steadily more difficult. The navy was like a gamekeeper who had to rush from one part of the estate to another scaring away poachers but was not allowed to arrest those whom he cornered.

By the beginning of 1745 it looked as though the British navy might soon have to let the Mediterranean and the Caribbean take care of themselves while it concentrated its forces in home waters. The polite fiction of Anglo-French neutrality, whereby the King of England fought in Austrian colours against Frenchmen who wore

[1] See above, p. 87.

the colours of Bavaria, had been abandoned in the spring of 1744 and the result had been an ominously successful French invasion of the Netherlands. This culminated in the French victory of Fontenoy at the end of April 1745, after which the greater part of the Netherlands, including the Channel ports of Ostend and Nieuport, passed into French hands. Many people feared that this was the prelude to an invasion of Britain. 'As we have now lost Flanders,' Newcastle wrote dolefully to Hardwicke, 'we may soon lose England and Holland too, for I don't know what can stop that victorious army. I'm sure ours in Flanders cannot.'

The invasion of Britain, when it came, did not take the form of a massed descent of French troops from Ostend and Nieuport. Instead, Charles Stuart arrived towards the end of July 1745 off the Isle of Eriskay in the Outer Hebrides. With him in the forty-four-gun frigate *Du Teillay* he had seven companions, a few thousand broadswords, some field-guns and muskets, and about £500 in French gold. He had been trying for the last few months to get French aid on a more effective scale, but without success. Only a month before his embarkation he had written to his father, the self-styled King James III, complaining of the 'scandalous usage' which he had received at the French court. The French had no intention of involving themselves in an unsuccessful Jacobite rebellion: they would wait to see how Charles did in Scotland before they decided whether to support him with an invasion of England from Flanders.

Charles did a good deal better in Scotland than most Frenchmen had expected. His standard was raised at Glenfinnan on 19 August 1745 and within a month he had occupied Edinburgh and proclaimed his father as King James VIII of Scotland. Sir John Cope collected together the scattered government forces in Scotland and landed them at Dunbar, hoping to march on Edinburgh and dislodge the Jacobites; but he was utterly defeated at Prestonpans on 21 September. Charles wanted to follow up this victory by marching south and falling on General Wade's army at Newcastle, but his advisers persuaded him to wait and consolidate his position in Scotland before moving into England. Many Scottish Jacobites were content to have thrown the Hanoverians out of Scotland and torn up the Act of Union; they did not want to hazard all that they had won in an invasion of England. But Charles's eyes were on the army of some 15,000 men that the French were assembling at Dunkirk. He knew that the French would not move as long as he remained in Scotland and he declared that he would go into England alone if necessary. When he finally moved south at the end of October he had an army of some 6,000 men, but desertions had reduced it to about 4,500 by the time he arrived in Manchester late in November.

Meanwhile George II and his ministers had hastily recalled most of the British forces in the Netherlands and these troops, commanded by the King's younger son the Duke of Cumberland, now stood between Charles and London. When part of the Jacobite force moved westwards, apparently with the intention of joining up with Sir Watkin Williams-Wynn and the other Jacobite gentlemen of North Wales, Cumberland allowed himself to be gulled into following them, thus leaving the main road to London open to Charles's advance. By 4 December Charles was in Derby, less than 130 miles from London, with only a few thousand scattered troops between him and the capital. The ministers in London realized that the situation was critical but, like Charles himself, they had their eye on Dunkirk rather than on Derby. They maintained two powerful naval squadrons in the Channel and Vernon engaged privateers from Dover to supplement this force. The French invasion force was unable to get out of Dunkirk. Without the French, few English Jacobites had the courage to come out into the open, and Charles was losing far more men in desertions than he was gaining in new recruits. By 6 December, when the news of his arrival at Derby reached London and caused considerable panic and a run on the banks, he had already been persuaded to turn back. His retreat was a sorry affair, with the Highlanders getting out of control and turning to plunder, but once back in Scotland he began to improve his position. By the middle of January 1746 he had amassed some 9,000 men and had inflicted a sharp defeat on the English at Falkirk. Meanwhile Cumberland himself had had to hurry back to London because of reports of renewed activities at Dunkirk. The French invasion threat, which had enabled Charles to come so near to success in England, now gave him a breathing space in Scotland.

The respite was not to last for long. By the end of January Cumberland was back in Edinburgh and Charles had to abandon the Lowlands and retreat to Inverness. There, early in April, he learnt that Cumberland was moving north from Aberdeen with an army nearly twice the size of his own. Charles's Irish advisers suggested that he should make up for the disparity in numbers by planning a surprise night attack on Cumberland's camp. Several of the Scottish

chiefs were opposed to the plan and the French ambassador went down
on his knees to beg that it should be dropped; but Charles insisted
on putting it into execution on 15 April. His men plodded wearily
towards the Hanoverian camp at Nairn, but by the time dawn broke
they were still an hour's march away from it and had to fall back
on their original positions on Culloden Moor outside Inverness.
Here they stood about for most of the morning of the 16th, exhausted,
starving and soaked to the skin by a ferocious gale of rain and sleet.
At last, shortly after one o'clock, they received the order to charge
into the punishing fire of Cumberland's eighteen heavy field-guns.
Less than an hour later the Jacobite army was broken and scattered,
its remnants escaping as best they could. Some 1,500 managed to
reassemble at Ruthven in Badenoch, only to get a message from
Charles telling them to disband. A few enthusiasts persisted in
thinking that all was not lost, but Charles Stuart himself knew well
enough that his bid to restore his father to the throne of Great Britain
had failed. His adventures during the next few months, as he was
hunted through the Highlands until he finally escaped to France in
September, were to provide an inexhaustible quarry for the romantic
writers of the next century; but they formed no part of the great
struggle between the House of Stuart and the House of Hanover.
That was over. The last echoes of the civil wars of the seventeenth
century were stilled at Culloden.

Cumberland, however, did not believe in taking any chances.
He was determined to terrorize the Highlands into loyalty to the
House of Hanover, so that the French would never again be able to
use Scotland as a bridgehead into England. 'All the good we have
done is a little blood-letting which has weakened the madness, not
cured it', he told Newcastle. 'I tremble for fear that this vile spot may
still be the ruin of this island and our family.' The Earl of Albemarle,
Cumberland's successor as commander-in-chief in Scotland, was
more specific. 'Nothing but fire and sword can cure their cursed,
vicious ways of thinking', he said of the Highlanders. Earlier in the
year clansmen had had their crofts burnt, their cattle stolen and their
heads broken by their chieftains if they showed any reluctance to
join the rebellion; now they suffered the same fate at the hands of the
authorities because they had joined it at all. One crofter in Lochbroom
had told his chief in March that he would rather die than join, but
he had been battered over the head with the butt of a musket and
carried off covered in blood. By June he was in the hold of a prison

ship at Tilbury, awaiting further sentence. Two authorities, the central authority of the government in London and the feudal authority of the Highland chieftains, confronted each other; and between them were ground ordinary men and women. When Parliament in Westminster passed the Disarming Act of 1746, banning the wearing of Highland dress, it was the ordinary clansmen who had to dye their plaids and get their wives to stitch their kilts up the middle. When the hereditary powers of the chieftains were taken away from them by another Act in 1747, it was the ordinary clansmen who suffered in the end. The old tribal pattern of Highland society was broken for ever and land which had once been held in trust for the clan by the chief was now exploited for his own personal profit. Clansmen were forced to leave their crofts and take ship for the plantations. The defence of the Hanoverian dynasty in 1745–46 had entailed the destruction of a whole way of life in the Scottish Highlands.

Back in London, the months of crisis had put the war in a new and clearer light. With the French in the Netherlands and the Protestant succession itself in danger, there seemed little point in arguing the relative merits of the Patriot War and the German War. Attacks on French and Spanish overseas possessions were continued, as were combinations of German princes to aid the Austrians, but both were now seen as integral and complementary parts of the struggle against the French. The death of the Bavarian Emperor, Charles VII, in January 1745 cleared the way to a settlement in Germany and in September of that year Maria Theresa at last secured the election of her husband Francis as Holy Roman Emperor. Then, having come to terms with Prussia, she turned her attention to Italy. She had the support of the British navy, which was always anxious to contest French and Spanish power in the Mediterranean, and by the end of 1746 it looked as though the campaign would culminate in the conquest of southern France and a joint attack on the great French naval base of Toulon. Early in 1747, however, the allied forces were pushed back into Italy. Meanwhile French advances in the Netherlands continued to menace British trade, British security and the future of the Hanoverian dynasty. By the autumn of 1747, when the French took the vital Dutch fortress of Bergen-op-Zoom and stood poised for a conquest of the United Provinces, ministers decided that the time had come to treat for peace. Even Pitt had lost a good deal of his fire now that the sober business of defending the dynasty had replaced the earlier excitements of Caribbean conquests; and Chesterfield, who had once been one of the noisiest of the Patriot spokesmen, was now more eager for peace than Newcastle himself.

The Peace Treaty, which was signed at Aix-la-Chapelle in October 1748, was singularly inconclusive. Apart from some minor Spanish gains in Italy and the retention of Silesia by Prussia, the provisions of the Pragmatic Sanction and the state of affairs before the war broke out were restored. France agreed, as she had done so many times before, to recognize the Hanoverian succession and to destroy the fortifications at Dunkirk. Thus an uneasy balance of power was restored in Europe, accompanied by one even more uneasy in the world beyond Europe. Louisbourg, a French fortress in Canada which had been taken by the British in 1744, was given back in exchange for Madras, a British fortress in India which had been taken by the French in 1746. Nothing was said about the French claims to the hinterland of North America, or about the Spanish right of search which had been the original cause of war back in 1739. But two years later, when the Anglo-Spanish Commercial Treaty of October 1750 upheld the right of search and also ended many of the privileges which the British had enjoyed in Spanish America since 1713, hardly a Patriot voice was raised in protest. This was partly because the years of war had shown how crude and over-simplified the slogans of 1739 had been; but it also had something to with the fact that many of the Patriots were by now members of the Pelhams' Broad-bottomed Administration. Their eagerness to rock the boat was diminished now that they themselves had climbed into it.

3 The Broad-bottomed Administration

The demand for a ministry constructed 'on a broad bottom' (that is, from a wide range of different political groupings) had originated as an opposition slogan in the 1730s, a way of attacking the 'narrow and rotten foundations' of Sir Robert's system. Pulteney and Boling-broke and Carteret had promised their followers that once they succeeded in pulling Walpole down they would end the iniquitous system whereby he had cornered all office and patronage for his own creatures. All men, whatever their political affiliations and con-victions, would come together to concert measures for the good of the whole country.

By 1746 something very like this had in fact been achieved, but not by

Pulteney and Bolingbroke and Carteret. Bolingbroke was by this time a dignified but ineffectual exile, while Carteret and Pulteney were the discredited favourites of the King. It was the Pelhams who had managed to widen the basis of their administration and combine Whig patronage with Patriot programmes. The idea of a broad-bottomed administration had been a weapon against Walpole, but the reality was a weapon in the hands of his friends and successors.

Having won their victory over the King in principle in February 1746, the Pelhams were not disposed to push it too far in practice. They insisted that he should demonstrate his confidence in them by making such changes as they recommended, but in the event very few offices changed hands. Pitt allowed himself to be slipped into the comparatively humble office of Vice-Treasurer of Ireland and three months later he was promoted to be Paymaster. This gave him a chance to win back, by a public show of integrity, some of the popularity which he had lost by taking office in the first place. Previous Paymasters had invested for their own profit the balances entrusted to them and had habitually taken bribes from the foreign rulers to whom they paid subsidies. By eschewing these practices and establishing a reputation for disinterested honesty, Pitt hoped to hold office without forfeiting the confidence of the independent members. Like all eighteenth-century politicians, he faced the eternal riddle of Court and Country, the problem of winning power without sacrificing popularity; and his solution was the pose of the honest office-holder, the man through whom the Commons might purify the Court, rather than the Court corrupt the Commons.

He certainly needed all the popularity he could get, for he was becoming more and more committed to the Pelhams. As well as accepting their policies in matters of peace and war, he found himself obliged at the elections of 1747 to accept their patronage. The very success of the Pelham policy of comprehension had driven their remaining opponents to desperation and the Prince of Wales had broken his uneasy truce with his father in order to lead a new opposition. Most of his followers were extreme Tories, crusty but undistinguished country gentlemen, or blatant careerists, but the fact that the throne would presumably revert to him in time put him in a powerful position. Henry Pelham wrote that Frederick had 'as much to give in present as we have, and more in reversion. This makes my task a hard one.' The Pelhams stole a march on the Prince by getting the King to dissolve Parliament in June 1747, a year before the expected date, and the elections were bitterly contested. Up to this time Pitt had sat for the family pocket borough of Old Sarum, an uninhabited collection of stones on Salisbury Plain; but now his elder brother, who had remained loyal to the opposition, refused to put the seat at his disposal.[1] Instead he was nominated for Seaford, a borough dominated by the Newcastle interest. When the opposition had the gall to put up a rival candidate, Newcastle himself travelled down to Seaford and sat beside Pitt on the hustings, scrutinizing the votes. This flagrant intimidation of the electors of Seaford ensured Pitt's election as their member, but it also involved him in bitter debates in the Commons about ministerial tyranny and corruption. The opposition had already been roused to fury by the premature dissolution, which they denounced as unconstitutional, and they now inveighed angrily against the methods by which the election had been won. Pitt, who in former years had been the mouthpiece of such attacks, now found himself at the receiving end.

The elections of 1747 gave the Pelhams and their supporters a majority of at least 125 in the new House of Commons. The hard core of the opposition was the Prince's own party, the 'Leicester House gang', numbering about thirty. With luck they could count on the support of the remnants of the Carteret and Pulteney followings, together with a section of the independent country gentlemen. A few days before the dissolution of Parliament the Prince had issued a declaration to the country gentlemen, promising that when he came to power he would remedy the chief grievances of the Country Party. But it was difficult, as difficult as it had been in the 1730s, to reconcile the independent squires with the career politicians of Leicester House. Prominent among these politicians was Sir John Perceval, second earl of Egmont, who deserted the Pelhams to join Frederick in March 1748. He was joined a year later by George Bubb Dodington, who resigned his place as Treasurer of the Navy in order to become 'Treasurer of the Chambers' to the Prince, a post specially created for the occasion. Bolingbroke once again put his particular blend of philosophy and journalism at the disposal of the opposition and in 1749 he published *The Idea of a Patriot King* and *Letter on the Spirit of Patriotism*. Ten years earlier he had been advocating a broad-bottomed administration, a coalition of all patriots, as the

---

[1] Two years later Thomas Pitt sold his rights of nomination at Old Sarum to the Prince of Wales for £3,000 down and a salary of a further £1,500 a year. See E. N. Williams: *The Eighteenth Century Constitution, Documents and Commentary*, p. 151.

only way of overthrowing the tyranny of Walpole; now he recommended the enlightened despotism of a Patriot King as the best cure for the corruption of a broad-bottomed Whig oligarchy. *The Remembrancer,* a weekly party journal which played the part previously played by *The Craftsman,* said that their aim was no longer to overthrow 'one over-grown minister', but to oppose the monopoly of all power and patronage by 'a party-coloured junto'. Egmont and the Prince drew up a plan which was to be put into operation as soon as George II died and which would ensure that the new King was not ensnared by the Whigs as his father had been in 1746.

By the beginning of 1751 this Leicester House vision of a new dawn of purity and patriotism was beginning to attract Pitt and his friends. Serious tensions were developing within the ministry, especially between Newcastle and his fellow Secretary of State, the Duke of Bedford. Like the Earl of Sandwich, First Lord of the Admiralty, Bedford owed his promotion largely to the patronage of the Duke of Cumberland; and Newcastle feared that Cumberland was gathering a party around him, possibly with the intention of making a bid for power on the death of his father. The Leicester House politicians certainly accused the Duke of harbouring such intentions and one of their pamphlets compared him to Richard III. Henry Pelham felt that his brother's fears about the Cumberland group were rather exaggerated, so that the two brothers were themselves on bad terms. Pitt, who was still uncomfortable about his conversion from Patriotism to Pelhamism, could see no future in staying in a ministry which seemed to be breaking up and might at any moment be destroyed utterly by the death of George II. Together with George Grenville and George Lyttelton, who had also been members of Lord Cobham's group of young Patriots in the 1730s, he opened negotiations with Leicester House and by March 1751 all three men were on the verge of leaving the ministry in order to join the opposition.

Then, on 20 March 1751, the whole situation was transformed by the sudden death of the Prince himself. His widow, who had always been uneasy about his opposition to the King, burned the plans which Egmont and Frederick had drawn up and dismissed Egmont himself from her household. The new Prince of Wales, Frederick's son George, was only thirteen and it was clear that it would be some time before he gathered a political party around him. For the time being the attractions of Leicester House as a political magnet were switched off. Pitt and his friends returned hastily to the ship which they had thought was sinking and prepared to repel boarders. The ministry drew together and the Pelham brothers made up their quarrels in order to push through a Regency Act. This provided that, in the event of George II dying before the young Prince of Wales came of age, the dowager Princess of Wales was to be Regent, while Cumberland was only to be President of her Regency Council, with very limited powers. Whatever truth there may or may not have been in it, the Leicester House picture of Cumberland as the potential wicked uncle had certainly served to reunite and revivify the Pelham ministry. The other Leicester House campaign, the attack on the Pelhams as corrupt Whig oligarchs who held their King in toils, seemed to die with Frederick. *The Remembrancer* ceased publication in June 1751 and six months later Bolingbroke himself was dead. But in fact the myth which he and the Leicester House politicians had so assiduously created, the myth of the wicked and corrupt Whigs who must be rooted out by a Patriot King and his Patriot Minister, was to be a powerful force in politics for many years to come.

While opposition politicians had been talking thus grandly about the future, the Pelhams had been doing what they could to make the present a little more orderly and efficient. In 1746 they had accepted a private Bill restoring to the Court of Common Council in the City of London some of the rights it had lost by Walpole's Act of 1725; and during the next few years Pelham deliberately wooed the Court of Common Council as a counterpoise to the three great Companies (the Bank of England, the East India Company and the South Sea Company) who were using their privileged position as government creditors to keep their interest rates unfairly high. By floating new loans which were open to public subscription he made the Companies realize that they must accept lower rates if they were to keep their special position. By 1751 the old stock, which had borne interest at 4 per cent, had all been converted into new stock paying 3 per cent, which was then the current rate. Two years later Pelham was able to bring the various different types of government stock into one consolidated fund which bore interest at 3 per cent. The 'three per cent Consols' which he thus created soon became a permanent feature of British life.

In London's twin city of Westminster the main problem was crime rather than financial management. Thomas de Veil,[1] who had made

[1] See above, p. 189.

some attempts to take crime detection out of the hands of private individuals, had died in 1746; but his work was taken up by Henry Fielding, a barrister, playwright and satirical writer who became justice of the peace for Westminster in 1748. In January 1751 he published his *Enquiry into the Causes of the late Increase of Robbers*, which stressed the need for a proper force of thief-takers, and a few years later he and his half-brother Sir John Fielding, who also became a justice for Westminster in 1751, formed such a force. Since it operated from the court in Bow Street its members came to be known as 'the Bow Street Runners'. In 1753 the Fielding brothers submitted to the Privy Council a plan for policing the City of Westminster, which was accepted in principle, and subsequently Sir John Fielding was able to persuade Newcastle to let him have £400 a year out of the secret service money to cover the costs of the plan. Meanwhile, the Gin Act of 1751 had helped to reduce drunkenness, one of the chief causes of crime and disorder in the metropolis. It stopped distillers from selling gin retail, and proved more effective than the Acts of 1736 and 1743. The consumption of gin, which had reached 8,495,000 gallons in 1751, fell to 5,946,000 in 1752 and by 1760 it was down to 2,100,000 gallons.

In 1752 the ministry provoked further desultory outbursts of disorder by its reform of the calendar. The Julian calendar, which was still used in Britain, had by this time fallen eleven days behind the more accurate Gregorian calendar which had been used in most European countries since 1582. An Act of 1752 provided that 2 September 1752 should be followed by 14 September and that from then on the Gregorian calendar should be used, with the year beginning on 1 January instead of 25 March. The riots that followed were not just inspired by childish fears that people were being robbed of eleven days of their lives: interference with the calendar seemed to presage interference with saints' days and other holidays, which were among the few bright spots in the harsh drudgery of a labourer's life.

In 1753 the Lord Chancellor, Lord Hardwicke, introduced a Bill to make clandestine marriages more difficult. It was a fair and sensible measure, which provided for the calling of the banns and insisted on residence qualifications. It also required that the consent of parents or guardians should be given in the case of minors. The opposition, however, attacked it ferociously as an invasion of the liberties of the subject and they were joined by Henry Fox, the

Secretary at War, who had always disliked Hardwicke, and whose own career had been founded on a secret marriage with Lady Caroline Lennox without her parents' consent. The Bill was passed, but the bitterness which it engendered between the Lord Chancellor and the Secretary at War made more difficult Henry Pelham's task of keeping his broad-bottomed ministry together. Then, on 6 March 1754, Pelham himself died. The broad-bottomed administration, and the carefully constructed façade of Whig unity on which it depended, were destined to die with him.

9

Uneasy Alliances
1754–1760

1 Pitt and Fox

Henry Pelham had been the keystone of the delicately balanced bridge between King and Country, between the Court and the Commons. As long ago as November 1743 Newcastle had written, somewhat peevishly: 'I do apprehend that my brother does think that his superior interest in the Closet and situation in the House of Commons gives him great advantage over everybody else.' Just how great that advantage had been was to become painfully apparent to those who now sought to replace him. The King himself was well aware that it would be hard to find another minister to manage his affairs in the Commons so efficiently. 'Now I shall have no more peace', he said mournfully when they brought him the news of Pelham's death.

Newcastle very soon decided that he would himself take over his brother's position of First Lord of the Treasury. This meant finding someone to take over his own place as Secretary of State for the North. If that someone was a commoner he could also take over the leadership of the House of Commons and defend in that House the policies of a ministry most of whose members would be peers; but Newcastle had no intention of allowing the management of patronage to pass to the Secretary of State. For him the leadership of the Commons and the control of patronage were two different things. The fact that they had been combined in the person of Sir Robert Walpole and again in that of Henry Pelham was, in his eyes, a fortunate accident. In fact, however, it was fast becoming a constitutional necessity. Henry Fox, who desired Pelham's place so desperately that he opened negotiations within two hours of his death and even apologized to Hardwicke for his opposition to the Marriage Act, refused it indignantly when he heard that he was not to be allowed control over patronage. 'How shall I be able to talk to members,' he asked, 'when some have received gratifications and others not?' His language was the language of the eighteenth century, but the truth which he glimpsed was one which was to be increasingly important in the future. The King's chief minister in the Commons would have to be the master, and not the servant, of his other councillors and courtiers.

The other man who might be persuaded to do Newcastle's business in the Commons was William Pitt. He was at Bath at the time of Pelham's death, recovering from a fit of the gout, but within three days he had received a message from Lord Chancellor Hardwicke hinting that the leadership of the Commons might be offered to him. Pitt, however, was more concerned with the future than with the present: he intended to be the King's chief minister eventually, but the King he would serve would be George III and not George II. For the moment the dowager Princess of Wales was on fairly good terms with her father-in-law, but it could not last. At any moment politicians might have to take sides as between the Court of St James's and Leicester House; and when that time came Pitt did not want to find himself caught on the wrong foot. He told Hardwicke that it would be impossible for him to lead the House of Commons unless he was given 'the protection and countenance of the Crown, visibly manifested by marks of royal favour at Court'. As he knew perfectly well that the old King still detested him for his attacks on Hanover, this was tantamount to an outright refusal.

Since neither Fox nor Pitt would serve their turn, Newcastle and Hardwicke fell back on lesser men. Sir Thomas Robinson, a skilled and experienced diplomat but no House of Commons man, was made Secretary of State and leader of the Commons, while Henry Legge, a friend and supporter of Pitt, took over Pelham's other job of Chancellor of the Exchequer. The arrangements were completed by the end of March and a few days later Parliament was dissolved. In the elections that followed the ministry won a sweeping victory. Even Fox and Pitt, though they were both rather put out by Robinson's appointment, remained loyal to the ministry of which they were still officially members. Fox accepted nomination for a government borough and Pitt was returned for Aldborough, a seat controlled by Newcastle personally. There was no repetition of the unpleasantness which had taken place at Seaford in 1747: Pitt did not even have to interrupt his convalescence in order to visit his constituency. But by the time the new Parliament met in November 1754 Pitt and Fox had decided to join together to attack Newcastle. Robinson's short-comings as a leader of the Commons became increasingly obvious as the session got under way; and both Pitt and Fox made it clear that they saw his appointment as an insult to the Commons. The House was fast becoming, said Pitt, 'a little assembly, serving no other purpose than to register the arbitrary edicts of one too powerful subject'.

This alliance between Pitt and Fox was a paradoxical and puzzling development, because they represented completely different approaches to politics. Fox had always been a ministerialist, a man who worked from the inside outwards, from the Court to the Commons. His refusal to lead the Commons without having control of patronage had not sprung from any concern for the dignity of the Commons, but from a concern for his own position at Court and in the Cabinet Council. Pitt, on the other hand, was essentially a House of Commons man: whatever position he might hold at Court or in the Cabinet would always be the result, and not the cause, of his prominence in the Commons. Moreover the two men had taken up completely different positions over the most pressing question of the hour, the future of the monarchy. Fox was a supporter of the Duke of Cumberland, who was suspected by many people of wanting to exercise a military dictatorship. As Commander-in-Chief of the army and a man with powerful supporters at Court and in the Cabinet, Cumberland might well come to wield very considerable power if George II were to become senile or if George III were to succeed before he came of age. Pitt hated standing armies, he hated Hanover, he hated everything Cumberland and Fox stood for; and yet he was prepared to make common cause with Fox in order to harass Newcastle. On the face of it, it made no sense at all.

In fact, it made a great deal of sense. Pitt's principal aim, now as always, was to be the minister of George III. When the old King died and the new dawn of purity and patriotism came, Pitt intended to be there to usher it in. Then all the contradictions of his previous career, his periods of Patriotism and his periods of Pelhamism, would fall into place as the necessary stages in the apprenticeship of the man destined to be the Patriot Minister of a Patriot King. But if Newcastle and Fox, Whig minister and Cumberland nominee, were allowed to come together they might prove strong enough to obscure the new dawn and continue into the new reign the ministers and the methods of the old. At all costs Pitt must keep Newcastle and Fox apart. The three of them—Newcastle the minister of George II, Fox the minister of Cumberland, and Pitt the minister of George III— formed an uneasy triangle. For each of them it was vital to stop the other two combining against him. Pitt could not isolate Fox by combining with Newcastle, since this would mean identifying himself with the existing regime and prejudicing his chances when George III came to the throne. He embarked, therefore, on the alternative policy of allying with Fox against Newcastle.

It failed. Whatever Pitt's long-range ambitions may have been, Fox was concerned with the present. He wanted to make sure that he and his patron Cumberland could continue their power from the old reign into the new; and to do this he needed to be in office. However ferocious his attacks on Newcastle might be, their main object was to put up his price, to make Newcastle think again about giving him what he wanted. Newcastle saw this as clearly as Fox himself and he therefore set to work to buy Fox out and thus separate him from Pitt. He very soon succeeded. By April 1755, when Parliament rose and the King left for Hanover, Fox was once again a firm supporter of the ministry. His office was still that of Secretary at War,[1] but he had been given a seat in the Cabinet and in the Council of Regency which, headed by his patron Cumberland, was to rule the country during the King's absence. To Pitt it seemed that his worst fears had been confirmed. The King, now a man of over seventy, was trundling around a Germany which was once again on the verge of a major war. At any moment news might come that he had been detained or taken prisoner or fallen ill. At home, all power was concentrated in the hands of the Commander-in-Chief and his lieutenant the Secretary at War, who were busily abetting the King's policy of raising hired German troops. Where would it all end? What chance was there of the young Prince George succeeding to his rightful inheritance? Throughout the summer of 1755, as rumours of subsidy treaties and other military commitments filtered back from Germany, Pitt drew closer and closer to Leicester House. From the beginning of June onwards he was in correspondence with Lord Bute, tutor to the young Prince of Wales, who had replaced Egmont as the leader of the Leicester House party. Together they discussed

---

[1] It is important to note that Fox did not become Secretary of State until the autumn of 1755. Professor Basil Williams, in *The Whig Supremacy* (p. 444) lists him as Secretary of State from November 1754; this error, continued in C. H. Stuart's revised edition of the book, can easily lead to confusion.

means of averting the dangers which they saw—or pretended to see —in the ascendancy of Cumberland.

The King returned safely in the autumn and the subsidy treaties which he had concluded with Russia and with Hesse-Cassel were passed by an overwhelming majority in the Commons. Pitt spoke vehemently against the treaties, against militarism and Hanoverianism, against the ascendancy of Cumberland, above all against the unnatural alliance between Newcastle and Fox by means of which all these things had been forced upon a reluctant country. It was a splendid display of oratory, but it availed nothing against the management of Newcastle and the leadership of Fox. Fox was now given the office of Secretary of State for the South, while Pitt was dismissed from the position of Paymaster which he had held for the past nine years. Once more he was in open opposition, the sturdy Patriot fighting for the independence of the Commons and the rights of the heir to the throne against those who sought to smother both in a miasma of Whiggery and militarism. He had failed to prevent Newcastle and Fox from coming together and now, it seemed, all he could do was to wait and to hope—wait for George III's accession and hope that Newcastle and Fox and Cumberland would not be able to dig themselves in sufficiently deeply to survive it.

2   Pitt and Newcastle

The alliance between the Newcastle Whigs and the Cumberland faction was nothing like as firm and formidable as Pitt seemed to think. Cumberland was an honest and an honourable man who did not intend to usurp his nephew's crown. Even if he had harboured any such wild ideas, Newcastle would certainly not have supported them. Like Walpole and Pelham, Newcastle saw subsidy treaties and hired troops as ways of buttressing Britain's security, not as the weapons of Hanoverian despotism or militarist conspiracies. Events in Europe and in the colonies were making it clear that war with France was imminent and the King's chief minister therefore did his best to keep on good terms with the Commander-in-Chief and with the Secretary at War. The Newcastle—Cumberland—Fox axis was concerned to plan the present, not to plot the future.

On the other hand, Newcastle had no desire to drift into war while Pitt and the Patriots were still in opposition. This would be to repeat the disastrous situation which had undermined Walpole in the years after 1739. Already Pitt was lashing out in the Commons, ridiculing the steps taken to protect Hanover and deploring the lack of action in America. At the end of January 1756 the ministry was goaded into offering the colonists £120,000 to help pay for the unofficial war which they had been waging against the French for the past year or more; but Pitt was not satisfied. He picked holes in the proposal and mocked at the quarrels between ministers, who were, he said, 'united only in corrupt and arbitrary measures'. By the end of March relations with the French were so bad that it was feared that they would launch an invasion. The ministers asked the Dutch to send troops to help defend Britain, but they were met with a refusal. The traditional alliance between Britain and Austria was breaking down and this in its turn jeopardized our alliance with the United Provinces. The Dutch did not want to fight the French if the Austrians in the Netherlands were not going to support them. The ministers therefore had to propose that Parliament should ask the King to send for Hanoverian troops. Once again Pitt poured a torrent of scorn on the incompetence and Hanoverianism of the King's ministers. When Parliament was told that the King had signed an alliance with the King of Prussia, a step which Pitt had himself advocated in the past, he attacked it as yet another measure to defend Hanover at the expense of Britain. Then, in the middle of May, news came that the French were attacking Minorca and war was at last formally declared. The decisive struggle with France at sea and in the colonies, to which Pitt and the Patriots had so long looked forward, had at last begun.

The progress of that struggle during the summer and early autumn underlined the incompetence of Newcastle's ministry. In the middle of June Pitt told Grenville that 'infinite distress seems to hem us in on all quarters. I am in most anxious impatience to have the affair in the Mediterranean cleared up. As yet nothing is clear but that the French are masters there, and that probably many an innocent and gallant man's honour and fortune is to be offered up as a scapegoat for the sins of the Administration.' Newcastle certainly intended to put the blame for the fall of Minorca, news of which came early in July, on to Admiral Byng, whose fleet had failed to assist the defence of the island. But it was not easy to find scapegoats for the other disasters which followed on the fall of Minorca. In India Calcutta fell to a French-supported prince, while in America the vital British fort at Oswego on Lake Ontario was captured by the French. Finally, at the end of August, Frederick of Prussia plunged Europe into war by invading Saxony. It certainly looked as though Newcastle's diplomacy in Germany had done more to endanger Britain's interests than to protect them. Pitt was appalled by the situation and he decided that the time had come for him to take control of affairs. For years past his political conduct had been guided by his hopes for the future, but now it must be governed by the needs of the present. 'I am sure I can save this country,' he told the Duke of Devonshire, 'and nobody else can.'

There can be little doubt that the chief reason for this change of attitude was Pitt's concern for the future of his country. As a politician, Pitt could be devious, unreliable, even dishonest; but he was a genuine patriot, passionately convinced of Britain's future greatness as a maritime and colonial power. In order to lay the foundations of that greatness he was prepared to be the chief minister of George II, even if it meant prejudicing his chances of being the chief minister of George III. On the other hand, it must be admitted that the prospects of his taking office without offending Leicester House had improved considerably in the last few months. The young Prince of Wales had come of age in June 1756 and his mother was no longer so obsessed with fears of a Cumberland usurpation. Early in October 1756 she succeeded in getting Bute appointed as Groom of the Stole to her son, in spite of George II's opposition to the idea. Leicester House was no longer committed to perpetual opposition, but was prepared to force itself on the old King in order to pave the way for the accession of the new King. If Pitt was ready to make a bid for office, he could do so with the blessing of Leicester House.

His opportunity came in the middle of October, when Fox handed in his resignation. The King saw that the alliance between the Whigs and the Cumberland faction could no longer manage his affairs for him in Parliament and he realized that he would have to turn to the only remaining alternative, an alliance between the Whigs and the Patriots. Now that he was on slightly better terms with the Patriots' backers at Leicester House, it was easier for him to face the prospect. Besides, the events of 1746–48 had shown how quickly Patriots reconciled themselves to Continental entanglements once they were in office. As soon as he heard that Fox wanted to resign the King authorized Newcastle to approach Pitt and tell him that he was prepared to take him into his favour as long as he supported his policies. By this, of course, George meant his Hanoverian policies as well as his British policies. Pitt, however, refused to be tied down. He insisted that he must have freedom to inquire into the ministry's past mistakes and to propose new and different measures. In particular, he wanted to bring in a Militia Bill which would create a local defence force officered by the country gentlemen and thus obviate the need for the importation of Hanoverian troops. Above all, he refused to serve with the Duke of Newcastle. He would have no more compromises between Patriotism and Pelhamism. If the old King was to be favoured with the Patriot ministry which had been intended for the new King, he must agree to rid himself of the last relics of Pelhamism. In the official negotiations which went on between Pitt and Hardwicke, the actual members of the proposed ministry were not listed; but in a private interview with the King's mistress Pitt suggested the Duke of Devonshire as First Lord of the Treasury, himself and Sir Thomas Robinson as the two Secretaries of State and a mixture of Patriots and nonentities in the lesser posts. Two years earlier he had been castigating Newcastle for ruling through obscure men like Robinson, but now he found that they had their uses after all.

The King was infuriated by Pitt's attempt to dictate his own terms and by his refusal to work with Newcastle. He also disliked being approached through his mistress. 'Mr Pitt shall not go to that channel any more,' he exclaimed angrily, 'she does not meddle and shall not meddle.' The outburst was unjustified: Lady Yarmouth, the mistress in question, had become an accepted part of the political scene since she had been brought over from Hanover after Queen Caroline's death. Both Fox and Newcastle had already consulted her and in doing the same Pitt was only trying to show, in his rather clumsy way, that he was prepared to come to terms with the Court and with things Hanoverian. He would not, however, come to terms with Newcastle or with Fox. He was prepared to court the favour of the old King, even to do his Hanoverian business for him if necessary, but he would not work with men who had so mismanaged the war and were associated with Cumberland and Hanoverian militarism.[1] Newcastle, for his part, had no desire to cling to office. He was scared by the popular clamour against him, which found expression in addresses and petitions demanding 'justice against persons however highly

[1] In order to underline the Hanoverian sympathies of the ministers, Pitt made great play with the case of the Hanoverian soldier who had walked out of a shop in Maidstone with two more handkerchiefs than he had paid for. Popular fury was aroused when he was tried by court martial instead of by the magistrates, but it was somewhat appeased when he was awarded 300 lashes.

dignified or distinguished.' He and Lord Hardwicke announced their intention of resigning late in October and the King tried to form some sort of coalition—anything to avoid bringing in Pitt alone and on his own terms. In the end he had to accept a ministry which was very like the one Pitt had originally suggested. Carteret, who since 1744 had held the title of Earl Granville, remained as Lord President of the Council and the Earl of Holderness kept his place as Secretary of State for the North. This was an important victory for the King because it meant that the affairs of Northern Europe, including Hanover, would be handled by a Whig minister whom he trusted and not by a supporter of Pitt. For the rest, Pitt's terms were accepted. He became Secretary of State for the South, Devonshire became First Lord of the Treasury and places were found for Legge (Chancellor of the Exchequer), Earl Temple (First Lord of the Admiralty) and Grenville (Treasurer of the Navy). It was not a completely clean sweep, but it was a cleaner one than the King would have liked. He was no longer in the hands of the Pelham Whigs, the trusted and experienced builders of patronage bridges between Court and Commons. He was delivered over to a Patriot minister, a man who based his position in the Commons and at Court on popularity rather than on connection.

The Patriot Minister proclaimed his intentions in the speech which he wrote for the King to deliver to Parliament when it met on 2 December. The King himself thought that a great deal of the speech was 'stuff and nonsense', but the country gentlemen and the merchants liked its promises of more vigorous action in America and the removal of Hanoverian troops from England. It was clear that Pitt was appealing over the heads of the professional politicians, the office-seekers and the borough-mongers, to the country as a whole and to its representatives in the House of Commons. On the whole his appeal was successful. A bad attack of gout early in 1757 prevented him from appearing in the Commons as frequently as he would have wished,[1] and at the end of February 1757 he courageously risked his popularity in an unsuccessful attempt to save Admiral Byng from being shot; but for the most part he remained the darling of the Country Party and of the City.

[1] A writer in the *Gentleman's Magazine* in February 1757 made the following comment on Pitt's illness:

> But heav'n (in mercy to the trembling foe)
> Bade the gout seize his senatorial toe.

He was not, however, the darling of the Court. George II remained completely unreconciled to the minister who had been forced on him, and his determination to be rid of him was strengthened by the knowledge that the great parliamentary following which had been built up by Walpole and the Pelhams was still in existence, waiting to help its King to break the Patriots and restore the Whigs. By February 1757 George II was already intriguing to replace Pitt. Newcastle refused to come back, so the King turned to Fox and to his patron Cumberland. Cumberland had just been asked to take command of the army which was being assembled in Germany to defend Hanover and help the King of Prussia, but he refused to leave England as long as Pitt was in power. He was not the wicked would-be usurper that Leicester House made him out to be, but he did not want to leave the country at a time when his enemies were in a position to control the old King and perhaps manage the succession of the new one. He demanded Pitt's dismissal and the King was only too glad to oblige. Early in April 1757 Pitt and Temple were dismissed and Grenville and Legge, the other two prominent Patriots in the ministry, resigned in sympathy. There was no question of a joint resignation of the whole administration. The King's other ministers sat back and waited for him to fill the gaps which he had made in their ranks.

The task proved far more difficult than the King had expected. For more than ten weeks, as the war in which he was engaged moved towards its climax, George II grappled with the most serious ministerial crisis of his reign. In his eyes and in those of most of his contemporaries it was a question of the old triangle of Pitt, Fox and Newcastle and of the three royal personages whom they represented —the Prince of Wales, the Duke of Cumberland and the old King himself. But behind this triangular problem there still stood the older and more straightforward problem of Court and Country. Newcastle and the Whigs had built up an alliance between the Court and the great party magnates, an alliance so strong that it had come to be regarded as almost irreplaceable. Pitt, on the other hand, had the support of the Country Party and of a large section of the City. He took his stand on prominence, on popularity, while Newcastle took his on patronage. In comparison with these two great forces, Fox was a negligible figure, his dependence on Cumberland a wasting asset. While the King dreamt of setting up an administration under the leadership of Fox, the City of London showed its preference for Pitt by presenting him with the freedom of the City in a gold box said to be worth £100.[1] Many other cities and towns followed London's example.

There was only one way out of this dilemma: Pitt and Newcastle must come together. Neither the alliance between Pitt and Fox nor that between Fox and Newcastle had been able to reconcile King and Country. If the bridge which had given stability to the administrations of Walpole and the Pelhams was to be reconstructed, its two halves, the patronage of Newcastle and the popularity of Pitt, must somehow be jointed together. The jointing would not be easy, since Pitt had expressed publicly and repeatedly his contempt for all that Newcastle stood for and his determination not to join any ministry of which he himself was not sole and undisputed head. But somehow the joint must be made, if the country was to have a government which could both stand and act, a ministry in which the First Lord of the Treasury could ensure stability while the Secretaries of State ensured efficiency.[2]

In the end the joint was made at Leicester House and the joiners were Lord Hardwicke, the wisest of the old King's advisers, and Lord Bute, the young Prince's tutor. It was agreed that Newcastle should be First Lord of the Treasury, Pitt and Holderness the Secretaries of State, Temple the Lord Privy Seal and Anson the First Lord of the Admiralty. The King was reluctant to go back on his promises to Fox and insisted that he should be made Paymaster. Thus Fox was able to console himself for his political failure with financial success. Pitt was by no means happy about the alliance with Newcastle and on 28 June 1757, after all the arrangements were at last completed, he told Bute: 'I go to this bitter, but necessary cup with a more foreboding mind . . . this is the wretch who draws the great families at his heels, and for whose elevation and power the pretended friends of the public have so loudly passed sentence on my inflexibility.' Bute was immensely relieved that Pitt's inflexibility had at last been overcome. The coalition between Pitt and Newcastle, which Pitt saw as an uneasy alliance, was in Bute's eyes the best guarantee of the Prince's peaceful accession to the throne. As well as being a bridge between the

---

[1] One satirist summed up the difference between Pitt's reputation and Fox's in verse form:

> The two great rivals London might content
> If what he values most to each she sent;
> Ill was the franchise coupled with the box;
> Give Pitt the freedom, and the gold to Fox.

[2] See above, p .31.

King and the Country, it was a bridge between the old reign and the new. 'If even the wreck of this crown can be preserved to our amiable young Prince,' he told Pitt soothingly, ''tis to your efforts, your abilities, my dear Pitt, that he must owe it.'

Pitt was indeed concerned with salvaging the wreck of the crown, but he saw his task in terms of securing victory overseas rather than satisfying the demands of Leicester House at home. During the next three years he made his uneasy alliance with Newcastle into a highly successful war ministry and he made the alliance with Prussia, which he had inherited somewhat reluctantly from his predecessors, into an integral part of his own effort on behalf of the colonists. But he did these things at the cost of weakening and eventually destroying his alliance with Leicester House. He waged and won the Patriot War but in doing so he mortally offended the boy who was determined to be a Patriot King.

3 Pitt and Prussia

The most important development in British foreign policy during the 1750s was the breakdown of the 'old Whig system' of European alliances. Ever since the Revolution Britain had sought to contain the threat presented by the Bourbon powers—first France alone, then France and Spain together—by allying with Austria and the United Provinces. The one exception to this policy, the period of Franco-British cooperation which had followed the Treaty of Utrecht, was seen as an unnatural departure necessitated by a Tory peace treaty. True Whig policy demanded close alliance with the Emperor and with the Dutch.

By 1749 the Emperor, or rather his wife Maria Theresa, was highly dissatisfied with the British alliance. Britain had let Austria down in 1748 by making peace just as the war was turning in Austria's favour and it was clear that British interests and Austrian interests were becoming more and more incompatible. British merchants wanted a balance of power in the Mediterranean, whereas Maria Theresa dreamed of turning the Mediterranean into an Austrian lake and Italy into an Austrian peninsula. Furthermore, British commercial interests in the Baltic and the policies of Britain's Hanoverian King both required a balanced situation in Germany, with neither Austria nor Prussia in complete control. Maria Theresa, on the other hand, intended to crush Frederick of Prussia and take revenge for his seizure of Silesia. Finally, and most important of all, there was the question of the Austrian Netherlands. Ever since she had acquired them in 1713 Austria had found the Netherlands more of a burden than an asset. Her one attempt to make them pay, the Ostend Company of 1722, had ended in failure and she had found herself saddled with the task of defending them as a buffer state against France. But a buffer for whom? It was the British and the Dutch, not the Austrians, who would suffer if the Netherlands were overrun by the French. The more they thought about it, the more Maria Theresa and her minister Kaunitz became convinced that the Austro-British alliance did more for the interests of Britain than for those of Austria.

The alternative, though staggering, had dazzling possibilities. It was nothing less than an alliance with France, the traditional enemy of the Habsburgs for the past five hundred years. For centuries the whole pattern of European war and diplomacy had revolved around the rivalry between Bourbon and Habsburg, between France and the Holy Roman Empire. Now Maria Theresa proposed to turn that rivalry into friendship. Once the improbable idea had been accepted its advantages became obvious. With France as her ally Austria would be in an almost impregnable position in Germany, and Prussia would be faced with a deadly three-pronged attack from France, Austria and Russia. Moreover, the knowledge that she could rely on French help in Germany would enable Austria to turn her attention more effectively to the Mediterranean and the Balkans, where there were almost unbounded possibilities for conquest and expansion. And the only price that need be paid for all these gains was the acceptance of French expansion in the Netherlands—something which menaced Britain and the United Provinces more than it menaced Austria. Austria would get all the benefits of the new arrangement, while the bill would be footed by her erstwhile allies who had deserted and betrayed her.

In 1750 Kaunitz was sent as Austrian ambassador to France and for the next few years he angled for a French alliance, while George II and Newcastle watched apprehensively from London. The Austro-French negotiations did not go very well, but they went well enough to scare George II's ministers into seeking some means of protecting Hanover in this new and dangerous situation. They found it, or thought they found it, in an alliance with Russia. By the Treaty of St Petersburg of September 1755 Russia agreed to station troops in Livonia ready to march into Germany if British interests there were threatened. In return she was to receive a British subsidy of £100,000 a year, which would be increased to £500,000 a year if war broke out. For George II it was a defensive treaty, aimed at shielding Hanover and avoiding a general war in Germany; but for Elizabeth, the Empress of Russia, it was merely a preliminary to the attack on Prussia which she had long been contemplating. Frederick of Prussia knew this only too well and he hurriedly came to terms with Britain himself. By the Convention of Westminster of January 1756 he and his uncle George II[1] agreed not to attack one another's territories and to resist any foreign power that tried to enter Germany.

Once again, George II's aims were entirely defensive. In his eyes the Convention of Westminister was just another in the long series of treaties which he had signed at divers times with divers princes for the defence of his Electorate. Pitt, with his eyes fixed on the coming colonial struggle with France, also saw it in these terms and distrusted it as a Hanoverian strategem which was irrelevant to Britain's real interests. But to the French it appeared in quite a different light. Their only ally in Germany had entered into a sinister combination with their great enemy across the Channel. They were threatened from both sides, by the military power of Prussia in the East and by the colonial and commercial ambitions of Britain in the West. The proffered Austrian alliance, which they had so far viewed without enthusiasm, now seemed to be their only safeguard. In May 1756 France and Austria signed a treaty of friendship and non-aggression and the reversal of alliances in Europe was complete. Instead of France and Prussia facing Britain and Austria, as in the previous war, France was now allied with Austria against Britain and Prussia. But the two great constants of European politics, the struggle between Austria and Prussia for the control of Germany and the struggle between France and Britain for the control of the world beyond the seas, continued undisturbed by the change of partners. The powers of Europe had changed their alliances, but not their enmities.

The treaty between France and Austria, like that between Britain and Prussia, was primarily defensive. The French knew that a colonial war with Britain was inevitable—indeed, it had already started— but they did not want a war in Germany on their hands as well. Whatever happened, their greatest danger lay in British sea power, the essential link between Britain and her allies on the Continent.

[1] George II's sister, Sophia Dorothea, had married Frederick's father, Frederick William I of Prussia.

If she could break that, France would have a good chance of fighting and winning a self-contained colonial war against one enemy, instead of being hemmed in by a war on two fronts. She therefore determined to attack the vital British naval base of Minorca. Early in April 1756 a force of some 15,000 troops left Toulon to capture the island. Newcastle had advance warning of the expedition, but he was hard put to it to find enough ships and men to defend Minorca, since there were also rumours that the French intended to invade Britain itself. A British fleet of thirteen ships with some four thousand troops on board finally arrived off Minorca towards the end of May, but its commander, Rear Admiral John Byng, had been present at the court martial which had condemned Admiral Mathews and had learnt his lesson from it. Whatever happened, he was determined not to break his line. When the van of his fleet turned down wind to engage the French he failed to follow it, in case by doing so he should break the line. Having thus thrown away the chance of defeating an inferior enemy fleet—the French only had twelve ships to his thirteen—he called a council of war, which decided that nothing more could be done for Minorca. The fleet sailed back to Gibraltar and at the end of June Minorca surrendered to the French.

The French commanders could hardly believe their eyes when they saw Byng sail away; and the British public could hardly believe its ears when it heard that the island had fallen because the man sent to relieve it had given up the attempt. There was a furious outcry for Byng's execution and in January 1757 he was condemned to death by a court martial at Portsmouth. After a last-minute attempt to save him had failed, in spite of the backing of Pitt, he was shot on 14 March. His behaviour during the actual engagement, which was the technical ground for his condemnation and execution, can be justified in the light of the Fighting Instructions; but there can be little doubt that he was culpable in sailing away and leaving Minorca to its fate. His death was no more tragic and no less tragic than those of the innumerable common soldiers throughout the ages who have been shot down for deserting in the face of the enemy.

Meanwhile the war in Germany which both Britain and France had tried to avoid was being precipitated by their allies. In concert with the Empress of Russia[1] and the Elector of Saxony, Maria Theresa

[1] After the signature of the Convention of Westminster, Elizabeth of Russia had repudiated her agreement with Britain and had invited France and Austria to join with her 'to reduce the King of Prussia within proper limits'

was planning a joint invasion of Prussian territory. At the end of August 1756 Frederick of Prussia anticipated her by marching into Saxony and capturing Dresden, where he found and published evidence of the conspiracy against him. George II was horrified to find that his alliance with Prussia, intended as a guarantee for Hanover, had instead endangered his Electorate by plunging Germany into war. He began to think of repudiating the Convention of Westminster and negotiating with Austria and France for the neutrality of Hanover; but Pitt, when he came into office in November 1756, persuaded him to drop this idea. The alliance with Prussia, which Pitt had originally seen as a purely Hanoverian measure, had now become an integral and essential part of the great global struggle with the French. At first, 'from an apprehension of going too far with the King of Prussia and from a remaining delicacy towards the House of Austria', George refused to go along with his new minister: the former Patriot, the unrelenting critic of Carteret's continental wars, had now become more eager for a German war than the King himself. But by the beginning of 1757 George had agreed to give proper assistance to Prussia.

That assistance could take various forms. The most obvious was the cash subsidy, Britain's traditional way of helping her continental allies. In February 1757 Pitt got the Commons to pass unanimously a vote of £200,000 for Prussia and a few weeks later the British ambassador in Berlin told him: 'The King of Prussia told me he had had such accounts of your behaviour in the House of Commons that he thought himself much obliged to you, and he desired me to acquaint you with it, and in his name return you thanks.' When he returned to office in the summer of 1757 Pitt was able to persuade the Commons to do even more for the King of Prussia. News of the great Prussian victory of Rossbach, over the French and the Austrians, arrived just before Parliament met in December 1757 and as a result Pitt got Parliament's approval for a new subsidy treaty by which Prussia received the quite unprecedented sum of £670,000 a year.

Another means of helping Prussia was to maintain an army in Germany, on the lines of the Pragmatic Army which Carteret had created in the War of the Austrian Succession. Here again Pitt had changed his views and was now the most vigorous advocate of such an army.[1] In February 1757, when he proposed the first Prussian

[1] Quite apart from anything else, it gave him an excuse to get the hated Hanoverian troops out of Britain and replace them with a local militia recruited under an Act passed in 1757. This Militia Act proved very unpopular and provoked widespread rioting.

subsidy, he also got Parliament to agree to maintain 12,000 Hessian troops. Together with 12,000 Prussians and 36,000 Hanoverians which George II was to provide at his own expense, they were to form an Army of Observation which was to be stationed in western Germany ready to move against the French if they invaded Germany. But when the French did march into Germany they defeated the Army of Observation, which was under the command of Cumberland, at Hastenbeck on the southern borders of Hanover. Cumberland fell back northwards until he was trapped in the Duchy of Bremen, with the river Elbe on his left, the Weser on his right and the North Sea behind. Here he signed, early in September 1757, the Convention of Klosterseven. This provided for the disbanding of his army in return for guarantees of Hanover's neutrality. It was an honourable and sensible way out of the impossible situation into which his father's half-hearted and contradictory orders had led him. George II was still toying with the idea of protecting Hanover by negotiation rather than by outright support of Prussia and he had encouraged his son to come to terms with the French instead of marching eastwards to join the Prussians. But when he heard the news of Klosterseven he raged against Cumberland who had, he said, 'ruined me and disgraced himself'. The country, which hated Cumberland as a symbol of Hanoverian militarism, was only too glad to accept him as a scapegoat for the King's indecision and cowardice. He resigned from his post of Commander-in-Chief and the Convention he had signed was repudiated. The Army of Observation—now renamed the Army of Execution, since its job was to act rather than to watch, now that the King had at last made his mind up—was reorganized and put under the command of Prince Ferdinand of Brunswick.

Prince Ferdinand did a good deal better than Cumberland. He cleared the French out of Germany altogether during the spring of 1758, drove them across the Rhine at the end of March and inflicted a crushing defeat on them at Krefeld on 23 June. By this time even the confirmed anti-Hanoverians of Leicester House had been converted to the German war and Pitt met with hardly any opposition when he proposed a vote of £1,200,000 for Ferdinand's army. But the opening of the next year's campaign was disappointing: the French drove Ferdinand back into Germany and took Minden, which dominated the upper Weser and the approaches to Hanover itself. On 1 August 1759 Ferdinand's army, which had been strengthened with some 10,000 British troops, attacked a numerically superior French army at Minden and defeated it. The bravery of the British infantry did a lot to win the battle, but the slackness of the British cavalry, which failed to charge when ordered to do so, gave the French a chance to make good their retreat. Lord George Sackville, the commander responsible for this astonishing piece of disobedience, was a Leicester House man and Pitt's refusal to shield him from punishment widened the breach between the would-be Patriot King and the man who had hoped to be his Patriot Minister.

For the rest of the war Prince Ferdinand's army managed to hold the French down in western Germany and prevent them breaking through to join in the attacks which their allies were making on Frederick of Prussia. Nevertheless Frederick's position was desperate by the end of 1759. He was severely defeated by the Russians a few days before Minden and on 13 August his main army was shattered by an Austro-Russian force at Kunersdorf. In November another Prussian army was trapped by the Austrians and forced to give itself up. The sledgehammer blows on Prussian territory continued throughout 1760 and 1761—at one point the Russians were in occupation of Berlin itself—and Frederick was only saved by the death of the Empress Elizabeth of Russia at the beginning of 1762. Her successor, Peter III, was an admirer of Frederick and made peace with him in May 1762. But by this time Pitt had fallen from power in Britain and those who had taken his place had reverted to the traditional Country Party distrust of continental entanglements. For a few brief years Pitt had reconciled the colonial war and the German war, had seen that they were complementary parts of the struggle against France; but when he fell the Prussian alliance fell with him and Britain once more turned her back on Europe.

4 Pitt and the colonists

The Patriot War which Pitt waged so successfully from 1756 onwards was something much more coherent and more ambitious than the Caribbean marauding recommended by the Patriots in 1739. Pitt saw, more clearly than any other man of his time, that Britain was in a position to dominate the world's shipping routes and thus to cut off her European rivals from their overseas possessions; and the greatest and most dangerous of those European rivals in his eyes was France. With extensive natural resources and a population three times that of Britain, France was already the dominant power in

Europe and might yet become the dominant power in the world. But she could only do this if her rulers were prepared to devote the greater part of her energies and her resources to building up her trade and her seapower. Fortunately for Britain and fortunately for the success of Pitt's policies, none of those who ruled France in the middle of the eighteenth century was ready to do so; and the opportunity which France let slip was seized by the British. It was sixteen years since London audiences had heard the song in James Thomson's masque *Alfred* which ended with the refrain: 'Rule Britannia, rule the waves.' Now Pitt was going to do his best to see that Britannia obeyed the exhortation.

British privateers had already been doing so for some years past. By the end of 1755 more than 300 French ships had been taken as prizes, the value of their cargoes running into millions of pounds, and about 6,000 French seamen were imprisoned in England. In spite of all the economies which had been practised since 1748, the British navy still possessed twice as many ships of the line as the French and our merchant fleets were correspondingly powerful. When war was formally declared in May 1756 merchants and shipowners at first took fright and overseas trade fell off, but it soon recovered again and began to expand at an unprecedented rate. In 1755, the last year of peace, British exports were valued at £11,065,000. By 1761, the year of Pitt's resignation, they stood at £14,873,000. The British navy controlled the high seas so effectively that few French merchants dared to send cargoes to sea and French shipowners had to turn to privateering for a living. Thus even the losses suffered by the British —over 800 ships were taken by French privateers in 1761—bore witness to the supremacy of British trade. By the time the Seven Years War ended in 1763 the Spaniards had shared the fate of the French and the vast majority of merchant ships at sea were British. Pitt had certainly earned the epitaph which Johnson later bestowed on him: 'The first statesman by whom Commerce was united with, and made to flourish by, War.'

Both Britain's allies and her enemies were well aware of the vital importance of her sea power. In the summer of 1757, before Pitt returned to office, Frederick of Prussia taunted the British ambassador with our failure to use our supremacy at sea properly; later, when Pitt used it to better effect, Frederick was quick to recognize his success. He saw that the blockade of French ports, the hit-and-run attacks which the navy made on the French coast and even the campaigns against the French in America and India and Africa all played their part in weakening the French offensive against Prussia. The French for their part sought desperately for a means of breaking the stranglehold of the British navy on their communications and their trade. The capture of Minorca, striking though it was, did not succeed in shaking Britain's control of the Mediterranean or her ability to keep the Toulon fleet bottled up in harbour. By the end of 1758 French naval forces were on the defensive all over the world, making only brief appearances when it was strictly necessary to support land forces and avoiding engagement wherever possible. The Duc de Choiseul, who took over the direction of the French war effort in November 1758, decided that there was only one way to break out of this situation. A full-scale invasion of Britain must be launched.

The invasion plan, timed for the summer of 1759, was more ambitious than anything that had been conceived by Britain's enemies since the days of the great Spanish Armada of 1588. From Dunkirk right round to the most southerly ports of Brittany thousands of workmen were employed building special flat-bottomed invasion boats, designed to carry 300 men each. Now that France was in alliance with Austria she could use the ports of the Austrian Netherlands as well as those along her own coast; and even the Dutch might be tempted to break their neutrality and give their support to the invasion. The British navy had shown little respect for the rights of neutral countries, who had had their trade interrupted, their cargoes searched and their ships seized. Pitt himself feared that at any moment the Dutch and the Danish fleets might appear in the Channel to help cover the invasion. Choiseul intended to land 50,000 men in England, as well as separate forces in Scotland and Ireland—and this at a time when the greater part of the British army was fighting overseas, either in America or in Germany. Pitt boasted that there were 40,000 men in arms in England to repel the invader, but many of these were inexperienced militiamen, recruited with difficulty under the Militia Act of 1757. If the French could once land a sizable force in Britain they might well be able to force the British government to come to terms.

But in order to land a sizable force in Britain the French had first to concentrate in the Channel a fleet large enough to give proper cover to such a force. Choiseul saw, quite rightly, that, for a country with fewer ships than the enemy, to disperse those ships all over the world was a foolish policy. If France was to make the best use of what ships she had she must bring them all together at one place in order to deal Britain a decisive blow. The English Channel was the obvious place for the decisive blow, but the concentration of French naval strength there was no easy matter. All through the summer of 1759 the invasion hung fire because the Toulon fleet was kept in harbour by an augmented British Mediterranean fleet under Admiral Boscawen. When he put into Gibraltar to refit, the French managed to slip through the Straits of Gibraltar into the Atlantic but he gave chase and dispersed them. Some of the French ships took refuge in Cadiz and the rest were pursued into Lagos and either captured or burnt, in spite of the fact that Portgual was neutral.

With the dispersal of the Toulon fleet and the successful bombard-ment, early in July, of the invasion flotilla in Le Havre, Brest became the centre of the invasion project. The Western Squadron, which had been made a permanent feature of British naval strategy by Anson,[1] ranged between the Isles of Scilly off Cornwall and the Isle of Ushant off Brittany, preventing enemy ships from getting out of Brest or into the Channel. Early in November a ferocious westerly gale forced Admiral Sir Edward Hawke, who commanded the Western Squadron, to run for shelter in Torbay, leaving only a few frigates to keep watch off Ushant. Conflans, the French admiral in command of the Brest fleet, realized that Hawke had left his station when a small French squadron from the West Indies was able to make its way into Brest and join him. He immediately made good his escape from Brest and sailed south, to chase off the British squadron which was blockading the ports of southern Brittany. Having done this, he intended to pick up the invasion transports which were lying in Quiberon Bay. On 16 November, as he sailed back to his station off Ushant, Hawke learnt of the whereabouts of the French fleet and gave chase. He came up with them on 20 November, with a westerly gale driving both fleets on to the jagged rocks of the south Breton coast, one of the most dangerous in the whole of Europe. In spite of the appalling risks involved, he followed the French through the rocks and shoals into Quiberon Bay itself and attacked them mercilessly. Five French ships were destroyed and

[1] Anson deserves to be remembered not just as a man who sailed round the world but as one of the greatest naval administrators of his time. During his period as First Lord of the Admiralty, from 1751 to 1756 and from 1757 to 1762, he improved the design and build of ships, introduced a proper system of classifying them, introduced uniforms, made tactics more effective and even began a system of retirement pensions.

four more broke their backs on the mud of the river Vilaine, where they took refuge. The rest escaped southwards to Rochefort, where they remained for the rest of the war. The Brest fleet had been effectively shattered in one of the most dramatic naval actions of the eighteenth century, a battle which contrasted vividly with the indecisive and cautious 'line' engagements of the textbook commanders.

The battle of Quiberon Bay ended the invasion threat once and for all, and it also ended any hopes the French might have had of challenging Britain's control of the seas. All over the world French colonies and trading stations were denied the reinforcements and the naval support which their British rivals obtained with relative ease. All the French stations on the West African coast, which supplied slaves to their sugar islands in the Caribbean, had already been captured in 1758; and in 1759 the sugar islands themselves began to fall to the British. Guadeloupe was taken in 1759, followed by Dominica in 1761 and Martinique, Grenada and St Lucia in 1762. When Spain joined in the war early in 1762 her colonies shared the fate of the French: both Cuba in the West Indies and Manila in the East Indies were captured by the British.

In India something greater than the piecemeal conquest of trading stations was at stake. Dupleix, governor of the French station at Pondicherry in the 1740s, had seen that by allying with the Indian princes he might establish French supremacy over the whole Indian continent and drive out the British altogether. Between 1749 and 1751 he set up puppet governments in the Carnatic, in the Deccan and in Hyderabad; but the French East India Company, like its counterpart in London, was concerned with trading rather than conquest. After the French-supported Prince of the Carnatic had been defeated in 1751-52 by a rival candidate supported by the British, the French East India Company repudiated Dupleix's schemes and brought Dupleix himself back to France in disgrace. Nevertheless, his achievements had been impressive and his fellow governors were tempted to copy his methods, especially since another major war with the British was obviously on the way. In Chandernagore, the French station in Bengal, the French intrigued with the young nawab, Suraj-ud-Daulah, and urged him to attack the British station at Calcutta. He did so in June 1756 and captured it, imprisoning the 146 captives whom he took in a small room eighteen feet by fourteen. They were kept there for a whole night and very few of them survived the ordeal. When the news of this atrocious 'Black Hole of Calcutta' arrived in Britain many months later, there was a furious demand for vengeance against the French and their Indian allies. It fact, vengeance had already been taken. Robert Clive, a clerk in the East India Company's service who had taken a commission in one of the Company's regiments and had distinguished himself in the campaigns in the Carnatic in 1751–52, led an expedition which recaptured Calcutta in January 1757 and took Chandernagore two months later. While the French had no assistance at all from the sea, Clive had been transported from Madras by a squadron under Rear-Admiral Charles Watson and this force continued to give him naval support right up to the battle of Plassey in June 1757, at which he defeated Suraj-ud-Daulah.

After his victory at Plassey Clive established his own puppet ruler, Mir Jafar, in Bengal. Whatever the Company's directors and share-holders in Britain might feel, he saw that it was necessary to play the French at their own game. Events were steadily pushing the East India Company into ruling India, rather than merely trading along its coasts. What happened in Bengal also happened farther south in the Carnatic. As long as both sides had effective fleets cruising in Indian waters, nothing very decisive happened on land; but when the French fleet sailed off in October 1759, leaving India to its fate, the French garrisons in the Carnatic found themselves in a desperate position. During the year 1760 Colonel Eyre Coote cleared the French out of the province altogether and by January 1761, when he received the surrender of the French station of Pondicherry, French influence in India was at an end. The East India Company had hoped for great things from Pitt's Patriot War—more trade, higher dividends, more security, less foreign competition. It had obtained all these, but it had also acquired something for which it had not bargained. It had won an empire; and now it must learn to rule it.

The acquisition of an empire, and the problems it brought with it, were on an even grander scale in North America. Pitt's ideas on America had developed considerably since his early speeches on colonial policy in the 1730s. Then he had been chiefly concerned with defending the West India sugar planters against the Spaniards, but now he was more worried by the threat which the French presented to the colonists on the mainland of North America. With the mouths of the St Lawrence and Mississippi rivers firmly in their hands, the

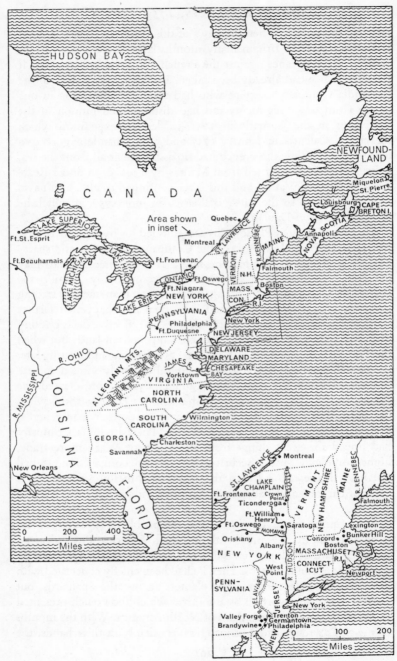

North America

French were in a position to hem in the thirteen seaboard colonies both from the north and from the south. What was worse, they were pushing steadily up both rivers into the hinterland of the North American continent. From their base of Quebec, established on the St Lawrence river as long ago as 1608, they had moved more than a thousand miles to the west and were now building strongpoints on Lake Superior. Their fortress of St Esprit, at the western end of that lake, was less than a hundred miles from the head waters of the Mississippi; and all down the length of that river, for a thousand miles from Fort Beauharnais in the north to New Orleans at the mouth, they had yet more forts. During the 1750s the threat had come even closer, as the French and their Indian allies laid claim to the river Ohio and the lands along its bank. The Ohio rose only a few miles south of Lake Erie and ran along the western side of the Alleghany Mountains to join the Mississippi. From their fortress at Fort Duquesne, built a little way down the river Ohio just at the point where the Alleghanies were at their narrowest, the French could pour across the mountains and sweep the colonists of Maryland and Virginia into the sea.

During the years after the Peace of Aix-la-Chapelle, the King and his ministers in London were reluctant to involve themselves again in war with France; and the colonists therefore had to rely largely on their own efforts. They formed companies—the Ohio Company of 1748 and the Loyal Company of 1749—to establish counter claims to those of the French and in 1754 they even sent a force against Fort Duquesne. This expedition, commanded by a young officer of the Virginia militia called George Washington, was ignominiously defeated and the home government found itself forced into action. Not only Pitt and his Patriots but even the Duke of Cumberland, commonly regarded as the champion of Hanoverianism rather than colonialism, pressed for a proper expedition to be sent to America. Accordingly, a force was sent out early in 1755 under General Braddock; but it failed to take Fort Duquesne and in the following year, after war had formally been declared, the French in Canada captured Fort Oswego on the southern shores of Lake Ontario. This meant that they were now in a position to advance down the Mohawk river into the New England colonies.

Pitt's return to office came too late to have much effect on the campaigns of 1757 in America. In August of that year a British expedition sent to take Louisbourg, the French strongpoint guarding the approaches to the St Lawrence, gave up the attempt because it did not have sufficient naval support, and a few weeks later the French captured Fort William Henry. Like Fort Oswego, Fort William Henry opened up a possible way into New England from Canada.

In 1758, however, Pitt put into execution a coordinated plan for an attack on French Canada. While a large British army under General Abercromby advanced up the Hudson river in order to attack 'either Montreal or Quebec, or both of the said places successively', another was to be landed at Louisbourg. The Louisbourg expedition, which consisted of twenty-three ships of the line under Admiral Boscawen and 12,000 troops commanded by General Amherst, was completely successful: the town fell on 26 July 1758 and the five French warships in the harbour were destroyed. But Ambercromby frittered away his opportunities and failed to take the French fort of Ticonderoga, the first outpost on the long road to Montreal. Although an advance column of colonial troops succeeded in capturing Fort Frontenac, at the eastern end of Lake Ontario, the essential part of the plan, the meeting of the two arms of the attack on the St Lawrence itself, had failed to materialize. Abercomby was recalled and replaced by Amherst, who in 1759 took Ticonderoga and advanced along Lake Champlain towards Montreal. Meanwhile a vast fleet of twenty-two ships of the line, 200 troop transports and many frigates and sloops, left Louisbourg on 4 June 1759 and made its way up the St Lawrence to Quebec, which it reached on 26 June. The admiral in charge of this astonishing feat of navigation was Sir Charles Saunders and the general in command of the troops was James Wolfe, a strange and neurotic young man of thirty-two whom Pitt had insisted on appointing over the heads of his fellow officers.

Quebec was built on the tip of a rocky peninsula which jutted out into the St Lawrence, with cliffs falling almost sheer for three hundred feet beneath it. All through July and August Wolfe tried unsuccessfully to find an effective means of attacking it and by the beginning of September the French Governor-General was convinced that the British plan had failed. But during the night of 12–13 September 1759 Wolfe led his men up the steep wooded cliffs to the west of the city. Shortly after nine o'clock in the morning he attacked the French army outside the walls of Quebec and routed it. He was wounded in the fight, first in the wrist, then in the stomach and finally in the lung; and he died on the battlefield, thanking God that he had conquered and could die in peace. By the end of the month Quebec had surrendered and an attempt to retake it in the following year failed because the British fleet still commanded the St Lawrence river. Montreal capitulated on 8 September 1760 and the French domination of Canada was at an end. Pitt had given the American colonists the security that they were seeking and he had won vast new territories for the British crown. He had turned the dream of a Patriot War into a triumphant reality.

Outwardly Pitt's association with the colonists was the most successful of the alliances made by this strange and lonely figure. He and Fox had had nothing in common but the desire to outwit Newcastle and to outwit one another, while with Newcastle he had made only a marriage of convenience which was already wearing very thin. He had a very real respect for Frederick of Prussia and Frederick had a very real respect for him; but each of them knew that the other was totally dedicated to his own schemes and would end the alliance as soon as it suited him to do so. Only with the colonists could he feel a genuine and lasting sympathy. His vivid and searching imagination, always hovering on the edge of self-dramatization and unreality, was fired by the thought of these sturdy pioneers working at the limits of the known world. He wanted to give them security and liberty and new opportunities for making money; but he did not want to give them independence. He worked for the advancement of Britain's trade, for the whole complex of merchants and planters and settlers which was the old colonial system, but in working for it he created a new and vaster British Empire which brought with it new and vaster problems. He never really understood these problems and he could never sympathize with the colonists' attitude to them. For this reason his relationship with the colonists was to be shot through with an increasing uneasiness, until at the end of his life he was to reproach them bitterly and demand that they should never be granted their independence.

It was not entirely Pitt's fault that all his alliances were uneasy, that he could never find a body of men with whom he could work consistently. Plenty of men more practical and less complex than Pitt were equally at sea in the political confusion which had followed Pelham's death; and most of them felt that they would continue at sea until the accession of the new King. Then there would be a clean sweep and politics would be given a new definition, a new clarity. Early in the morning of 25 October 1760 George II felt a sharp pain in the heart and within a few minutes he was dead. The new reign, of which so many hoped so much, had begun.

10

The Search For a New Formula
1760–1770

1 The Patriot King and the Patriot Minister

Nobody expected Newcastle and Pitt to survive George III's accession in the way that Walpole had managed to survive that of George II. This time there would be no miracle: the natural laws of politics would assert themselves and there would be an exit of the 'Ins' and an entry of the 'Outs'. Those who had made the short-term investment of supporting the old King had had their day and now it was the turn of the men who had pinned their hopes on the future. The whole pattern of eighteenth-century politics implied the accession to power of the Reversionary Interest now that the crown had in fact reverted to the Prince they served.

The very fact that the young King was concerned with more than just the triumph of the Reversionary Interest seemed to make that triumph all the more probable. George II in 1727 had simply wished that those who had served him as Prince should continue to do so now that he was King, but George III in 1760 wished to bring about a 'reformation in government'. All the old Leicester House cries—the need to purify politics, to purge corruption, to free the crown from the grasp of the great Whig magnates, to end the German war—were, for him, much more than mere political slogans. The hard-headed politicians who had grouped themselves around Prince Frederick and Lord Egmont in the 1740s had certainly not been taken in by Bolingbroke's pseudo-philosophical rendering of their catch-phrases, but things had changed since Frederick's death. When his widow turned from Egmont to Bute the whole atmosphere of Leicester House became more idealistic, more moralizing. The young Prince was kept from the company of his contemporaries among the aristocracy, who were held up to him as terrible examples of vice and depravity. Whether or not he had read *The Idea of a Patriot*

King[1] he would certainly have echoed its condemnation of kings who were surrounded by 'the pandars, parasites and buffoons of a voluptuous court'. His own Court would be very different. The men who surrounded him would be chosen for their purity, their honesty and their readiness to accept Bolingbroke's maxim that 'the good of the people is the ultimate and true end of government'. He would indeed be a Patriot King and his reign would see not just the triumph of Leicester House but the triumph of good over evil.

If he was to be a Patriot King he would need a Patriot Minister, a man who would be prepared to work with him to break the Whig cliques, to end the sacrificing of British interests on the altar of Hanover, to govern in the interests of the whole country rather than in that of the party magnates. The obvious man for the job was Pitt himself, the greatest of the Patriots, the man who had shown that he was ready to take his stand on public confidence rather than on private connection. He had come into power in 1757 as a Leicester House man and if he had succeeded in retaining the confidence of Prince George between then and 1760 the only thing that would have been necessary at the beginning of the new reign would have been the dismissal of Newcastle and the old Whigs. Then Patriot King and Patriot Minister could have gone forward hand in hand to cleanse and purify British political life. But, unfortunately, the interval between Pitt's coming into office and the beginning of the new reign had been longer than anyone had expected—long enough for George II's minister to become objectionable in the eyes of the future George III. George II had lived too long. If he had died in 1757 or early in 1758 there might have been a chance of Pitt's ministry continuing smoothly into the new reign; but as it was, Pitt had ruined his chances by putting his responsibilities as a minister before his obligations to Leicester House. When, in December 1758, he renewed the subsidy treaty with Prussia without consulting Leicester House, the Prince told Bute that they had been treated like a 'parcel of children', and that Pitt seemed to forget that 'the day will come when he must expect to be treated according to his deserts'. In 1759 relations grew even worse, after Pitt had failed to coax George II into letting his grandson join the army and had refused to shield Lord George

[1] It is doubtful whether the old Whig charge that George III was brought up on *The Idea of a Patriot King* will ever be conclusively disproved. What is certain is that the charge was never worth making: the book is in no sense an attack on the idea of limited monarchy.

Sackville after the battle of Minden. By August 1759 Bute himself told Pitt: 'I will not be responsible for the consequences of this treatment.' Pitt had committed the unforgivable sin, in the eyes of George III, of daring to be a Patriot in the service of George II.

George III himself did not regard the breach with Pitt as particularly important. He hoped to manage perfectly well without Pitt and his party, for the simple reason that a Patriot King did not need a party at all. All he had to do was to make clear his pure and lofty intentions and all men of good will would rally round him, forgetting their party connections. Accordingly, he started his reign by lecturing the Privy Council on the evils of 'this bloody and expensive war', announcing that he 'gloried in the name of Briton' and issuing a Proclamation 'for the encouragement of Piety and Virtue and for the prevention and punishing Vice, Profaneness and Immorality'. At the same time he let it be known that he was determined to put an end to corruption and would not allow Treasury money to be spent on the forthcoming elections. These gestures, he felt, would be sufficient to draw to him such an overwhelming measure of popular support that all the professional politicians, whatever their colour, would be left high and dry.

Bute, who was closer to political realities, was less optimistic. He saw that any king, however lofty his aims, needed ministers who could manage Parliament and that he himself, since he did not sit in either House,[1] could not perform this function. If George was going to do without either Pitt or Newcastle, if he was determined to reject both the man of prominence and the man of patronage, then he must build up a party of his own. This was a perfectly constitutional thing for a King to do and it should not prove unduly difficult; but it would take time and so, for the time being, the King must put up with the existing ministers. George wanted Bute to take over the ministry forthwith, but at first he agreed only to being made a Privy Councillor and Groom of the Stole. It was not a very satisfactory arrangement, because everyone knew that his influence in the Closet was out of all proportion to the importance of his office. Finally, in March 1761, he agreed to come into the ministry officially as Secretary of State for the North.

Even when he came into the ministry, Bute was by no means ready to satisfy George III's desire to end the 'bloody and expensive

1 Bute was a Scottish peer and did not sit in the House of Lords.

war'. He insisted on the need to cooperate with Pitt and win the war rather than abandon it. Pitt himself was beginning to be less confident: 'I am little equal to a situation of things, where difficulties are daily growing,' he wrote on 22 October 1760, 'and clouds gathering in the midst of prosperity and glory.' In March 1761 he told Bute that he was ready to give up the war on the Continent if that was the King's wish. With the approval of Frederick of Prussia, Franco-British peace talks were started, but they reached deadlock over the question of French fishing rights off Newfoundland. An increasingly powerful group within the ministry, led by the Duke of Bedford, felt that this point should be conceded. Early in July Bedford told Bute that Pitt's idea of depriving France of any kind of sea power was 'against nature and can tend to do no good to this country'. Bute, however, continued to support Pitt and the ultimatum sent to France at the end of July insisted on the exclusion of the French from the fishing grounds. In August the pacifists won their point: Pitt was out-voted and the Cabinet agreed to concede the fishing rights and also to give the French the island of St Pierre as a base for their fishing-boats.

It was too late. In France, Choiseul had given up all hope of a reasonable peace and had turned instead to the idea of a Spanish alliance. In September Pitt produced in Cabinet certain secret papers which had been intercepted by his agents and which showed that the Family Compact between France and Spain had been revived. The Cabinet agreed to send an ultimatum to the Court of Madrid, but Pitt insisted that this was not enough: it was essential for us to anticipate the Spaniards and declare war on them before their treasure fleets arrived in Cadiz from the new world. Not only Bedford but also the Newcastle Whigs and even Pitt's own military and naval advisers were against him. Anson declared that 'our ships were not in condition to enter immediately into any material operations against Spain'. But Pitt continued to urge war and in October, after a stormy Cabinet meeting at which he said that he would go on no longer since his advice was not taken, he went to the King and resigned. George was gracious to him—so much so that Pitt, always very susceptible to the aura of monarchy, dissolved into tears—but he made no attempt to dissuade him. The dream of a Patriot King ruling through a Patriot Minister, appealing from the narrow world of Whig politics to a wider basis of popular support, was shattered. It was a dream which, in any case, would have been difficult to translate into reality: both George III and Pitt were very unstable characters and they had little in common except a dislike of the Whig cliques. Nevertheless, its shattering was the turning point of George III's early years and was to turn his 'reformation of government' into a nightmare of ministerial instability and confusion.

As yet, however, George felt nothing but elation at Pitt's fall. Only Bute felt apprehensive, speaking of the 'most dangerous and difficult work' of taking over from him, and worrying especially about the sharp reaction which came from the City of London. Pitt's popularity there fell temporarily when he accepted a pension of £3,000 a year from the King, together with a peerage for his wife, but it soon regained its old level. When he went to the Lord Mayor's banquet he got a tremendous reception while Bute was hissed and pelted. To George the fall of Pitt simply meant that they had cut off one head of the political hydra, the head labelled 'Treachery', and could now go on to attack the one labelled 'Corruption'—the Newcastle Whigs. But Bute saw that the more heads they lopped off, the more they would have to rely on the heads that were left. It is significant that it was Bubb Dodington, one of the seediest of the old Leicester House gang, who wrote delightedly to Bute on the day after Pitt's resignation, congratulating him 'on being delivered of a most impracticable colleague'. He had reason to exult: if the King was not going to rely on Pitt in his crusade against the old Whigs he would have to turn to men like Dodington. By breaking with Pitt, George committed himself to building a party of his own and at the same time left himself with none but the most unsatisfactory materials to build it with.

Not that this 'King's Party' would need much building—indeed, it would almost build itself. There had always been a hard core of politicians who saw themselves as the servants of the King rather than the followers of any particular minister. For the most part they were hard-working and honourable men who deserve to be remembered not as slavish courtiers but as forerunners of the modern civil service. Around this nucleus of King's Servants gathered the King's Friends. All those groups in Parliament that were neither Patriots nor Whigs began to turn to the King and to the men who were known to enjoy his confidence. As always, the patronage of the Crown was the greatest single force in politics and few people felt inclined to challenge the King's right to appoint whomsoever he pleased as his minister. If anything was unconstitutional, it was not the King's right to choose his ministers but the politicians' habit of opposing them. Hardwicke, the most statesmanlike of the Whig lords, thought that organized and deliberate opposition was inadmissible and even Pitt, when he resigned, gave a pledge not to embarrass his successors. The one thing which limited the power of the Crown and gave the idea of permanent opposition some semblance of respectability was the existence of Leicester House. The fact that politicians, and especially young politicians, could oppose the present régime secure in the knowledge that they would obtain office in the future had had the effect of dividing the Crown's patronage against itself and thus neutralizing its effects.

And now there was no longer a Leicester House interest. It was Hardwicke who saw the significance of this fact when he wrote: 'There is now no *reversionary* resource. Instead of an old King and a young successor, a young healthy King and no successor in view.' There was no longer any shelter to which a politician could run if he decided to risk the King's displeasure. George had only been married for a month or so and it would be a very long time before there would be a Prince of Wales old enough to have an establishment of his own. It would be a very young man, and a very patient man, who settled down to wait for office in the next reign. It did not take much to make men King's Friends now that the only alternative was exclusion from office for an apparently indefinite period. On 12 November, the night before Parliament met, Newcastle urged his followers to support the administration; but his exhortations were rather redundant now that the balance between the aristocratic patronage which he represented and the royal favour which Bute represented was swinging steadily in favour of the latter. It was not a question of supporting the King as long as Newcastle advised it, but of following Newcastle as long as the King approved of him.

And it became increasingly apparent that the King did not approve of him at all. Within the administration the real power lay with Bute. Newcastle found that he was being bypassed and ignored and he complained bitterly that Bute dealt directly with the Treasury instead of going through him. This, he said, was 'an indignity never heard of before'. The climax came in May 1762, when Bute and the King cut by half his proposed vote of £2,000,000 for the German and Portuguese campaigns. Newcastle was particularly angered to find that some of the other Lords of the Treasury were against him on this issue and this led him to suspect that there was a cabal of King's Friends working against him within the ministry. These suspicions were subsequently inflated by Burke into the charge that George III introduced a system of 'double Cabinet', whereby an inner ring of courtiers held the real power and ministers were only a façade. But in fact such tensions within an administration were normal and inevitable. Eighteenth-century governments consisted of a series of circles, sometimes concentric and sometimes overlapping, and relations between them were very complex. Boards and committees, formal and informal Cabinets, audiences in the Closet and informal discussions between ministers—all combined to make up a jarring and inefficient machine.

At the end of May, after a month of crisis and recrimination, Newcastle resigned. Unlike Pitt, he refused to give any undertaking not to go into opposition. Within a few months he was making overtures to Pitt to see if they could join together in attacking the ministry; and he tried to encourage a 'campaign of resignations' on the part of his followers. As the Newcastle Whigs went out, George filled up as best he could with the rather undistinguished men he had gathered around him. Dodington did not come in, because he was dying; but his friend Sir Francis Dashwood, a rake and an amateur of black magic, became Chancellor of the Exchequer. For the rest, the new ministry was an unconvincing mixture of old Leicester House men, Hanover Tories (Lord Egremont, one of the Secretaries of State, was a son of the Sir William Wyndham who had led the Tories against Walpole), ex-Patriots who had broken with Pitt, ex-Whigs who had broken with Newcastle, and a few genuinely efficient King's Servants such as James Oswald, one of the Lords of the Treasury who had opposed Newcastle on the army vote. George imagined that in breaking the Whigs he had put an end to the confusion and instability that had bedevilled politics for so long, but he was sadly mistaken. The Whigs had themselves created what stability there was, based on an uneasy combination of royal favour and their own patronage; and the only feasible alternative was a combination of royal favour and public confidence. If George was shocked by the men who were in politics for what they could get out of it, he must turn to those who were in it for what they could put into it. Such men were rare indeed, but until he could find them and work with them his struggle to end corruption and instability would bring him nothing but corrupt and unstable ministries.

2 Towards a new Toryism

Meanwhile, the 'bloody and expensive war' that George had denounced so roundly at his accession still dragged on. Annual expenditure had risen from £7,119,000 in 1755 to £21,112,00 in 1761 and revenue had totally failed to keep pace with it: although the Land Tax had been kept for five years at the exceptionally high rate of four shillings in the pound, the government had only managed to collect £9,594,000 in 1761 as against £6,938,000 in 1755. This meant government borrowing on an unprecedented scale. The National Debt now stood at £114,200,000 and cost nearly £4 million a year in interest charges—twice what the Land Tax produced, even at four shillings. To the country gentlemen this seemed a disastrous and scandalous state of affairs: not only were they required to pay a large part[1] of the cost of a war which was being fought in the interests of colonists, planters, merchants and Hanoverians, but they were also doomed to go on paying for a debt which had been contracted by corrupt Whig politicians in order to line the pockets of their friends among the London financiers. Over a hundred of these country gentlemen sat in the Commons, traditional friends of the Crown and implacably opposed both to the Whig factions and to Pitt's vociferous monied supporters from the City of London. Some of them, it was true, had a lingering nostalgia for the Stuarts; but they were not active Jacobites, and George III was far more likely to command their loyalty than George II had been. If he and Bute could gather such men around them they might yet transform their collection of Leicester House remnants into a new Tory party strong enough to challenge both Newcastle and Pitt. But the first necessity, if they were to secure such support, was to put an end to the war and to the inflated government expenditure it had brought with it.

In fact 1762 had seen an extension of the war. With her treasure ships safely arrived in Cadiz, Spain had refused to give any assurances as to the peaceful intentions of the renewed Family Compact[2] and Britain declared war on her on 4 January 1762. Frederick of Prussia wrote to Bute congratulating him and saying that this would give

---

[1] It was true that the bulk of the revenue came from the customs and excise—the Land Tax, even at 4s, only produced £2 million. But the squires could argue that they paid their share of the customs and excise too.

[2] In fact it bound her to declare war on Britain on 1 May 1762.

opportunities for yet more victories. He was right. By the autumn Spain had lost Cuba and the Philippines, as well as two great treasure fleets valued at some seven million dollars. Her possessions in Panama San Domingo and Florida were threatened, her Caribbean fleet smashed, her invasion of Portugal repulsed. So far from rescuing France from defeat, she shared it and indeed made it worse—Spanish neutrality had protected French privateers operating in the Caribbean and in 1762 these were put out of action and their base, Martinique, was captured together with Grenada, St Lucia, St Vincent and Tobago.

Bute's first reaction to the Family Compact had been to make overtures to Austria to see if he could detach her from her French alliance. It seemed to him that the Franco-Spanish combination threatened such a major upset in the European balance of power that Austria would be frightened into throwing her weight into the other scale, thus returning to her traditional policy. If so, such a move might be used as a basis on which he might build a general settlement of Europe. But Austria stood firm and the only result of his manœuvre was that Frederick got wind of it and began to think that Britain was betraying him. His suspicions were intensified a few weeks later when he found out that Britain was actually asking Russia to keep her armies on his territory so that he could be forced into making peace. Up to this time it would not have needed a request from us to make Russia keep troops on Prussian soil; but on 5 January 1762 Elizabeth of Russia had died and had been succeeded by Peter III, a fervent admirer of Frederick who was busy reversing Russian policy and seemed about to enter Germany with a Russian army in support of Prussia against Austria. Furthermore, it was known that Peter had designs on Denmark and Bute suspected that Frederick was encouraging him. In short, the European war, which had seemed to be grinding to a standstill, suddenly took on new and alarming proportions. Just as he was beginning to dream of imposing a general settlement on Europe, Bute found himself faced with horrifying and apparently limitless possibilities of further conflict.

He reacted sharply. On 9 April 1762 he told Frederick that he would not renew his subsidy if it was to be used for the extension or prolongation of the war; and at the end of the month, after Frederick had failed to give the required assurances, the subsidy was stopped. The Newcastle Whigs protested strongly, arguing that we had supported Prussia when she was doing badly and it was absurd to drop her now that she was doing well. Even when they had resigned, Bute's difficulties were by no means over. Frederick tried to stir up Pitt and his friends in the City against the ministry, and even within the Cabinet Grenville demanded the retention of Guadeloupe and better territorial guarantees for Prussia. His attitude hardened at the end of September, when news came of the capture of Cuba, and in October Bute took action against him. He was demoted from Secretary of State to First Lord of the Admiralty and Henry Fox was brought in to take his place as leader of the Commons. Fox was given a seat in the Cabinet but refused to become Secretary, preferring to hang on to his offices of Paymaster, writer of the tallies and clerk of the pells in Ireland.

This list of sinecures spoke for itself. Fox was the very epitome of the corruption that George was trying to root out. The King was horrified at having to employ such a man, but Bute insisted that they must have someone who could beat Newcastle at his own game of 'managing' the House of Commons. For his own part, Fox remarked: 'I don't care how much I am hated if I can say to myself, I did His Majesty such honest and essential service.' It may or may not have been honest, but it was certainly essential. It was not just a question of getting the peace preliminaries through the Commons—indeed, many of Fox's most vigorous measures were taken *after* the vote, not before it—but of convincing men once and for all that it was the King and not Newcastle who could grant or withhold office. Few people in politics could remember a time when Newcastle had not had control of Crown patronage and it was only too easy—especially for Newcastle himself—to mistake the channel for the source. Like Walpole in 1733, Fox devoted some of his energies to removing from the King's service those who had voted against the King's ministers; but much more important was the task of providing leadership and cohesion in the House itself, moving from member to member and making each feel that he was the particular object of the King's attention. Fox himself commanded little respect, but his appeals for loyalty to the King against the factious Whigs won over many of the independent members.

Preliminaries of peace between Britain, France and Spain were signed at Fontainebleau on 3 November 1762. In America France gave up Canada, Cape Breton Island and the Caribbean islands of Grenada, Dominica, St Vincent and Tobago; in Africa she ceded Senegal; in India she received back her factories but had to recognize the supremacy of the British East India Company and the native princes whom it supported; in Europe she restored Minorca and all her conquests in Germany. Spain gave up Florida and got back Cuba. When these terms came before the Commons in December they were bitterly attacked by Pitt. First he argued that what France had *not* given up—the Newfoundland fishing rights and the sugar island of Guadeloupe—was of more significance than what she *had* given up: 'France is chiefly, if not solely, to be dreaded by us in the light of a maritime and commercial power . . . the fishery trained up an innumerable multitude of young seamen; and the West Indies trade employed them when they were trained . . . our conquests in North America are of very little detriment to the commerce of France.' Secondly, he denounced the desertion of Prussia, which would leave us isolated in Europe. He had forgotten, apparently, that he had himself been ready in 1761 to give back Guadeloupe[1] and end the German war. In fact, Frederick of Prussia concluded a satisfactory peace with Austria at Hubertusburg in February 1763, soon after our own treaty with France and Spain was signed in Paris; but Europe as a whole was bitterly resentful of Britain's determination to monopolize all maritime and commercial power. Maritime supremacy could only be achieved at the cost of European hostility—this was one of the reasons why the old Whigs, with their concern for the European 'system', had always been suspicious of Pitt and his Patriot ideas. The country gentlemen, for their part, had no desire to go on footing the bill for his dreams of grandeur: they listened patiently and respectfully to his long, rambling and often inaudible speech, but they nevertheless voted for the preliminaries, which were carried by 319 to 65. The formal Treaty of Paris was signed the following February, with only slight changes in the terms: France agreed to give Louisiana to Spain, thus easing our fears of French control of the Mississippi, and Spain also received back the Philippines, the news of whose capture had arrived after the Preliminaries were signed, in return for a payment of £500,000.

It was a great victory for the King and his ministers, but it was a victory over the Whigs rather than over Pitt. Newcastle stood revealed as an empty vessel, a patron robbed of his patronage; but it

1 Israel Mauduit, in *Considerations on the War* (1760), suggested that Pitt's friends among the West Indian merchants feared competition from the French sugar islands if they fell into British hands and that Pitt was therefore deliberately lukewarm in his attempts on them.

was not so easy to rob Pitt of his prominence. The City of London still worshipped him and in the Commons he could still cast a spell that made men accept him as the voice of the nation itself, even though in their more cynical moments they might suspect that the voice was only that of the commercial interest. When, in November 1763, he exhorted members to forget their party allegiances and rally to the support of the King and of the Peace of Paris, one member of the administration remarked: 'If £50,000 had been given for that speech, it could have been well expended. It secures us a quiet session.' It was an impressive tribute to Pitt's political stature and it underlined the fact that if the King could not work with him, then at least he must outbid him. He must produce a minister who could show that the real voice of the nation was not that of the merchants but that of the squires and who could provide the sort of government that they wanted—unambitious, efficient and above all cheap.

But the ending of the war did not produce an automatic drop in government expenditure, which was still running at well over twice its prewar figure. So far from being able to bring down the level of taxation, the ministers were forced to propose a new tax—an excise of 4s on every hogshead of cider and every bin of wine. Immediately all the old cries that Walpole had met in 1733 were raised again. Bute was already unpopular because of his Scottish origins and his supposed association with the dowager Princess of Wales; and now, it seemed, the foreign favourite was trying to enslave freeborn Englishmen in the foreign tyranny of the hated excise. Caricaturists found a ready sale for their prints showing a tartan-clad Bute and his royal mistress riding jackbooted[1] over English liberties; and in the Commons Pitt painted in horrifying detail the picture of a country swarming with excise inspectors. Whigs and Patriots, country gentlemen and City merchants, all seemed united against the ministry. And yet, when it came to a vote in the Commons, the Cider Bill was carried by a majority of 106 to 55 in a very thin House. Those gentlemen who made up what Hume once called 'the honest and disinterested part of the House' disliked Bute and the excise, but they were reluctant to join in a Whig opposition which they regarded as opportunist and factious. One of their number remarked that they were not going to 'make ladders for tyrant Whigs to mount by'.

Nevertheless, the outcry against Bute had convinced him that he

---

[1] The jackboot had come to be used as a symbol of Bute, in punning reference to his name.

must go. George was very distressed and it seems to have been decided between them that Bute would continue to advise the King in private, even though he no longer served him in public. After several days of negotiations, during which approaches were made both to Pitt and to Newcastle, the ministry was finally reconstructed under George Grenville, who became First Lord of the Treasury with Halifax and Egremont continuing as the two Secretaries of State. When the crisis was over, George wrote to Bute: 'Tho' young I see but too much that there are few very few honest men in this world; as my Dear Friend has quitted Ministry I don't expect to meet with it there again; I shall therefore support those who will act for me and without regret change my tools whenever they act contrary to my service.'

The chief reason for this outburst was the behaviour of the New-castle Whigs. Throughout the crisis they had maintained their unity as a party and had refused to come in at all unless they came in together. George thought that they could not serve him loyally unless they forgot their party allegiances; they thought that they could not serve him efficiently unless they preserved them. This was, in fact, the central question in politics: was 'party'. a factious and unconstitutional attempt to put pressure on the King, or was it the essential means of giving cohesion and stability to a ministry and enabling it to com-mand an effective following in Parliament? George Grenville had no doubt as to his answer. Party was an unconstitutional device and it was his duty to save the King and the country from it. 'I told His Majesty that I came into his service to preserve the constitution of my country,' he said, 'and to prevent any undue and unwarrantable force being put upon the Crown.' Rule by Newcastle meant the oligarchy of the Whigs, rule by Pitt stood for the dominance of the City interest, rule by Bute was based on nothing but royal favour unadulterated and unsupported. Only rule by Grenville could give the country disinterested and efficient government.

Grenville had already identified himself with the demand for government economy by pressing for an inquiry into the way public money had been spent during the war.[1] He was known as the enemy both of the corruption associated with the Whigs and of the grandiose and expensive policies of Pitt; and his enthusiasm for thrift and

---

[1] On the other hand, he risked unpopularity by supporting Bute's cider excise. He ended his speech by asking members to tell him where they could find another source of revenue: 'Tell me where!' Pitt hummed the tune of a popular song called *Gentle Shepherd, tell me where,* and from then on Grenville was dubbed 'The Gentle Shepherd'.

efficiency was backed by a tremendous capacity for hard work. Burke said of him that his ambition was 'to raise himself not by the low pimping politics of a court, but to win his way to power through the laborious gradations of public service', while even Pitt, who had quarrelled violently with him, admitted that he was 'universally able in the whole business of the House . . . certainly one of the very best parliament men in the House'. Here, it seemed, was a minister eminently well qualified to manage both the country and the Commons.

But managing the King was another matter. With his 'Dear Friend' gone George was on his own for the first time, desperately unsure of himself but determined to control his ministers and not be controlled by them. From the beginning he resented Grenville's attempts to gather all patronage into his own hands and when Egremont died in August 1763 he took the opportunity to consult Bute about a possible reconstruction of the ministry. Bute approached Pitt and a few days later Grenville was surprised and horrified to see Pitt's sedan chair[1] parked outside the Palace. But George's negotiations with Pitt broke down and he had to fall back on the Bedford group, one of the most disreputable of all the political cliques. Bedford himself came in as Lord President of the Council and his associates Sandwich and Gower became Secretary of State and Lord Chamberlain of the Household respectively. To Grenville at least the moral of the episode was plain: by failing to give his ministers his full confidence the King had strengthened rather than weakened the forces of faction. As long as men suspected that Bute was the 'minister behind the curtain', the ministry would not have the strength and authority which it needed if it was to rescue the Crown from its dependence on the Whig cliques. Accordingly, Bute gave an undertaking to 'absent himself from the King for a time, till an Administration, firmly established, should leave no room for jealousy against him'. George resigned himself to making the best of a bad job, at any rate for the time being, and Grenville went back to his task of devising economies to please the gentry.

Although some of his economies were short-sighted—his running down of the navy was to have disastrous consequences during the War of American Independence—and others were rather pettifogging, most of them were based on genuine improvements in government efficiency. The collection of customs duties was made

---

[1] It was unmistakable, being specially constructed to enable him to stretch his gouty legs straight out in front of him.

more effective, especially in the colonies where the new duty of threepence a gallon on imported molasses, brought in in 1764, was made to yield far more than the old duty, of sixpence a gallon, had ever done. An attempt was made to limit expenditure on the colonies by prohibiting their further expansion beyond a definite line fixed by a Proclamation of 1763; and when it became clear that they were still costing the Exchequer more than it got from them in taxes, the Stamp Act was introduced. This Act, which imposed a stamp duty on legal documents in the colonies, was welcomed not only by the country gentlemen, anxious for a reduction of the Land Tax, but by most of the other groups in Parliament also; and in March of 1765 it passed through the Commons with an overwhelming majority. Most of the forty-nine members who voted against it were members of the West India sugar interest. It was only later, when the colonists started to use the weapon of boycott, that the monied interests as a whole turned against the Act. For the most part, the Commons was reasonably well satisfied with Grenville. The Wilkes affair[1] had caused him some of his worst moments—in February 1764 in the debate on the legality of General Warrants his majority had fallen to fourteen (232:218) and more of the independent country members had voted against than for him. He insisted on the dismissal of Conway from his colonelcy and his position in the Bedchamber for voting against the government on this issue; and this display of firmness did a lot to win back support.

Grenville's real troubles started when the King had a nervous breakdown in the spring of 1765. He soon recovered, but it was clearly necessary to make provisions for a regency in case the same thing happened again. Having reluctantly accepted his ministers' advice to omit his mother from the Regency Council because of her unpopularity, the King was furious to find that the opposition in the Commons had brought in an amendment to include her name. He had been loyal to his ministers against his better judgment, only to find himself in a false and embarrassing position—and this at a time when the ministry itself was seriously threatened by internal and external tensions. Bedford had persuaded the Lords to throw out a Bill of Grenville's for the protection of the silk industry and there were serious riots in London: a body of angry silk weavers stoned Bedford's coach and laid siege to his house. The King decided that this was an emergency: he ordered troops up to London,

1 See below, p. 282.

set up alarm posts and guards and asked his uncle Cumberland to act as Captain-General if necessary. In spite of protests from the Secretaries of State, who expatiated on the wickedness of those who were advising the King to change his ministers under pressure from a 'lawless mob', he also sent Cumberland down to Hayes, escorted by a troop of cavalry, to negotiate with Pitt. Once again the negotiations failed and he was forced to take back Grenville, who made him promise not to see Bute again.[1] He kept his promise, but he was still determined to get rid of Grenville at all costs. 'I would rather see the Devil in my Closet', he said, 'than Mr Grenville.' At the beginning of July, after another approach to Pitt had failed, he authorized Cumberland to ask Rockingham, a Whig in the Newcastle tradition, to form a government. Rockingham's attitude was moderate and accommodating: he did not demand the reinstatement of those Whigs who had been dismissed from office for voting against the Peace of Paris (although Newcastle pressed him very strongly to do so) and he was prepared to work with Egmont and Northington, both of whom could be considered as 'King's Friends', as well as with the 'men of business' like Elliot and Oswald. But there was no disguising the fact that when the Rockingham group took office on 12–13 July 1765—Rockingham himself as First Lord of the Treasury, Winchelsea as Lord President of the Council, Newcastle as Lord Privy Seal, Grafton and Conway as Secretaries of State, William Dowdeswell as Chancellor of the Exchequer—they did so as a party. But it was not the same party that Newcastle had commanded so confidently in the previous reign. George II had not succeeded in breaking down party distinctions but he—and the events of his reign—had certainly succeeded in changing their nature.

3 John Wilkes and the New Whiggery

There had always been divisions in the Whig party, because Whiggery had always been a nebulous and even self-contradictory idea. But during the period from 1760 to 1794 these divisions became so sharpened and clarified that men began to distinguish between 'New' Whigs and 'Old' Whigs. When Burke wrote his *Appeal from the New to the Old Whigs* in 1791 he was using terms that were already in common use. The essential thing about a New Whig was that he

[1] This view of the Regency Crisis was the one generally accepted at the time this book was written. For a fuller and more recent treatment see my forthcoming article in the *English Historical Review*.

was prepared to seek popular support, while an Old Whig regarded this as a dangerous, irresponsible and ungentlemanly thing to do. Newcastle made his attitude to the New Whigs clear in 1764, when he wrote: 'As to being at the Head of such a Sort of Opposition as I am afraid this must be, his Royal Highness[1] thinks it below Him, and was pleased to say that it was below me also. But he will have no objection to the Young Men going on as they please.' To the 'Young Men' it seemed that Newcastle was simply refusing to face facts. Political success had always been based on three things: royal favour, a following in Parliament and a measure of popular support. Now that circumstances enabled the King to assert his own undivided control of patronage and thus ensure that only those who had his favour had parliamentary followings, what was there left but popular support? If the Court rejected them, then they must remember their historic role as the spokesmen of the Country. Pitt had already shown that the man of prominence could force himself on the men of patronage and now the Whigs must take a leaf out of his book. If they did not want to become a party of little courtiers, they must become a party of Great Commoners.

But even the Great Commoner himself was anxious not to go too far in his search for support 'out of doors'. Although he disliked the narrow and aristocratic nature of the Whig cliques, he did not want to appear as a demagogue stirring up the forces of riot and disorder against his King; and he had been more embarrassed than gratified in November 1761 when the City had cheered him and hissed the King. In June 1762 one of his supporters in the Commons, John Wilkes, decided to start a journal called *The North Briton* in opposition to Bute's paper *The Briton*, edited by Smollett. Even though the paper was largely dedicated to propagating Pitt's views on the peace negotiations, it was Pitt's brother-in-law Earl Temple who provided the financial backing, not Pitt himself. As Wilkes's attacks on the Court became more and more ferocious and impertinent, even Temple became alarmed. In October 1762 he wrote: 'Mr Pitt and I disapprove of this paper war.' But however much they may have disapproved, they did not take any positive action to stop it. And at the end of April 1763 it turned from a paper war into a major political crisis.

In No. 45 of *The North Briton*, published on 23 April 1763, it was declared that the King's Speech, describing the Peace of Paris as

---

[1] This refers to the Duke of Cumberland, to whom Newcastle was trying to attach himself, because he represented the nearest thing there was to a Reversionary Interest.

'honourable to my Crown and beneficial to my people', was a falsehood. Since the paper was published anonymously, it was necessary to proceed by means of a General Warrant for the arrest of 'the authors, printers and publishers'. When it was found, from the printers and publishers, that the author was Wilkes, a Member of Parliament, the ministers consulted the Attorney-General, who gave it as his opinion that this was a case of seditious libel and that Wilkes's privilege as a Member of Parliament therefore did not exempt him from arrest. He was then arrested, but when he was brought before Sir Charles Pratt, the Chief Justice of the Common Pleas and a supporter of Pitt, he was released on the grounds that he *was* covered by privilege of Parliament; and in a further series of legal actions lasting from July to December Pratt ruled that General Warrants were illegal and awarded Wilkes and the others who had been arrested over £4,000 in damages against the government. Having been baulked in the law courts, the government proceeded against Wilkes in Parliament: in November the Commons voted that No. 45 was a false, scandalous and seditious libel, ordered it to be burnt by the common hangman and resolved that parliamentary privilege did not cover the case. Wilkes was further discredited by the production in the Lords of an obscene and blasphemous poem, allegedly by him, called *An Essay on Woman*[1] and in due course he was indicted before the Court of King's Bench for seditious libel and obscenity. He failed to appear to answer the charge, having fled to Paris, and in November 1764 he was pronounced an outlaw. In the meantime the government had confirmed its victory in the Commons: the House voted in January 1764 to expel Wilkes and in February to declare the legality of General Warrants, in defiance of Pratt's decision.

From the beginning the Wilkes affair had divided and embarrassed the Whigs. Temple, who at first supported him and was deprived of his lord-lieutenancy of Buckingham as a result, later became more cautious and tried to stop him reprinting *The North Briton* articles. At his first trial Wilkes claimed that he stood for the liberties not only of gentlemen but also of 'the middling and inferior sort of people, who stand most in need of protection', and such people gave him

---

[1] It was brought before the Lords by Sandwich, who had been an associate of Wilkes in Sir Francis Dashwood's Hell Fire Club at Medmenham. The spectacle of one rake solemnly accusing another of obscenity caused much amusement and Sandwich was henceforth known as 'Jemmy Twitcher', in reference to the character in *The Beggar's Opera* who betrays his fellow thieves.

increasingly vociferous and even violent support: on 3 December 1763, at the ceremonial burning of No. 45, a large crowd pelted the sheriffs, rescued the journal from the fire and burnt in its place a jackboot, symbol of Bute and the tyranny of the Court. Even the most enthusiastic New Whig could see that it would do him no good to be associated with this kind of mob violence. Not only the country gentlemen in the Commons but also men of substance throughout the realm still had a healthy fear of the 'many-headed multitude'. But they might well be induced to vote against the ministry if emphasis could be put on the issues at stake in the case rather than on Wilkes himself. It was Pitt who led the way here: he described Wilkes as 'the blasphemer of his God and the libeller of his King', said he was not fit to be numbered among the human species, dismissed his writings as 'illiberal, unmanly and destestable' —but insisted that the liberties of all Englishmen would be in jeopardy if the government's hounding of him was successful. On the first issue—whether privilege of Parliament extended to seditious libel— he did not get much support. The Attorney-General who had advised Grenville on this point was Charles Yorke, a son of Lord Hardwicke and also a personal rival of Pratt. It was hardly to be expected, therefore, that the Old Whigs would join forces with Pitt on this issue and the independent members, though sensitive about their privileges, did not want to appear to condone sedition and libel. But when it came to the legality of General Warrants, things were different. Charles Yorke said he had not been consulted on this point, the Whigs closed their ranks, the squires thought they heard echoes of seventeenth-century arbitrary government. As a result, the government only scraped home by a majority of fourteen in the final division. The Whigs and the Patriots had succeeded in producing a united opposition based not on patronage but on principle.

It was an impressive achievement, but it did not represent the triumph of the New Whigs over the Old. Although the latter had their ranks thinned in 1764 by the deaths of Hardwicke, Legge and Devonshire, their concern with the politics of patronage still dominated the party. Newcastle was far less interested in the question of General Warrants than he was in getting the new Earl of Hardwicke elected to his father's office of High Steward of Cambridge University. Rockingham himself was an ambiguous figure: he had been connected with the group of New Whigs who had been meeting at Wildman's Tavern in Albemarle Street and had taken one of their number, Edmund Burke, as his private secretary; on the other hand he came from an Old Whig family which owned great estates in Yorkshire and Ireland and wielded very considerable territorial influence. When he came into power in July 1765 he brought with him a party which was changing, but few of its members were fully convinced of the need for change and fewer still were sure what direction it should take. And the problems that awaited them were more likely to increase their uncertainty than reduce it.

The most serious of these was the problem of the American trade. It was clear, even after only two years, that Grenville's policy of imposing efficient government on the colonies might well have disastrous consequences for the merchants who traded with them. Already his tightening up of customs regulations had led to severe losses—British exports to Jamaica alone fell by £168,000 between 1763 and 1765—and it now looked as though the Stamp Act would have even more unfortunate results. In August the colonists began rioting against it and in October they started to make non-importation agreements and boycott trade with the home country. Merchants in London and the other ports became seriously worried; most of them were owed large sums of money by their clients in the colonies and they were faced with the prospect of bad debts as well as loss of trade. William Reeve, a merchant of Bristol, who had been used to doing business to the value of £100,000 a year with the colonies, reported that the trade was now totally stagnated. In Bristol, Manchester and Liverpool there were riots, and in London a group of merchants set about organizing a national campaign against the Act. They were determined that the American trade, worth millions of pounds a year, should not be put in jeopardy for the sake of a few hundred thousand pounds of revenue.

But to the country gentlemen, worried as usual about the Land Tax, the few hundred thousand pounds of revenue were vitally important. They supported the demands of Grenville and the Bedfords for strict enforcement of the Act, by force if necessary. Rockingham was thus in a desperately difficult position. It was all very well for the New Whigs to talk about appealing beyond patronage politics to a wider public, but to which wider public should they appeal? To the merchants or to the squires? They were in fact already committed to the merchants: the campaign for repeal, which resulted in dozens of petitions pouring into Parliament from all over the country, was being organized by Barlow Trecothick, one of Rockingham's supporters in the City, and Rockingham himself helped to draw up the circular letter which Trecothick's committee sent to merchants in the outports. But ministers dared not admit publicly that they were doing this, for fear of alienating not only the independent country members but all those in Parliament who distrusted clamour 'out of doors'. The techniques of the New Whiggery might be used in office as well as in opposition, but only with the greatest discretion and in the deepest secrecy.

On 21 December 1765 Shelburne wrote to Pitt: ''Tis you Sir alone in everybody's opinion, can put an end to this anarchy, if anything can.' He was not exaggerating. Everyone from the King down was looking to Pitt for a lead. George was deeply conscious of the gravity of the situation, but was undecided as to what should be done. He authorized an approach to Pitt, but Pitt would neither advise the ministry nor join it. However, when Parliament reassembled in January 1766 he did give a lead—he came out vigorously for the repeal of the Stamp Act. 'I rejoice that America has resisted', he said. 'Three millions of people so dead to all the feelings of liberty, as voluntarily to submit to be slaves, would have been fit instruments to make slaves of the rest.' It was a powerful argument: as in the case of General Warrants he had managed to show that the question concerned the fundamental liberties of Englishmen and had thus sounded the only note that might make the squires forget their concern over the land tax. Rockingham was impressed by 'the amazing power and influence which Mr Pitt has', and told the King that he must be persuaded to join the ministry. Once again Pitt was approached and once again he refused. Rockingham decided to go ahead without him. Having first put through a series of resolutions asserting Parliament's right to tax the colonies and declaring that the resolutions of the Colonial Assemblies were illegal, the ministers moved to repeal the Act and were victorious by 275 to 167. In March the two measures, the Declaratory Act asserting Parliament's right to tax and the Act for the Repeal of the Stamp Act, were passed through Parliament without any further trouble. Pitt thundered against the Declaratory Act, but he got little or no support. It seemed that Rockingham had managed to please both sides: the merchants had got their trade back and the independents had been reassured by the Declaratory Act.

The ministers went on to reverse most of the other unpopular measures of Bute and Grenville. The right of the cider excisemen to search private houses was abandoned and General Warrants were declared illegal. A new and very successful Revenue Act was brought in which solved the problem of the West Indian trade by reducing the duty on molasses to one penny per gallon and making British molasses as well as foreign pay it. In this way the smuggling trade was killed—because it was no longer profitable—without the economy of the Sugar Islands being upset. The Act raised more revenue in the colonies than any other Act ever passed by Parliament. Thus, while the less reputable aspects of New Whiggery were kept firmly in check (when Wilkes appeared in London in May Rockingham refused to see him and he was forced to return to his exile), its positive achievements were considerable. Rockingham and his friends had managed to appear not as a narrow Whig clique but as a popular party which had saved the country from the dark designs of Bute and Grenville. Even the old Duke of Newcastle was persuaded to ride the wave of popularity and attend a public dinner organized by Trecothick at Drapers' Hall to celebrate the repeal of the Stamp Act.

But the more the Whigs moved away from the narrow basis of patronage politics, the more surely they pushed themselves into the arms of Pitt. Rockingham's desperate attempts to get him into the ministry showed how clearly he recognized this and by the end of February he was even prepared to serve under him—he told Thomas Nuthall that 'he wished to God Mr Pitt would fix up some plan for carrying on administration and putting himself at the head of it'. He wanted Pitt not only as a popular hero but also as an ally against the King's Friends. The death of Cumberland at the end of 1765 had severed one of his few personal links with the King and now, like Grenville before him, he had come to believe in the existence of an inner cabal working against him. Bute himself had agreed not to see the King during the parliamentary sessions, but there were many men in the ministry whom Rockingham regarded as Bute's minions. Northington, the Lord Chancellor, made it clear that he thought it his duty to report to the King on what went on at informal meetings of ministers; and there were many others who showed the same distressing tendency to put loyalty to their King before loyalty to their colleagues. When fifty-two of these men voted against the ministry over the repeal of the Stamp Act and the King refused to dismiss them for doing so, Rockingham's suspicions seemed to be confirmed. George, it seemed, was withholding his confidence from his official ministers and giving it to a group of courtiers. By widening their 'connection' and bringing in Pitt, the Rockinghams would be able to smash this group and force the King to accept a united and harmonious ministry, bound together by friendship and mutual trust,[1] instead of one divided against itself. Pitt would save them—and the country—from the King's Friends.

Pitt, however, saw the situation in a different light. To him, the important thing was to save the King and the country from the Whigs and the evils of party government.

4 The failure of non-party government

Although he felt some distaste both for their persons and for their policies, George had been prepared to support the Rockinghams as long as they seemed able to carry on his government. But by January 1766, when they began to cry so desperately for Pitt, he had come to think that they could not carry on much longer and he therefore thought it his duty to see what alternative arrangements could be made. He turned first to the men of whom Rockingham was so suspicious—the nucleus of professional administrators and 'men of business' around whom every ministry for the last twenty years had been constructed. A group of these men, describing themselves as those 'who have always acted upon the sole principle of attachment to the Crown', met to consider what should be done. They were unanimous in denouncing the party leaders who tried to prevent the King from having 'the free choice of his Servants', but they confessed ruefully that they themselves, although they could provide the administrative capacity, could not provide the 'great names' without which no ministry could survive. For a while the King toyed with the idea of doing without the great names and he even drew up a tentative scheme for a purely 'King's Friend' ministry under Northington. But it soon became obvious that this wouldn't do. When Grafton resigned in May, saying that he wouldn't serve in any ministry that didn't include Pitt, it was pretty clear which great name the King must look to. He approached Pitt once more and asked him to 'give his aid towards destroying all party distinctions, and restoring that subordination to Government, which can alone preserve that inestimable

[1] This was where Rockingham differed from Grenville, who resented the King's Friends because they stood in the way of his own personal ascendancy. Rockingham saw his job in terms of consultation and cooperation rather than control, and Shelburne once described his ministry contemptuously as 'a round-robin administration'.

blessing, Liberty, from degenerating into Licentiousness'. This time the negotiations were successful. By the end of July Rockingham and Newcastle were out of office and Pitt, now created Earl of Chatham, stood at the head of an administration dedicated to the abolition of party distinctions. Patriot King and Patriot Minister had come together at last.

Earlier that year Pitt had declared proudly in the House of Commons: 'I stand up in this place single and unconnected.' This lack of connections, of attachment to any particular group, which others saw as his weakness, he claimed as his great strength. It had set him apart as a kind of Olympian figure, towering over the petty party politicians, and he was convinced that it would continue to serve him in good stead now that he was in power. For this reason he took a peerage and the office of Lord Privy Seal, so that he could survey the whole field of ministerial activity rather than be bogged down in the work of any particular department. He became a lord in order to be an overlord. Unfortunately his elevation to the peerage lost him a good deal of that prominence and popularity on which his special position was based. The Earl of Chatham was never able to catch the public imagination in the way that the Great Commoner had done and, furthermore, he was no longer in the position to dominate the House of Commons. But to his new colleagues he was certainly a commanding and awe-inspiring figure. Charles Townshend, the Chancellor of the Exchequer, by no means a man given to underestimating his own abilities, said that Chatham made them all feel like inferior animals; and Thomas Bradshaw said he issued instructions to other ministers 'like an Adjutant-General to the Regimental Adjutants'. Something of the sort was certainly necessary if any cohesion was to be given to this very disparate collection of ministers. Having insisted on breaking down the party connections and bringing men in as individuals, he was left with an administration which would have to have unity imposed on it.

The obvious way to do this was to embark on a definite policy which should command the support of all his colleagues, so that they might be united in pursuit of a common aim. The politics of patronage must be replaced by the politics of programmes. 'Measures, not men' was to be the rallying cry. Ministers must not think of themselves as followers of Rockingham or Grenville or Bedford or even of Chatham: they must think of themselves as supporters of this or that measure. As to what the measures should be, this was clear: they should be such as would win for Great Britain the glory, security and commercial supremacy for which she had fought in the Seven Years War and which had been frittered away by Bute and Grenville and Rockingham. He was convinced that Choiseul in France was planning a war of revenge[1] and his first aim was to secure a Triple Alliance of Great Britain, Russia and Prussia to guard against such a possibility. His first Cabinet Council was devoted to drawing up plans for this and envoys were sent off to St Petersburg and Berlin forthwith. The following day the Cabinet discussed the continuing troubles in the American colonies, where there was resistance to the billeting of troops. Chatham was convinced that American discontent would die out of its own accord once the colonists learnt that he was at the head of affairs, and it was decided to continue existing policies and to enforce them firmly. On the other side of the world, in India, the problem of how best to reap the rewards of victory was a rather more difficult one. As early as January 1759 Pitt had been told by Clive that the new territorial authority acquired in Bengal 'may possibly be an object too extensive for a mercantile company', and now, in 1766, he learnt that revenues of over two million pounds a year were expected. There seemed to be a case for state intervention—after all, the East India Company had been given a charter to trade with India, not to rule it. At a Cabinet meeting at the end of August it was decided to bring in a motion in the coming parliamentary session for a committee to inquire into the affairs of the Company. It seemed that the Patriot Minister was going to make a serious effort, both in Europe and overseas, to deal with the complex heritage of the Patriot War.

Within six months this Patriot programme had collapsed in confusion and Chatham's ministry was left without any cohesion, either of men or of measures. The attempts at alliance with Prussia and Russia were rebuffed; Beckford found his frontal attack on the East India Company in Parliament sabotaged by negotiations which both Townshend and Shelburne undertook separately with the Directors of the Company; and Shelburne's plans for the conciliation of America were undermined by Townshend's duties of March 1767.[2] After all their high hopes, ministers were left with nothing but

---

[1] He was right. Choiseul sent a group of officers to England in order to survey the ground for a future invasion; and between 1767 and 1773 they produced a series of very detailed reports and maps.

[2] See below, p. 302.

increased discontent in America (in July 1767 they had to take the drastic step of suspending the Assembly of New York colony) and a compromise settlement with the East India Company whereby the Company agreed to pay the Crown £400,000 a year. To Chatham's old friends in the City it seemed that he was allowing men like Townshend to turn his administration from a Patriot Ministry into a Tory one. For their part, the Rockinghams made still graver charges. The bad harvest of 1766 had caused an acute corn shortage and serious riots—in October, Shelburne reported that Oxfordshire and Leicestershire were 'in a most disorderly state'—but when Chatham prohibited grain export by an Order in Council they accused him of reviving prerogative government. When he dismissed one of their friends, Lord Edgcumbe, from his post as Treasurer of the Household, they countered with a campaign of resignations and then, when he still refused to come to terms with them and filled up the vacant places with men like Charles Jenkinson and Lord Le Despencer[1] they denounced him as a King's Friend and a traitor to the popular cause. Newcastle said that 'my Lord Chatham had thrown off the mask and publicly owns and courts my Lord Bute's friendship and support'. Chatham remained unperturbed. 'Faction', he said, 'will not shake the closet or gain the public.' He could rely on George III to see that it did not shake the Closet, but unless he himself recaptured some of his old fire it might well gain the public.

The likelihood of the old fire being recaptured steadily dwindled. At the beginning of 1767 he was in Bath with a severe attack of gout and when he tried to travel to London he only got as far as Marlborough. There he shut himself up in his room at the Castle Inn and insisted on all the potboys and ostlers of the inner being dressed in his livery of blue and silver. Frantic letters arrived from his quarrelling colleagues in London and Grafton, the First Lord of the Treasury, wrote that 'without you we shall see great confusion'; but still he was unable either to come to town or to give a lead on the vital questions of the hour. As to the crucial issue of the East India Company, he merely said that 'his fixed purpose has always been and is not to be a proposer of plans but, as far as a seat in one House enables, an unbiased judge of them'. This was hardly the language of a leader, or of

[1] Charles Jenkinson, who had been secretary to the Treasury under Grenville, was regarded by Horace Walpole as Bute's successor in the leadership of the 'Court' party. Lord Le Despencer had been Sir Francis Dashwood before succeeding to the title.

the man who talked about 'measures, not men'. He finally got to London at the beginning of March, only to be prostrated again. For a long time he would see nobody, and when the King finally prevailed upon him to grant Grafton an interview the latter was appalled at Chatham's condition. There could be no disguising the fact that the Patriot Minister was now in a state of melancholia and nervous collapse which bordered on madness. Grafton and the King tried to keep things going, although by now they had come to regard Charles Townshend as openly disloyal and Shelburne as secretly so. Townshend died in September 1767 and Shelburne, whose duties as Secretary of State for the South had included responsibility for the colonies, was shorn of this in January 1768 when a new Secretaryship of State for the Colonies was created and given to Lord Hillsborough. The same reshuffle saw the exit of Conway and the entry of three of the Bedford gang. It was clear that the ministry was no longer Chatham's either in its content or in its intentions, although the King told him that 'your name has been sufficient to enable my administration to proceed'. In October 1768, when Shelburne resigned what was left of his Secretaryship, Chatham felt that he too must go. He gave up the Privy Seal and Grafton took over the leadership of the ministry. Chatham promised the King that 'should it please God to restore me to health, every moment of my life will be at your Majesty's devotion'. But by the time he had been restored to some semblance of health the affair of John Wilkes and the Middlesex election had so changed the political scene that he found himself devoting most of his moments to opposing the King's government.

When Wilkes returned to London in February 1768 the government wisely decided to ignore him: his letter craving pardon remained unanswered but no proceedings were instituted against him. But Wilkes would not be ignored. He determined to stand for the new Parliament that was being elected that spring, and after an unsuccessful attempt in the City of London, where he came bottom of the poll, he was elected for the county of Middlesex amid tremendous popular enthusiasm.[1] For several years past there had been increasingly serious riots among silk weavers, coal heavers, tailors, sawyers, sailors and other artisans, mainly directed against the lack of

[1] An eighteenth-century general election was a protracted affair: different constituencies went to the polls at different times and the poll often remained open for several days.

work or the high price of bread;[1] and now Wilkes provided a focus for this discontent which turned it from economic into political channels. Almost every night from his election at the end of March 1768 until the opening of Parliament in the middle of May there were ugly riots in London, and men whose real grievances were economic sought to express them by crying 'Wilkes for ever!' or chalking 'No. 45' on doorways. Wilkes himself was careful to act the part of the dutiful subject. He submitted to the law, resisted various attempts of the mob to release him, and was finally sentenced to twenty-one months in prison and a fine of £1,000 for his various misdemeanours. In prison he lived comfortably in rooms overlooking St George's Fields, receiving his supporters and managing to be a political martyr and a political organizer at one and the same time.

And he was still a member of the House of Commons—his outlawry, which might have rendered him incapable of sitting, had been reversed by King's Bench. The King was determined that he should not remain an M.P. As early as April 1768 he wrote that 'the expulsion of Mr Wilkes appears to be very essential and must be effected' and by the beginning of 1769, when it finally came before the Commons, he was speaking of it as 'a measure whereon almost my Crown depends'. On 3 February 1769 the Commons expelled Wilkes by 219 votes to 137, only to find him readopted and returned unopposed by the electors of Middlesex. Again he was expelled and again he was returned unopposed. At last the Court put up a candidate against him, Colonel Luttrell, who received 296 votes as against Wilkes's 1,143. Nevertheless the Commons declared Luttrell duly elected as the member for Middlesex; and it was this open defiance of the principle of representation that brought Chatham, Temple, Rockingham and even George Grenville together in an attempt to create a truly national opposition to Grafton's government. Between May 1769 and January 1770 dozens of petitions were presented to the King, containing between them some 60,000 signatures—about a quarter of the total voting population of the country. For the most part they came from London and the home counties, where Wilkes's radical supporters had direct influence, from Rockingham's sphere of influence in the northern counties or from Buckinghamshire and Kent, areas dominated by the Pitt–Grenville family; but there were also petitions from the cities of Bristol and Exeter, from Worcestershire and Herefordshire where the Dowdeswell family exercised considerable control

[1] Bread was 2d a pound in London in 1768. In normal years it was 1¼d or 1½d.

and from many western counties. As well as protesting against
Luttrell's admission, the petitioners called for the dismissal of the
ministry and the dissolution of Parliament. Many independent gentlemen, horrified by this combination of Whiggery and mob rule, sent
loyal addresses to their King. But in spite of this counter demonstration there could be no doubt that the Whigs had gone a long way
towards uniting the country against the ministry. The King who had
set out in 1760 to rescue his country from the Whigs found that by
1770 it preferred to be rescued by the Whigs from him.

When he initiated his 'reformation in government' George had
been concerned merely to contest the Whig notion of how a government should be formed. Whereas they thought that those who had
patronage, prominence and unity among themselves should also have
royal favour, he was determined that those who had royal favour
should have patronage, prominence and unity. He could give them
patronage and, by dint of an appeal to the independent country
gentlemen, a degree of prominence as well; but unity was much more
difficult. The only alternative to the unity given by family and
'connection' was a unity based on a programme of legislation—but
what programme? The New Tory programme had proved insufficient, the Patriot programme seemed fitted only for wartime
conditions. All that remained was the simple idea of 'attachment to
the Crown', a belief that the King's government must be carried on
at all costs. By 1770 there was a large body of men who took their
stand on this principle and Lord North, who took over the leadership of the ministry in February 1770 on the resignation of Grafton,
was one of them. He and his colleagues, whether they were Courtiers,
King's Friends or embryonic civil servants, succeeded in carrying on
the King's government in the face of mounting difficulties for the
next twelve years; but in the long run their 'attachment to the Crown'
was not enough. Just as their Whig opponents had to show that they
really stood for freedom and not just for aristocratic privilege, so they
had to show that they really stood for efficiency and not just for royal
absolutism. The first ten years of George III's reign had broken down
patronage politics and had ensured that mere 'connection' would
never again be sufficient to give unity either to a ministry or to an
opposition. But it was to be a long time before the politicians learnt
how to base either their government or their opposition on principles rather than patronage.

PART IV

The Rise of a New Toryism
1770–1789

II

The Collapse of Management
1770–1782

1 The problem of the American colonies

In 1764, when the problem of the American colonies was just
beginning to make itself felt, a writer in the *London Chronicle* insisted
that 'the colonies were acquired with no other view than to be a
convenience to us, and therefore it can never be imagined that we are
to consult their interest preferably to our own'. For the next twenty
years, while the problem turned into a quarrel, the quarrel into
a war and the war into a great national humiliation, this basic
attitude continued to be held by most people in the home country,
however much they might disagree about the policies that ought to be
adopted towards the colonists. Even when Josiah Tucker recommended separation in 1774, he did so on the grounds that what had
been meant as an asset had become a liability and as such should be
abandoned. The colonists themselves might think in terms of right
and wrong, freedom and tyranny, but the British thought like shopkeepers deciding whether or not to close down a branch that was
losing money.

In what ways were the colonies supposed to be a 'convenience'
and a source of profit? In the first place, they provided work for
the unemployable. Queen Elizabeth had ordered her overseers of the
poor to give paupers 'a convenient stock of ware and stuff' so that they
might provide for themselves by their labour; and in the colonies
the ware and stuff lay ready to hand, provided by nature herself. Not
all the 300,000 or so people who emigrated from Britain to America
during the colonial period were paupers and they were certainly not
all convicts, as Dr Johnson once averred, but many of them came
from those classes described by Gregory King as 'decreasing the
wealth of the country'. The mercantilist, always anxious to create

employment, was delighted that the paupers could be thus trans-
planted to areas where their labour might benefit the country—
especially if they made themselves doubly useful by producing raw
materials which otherwise would have to be obtained from hostile
or potentially hostile powers. At the beginning of the eighteenth
century Britain had been almost totally reliant on Sweden for her
essential supplies of tar, importing 43,000 barrels a year from her and
only about 800 from the colonies. By 1770 the British Empire was
self-sufficient in this respect: 103,000 barrels a year came from the
colonies and none from Sweden. The Carolinas, with their great
pine forests, benefited especially from this trade. Sugar and tobacco,
though hardly as essential for British sea power as tar, were almost
equally welcome since they could be very profitably re-exported to
the European markets. William Burke pointed out that 'those sugar
islands who supply to the home Consumption purvey to our Luxury:
those who supply the foreign markets administer to our Wealth and
to our Power'.

While the colonists thus busied themselves providing raw materials,
'the unimproved Product of the Earth', the home country concerned
itself with producing manufactured goods, since here the value of
the labour was higher and the employment therefore more profitable.
The colonists then accepted these commodities in exchange for the
raw materials they sent us, thus benefiting home industry and
providing yet more employment. Sir William Keith remarked with
satisfaction in 1740 that 'the Colonies take off and consume above
one Sixth part of the Woollen manufactures exported from Britain,
which is the chief staple of England'. Finally, the ships that carried
all this lucrative trade backwards and forwards across the Atlantic
were built by British craftsmen, manned by British seamen and
operated by British merchants. Not only did this great circle of trade
ensure rich profits for all who took part in it; it also created and kept
in being a powerful shipping fleet which could be turned to good use
in time of war. The first British Empire was a great national investment designed to yield a general dividend of prosperity and power
for the country as a whole, as well as handsome returns for the
individuals who put their money into it.

In order to ensure the smooth working of this complex system,
there existed a framework of legislation. The Navigation Laws laid it
down that all trade should be carried in British ships; the Enumerat-
ing Laws listed articles that could not be exported from the colonies

to foreign markets;[1] the Staple Act prevented the import of nearly all goods direct from Europe to the colonies; and a series of further laws restricted the development in the colonies of manufacturing industries liable to compete with those at home, such as the woollen and iron industries. Many nineteenth-century writers, influenced by theories of Free Trade, saw the whole system as a cruel straitjacket: but to contemporaries the garment, though perhaps a little cumbersome, seemed to provide essential support. The Virginia tobacco planter might complain because he could not load his tobacco on to Dutch ships, but the New England shipbuilder was growing rich as a result. And after 1783 the tobacco planters themselves were to lament the loss of their protected markets in Britain. Despite the touching pictures which are sometimes drawn by Free Trade writers, of gaunt and bankrupt colonists weighed down by layers of British cloth they did not want and could not pay for, the mercantilist system worked. For a hundred years it kept the first British Empire together as an effective economic unit.

What is more, it was still working when North came to power. During the year 1770 Britain exported to her colonies and plantations in the New World goods worth £3,613,361 and took from them imports to the value of £4,261,541: the colonists had a favourable balance of trade of more than half a million pounds with the home country. It is true that it was very unevenly distributed—while the West Indies had a credit balance of nearly two million, the New England colonies had an adverse one of well over half a million— but this was not so sinister as it appears, for the seaboard colonies helped to pay for their imports by exporting to the West Indies. The latter contained very few white men (Jamaica in 1770 had about 18,000 and nearly ten times that number of black slaves) and they were certainly not going to bother their heads, soil their hands and risk their health by attempting to produce all the necessities of life for themselves. They concentrated on one thing only, the cultivation of sugar by means of slave labour; and the timber for their buildings, the horses for their transport, the flour, beef, pork and fish for their food were all imported from the mainland colonies. The New England colonies carried on a particularly profitable trade in fish— which was at no time an enumerated commodity—and their 'refuse' fish, which they could not sell even on the markets of southern

---

[1] From 1722 onwards, the Enumerated List included ginger, sugar, cotton, tobacco, wool, indigo, fustic, rice, naval stores, copper, and beaver skins.

Europe and the Canary Islands, went to the West Indies as the staple diet of the slaves. Even the slaves themselves were often provided indirectly by the New Englanders. The molasses which they imported from the West Indies in part payment for their goods were distilled into rum, which was then taken to the slave coasts of West Africa and bartered for slaves who were subsequently sold in the West Indies. In the early years of the eighteenth century Rhode Island was one of the chief centres of the slave trade and even when Bristol and Liverpool succeeded in cornering a large part of it later in the century they continued to rely on the colonists' rum as a useful form of currency in West Africa.

Thus the British sold to the Americans, the Americans sold to the West Indies, the West Indies sold to the British. And everybody prospered. The game of colonial trade, like many other games, was played according to curious and arbitrary rules, but most people seemed to find it well worth playing for all that. Yet, like most games, it needed an impartial umpire—especially at a time when everyone was accusing everyone else of breaking the rules, as they were in 1770. The intricate arts of management, of weighing one interest against another, were nowhere more important or more difficult than in colonial affairs. When, during the controversy over the Peace of Paris, Wilkes published a lampoon on Bute, representing him lamenting 'O, that I must be doomed to watch over the caprices of furriers, sugar-boilers, cod-merchants, planters, rum-distillers, freighters, importers and haughty East Indian directors!', he was begging the question. Bute knew as well as any other minister that his job was to watch over these interests. The difficulty was not to watch over them, but to decide between them.

Faced with the continual need to placate the House of Commons, 'that confused and scuffling bustle of local agency' as Burke once called it, it was very hard for ministers to give proper consideration to those interests that were not represented there. Some transcendent authority, surveying with Olympian gaze both Parliament in West-minster and the Assemblies in the Colonies, able to consider im-partially the claims of London merchants and Virginia tobacco planters, New England rum distillers and West Indian sugar growers, might have arrived at an equitable solution. But, though in theory all the corporations and companies and colonies that made up the British Empire were ruled over by the King, in practice the King's government was chained to Parliament. It could well be argued that the American colonies were lost not because George III tried to rise above parliamentary factions, but because he failed to do so. A Patriot King might have kept the Empire together; a ministry harassed by the vociferous pressure groups in London certainly could not.

The final irony of the situation lay in the fact that the more populous a colony became, the less likely it was to be represented in Parliament. The proprietors and planters of those colonies which were mere producers of raw materials or simple trading stations still regarded Britain as their home. The tremendous sugar boom of the 1730s and 1740s (raw sugar, which was worth 16s 11¼d a hundred-weight on the London market in 1733, was worth 42s 9½d by 1747) meant that many of the West Indian sugar planters retired very early in life and took up the life of an English country gentleman while still retaining their financial interests in the West Indies. By 1770 a score or so of them sat in Parliament and, together with the merchants with whom they dealt, represented a formidable 'West India interest'. The mainland colonists, numerically far more significant, had difficulty in making themselves heard at all. The original empire of proprietors and traders envisaged by the seventeenth-century venturers could and did speak from London, in Parliament and in the Board of Trade; but the vastly more populous empire of settlers and pioneers had grown away both from its trading origins and from its connections in London. Originally conceived as a commercial enterprise it had become a problem in government. Horace Walpole glimpsed the nature of the problem, as well as the difficulties of solving it within the existing framework of jarring pressure groups, when he wrote to Sir Horace Mann in 1767: 'Is not this magnificent? A senate regulating the Eastern and Western worlds at once; the Romans were triflers to us; and yet our factions and theirs are as alike as two peas.'

Contemporary opinion regarded with some alarm this appearance of a vast empire in the place of a network of trading stations and plantations. It seemed to justify the fears which had been expressed back in 1761 about the acquisition of Canada: 'Are we not the only people on earth, except Spain, that ever thought of establishing a Colony ten times more extensive than our own country . . . and yet imagine that, when it comes to maturity, it will still depend on us, or be of any kind of advantage to us?' This was overstating the case: the problem did not appear overnight as the result of the conquest of Canada. After all, the population of Canada at this time was less than 100,000, compared with more than 2,000,000 in the thirteen colonies. But the removal of the French threat from Canada and Louisiana certainly helped to turn the American colonies from a static to an expanding area. Pioneers picked their way through the hinterland on the far side of the Alleghanies, developing the land, opening up trade with the Indians and breaking still further, to the horror of the merchants back home, the set pattern of the old colonial empire. Nor were the merchants the only ones to be alarmed: the landed gentlemen saw that all this meant higher taxes at home. In 1764 the cost of controlling these hinterland territories was reckoned at £370,000; and by 1767 the total colonial charges of £428,000 represented an extra shilling in the pound on the Land Tax. There was a general feeling in the home country that the colonists must be forced not only to stop their giddy expansion and allow themselves to be fitted back into the old system, but also to pay for their own upkeep.

Grenville tried to achieve the first aim by the Proclamation of October 1763, which laid it down that the newly conquered lands should be used for the cultivation of raw materials and for the expansion of manufactures, while at the same time forbidding indiscriminate colonization beyond the Alleghanies. The second he hoped to achieve by the Stamp Act; but the fury of the merchants whose trade was adversely affected by that Act, and the efficiency with which they brought pressure on Parliament to secure its repeal,[1] showed how difficult it was to solve the colonial problem to the satisfaction of the interests at home. Just as Grenville's plans of 1763–64 were frustrated by the merchant interest, so Shelburne's of 1767 were frustrated by the landed interest. In March of that year he was busy drawing up a scheme whereby controlled expansion into the hinterland was to be allowed and was to be made to pay for itself by a system of quit-rents. It is doubtful if his scheme in its original form would have solved the problem; but at least it showed a realization of the basic need to produce an empire which could transcend the old system without being a charge on the home country. But after his colleague Charles Townshend, without consulting him, had promised the Commons in January that he would raise in America a revenue sufficient to meet the colonial charges, the 'independent' members who usually supported the government of the day had voted for an opposition motion to reduce the Land Tax by a shilling in the pound. This was carried and the ministry was thus robbed of

1 See above, pp. 285–6.

£500,000 at a stroke. Townshend's duties on glass, lead, paint, paper and tea, proposed in his budget in March, represented little more than a token attempt to redeem his promise of January, since they went nowhere near making up the deficit. This had to be covered by an extensive raid on the sinking fund. But the duties, insufficient though they were, were enough to undermine the goodwill needed for the functioning of Shelburne's plan and to carry the argument with the colonists on to new and much more dangerous ground.

Previously everyone had recognized Britain's right to impose duties on the colonies for the purposes of regulating trade. It was only the direct raising of revenue which was in dispute. Pitt had made this distinction between 'external' and 'internal' taxation the basis of his attack on the Stamp Act, and a similar doctrine lay behind the Declaratory Act. Regulation was an essential and accepted part of the mercantilist system, while the raising of revenue internally was quite a different thing and could only be done with the consent of an assembly in which the colonists were represented. By using what were technically regulating duties for purposes of revenue Townshend sought to exploit this distinction; but if he thought the colonists were going to admire his subtlety, admit that they had been caught, and pay up like gentlemen, he was sadly disappointed. Instead they reacted by denying Britain's right to levy *any* taxes, external or internal. It was no longer a question of particular grievances: the whole nature of the relationship between the colonies and Great Britain, the whole structure of the mercantilist system, was brought under attack. The Americans began to talk in terms of political theory rather than business expediency. To the merchants at home, threatened with non-importation agreements by the colonists, it was a question of trade; but on the other side of the Atlantic it was swiftly becoming a question of sovereignty.

North's first step was a conciliatory one: he abolished all Townshend's duties except that on tea. In any case, the campaign of non-importation was becoming less fervent and less effective and, now that the postwar trade depression which had helped to exacerbate the crisis was passing, tension was reduced. A fresh wave of radical agitation in Boston in March of 1770, resulting from the shooting of five people in a riot, served only to emphasize the gulf between the extremists and the men of substance in the colonies. In New York the moderates were so scared by the violence of the radicals and the menace of mob rule that they called off the non-importation agreement and opened the port to tea forthwith. In London merchants found that trade was picking up, so that they were not prepared to support the colonists in the way they had done in 1764 and 1765. It began to look as if tension between the different groups, which had threatened to split the old system apart, might yet serve to hold it together.

But Sam Adams and the other radical colonial leaders continued to busy themselves setting up Committees of Correspondence throughout the thirteen colonies. These committees not only spread the gospel of independence but also organized the intimidation of loyalists and moderates. The barrels of tar mentioned earlier now began to be used, in conjunction with supplies of feathers, for purposes not purely naval. The burning of the revenue ship *Gaspee* in 1772 showed that the crisis had not passed; much more serious was the affair of the Hutchinson letters in 1773–74. Hutchinson, Governor of Massachusetts Bay, had written a series of letters to Whateley, a member of Parliament in England, stressing the need for sterner measures against the New England radicals. These were stolen and published, upon which the Assembly of Massachusetts petitioned the Privy Council for Hutchinson's removal. The petition was rejected as being 'false, scandalous and seditious', and Benjamin Franklin, who had been involved in the publication of the letters, was dismissed from his post of Postmaster-General of the Colonies. As well as driving into the radical camp a man who had been an important moderating influence (for Franklin had consistently worked for the retention of the link with Great Britain), the episode increased feeling at home against the colonies. The apparent lessening of tension had been deceptive, since behind it lay a grim determination, on one side to enforce the existing system and on the other to break it once and for all if the home government gave any further provocation.

The provocation, when it came, was absurdly trivial. North could be forgiven for thinking that his scheme of April 1773, to allow the East India Company to send tea direct to America without paying the British duty on it, would please everyone. It was a particularly ingenious example of the traditional technique of reconciling different interests—and it would, after all, mean that tea would sell in America at half its previous price. It was rather ironic that this well-meant evasion of the mercantilist system should have precipitated its collapse.

When the Bostonians had tipped the tea into the harbour in their notorious Tea Party of December 1773, it seemed reasonable to assume that condign punishment of these radicals would rally the moderates and loyalists to the British cause, as it had done in 1770. North's punitive measures—the revision of the Massachusetts Charter, the quartering of troops in Boston and the closing of the port until reparation had been made—were widely supported at home. Even Chatham denounced the Tea Party; and outraged merchants and exasperated squires alike were convinced that the time had come to teach the Americans a sharp lesson. But the radicals had done their work well and there was a general fear throughout the colonies that this was only the beginning of a determined policy of repression by the home government. With the passing of the Quebec Act in 1774 their fears seemed to have been justified. It set up a French and Catholic Canada which was to be allowed to extend its boundaries down to the Ohio. As well as checking their westward expansion, this seemed to threaten the colonists with the re-emergence of that strong Catholic menace which had done so much to keep them dependent on the home country, and reliant on its protection, before 1760. Instead of being deserted by all sensible men as North had hoped, the radicals found themselves riding a great wave of united opposition to Britain at the Continental Congress of 1774, to which all the colonies except Canada, Florida and Georgia sent delegates. Its enactments amounted to a total rejection of the supremacy of Parliament over the colonies—though whether this was intended to involve complete independence or equality under the Crown was not clear.

To the wrangling pressure groups at home, temporarily united in their determination to discipline this recalcitrant member of the team, it did not seem to matter. Chatham and Burke, in their different ways, glimpsed the true nature of the problem. But for all their talk of Imperial Federations and Great Empires they both had their feet too firmly entrapped in the meshes of the old system to see clearly and steadily the need to rise above it. Chatham had fought his Patriot War to extend mercantilism, not to supersede it, while it was to take the French Revolution rather than the American to make Burke abandon at last the old Whig scheme of politics.

Meanwhile the skirmish at Lexington had turned North's problem into the War of American Independence.

2 The War of American Independence

The paradoxical thing about the war, and the thing which explains many of the difficulties the British were to encounter in waging it, is that the Americans were independent before it started. It was not up to them to win their independence: it was up to. us to destroy it, to bring them into obedience and submission by imposing upon them an effective and centralized system of administration that could be operated from London. This was to be no ordinary war of liberation in which the rebels would have to tear down an existing tyranny. The British could only win the war if they were prepared to conquer America anew, creating strong government as they went. For, in spite of the apparently high-handed and paternalistic laws of the mercantilist system, in spite of the power exercised by the Crown and the Board of Trade through the colonial governors and their councils, government in the colonies was in the last resort local self-government—as, indeed, it was at home also. Walpole had seen that he could not continue with his Excise Scheme if the local gentlemen, in their capacity as justices of the peace, were unwilling to enforce it. He would have been horrified at the prospect of imposing it on a countryside where almost every family possessed firearms and the skill to use them effectively, where discontent could produce not just a mob but a militia, and where distances were so enormous that the task of controlling the country from the existing centres of administration was like trying to discipline Lancashire, Oxfordshire and Norfolk by occupying the Tower of London. If on the top of all this it had been suggested that he should operate with 3,000 miles of water separating him from his task, so that it often took two months for news of an event to reach London or for orders from London to reach armies in the field, he would have dismissed the idea as totally impracticable. The techniques of Whig government were never meant to be stretched to such extremities: they were intended for the management of society, not for the creation of an imperial machine of government.

But things did not seem as black as this when hostilities started in the spring of 1775. It was reasonable to assume that the uprisings in New England and Virginia represented the beginnings of a civil war within the colonies, between the radicals and the loyalists. It was true that the former had seized the initiative in an alarming way and that they were organized and militant while the loyalists were disunited and hesitant. None the less, it should not be too difficult to contain and punish the radical uprisings while encouraging, reassuring and protecting the loyalists. In this way law and order could be restored. And even if the Continental Congresses should prove successful in creating a united revolt of all the colonies, they could always be brought to their senses by economic pressure, without the need for an ambitious plan of reconquest on land. If the British could hold the chief ports—Boston, Rhode Island, New York, the Delaware and Chesapeake rivers, Wilmington and Savannah—then no amount of fervent organization within the colonies could prevent their commercial and financial life from falling into such decay and disruption that they would have to sue for peace.

Unfortunately these two solutions were mutually incompatible. If the government was going to intervene in a civil war, strengthen centres of loyalty and isolate centres of rebellion, then it could not afford to let its forces sit smugly in the ports of the Atlantic Coast waiting for the blockade to take effect; if it was going to concentrate on a blockade, it could not afford to squander its resources and its manpower in vain campaigns on land. A clear-cut decision had to be made one way or the other. That it was not made was not only the result of muddled thinking and hesitancy in the ministry, but also because in its early stages the problem stubbornly refused to reveal itself in its true colours. By the time it had come out into the open as one of united rebellion rather than civil war, the entry of France into the war had made both solutions out of date.

To General Gage, seeking to assert his authority as Governor of Massachusetts in the spring of 1775 with a force of only 2,000 men, it was a purely local problem. He wrote insisting on the imperative need for reinforcements, at least 20,000 of them, to forestall or contain a possible rising. They failed to arrive; instead, he received alarming reports that a local militia was being recruited and that secret stores of munitions and supplies were being built up. On the night of 18 April 1775 he sent off a detachment of 800 men from Boston to seize one such store at Concord, some twenty miles away; and in the early morning of the 19th, at Lexington, they had an encounter with the colonial militia in which shots were fired and some of the colonists killed. The troops pushed on to Concord and made some show of destroying the store, but their march back was one long agony, as the colonial marksmen gathered in the hills and woods along the road and picked off the British redcoats as though they had been brightly plumaged game birds. By the time the force got back to Boston it had lost well over a quarter of its men in killed, wounded or missing. This was a very serious loss, since the Boston garrison only totalled 2,000 and now found itself besieged on the landward side by a force amounting to 20,000 men. Even when reinforcements arrived under General Howe in May and June they failed to break the siege. One of the heights commanding the town, Bunker Hill, was recaptured from the colonists in June, but only at the third attempt and with the loss of over a thousand men. After this, Gage and Howe settled down to the defensive.

They had certainly failed to contain the New England rising. It was beginning to look like a united rebellion which would contain them. Not all the delegates at the second Continental Congress which met at Philadelphia on 10 May 1775 were as fiery as the New England radicals; and the Congress sent a petition to George III disclaiming any intention of separating from Britain and asking for his protection against the unwarranted exactions and pretentions of the Parliament at Westminster. But it also voted for the raising of more troops and gave to the collection of militia men surrounding Boston the title of the 'Continental Army'. To underline the fact that this was more than just New England's war, a Virginian farmer, George Washington, was appointed its commander. Even in those colonies which had so far been little affected by radical enthusiasm, it was becoming increasingly dangerous to be known as a loyalist. In July Governor Martin of North Carolina wrote to the Secretary of State confessing the 'impotence' of royal government there; and by the autumn all the governors had been driven out. Lord Dunmore, Governor of Virginia, took up his headquarters on a man-of-war and began a privateering campaign against the colonists' commerce. Meanwhile George III declared a general blockade of all ports in the thirteen colonies and a British naval force attacked and destroyed the port of Falmouth in Maine. It looked as though the home government, faced with a united rebellion, was prepared to leave the colonists to do their worst on land while it concentrated on blockading them from the sea.

But the thirteen colonies were not content just to underline their own unity: they sought to spread the rebellion into Canada. In May armed bands from Vermont took the important fortresses of Crown Point and Ticonderoga, which commanded the route from the Hudson valley into Canada as well as containing three hundred guns and other important supplies. In the autumn a force advanced from these strong points down into Canada, took Montreal and in December appeared before Quebec, where it was joined by another force under Benedict Arnold which had gone by sea from Massachusetts to the Kennebec River in Maine and had then pushed its way through very difficult country to the St Lawrence. But the combined force failed to take Quebec and retreated to Ticonderoga the following spring. Though they had not succeeded in taking Canada, the colonists had succeeded in making the British think again as to the wisdom of leaving the rebellion to wither away. When, early in 1776, Washington set up batteries of the heavy guns from Ticonderoga on heights overlooking Boston and compelled the evacuation of the city, Howe (who had succeeded Gage as Commander-in-Chief) became even more convinced of the need to undertake military operations to split up the colonial forces—preferably by seizing New York. But owing to lack of supplies, transports and reinforcements (six battalions had been diverted from him to help an abortive Loyalist rising in North Carolina) he had to make for the relative safety of Nova Scotia instead. By 4 July, when Congress passed the Declaration of Independence, there were no British troops left on American soil. The civil wars in New England had turned into a militant united rebellion of all the thirteen colonies; and Britain seemed unable to implement either the military solution of intervention or the naval solution of blockade.

Even after they had taken up arms against the British, the Americans had continued to cling, with varying degrees of sincerity, to the theory that they were appealing to the supreme authority of the King as against the partial authority of Parliament. They were convinced, or pretended to be convinced, that once he was informed of the true nature of the case he would exercise his royal prerogative to squash the self-interested designs of Parliament. He would see that it was as absurd to submit the Americans to the jurisdiction of Parliament as it would be to put the British under the authority of the Massachusetts assembly—and that both were inroads on his own royal power. Instead, George III used his royal prerogative to proclaim the Americans traitors. Tom Paine's pamphlet *Common Sense*, which appeared in January 1776, cut through the legal and constitutional tangles into which Congress had talked itself: not only did he attack monarchy in general and George III in particular, but he also insisted that the idea of Britain and her colonies existing side by side with equal rights under the benevolent rule of the King was an illusion and a fiction. George III was 'the royal brute of Great Britain' and would always be the instrument, not the curb, of her tyrannous designs. The work had a remarkable impact on the colonists and undoubtedly made possible the acceptance of the Declaration of Independence. The Americans hastened to follow his advice and repudiate royal authority. In New York the gilded leaden statue of the King was melted down and moulded by the ladies of Litchfield, Connecticut, into 42,000 bullets to be fired at the soldiers of the King.

The government remained convinced that this united front could be broken down by playing on the loyalist sympathies of the central colonies—Pennsylvania, Maryland, New Jersey and New York. Accordingly, a force of some 20,000 men, mostly German mercenaries, commanded by Howe and carried by a naval force under his brother, Admiral Lord Howe, appeared off New York in August. The brothers were empowered to open negotiations on the basis of the dissolution of Congress and compensation for loyalists; but an abortive conference on Staten Island showed that American unity could only be broken down by seizing the central colonies, not by wooing them. By the middle of September New York was in British hands, though Howe seems to have shown a certain lack of determination in pressing home his victories. Whether this was the result of incompetence or of a lingering belief in the possibility of conciliation is uncertain; but it enabled Washington to withdraw in good order to the far side of the Delaware River in order to defend Philadelphia. The further the British advanced, the more it was brought home to them that they were conquering the map and not the rebels; even the loyalists were more often a hindrance than a help, since the deployment of troops had to be governed by the need to protect them rather than by the strategic demands of the campaign. Sir Guy Carleton's attempt to complete the isolation of New England by an advance from Quebec down the Lake Champlain–Hudson River route was frustrated by a successful delaying action fought by a small flotilla of colonial ships on Lake Champlain. The year 1776 was a disappointing one for the British commanders and it was crowned by the affair at Trenton on Boxing Day, when Washington took advantage of the German devotion to Christmas festivities to fall upon a force of Hessians and kill or capture over three-quarters of them.

These were only minor setbacks. The colonists were running into great difficulties in raising revenues, recruiting armies and maintaining the credit of their government. Serious depreciation of their currency threatened their financial stability, intercolonial rivalries threatened their political unity and large-scale desertions threatened their military effort. The British were still confident of their ability to end the war in 1777 by means of a plan to divide the colonies. This time it was to be elaborated: one force, under Burgoyne, was to move down the Lake Champlain route, another under St Leger was to start from Fort Oswego on Lake Ontario and advance down the Mohawk River, while Howe was to come up the Hudson River from New York. The three armies would converge on Albany, whereupon New England, separated from Washington's continental army by overwhelming British forces and by the solid loyalism of the central colonies, would be forced to submit. The revolt in the South would then collapse. But even as the Secretary for the Colonies, Lord George Germain, busied himself with the organization of this plan, Howe began to have doubts about it—chiefly because it meant that he must waste the whole summer waiting for Burgoyne. He believed that if only he could tempt Washington into a pitched battle by attacking Philadelphia he could break the Continental Army altogether; and he wrote to Germain suggesting this. The Secretary sent his approval and then proceeded to make nonsense of his decision by writing to Burgoyne to say that he would duly meet Howe in Albany as planned. He did not bother to send a copy of this last letter to Howe, who would never have known about it had not the Deputy Secretary at War made it his business to inform him. Nevertheless Howe put to sea with the bulk of his forces, leaving only 9,000 men in New York. He was unable to land in the Delaware estuary as he had planned and had to sail right round to Chesapeake Bay. Although he defeated Washington at Brandywine and Germantown, neither battle was the decisive victory he had hoped for; and it was late in September by the time he had established his control of Philadelphia, much too late for him to get back to meet Burgoyne at Albany. St Leger's advance down the Mohawk had been turned back at Oriskany in August, so that when Burgoyne got to the Hudson he found himself alone. The whole countryside was in arms and his force was surrounded by bands of militiamen who harassed it mercilessly. At Saratoga on 17 October he surrendered his whole force to the American commander Gates.

Saratoga demonstrated the superiority of the guerrilla tactics of the militiamen over the formal evolutions of European warfare; it showed the dangers of Burgoyne's over-confidence and Howe's impatience; above all it indicated the fatal consequences of hesitant and confused planning at home. If Lord George Germain really thought that Howe could take Philadelphia and still be back in time to meet Burgoyne he was guilty of the most ludicrous miscalculation. If he did not, then he was guilty of plain neglect of duty. The shock of Saratoga and the realization of the impossibility of reconquering America with the forces available drove the ministry back upon the plan for a naval blockade, while the fear that France might now be encouraged to intervene led them to think in terms of conciliation. But it was too late, either for blockade or for conciliation. On 6 February 1778, eleven days before North's Conciliatory Acts were passed by Parliament, Benjamin Franklin in Paris signed a treaty of alliance between the Americans and France. The War of American Independence had become a French war of revenge for the humiliations of the Seven Years War. Spain also was waiting for a chance to avenge the defeats inflicted on her during that war and in the Falkland Islands,[1] but she had an extensive colonial empire of her own and was reluctant to support colonial rebellion. However, after Britain rejected her offer of mediation in 1779 she joined in the war.

When fears of French and Spanish intervention had first been expressed, in November 1777, Lord Sandwich, First Lord of the Admiralty, had boasted that the British navy was more than a match for the whole House of Bourbon. On paper, his claim seemed iustified, for Britain had 150 ships of the line, France 80 and Spain 60; but both France and Spain had made intensive efforts to improve their navies since 1763 and many of their ships were larger, more heavily armed and in better condition than their British equivalents. For the first time in the eighteenth century British naval supremacy faced a really serious challenge—a challenge which came from the neutrals as well as by our enemies. Remembering with resentment Britain's high-handed treatment of neutral shipping during the Seven Years War, they insisted on their right to trade with the colonists —a very profitable trade, since the Prohibitory Act of 1776 excluded the colonists from British ports. This insistence led the Dutch into war with Britain in December 1780, and the Baltic powers into an Armed Neutrality earlier in the same year. The overwhelming success of Pitt's Patriot War had united the powers of Europe in their dislike

[1] See below, p. 317.

of British commercial supremacy: the feeling against the usurping 'nation of shopkeepers', which Napoleon later sought to use for his own ends, first took definite shape in the War of American Independence.

But the entry of France, though it boosted the colonists' morale and encouraged them to reject North's peace moves of early 1778, did little to improve their immediate prospects. During the winter of 1777–78, while American farmers had unashamedly sold their best produce to the British in Philadelphia, Washington had had the greatest difficulty in keeping his army together in its miserable winter quarters at Valley Forge, and it was doubtful whether the American war effort could be kept going long enough for French financial and military aid to take effect. But instead of striking a decisive blow at this point the British went on to the defensive. Philadelphia was evacuated and Washington was allowed to advance to the Hudson River, where he established a strong fortress at West Point. In the interior George Rogers Clark pushed down the Ohio River as far as the Mississippi, where he established American claims. Not until December, when they attacked and took Savannah in Georgia, did the British make a positive move. From now on they were to pin their hopes on a campaign in the southern colonies, where the loyalists were stronger than in the north. Besides, forces deployed in the south could be more easily diverted to defend the West Indies against French or Spanish attack. For now that the indecisive action off Ushant in July 1778 had marked Britain's failure to keep the French fleet bottled up in home waters it was free to cruise either along the American seaboard or in the Caribbean. After a brief and ineffective appearance off New York, the French concentrated on the Caribbean, where they took Dominica. However, British forces captured the French island of St Lucia.

1779 was a year of desultory and indecisive campaigns, but by 1780 events began to move towards a climax. Now that Spain was in the war the British navy had to defend Gibraltar and guard against a possible invasion of England, as well as controlling the Atlantic and Caribbean and enforcing the inspection of neutral shipping throughout the world: the strain was beginning to tell. Although Rodney won a decisive victory over the Spanish off Cape St Vincent at the beginning of the year and went on to out-manœuvre the French in the West Indies, he failed to maintain the British control of the American coast. In July 1780 the French landed a force of 6,000 men under Rochambeau at Newport, Rhode Island. Rodney appeared off the New England coast in the autumn but left again without making any attempt to dislodge the French, who remained in control of Newport, thus tearing a significant hole in the British blockade and providing an invaluable base for American privateers. Clinton, the British commander in New York, hoped to prevent Rochambeau from joining up with Washington by extending his control of the Hudson as far up as West Point, which its American commander, Benedict Arnold, was prepared to betray into his hands. Unfortunately the plan was prematurely revealed in September 1780, when Major André, his emissary to Arnold, was captured behind the American lines in disguise and hanged as a spy.

But British operations in the southern states continued to prosper. In May 1780 a seaborne attack on Charleston, the chief port of South Carolina, resulted in its surrender, together with a force of 5,000 Americans. This was followed by Cornwallis's rather circuitous but successful campaign in the Carolinas. By the beginning of 1781 the American position in Virginia was threatened from two directions— one invasion from the Carolinas under Cornwallis and another up the James River. This latter was led by Benedict Arnold, who had managed to escape after the capture of André and was now fighting for the British. By May 1781 the two had joined forces and by August they had established a strong defensive position at Yorktown on Chesapeake Bay. Washington sent a detachment under Lafayette to contain the situation in Virginia, but he concentrated his main forces in a march north to join Rochambeau and launch an attack on New York. However, the French admiral in the West Indies, de Grasse, decided that he could use his fleet more effectively by sailing against Cornwallis in Yorktown rather than against Clinton in New York. As soon as they were informed of his decision Washington and Rochambeau hurried south, leaving only 4,000 men behind them to deceive Clinton as to their intentions on New York. De Grasse anchored in Chesapeake Bay at the end of August and by the middle of September the British naval forces under Graves and Hood had not only failed to dislodge him but had also permitted another French fleet under de Barras to sail in from Newport, carrying Rochambeau's heavy siege artillery. With the arrival of Washington and Rochambeau the siege of Yorktown began in earnest at the end of September. Cornwallis was ringed round by the combined forces of Washington, Rochambeau and Lafayette, as well as by the whole strength of the Virginia militiamen and two French fleets—probably about 15,000 men all told. With no hope of relief from the land or the sea, he surrendered his entire force of some 7,000 men on 19 October 1781.

It was a shattering disaster, but it need not have meant final defeat for the British. They still held Charleston in the South and New York in the North; the Americans were still experiencing crippling economic and political difficulties; and the French command of the sea which had sealed Cornwallis's fate was broken once and for all by Rodney's great victory at the battle of the Saints in April 1782. But the surrender at Yorktown dealt the last blow to North's already faltering confidence in his own ability to win the war. He devoted his remaining energies not to further plans for the reduction of the Americans but to the increasingly difficult task of keeping together his majority in the Commons. By the time Rodney won the battle of the Saints North's ministry had already fallen. His successors might or might not be able to restore British fortunes in the war against France, Spain and Holland, but one thing was certain: they would have no stomach for the fight against the American colonists.

3 Lord North and the Opposition

The ministry North took over in February 1770 was facing a truly formidable opposition—an opposition which claimed to represent not a mere political faction but the country as a whole. The Middlesex Election affair had made it seem as though the government were bent on destroying the civic rights and liberties of Englishmen, while the crisis in the colonies lent colour to the charge that they were also neglecting their economic duties. The Old Whigs, in spite of the King's success in turning their weapons of patronage against them were still reluctant to carry the fight 'out of doors', into the country as a whole; but they found themselves swept along by the Chathamites, who now came forward as the leaders of a united and 'national' opposition. Warning Rockingham of the limitations of his moderate 'Old Whig' ideas, Chatham wrote: 'The *whole* alone can save the *whole* against the desperate designs of the court.' His theme was still the Patriot one, of the need to save the country from the evils of government by factions, but he had ceased to believe that it could be brought about by the King. The King's following, in his view, had now become nothing more than a faction itself: the Patriot Minister, therefore, must turn from the support of the Patriot King to the formation of a Patriot Opposition—an opposition which should carry with it not just the great lords of Parliament, not just the commercial pressure groups he had courted so successfully in the past, but the whole country.

In France the same thing was happening at the same time: as North took over in London, Maupeou and Terray took over in Paris to find themselves facing furious opposition from the privileged classes who claimed, as did their opposite numbers in Britain, that they stood for the whole country against the tyrannous designs of the Court. In the long run both countries were to face the same problem: the need to transcend the existing system. It is true that the problem was far more urgent in France, where the clash between the local power of the privileged classes and the needs of central government had produced not just inefficiency but administrative deadlock and financial chaos. It was also true that the solutions offered by Maupeou and Terray for the evils of the *Ancien Régime* were more positive than those offered by George III for the inadequacies of Whig management: they wanted a strong central government with a policy of fiscal reform and effective bureaucratic control, while George seemed to regard the strengthening of government as an end in itself. But in both cases the alternative solution, that of the nobility leading a popular revolt in the name of freedom, seemed unconvincing. In 1789 the French nobility were to find out—too late—that they had more in common with the King they sought to weaken than with the people they sought to lead against him. Perhaps it was as well for the Whigs that they were never put to this extreme test.

Burke, who was to be the first to recoil in horror at the sight of the sovereign people in action at the time of the French Revolution, was very ready to appeal to them in 1770. On 23 April, when the attack on North was at its height, he published *Thoughts on the Cause of the Present Discontents*, in which he stated categorically that the only remedy for a situation in which Parliament was being enslaved by the wicked designs of the court was 'the interposition of the body of the people itself'. Burke and the Rockingham Whigs were in some disagreement with Chatham as to how far they might decently go in calling forth this interposition. They joined with him in harrying North over the Wilkes case and they supported the petition of 14 March in which the City of London attacked the King's government in the most violent terms; but when, in May, Chatham pressed the appeal to the forces outside Parliament to its logical conclusion by demanding electoral reform, he found himself alone. The Old Whigs were prepared to contest with the Crown the control of the existing patronage system and to accept the plaudits of the people for doing so; but they were not so happy about letting the people remould the system nearer to their heart's desire.

By the early summer of 1770 the prospect of a really national opposition to North was already fading. Chatham's old friend Beckford, who as Lord Mayor of London had done much to stir up opposition in the City, died in June and much of the City's petitioning enthusiasm died with him. Whig fears that in supporting Wilkes they were encouraging a demagogue rather than espousing a cause were intensified when he tried to divert the funds of the Society of the Bill of Rights, formed to support him, to his own uses. In 1771 a section of the Society broke away to form the rival Society for Constitutional Information, which continued to receive the support of Shelburne, but the Rockingham Whigs turned away from the popular movements in distaste. Even Chatham lost his enthusiasm for dangerous domestic issues when news arrived of a Spanish landing in the Falkland Islands. Here was a more effective stick to beat the ministry with, a stick he could handle superbly well. To plot the Patriot course in home affairs was a delicate and uncertain business, but abroad it was clear and straightforward. In a rousing speech he demanded vigorous action against this new piece of Bourbon impertinence and attacked the government for its neglect of the navy. But any hopes he might have had of bringing down the ministry on this score were ended when Spain, denied the French support she had expected, backed down in January 1771 and agreed to withdraw her forces.

The Whigs might be anxious to drop Wilkes, but Wilkes was equally anxious not to be dropped. In March 1771, with two other Aldermen of the City of London (one of them the Lord Mayor, Brass Crosby), he refused to convict a printer accused of printing accounts of the debates in the Commons. North quietly allowed the case against Wilkes to lapse, but the other two were sent to the Tower of London for committing a breach of parliamentary privilege. Fundamentally, the issue was that raised by the Middlesex election: was Parliament for the people or against them? But now it was raised in a new and acute form, since Parliament could hardly claim to be the mouthpiece of the people if it would not even allow them to read accounts of its debates. Glynn, a member of the Wilkes group among the opposition, pointed out the dangers of asserting the supremacy of parliamentary privilege over the common law: 'In laying the whole nation, therefore, at our mercy, we lay it at the mercy of the Crown.' But the Whigs remained embarrassed and uncertain in their attitude and the only thing they could agree upon was the proposal to pay a formal visit to the prisoners in the Tower. It was a rather meagre and unconvincing expression of their claim to lead a truly national opposition.

Meanwhile North had been steadily establishing his own claim to lead a truly national government. The ministry he had taken over in 1770 had never been a mere collection of King's Friends but a continuation, albeit in a very attenuated form, of Chatham's much-vaunted national government of 1766; and by 1772 he had included in it members of the Bedford connection, the Grenvillites (Grenville himself died in 1770) and even the Rockingham Whigs, in the person of Dartmouth, Secretary for the American colonies from August of that year. It was difficult to dismiss such an impressive array as a mere court faction; and when the ministry brought forward the Royal Marriages Bill of 1772, preventing members of the Royal Family from marrying without the sovereign's consent, opposition attempts to depict them as slavish courtiers enforcing the personal whims of the King fell very flat. Sir George Savile's Bill for the relief of Dissenters seemed to offer more encouraging material, since the Whig connection with dissent fitted in both with traditional policy and with the new bid for popular support. But North, secure in the knowledge that the bishops would kill the Bill in the Lords, refused to make a fight of it in the Commons. Once again the Whigs were denied the chance to close their ranks in support of a really major issue of principle.

In 1773 a major issue of principle did arise, over the affairs of the East India Company; but it was hardly one calculated to unite the opposition. The Rockingham Whigs, with their passionate concern for the rights of chartered companies and their determination to prevent North from cornering a valuable source of patronage, could hardly be expected to see eye to eye with Chatham over India. They had attacked his suggestion of 1767, that the Crown should claim sovereignty over all the territories conquered in India, as a typically self-interested move on the part of a man whose connections lay with the West Indian interest rather than the East Indian. It was certainly true that it was the West India merchant Beckford who wrote to

Chatham in 1766 insisting that 'we must look to the East and not the West', for an imperial revenue, but the scheme was more than the petulant gesture of a pressure group politician. It was a recognition, however uncertain, that the Indian problem was one of government, not merely one of the regulation of trade and the reconciliation of interests.

By the end of the Seven Years War the Company found itself virtual ruler of Bengal, the Carnatic and much of the coast in between. In 1764 Munro's victory at Buxar marked a new policy of conquering the Indian princes themselves instead of just using them against the French, a policy which led inevitably to the extension of Company influence into Mysore, Hyderabad and Oudh. Shareholders at home might think they were investing in a rich trade whose prospects were immeasurably brightened by the acquisition of the new territories, but in fact they were committing themselves to the government of a subcontinent. The system of dual control whereby the routine business of administration was left to the princes and their agents did not lessen the cost of the task, as Clive had hoped. On the contrary, it vastly increased it because of the corruption which it encouraged both among the Company's servants and among the Indians themselves. In the period from 1767 to 1771 corruption and famine between them produced a drop of £400,000 a year in the Company's revenues, while its expenses rose steadily—military costs alone increased by £160,000 in the same period. Trade, as well as administration, was running at a loss because it was increasingly hard to pay in British manufactures for the goods bought in India—the sale of heavy woollen textiles did not go with a swing in the Indian climate. Instead, the Company paid the Indians in bonds drawn on London and thus ran itself steadily into debt at home. By 1773 the mighty East India Company, which was popularly supposed to hold the gorgeous East in fee, was on the verge of bankruptcy. Many people at home, seeing only the wealth and ostentation of the retired company officials or 'nabobs', concluded that all the trouble was caused by dishonest and grasping individuals. This was particularly true of Burke and the Old Whigs: as always, they were only too ready to believe that the wrong people were controlling the system rather than that the system itself was wrong.

Nor was North the man to create a new system. He was concerned to please all parties, not to bring about a radical reform. The Company's charter was due to expire in 1780 and it should be possible to patch things up until then. A loan of £1,400,000, together with the ill-fated decision to allow the export of tea direct to the colonies, helped to restore the Company's credit, while the Regulating Act of 1773 set out to supervise, rather than to supersede, its rule in India. A governor-general was established in Calcutta with an ill-defined authority over the other two presidencies at Bombay and Madras. He was to be advised by a Council nominated partly by the Company and partly by the government, while the whole structure was to be answerable to the Company but subject to government inspection and supervision. The system never worked very well and it says a good deal for the abilities of Warren Hastings (first governor-general, 1773–85) that it worked at all. In spite of the difficulties of his position he managed to put Indian administration on a better footing, as well as fighting off the French-inspired attempts of the Mahrattas and of Hyder Ali of Mysore to contest British rule in India.

The same reservations that prevented the Whigs from uniting to exploit North's difficulties over India made it equally hard for them to produce a consistent and convincing policy towards the American colonies. Burke and Chatham might thunder and theorise about the need to rise to the occasion and forge a really effective imperial government, but they found it impossible to square this with their stock political attitudes and those of their followers. North exposed their dilemma neatly when he asked whether, since their sole remedy for the trouble was a change of ministry, he should give way to those who had passed the Stamp Act or to those who had repealed it. Each section of the opposition was connected in some way or other with groups having trading interests in America; and more and more of these groups came to feel that the government must be supported in its efforts to discipline the colonists. By 1775 the opposition could only muster seventy-three votes in the Commons and in November 1776 many of the Rockingham Whigs seceded from Parliament. This was because they felt that opposition to the American War was not only unpopular and unavailing but even dangerous. In 1776 Richard Price published *Observations on Civil Liberty*, in which the arguments in favour of the colonists were extended to justify the demand for radical reform at home as well. If support for the colonists was to be construed as encouragement of subversive agitation, then the Whigs preferred to remain silent. In October 1777 Burke wrote in despair to Fox: 'We must quietly give up all ideas of any settled preconcerted plan.' With the entry of

France into the war at the beginning of 1778 the prospect became even blacker, for many people felt, with Chatham, that by allying with the hated Bourbon the Americans had forfeited any right they may have had to sympathy at home. The immediate result of the French declaration was an attempt to bring Chatham into the ministry. But it was too late. After a speech in the Lords condemning the colonists at the beginning of April he collapsed, and a few weeks later he was dead. Shelburne, generally recognized as his political heir, was a man distrusted by his fellow politicians for his links with radicals and Dissenters and for the uncertainty of his party loyalties, so that his succession to the leadership of the group did little to help either its own unity or its relations with the Rockingham Whigs.

It was still possible, however, for the opposition to attack the conduct of the war rather than the war itself. Both Burke and Chatham spoke vehemently against the government's policy of raising the Indians against the colonists (though Chatham had sanctioned the use of Indians against the French in the Seven Years War) and popular caricatures appeared showing George III feasting on human flesh in the company of his savage allies. The shortcomings of Lord Sandwich, First Lord of the Admiralty, were also exploited to the full: he had suffered much discredit in 1778 when the brilliant advocacy of Thomas Erskine secured the acquittal of one Captain Baillie on charges of corruption at the naval hospital at Greenwich; and by their noisy championing of Keppel when he was court-martialled for his failure off Ushant the Whigs ensured that the same thing happened again in an even more spectacular and resounding fashion. The court acquitted Keppel in 1779 and described the charges against him as 'malicious and ill-founded'.

North countered these attacks on particular ministers—on Suffolk for sanctioning the use of Indians, on Sandwich for the deficiencies of the navy, on Germain for military failures—by enunciating the doctrine of collective responsibility: 'The measures ... were measures of state, originating in the King's counsels, and were of course no more the noble Lord's measures than they were of any other member of the cabinet: the crimes or faults, or errors committed there, were imputable to the whole body, and not to a single individual who composed it.' But collective *action* was a thing much more difficult to achieve, as long as the cement of politics was 'connection' rather than principle, as long as politicians grouped themselves around men rather than measures. George III and Chatham and North himself might assert the need for government to cut across the various political groupings, but the task of keeping such a government together was tremendously difficult. In the later years of his ministry North became increasingly worried lest it should become either so wide that it fell apart or so narrow that it lost its majority in the Commons. The problem of whom to ask in and whom to keep out weighed on him more and more, until in the spring of 1779 the death of Suffolk, Secretary of State for the North, paralysed him to such an extent that it was October before a successor was chosen. Meanwhile all around him his colleagues threatened and combined and intrigued to secure their own advancement or the admission of their friends. The more they intrigued, the more frightened and indecisive he became; and the more indecisive he became the more they intrigued. The King's reaction to the situation was to enter into an increasingly confidential correspondence with Robinson, the Secretary of the Treasury, and Jenkinson, Secretary at War. His object was to supplement North's management of his ministry, not to supplant it: but the exchanges, whose existence was suspected both by North and by the opposition, gave rise inevitably to the old charges of 'closet influence'. Either from a sense of duty or because of some promise George may have extracted from him when he settled his personal debts for him at the end of 1777, North consented to remain in office and do his best to hold together his disintegrating ministry. It was an unenviable task. Perhaps it was even an impossible task—at least until men learnt to accept a new view of politics. Not until the politics of programmes came to replace the politics of patronage would it be possible to maintain a government irrespective of 'connection'.

But in 1779 it was not the ministry but the opposition that had a programme: the programme to which Burke gave the impressive title of 'Economical Reform'. In the early years of his ministry North had prided himself on his success in reducing government expenditure and in paring down the National Debt, but the American War had swept away all his economies and by 1779 the Debt stood at £153,000,000. As the war went from bad to worse the country gentlemen upon whom fell a large part of the burden of taxation became increasingly incensed at the apparent waste or misuse of their money. Defeat in America was depressing enough, but by 1779 the government had presented them with danger at home as well. American privateers had actually made a landing in Scotland in 1778 and in the summer of 1779 the local tradesmen of Falmouth, putting out in small boats to sell provisions to the men-of-war cruising in the bay, found to their horror that it was not the British fleet but a combined Spanish and French force which was sailing unchallenged up and down the British coast. The possibility of a French invasion of Ireland as well as the need to free regular troops from the Irish establishment for service in America, had led to the formation of a force of Irish volunteers, which by the summer of 1779 numbered over 8,000; and, now that the government found itself involved in economic and constitutional quarrels with the Irish that bore an alarming resemblance to those with the American colonists,[1] it looked very much as though the Volunteers might become more of a danger than a protection. At any moment, it seemed, the country might be faced with a Bourbon invasion and with a full-scale rebellion in Ireland as well.

To the independent members, representatives in Parliament of the country interest, it seemed that they had paid for victory and been given only defeat. Suspicious, as always, of the smooth, scheming Whig politicians, they had trusted North: and now he had let them down. Their first reaction was to mobilize their own forces against the ministry, without recourse to allies either among the Whigs or among the popular movements. The independent landowners of Yorkshire, led by Christopher Wyvill, a prosperous squire who was also an Anglican parson, formed an association of independent gentlemen of substance, 'equally unconnected with the leaders of Administration and their opponents', to protest against the waste of public money and to demand parliamentary reform. It was not to be the sort of reform the radicals wanted, the representation of the whole body of the people on a numerical basis, but simply an increase in the number of county members, in order that those sturdy representatives of property should no longer be swamped by the professional politicians who sat for the boroughs. Nevertheless, the Yorkshire Association found itself swept into alliance with radicalism. At a great meeting in Westminster Hall at the beginning of 1780 Wyvill and his friends had to rub shoulders with men who were avowed enemies not only of the ministry but of the squirearchy and the Anglican Establishment as well—men like Jebb and Cartwright and even Wilkes himself. In their attempt to breathe new life into the 'country' interest the gentlemen of England had aroused something much more significant: the 'popular' interest.

[1] See below, p. 376 for a fuller account.

While Fox came forward to ride the wave of popular feeling and win for himself a reputation as 'the Man of the People', Burke set himself to work out a programme which should be sufficiently constructive to satisfy the aspirations of the radicals, sufficiently conservative to please the country interest and sufficiently practical to suit the need of the Whigs themselves—the need to wrest from North and the King the control of patronage. He proposed not electoral reform but economical reform: Parliament was to be purified not by altering its composition but by stemming the flow of sinecures and pensions by which it was corrupted. The plan had many advantages. It satisfied the need of the time for economy and retrenchment in view of the expensive failures of the American War; it pleased those who still thought in seventeenth-century terms of the need to preserve the independence of Parliament from the executive at all costs; it helped to neutralize the old Whig weapon of patronage now that the King had turned that weapon against the Whigs themselves; it paved the way for more efficient government and a new view of offices as jobs to be done rather than investments to be enjoyed. Above all it avoided concessions to the manyheaded monster of popular agitation.

But it did not succeed in bringing down North. All through February and March the Whigs went from success to success, forcing upon the government measures to set up commissions of accounts, publish details of payments from the Civil List, reduce or abolish sinecures. On 6 April the onslaught reached a triumphant climax when Dunning's motion, 'That it is necessary to declare, that the influence of the Crown has increased, is increasing, and ought to be diminished', was carried by eighteen votes. But for all his moderation Burke had not succeeded in overcoming the misgivings of the country gentlemen. They viewed with alarm and apprehension the campaigns conducted 'out of doors' by Fox and Richmond, in which ideas of universal manhood suffrage and equal electoral districts were being openly canvassed, and when in June the Gordon riots brought home the dangers of mob rule, they began to turn back to the support of North. These very ugly riots, which held London in their power from the 2nd to the 12th of June, were the results of popular hatred of the Catholics and of recent measures for their relief. They had no connection with the movements that had produced the opposition to North in Parliament, but they convinced independent gentlemen and Whig leaders alike of the risks of stirring up popular discontent. At the general election of September 1780 North retained his majority and after an uneventful session in 1781 it was the old charge of a war improperly conducted rather than any programme of reform that brought him down in the spring of 1782. Motions condemning the war were carried at the end of February and the beginning of March, and on 15 March a vote of censure on the government was defeated by only nine votes. A few days later North resigned.

That last vote of censure was not moved by one of the Whig leaders but by a typical Tory country gentleman, Sir John Rous. If Burke and the Rockingham Whigs thought they could take up where they had left off in 1766, they were to be quickly disillusioned. The last sixteen years had demonstrated not the wickedness of the King's Friends but the inadequacies of Whig government; and now a new approach was needed. It might take the form of a new Toryism or a new Whiggery. It might find a leader in Shelburne, the follower of Chatham and the patron of the Philosophical Radicals, or in Fox, the 'Man of the People'; in Burke, the conservative Whig, or in Pitt, the progressive Tory. But whatever its label and whoever its leader, it would have to represent new interests and concern itself with new problems. While the politicians had been absorbed with the changes in political alignments brought into being by the Patriot War and the Patriot King, a new society had been growing up around them. And that society would need more than management: it would need government.

12

New Problems

1 The end of self-sufficiency

In 1761 a pamphleteer arguing against the retention of Canada prophesied that 'if it does not become our master it may soon, very soon, stand our powerful rival in all branches of our trade'. It was a warning which traders and manufacturers must have pondered, but it probably did not mean much to the average country gentleman. To him the overseas possessions were expensive luxuries which if properly selected and firmly managed might make Britain more powerful and more prosperous, but they were not necessities. If some branches of our trade were to suffer because the mercantile interests overreached themselves it would be a pity: gentlemen might lose their dividends, merchants might be ruined, workers might be put out of a job. But the country would survive. It would survive even if it lost all its colonies, all its trade, all its foreign markets, all its sources of foreign raw materials. It would survive because in the last resort it was still self-sufficient, because the land could still feed and clothe and shelter its inhabitants. It must have comforted the squires to reflect that when all the wrangling merchant interests were forgotten they or their successors would still be providing the country with its daily bread.

It would not comfort them much longer. From being a country that fed itself and used its surplus energies to create extra wealth by industry and trade, Britain was to become a country dependent on these things for its very existence, selling manufactured goods abroad in order to buy essential foodstuffs. The country gentlemen of 1761 might dismiss the pamphlet war over Canada as being no concern of theirs, but their descendants were to find themselves competing with cheap imported Canadian grain. The nation of farmers, having once consented to use trade as a sort of auxiliary engine for their rather lumbering agrarian economy, now found that it was in full control and was carrying them along at an increasingly frightening speed.

Some of them still hoped that it would slow down again so that they could get out and walk, but the majority accepted the new acceleration and set themselves to master its problems and control its direction.

One of those who would have liked to slow things down was Oliver Goldsmith. His poem *The Deserted Village*, published in 1770, painted an idyllic picture of traditional village life and suggested that it was being undermined by the new 'improving' agriculturalists. Once upon a time, he argued, landlords had seen themselves as trustees and had ensured that the land supported the community; but now they thought and acted like tradesmen. What had been a way of life had become merely a means of making money: 'wealth accumulates, and men decay'. In fact, men were by no means decaying, since the new developments were to enable the country to support a larger population than ever before. But Goldsmith, in spite of his absurdly idealized and romanticized view of rural life,[1] had put his finger on the root cause of the change: the accumulation of wealth. Behind the new economy stood a new attitude of mind, a new approach to the whole business of man's labour here on earth and to the riches that his labour could produce.

The self-contained and static society of the past had been based on the idea that man's destiny was to live by the sweat of his brow. Diligence was therefore a virtue and sloth a sin, but only because work was a necessity if the community was to survive. Men laboured to provide for themselves and their families, and if they produced more than they needed they sold it for money, with which they subsequently bought the fruits of other men's labours. Money was purely a means of exchange, a bridge between the commodity you wished to dispose of and the commodity you wished to acquire. It was sensible and provident to keep a store of it, but only in order that it should eventually be spent. The spendthrift might be reproached, but the miser was despised.

Though still held by many, this view was steadily being ousted by another, which was the real driving force behind the changes that took place in eighteenth-century Britain. It was a view that tolerated the miser and despised the spendthrift, that saw the accumulation of money as an end in itself, that regarded work as a self-justifying activity whether it was necessary or not. In the past men had never forgotten that in Paradise work was unnecessary. But now, to the

---

[1] Crabbe's poem, *The Village*, published in 1783 as a protest against Goldsmith's view, gives a more sombre and more accurate account of village life.

bustling money makers of the new age, infinite bliss and infinite leisure seemed to go ill together. A man's efforts were no longer to be limited by the needs he was seeking to provide for—indeed, those whose needs were already provided for were often those who worked hardest. What money they had must be intelligently and industriously used so that it yielded yet more money. Instead of money being the means of buying commodities, commodities were the means of making money. Money was no longer just a means of exchange: it was capital.

This capitalist attitude of mind did not emerge suddenly in the eighteenth century. To some extent it had been present throughout human history, although the morality of the Middle Ages had tended to hold it in check. What was relatively new and relatively sudden was the increase in the amount of capital available for invesment— money which men had accumulated, usually from trade, and which they could not or would not spend. Some of them, especially the Dissenters, felt that indiscriminate spending was self-indulgent and sinful. Others lacked the education which was necessary in order to acquire really expensive tastes, or were so conscious of their inferior social position that they shrank from imitating their superiors. Even among the upper ranks of society there were many who had ceased to feel that it was their duty to spend lavishly and live ostentatiously and had turned instead to the 'improvement' of their land or resources. Noblemen, gentlemen, tradesmen, merchants, manufacturers—all had money which they wanted to invest. Their search for profitable investments was to transform British life.

For the landowners the obvious use for their capital lay in the improvement and extension of their estates. The rather haphazard planting of root crops and new grasses which had passed for agrarian improvement in the early eighteenth century had developed into something much more systematic by the 1770s. Advocates of the 'new husbandry' practised a four-year rotation of wheat, turnips (to clean the soil and to provide winter fodder for livestock), barley (or sometimes oats) and clover. Instead of scattering their seed broadcast and resigning themselves to seeing some of it choked by weeds, they sowed in rows at a controlled depth and they used horsedrawn harrows and hoes to break up the soil and keep it free of weeds. They tried out new methods of drainage and fertilizing and most of them took a lively interest in the selective breeding of livestock, now that the increased supplies of fodder enabled them to keep their herds intact from year to year. Robert Bakewell's new Leicester sheep were already well known and by 1770 the rams he had bred with such care were earning him three thousand guineas a year in stud fees. Not everybody approved of the new sheep—Thomas Bewick said that their mutton tasted like blubber—but nobody could deny that they were profitable. Similar advances were made in cattle breeding and Charles Colling's 'Ketton Ox', which weighed 3,000 lb at four years of age, was generally regarded as a perfect example of its kind.

As well as increasing the farmer's profits, the new husbandry put up the value of the land itself; this meant that a man was unlikely to put his capital into agricultural improvement unless he owned his land or at any rate held it on a long lease. Enclosure, which had always been advocated by improvers as a means of bringing waste land under cultivation and breaking down the inefficient open field system, was now seen as a way of redistributing land so that it was held by men who could and would improve it and in units large enough to make improvement practicable. One writer, after listing the heavy expenses which the new methods involved, asked scornfully: 'What mind can be so perversely framed as to imagine for a single moment that such things are to be effected by little farmers?' In the early part of the century most enclosures were the result of mutual agreement on the part of everybody concerned; but now it became customary to enforce enclosure on reluctant smallholders by means of private Acts of Parliament. Between 1700 and 1760 there were just over 200 of these Acts, affecting some 300,000 acres of land, but from 1760 to 1800 there were more than 1,900, affecting over three million acres. As long as the promoters of the enclosure could show that the owners of 75 per cent of the land concerned supported it, they had little difficulty in getting their Act passed. Even if the owners of the remaining 25 per cent objected to the loss of their land, they were unlikely to be rich enough to hire lawyers or bring pressure to bear on Parliament. While earlier enclosures had worked against the open field system and against squatters on the common lands, the new wave worked against smallholders in general. Those who could raise the necessary funds to buy a larger holding might survive in the new world of competitive capitalistic farming, but the rest would become hired labourers. Rural life no longer centred on the division between landlord and tenant but on that between employer and employed.

While landowners devoted their capital to the improvement of agriculture, other men turned their attention to industry. As early as the 1700s the merchants of Bristol had invested in Abraham Darby's ironworks at Coalbrookdale and now the merchants of Liverpool also had considerable sums to invest, sums which went to finance the expansion of the cotton industry. Even great noblemen like the Duke of Bridgewater and the Duke of Devonshire poured vast sums into the development of the mineral resources of their estates, while others went into partnership with industrialists. James Corbett, ironmaster at Wigan at the end of the century, relied on his partner the Earl of Balcarres for much of his capital. Those merchants and manufacturers who did not launch out into industrial enterprises of their own often put their money into industry indirectly by founding local banks: there were some three hundred provincial banks by the 1790s, including those founded by the ironmaster Sampson Lloyd and the brewer James Barclay. Some were unsound and perished in the credit crises of 1793, 1797 and 1810; but many stood firm and provided the essential credit facilities without which industrial expansion could not have taken place.[1]

Just as those investing in agriculture looked to the new husbandry to bring them increased returns, so the industrial capitalist interested himself in new methods and labour-saving devices. The self-employed worker, small craftsman or domestic weaver, regarded such things with suspicion since they lessened the value of his labour and threatened his livelihood; but to the capitalist they meant reduced labour costs and increased output. Domestic weavers might protest, but those clothiers who had sunk their capital in building workshops and employing hired weavers found that refinements like the flying shuttle paid for themselves by stepping up production and cutting down overheads. The spinners, when they saw that the expansion of the weaving industry created an increased demand for yarn, began to seek ways of speeding up their own processes. Hargreaves's Spinning Jenny, patented in 1770, drove several spindles from one wheel, and later developments by Arkwright and Crompton resulted in massive and efficient spinning machines driven by water power. When Arkwright's patents were cancelled in 1785 power spinning became general, especially in the cotton industry. Machines to spin were followed by machines to weave: Cartwright invented the power loom in 1784 and patented it the following year. At about the same time steam power came to supplement water power. The steam

[1] In County Durham in the early nineteenth century, the notes issued by Backhouse's bank in Darlington were preferred to those of the Bank of England itself.

engines developed by Savery and Newcomen in the 1690s had been at work ever since, pumping water out of mines; but now the demand was for an engine that would turn a wheel, since reciprocating motion could not easily be transmitted from one machine to another. Watt's 'sun-and-planet' device, patented in 1782, solved this problem, while his invention of the separate condenser made possible an efficient and economical steam engine for use in conjunction with the new machines. During the last quarter of the eighteenth century the firm of Boulton and Watt turned out nearly 500 steam engines. Standing at the centre of the process which was transforming the workshops of the eighteenth century into the factories of the nineteenth, the two men provided a perfect epitome of the whole process: Boulton, capitalist and businessman, saw what was needed and Watt, technician and inventor, saw how it could be produced. Necessity was the parent of invention and investment was its grandparent.

Machines bred more machines. Faster spinning and weaving necessitated faster printing—by the late 1780s Thomas Bell's revolving press for cloth printing was in general use—while the demand for dyestuffs and for the new bleaching powders stimulated the growth of a large-scale chemical industry. All this meant more iron and also more coal, especially after the development of coal gas lighting by William Murdoch in the 1790s. Boulton and Watt's works were lit by gas in 1803 and by 1815 it was in general use for street lighting in London. Coal production rose from about six million tons in 1770 to over ten million tons at the end of the century, while the increase in iron production was even more dramatic—from 65,900 tons in 1788 to 258,206 in 1806. Even so the British iron industry could not always keep pace with the soaring home demand and iron sometimes had to be imported—as much as 64,200 tons of it in 1792.

Expansion of heavy industries and of mining and quarrying was also assisted by the new enthusiasm for better communications. The new roads, which were pioneered by turnpike trusts employing such men as John Metcalfe, Thomas Telford and John McAdam, helped postal and passenger services rather than carriers of heavy goods,[1] but the new canals played a vital part in the industrial boom. In 1759 the Duke of Bridgewater had obtained an Act of Parliament allowing him to build a canal from his collieries at Worsley to Manchester;

[1] Even by 1776 the journey from London to Edinburgh by coach had been cut from twelve days to four; and by the early nineteenth century it was possible to get from London to Bath in a day.

and the result was Brindley's canal, opened in 1761, which cut the price of coal in Manchester by nearly a half. Liverpool merchants and inland manufacturers were quick to see the possibilities of canals joining the Mersey with Lancashire, the midlands and the West Riding of Yorkshire. Josiah Wedgwood, the Staffordshire potter whose ambition was to be 'Vase Maker General to the Universe', joined with Liverpool and Birmingham businessmen to finance a canal from the Mersey to the Trent so that he could bring his china clay all the way from Cornwall by water. Opened in 1777, the canal benefited the salt works of Cheshire, the metal industries of Birmingham and the brewing and textile industries of Derbyshire as well as the Staffordshire potteries. The Leeds and Liverpool canal, an immense 127-mile undertaking which took nearly fifty years to build, provided the northern side of the great triangular system of inland waterways which, by the early nineteenth century, bound together the new industrial regions of the north and the midlands. Many canals serving industrial areas paid very well indeed: the Worsley–Runcorn canal yielded dividends of up to 37 per cent and the value of shares in the Mersey and Trent canal went up by twenty-three times in less than fifty years. But in other parts of the country, and especially in agricultural regions, investors were less fortunate and the three canals built to connect the Thames and the Severn were all financial failures. British agriculture was by no means in decline, but when compared with the explosive boom in industry its progress was hesitant and uncertain.

The cotton spinning industry, though it cannot be seen as the only cause of the industrial boom, certainly set the pace for it. By 1784 there was more than half a million pounds invested in cotton spinning in Lancashire and the spinners were selling their yarn for six times the price they paid for raw cotton from America. Competition tended to bring selling prices down but this was partly offset by the adoption in America of Whitney's cotton gin, which reduced the price of raw cotton still further. John Horrocks, who went into cotton spinning in 1786 at the age of eighteen, was worth three-quarters of a million pounds when he died in 1804; and Arkwright made such a colossal fortune that he even boasted he would personally pay off the National Debt. By 1815 Britain was exporting £22,555,000 worth of cotton goods, three times as much as her export of woollens.

Although the eighteenth-century woollen industry had been to some extent dependent on finding markets abroad, it had at least been a truly native industry, an extention of British farming. But the cotton industry stood fairly and squarely on the shoulders of foreign and colonial trade. Trade had provided much of its initial capital, trade was providing all its raw materials, trade must provide the greater part of its markets. The central part which it now played in Britain's economy meant that the sea could never again be regarded simply as a 'moat defensive to a house'; it was now a highway and a lifeline, essential both to prosperity in peace and survival in war. When war came in 1793 statesmen and farmers alike saw Britain's dependence on foreign food supplies as her greatest danger. Strenuous efforts were made to boost home agriculture and a Board of Agriculture was set up with Arthur Young, a prolific writer on agricultural improvement, as its first Secretary. But in spite of all that could be done, wheat imports for the war years averaged over 500,000 quarters a year, whereas a hundred years earlier, during the War of the Spanish Succession, wheat had only once had to be imported—in the year 1709—and then only to the extent of 2,000 quarters. Even the improvements in agriculture, though they produced more food, meant more horses and thus increased Britain's reliance on foreign supplies of fodder. The import of oats, which only started in the last quarter of the eighteenth century, had reached a million quarters a year by 1815. It was clear that Britain could no longer feed herself.

But the end of self-sufficiency was not just a matter of dependence on foreign food. It also meant dependence on foreign markets. As more and more capital was poured into the manufacturing industries and as an ever increasing proportion of the population came to depend on them for its livelihood, it became obvious that the country would face appalling financial dislocation and social distress if the products of these industries could not be profitably sold. It was impossible for the home market to absorb all that was being made, since wages were too low. By 1815 an extra expenditure of £3 10s on the part of every man, woman and child in the country would have been necessary if all that was being sold abroad had had to be sold at home instead. With a large part of the population living only a little above subsistence level this was clearly out of the question. Britain had to sell her goods abroad or perish: cut off from their foreign markets her industries would shrivel and die. Faced with this inescapable fact, industrialists and businessmen set themselves to bind those markets closer to them while statesmen prepared to defend, by force if necessary, their right to do so. If Britain was to

333

depend on the world, then the world must be made to depend on Britain.

2   The unsettled society

In 1709, when the parish authorities of Cowden in Kent were asked to take in refugees from the Palatinate, they replied that they could not, 'for wee Have more of ouer one Poor than we can imploy, nither Have we any Housing to Pott them in'. The reply summed up the early eighteenth-century view of society. It was a static view, a settled view, a view which refused to think in terms either of the growth or of the movement of population. Each parish was a fixed and stable community, with employment and accommodation for a certain number of people. As old men became enfeebled, so young men grew up to take their place. What death took away, birth gave back. Men might not always have to wait to step into dead men's shoes, but they often had to wait to step into dead men's cottages. A young man who wished to marry and raise a family had to wait until he could find 'Housing to Pott them in'; and parish constables were anxious to see that no new cottages were erected. They were equally anxious to ensure that those bringing new 'inmates' into the parish accepted full responsibility for their relief should they become pauperized, and that all casual labourers entering the parish brought settlement certificates with them. Since these certificates bound the parish that issued them to take back the man in question—and pay the cost of transporting him—should he become a pauper, they were only given reluctantly and usually only for fairly short journeys. Everything possible was done to prevent the movement of population and to preserve the settled, static nature of society.

Yet movement took place. 'We daily see manufacturers leaving the places where wages are low and removing to others where they can get more money' said Josiah Tucker in 1752; and by 1788 John Howlett was speaking of agricultural labourers who 'ranged from parish to parish and from county to county unthinking of and undeterred by the laws of settlement'. Instead of looking for work where their homes were, men were prepared to make their homes wherever they could find work. The settled society was breaking up.

At first the movement was no more than the drift into the towns from the surrounding countryside which had been noted—and deplored—for many years past. Sheffield, which increased its population from 2,695 in 1736 to 12,571 in 1755, took more than

334

three-quarters of its new inhabitants from villages within a twenty-mile radius. But during the second half of the century it was no longer a matter of short journeys authorized by reluctant parish overseers, but of large-scale migrations over considerable distances. In the new cotton towns of Lancashire, Cheshire and Derbyshire, where expansion came a generation or so later than that of Sheffield, parish authorities were non-existent or ineffective. Factory owners, faced with the problem of building up a large, reliable and disciplined labour force in a short time, were not likely to ask awkward questions about settlement certificates; and parish overseers in other parts of the country soon came to regard Lancashire as their predecessors had regarded the American colonies—as a newly developed area which could absorb their unwanted paupers. By 1787 the parish of St Clement Danes in London was advertising in the Manchester papers, offering its pauper children as 'apprentices' to the cotton manufacturers. By the end of the century workers were pouring into Lancashire at the rate of more than 15,000 a year. Some came involuntarily, parish children transported in batches under contract, while others came voluntarily, drawn by ambition or driven by hunger. The new roads facilitated their movement and helped to make the migration of labour a familiar and widespread feature of the nation's life. While the canals brought the new industrialists their raw materials, the roads brought them their labour force.

Those who regretted the passing of the old order sometimes imagined that labourers were being driven off the land, that the new agricultural methods were producing mass unemployment and thus forcing men to look for work in the new industries. In fact, it seems that the changes increased rather than reduced the demand for labour. New land had to be prepared, drainage and irrigation schemes undertaken, hedges, fences and ditches made, and all this meant more labourers. The new horse-drawn appliances had to be forged and repaired, while the horses that drew them had to be looked after. Increased cultivation of root crops required more men to hoe them and to lift them. If prosperity was to be measured purely by the number of men in work and the amount of food that their labour produced, then the new husbandry brought prosperity to many rural districts. Gilbert White paid tribute to its beneficial effects in 1773 when he observed that 'such a run of wet seasons as we have had the last ten or twelve years would have produced a famine a century or more ago'.

BRITAIN, 1688-1815

But the new methods, as well as creating more employment and more bread, also created a class of agricultural labourers for whom these two things were more immediately and more relentlessly connected than ever before. The cottagers who had made up the bulk of the population earlier in the century had never been entirely dependent on their daily employment for their daily bread: the beasts that they grazed on the common land, the fowls that pecked and scratched around their cottages, the crops that they raised on their plots of land, all helped to feed them and their families. Their wives and children could go gleaning in the fields after the harvest, or collect firewood, or do a little spinning to help things out. In bad times these things might make the difference between starvation and subsistence, while in good times they could make men sufficiently sure of themselves to bargain for higher wages—eighteenth-century employers frequently found that cheap food put wages up instead of bringing them down. The cottager's resources had been slender, but they had helped him to survive and sometimes even to welcome those periods of unemployment which the seasonal nature of work on the land made inevitable. For the landless labourer there was nothing to fall back on except parish relief: he was totally dependent on his employer and on the charity of his neighbours. So far as he was concerned, the end of national self-sufficiency was reflected in the loss of his own self-reliance. It was this change of status, rather than widespread unemployment, that produced the migration from the countryside to the new towns.

It also produced a crisis in the administration of parish poor relief. The total reliance of the poor on money wages meant that any rise in the price of bread would drive more and more people to seek relief just when it cost most to provide it. At first the problem was an occasional one, asserting itself locally and in times of bad harvests; but as wheat prices climbed steeply and inexorably, from an average of 46s a quarter in the 1780s to 83s 8d a quarter in the 1800s, it became general and permanent. Even those labourers who were in work found it difficult to buy enough bread for their families and joined the unemployed in seeking parish relief. Poor rates soared from just over £1½ million in 1776 to nearly £8 million in 1818, and many farmers found themselves paying several shillings a year in poor rates for every acre they farmed. With their profits and sometimes even their solvency threatened, they tried to save themselves by reducing wages; and the 'Speenhamland system' provided them with a justification and even an incentive to do so. This system, devised by the Berkshire justices in 1795 and subsequently adopted in most parts of southern England, involved laying down standard wage rates which were worked out according to the current price of bread and the size of the labourer's family. Any man earning less than the accepted rate was entitled to have his wages made up to that level out of the poor rates. Unscrupulous employers were thus enabled to offer lower wages without losing their workers, while labourers had no incentive to work hard since they would get no more and no less than the standard rate in any case. Farmers who were honest enough to offer fair wages still had to subsidize, through the poor rates, their neighbours' wages bills. In a last desperate effort to hold down rates, parish overseers started to hire out pauper labour at cheap rates; but this only accelerated the spiral of falling wages and rising poor rates, since some employers deliberately laid off their workers in order to hire paupers. The new husbandry had made possible a more efficient use of the land, but it had certainly not produced a more efficient use of the labour force.

The problems which faced parish and municipal authorities in the newly industrialized areas were different from those in the country but no less daunting. Some parishes in Lancashire which covered more than a hundred square miles each and had been difficult to run even at the old levels of population now became quite unmanageable. The justices of the peace and the parish officers were scarcely able to maintain law and order, let alone watch over the moral and social welfare of the vast new populations entrusted to their care. Sometimes the factory owners themselves took part in local government —one of the two justices who struggled with the problems of Merthyr Tydfil's 30,000 inhabitants was the proprietor of the local iron works— but for the most part they had neither the leisure nor the social standing to take their places on the bench. Instead they ruled their workers by means of private regulations of their own, enforced by a system of fines. The practice of fining workers for such offences as smoking or swearing was already well established and had been extensively used by Sir Ambrose Crowley, who had built up a £200,000 iron manufacturing business at the beginning of the eighteenth century. It was now extended, especially in the cotton mills, to form a rigid system of industrial discipline. Men and women who had been used to spinning or weaving in their own cottages and determining for themselves their hours and conditions of work

337

found that when they came to work in the factories they were fined for unpunctuality, for talking at their work, or even for opening a window. The damp and stuffy atmosphere of the mills, however unwelcome it might be to the workers, was essential for the proper functioning of the machines which ruled and regulated and dominated their lives. Child workers in particular found it difficult to keep pace with the relentless and tireless motion of the machines they served. For them penalties were usually physical rather than financial: overseers like Robert Woodward of Litton Mill, who hung up children by their wrists over their machines, were no doubt exceptional, but there were many factories in which children were treated with sickening cruelty. William Hutton said of his time as an apprentice at a silk mill in Derby: 'The confinement and the labour were no burden, but the severity was intolerable, the marks of which I yet carry and shall carry to the grave.'

Men and women had been overworked and apprentice children ill-treated long before the factory system became general. It took the London bookbinders forty years and an indictment for conspiracy to get their working day reduced from fifteen hours to thirteen; and Jouveaux, the London embroiderer who worked parish girls from five in the morning until midnight and fed them largely on bread and water, was probably not unique. But whereas the earlier workshops had been established in places where the municipal and parish authorities were reasonably competent and vigilant, so that a harsh employer ran a real risk of exposure and punishment, the new factories were often far beyond the reach of all authority but that of their owners. Where they were able, local authorities would still sometimes take action. The Manchester magistrates decided in 1784 not to apprentice children to mills that worked them more than ten hours a day; and in 1801 Thomas Watson shot himself after inquiries by parish officers had revealed that the apprentice children in his silk mills at Watford were half-starved. But in many of the new industrial areas the existing structure of local government was completely swamped by the sheer magnitude of the problems thrust upon it, so that all power passed into the hands of the industrialist. His workers were utterly dependent on him for their livelihood and in many cases he also owned the houses they lived in and the shops from which they bought their food and other necessities. Some of the industrialists of the early eighteenth century, like Sir Ambrose Crowley or the Quaker copper manufacturer William Champion, had organized schemes of social welfare or built model villages for their employees; and some of the new men carried on this paternalistic tradition. In 1793 John Curwen of Workington Hall in Cumberland set up a fund for pensions and accident benefits and later on, in the years of high food prices, he sold supplies to his workpeople from his own store at reduced prices which left him out of pocket.

Unfortunately men like John Curwen were rare. More typical was William Sidgwick, who told a committee of the House of Commons in 1816 that the hours worked in his mill depended entirely on the demand for cotton yarn and the availability of water power. When asked what there was to stop him working his employees day and night, he replied: 'I know of no law to restrain me for so doing: I never heard of any.' Men like this arranged every aspect of the society that they ruled in such a way as to increase their own profit rather than to promote the welfare of their workers. The living conditions of the apprentice children, the hours and conditions of work in the factory itself, the rents paid for hastily erected tenements, the prices in the factory store—all helped to lay up treasures upon earth for the owner. To compare him to a West Indian planter, as some contemporaries did, was misleading, but only for one reason. Whereas the planter had paid for his slaves and had a financial interest in keeping them alive and reasonably healthy, the factory owner had only hired the men, women and children whose lives he ruled. Thus there was no incentive for him to protect them from the injuries, disease and malnutrition which were such familiar features of the world he had created for them.

By the end of the eighteenth century every social unit in the country, from the smallest rural parish to the largest factory community, bore witness to the passing of the settled society of the past. The problems of the landless agricultural labourer and the rootless industrial worker strained existing institutions to the limit and beyond, while the shift in population made existing administrative divisions obsolete. Lancashire, which had been one of the most thinly populated of the English counties in 1700, now had 673,000 inhabitants—about one-thirteenth of the total population of England and Wales. Many other northern counties had grown at a similar rate, so that the area of the densest population, which had previously stretched across the centre of England from Somerset to Suffolk via the midlands and the Home Counties, now lay between Birmingham and Barrow-in-Furness. South Wales had been transformed from a sparsely populated and mainly pastoral area into a rapidly developing centre of iron and coal mining: between 1788 and 1806 its iron production went up by more than six times. In the lowlands of Scotland, and especially in Lanarkshire, the expansion of the textile and mining industries had brought an equally dramatic growth in population.

The growth of the new industrial areas did not take place at the expense of the countryside. What was taking place was not simply a large-scale movement of the existing population but a rapid and unprecedented increase in the population as a whole. Apart from the Orkney and Shetland Islands, there was not a single county in the whole of England, Wales and Scotland where the population was not increasing in the first years in the nineteenth century. The first official census, taken in 1801, showed a total population of 10,501,000 —8,893,000 in England and Wales and 1,608,000 in Scotland. Ten years later the total had risen to 11,970,000 (10,164,000 and 1,806,000). In Ireland the first census was not taken until 1821, when it revealed a population of 6,802,000. Back in 1696 Gregory King had reckoned that the population would double itself in six hundred years, by about the year 2300. In fact, it had done so in little more than a century.

This steep rise in population, which seems to have begun in the 1780s, caught most politicians and writers unawares. Many of them were convinced that it was not happening and both Chatham and Shelburne spoke of the disastrous implications of what they took to be the current *decline* in population. As late as 1777 Richard Price in his *Essay on the Population of England and Wales* convinced himself that the population had fallen by 25 per cent in less than a century and that it was still falling. However, as the expansion of both industry and agriculture became more and more obvious in the 1780s and 1790s, most people became convinced that the population must be increasing. 'The increase of employment', wrote Arthur Young, 'will be found to raise men like mushrooms.' In other words, a greater demand for labour meant earlier marriages and more children. In fact, the increase seems to have been produced more by a falling death-rate than by a rising birth-rate. It has been estimated that the birth-rate remained fairly steady at about 34 or 35 per 1,000 from the middle of the eighteenth century to the beginning of the nineteenth, while the death-rate fell sharply from 33·4 per 1,000 in 1730 to 19·98 per 1,000 in 1810. Improved medical services helped to account for the drop, but for the most part it was the result of better living conditions, a more varied diet (far more vegetables were being eaten and fresh fruit was no longer regarded as a dangerous food), and more scrupulous standards of personal hygiene. The advances in the textile industries made cheap washable cottons available to all but the very poorest and this played an important part in reducing the level of infant mortality. The new town houses, at any rate in the early years of industrialization and urbanization, were probably healthier and drier than the damp and draughty hovels in which the greater part of the population had lived in the early eighteenth century. It was not until about 1810 that overcrowding, lack of sanitation and unhealthy working conditions began to take their toll in the factory areas. From that date onwards the death-rate started to rise again, while the birth-rate fell steadily until by 1830 it stood at 32·36 per 1,000—lower than it had been since the 1730s. It seemed that the balance of nature was reasserting itself: the process of industrialization which had helped to increase the population was now tending to reduce it again.

Many people believed that this redressing of the balance, even if it was brought about by poverty and suffering and hunger, was a necessary and inevitable process. Thomas Malthus, in his *Essay on the Principle of Population as it affects the Future Improvement of Society*, published in 1798, insisted that all attempts to alleviate poverty and disease were misguided and harmful. Writing at a time of rising food prices and rising poor rates, he prophesised disaster if the population was allowed to go on increasing. Well-intentioned but short-sighted people were enabling more and more people to stay alive and more and more children to be born, with the result that in the end the population would outrun the means of subsistence and the whole society would be reduced to destitution and starvation. Men must be cruel only to be kind: they must close their eyes and ears to the sufferings of the poor and allow the natural checks to population growth—poverty, illness, premature death—to operate freely. Although his book was widely read, most men of good will were unable to resign themselves to the prospect of widespread starvation and disease. In spite of all the difficulties, the parish system of poor relief continued to be operated and the fight against disease went on. In 1796 Manchester set up a Board of Health to inquire into food pollution, overcrowding and problems of sanitation, and in 1798 the development of Jenner's technique of vaccination, by which the patient was given a dose of the harmless disease known as cowpox in order to render him immune from smallpox, marked a decisive advance in the campaign against diease. Whatever the Malthusians might think, the population increase had come to stay. Like all the other aspects of the unsettled society it posed problems which necessitated a drastic re-thinking of the whole purpose and function of the King's government.

3 The need for Government

The need for a more positive and more professional approach to administration manifested itself first at the local level. The transformation of Quarter Sessions from County Courts into County Councils was accentuated and accelerated, involving the appointment of more and more salaried officials. Professional county treasurers and county surveyors became the rule rather than the exception and even officers like criers and marshals were employed in an administrative rather than a purely ceremonial capacity. The appointment of salaried justices, which had previously been restricted to exceptionally populous areas like the City of Westminster and the County of Middlesex, began to be customary in other places as well. Even where the justices themselves were still unpaid amateurs they came to rely increasingly on professional assistants: as early as 1764 Shenstone remarked that 'a Justice and his Clerk is now little more than a blind man and his dog'. Parish officers, too, found that the new problems could not be solved by the old methods. One farmer who was appointed Overseer of the Poor in the early nineteenth century was so unfamiliar with book-keeping that he kept his accounts in a pair of boots—one for the money he got in and the other for the receipts for what he paid out. At a time when the whole administration of the poor law was in a state of continuous crisis, easygoing amateurism of this sort did not make for greater efficiency. Professional deputy constables and overseers, hired by those elected to parish offices, joined the professional county officials and the growing army of magistrates' clerks in turning local government from a spare-time occupation into a full-time business. Since the new professionalism was still unofficial and unrecognized, its standards were often very low. Mr Unite, a hired deputy constable who practised in Manchester in the 1790s, was so corrupt that he was even prepared to lock up troublesome wives as lunatics on receipt of the appropriate bribe from their husbands.

Associated with the passing of amateurism and the coming of professionalism was a general widening of the scope of local government. Between 1761 and 1765 the city of Westminster had promoted a series of private Acts of Parliament which gave it powers to collect rates from householders for the purpose of paving and lighting the streets; and by the 1780s and 1790s most of the new and expanding towns of the industrial regions, as well as many of the older towns, were securing for themselves similar powers. Between 1785 and 1800 over two hundred of these 'Improvement Acts' were passed and they made possible civic amenities and social services of all kinds. Municipal buildings were erected, town centres planned, streets paved and widened, hospitals founded and water supplies provided. In many places, and especially in Birmingham and Manchester, the literary societies and cultural institutions started by the Dissenters earlier in the century provided the impetus for the new burst of civic activity.

While county and municipal authorities did their best to adapt the institutions of a static society to the needs of a society which was expanding and changing at an unprecedented rate, the attitude of Parliament and of the central government remained essentially negative. The Improvement Acts, like the Acts that made possible enclosures or canals, were permissive rather than mandatory: instead of initiating change they merely consented to it. Two hundred years earlier, the Parliaments of Queen Elizabeth I had passed a series of remarkably positive and far-reaching Acts which sought to direct and control the whole economy of the country. The Parliaments of George III, however, were so determined to put freedom before efficiency that they could hardly bring themselves to repeal old Acts, let alone provide a new and more relevant system of legislation. The apprenticeship clauses of the 1563 Statute of Artificers, which served at one and the same time to cover up abuses in the factory system and to prevent its proper development—one factory in 1800 was said to have two workmen and sixty apprentices—were not repealed until 1814. Most of the other Elizabethan Acts remained in force until well into the nineteenth century. After weighing up and considering the petitions presented to it by different interests and groups, Parliament might be prepared to permit change, but it was not ready to initiate a comprehensive programme of legislation designed to solve the problems which the social and economic changes had created.

Yet there was a desperate need for such a programme. More than ever before, the country needed a statesman who would implement

Chatham's old slogan of 'measures, not men'. And he must be prepared to go much further than Chatham had gone. It was not enough simply to submit problems to Parliament and wait for Parliament to come up with an answer to them, as Chatham had done over the East India question in 1766–67; definite programmes of legislation must be drafted and guided through the two Houses. In spite of the long-standing prejudices against a 'prime' minister, and against any attempt by the executive to control the legislative, there must be a definite lead from the top. The prime minister must lead the Cabinet, the Cabinet must lead Parliament and Parliament must lead the country. Management must give way to government.

As well as implying a new view of the relationship between the King's ministers and Parliament, between the executive and the legislative, this meant a new view of the executive itself. Ministers and other government officials must do more and know more than ever before. The central government, like local institutions, must be in the hands of professionals rather than amateurs. As late as 1822, Thomas Bewick still thought that the country's interests would best be served by extending the system of amateur government upwards. 'Justices of the Peace', he said, 'take the very great trouble of acting their parts gratuitously; churchwardens and overseers do the same; and why do not the great and rich men of the land follow their praiseworthy example?' As a protest against the corruption of patronage politics and against the iniquitous practice of fee-taking, his outburst was justified and understandable. But to suppose that the complex governmental machinery of a modern state could be run by unpaid amateurs was naïve and unrealistic. Patronage politics would have to be replaced not by an easygoing amateurism but by a properly trained and properly paid civil service. Places under the Crown would have to be thought of as offices rather than beneficies, as jobs to be done rather than as opportunities to be exploited.

Such a change was unlikely to be popular. Even the Whigs, who had campaigned so strenuously for 'Economical Reform', were more concerned to reduce the power of the Crown than to end the patronage system itself. To most of them it seemed right and proper that the government of the country should be in the hands of men who had bought their places and intended to profit from them, just as to a later age it was to seem right and proper that the development of the country's economic resources should be in the hands of men who had bought stocks and shares and looked for dividends and capital appreciation. Anyone who sought to end the patronage structure and abolish sinecures would have to face charges of interfering with freedom of investment. To the career politicians his schemes would appear as threatening and tyrannical as 'nationalization' appeared to the businessmen of a later age.

13

New Ways of Thinking

1 The old way: Natural Religion and Natural Law

To the seventeenth century the conflict between human reason and
the Word of God had been a very real thing. While some believed
that man could and should use his reason in order to reach an understanding of the world around him, others considered that this was
presumptuous and irreverent. For them, revelation and not reason
provided the key to the mysteries of God's creation and man's life
here on earth. A man who finds himself in a carpenter's workshop
does not seek to understand the meaning of the pieces of wood
around him by weighing them and measuring them, but by asking
the carpenter: he and he alone can reveal the true purpose of his
creation and the true nature of his work. In the same way, they
argued, God and God alone could provide an explanation of His
work. Only by studying God could man understand the universe that
God had created. The gateway to all knowledge of men and things
was theology, the study of the nature of God and of the way in
which He had revealed Himself through the prophets and in the life
and teaching of Jesus Christ.

Isaac Newton, member of Parliament in 1689 for the University
of Cambridge and subsequently Master of the Mint and President
of the Royal Society, did more than any other man to resolve this
conflict. He did so by demonstrating, to most men's satisfaction, that
it simply did not exist. His *Mathematical Principles of Natural Philosophy*, published in Latin (the traditional language of theology) in
1687, suggested that the whole universe was governed by natural
laws which were themselves intelligible and reasonable. The purpose
of his work was as much theological as scientific. Like Milton, he
sought to 'justify the ways of God to men'; and to most people it
seemed that he had succeeded. There was now no more mystery
and therefore no more conflict. Whether man looked inwards into
the workings of his own mind or out to the remotest regions of

interstellar space, he would find the same answer and hear the same voice: the voice of God, which was also the voice of reason. Newton himself hoped that the natural laws which he had revealed would in due course be seen to explain all the aspects of God's creation. 'I wish we could derive the rest of the phenomena of Nature by the same kind of reasoning from mechanical principles,' he said, 'for I am induced by many reasons to suspect that they may all depend upon certain forces by which the particles of bodies, by some causes hitherto unknown, are either mutually impelled towards one another, and cohere in regular figures, or are repelled and recede from one another.' Roger Cotes, his friend and collaborator, was even more enthusiastic: 'The gates are now set open,' he wrote, 'and by the passage he has revealed we may freely enter into the knowledge of the hidden secrets and wonders of natural things . . . and, which is the best and most valuable fruit of philosophy, be thence incited the more profoundly to reverence and adore the great Maker of all. . . . Newton's distinguished work will be the safest protection against the attacks of atheists, and nowhere more surely than from this quiver can one draw forth missiles against the band of godless men.'

The Church of England, under attack in 1689 both from High Church Tories and from Dissenters, lost no time in using the missiles with which Newton had provided her. When Richard Bentley lectured in 1692 against atheism he based his arguments on 'The Advantages and Pleasures of a Religious Life, the Faculties of Humane Souls, the structure of Animate Bodies, and the Origin and Frame of the World'. God was no longer thought of as moving in a mysterious way His wonders to perform, but as the reasonable Creator of a reasonable universe from which reasonable men could deduce the sort of religion He intended them to follow. There was no room in such a religion either for the 'superstition' of the High Churchmen or for the 'enthusiasm' of the Dissenters. Since human institutions, like everything else, must be judged by the light of reason and by the laws of nature, the Tory charge that the Church of England had deserted her rightful anointed King could be shown to be mere superstition, while the Dissenters' insistence on the right of each man to bear witness to his own personal experience of God was enthusiasm, a perverse rejection of the universal dictates of reason. 'An Enthusiast', said one writer in 1704, 'thinks everything that comes into his head not only lawful but the Inspiration of God.'

Both extremes were equally repugnant to reason and therefore to God. Because they were unreasonable they must also be unnatural. Edmund Gibson, bishop of London from 1720 to 1748, remarked that 'it is universally acknowledged that revelation is to stand or fall by the test of reason'. Christianity was a reasonable religion, a natural religion. In the past men had worshipped God because He was beyond their comprehension, but now they worshipped him because He was within their comprehension. Since it seemed that He had designed a universe that measured up to their standards of orderliness and reasonableness, they were prepared to believe in His existence.

The creations of men, like the creation of God, must be governed by reason, order and symmetry. Sir Christopher Wren, who had been appointed surveyor general and principal architect for the rebuilding of the City of London after the Great Fire of 1666, had been a professor of astronomy before he was an architect; and the classical laws of proportion on which he based his work were for him as absolute and incontrovertible as the Laws of Nature. 'Natural Beauty', he said, 'is from Geometry.' The new St Paul's Cathedral, which he built between 1675 and 1716 to replace the medieval building which had been damaged and weakened by the fire, was a symbol of men's determination to sweep away what they regarded as the superstition and obscurantism of the past. The benighted and priest-ridden papists of the Middle Ages might have been content to worship in a dark Gothic church, but the enlightened rationalists of the new age must have a building that reflected the order of the universe and the order in their own minds. The new cathedral was essentially a 'classical' building, relying for its effect on symmetry and proportion, although its detail and decoration showed that Wren had been to some extent influenced by the 'baroque' style which was then fashionable throughout Catholic Europe. Whereas the classical style was concerned to reflect coolly and serenely the order of the universe itself, the baroque sought to overawe the beholder by its sheer power and splendour. In the eyes of most Englishmen it was an ostentatious and flamboyant style, better suited to the palaces of vainglorious foreign kings than to the houses of reasonable men living in harmony with nature. The years of war against Louis XIV intensified this feeling, so that when Sir John Vanbrugh began to build Blenheim Palace in 1705 on a truly colossal scale many people felt that he was offending against reason and nature as well as against

348

good taste. Vanbrugh's splendid and ponderous buildings came nearer to pure baroque than anything else produced in Britain in the eighteenth century; and the contemporary verdict on them was summed up neatly in Abel Evans's often quoted epitaph:

> Under this stone, Reader, survey
> Dead Sir John Vanbrugh's house of clay.
> Lie heavy on him, Earth! for he
> Laid many heavy loads on thee!

Alexander Pope, the poet and satirist, was one of Vanbrugh's most outspoken critics. He regarded Blenheim and other baroque palaces as unnatural monstrosities and he also disliked the gardens in which they were usually set. Modelled on the gardens of the French King's palace at Versailles, they consisted of long, straight, level avenues running between geometrical flower beds and carefully clipped hedges. While the palaces themselves lay like heavy loads upon the earth, the formal French gardens around them sought to roll and carve and clip the surrounding countryside into an unnatural subordination. This was not man in tune with nature: it was man shaking his puny fist at her and making himself despicable and ridiculous as a result. When Pope came to lay out gardens for his house at Twickenham in 1719 he was helped by William Kent, who was making a name for himself under the patronage of Pope's friend Lord Burlington. Kent, who was a painter and an architect as well as a garden designer, produced buildings which were very formal and symmetrical, based on the 'laws' of classical architecture laid down by the Italian architect Andrea Palladio in the sixteenth century; but the gardens in which he placed them were informal and undisciplined, intended to blend with the landscape rather than to dominate it. Kent's successor in the art of 'landscape' gardening was Lancelot Brown, who insisted that it was the gardener's job to work with his site rather than against it, to seek out and develop the underlying features or 'capabilities' of a landscape. It was for this reason that he was nicknamed 'Capability Brown'.

What Newton had done in the realm of philosophy, Kent and his followers did in the realm of taste: they reconciled the creations of man's mind with the natural order. Their elegant and beautifully proportioned Palladian houses, set among gardens that merged effortlessly with their surroundings, seemed the outward and visible signs of a society at one with nature and nature's laws. Proud foreign potentates might twist and torture God's creation to make it conform to their tastes, like superstitious savages hacking out clearings in the primeval forest; but in Britain reasonable and enlightened men had come to terms with a reasonable universe. Already their insight into the real nature of things had resolved the conflict between faith and reason and between nature and art. Who could doubt that in time they would be able to illumine such dark corners as still remained and learn all that men needed to know on earth? It was in this confident and even complacent atmosphere that Pope set out in 1731 to write a summary in verse of human nature and human knowledge, based on the philosophical ideas of Lord Bolingbroke. The project was never completed, but parts of it appeared, including an *Essay on Taste* and an *Essay on Man*. The latter included a triumphant avowal of faith in natural law:

> All Nature is but Art unknown to thee,
> All Chance, Direction which thou can'st not see;
> All Discord, Harmony not understood;
> All partial Evil, universal Good;
> And, spite of Pride, in erring Reason's spite,
> One truth is clear, Whatever Is, is Right.

It was a comforting thought. But there were still one or two unanswered questions which gnawed at the bland optimism of Pope and his contemporaries. Natural disasters, in particular, presented a tricky problem. How could earthquake and pestilence be fitted into the benign plan of the Great Craftsman? In the spring of 1750 two slight earth tremors and the prophecy of a third produced an extraordinary panic in London. Roads out of the city were jammed with refugees and women made themselves special 'earthquake gowns' to keep them warm while they sat out in the fields waiting for the destruction of London, as Jonah had waited for the destruction of Nineveh. Like Jonah, they felt rather foolish when nothing happened. As the refugees slunk back into London they were met by a chorus of mockery and reproof from the rationalists, who had been shocked at this mass exhibition of 'superstition'.

But in fact it was the rationalists themselves who were playing the part of Jonah and claiming, as he had claimed, a particular insight into the workings of providence. Their optimism might be strengthened by the earthquakes that did not happen, but it was not proof against those that did. On 1 November 1755 the city of Lisbon in

influence of
Lisbon quake

Portugal was devastated by a series of earthquakes which were accompanied by tidal waves and extensive fires. Thousands of people were crushed or drowned or burned to death; and all over Europe philosophers began to question their easy assumption that nature was reasonable and reason natural. If the universe really was governed by immutable laws, then those laws must be a good deal more mysterious than had been thought. It might well be that superstition and even enthusiasm had a part to play in justifying the ways of God to men and in regulating the attitude of men to God.

2 *A new approach to Religion*

People in Britain were shocked and horrified by the news from Lisbon. Gifts of money, food and clothing were sent to Portugal and on 18 December 1755 George II issued a special Proclamation. It began by observing that 'the Manifold Sins and Wickedness of these Kingdoms have most justly deserved heavy and severe Punishments from the Hand of Heaven', and went on to point out that 'some Neighbouring Countries, in Alliance and Friendship with Us, have been visited with a most dreadful and extensive Earthquake, which hath also, in some Degree, been felt in several Parts of Our Dominions'. The King therefore ordered that 6 February 1756 should be observed as a general Fast Day, when all his subjects were to repent of their sins and pray that their country might be spared from the wrath of God.

Some of the sermons preached on the Fast Day suggested that God had punished the Portuguese for their popish superstition, and one or two preachers made much of the fact that the only Protestant chapel in Lisbon had been miraculously preserved amidst the general ruin. But most clergymen were more concerned to castigate their congregations than to reassure them. From pulpits all over the country came denunciations of the godlessness and debauchery of the times. Dancing, drunkenness, theatre-going, neglect of the Sabbath, mockery of religion and sexual immorality all came in for their share of condemnation. They were particularly rife, it was alleged, among the upper ranks of London society. 'It is almost a fashion to be thought wicked!' thundered the Dean of York.

Wickedness for its own sake was not as fashionable as the Dean imagined. It was over thirty years since the Privy Council had had to issue orders for the suppression of Satanist societies in London[1] and when Sir Francis Dashwood and his associates at Medmenham revived such practices they did not meet with much approval. But the easy optimism of the rationalists and the current fear of 'enthusiasm' in any form had certainly led the world of fashion to look askance at any display of religious fervour. 'Religion', remarked the Earl of Chesterfield to his godson, 'is by no means a proper subject of conversation in a mixed company.' When they went to church, gentlemen expected to hear comforting addresses on the advantages of Christianity, not passionate harangues dwelling on the sins of the congregation and on the need for amendment of life. Many of them, like Sir Roger de Coverley, were only too glad when preachers gave up the attempt to compose their own sermons and relied instead on those which were available in published form.

Nevertheless, religious enthusiasm and the type of preaching with which it was associated were not entirely unknown in the early eighteenth century. Long before the appalling news from Lisbon in 1755 produced its crop of Fast Day sermons, many preachers were in the habit of lashing their congregations with fiery and uncomfortable words. Griffith Jones, who held various livings in Carmarthenshire from 1709 until his death in 1761, began a religious revival which spread from Wales into England. In Scotland the old Puritan tradition of marathon sermons to large and enthusiastic gatherings was still carried on by men like John Hepburn. On one occasion he preached for nearly seven hours to some 7,000 people, many of whom had come fifteen miles on foot to hear him. Even in London itself, John Henley began to give open-air addresses in Newport Market in 1726, after he had quarrelled with his bishop and lost his chances of preferment.

It was in Bristol in 1739 that the new approach to religion, the approach of enthusiasm rather than of reasonableness, was really launched. On 17 February of that year George Whitefield, a powerful young preacher whose first sermon was said by hostile critics to have driven fifteen people mad, gave an open-air address to the colliers in the Kingswood area. Like the workers who were to pour into the industrial north later in the century, the Kingswood colliers were not

[1] In the spring of 1721 there were three of these 'Hell-Fire Clubs', one meeting in Somerset House, another in a house in Westminister and a third in Conduit Street, Hanover Square. Their members included 'upwards of forty persons of quality of both sexes'.

properly covered by the existing parish system and lived 'as sheep having no shepherd', in Whitefield's own words. His friend John Wesley, who had at first regarded open-air preaching as a dangerous innovation which might subvert all decency and order, decided a few weeks later to follow his example and preached to a crowd of three thousand on a hillside just outside the city. By the summer the two men were drawing large congregations, both in Kingswood and in the city itself, and were building chapels and meeting houses to accommodate them. From open-air preaching to itinerant preaching was an easy step: 'Seeing I have now no parish of my own, nor probably ever shall,' Wesley wrote to a friend in June 1739, 'I look upon all the world as my parish; thus far I mean, that, in whatever part of it I am, I judge it meet, right, and my bounden duty, to declare unto all that are willing to hear, the glad tidings of salvation.' By the time he died in 1791 he had himself covered nearly a quarter of a million miles and preached 40,000 sermons. Whitefield, who died in 1770, preached 18,000; and hundreds of their followers, both clergymen and laymen, developed and extended the work. It soon became clear that the new approach had grown into a new movement, known to friends and foes alike as 'methodism'. At Oxford earlier in the 1730s Wesley had been the leader of a group—including his brother Charles, the future hymn-writer, and Whitefield himself—devoted to a strict and regulated life of prayer and good works. They had been dubbed 'methodists' by other members of the university and now the same name was used to describe the great national movement of religious regeneration which they had founded.

Men of substance everywhere were outraged by the movement. Country gentlemen and respectable tradesmen might not approve of the sceptical and half-mocking attitude to religion which was fashionable in London, but they were certainly not going to let un-licensed enthusiasts usurp the functions of the clergy. 'Itinerant Preachers', said one shocked writer in 1740, 'run up and down from Place to Place, and from County to County, drawing after them confused Multitudes of People, and leading them into a Disesteem of their own Pastors, as less willing or less able to instruct them in the Way of Salvation.' Local authorities often refused to protect Method-ists against rioters and in some cases they even encouraged trouble-makers to break up the meetings. Wesley's journals contain accounts of some sixty riots and at Sheffield in 1743 his brother Charles was viciously stoned, as well as being threatened with a drawn sword by the captain of a detachment of soldiers. When the rioters started to pull down the meeting-house and the local Constable was called, he merely ordered Charles to leave the town, saying that he was 'the occasion of all this disturbance'. Some justices resorted to the Act of 1703, which empowered them to press into military service 'all able-bodied men as had not any lawful calling or employment'. John Nelson, a Yorkshire stonemason who was one of the most vigorous and persuasive of Wesley's early lay preachers, was pressed for the army and only released from his regiment after Charles Wesley had managed to find a substitute to serve in his place. The same device was used against Thomas Maxfield when he was preaching in Cornwall in 1745: the justices of Marazion handed him over to the military authorities, in spite of John Wesley's intercessions on his behalf, and he was forced to serve as a soldier for a number of years.

Some of the ecclesiastical authorities wanted to discipline the Methodist clergymen as severely as the justices disciplined the lay preachers. Bishop Gibson of London insisted that they were breaking the law, because 'they have the boldness to preach in the Fields and other open Places, and by publick Advertisements to invite the Rabble to be their Hearers; notwithstanding an express Declaration in a Statute'. Others viewed them with more favour,[1] and in the end no prosecutions were initiated, although many bishops refused preferment to clergy who became involved in the movement. Preachers who were branded as 'enthusiasts' were often forced to resign their places, even when they had no direct connection with the Methodists. The fashionable congregation at St George's, Hanover Square, were scandalized when their additional morning preacher, William Romaine, started to preach fervent sermons which attracted large crowds to the church. At St Dunstan's in the West, where he also held a preaching appointment, things were even worse: outraged parishioners complained that they had to make their way to their pews through a 'ragged unsavoury multitude' and the rector himself prevented Romaine from entering the pulpit. He had to resign his appointments at both churches and for several years he was unable to obtain further preferment. Finally he secured the living of St Anne's, Blackfriars, but only because it was in the gift of the parishioners and not of the bishop. The people of Blackfriars, unlike those

[1] Bishop Benson of Gloucester, when told of the fifteen people who were supposed to have been driven mad by Whitefield's first sermon, remarked that he hoped the madness would continue.

at St George's and St Dunstan's, evidently liked their religion laced
with enthusiasm.

Among those who tried to break down the stony hostility with
which Methodism was met in fashionable circles was Selina Hastings,
Countess of Huntingdon. After the death of her two sons in 1743 and
of her husband in 1746 she devoted the rest of her life to the movement. In 1748 Whitefield became her chaplain and she opened her
house in Park Lane for him to preach twice a week to such members
of the nobility as she could persuade to attend. As a peeress she could
appoint as many chaplains as she liked and she used this right to
protect clergymen like Romaine who were out of favour with their
bishops. She never ceased to denounce the immorality of London
society—she would not let her daughter be a maid of honour because
of the Sunday card parties at Court—and she established chapels in
fashionable resorts like Bath, Brighton and Tunbridge Wells in order
to convert the upper ranks of society to Methodism.

On the whole the upper ranks of society were not impressed. The
Duchess of Buckingham thought that the doctrines of the Methodists
were 'strongly tinctured with impertinence and disrespect towards
their superiors'. 'It is monstrous', she wrote to the Countess of
Huntingdon, 'to be told that you have a heart as sinful as the common
wretches that crawl the earth. I cannot but wonder that your lady-
ship should relish any sentiments so much at variance with high
rank and good breeding.' Religion that harped on sin was distasteful,
especially when the sin in question was that of the nobility and
gentry; and when Joseph Trapp preached a series of sermons against
Methodism in 1739 it was noted with satisfaction that he castigated
them for being 'righteous overmuch'.

While some accused the Methodists of radicalism, of encouraging
the lower orders to dwell upon the sins of their betters, others saw
them as secret papists. Hogarth produced a caricature of a Methodist
preacher with his wig pushed aside to reveal the shaven head of a
monk; and as early as 1741 Wesley's sermons were interrupted by
cries of 'Popery, popery!' In 1749 Bishop Lavington of Exeter published *The Enthusiasm of Methodists and Papists Compared* in which he
suggested that this new outburst of religious fervour was nothing
but the crude superstitions of popery and even of paganism under a
new guise. If it was 'superstition' to think and act on the principle
that man cannot live by reason alone, then Wesley was indeed
superstitious, as were all the other opponents of the easygoing

355

latitudinarianism[1] of the eighteenth-century Church. Catholics, Non-jurors and High Church Tories, as well as Methodists, were distressed and worried by the worldliness of a Church which valued reasonableness more highly than righteousness. Wesley was deeply influenced by the works of the non-juror William Law; and in this respect his fellow enthusiast was that unrepentant high tory, Dr Johnson. Like Wesley, he thought of religion as a real spiritual force and not just as a reasonable commentary on the natural order.

In the atmosphere created by the Lisbon earthquake, spirituality, righteousness and even enthusiasm began to come back into fashion. Wesley published a pamphlet called *Serious Thoughts occasioned by the late Earthquake at Lisbon*, addressed to 'the learned, rich, and honourable heathens, commonly called Christians' and it ran into six editions. Even Horace Walpole, a man of fashion who was much given to sneering at the Methodists, paid grudging tribute to the new state of affairs. 'Between the French and the Earthquake,' he wrote in February 1756, 'you have no notion how good we are grown; nobody makes a suit now but of sackcloth turned up with ashes.' The new enthusiasm for righteousness was still strong enough in 1757 to make the government drop its plans for exercising the militia on Sundays, and in 1760 it was given a new impetus by the accession of George III. He began his reign by issuing a Proclamation against profanity and immorality and set a personal example of piety and domestic virtue, discouraging the Sunday card parties which so shocked the Countess of Huntingdon and taking swift action when she complained to him about the Archbishop of Canterbury's extravagant festivities at Lambeth Palace. The gossipwriters and caricaturists were quick to make fun of the new King's simple piety, his down-to-earth domesticity and above all his thriftiness; but to most of his subjects these traits were more endearing than those of London society. As well as making the monarchy more popular than it had been since the days of Queen Elizabeth, he also made it less disreputable. Professional courtiers may have found him over-righteous and professional politicians may have found him over-

[1] A latitudinarian was one who followed Bishop Hoadly of Bangor in denying the need for strict doctrinal conformity in the Church. Preaching before the King in 1717 on the text 'My kingdom is not of this world', he had argued that the Church on earth could have no real spiritual or moral authority because the laws of Christ were not of this world. Non-jurors and High Churchmen disputed this Whig point of view hotly, provoking the notorious Bangorian controversy.

enthusiastic, but the country as a whole was glad to have such a pious and homely monarch.

Strengthened by this example of kingly piety, Methodism came to be tolerated and even welcomed by the propertied classes: when Wesley preached at Grimsby in 1764 he was gratified to find that 'the mayor and all the gentry of the town were present'. Richard Graves's satire on him, *The spiritual Quixote, or, the summer's ramble of Mr Geoffrey Wildgoose*, published in 1773, had a certain amount of success and London society continued to regard him with amused contempt. 'I wonder these madmen and knaves do not wear out,' wrote Horace Walpole in 1776, 'as their folly is no longer new.' Outside London, however, landowners and industrialists alike found that Methodism had a steadying effect on the labouring classes. Wesley was a staunch supporter of the existing social order and his denunciation of the colonists during the War of American Independence made him even more respectable and acceptable. By 1785 he could write: 'I am become, I know not how, an honourable man.' In Leicester, where militant working class movements were particularly strong at the end of the eighteenth century, the local Methodists would have nothing to do with them; and the same was true in the great Methodist strongholds of Cornwall and Yorkshire. By the turn of the century there were some 150,000 Methodists in the country and most of them were convinced that their chances in the next world depended, at least in part, upon a dutiful and humble acceptance of the established order in this one.

They were not, however, members of the Established Church. From the beginning the Methodist leaders had seen the danger of their movement breaking away from the Anglican communion and had striven to avert it. When Susannah Wesley asked Whitefield in 1739 'if her sons were not making some innovations in the church', he replied that 'they were so far from it that they endeavoured all they could to reconcile Dissenters to our communion'. Nevertheless, Whitefield himself moved closer and closer to the Calvinistic doctrines of the Dissenters and after his death the Countess of Huntingdon continued the process. From 1779 onwards her chapels were registered as dissenting meeting houses and by the time she died in 1791 she had ceased to regard herself as an Anglican. Wesley, however, was bitterly opposed to the Dissenters, both on theological grounds and because he thought they were more concerned with the things of this world than with their prospects in the next. He refused to countenance the idea that Methodism might become just another dissenting sect and when he died, also in 1791, he died an Anglican. But all his protestations of conformity could not conceal the essential nonconformity of Methodism. Methodist communities were based on Church membership, but their activities and their organization stood apart from the Anglican Church. They were grouped into Classes, each with a Class leader who collected subscriptions (a penny a week per member) and organized weekly meetings. Above them stood the Stewards and the Annual Conference, which decided matters of policy and doctrine. The vital thing which all this had in common with the Dissenters was its congregationalism—its implicit assumption that authority came from below, from the congregations, rather than from above, from the King and the hierarchy of bishops. Wesley himself took the crucial step which was to lead the movement away from the Church when in 1784 he laid hands on Richard Whatcoat and Thomas Vasey and ordained them as presbyters for the Methodist mission in America. After his death Methodism broke away from the Church of England completely and some of its offshoots, such as the New Methodist Connexion founded by Alexander Kilham in 1797 and the Primitive Methodists established by Huge Bourne and William Clowes in 1810, gave still more authority to laymen and even became associated in some areas with political radicalism.

Though they parted from her in the end, the Methodists had a great and lasting effect on the Church of England. The evangelical revival with which they were associated led many parsons to concern themselves more than ever before with the spiritual life of their parishes. Some, like Henry Venn, vicar of Huddersfield from 1759 to 1771 and rector of Yelling in Cambridgeshire from then until his death in 1797, resented Wesley's intrusions into the parish; but most of them were content to have him as an ally in the fight against apathy, even though they did not join his movement. Among those who were on good terms with him were William Grimshaw, the formidable Yorkshire parson who used to leave his congregation to sing the 119th Psalm while he routed out the ungodly from the alehouse with a horsewhip, and John Fletcher, who worked for twenty-five years in the tough industrial parish of Madeley on the borders of Cheshire and Shropshire.

Like the Methodists, the evangelicals within the Church of England were firm supporters of the social order. Reformation of manners, not reformation of social evils, was their main concern; and to most

of them righteousness and radicalism seemed to go ill together. This
was especially true of the group of rich evangelical laymen known
as the Clapham Sect.[1] When Paine's *Age of Reason* appeared in
England they pursued its publisher with relentless ferocity and ruined
him, even though he and his family were found starving in a garret
and ill with smallpox. When they founded a Society for the Suppression of Vice in 1802, Sydney Smith referred to it bitterly as 'the
Society for the Suppression of Vice among those with less than £500
a year'. On the other hand the anti-slavery movement and the
campaign for prison reform owed a lot to the evangelicals, and in the
field of education their efforts were particularly important. By the
end of the Napoleonic wars nearly a million children were being
educated in day schools and Sunday schools up and down the country,
thanks largely to the work of such evangelical enthusiasts as Robert
Raikes and Hannah More. Religious enthusiasm was leading men,
whether they liked it or not, to a new consciousness of social problems.

3 A new approach to Law

In 1758 the University of Oxford appointed William Blackstone as
its first Vinerian Professor of English Law. Although he had other
commitments—from 1761 onwards he was a member of Parliament
and also principal of New Inn Hall, and from 1763 he was solicitor-
general to the Queen—he lectured regularly in the university and
between 1765 and 1769 he published his lectures in four volumes
under the title of *Commentaries on the Laws of England*. Ever since the
1688 Revolution there had been a growing tendency to see the
British constitution, with all the laws which had produced it and
which it had produced, as something sacred and inviolable. In
Blackstone's work this tendency reached the point of idolatry. At
the heart of the constitution he saw the mystery of the trinity, the
three forces of King, Lords and Commons which were separate and
yet united. 'Like three distinct powers in mechanics,' he wrote, 'they
jointly impel the machine of government in a direction different
from what either, acting by itself, would have done; but at the same
time a direction partaking of each, and formed out of all; a direction
which constitutes the true line of the liberty and happiness of the

[1] Henry Venn's son, John, was rector of Clapham from 1792 to 1813 and the group
grew up around his church. Its members included William Wilberforce, Isaac Milner,
Henry Thornton and Zachary Macaulay.

community.' Reflecting at one and the same time the universal principles which governed the universe and the rational intelligence of the men who created it, the constitution was a supreme example of the works of man harmonizing with the works of God. The laws of England, because they were the product of this natural and rational constitution, were bound to echo the laws of nature. Of them it could be said, as of the universe itself, that 'whatever is, is right'.

Not everybody felt inclined to join Blackstone in his prostrations at the altar of the constitution. Some people felt that the law should concern itself not with what is, but with what ought to be; and the really important person in their eyes was not the lawyer who expounded the law but the legislator, the man who was prepared to change it. Like the politicians who thought in terms of 'measures, not men', and the administrators who saw the need for more government, they wanted new laws, whole programmes of legislation if necessary, in order to create a new and better society. Traditionalists and pessimists distrusted their enthusiasm and Dr Johnson wrote dourly:

> How small, of all that human hearts endure,
> The part which laws or kings can cause or cure!

But they were not discouraged and they continued to develop and propagate the idea of law as something which could and should change the lives of men. In the end they were to be proved right: their new approach to law did more even than the new approach to religion to transform life in Britain.

Enthusiasm for legislation, unlike religious enthusiasm, was the logical outcome of those ideas of natural law which had played such an important and formative part in early eighteenth-century thought. Students of natural law soon found themselves thinking more about what ought to be than about what was and they distrusted the cry, 'whatever is, is right'. Newton's conviction that everything in nature could be interpreted by means of rational and mechanical principles did not necessarily mean that whatever existed was to be justified. Many things in human society, including laws and constitutions, might well be the products of superstition, bigotry or prejudice and as such they must be examined and if necessary rejected in the name of reason and nature. Locke, for all his emphasis on natural law, had argued that constitutions were the work of men and not of nature. They were not living things but mechanical constructions, which should be dismantled and rebuilt if they didn't work properly. If they had been made by reasonable and natural men, according to the principles of reason and nature, they would be acceptable to other reasonable and natural men. If not, they must be scrapped. Belief in natural law did not entail a readiness to believe that all laws were natural.

From this it followed that those who wished to create a society based upon natural law must first study human nature itself. Only when they had understood the workings of the human mind would they be able to sweep away the superstitions and prejudices which had bedevilled mankind for so many centuries and create a reasonable world in which all reasonable men would be happy to live. It was for this reason that men felt, with Pope, that 'the proper study of mankind is man'.

Locke, in his *Essay concerning Human Understanding*, published in 1690, had provided a basis for this study by suggesting that the human mind was something constructed by human reason out of the raw materials provided by the senses. A child felt pain when he touched a nettle and as a result his reason registered the fact that nettles were bad things; he experienced pleasure when he was nursed by his mother and his reason noted that the mother was a good thing. In this way, slowly and painfully, like a marooned man building his hut from such flotsam as the sea cast up on his shores, the sovereign power of reason erected the whole elaborate structure of the mind. Loves and hates, hopes and fears, even those impulses which seemed most irrational, were end products of reason acting upon the impressions received through the five senses. Reason itself was natural and divine, an echo of the reason that ruled the universe, but what it built was dependent on the impressions it received. If they were determined by bigots and fanatics, then the child could be turned into a credulous moron, fit material for tyranny and priestcraft. If they were regulated by reasonable and enlightened educators, so that reasonable actions were rewarded by pleasant sense impressions and unreasonable ones by those which were less pleasant, he could be turned into a reasonable and natural man, ready to be governed by reasonable and natural laws.

It was an exciting prospect. Newton had revealed the laws which governed the physical universe and now, it seemed, Locke was pointing the way to an understanding of the moral universe as well. By working along the lines he had laid down men would be able to explain not only the behaviour of things but also the behaviour of people. And once they were in a position to explain them they would be able also to control them. Humanity would take its last and definite step in its long progress from primeval darkness to a perfect world in which reasonable educators produced reasonable men to live in a reasonable society under a reasonable constitution.

There was still one great difficulty. Even if men could prove to their own satisfaction that they were by nature reasonable creatures did it necessarily follow that their reason worked for the good of society as a whole? What if a man's reason taught him to covet his neighbour's house or his neighbour's wife? Before reason could be accepted as an infallible guide in the construction of the ideal society and in the formulation of ideal laws, it had to be shown to be a social and not an antisocial force. Once natural man could be shown to be a social creature as well as a reasonable creature, then it might be safe to demolish existing laws and build anew in the light of reason and nature.

The third Earl of Shaftesbury, grandson of the Whig leader of the 1670s and 1680s, tried to solve the problem in his *Inquiry concerning Virtue*, published in 1699. His method was to assume what he was supposed to be proving: he argued that because man was by nature a gregarious animal, his reason when left to itself was bound to make him behave in a sociable and cooperative way. Men whose minds had been formed in an unnatural and irrational way might be torn between selfish and unselfish desires, but for reasonable men there was no such conflict: they desired for themselves what was in the interests of society as a whole. In spite of its rather shaky reasoning the book was very popular and influential and it led a whole generation of optimistic thinkers to accept Pope's dictum that 'true self-love and social are the same'. David Hartley's *Observations on Man*, published in 1749, put forward a more complex and more beguiling version of the same argument. He saw the human mind as a place where sensations worked upon the brain in such a way as to produce ideas while the reason, working by means of the association of those ideas one with another, led the mind on from simple to complex concepts and from selfish to social desires. As a man became more reasonable he saw more clearly the essential identification between his own interests and those of society.

Hartley's book was by implication a blueprint for the ideal society. If his picture of the human mind was correct, then all that remained was for the educators to see that all minds developed naturally in a reasonable way and for the legislators to see that the law allowed reasonable men to pursue their interests freely. The rest could safely be left to the workings of the laws of nature. The philosophers from Newton to Hartley had plotted the path to the ideal society and now it was up to the next generation to hack their way along it, rooting out anomalies and injustices and obsolete traditions as they went. They would need to have something of the philosopher in them, so that they could see the way ahead, and something of the radical, so that they could root up the obstacles without compunction; but above all they would have to be lawyers, so that they could provide the legal framework for the new society. The new generations of radicals would be philosophical radicals, but they would also be legislators.

There was a certain amount of radicalism about at the time when Hartley wrote, but it was not of the kind that was easily linked with a forward-looking and idealist philosophy. Thomas Hollis of Lincoln's Inn and his adopted heir Thomas Brand Hollis, two of the most active radicals of their day, were more concerned to revive the republicanism of the seventeenth century than to plan the ideal society of the future; and it is significant that even the supporters of John Wilkes chose to call themselves by the relatively traditionalist title of 'The Society for the Defence of the Bill of Rights'. The Dissenters, with their vision of a society in which the religious prejudices of the past would be swept away and civic and political rights given to all men irrespective of their beliefs, were readier to follow up Hartley's work and it was a Dissenter, Joseph Priestley, who worked out some of its political implications in his *Essay on the First Principles of Government*, which appeared in 1768. He broke completely with the nostalgic and backward-looking radicalism of the past and looked forward instead to the perfect society of the future, in which reasonable laws would ensure that all men behaved reasonably. Another Dissenter, Richard Price, developed a similar argument in *Observations on the Nature of Civil Liberty*, published in 1776.

By this time the cause of radicalism had become identified with that of the American colonists; and by far the most important radical utterance among the many that were produced in the year 1776 was the American Declaration of Independence itself:

'We hold these truths to be self-evident, that all men are created equal, that they are endowed by their Creator with certain unalienable Rights, that among these are Life, Liberty, and the pursuit of

Happiness. That to secure these rights, Governments are instituted among Men, deriving their just powers from the consent of the governed. That whenever any Form of Government becomes destructive of these ends, it is the Right of the People to alter or to abolish it, and to institute new Government. . . .'

While this majestic vision of the new society was being proclaimed on the other side of the Atlantic, radicals in Britain were producing blueprints for various parts of the new structure or were urging the demolition of the dangerous parts of the old. John Cartwright, a respectable country gentleman and a major in the Nottinghamshire militia, came out with a startling pamphlet called *Take Your Choice* in which he advocated annual elections, secret ballot, votes for all men over eighteen and payment of members of Parliament. At one bound he took the cause of parliamentary reform out of the hesitant and cautious world of Wilkes and Chatham, where men proposed to tinker about with the existing system in order that a few more freeholders should be represented or a little less corruption permitted, into a world in which a body of representative legislators would be elected *by* all the people so that they could frame laws *for* all the people. Cartwright saw Parliament not as a kind of Grand Jury, where men with a stake in the country could call ministers to account, but as a positive law-making body; and he was convinced that once it was reconstituted in this way its legislative activities would automatically do away with all the evils of the time, from the National Debt to prostitution.

The year 1776 also saw the appearance of *An Inquiry into the Nature and Causes of the Wealth of Nations*, by Adam Smith. Like many other eighteenth-century thinkers, Adam Smith had been led from the study of human nature and human conduct to the study of the laws that governed—or ought to govern—human societies. He had been successively Professor of Logic and Professor of Moral Philosophy in the university of Glasgow and his first important work had been on 'the theory of moral sentiments'. Now he moved from sentiments to motives, the motives that lay behind men's economic activities, and to a consideration of the laws that ought to be framed to control and direct them. He was convinced that the saying 'true self-love and social are the same' was particularly applicable to economic affairs: 'The natural effort of every individual to better his own conditions, when suffered to exert itself with freedom and security, is so powerful a principle, that it is alone, and without any assistance, not only capable of carrying on the society to wealth and prosperity, but of surmounting a hundred impertinent obstructions with which the folly of human laws too often encumbers its operations.' He exploded one after another the fallacies of the mercantilist system and he was especially scathing about its bullionism, its conviction that the accumulation of gold was a way of increasing the wealth of the country: 'To attempt to increase the wealth of any country, either by introducing or by detaining in it an unnecessary quantity of gold and silver, is as absurd as it would be to attempt to increase the good cheer of private families by obliging them to keep an unnecessary number of kitchen utensils.' The wealth of a nation, he concluded, lay in the expansion of its trade and industry; and this was to be achieved by demolishing the misguided and restrictive regulations of the past and bringing in laws that would encourage men to make themselves and their country rich.

Adam Smith's idea

Yet another radical work appeared in 1776—one of the shortest but one of the most significant of them all. It had the rather formidable title of *A Fragment on Government; being an examination of what is delivered, on the subject of Government in General in the introduction to Sir William Blackstone's Commentaries: with a preface, in which is given a critique on the work at large,* and it was by an unemployed and unsuccessful barrister called Jeremy Bentham. His career at the bar had been stillborn, not because of any lack of talent but because of his implacable hostility to the whole structure of the law and his desire to reform it from top to bottom. So far from seeing it in Blackstone's terms, as the repository of the wisdom of the ages, he regarded it as a vast rubbish dump, the tangled and meaningless residue left behind by countless generations of dishonest lawyers who had conspired to cheat and confuse their clients. Instead of being available to all men in an accessible and intelligible form, it was deliberately kept hidden away in obscure Statute Books, full of barbarous French and worse Latin, and in even more obscure reports of past cases. The whole idea of case law, whereby the law was built up gradually upon the decisions of judges in particular cases, offended his orderly and scientific mind; and he even had his doubts about the jury system, which most lawyers saw as one of the great bulwarks of British liberty. 'When I get to heaven,' he wrote to a friend some years later, 'I will make as many tribunals as I please and I'll promise you they shall every one of them have cognizance of everything and hold none of them more than one Judge. . . . As for Juries, I will have none of them, though the twelve Apostles offer themselves to make the first.'

This sweeping attack upon Blackstone and upon the traditional idea of the Law was followed up and developed in Bentham's next major work, *The Principles of Morals and Legislation*. In it he proclaimed his faith in legislation as the greatest of all sciences, the thing which could and would produce the perfect society of which men had dreamed for so long. Like Locke, he assumed that men were reasonable creatures and that their ideas and actions were determined by the pains and pleasures which they received by way of their senses. Like Shaftesbury, Pope, Hartley and Adam Smith, he believed in the principle of the identity of interests—the complete compatibility of selfish and social desires, when both were properly regulated by intelligent legislation. From Priestley he took the phrase in which he summed up the ultimate aim of all legislation: 'the greatest happiness of the greatest number'. On these foundations he built a science of lawmaking which he believed to be infallible.

Like most men who think they have a final and complete answer to the problems of mankind, Bentham was by inclination a despot. Having reduced legislation (and therefore, by implication, all political and constitutional problems) to a science as exact as mathematics, he tended to dismiss other points of view rather as a man might dismiss the idea that two and two might possibly add up to five. He found it difficult to understand why all enlightened and well-intentioned men did not adopt his ideas in their entirety; and he easily lost patience with parliaments and with parliamentary politicians. When he was working at his *Principles of Morals and Legislation*, his first instinct was not to submit it to Parliament but to get his brother Samuel, who was at that time in Russia, to press it upon that enlightened but despotic ruler, the Empress Catherine the Great. 'You must spy on her in the road,' he wrote, 'you must bow down before her; and when you have eaten as much dust as you feel inclined you must thrust my note under her nose, or else at her breast.' Towards the end of his life, after a series of disappointments and frustrations had shown how over-optimistic and over-simplified his schemes really were, he could still produce a picture of himself as the world's supreme legislator which, for all its whimsicality, had an element of seriousness in it. 'We shall go hand in hand', he wrote to Dumont[1] in November 1821, 'through all future ages, doing good, diminishing pains, everlasting pleasures, all the way, and all the while, as we go; all the way, and

1 Etienne Dumont, 1759–1829, a talented and versatile Genevese who devoted a large part of his life to editing Bentham's manuscripts for publication.

(not to speak of the moon) our way will cover the whole earth. We shall for we will be despots of the moral world: Locke and Helvetius,[1] offering incense to us every morning, both of them on their knees.'

By the time that letter was written many political philosophers and many political events had combined to undermine the optimistic view of man as a reasonable creature who could be made happy by reasonable legislators. Even in the middle of the eighteenth century, a new view of nature and of man's place in it was coming to challenge that of the rationalists; and the philosophic radicals and the supreme legislators, like the enthusiasts and the evangelicals, would have to take account of it if they were to be politically effective.

4   *A new approach to Nature*

Among the writers who proclaimed the reasonableness of man and of nature during the first half of the eighteenth century, none was more influential than Bolingbroke. He was not a very profound or a very original thinker but he was an effective popularizer, especially after his ideas had been put into verse form by Pope; and by the time his collected works were published in 1754, three years after his death, his name had become synonymous with rationalism and optimism. Anyone who felt disposed to challenge these things, anyone who had doubts about the reasonableness of man and of nature, would first have to challenge Bolingbroke.

One of the first people to do so was Edmund Burke. In 1756 he published a satirical parody of Bolingbroke's work under the title of *Vindication of Natural Society*. With savage irony he showed up the absurdities that resulted from pushing rationalism to its logical conclusion; and he developed instead a point of view which he was to hold with growing conviction all his life and which was to provide the basis for that great reaction against rationalism which came to be known as the Romantic Movement. Its influence was so far-reaching that by 1790, when he came to give it its fullest expression in his *Reflections on the Revolution in France*, he could write with some pride and with considerable justification: 'Who now reads Bolingbroke? Who ever read him through? Ask the booksellers of London what is become of all these lights of the world.'

[1] Claude-Adrien Helvetius, 1715-71, a rich French revenue officer who threw up his office in order to write radical philosophical works. His *De l'esprit* (1758), which was publicly burnt by the authorities, argued that reason and not religion was the true basis of all morals and legislation. Bentham took most of his ideas from Helvetius.

In its simplest form, the new view of man and of nature which Burke was advocating and which was so successfully eclipsing the lights of the rationalist world boiled down to one observation: man cannot live by reason alone. The reasonable man, the predictable automaton for whom the rationalists had designed such splendid patterns of behaviour, was only a part and a relatively unimportant part of the whole man. To interpret men purely in terms of reason was like interpreting plants in terms of that part of them which showed above the ground. The rationalist, if he was allowed his way, might well succeed in rearranging the human scene in a neat mathematical fashion, just as a carpenter let loose in a garden might make it more orderly by planing down some plants and jointing others together. In both cases the results would be disastrous because men, like plants, were living and growing things. Their roots, deep down in the dark soil and often strangely twisted, were as important as that reasoning part of them which showed above the ground and about which the rationalist made such rash generalizations.

Human societies, like individual human beings, were living and growing things with roots that stretched far back into the past. Once those roots were cut, the societies would wither and die. 'People will not look forward to posterity,' wrote Burke in the *Reflections*, 'who never look backward to their ancestors.' Jeremy Bentham and his circle of would-be legislators tended to regard the study of the past and the desire to cherish its traditions as a superstitious and unenlightened waste of time; and one of them, Samuel Romilly, once made a violent attack on the Society of Antiquarians for its interest in 'the rude utensils and implements of barbarous times'. For Burke, however, the past held the key to the present. No gardener in his senses would rely on a drawing of a plant at a particular stage of its growth to tell him all he needed to know about its whole life cycle, yet Bentham and his friends expected a cross-section of human knowledge, made at a particular time, to tell them all they needed to know about the whole process of human history. The proper study of mankind was indeed man, but it was the whole man that must be studied and not an artificial abstraction uprooted from his past.

This anti-rationalist view of man implied not only a different approach to politics but also a different approach to the arts and to literature. Once again it was Burke who pointed the way, in a treatise called *The Philosophical Inquiry into the Origin of our Ideas on the Sublime and the Beautiful*, also published in 1756. It was concerned with a question which most of the rationalists had ignored: why was it that things which were neither beautiful nor reasonable nor pleasing could still move men to the depths of their being? It was no good pretending that all those who devoured accounts of the Lisbon disaster so avidly were prompted by scientific curiosity or by sympathy for the victims. Rationalists might insist that man's search for beauty, like his search for truth, was conditioned purely by his reason; but the fact remained that things which were horrifying and utterly irrational had a compelling power over the human mind. They might not be beautiful—even Burke could not think of beauty except in terms of order and proportion—but they were, he thought, sublime. 'Whatever is fitted in any sort to excite the ideas of pain and danger,' he wrote, 'that is to say, whatever is in any sort terrible . . . is a source of the sublime.' The overwhelming grandeur of untamed nature and the appalling spectacle of human agony could thrill and even gratify something in man which lay deeper than reason. 'I am convinced', said Burke, 'that we have a degree of delight, and that no small one, in the real misfortunes and pains of others.' Somewhere inside the tasteful and sophisticated eighteenth-century gentleman was his remote primeval ancestor, responding to the mysterious rhythms of the natural world and living out his life in terms of myth and ritual and taboo.

During the second half of the eighteenth century poets and artists, as well as philosophers, began to interest themselves in this strange savage who inhabited the inner recesses of the human mind. The rationalists had assumed that he would lose his power as soon as the mind which he had once controlled became properly enlightened; but now men began to think of him as very much alive and capable of wreaking vengeance on those who tried to ignore him. His kingdom, the twilight kingdom of magic and mystery and violence, became once more an area where respectable scholars and writers could allow themselves to be seen. Thomas Gray, whose poetry had always contained an element of melancholy and of dissatisfaction with the values of the enlightenment, turned in his later years to those ancient myths and legends which the rationalists had dismissed as childish absurdities. He was fascinated by Celtic and Scandinavian mythology and by the wild mountain country which was its natural setting; and when James Macpherson produced in 1762 poems which he claimed were translations from a third-century Gaelic bard called Ossian, Gray was full of admiration for them and tried desperately to believe in their authenticity, which was questioned by Johnson and other critics. Macpherson survived these attacks, but a later and more talented fabricator of imitation medieval poetry, Thomas Chatterton, ended by taking his own life in 1770. A few years later his forgeries were exposed by Thomas Tyrwhitt.

The fashion for exotic literature continued. Icelandic eddas, Germanic and Scandinavian sagas, British ballads and folk stories, even Chinese poems, were collected and translated and edited. Instead of being satisfied with works that reflected the reasonableness of the universe as a whole and of man in particular, the reading public clamoured for echoes of the superstitious past. The word 'gothic', which earlier in the century had been used to sum up all that was primitive and barbarous and uncouth, now became respectable again. Horace Walpole pointed the way in 1764 with his *The Castle of Otranto, a Gothic Story* and by the end of the century writers like Ann Radcliffe and Matthew Lewis had made the gothic novel, with its ghosts and dark castles and fiendish medieval cruelties, into a highly successful literary form. In the early nineteenth century it was taken up by Walter Scott, along with the traditional ballad and the whole apparatus of medievalism, and used as the basis of a new and very influential type of romantic literature.

Horace Walpole set a fashion in gothic architecture as well as in gothic literature. In 1750 he rebuilt his house at Strawberry Hill in the gothic style; and within a few years it had become fashionable for gentlemen to embellish their houses with gothic facades and their gardens with gothic ruins. Other excursions into the exotic, such as Chinese pagodas and imitation grottoes—sometimes occupied by paid hermits, engaged specially to provide local colour—took their places alongside sham castles and summerhouses built to look like gothic chapels. Few people regarded such things as anything more than amusing trifles and Walpole himself spoke of the 'whimsical air of novelty' which the gothic style imparted; but by the 1790s, when William Beckford commissioned James Wyatt to build him an enormous gothic abbey at Fonthill in Wiltshire, it was becoming clear that the gothic revival in architecture, like its counterpart in literature, was much more than a passing craze. It was an integral part of the Romantic Movement, that immensely important complex of ideas which was to transform the whole of European thought within little more than a generation.

Considered as a political or philosophical movement, or as a thread on which to string a selection of poets and artists, the Romantic Movement is a puzzling and elusive thing. It can be seen at work on both sides of the debate on the French Revolution, in the ecstatic approval shown by the younger poets as well as in the passionate hostility of Burke. It stood for liberty and also for tyranny, for change and for conservatism, for reform and for reaction. Since it emphasized sensibility rather than reason and virtue rather than intelligence, it could sometimes provide the motive force for humanitarianism and philanthropy; but it could also induce a melancholy acceptance of the world's ills, the kind of mood that led Robert Southey to write in 1797: 'There was a time when I believed in the persuadability of man, and had the mania of man-mending. Experience has taught me better . . . the ablest physician can do little in the great lazar house of society.' It was romanticism of a sort that led eighteenth-century travellers to enthuse over the awe-inspiring spectacle of early industrialism, but it was also romanticism that made Blake cry out against the 'dark Satanic mills'. While some romantic poems and drawings set out to capture the exotic fantasies of a dream world, others reproduced faithfully the familiar and even humdrum world of daily experience. Blake could produce the moving simplicity of *The Chimney Sweeper* as well as the weird images of the *Prophetic Books*; and the collection of poems published by Wordsworth and Coleridge in 1798 under the title of *Lyrical Ballaas*, which has often been seen as the key work in the development of romanticism, included the down-to-earth realism of *Simon Lee the Old Huntsman* as well as the nightmarish horrors of *The Ancient Mariner*.

Romanticism produced these widely differing attitudes and styles because it was at bottom a quest rather than a statement. The romantic was not a man who had bound himself to a particular political or philosophical programme, but a man in search of himself. He sought to throw off the artificial conventions of his time because he felt that somewhere buried underneath them was something more basic, more real, more natural. Other men might be satisfied with outward appearance, but he was determined to discover his inner self, the real kernel of his personality.[1] He tore away the useless outer husks of

---

[1] Not everybody accepted this picture of the human personality as a nut whose kernel could be found once the outer shells were stripped away. In 1867, when the Romantic Movement had run its course, the Norwegian dramatist Henrik Ibsen wrote a bitter and terrifying epitaph on its search for self-knowledge. His hero, Peer Gynt, symbolizes his quest for his true self by peeling not a nut but an onion: and at the end he is left empty-handed, since an onion is nothing but a series of skins.

worldliness and reasonableness and thought that what he glimpsed beneath them was ultimate reality. It might present itself in terms of a consciousness of the past, a need for roots, or as the clear and un-spoiled vision of childhood, or as the dynamic and creative power of the imagination; but whatever form it took, he accepted it as a revelation of the true meaning of nature and of man's relation to nature. Whereas the rationalist saw reason as something by which nature might be understood, the romantic saw it as something by which she was obscured and hidden.

This essential opposition between rationalism and romanticism was not always appreciated at the time, even by the opponents themselves. Burke understood it and his uncompromising hostility to rationalism, his insistence that reason alone could never provide the answer to the problems of mankind, was the keynote of the whole Romantic Movement; but many of those who were at heart romantics thought of him as an enemy rather than an ally. In their eagerness to tear down the citadels of artificiality and create a world fit for men of sensibility to live in they thought of themselves as radicals rather than tradition-alists. In the final analysis they were wrong: romanticism was not an uprooting movement at all, but one which insisted on the need for roots. Bentham and the other would-be legislators could afford to rearrange human beings and human institutions according to the laws of reason because they believed that these laws were all that men knew on earth and all that they needed to know; but to the romantics rearrangement meant uprooting, and uprooting meant death to the things which lay too deep for reason. Although the new approach to nature and the new approach to law came together in the 1780s to form a more or less united radical movement, they were destined to be driven apart again by the shock of the French Revolution and by the intractable problems posed by a rapidly changing society. If they were to survive that shock and deal with those problems, politicians would have to take account of all the new ways of thinking. Those who bound themselves exclusively to any one of them, or tried to knit them all together into a comprehensive radical programme, would fail. Those who knew how to select ideas and slogans judic-iously from each of them might have some hope of success.

14

New Men
1782–1789

1 *Edmund Burke*

The Whigs greeted the fall of North as enthusiastically as the Patriots had greeted that of Walpole forty years before. Like Walpole, North had maintained himself in power long enough to build up an effective 'corner' in the patronage market; but, unlike Walpole, he had done so in flat defiance of the great Whig families. For the last sixteen years, as Chatham had given way to Grafton and Grafton had given way to North, the King's ministers had appealed to many things: to the desire for non-party government, to the aspirations of City merchants and country gentlemen, to the loyalty of the Court Party. But they had not appealed to the party magnates, to the powerful alliance of great borough-mongering families which had been forged by the Pelhams and was now led by the Marquis of Rockingham. For sixteen years these families had been excluded from office, but they had preserved their connections one with another and their unity as a political party. Now they were determined to use that unity as a means of forcing their way back into power. George III tried desperately to reconstruct his ministry on a Patriot basis, either under Grafton or under the Earl of Shelburne, the political heir of Chatham; but he found that he could not do without the Whigs and that the Whigs would not be divided. They insisted on coming in as a party and thus undoing all that he had done over the last sixteen years to discredit 'party' as a political weapon. The King who had once invited Chatham to help him destroy all party distinctions was now forced to surrender to party government. By the end of March 1782 Rockingham had taken over as First Lord of the Treasury and was in the process of creating a united Whig ministry, a practical demonstration of the King's dependence on the great Whig families.

At first the new ministry enjoyed a good deal of popular support:

the long years of opposition to North had enabled the Whigs to pose as the defenders of liberty against the tyranny of the Court. But there was very soon a reaction against them. The caricaturists, led by Gillray, attacked them as republicans. One print, entitled *The Captive Prince, or Liberty run Mad*, showed Rockingham walking off with the Crown jewels while his colleagues in the Cabinet fastened manacles on the King. Another showed the King with the crown and sceptre bundled up in a sack, in preparation for flight to Hanover. George had certainly toyed with the idea of abdicating and he had even drawn up a message to Parliament announcing that 'His Majesty therefore with much sorrow finds he can be of no further Utility to His Native Country which drives Him to the painful step of quitting it for ever'. The message was never sent, but if the Rockingham Whigs pushed the King too far they might well find the threat of abdication used against them, to rally both Court and Country around the King they had used so harshly. In order to prevent this happening and to win public opinion to their side they needed a new leader, a man who could prove that the Whig party was not a dangerous republican oligarchy but a genuinely reforming party.

Edmund Burke, the man who had been so successful in organizing the campaign against the Stamp Act in 1765 and the campaign for Economical Reform from 1780 onwards, was the obvious man for the job. He believed passionately in the great Whig families and in their historic mission to safeguard the constitution of 1688 by combining to provide a counterbalance to the power of the Crown. His *Thoughts on the Cause of the Present Discontents*, published in 1770, had been largely devoted to a defence of party in general, and the Whig party in particular, against the attacks of the Patriots and the King's Friends. In 1777, when his constituents in Bristol had questioned the legality of his opposition to Lord North's administration, he had told them proudly that he venerated the constitution 'in company with the Saviles, the Dowdeswells, the Wentworths, the Bentincks; with the Lennoxes, the Manchesters, the Keppels, the Saunderses; with the temperate, permanent, hereditary virtue of the whole House of Cavendish'. No man revered the great territorial magnates more and no man was better qualified to act as their apologist and their publicist.

Rockingham and his friends were quite prepared to accept Burke as a publicist, but they were not so keen on having him as a colleague in the Cabinet. To them he was a useful mouthpiece, a tame intellectual who could work out policies and devise attractive slogans, but he was not a man with whom they could associate on equal terms. The high-born territorial magnates, the great Whig families whose names Burke himself had recited with such satisfaction, considered that this adventurer from Ireland was amply rewarded by the comparatively humble office of Paymaster, which did not carry with it a seat in the Cabinet. His son and one of his friends were made Joint Deputy Paymasters, each with a salary of £500 a year, while his brother Richard Burke drew another £3,000 as Secretary to the Treasury. William Burke, a distant relative but a very close friend, got something approaching £2,000 a year as Deputy Paymaster in India. As if this was not enough, Burke made strenuous efforts to obtain for his son the even richer sinecure of the Clerkship of the Pells. He was as energetic on behalf of his friends as he was on behalf of his family and in the following year, when he obtained for Dr Charles Burney the post of organist at Chelsea Hospital, Dr Burney's daughter noted that 'nothing could be more delicate, more elegant, than his manner of doing this kindness'.

Neither Burke himself nor the majority of his party saw anything hypocritical or inconsistent in this grasping of sinecures by the man who proclaimed himself the champion of 'Economical Reform'. The Whigs were not concerned to end the patronage system, which they saw as a necessary part of political life, but to reduce the power and influence of the Crown. Even Dunning, the author of the famous resolution of April 1780 'that the influence of the Crown has increased, is increasing and ought to be diminished', allowed himself to be slipped into the remunerative office of Chancellor of the Duchy of Lancaster. The original Whig proposals had provided for the abolition of this office, but it now proved necessary to retain it for the benefit of the very man who had coined the catchphrase of 1780. Other modifications of the original scheme were also made, either by Burke himself or by the Cabinet, and the Act which was eventually passed later in 1782 was concerned largely with abolishing archaic Household offices like the Clerks of the Board of Green Cloth and the Master of the Stag Hounds. Its other provisions, such as the limitation of the secret service money and the stipulation that all pensions should be paid publicly at the Exchequer, showed that it was aimed against the Crown rather than the patronage system. It also provided for the abolition of the Board of Trade, a curiously short-sighted step to take at a time when the need for government control over the country's trade was greater than ever before.[1] The preamble to the Act, which called it 'an Act for enabling his Majesty to discharge the Debt contracted upon his Civil List Revenues, and for preventing the same from being in arrear for the future', emphasized its purpose as an economy measure, intended to appeal to those country gentlemen who looked for a reduction in the Land Tax. It was accompanied by two Place Acts, one to prevent revenue officers from voting at parliamentary elections and the other to prevent government contractors from sitting in the Commons. The whole programme was essentially a Country Party programme, intended to secure the independence of Parliament and the reduction of government expenditure. Like Pitt in 1746, Burke used his position as Paymaster to demonstrate his own altruistic incorruptibility: measures were brought in to regulate the Paymaster's salary and to prevent him from using the balances in the Pay Office for his own profit.

While Burke busied himself with economic reform, winning over the Country Party and weakening the Court, his superiors in the ministry had to concern themselves with the problems of Ireland and America. The Volunteers in Ireland were still ostensibly loyal to the British Crown, but they were determined to support the demand for legislative independence for Ireland. Henry Grattan and Henry Flood, the leaders of the independence movement in the Irish House of Commons, were given solid support by a great meeting of the Volunteers at Dungannon in February 1782; and the Rockingham ministry decided to yield to their demands. On 17 May 1782 both Houses of Parliament at Westminster passed resolutions abdicating their right to make laws to bind Ireland. Ten days later the Duke of Portland, the Rockinghamite Lord-Lieutenant of Ireland, informed the Parliament at Dublin that the King intended to repeal all those Acts which gave the English Parliament or the Privy Council control over Irish legislation. The Irish Parliament then voted an address of thanks to the King, together with a sum of £100,000 to raise Irish seamen for his navy. The events of the next few years were to show that the Irish problem was far from being solved, but for the time being relations between the two countries were reasonably cordial.

The problem of America was even more pressing and even more difficult. A large section of the Whig party was already committed

1 Four years later the Board had to be re-established, as a Committee of the Privy Council.

to the proposition that the war could not be won and that full independence must be granted to the colonists. George III was convinced that France was on the verge of bankruptcy and that the war could still be brought to a successful conclusion. He regarded many of the Whigs as little better than traitors, men who had given support and encouragement to revolutionaries in America and radicals at home. When he had been forced to take in the Rockingham Whigs he had promised, very grudgingly, that he would not veto the grant of independence to the American colonists; but he did not expect that independence to be granted straight away. He expected his ministers to prosecute the war vigorously and to hold independence in reserve, as something which must be bargained for at the conference table. The new ministry's efforts to prosecute the war were neither convincing nor successful. Early in May they decided to send Admiral Hugh Pigot out to the West Indies to replace Rodney, but the decision was no sooner made than news arrived of Rodney's victory at the battle of The Saints, the greatest naval success of the war. The satirists and the caricaturists accused the Whigs of sacrificing the country's security for the sake of their own patronage politics: Gillray produced a print showing Rodney slaying the dragon of Bourbon power while Charles James Fox, Foreign Secretary in the Rockingham ministry, ran towards him with a coronet, crying, 'Hold, my dear Rodney, you have done enough. I will now make a Lord of you, and you shall have the happiness of never being heard of again.'

Meanwhile, the American problem had been transferred from the battlefield to the conference table. As soon as they had come into office the Whigs had sent Richard Oswald, a retired merchant who had once lived in America, to contact Benjamin Franklin, the American minister in Paris. Peace negotiations got under way early in May, but they soon ran into difficulties owing to quarrels between the two Secretaries of State. The secretaryship for the colonies, created in 1768, had been abolished as part of Burke's economical reforms and colonial affairs were now the concern of the Home Secretary. Rockingham had insisted on having a Home Secretary and a Foreign Secretary, instead of a Secretary for the North and a Secretary for the South, and this new and more sensible division of responsibilities should have made for greater efficiency. Unfortunately it came at a time when the greatest issue in politics could be seen as the province of either Secretary. Charles James Fox, the Foreign

Secretary, wanted to recognize the independence of the colonies forthwith, so that both the negotiations with the French and those with Americans would be his concern. The Earl of Shelburne, Home Secretary, envisaged some kind of federal union between Britain and the colonies and wanted to grant independence only as a last resort, as the epilogue rather than the prelude to a general peace. By the end of June relations between the two Secretaries were so bad that Fox had decided to resign.

Then, on 1 July 1782, the Rockingham ministry was brought to an end by the death of Rockingham himself. The members of the Cabinet sent a message to the King asking him to appoint the Duke of Portland as Rockingham's successor. Portland was a dull man, but he was a great territorial magnate and an ideal figurehead for a ministry based on Whig ideas of party and patronage. He was also associated by marriage with that same house of Cavendish whose permanent and hereditary virtues had been praised so ecstatically by Burke. The King, however, was determined to rid himself of the Rockingham Whigs and he resented their attempt to dictate to him the choice of his own ministers. He asked Shelburne to form a ministry and as a result Fox handed in the resignation which he had already been contemplating before Rockingham's death. He was followed by Burke, by Portland, and by the Chancellor of the Exchequer, Lord John Cavendish; but many important members of the ministry refused to resign. The Duke of Richmond, head of the house of Lennox, stayed on to serve under Shelburne and so did Viscount Keppel, the First Lord of the Admiralty. The truth was that the great Whig party, the association of noble families which was to have held in check the power of the Crown, was divided against itself. Four months earlier it had entered the promised land with high hopes of a long period of office, but now it was left without a leader and without a policy. With Rockingham to lead them and Burke to advise them the Whigs had been ready to impose themselves on the King and upon the country; but now they were uncertain of their aims and divided in their allegiance.

Fox later made the sardonic comment that on Rockingham's death the crown had devolved on the King. It was certainly true that without Rockingham the power of the Whig party, its ability to force itself on the King, was fatally weakened. But the principles of the Whig party lived on in the political philosophy of Edmund Burke. Although he was too humbly born to lead it, he understood the Whig party better than any of its members. He valued liberty and justice above all things and he believed that they could best be preserved in a balanced constitution which allowed great noblemen, men who had the disinterested detachment which only wealth and leisure could bestow, to hold in check the power of the central government. He was always a conservative, ready to defend society and the constitution against those who wanted change of any sort. When he supported reform it was in order to undo real or imaginary errors, to restore the constitution to its ancient purity. In May 1782, when Chatham's son William Pitt proposed that the House should consider the question of electoral reform, Burke was his most formidable opponent. 'It is for fear of losing the inestimable treasure we have', he cried, 'that I do not venture to game it out of my hands for the vain hope of improving it. I look with filial reverence on the constitution of my country, and never will cut it in pieces, and put it into the kettle of any magician, in order to boil it, with the puddle of their compounds, into youth and vigour. On the contrary, I will drive away such pretenders; I will nurse its venerable age, and with lenient arts extend a parent's breath.'

It was the authentic voice of Whiggery, of the men who for nearly seventy years had managed both King and Country and had made the Revolution Settlement the framework for a tolerant, an easygoing, an essentially amateurish system of administration. Like the Whig party which he served so well, Burke could not bring himself to believe that the 'lenient arts' of management were no longer sufficient and that the country stood in need of something more positive and more drastic. At fifty-three, Burke was still young as politicians went and he might yet have a great future; but he would never inherit that future as long as he continued to worship the past.

2   The Earl of Shelburne

The best thing about the Rockingham ministry from the King's point of view, and the worst thing about it from the Whig point of view, had been the presence in it of the Earl of Shelburne. He had begun his political career as President of the Board of Trade under Grenville in 1763, but he had very soon attached himself to Chatham and most people saw him as the heir to the Patriot tradition, with its emphasis on 'measures, not men' and its dislike of party politics. Like Chatham, he had opposed both Grafton and North, and after Chatham's death in 1778 he had even made common cause with the Rockingham Whigs, refusing to come into office without them. But the experience of sharing office with them for four months had cured him of any desire to be a traditional Whig. The Rockingham group had come to distrust him intensely because he put his own ideals and his own schemes before his loyalty to the party, while he for his part had come to despise them for their 'party' attitude to political problems. In the crisis that followed Rockingham's death George III turned to Shelburne as the man who would save him from the Whigs and from the horrors of party government. By the time Parliament adjourned for the summer recess on 11 July 1782 Shelburne had taken over as First Lord of the Treasury and had formed a ministry which, like Chatham's ministry of 1766, aimed at transcending and destroying party distinctions. He told the House of Lords proudly that he stood by 'all those constitutional ideas which for seventeen years he had imbibed from his master in politics, the late Earl of Chatham'. George III could flatter himself that he had once again got a Patriot Minister.

Shelburne, however, was more of a radical than the King realized and the phrase 'measures, not men' meant far more to him than it had ever meant to Chatham. In May 1771, shortly after he had been engaged in stirring up a united national opposition to Lord North's ministry, he had set off on a tour of France and Italy which he saw later as the turning point of his life. He had spent some time at the house of Trudaine, an intelligent and enlightened French government official, where he had met many of the most advanced writers and thinkers of the time. Most of them were reformers, men who dreamt of building in France a new and better society, but they were no friends to the privileged classes who claimed to stand for freedom. They could see that the French monarchy, the monarchy which Trudaine himself served, offered a better hope of genuine reform than the aristocrats who opposed it. France could be regenerated by means of an enlightened and efficient central government, rather than by the policy of checks and balances which was advocated by the privileged classes. The great noblemen of France had dreams of weakening the monarchy and taking a greater share in government themselves, like their counterparts across the Channel; but their dreams were not shared by the real radicals of France, the revolutionary philosophers who were planning the new society.

Shelburne saw that what was true of France was also true of

Britain. Chatham had been right in condemning Whig opposition to the Crown as irresponsible and dangerous, but he had not gone far enough. What was needed was an alliance between the government and the forces of change, between the King's Servants and the philosophical radicals. Patriot Kings and Patriot Ministers must do more than defend the central government: they must reform it. Rule by the Whigs meant clinging blindly to the patronage system, to the management of public affairs by gentlemenly amateurs, to the sacrifice of efficiency for the sake of liberty. The alternative, therefore, must be a programme of reform designed to rally to the King's side all those who looked for a better organized and more just society. Since his return from his continental tour Shelburne had deliberately patronized radical writers and thinkers. Joseph Priestley, the author of *An Essay on the First Principles of Government*, was his librarian from 1773 to 1780 and later wrote: 'My office was nominally that of librarian, but I had little employment as such . . . in fact, I was with him as a friend.' Clearly Shelburne was his patron rather than his employer. Several other progressive thinkers enjoyed Shelburne's hospitality at his country house at Bowood in Wiltshire and by 1782 he had built up around him a group of men to whom he could turn for ideas on all aspects of political and social reform. The Constitutional Information Society, founded in 1780 to promote the cause of parliamentary reform, owed much to the efforts of members of this Bowood group and in the summer of 1781 Jeremy Bentham spent some time at Bowood and showed the drafts of his *Introduction to the Principles of Morals and Legislation* to Shelburne and to his political friends.

When he became First Lord of the Treasury, Shelburne started to apply in practice the reforming ideas he had evolved in his discussions at Bowood. He continued and extended the reform of Civil List expenditure, which had already been inaugurated under the Rockingham administration, and he also embarked on a reorganization of the Treasury, the Navy Board and other government departments with a view to promoting greater administrative efficiency. He proposed to cut down fees, redistribute offices, overhaul methods of accounting and simplify taxation. Adám Smith had been one of the radical thinkers with whom he had associated and as a result he was anxious to encourage trade by revising and reducing rates of duty. Finally, he promised to bring forward a plan for parliamentary reform.

His reforming zeal carried him through the summer and autumn, but by the end of the year it was clear that he was going to run into serious difficulties when he met Parliament. Most people had expected him to devote the long summer recess to political manœuvring, winning over the waverers in order to make the mangagement of Parliament easier. Instead he had concerned himself with his plans for reform, with measures rather than men. Nor were the measures calculated to win him support in the House of Commons. The professional politicians, the followers of the great borough-mongers, could not be expected to back a drive for administrative efficiency which threatened to undermine the patronage system; and the independent gentlemen of the Country Party were not interested in complex details of Treasury organization. They wanted to weaken the power of the central government, not to make it more effective. When Parliament met on 5 December 1782 the debates on the King's Speech made it clear that the Whigs were determined to oppose the new ministry vigorously. Lord North's party, still the most powerful and best organized group in the Commons, held its fire. Since it had waged the war against the American colonists, its attitude to Shelburne's·ministry would depend on the sort of peace that ministry made to end the war.

Shelburne saw only too clearly that the peace treaty was the most vital measure of all, the thing on which the survival of his ministry and the future of his reforms would depend. Hard bargaining had been going on throughout the summer, at Versailles and at Paris and even at Bowood, and by September he had become convinced that he would have to give in and recognize American independence prior to the signature of a treaty. Only by doing this would he be able to get the colonists to desert their European allies and sign a separate peace. The recognition was accordingly given and early in October a draft treaty was submitted to the Cabinet. It provided for an independent United States of America stretching northwards to the Great Lakes and westwards to the Mississippi; and it also proposed free trade between Britain and America. Shelburne himself had some sympathy with the theory of free trade, but he knew that the powerful West Indian interest in the Commons was determined to exclude the colonists from the trade of the Caribbean. After further negotiations he got the free trade clauses removed from the treaty, although the Mississippi trade was to be open to all comers. Minor boundary changes were also made, giving more territory to Canada and less to the United States. The revised treaty was signed at the end of November and in January 1783 preliminary articles of peace with France and Spain were signed. There was a general restoration of conquests in the West Indies and France also received Tobago, which had been in British hands since 1763. French fishing rights off Newfoundland were fully recognized and the French slaving station of Senegal in Africa was restored. Minorca and Florida were ceded to Spain, but Gibraltar, which had been besieged almost continuously ever since Spain had entered the war, was retained.

When the debates on the peace treaty opened in the Commons on 17 February 1783 it soon became apparent that North had decided to join with the Whigs in attacking the ministry. A Whig amendment to the Address of Thanks, moved by Lord John Cavendish, was accompanied by one proposed by North himself, deploring the failure to obtain proper guarantees for the Loyalists in America. Early in the morning of the 18th, after a long and fierce debate, the amendments were carried by 224 to 208. In spite of their doubts about the peace terms, the majority of the independent country gentlemen voted with the ministry: they were not wholeheartedly behind Shelburne's programme of reform, but they resented the efforts of the Whigs and North to force themselves on the King. The Court, on the other hand, preferred North to Shelburne. and the majority of the placemen, serving officers and government contractors voted against the ministry.[1] It was a dramatic reversal of the usual position. All those with an interest in the patronage system, whether office-holders or office-seekers, banded together to bring down a minister whom they saw as an enemy to party, to patronage and to all that they held dear. On the other hand the Country Party, together with some of the more radical elements in the City,[2] were prepared to accept a peace treaty they distrusted in order to save a minister whom they saw as their only shield against the party magnates.

But the Country Party and the City, even if they had been more united and determined than they were, could not have held back the onslaughts of Lord North and the Whigs. On 21 February Lord John Cavendish moved a series of resolutions which had been worked out jointly by the Whigs and by North's party. They pledged the Commons to accept and support the peace, but deplored the

[1] See John Norris: *Shelburne and Reform* (London, 1963), pp. 267–8 and 295–307, for an invaluable analysis of the vote of 18 February.

[2] John Wilkes, now a member for the City of London, voted for the ministry.

concessions to the enemy as being 'greater than they were entitled to, either from the actual state of their respective possessions, or from their comparative strength'. After the resolutions had been carried against him by 207 votes to 190, Shelburne went to the King and insisted on resigning. He seems to have imagined, quite wrongly, that the King could have done more than he had in fact done to ensure him the support of North and the Court Party. Preoccupied with his radical reforming schemes, with measures and not with men, Shelburne had consistently underrated the power of the patronage structure and its ability to act independently of the King and his ministers. George III, for his part, felt that Shelburne was running away from his responsibilities and that he ought to carry on even though he had temporarily lost control of the Commons. After a good deal of mutual recrimination they parted on 24 February, the King to fight off the Whigs as best he could and Shelburne to retire to Bowood and his circus of tame intellectuals.

He was still only forty-five, a politician in the prime of life and an experienced administrator, but he was destined never to return to public life. He had incurred the hatred both of the Whigs and of the King, while his patronage of Dissenters and other radicals made him increasingly distrusted by those independent country gentlemen who had rallied to him in the crisis of February 1783. He went abroad again, renewed and extended his contacts with the radical thinkers in France, and took into his service Etienne Dumont, a young Genevese who was later to act as his observer in Paris during the early stages of the French Revolution. A group of radically minded young lawyers who were introduced to the Bowood circle in the 1780s included Samuel Romilly, the future penal reformer. In 1788 Shelburne, who had been created Marquis of Lansdowne four years earlier, introduced Bentham to Dumont, who was later to make himself responsible for the editing of the major part of Bentham's works. At about the same time the Bowood group started a journal, *The Repository*, to act as a mouthpiece for their ideas. Its editor was Benjamin Vaughan, who had been a pupil of Priestley's at the Dissenting Academy at Warrington and had later acted as Shelburne's agent in the peace negotiations of 1782. *The Repository* was not successful—it ceased publication in January 1789—but in May 1789 the beginnings of the French Revolution encouraged the Bowood radicals to think that their ideas might be applied in France and, as a result, in Britain as well. From Paris Dumont sent long and enthusiastic reports back to Bowood, telling his patron of 'events so much in accord with your views, so consonant with your principles, so effective as milestones in that march of progress which you observe with such interest'. Early in 1790 Romilly published his optimistic *Thoughts on the Probable Influence of the French Revolution on Great Britain*, in which he predicted that the example set by France would shame Britain into reforming the poor law, introducing free trade, changing the electoral system, abolishing the slave trade, abolishing the death penalty for theft and generally implementing the radical programmes drawn up at Bowood.

By 1792, however, the French Revolution had become so extreme and so violent that all those who had sympathized with it were regarded with great suspicion. In May 1792 an under-secretary at the Foreign Office told his friend scornfully that the new French envoy 'is intimate with Paine, Horne Tooke, Lord Lansdowne, and a few more of that stamp, and generally scouted by everyone else'. Lansdowne still spoke to his friends of his hopes of bringing about 'an interesting conclusion to his political career', but he was becoming increasingly irritable as the knowledge of his failure was borne in on him. Throughout the 1790s he continued to oppose the war against the French Revolution and the steps taken by the government to prevent revolution in Britain, but he was fighting a losing battle. He died in May 1805. He had never learnt to manage men and as a result he was never given a chance to implement his measures; but the radical ideas which had been developed at Bowood under his patronage were destined to dominate the political thinking of the next generation. He had been defeated by the politics of patronage, but he had played a great part in moulding the politics of programmes which was to replace it.

3 Charles James Fox

For several weeks after Shelburne's resignation the Whigs and Lord North's party haggled over the distribution of offices. The Duke of Portland, titular head of the Whig party, was so sure of himself that he refused at first to let anyone from North's party have either of the Secretaryships of State. The great party magnates were so intoxicated with their victory over Shelburne that they seem to have forgotten that North, the King's Friend whom they had attacked and despised for over twenty years, had won it for them. In their eyes it was a victory of principle, a vindication of the right of all men of substance to deal freely in the patronage market and share in the fruits of office. In order to defeat one King's Friend, Shelburne, they had had to make use of another, North; but they hoped that they would be able to discard him once he had served his purpose. North, however, would not be discarded. He had a following of some 130 or 140 members in the Commons and he knew that if he wanted to keep it he must return to office. If he stayed in opposition much longer his party would melt away. In the middle of March Portland gave way and agreed that North himself should be Home Secretary and that his friend Lord Stormont should be Lord President of the Council. He himself was to be First Lord of the Treasury, Fox was to be Foreign Secretary, Carlisle Lord Privy Seal, Keppel First Lord of the Admiralty and Lord John Cavendish Chancellor of the Exchequer. Armed with this list of seven names, his proposed Cabinet, he went to see the King and asked to be appointed as his minister.

George III was furious. It was bad enough that the Whigs should force themselves on him again, but it was quite intolerable that they should have the impertinence to present him with a *fait accompli*. He refused to look at Portland's list and told him that there must be full consultations about the whole administration. Portland insisted on having a free hand in the distribution of lesser offices, and the King broke off the discussion. He approached North and tried to detach him from the Whigs, but without success. He turned to the young William Pitt, who had been Chancellor of the Exchequer in Shelburne's ministry, and asked him for the second time to take over the Treasury and form a ministry. Pitt refused. The King had wild ideas of abdicating, or of making a solemn appeal to Parliament to rescue him from the Whig conspiracy; but in the end he surrendered. He gave Portland blank warrants of appointment to be filled up at the discretion of the Whig leaders, and retired into a sullen silence. At last, on 2 April 1783, the Portland ministry took office.

What made the King even angrier was the knowledge that Portland was only a figurehead in any case. It was Charles James Fox, and not the Duke of Portland, who had been the effective leader of the Whig party since Rockingham's death, and George III's hatred of the Whigs in general was a mild thing compared with his hatred of Charles James Fox in particular. He had always regarded the Fox family as a set of corrupt and unprincipled politicians, and when

Charles James, the younger son of Henry Fox, had first appeared in Parliament in 1768 at the age of nineteen he had epitomized all those aristocratic vices which the King disliked so much. His father had taken him away from Eton at the age of fourteen in order to introduce him to the gaming rooms of the Continent, and by 1768 he was an experienced man of the world and a notable dandy, affecting red-heeled shoes and blue hair powder. But at first he had at any rate supported the Court and opposed the 'New Whiggery' which sought to appeal from Lord North to 'the voice of the people'. 'I pay no regard whatever to the voice of the people', he had declared disdainfully in 1771. 'I will not be a rebel to my King, my country, or my own heart, for the loudest huzza of an inconsiderate multitude.' A few years later, however, after he had been rolled in the mud by an angry mob, twice appointed to North's ministry and twice dismissed, he changed his tune and became a supporter of the popular cause. 'That young man has so thoroughly cast off every principle of common honour and honesty,' grumbled the King, 'that he must soon become as contemptible as he is odious.' Fox spoke vehemently in support of the American colonists and gave up his dandified clothes to wear the plain blue coat and buff waistcoat which were associated with Washington's army. By 1779 he was comparing George III publicly to Henry VI, the weak-minded and incompetent King during whose reign the British possessions in France were lost, and in the following year he further disgusted the King by taking the chair at radical meetings in Westminster.

Worst of all, in the King's eyes, was his influence over the Prince of Wales. George III had hoped to shield his sons from the vices of the fashionable world and to inculcate in them the simple piety which he himself valued so highly. The Prince and his brother, Frederick Duke of York, had been brought up in Spartan seclusion at Kew and had even been made to dig their own plots of land to teach them the value of honest toil. But in 1781, as soon as the Prince was given an establishment of his own, he threw himself into all the pleasures of the town with great enthusiasm and with Fox as his friend and companion. The King did not stop to consider whether this might not be a natural reaction against the strictness of the Prince's upbringing. All he knew was that Fox had corrupted his son and was now in a position to corrupt his Court and his country as well. He saw Fox's victory in April 1783 not just as the triumph of the Whigs but as the triumph of wickedness.

George III misjudged Fox. He was not unprincipled and he was certainly not wicked. He had a great zest for life and a healthy contempt for everything that was narrow-minded and mealy-mouthed, but he was not a mere playboy. He was well aware that his alliance with North was violently unpopular, that the pamphleteers and caricaturists represented it as a shameless and hypocritical union of opposites,[1] but it was the only way of bringing the Whigs back into power and for that reason it seemed to him justified. His main quarrel with North had been over the American war and that was now over and done with. He was convinced that the Whig party, and the Whig party alone, could liberalize the constitution without bringing about a dangerous increase in the power of the central government. He distrusted professional bureaucrats and he distrusted the sweeping generalities of Shelburne's tame philosophers; only civilized Whig gentlemen, tolerant and broad-minded amateurs, could solve the country's problems. Officially he was only Foreign Secretary, but North was quite prepared to let him concern himself with home affairs as well. He set himself to study the questions of the hour and to find answers to them.

Since the ministry did not take office until April, there was not time to do much in the present session of Parliament. Early in May William Pitt brought forward resolutions for the reform of Parliament. They were opposed strenuously by North and his party, but Fox spoke in their favour and said that in his view 'the right of governing was not property, but a trust'. The phrase was a crucial one, since it pointed the way from the Old Whiggery to the New. The Old Whigs had seen office and power, seats in Parliament and sinecures at Court, as part of the property which had been guaranteed to the gentlemen of England by the Revolution of 1688; but Fox saw these things as duties to be undertaken for the good of the people. Pitt's resolutions were defeated by 293 to 149 and they served to reveal—as they were intended to—the gulf between North and Fox; but they also gave Fox a chance to enunciate the principles on which the rest of his political life was to be based.

During the summer recess Burke, who had once again become Paymaster, consulted with Fox on the problem of India. Ever since North's stopgap measure of 1773, successive ministries had turned

---

[1] The flood of hostile comment was so ferocious that Horace Walpole said of the ministry on 25 April 1783. 'If satiric prints could despatch them, they would be dead in their cradle.'

over possible schemes for the government of India and Burke had been passionately interested in them all. His interest was partly financial, since his family had speculated heavily and unsuccessfully in East India Company stock, but it was also humanitarian. In 1772 a Select Committee set up to examine the Company's efforts to govern the Indian continent had spoken of 'the most atrocious abuses that ever stained the name of civil government', and Burke had become more and more convinced of the utter incompetence of the East India Company as a governing body. On the other hand, his Whig principles made him revere the rights of chartered companies and fear any extension of the influence and patronage of the central government in Whitehall. India presented a problem in government, but it also presented a challenge to the fundamental tenets of Whiggery. And if it was a challenge to the Old Whiggery of Burke, it was even more of a challenge to the New Whiggery of Fox. If the right of governing was a trust and not a piece of property, then the Whigs who had inherited that right must do what they could for the people of India who had been entrusted to their care. Fox knew that it would be rash to bring forward anything as controversial as an East India Bill while his ministry was still so insecure, but he felt that the risk must be taken 'when the happiness of so many millions was at stake'.

When Parliament met again on 11 November the King's Speech mentioned the need for an immediate consideration of the Indian question and Pitt called upon the ministry to bring in an India Bill without delay. If he hoped to catch the ministers unprepared he was disappointed: Fox immediately announced his intention of bringing in not one Bill but two. The first vested the government of India in a Board of seven commissioners and nine assistant commissioners, while the second subjected the authorities in India itself to the tightest possible control by the Board in London. From the practical point of view the second Bill was more open to criticism than the first: it took months for instructions to reach India from London and a Bill which left nothing to the discretion of the men on the spot would make good government almost impossible. But the whole weight of the opposition's attack, both in Parliament and in the Press, was directed against the first Bill. The commissioners and assistant commissioners named in it were all Foxites; and the commissioners were to hold office for four years, during which time the King could only dismiss them if he was asked to do so by an Address of both Houses of Parliament. Future assistant commissioners were to be elected by the shareholders of the East India Company, but it was alleged by the opposition that in the four years at their disposal the commissioners would be able to establish such complete control of East India patronage that no shareholder would dare to defy them. Sayers's famous print of *Carlo Khan's Triumphal Entry into Leadenhall Street*, showing Fox riding on an elephant into East India House, summed up the popular view of the East India Bills. The elephant, who had the face of Lord North, looked somewhat anxious; but Carlo Khan and his attendant—an Indian with the face of Edmund Burke—were beaming with satisfaction. If Fox and Burke[1] expected to be given credit for shouldering the burden of Indian government, for concerning themselves with 'the happiness of so many millions', they were sadly disillusioned. They were seen only as grasping politicians who wanted to corner East India patronage for all time.

George III was quite prepared to use the outcry against the East India Bills as a means of getting rid of the ministers he hated, but he could not shake their position in the existing House of Commons, where the Bills were carried by 208 votes to 102. He might be able to get the Bills defeated in the Lords and use this as an excuse to dismiss his ministers, but he must first ensure that he could produce an alternative administration and that he could guarantee that administration a majority in a new House of Commons. While the Bills were still before the Commons the East India Company approached the King discreetly through one of its directors called Richard Atkinson and offered to make a substantial contribution to the King's election expenses if he decided to dismiss the ministry and dissolve Parliament. John Robinson and Charles Jenkinson, two King's Friends who had had considerable experience of managing elections, were called in to advise the King and they assured him that with the money promised by the Company at least 116 seats could be won over from Fox and North. William Pitt was then approached and, after a secret meeting at which he vetted the plans for the proposed election, he agreed to take office. Earl Temple, Pitt's cousin and son of that George Grenville who had come to the King's aid twenty years before, was given a letter in which he was authorized to say

[1] Fox left the actual drafting of the Bills to Burke—not just out of idleness but because it was the only way to get his full cooperation. He said later that Burke was 'a most impracticable person, a most unmanageable colleague; that he would never support any measure, however convinced he might be in his head of its utility, if it had been prepared by another'.

that any member of the House of Lords who voted for the India Bills would be considered as an enemy to the King. As a result the Lords rejected the Bills by ninety-five votes to seventy-six on 17 December and the Fox–North ministry was dismissed the following day.

Among the members of the House of Lords who decided to brave the King's enmity and vote for the Bills was the Prince of Wales. He joined vociferously in the Whig chorus of horror at his father's allegedly 'unconstitutional' actions. Once again, as in the 1740s, politicians could choose between a King who wielded the patronage of the present and a Prince who would wield the patronage of the future. Once again, those who chose the Prince accused the King of corruption and tyranny and promised to bring in a better and purer system of politics when they came to power. This time, however, the promises were more specific: the Prince was not advised by Bolingbrokes and Egmonts, men who talked in vague terms of 'Patriotism', but by Charles James Fox, the 'man of the people' and the advocate of parliamentary reform. Fox was destined to spend the next twenty-three years in opposition and during that time he would have to reconcile his own reforming zeal with the service of a Prince who became steadily less popular and less interested in 'the voice of the people'. It was a task that was to become increasingly difficult. Fox the man of pleasure, the link between the Whigs and the Prince, was to find it hard to live with Fox the man of the people, the link between the Whigs and reform.

4   *William Pitt the Younger*

Second son of the great Chatham, William Pitt had inherited all his father's superb self-confidence and much of his hatred of party politics. When he took office in December 1783 he was sure, as sure as his father had been in 1756, that he could save the country and that nobody else could. The enemy, however, was no longer France but the Whigs. Pitt believed in the balance of the constitution and he saw that balance threatened by the arrogant ambitions of Fox and Burke and North. In 1688 it had been necessary to prevent the executive swallowing up the legislative; now it was necessary to prevent the legislative swallowing up the executive. If Fox was allowed to have his way King and Country alike would be led captive by an unholy alliance of office-holders and office-seekers, the placemen created by North and the party magnates led by Portland. Whiggery, which had once stood for the efficient management of the King's affairs in Parliament, now stood for the subordination of the King's government to the needs of the patronage system. Like his father, Pitt believed in 'measures, not men' and he opposed the notion that mere 'connection' and mutual confidence entitled a group of men to run the country; but, unlike his father, he had clear and positive ideas as to how the country should be run, what the measures should be. He understood finance as well as foreign policy, the needs of peace as well as the aims of war. For this reason he was to succeed where his father had failed and make himself the effective Patriot Minister of a Patriot King.

When he first took over the Whigs treated his ministry with ridicule and believed, or pretended to believe, that it could not last longer than the Christmas recess. He was not yet twenty-five, exceptionally young for a First Lord of the Treasury; he was dubbed 'Master Billy' and assailed with lampoons about his youth and inexperience. But when Parliament met again on 12 January 1784 he was still in office and the Whigs began to realize that it would not be so easy to dislodge him, in spite of their majority in the House of Commons. In a debate on the state of the nation and on the measures to be taken to counter the threat of dissolution, they defeated him by thirty-nine votes—little more than a third of their majority in December. When they brought in a resolution demanding a ministry which had the confidence of the Commons, Henry Dundas[1] neatly revealed the weakness of their position by proposing an amendment which spoke of the confidence of 'the Crown, the Parliament and the people'. It was rejected, but it served to remind the Whigs that there was more to the constitution than a temporary majority in the House of Commons. Even that temporary majority was dwindling steadily: on 23 January, in a division on Pitt's India Bill, it was down to eight.

Pitt remained blandly indifferent to votes of censure and charges of unconstitutional behaviour. He challenged the Whigs to impeach him if they really thought he was acting illegally by staying in office against the wishes of the majority of the Commons. He knew perfectly well that they dared not use this extreme weapon, any more than they dared to risk a headlong collision with the King by voting

[1] Henry Dundas was a typical King's Servant, a hardworking administrator who now resumed the post of Treasurer of the Navy which he had held in Shelburne's ministry. All Pitt's Cabinet colleagues were peers, so that Dundas was one of his few supporters in the Commons.

against the Land Tax Bill or the Mutiny Bill. The City had already presented its freedom in a golden casket to Pitt the son, as it had once done to Pitt the father, and the Country Party was also turning against the Whigs: the independent members had tried to bring about a coalition of Pitt and Fox and most of them blamed Fox's intransigence for the failure of the attempt. Extreme measures would not only lose the Whigs support among moderate members of the existing House of Commons, but would also increase the chance of their having to face a new one. The King and his advisers had intended all along to dissolve Parliament and hold an election, but Pitt withheld this information from the Commons and so kept the Whigs guessing until the last moment. At last, when he had whittled the opposition majority down to a single vote, he announced the dissolution of Parliament at the end of March. The Whigs protested violently and Burke spoke of 'a Parliament sentenced, condemned and executed . . . a settled plan to destroy not the form but the essence of the House of Commons'. But the Whigs could not really argue that the dissolution was unconstitutional. It was true that the current Parliament was only just over three years old and that most Parliaments since the passing of the Septennial Act had lasted for six or seven years; but the Act only prescribed a maximum life for Parliaments, not a minimum. George III was quite within his rights in dissolving and the Whigs knew it.

The election was a great triumph for Pitt and the King. Instead of the 116 seats that Robinson had promised, no less than 160 were won over by the government. It was a victory for royal influence and East India money, but it was also to some extent a victory for public opinion. Rather to his surprise, Robinson found that his candidates were successful in several constituencies where the electorate was too large to be managed by the usual means. Nobody could say where the power of royal patronage ended and the effects of royal popularity began. Not even the electors themselves could say for certain who had voted out of hatred for the Whigs and who had voted out of a desire to profit from the new régime and its distribution of favours. What was clear was that the King had turned the Whig weapons of patronage and popularity against them. Men had said of the elder Pitt that the House of Commons had given him to the King; but now the King had not only given the younger Pitt to the House of Commons but had also given a new and more amenable House of Commons to the younger Pitt.

Pitt was determined to use it in order to give the country a period of stable and efficient government. For more than forty years successive administrations had had to contend with party confusion, ministerial instability and expensive wars. Now, at last, there was a prospect of at least seven years of peace and stability. Pitt's majority in the new Parliament was large enough to enable him to defy both office-holders and office-seekers, both the Court and the party magnates; and only a minister who was ready to defy these groups could undertake the administrative reforms which the country needed so badly. He now possessed what Dundas had spoken of in January: the confidence of 'the Crown, the Parliament and the people'. He was in the position to transcend patronage and management and to create government.

He turned his attention first to the problem of governing India, the problem which had precipitated the crisis of the last few months. His India Act, passed in August 1784, was based on the Bill which he had failed to carry in the previous Parliament. Overall control of Indian affairs was given to a board of six Privy Councillors appointed by the King, but patronage remained in the hands of the East India Company. The Governor-General in Calcutta and the members of his Council were to be appointed by the King, however, and they were to have far more power than they had been allowed by Fox's Bills. In 1786 a further Act gave the Governor-General the right to over-ride his council. Fox and Burke attacked the measures vehemently, saying that they would permit Governor-Generals to become un-trammelled tyrants and that the system of 'dual control', of separating government and patronage, was unworkable. In fact, it worked until 1858.

Whig criticisms of the Act were not merely perverse. For many years past there had been a growing feeling in the country that the officials who ruled India were practising extortion and cruelty and that it was the duty of politicians at home to protect the natives of India against them. Burke had felt this more strongly than most and he had been particularly influenced by his association with Philip Francis, a member of the Governor-General's Council from 1774 to 1780. The Governor-General in question had been Warren Hastings, who had done great things for India. He had reorganized and reformed the government of Bengal and he had helped the Nawab of Oudh, a native ruler to the north-west of Bengal, to resist the incursions of a plundering tribe called the Rohillas. Francis,

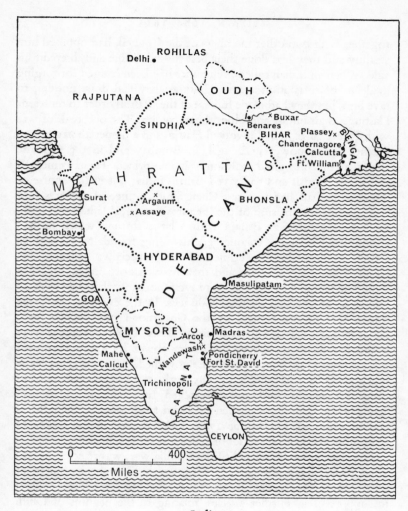

India

together with two other members of the Council, had opposed him steadily and they had done their best to undermine and discredit his rule. When an Indian called Nuncumar had been hanged for forging evidence of corruption against Hastings they had done nothing to save him, but they had made full use of the affair in order to represent Hastings as an unjust and bloodthirsty tyrant. The outbreak of war with France in 1778 had involved Hastings in a desperate struggle to defend British power in Bengal, in Bombay and in the Carnatic against a French inspired coalition of Indian princes. He had emerged victorious from it and had saved British India; but in the course of doing so he had had to arrest Chait Singh, prince of Benares, and seize part of the treasure of the 'begums', or royal ladies, of Oudh. Francis, now back in Britain with a large fortune which he had accumulated in India, encouraged his Whig friends to view these actions as unpardonable crimes. Burke, especially, believed that Hastings had been a tyrant and that his successors under Pitt's Act would be tempted to be even more tyrannical now that they were no longer to be checked by their Councils. In the event it was to be shown that tighter control by the Governor-General made for a better and less corrupt government in India; but the Whigs always found it difficult to believe that more power for the government might mean more happiness for the governed. When Warren Hastings arrived back in London in 1785 Burke and Fox opened a violent campaign against him and threatened impeachment. Hastings's agent in the Commons challenged them to implement their threat and they did so. On 1 June 1786 Burke moved in the House of Commons the first of a series of articles of impeachment.

The charge, which related to the Rohilla war, was rejected by 119 votes to 67; but a subsequent charge concerning the treatment of Chait Singh was accepted by 119 to 79 after Pitt himself had spoken in support of it. Further articles, relating to the begums of Oudh and other matters, were then accepted and the trial of Warren Hastings before the House of Lords opened in Westminster Hall on 13 February 1788. At first the fashionable world flocked to hear the impassioned eloquence of Burke and the other Whig managers of the trial; but as the speeches grew longer and longer and the progress of the trial slower and slower interest waned. By the time Hastings was finally acquitted in 1795 the impeachment had become boring and unpopular. Burke declared that the acquittal was in reality a 'barbarous and inhuman condemnation of whole tribes and nations', and that a rump of the House of Lords had betrayed its trust and endangered the constitution itself. They were brave words, but they could not disguise the fact that the Whigs had made fools of themselves. Their attempt to stand forth as the champions of freedom against the tyranny of governors and governments had failed dismally.

Meanwhile Pitt had moved on from the problems of governing India to the problems of governing Britain. The crucial and central problem was that of finance. Year by year ever since 1776 government expenditure had exceeded government income by a steadily increasing margin; and by 1784 the National Debt stood at £242,900,000. There was a general lack of confidence in the government's ability to repay it or even to bring it within manageable bounds; and as a result £100 worth of government stock was only worth £56. In his budgets of 1784 and 1785 Pitt had to allow for the repayment of large military and naval debts incurred in the American war, but from 1786 onwards he kept expenditure and income fairly evenly balanced. By February 1792, when he came to introduce what proved to be his last peace-time budget, he could point to an increase in revenue of some 45 per cent over 1783 figures.[1] To some extent this had been achieved by inventing new and ingenious taxes: all manner of things from hats and ribbons to horses and servants were taxed and in some cases the taxes did more harm than good. The window tax not only harmed the glass industry, but also helped to make the new factory buildings even more sunless and airless than they would otherwise have been. Duties on linen and cotton, imposed in 1784 and later removed, also had an adverse effect on the new industrialism.

But the greater part of the increase in revenue had been produced not by raising but by lowering taxes. Something like two-thirds of the government's income came from customs and excise and by the time Pitt took over in 1783 this source was being eaten away by a vast and terrifying growth in large-scale smuggling. 'Will Washington take America, or the Smugglers England first?' Lord Pembroke had asked in 1781. When Burke had come back into office in the spring of 1783 he had called for a report on smuggling from the Board of Customs; and the Board had estimated that smuggling had increased threefold during the previous three years and that over

[1] Contemporary estimates of revenue were seldom exact. Pitt reckoned the revenue for 1791 as £16,690,000; in fact it was £18,506,000. In 1783 it had been £12,677,000. Compare *Speeches of William Pitt* (1806), vol. ii, p. 25, and *Abstract of British Historical Statistics* (1962), p. 388.

21,000,000 lb of tea were brought into the country illegally every year. Things had got so bad that Richard Twining, a tea and coffee merchant of London, had set up an association to protect the interests of those few traders who refused to deal in smuggled goods. Burke had recommended a drastic reduction in the duty on tea, in order to cut the ground from under the smugglers' feet by making their activities less profitable. Pitt implemented his suggestions in 1784 by sweeping away the heavy and complex tea duties, which amounted to about 119 per cent, and substituting a single duty of 12½ per cent which was to be collected through the agency of the East India Company. At the same time the excise system was tightened and in 1786 it was extended to wines. Finally, in 1789 and 1790, Pitt extended it to tobacco as well, thus completing the programme which Walpole had failed to bring in in 1733.

The reduction in tea duties was followed by further reductions and simplifications of the customs tariff in 1787; and by 1792 the customs and excise were bringing in more than half as much again as they had done in 1783. Vigorous efforts had been made to smash the smugglers: in 1784 no less than eight regiments were stationed along the coasts to deal with them and an Act was passed enabling the authorities to board and examine vessels hovering suspiciously near the coast. But the increase in revenue was not only the result of the campaign against smuggling and the reduction in rates of duty: it was also a reflection of a steady rise in the volume of trade and in the general level of national prosperity. Pitt appreciated this fact and he saw that the continued success of his policies depended on the efforts of the industrialists and the merchants and the financiers. His speech of February 1792 attributed the improved state of the nation's finances to 'the exertion of genius and labour, the extent and solidity of credit, the circulation and increase of capital'. But for all his reliance on the City and the country rather than on the potentates of the patronage system, he was still enough of a traditional politician to resent any attempt by the industrialists to take a hand in government themselves. When Josiah Wedgwood and other manufacturers tried to form their local Committees of Commerce into a General Chamber of Manufacturers, Pitt warned them not to stray into 'the paths of legislation and government'. He was prepared to take the new forces into consideration, but he was not prepared to take them into partnership.

As well as seeing that the government collected money more

effectively, Pitt saw that it spent it more efficiently. In 1780 Lord North had appointed six Commissioners to 'Examine, Take and State the Public Accounts of the Kingdom' and the reports of these commissioners, made over a period of seven years, were used by Pitt as the basis for a good deal of unobtrusive but important administrative reform. A proper system of auditing the public accounts was introduced in 1785 and in the same year Pitt appointed Commissioners to inquire into fees and gratuities received by public servants. There was no drastic purge of sinecurists, but unnecessary offices were gradually abolished, and those officials who remained found their work increased and their opportunities for taking fees and other perquisites steadily reduced. By 1789 more than 700 offices had been done away with in the revenue service alone. Less obvious aspects of the patronage system were also reformed: whereas the Rockinghams had dealt with government contractors by excluding them from the House of Commons, Pitt dealt with them by putting government contracts out to competitive tender. Burke had been concerned to reduce government influence, but Pitt was concerned to reduce government expenditure. In 1786, after setting up yet another committee on finance, he decided to set aside the money that was being saved for the purpose of reducing the National Debt. A Sinking Fund was established, administered by commissioners who were independent of the Treasury. The government was to pay them £1,000,000 a year, which they were to devote to buying up government stock, below par if possible. In this way the government would gradually become the owner of its own stock and would use the interest it paid itself in order to buy yet more stock. It was a good idea when it was launched, even though the exceptional conditions of war finance were later to render it absurd.

The scheme for a Sinking Fund was partly based on the ideas of Richard Price, a dissenting minister and a member of Shelburne's circle of radicals at Bowood. Although Pitt had not invited Shelburne to join his administration, he often visited Bowood and made good use of the ideas that he encountered there. He was particularly impressed with the Free Trade theories of Adam Smith[1] and in 1787 he set up a system of free ports in the West Indies in order to make trade with the United States easier. By 1792 British exports to the United

---

[1] One of Bentham's friends told him in July 1787 that Adam Smith was 'much with the ministry'. 'I am vexed that Pitt should have done so right a thing as to consult Smith', he added.

States stood at £4,271,000, more than they had ever been before the War of Independence and over four times the 1783 figure. Negotiations were started for commercial treaties with France, Spain, Portugal, the United Provinces, Russia and several other countries. Most of them were abortive, but in 1786 a treaty was signed with France by which import duties on French wine were reduced in return for reductions on British textiles and hardware going into France. Pitt also supported the campaign for the abolition of the slave trade, a cause which aroused the hostility of vested mercantile interests even more than Free Trade did. He was a close friend of William Wilberforce, the rich evangelical who championed the cause of abolition in the House of Commons, and he regularly spoke in support of Wilberforce's unsuccessful attempts to get the trade stopped. Yet he was never able to bring in a government Bill for abolition and many of his closest supporters on the Treasury bench, including Dundas, were ardent defenders of the trade.

This cleavage between Pitt the reformer and the conservatively minded administration which he led was even more marked when it came to the question of parliamentary reform. In April 1785 he brought in a relatively modest proposal to disfranchise thirty-six rotten boroughs and to transfer the seats to the counties and the new industrial towns. Even though he proposed to give compensation to the owners of the boroughs, the measure was much too radical for the taste of the King, who refused to instruct the placemen to vote for it. 'Mr Pitt must recollect', he wrote, 'that . . . I have ever thought it unfortunate that he had early engaged himself in this measure.' A great part of the government party voted against the measure, which was defeated by 248 votes to 174. It was a sharp reminder to Pitt that the King had given him his position in the Commons and that the King could take it away. In May 1788 an experienced manager of the House reckoned that the party of the Crown, 'those who would probably support His Majesty's Government under any Minister not peculiarly unpopular', numberd 185; Pitt's personal following he put at fifty-two, of whom 'were there a new Parliament, and Mr. P. no longer Minister, not above twenty would be returned'. Like his father and like Shelburne, Pitt was better at framing measures than managing men. As a result he still had no party of his own, even after more than four years of power. He could defy the party magnates only as long as his measures were popular enough to please the country but moderate enough to please the King.

Throughout the summer and autumn of 1788 George III was unwell and by the beginning of November it was known that his illness had affected his mind.[1] His physicians, in an attempt to 'draw out the humours' from his brain, applied hot poultices to his shaven head; and the appalling agony occasioned by this treatment helped to turn a nervous breakdown into a fit of temporary insanity. The Whigs were delighted: at last the King who had baulked them was unfit to reign and the Prince whom they served would come to power and bring them into office. The opposition press broke into verse:

> If blisters to the head applied
> Some little sense bestow
> What pity 'tis they were not tried
> Some twenty years ago.

The Prince, assuming that his father's condition was permanent, sent a message to Fox, who was holidaying in Italy, and settled down to make arrangements for his regency. Lord Thurlow, who had been Lord Chancellor almost continuously ever since 1778 and was the epitome of the Court Party, deserted Pitt and opened negotiations with the Prince. At first Pitt was convinced that he must fall, but by early December things looked more hopeful. Dr Willis, who had had considerable experience in dealing with insanity, took charge of the King and predicted a recovery. Pitt insisted that Parliament must authorize the regency and prepared a Bill which put important restrictions on the Prince's power. These were designed to prevent the Whigs using a period of regency in order to build up a majority in the Commons strong enough to defy the King in the event of his recovery; but Fox and Burke claimed that they amounted to a plot against the constitution. The Prince, they argued, should take over complete power immediately, without any authorization by Parliament: only in this way could the 'anarchy of elective government' be avoided. When the King recovered his senses in February 1789 they refused to credit the news. Burke spoke darkly of lunatics who had apparently got well and had then committed suicide or had butchered their sons. He told the Commons that George III was 'a monarch smitten by the hand of Omnipotence ... the Almighty had hurled him from his throne'. But most people were relieved and were grateful to Pitt for having held the Prince and the Whigs at bay.

[1] Recent medical research has shown conclusively that George III's periods of mental derangement were physical rather than emotional in origin. See: *Porphyria—a Royal Malady: articles published in or commissioned by the British Medical Journal*, London, 1968.

'The national acclamations already echo the name of Pitt!' wrote one pamphleteer. 'At the very sound PATRIOTISM rises from her seat to pay the tribute of obeisance.'

The use of the word 'patriotism' was significant. Like his father, Pitt had won for himself the reputation of a Patriot Minister who would defend both King and Country against the factious party magnates. Just at the time when Fox was trying to turn the Whig party into a popular and progressive party, its unsavoury inner nature had been dragged into the light of day. It was clearly a party more interested in the patronage of the Prince than in the power of the people. But if the Regency Crisis has made it difficult for the Whigs to pose as a reforming party, it had had an even greater effect on Pitt himself, for it had made him realize his utter dependence on the King and on the King's mental stability. 'Though I am recovering,' George told him in April 1789, 'my mind is not strong enough as yet to stand little ruffles.' Any attempt at radical reform would certainly distress the King and might well lead to another attack of insanity. The King's support had enabled Pitt to revive his father's concept of non-party government, of measures rather than men, and to make it both popular and efficient, but it would not stretch to a programme of reform. By turning Patriotism from an idea into a reality, from a war cry into a peace policy, Pitt had laid the foundations of the New Toryism; but the fear of the King's renewed madness prevented him from making it a radical party. During the next few years the fear of revolution was to drive him even further into conservatism.

PART V

The Years of War and Toryism
1789–1815

15

Revolution Averted
1789–1801

1 The War against the French Revolution

When Pitt took office in December 1783 the problems that faced him
in the field of foreign policy[1] were as daunting as those at home.
The War of American Independence had underlined Britain's
dangerous isolation in Europe and the resentment which the European
powers felt at her colonial and commercial supremacy. Fox, during
his brief periods of office as Foreign Secretary, had made attempts to
renew the Prussian alliance, but he had met with nothing but polite
words. Pitt initiated a series of commercial negotiations designed to
get the countries of Europe to accept the idea of expanding overseas
trade to which Britain herself was committed, but he was not very
successful. Most European governments still thought in terms of
fixed, static economies and protective trade policies. They regarded
Britain's unprecedented expansion as something unnatural and
unhealthy, something to be distrusted rather than accepted.

For Pitt, as for his father before him, the danger of this isolation
lay in the fact that France might profit from it. Bourbon aggression,
he thought, lay at the root of Europe's troubles and Britain's dangers.
In 1785 the French took advantage of Austrian threats against the
United Provinces in order to establish an alliance with the Dutch, an
alliance which represented a very real threat to British commercial
interests and to British security. In Parliament Pitt was attacked
bitterly for tamely negotiating a trade treaty with France at a time
when a Franco-Dutch combination sought to dominate the Channel.
In 1787, however, he scored a considerable diplomatic victory when
the King of Prussia sent troops into the United Provinces in order to

[1] The Foreign Secretary, the Marquis of Carmarthen, was a nonentity and Pitt had
effective control of foreign policy. Sir James Harris reported that at a Cabinet dinner
he attended in May 1787 the Foreign Secretary was the only person who said nothing
about foreign policy.

overthrow the pro-French party there. Pitt supported him and threatened to go to war if France intervened in the United Provinces. The French backed down and by the summer of 1788 Britain, Prussia and the newly restored pro-Prussian régime in the United Provinces had formed a Triple Alliance to guarantee Dutch security and to resist French aggression. The traditional pattern of British foreign policy, the pattern which had made possible Chatham's victories, had been re-established.

Pitt was well aware that the reason for his success lay not in the strength of Britain but in the weakness of France. He had been able to do little to maintain British military strength; and the Country Party, with its desire for economy at all costs, had helped to defeat a proposal to fortify the dockyards at Portsmouth and Plymouth. But if Britain was ill-prepared for war, France was in a far worse state. Her financial system had been given its death-blow by the War of American Independence and Louis XVI's ministers knew that the only way to set the country on its feet again was to impose new taxes, taxes which would bear upon the nobility as well as on the classes beneath them. The nobility, who had hitherto been exempt from most taxation, managed to represent such proposals as despotic, as a threat to popular liberty as well as aristocratic privilege. Backed by popular opinion, they demanded that any new scheme of taxation should be first submitted to a meeting of the Estates General. The Estates General, which had not met since 1614, was the nearest equivalent in France to the British Parliament and the nobility hoped to use it to establish a system of government similar to that in Britain, a system of checks and balances in which the aristocracy could once again play its part in running the country. In 1788 Louis XVI gave way to their demands and agreed to summon an Estates General.

When the Estates General met at Versailles in May 1789 it soon became clear that the French nobility were to be consumed by the flames they had fanned. The popular party in the Estates formed itself into a National Assembly, pledged to give France an entirely new constitution. An aristocratic revolt had become a radical revolution. If Bourbon aggression really was at the root of Europe's troubles, then those troubles could now be ended, since the Bourbons were too weakened and distracted by the French Revolution to take an active part in European affairs. In May 1790, when Pitt threatened to go to war with Spain over Britain's claim to Vancouver Island, the King of France made ready to help his Spanish cousin; but the

National Assembly repudiated his actions and asserted its own right to decide on questions of peace and war. In the end the Spaniards had to give way and Pitt secured recognition of British rights in what were later to be the western provinces of Canada.[1] He also played an active part in the diplomacy of Eastern Europe, mediating between Prussia and Austria and breaking down the alliance between Austria and Russia. But in the spring of 1791, when he threatened to make war on Russia unless she returned the Turkish naval base of Oczakov on the Black Sea, he found that he had overstepped the mark. His majorities in the Commons started to fall and he found his policy opposed both in the Cabinet and in the City of London. He doubted his ability to get the country gentlemen to pay for a war against so distant an enemy as Russia and he therefore abandoned his warlike policy and allowed Russia to keep Oczakov.

In spite of his humiliation over the Oczakov affair, Pitt was convinced that the situation in Europe was favourable to Britain. 'Unquestionably there was never a time in the history of this country', he declared in his budget speech of February 1792, 'when, from the situation of Europe, we might more reasonably expect fifteen years of peace, than we may at the present moment.' Few prophecies have proved so dramatically and so disastrously mistaken. Two months later the monarchs of Europe had undertaken a war of intervention against the French Revolution, a war in which Britain was soon to become involved and which was to last for more than twenty years.

The basic reason for Britain's involvement was the fact that the French Revolution came to have ambitions which threatened the balance of power in Europe, and therefore the security of Britain, even more than those of the French Kings in the past. In August 1792 the French monarchy was overthrown altogether and a National Convention was elected which waged the war with relentless and unprecedented fury. To the members of the Convention it was not just a war against particular kings but a war against kings in general, a challenge to the whole existing order. They were given new confidence by the battle of Valmy in September 1792, when for the first time the untrained and scantily armed revolutionary levies turned back an experienced and properly disciplined professional army. 'Here and now', said the poet Goethe, who was present at the battle, 'begins

[1] In 1791 Pitt passed a Canada Act which sought to prevent racial friction by dividing Canada into two provinces, one mainly British and the other mainly French. Each province had a Council appointed by the King and an Assembly elected by the colonists.

a new age in the history of the world.' To the limited wars of kings, waged by professional armies for specific objectives, the Revolution opposed the concept of total war, of a whole people in arms fighting to change the world. On 19 November 1792 the Convention offered 'brotherhood and assistance' to all peoples who sought to overthrow their kings. 'We cannot rest', said one speaker, 'until all Europe is ablaze.'

Pitt was still cautious. He had no desire to involve Britain in a crusade on behalf of the French monarchy, but he could not afford to accept tamely a régime which repudiated the past and all that had been done in the past. The balance of Europe and the interests of Britain were guaranteed by a complex and delicate structure of treaties and alliances, all of them signed by the kings whom the Revolution sought to dethrone. Were all these to be swept away in the name of the new order which the Revolution hoped to establish? If so, war against the Revolution would be the only way of asserting Britain's determination to have a hand in the affairs of Europe for the sake of her own security. By the end of the year French forces had overrun the Austrian Netherlands and had announced their intention of opening the river Scheldt to navigation, in defiance of repeated treaty promises made by past French kings. The Dutch, who, like the British, regarded the closure of the Scheldt as essential to their commerce and to their security, appealed to Pitt for help. He was still hesitant, but on 1 February 1793 the Convention took matters out of his hands by declaring war against Britain and the United Provinces. A declaration of war against Spain followed a week later. The war against the Emperor and some of the German princes, in which the Revolution had been engaged since April 1792, had now become a war against almost the whole of Europe. Only Russia, preoccupied with her ambitions in the Baltic, the Black Sea and Poland, stood aside.

The British army at the outbreak of war numbered little more than 13,000 men. It was, as usual, augmented by Hanoverians and Hessians; but even so it was clear that Britain could not undertake any major military operations on the Continent. A small expeditionary force was assembled—so small that the whole force could be drawn up on the Horse Guards Parade for its commander, the Duke of York, to review—and sent to the Netherlands. The allies held a conference at Antwerp early in April, at which they agreed to reconquer the Netherlands; but they could not agree on much else. Allied efforts along the whole front, from Dunkirk in the north to the Swiss frontier in the south, were weakened by jealousies and divisions. By the end of the year the French had stemmed the allied advance in the Netherlands, held off the Duke of York's attempt to take Dunkirk and pushed the Prussians back across the upper Rhine into Germany. Pitt negotiated a series of subsidy treaties with his allies, spending over £800,000 in 1793 and more than £2,500,000 in 1794, but the run of defeats continued. By the end of 1794 the French had conquered not only the Netherlands but most of the United Provinces as well.

The navy was in much better shape than the army. Since Pitt's accession to power naval expenditure had been running at about £2,500,000 a year, a very modest figure; but the administrative genius of Sir Charles Middleton, Comptroller of the Navy from 1778 to 1790, had ensured that the country got the best possible value for its money. There were 113 ships of the line, most of them ready for service. The Mediterranean fleet under Lord Hood sailed in June 1793 and blockaded Toulon, where there was a royalist uprising later in the summer which handed the town over to the British. By December, however, the revolutionary forces had recaptured the town and Hood was driven off. Attempts to give help to royalist risings in the west of France also failed. This was partly because the allies themselves were uncertain whom they wanted to help: Pitt was anxious to support the moderates who wanted to restore a constitutional monarchy, but most of his allies were committed to the extremists, the exiled noblemen of France who were determined to destroy the Revolution completely. As a result neither the British navy nor the allied armies took proper advantage of the civil war which tore France apart in 1793. By the middle of 1794 the opportunity had gone and the Convention was once again in control of most of France. An attempt to land a force of exiled noblemen in Brittany in June 1795 was a miserable failure.

If British seapower could not influence the course of events in France itself, it could at least ensure the seizure of French overseas possessions and the blockade of French trade routes. In November 1793 Admiral Jervis took a force to the Caribbean, where most of the French islands were soon captured, and in the Mediterranean Hood and Nelson made possible the conquest of Corsica from the French in the summer of 1794. By this time the British blockade was making itself felt and France was extremely short of food, so much so that the main Brest fleet ventured out of port at the end of May in order to provide an escort for a convoy of vital grain ships from America. It was chased by the British Channel fleet under Lord Howe, who came up with it some 400 miles west of Ushant on 28 May. Ignoring the Fighting Instructions he divided his fleet, attacked the French from both sides and eventually succeeded in getting to windward of them so that he could force an action. Four days later the battle which came to be known as 'the Glorious First of June' was fought. Howe deliberately broke his line and inflicted heavy casualties on the enemy. Although the grain ships finally got into Brest, the Brest fleet itself was broken: six French ships were captured, one sunk and several more dismasted or crippled.

During the next two years, however, French victories on land were so dramatic that the British navy was thrown back on to the defensive. The United Provinces were finally conquered in the early months of 1795 and the British army which had been sent to defend them was driven back into Hanover, to be shipped back to England in March. The Netherlands became part of France and the United Provinces became the Batavian Republic, a satellite of the French Republic and a token of the new order which the Revolution intended to impose upon Europe. The King of Prussia, who had quarrelled with Britain in the autumn of 1794, made his peace with France in April 1795 and Spain followed suit three months later. General Bonaparte, one of the most brilliant of the young revolutionary officers, took command of the French army of Italy in March 1796 and a month later he imposed a humiliating armistice on the Duke of Savoy. By the autumn he had swept the Austrians out of north Italy and his success was made even more threatening, from the British point of view, by the entry of Spain into the war on the French side in October 1796. The Revolution was now in control of the three greatest navies in Europe—the French, the Dutch and the Spanish— and Britain's whole position as a Mediterranean power was in jeopardy. Reluctantly, Pitt ordered the Mediterranean fleet to abandon Corsica and retire to Gibraltar. Things looked so bad that he decided, much to the King's disgust, to sue for peace. Lord Malmesbury was sent to Paris to offer the restoration of all the colonial possessions which Britain had seized, in return for a French evacuation of the Netherlands. The offer was brusquely refused and Malmesbury returned to London at the end of December 1796. The war continued and by April 1797 Bonaparte had gained control of the whole of

Italy and forced Austria to sign an armistice. Britain's last continental ally had deserted her and she stood alone against the Revolution.

The peace negotiations of December 1796, short and abortive though they were, contained the clue to the whole nature and purpose of the war. To the extremists on both sides they meant nothing: George III and the conservatively minded gentlemen of England were determined to fight on until the Revolution was crushed, while for the fiery idealists in France the only good monarchist was a dead monarchist. But the bargain which Pitt offered, the exchange of colonial conquests for the Netherlands, summed up British foreign policy in the eighteenth century. Pitt, like his father, thought of Britain as a commercial and colonial power, a power concerned with the Atlantic rather than with Europe. But he also considered it vital for British security that no one power should ever control the opposite shore of the English Channel, from Brittany to the Frisian Islands. In order to prevent this happening, Britain must be prepared to demand a voice in the affairs of Europe and to use her seapower as a lever to obtain it. What made the French intractable, from his point of view, was not the fact that they were revolutionaries but the fact that their determination to secure 'the natural frontiers of France' made them tear up existing treaty agreements and advance their power to the Rhine. Pitt was ready to envisage coexistence with a revolutionary France, but not with a France which endangered Britain's safety by occupying the Netherlands and the mouths of the Rhine.

By 1797 the British navy was no longer concerned with supporting an invasion of France, as at the beginning of the war, but with preventing a French invasion of Britain. For the first time since the battle of Beachy Head in 1690 it was conceivable that enemy fleets might seize control of the English Channel. The Spanish fleet set sail from its Mediterranean base of Cartagena on 1 February 1797 with the intention of joining the French fleet at Brest, and on 14 February Admiral Jervis brought it to action off Cape St Vincent. He only had fifteen ships to the Spaniards' twenty-seven, and his ships were much smaller and less heavily armed; but he nevertheless won a magnificent victory. Ably assisted by two of his subordinate captains, Nelson and Collingwood, he broke up the enemy fleet and captured four of its ships. The remaining Spanish ships made for harbour and gave up any idea of joining the French.

But there were still the French and Dutch fleets to be reckoned with; and the British ships which should have been dealing with them were still in harbour at Spithead and the Nore, incapacitated by mutiny. The Duke of York had recently secured an increase in soldiers' pay from $8\frac{1}{4}d$ to $1s$ a day, but the pay of ordinary seamen remained at $19s$ a month, the figure at which it had been fixed in the reign of Charles II. It was not paid in cash but in the form of a ticket which had to be redeemed at the Pay Office on Tower Hill, where unscrupulous clerks cheated the sailors out of part of their money. Anonymous petitions to Lord Howe, although faithfully forwarded by him to the Admiralty, had had no effect; and on 15 April 1797, when the Spithead fleet was ordered to put to sea, the crews seized control of the ships and refused to sail until their grievances had been redressed. They complained of low rates of pay, poor food and lack of shore leave, but they did not mention the most brutal aspects of contemporary naval life, the activities of the press gang and of the cat-o'-nine-tails. The Admiralty sent down commissioners to negotiate with them and by the middle of May the mutiny was over. All the men's demands had been met and guaranteed by Act of Parliament, while a royal pardon was extended to all the mutineers. These concessions helped to encourage another and much uglier mutiny at the Nore, where the mutineers even went to the extent of blockading the Thames. This second mutiny was forcibly suppressed in July, and in October this same fleet sailed from the Nore to smash the Dutch invasion fleet off Kamperduin, at the entrance to the Zuider Zee. Nine of the sixteen Dutch ships were captured and the victory, anglicized as Camperdown, produced a new wave of confidence throughout Britain.

New confidence was certainly needed, for even Pitt had been reduced almost to despair by the events of the past few months. In the face of strong opposition from George III and from the Foreign Secretary[1] he sent Malmesbury to negotiate with the French again in July 1797, authorizing him to offer a recognition of French sovereignty over the Netherlands. Pitt the Patriot, the heir to his father's proud enmity towards France, was now ready to contemplate French control of the vital coastline between Dunkirk and the mouths of the Rhine. The French, however, broke off the negotiations and went ahead with their plans for the invasion of Britain. When

---

[1] Carmarthen had resigned in 1791 and had been replaced as Foreign Secretary by Lord Grenville, youngest son of George Grenville. He was much more vigorous than his predecessor and became identified with the war party within the ministry.

General Bonaparte returned to France at the end of the year, after his triumphs in Italy, he was put in charge of the invasion preparations. He spent several weeks on an intensive study of the whole project and then, at the end of February 1798, he submitted a report to the French revolutionary government in which he condemned the idea of an invasion as completely impracticable. Instead he suggested attacking British commerce and Britain's route to India by sending an expedition to Egypt. The politicians accepted his scheme and on 19 May he set sail from Toulon with a force of some 45,000 men.

Bonaparte's Egyptian campaign was to be an important turning-point, both in his own career and in the war between France and the powers of Europe. Until now the kings of Europe had thought that the Revolution's territorial ambitions were reasonably limited, even though its political complexion was highly distasteful. It had concerned itself with the Netherlands, with north Italy and with the Rhineland—all of them traditional French spheres of influence. It was Britain, not France, who threatened to ring Europe round with her commercial ambitions in the Mediterranean and the Baltic and with her colonial supremacy in America and Africa and Asia. But now, it seemed, the Revolution had moved beyond mere questions of 'natural frontiers' and saw itself as a world power. It was all very well for Bonaparte to talk about the conquest of Egypt as an indirect threat to Britain, but it was also an indirect threat to Austria and Russia. If Bonaparte took Egypt, an outlying province of the Turkish empire, he might well go on to take the Holy Land, Syria, even Turkey itself and Constantinople. Austria might find herself faced with French influence in the Balkans and Russia might be attacked on her southern flank and shut out of the Mediterranean. Even before he reached Egypt, Bonaparte had captured Malta, an island which belonged to the Knights of St John but which Russia regarded as being under her special protection. Within a few weeks of its fall Russia sent ships into the Mediterranean and made approaches to Britain with a view to entering the war against France. Britain's period of perilous isolation was at an end.

When he reached Egypt, early in July 1798, Bonaparte was at first brilliantly successful and the country was in his hands by the middle of August. In the spring of 1799 he advanced northwards through the Holy Land towards Syria, but he was halted at Acre, the defence of which was assisted by a British naval squadron under Sir Sidney Smith. After a desperate but unsuccessful attempt to take the town the French fell back into Egypt, where they remained until 1801. Bonaparte, however, left his army in August 1799 and sailed back to France in order to further his political ambitions. By the end of the year he had overthrown the existing government and made himself master of France, with the title of First Consul of the French Republic.

Though the military results of the Egyptian campaign were meagre, the diplomatic repercussions were far-reaching. The British navy had re-entered the Mediterranean in the spring of 1798 and before long the Austrians and Russians were further encouraged to take arms against the French when they heard the news of the Battle of the Nile, fought on 1 August. After a long and frustrating chase, Nelson's squadron had found Bonaparte's fleet anchored in Aboukir Bay at the mouth of the Nile. In spite of dangerous shoals Nelson sent some of his ships in between the enemy and the shore, so that the French found themselves attacked from both sides. Of their fleet of seventeen ships, thirteen were captured, burnt or sunk. Nelson then sailed to Italy, to give the King of Naples support against the French, while another British squadron took Minorca from the Spaniards. The Russians threw away their last doubts in December and accepted a subsidy of £825,000 from Britain, while in March 1799 Austria reopened the war. By November 1799 the Austrians and the Russians, helped by British naval support, had thrown the French out of Italy. But throwing them out of the United Provinces proved a more difficult business—too difficult for the joint Anglo-Russian expedition which landed in the north of the country, at the entrance to the Zuider Zee, in the autumn of 1799. Its commander, the Duke of York, had been assured by Pitt that 'the Dutch are so exceedingly discontented with the French that if a body of troops could be sent there it could be easy to seize upon Flushing'; but in fact he got no cooperation from the Dutch and very little from the Russians. He struggled forward as far as Alkmaar, less than thirty miles from his point of disembarkation, and there he made a convention with the French whereby he evacuated the United Provinces. The one positive result of the adventure was the seizure by Britain of the Dutch fleet.

In June 1800 Bonaparte's victory over the Austrians at Marengo transformed the whole European situation. The Austrian armies retreated from Italy and by December two powerful French forces were converging on Vienna from north Italy and from Bavaria. Faced with this dual threat the Emperor made peace with France at Luneville in February 1801. He recognized the satellite French republics in Italy, Switzerland, the Rhineland, the Netherlands and the United Provinces, and he also agreed to give France a free hand in reorganizing Germany. Meanwhile, Russia had tired of her British allies and had been offended by Britain's capture of Malta in September 1800. She went over to the French side, forming a second 'Armed Neutrality'[1] of the Baltic powers against British trade. The murder of the Czar of Russia, together with Nelson's destruction of the Danish fleet in Copenhagen harbour, had put an end to this Baltic league by the summer of 1801, but there was no disguising the fact that the French were supreme in Europe and that Britain could do little about it. Pitt had left office in March 1801 and his successors decided to come to terms with France, using British overseas conquests as levers to get what guarantees they could for the balance of power in Europe.

Conquests overseas had been considerable. Apart from the French recapture of Guadeloupe, early successes in the Caribbean had been maintained, though at the cost of heavy losses from disease. The entry of the Dutch into the war against us had resulted in the capture of their possessions in the Cape of Good Hope, Ceylon and the East Indies. In India itself Tipu Sahib, a prince of Mysore who had received encouragement but little else from the French, had been defeated and killed in 1799; and by 1801 the last shadow of French influence in India had gone. When they first opened negotiations with the French in 1801, the new ministers proposed that Britain should retain most of her conquests, but when the French threatened to resume the war they gave in. By the Treaty of Amiens, signed in March 1802, Britain gave back everything except Ceylon and Trinidad and recognized the French Republic. In return the French agreed to evacuate southern and central Italy. It was the old game, guarantees in Europe in return for restorations overseas. But Britain was soon to find that the French had invented new rules.

2 Fears of a British Revolution

In 1788 and 1789, when the French first embarked upon the experiment which was to end in revolution, the English were celebrating the centenary of their own Revolution. The Dissenters in particular had always looked back to William III as their deliverer and had

---

[1] The first had been formed during the War of American Independence. See above, p. 312.

regularly observed the anniversary of his landing at Torbay. They had also been diligent in pointing out that the Revolution was still not completed and that the toleration for all Protestants, which William III had desired, had still not been achieved. As the hundredth anniversary of his landing approached they suggested that the best way to celebrate it and to pay tribute to his memory would be to repeal the Test and Corporation Acts and thus remove the remaining disabilities imposed upon Dissenters. A motion to that effect was introduced into the Commons on 28 March 1787, but it was defeated by 178 votes to 100. The next day the King wrote to Pitt expressing his satisfaction and saying that if such a proposal was ever raised again 'my coronation oath as well as my conviction of the temper ever shown by the Church of England will oblige me in the most public manner to shew it my discountenance'. A more moderate motion, which merely proposed to set up a committee to 'take into consideration' the Test and Corporation Acts, was rejected by 122 votes to 102 on 8 May 1789, just as the first accounts of the great events in France were coming through. Thus the Dissenters were still second-class citizens, barred from full participation in public life, when they first read the revolutionary 'Declaration of the Rights of Man and of the Citizen' which the French National Assembly proclaimed in August 1789 as the basis of their new constitution. While in Britain the natural rights of human beings were sacrificed to traditional respect for the constitution, the French were preparing to build a constitution which would secure justice and liberty for all men.

In these circumstances it was hardly surprising that the Dissenters moved from veneration of past events in Britain to admiration of present events in France. The Society for Commemorating the Revolution in Great Britain, a body formed by dissenting congregations in London, became in fact a society for the encouragement of the revolution in France. It entered into enthusiastic correspondence with the popular party in France and in November 1789 Richard Price, author of *Observations on the Nature of Civil Liberty* and friend of both Shelburne and Pitt, preached before it a sermon in which he compared the British and French revolutions. In 1689, he said, the British had established the right 'to choose our own governors; to cashier them for misconduct; and to frame a government for ourselves'; now the French were claiming the same right. The result would be the defeat of tyranny and despotism all over the world. 'Tremble all ye oppressors of the world!' he cried. 'You cannot now hold the world in darkness. Struggle no longer against increasing light and liberality. Restore to mankind their rights; and consent to the correction of abuses, before they and you are destroyed together.'

Price's sermon turned the French Revolution from an exciting foreign spectacle into a burning domestic issue. This was partly because there was a general election in the offing and the Dissenters were again campaigning for the repeal of the Test and Corporation Acts. Anglican country gentlemen raised the old cry of 'the Church in Danger!', which had not been heard since the days of Queen Anne, and they pored with satisfaction over satirical prints showing Price as the prophet of anarchy and disorder and the enemy of 'all rank and Subordination in civil Society'. When the motion for repeal was brought forward yet again in March 1790, this time by Fox himself, the Country Party turned up in force to vote against it and it was turned down by 294 votes to 105. Although Fox in his opening speech declared that French politics had nothing to do with the question, it was clear that events in France were at the back of everyone's mind. They were very much to the fore in Burke's mind: a few months earlier he had written to Fox saying that the Whigs must conciliate the Dissenters and the Bowood radicals in view of the impending election, but now he was in full cry against anyone who dared to approve of the French Revolution. He had already told Philip Francis that he meant to oppose 'Dr Price, or Lord Shelburne, or any other of their set' and to 'set in full view the danger from their wicked principles and their black hearts'. He spoke vehemently against Fox's motion and in November 1790 he published his *Reflections on the Revolution in France and on the Proceedings of Certain Societies in London relative to that Event*. It was to become one of the most important books of its time, influencing the political thinking of a whole generation.

Its real greatness lay in its masterly exposition of Burke's political philosophy, of his belief in the living and growing nature of human society,[1] but its immediate impact derived from its comparison of the revolutionaries in France and the radicals in Britain. Burke expressed at great length his horror and disgust at what had happened in France, but he also criticized and ridiculed 'the proceedings of certain societies in London'. He declared roundly that the

[1] See above, p. 367

417

Revolution of 1688 was not at all what Price thought it was, that it had not established government by consent and that Price's idea of abstract liberty and natural rights was the contradiction, not the fulfilment, of the principles of 1688. The notion that men could decide for themselves what were their rights, and then tear down any government that did not respect them, was the 'reverse of true Whiggery. The Whigs had stood, and must stand, for the balance of the existing constitution and not for the empty promises of an imaginary one. Discontent with the existing order and the Utopian search for a better one was already producing anarchy and violence in France and might yet give rise to these things in Britain as well.

Men of substance and property all over the country were delighted with the book. Those who remembered the Burke of twenty years ago, the fiery young Whig who had insisted that 'the interposition of the body of the people itself' was the ultimate remedy for bad government, were glad to find that he had matured and become more sensible. Even George III found it in him to praise the Whig leader whom he had disliked for so long: the *Reflections* was, he admitted, 'a good book, a very good book; every gentlemen ought to read it'. Most gentlemen did read it and found it good. Both King and Country were won over by the man whom they had once regarded as an unscrupulous adventurer, an agitator ready to stir up colonists and merchants alike in the interests of the party magnates who employed him.

To Fox, Burke's conservative attitude seemed not only misguided but politically dangerous. It was clear that the King and Pitt between them had complete control of the existing system: patronage and influence, once the weapons of the Whigs, had now been turned against them. The Whigs would never get back to power within the framework of the present system: their only hope lay in appealing to the forces of change, to the future and not to the past. If patronage politics worked against them, then patronage politics must be done away with. The Whig party must stand for reform. If they did not, they would soon stand for nothing. They must seize on the new forces, the forces of radicalism and perhaps even of industrialism, before those forces were swallowed up, like everything else, in the frightening efficiency of William Pitt and the rejuvenated central government he was creating. Fox opposed Burke's views vigorously and by the spring of 1791 the rank and file of the Whig party were becoming very alarmed by the split between their two leaders. Just before the Easter recess, when it seemed that they were about to argue out their ideas about the French Revolution on the floor of the House of Commons, a Whig backbencher tried to stop them by threatening to call to order anyone who discussed general principles of government or the constitutions of other countries. But when the House reassembled on 6 May 1791 Burke immediately launched into a tirade against the French Revolution, on the grounds that the House was discussing what sort of government to give to Canada[1] and should therefore know what to avoid. Fox defended the Revolution and after a highly emotional scene the two men parted for ever. It was two years and a day since the opening session of the Estates General. An event in a foreign country had done in two years what events in Britain had failed to do in two generations: it had split the Whig party from top to bottom.

As soon as the parliamentary session was over Burke hurried off to Margate, where he settled down to compose a justification of his conduct. It was called *An Appeal from the New to the Old Whigs* and it argued that all true Whigs must renounce the dangerous tenets of demagogues like Fox and defend the British constitution, the balanced and conservative constitution of 1689, in its hour of peril. In June 1792, while the people of Paris were forming a revolutionary army and moving towards an open breach with King Louis XVI, the Whig leaders were preparing to rally round King George III. Thurlow, the Lord Chancellor who had been for so long one of the key men in the Court Party, quarrelled with Pitt in the spring and was dismissed by the King on 15 June. Portland could not believe that Pitt would survive this crisis and he called together Burke, Fox and the other Whig magnates in order to discuss the terms on which they should form a ministry. They conferred together excitedly for most of the summer recess, Fox holding out for a coalition with Pitt on equal terms and Burke insisting that they must rush to the King's aid at all costs and on any terms. 'It should be declared by the Duke of Portland, etc.,' he said, 'as the heads of the great Whig Party, that all systematic opposition was at an end.' All men of good will must stand together to form a national government.

The discussions were curiously unreal, because Pitt stood in no need of support from the Whigs. After more than eight years in office he was no longer the manager of a ministry but the head of a government. He refused to negotiate with Portland for the formation

[1] See above, p. 407, n. 1.

of a new ministry and in the end the Old Whigs made what terms they could with him, joining his ministry one by one. By July 1794, when Portland himself became Home Secretary, the Old Whigs had become merged with the party of Pitt. As yet that party had no official name: it was a compound of the Court Party, the King's Friends and the Patriots. It was to be in the end the basis of the Tory Party of the nineteenth century, and the junction with the Old Whigs, the most conservative force in politics, made sure that its Toryism would be more conservative than radical. Burke, now the oracle of conservatism and respected throughout the courts of Europe as a prophet justified, lived on for three more years. In July 1797, when Fox heard that Burke was mortally ill with cancer of the stomach, he tried to visit him; but Burke still refused to see the man whose democratic principles he regarded with such loathing. He died on 9 July 1797. 'There is but one event,' wrote George Canning, the man who was to be the bridge between Pitt and nineteenth century Toryism, 'but that is an event for the world: Burke is dead.'

Fox, with the small band of New Whigs who still remained faithful to him, did his best to prevent the reaction against the French Revolution from turning into an attack on British liberties. In 1791 he had introduced, with Pitt's approval, a Bill to enable juries in libel cases to decide not merely whether the accused had published the passage in question but whether it was or was not a libel. After some delay the measure became law in 1792, in time to be of some help to the large number of radical writers who were now to find themselves haled before the courts for seditious libel. The first of them, and the greatest, was Tom Paine, whose *Rights of Man* appeared in two parts in 1791 and 1792 as an answer to Burke's *Reflections* and a vindication of the French Revolution. It had a tremendous circulation, running through eight editions in a year and being translated into Gaelic, Erse and Welsh. It proclaimed that all hereditary government was tyrannous and that the only legitimate government was one which dedicated itself to abolishing poverty and ignorance and distress. The King, who remembered the part Paine had played in the American Revolution,[1] was determined that he should not be allowed to promote a revolution in Britain. A Proclamation was issued against seditious writings and proceedings against Paine were started. In order to escape certain conviction he fled to Paris, where he became a member of the Convention. But many of those

[1] See above, p. 309.

who stayed in Britain suffered for what they wrote or what they said: a Scottish lawyer called Thomas Muir was sentenced to fourteen years' transportation for recommending people to read the *Rights of Man*.[1] The Attorney-General later boasted that there had been more prosecutions in 1793 and 1794 than in the previous twenty years.

The government's fears of revolution were not entirely groundless: there was a severe depression in 1793 and by May of that year thousands of workpeople were destitute and unemployed in Manchester. In Scotland it was reported that the manufacturers had 'discharged great numbers of their workmen' and all over the country workmen in the new industrial towns formed themselves into societies to press for reform. The London Corresponding Society, a working-class body founded by a shoemaker called Thomas Hardy, was soon in correspondence with agitators in Manchester and Sheffield, as well as with the Convention in Paris. Previously, artisans in the towns had been hostile to the radicals and to the French Revolution: in July 1791 a Birmingham mob shouting for 'Church and King' had destroyed the houses of Priestley and other Dissenters because they had had the temerity to celebrate the second anniversary of the fall of the Bastille. But now the mood was different. In Edinburgh a Scottish National Convention, representing eighty different local societies, sent congratulatory addresses to the Convention in Paris, while in England the radicals in Sheffield were able to get no less than 8,000 signatures for a petition for parliamentary reform. Even innocent discussion groups, such as the one which met at the Black Boy Inn at Newcastle, became transformed into radical political groups. In May 1794, after a few arms and some radical papers had been seized in Edinburgh, Hardy and other prominent members of the radical societies were arrested. A secret committee of the Commons reported that an armed insurrection was being planned. The Habeas Corpus Act was suspended[2] and Hardy and the other prisoners were put on trial not for sedition but for treason. They were all acquitted.

The worst of the depression was over by 1795 and there was less unemployment, but discontent continued owing to the very high price of bread and other foodstuffs. 'Wherefore, in the midst of

[1] The sentences imposed in Scotland were much more ferocious than those in England and many anecdotes were told about the savagery of Lord Braxfield, one of the Scottish judges. But his severity may have been the product of ignorance rather than cruelty: he later admitted that he had no idea what transportation involved.

[2] It remained suspended until 1801.

apparent plenty, are we thus compelled to starve?' demanded the speakers at an angry demonstration in London, 'Why, when we incessantly toil and labour, must we pine in misery and want? Parliamentary Corruption . . . like a foaming whirlwind, swallows the fruit of all our labours.' At the state opening of Parliament in October 1795 the King's coach was attacked, with cries of 'No war, no Pitt, no King!' Pitt hurried through Parliament the Treasonable Practices Bill and the Seditious Meetings Bill. The first extended treason to cover the speaking or writing of anything calculated to bring the King or the government into contempt, while the second gave justices of the peace extensive control over public meetings. Fox fought both measures tooth and nail, telling the House bitterly: 'Say at once that a free constitution is no longer suitable to us, but do not mock the understandings and the feelings of mankind by telling the world that you are free.' He was no longer playing politics: his parliamentary position was now hopeless unless he gave up his democratic ideas and joined in the general enthusiasm for 'Church and King'. But he would not. A few months later he wrote to his nephew, almost in despair, saying that the radical elements in the country 'being wholly unmixed with any aristocratic leaven, and full of resentment against us for not joining them, will go probably to greater excesses'. He sought to be a 'man of the people', to build a bridge between the old forces and the new forces, because he wanted to preserve the balance of the constitution and not, as Burke thought, because he aimed to destroy it. He was convinced that if all the men of property ranged themselves on one side and all the poor and the discontented gathered on the other there could only be two possible results: despotism or revolution. But he was a voice crying in the wilderness and in 1797, after a Reform Bill brought in by his chief supporter Charles Grey had been overwhelmingly defeated, he determined to cry no longer. He and the majority of his followers gave up attending Parliament.

For the next four years, while the New Whigs maintained a despairing silence and the Old Whigs gave him their open support, Pitt worked to give the King and the Country Party what they wanted: strong and efficient government. Gone were the days when the country gentlemen had distrusted every extension of the executive's power. When Pitt weathered another credit crisis in 1797, even worse than the one of 1793, by suspending cash payments from the Bank of England, they gave their grudging consent. In December 1798, when he introduced an income tax of 2s in the £ on all incomes over £200 a year, they grumbled but they paid. In 1799 they were able to applaud further measures for restricting the activities of revolutionary societies and radical journalists. Above all they welcomed the Combination Act, passed in 1799 to prohibit workmen forming combinations in order to press for higher wages or better conditions. In 1800 this Act was amended in order to prevent workmen being sentenced by justices of the peace who were themselves masters in the trade concerned; but the amendment did little to mitigate the severity of the Act, which effectively held back the development of the trade union movement for a generation. Although the Act mainly benefited the new industrialists, the landowners also regarded it as a useful weapon to hold in reserve: agricultural wages had risen steeply since 1793 and the gentlemen of Britain were determined that they should rise no further. In defence of property and good order, high dividends and cheap labour, they were prepared to make common cause with the owners of factories and mills. The rich men of Britain, as well as those furnished with abilities which they hoped would make them rich, intended to go on living peaceably in their habitations. Only Fox and a few others wondered and worried about what would happen to the poor, cut off and 'wholly unmixed with any aristocratic leaven'.

3 Consequences of an Irish Rebellion

Most people in England had hoped that the legislative independence granted to Ireland in 1782 would solve the Irish problem. While Fox declared grandly that he 'would rather see Ireland totally separated from the crown of England than kept in obedience by mere force', less liberal men talked of Ireland as a ship on fire, which must be cut loose before it set the rest of Britain ablaze. As in the case of the American colonists, so in the case of the Irish: those who admired them wanted to free them, while those who did not wanted to be rid of them.

But the Irish question could not be answered thus easily. The Irish Sea was a lot narrower than the Atlantic, and neither the grandiose gestures of the Rockinghams nor the petulant indifference of the Country Party could make it any wider. Earlier in the century Englishmen had feared that Ireland might become a weapon in the hands of the French, a dagger held at the back of Britain by her continental enemies; and this fear still existed. The country which had supported the colonists against us might still support the Irish against us, and with even more serious results. Before Ireland could be cut loose it was essential to make sure that she could stand on her own feet and that her troubles would not lead her into seeking foreign support.

For the first few years of Pitt's ministry it seemed that the troubles of Ireland were indeed on the way to being solved. The country became more prosperous than ever before and her exports of linen, cattle and corn rose steadily. Her exports to the rest of Britain, which were worth £1,612,000 in 1783, had risen to £3,114,000 by 1797. Landlords found it easier to get their rents and labourers found it easier to get work. Pitt saw in this increased prosperity the best hope of an answer to the Irish question. In February 1785 he proposed to the Irish Parliament that there should be free trade between Ireland and the rest of Britain and that Ireland should be allowed to participate fully in colonial trade in return for a small contribution to Britain's naval expenditure. In Dublin both Houses of Parliament accepted the scheme, but in Westminster there was violent opposition. Fox attacked the proposals as being harmful to manufacturers in England and Scotland, who would be undercut by the cheap labour costs of Irish industry; and later, when Pitt revised the plan so as to give guarantees to English merchants and industrialists, Fox attacked it again as an attempt to 'barter English commerce for Irish slavery'. Nevertheless Pitt carried his revised scheme in the British House of Commons; and in the Irish House of Commons, in spite of violent opposition, it was passed by 127 to 108. But the majority was too small for safety and the feeling in Ireland against the new proposals, which limited Ireland's share of the colonial trade and also gave the British Parliament effective control over Irish commerce, was so strong that Pitt decided to drop them. His attempt to provide an economic solution to the Irish question had failed.

A few years later the political aspect of the question showed itself in a particularly uncompromising form. In February 1789, while Pitt was carrying through the British Parliament his scheme for a limited regency, the Irish Parliament passed by a large majority an Address to the Prince asking him to 'assume the government of this nation during his Majesty's indisposition, under the style of Prince Regent of Ireland, and to exercise the prerogative of the Crown'. After the Lord-Lieutenant had refused to have anything to do with the Address it was taken by a deputation to London, where the Prince agreed to receive it. Fortunately the King was already on the way to recovery; but if his illness had continued the action of the Irish Parliament would have raised very thorny constitutional questions. The motives of Grattan and Flood, the main opposition leaders in the House of Commons in Dublin, were entirely political: they believed, rightly or wrongly, that the accession to power of the Prince and his Whig friends would mean the end of the 'Dublin Castle interest', the group who formed in the Irish Parliament the equivalent of the Court Party at Westminster and monopolized all patronage. But in their desire to solve the political problem of patronage, they had revealed a constitutional problem of the first order. If the Irish legislative was fully independent, what was to stop it offering the crown of Ireland to a Pretender as easily as to a Prince? Why should it not do for itself what the British Parliament had done in 1689? And, now that Revolution of a more radical nature was in the air, who could be sure that an Irish Revolution in the 1790s would be as moderate as the British Revolution of the 1680s?

Considerations of this sort made Pitt more and more convinced that the solution to the Irish problem lay not in a cutting operation but in a binding one. The Irish must first be united among themselves and then they must be united with the rest of Britain on terms acceptable to both sides. Already there were signs which suggested that such a solution might be possible. The Volunteers, at their famous meeting at Dungannon in 1782, had resolved that 'as Men and as Irishmen, as Christians and as Protestants, we rejoice in the relaxation of the Penal Laws against our Roman Catholic fellow-subjects'; and the United Irishmen, a society founded in Belfast in October 1791 by Wolfe Tone, Napper Tandy and other Episcopalians, sought to break down still further the barriers between Catholics and Protestants. The United Irishmen became increasingly anti-English and revolutionary in their aims, but at least by clarifying the discontent they clarified also the lines along which it might be remedied. The government in London must take the initiative in uniting the Irish before the Irish themselves united against London.

Pitt took the first step in 1793, when he prodded the reluctant Protestant magnates of Dublin Castle to give their grudging support to a Catholic Relief Act. This allowed Catholics to carry arms, sit on juries, vote in parliamentary elections and hold minor civil and military offices. It did not, however, permit them to sit in Parliament.

Later in 1793 a Pensions Act and a Place Act were passed by the Irish Parliament, as further indications that the supremacy of Dublin Castle and its ability to pack Parliament were under attack from London. In December 1794, after Pitt's junction with the Portland Whigs, Lord Fitzwilliam was appointed as Lord-Lieutenant of Ireland. He was a man of twenty-six, nephew to Rockingham and an ardent young Whig. Even before he arrived in Ireland he wrote to Grattan and told him that he intended to declare open war on Dublin Castle and the Protestant ascendancy. When he arrived in Dublin he plunged straight into the fight, dismissing ministers and promising full and immediate Catholic emancipation. He aroused the violent hostility of the Protestant magnates, as well as the religious prejudice of George III, and even Pitt and Portland were horrified by the storm he had created. He was recalled and left Dublin on 25 March 1795, having stirred up more hatred between Catholics and Protestants in two months than the most bigoted reactionaries had produced in two generations.

Fitzwilliam's recall convinced the extremists in Ireland that reform was impossible and revolution indispensable. Wolfe Tone went off to America and later to France, where he conferred with the revolutionary government. In December 1796 he returned to Ireland aboard a French fleet of seventeen ships of the line and thirteen frigates, with 15,000 French troops and a quantity of arms and ammunition for distribution to the Irish revolutionaries. Only a violent storm, which dispersed the French fleet at the entrance to Bantry Bay, prevented a landing which would have faced the Irish authorities with a very serious problem indeed. Conscious that the mutinies at Spithead and the Nore had left them without proper naval protection, they took drastic steps, especially in Ulster, to prevent an uprising. The local militia was called up and thousands of muskets and pikes were seized from potential rebels, who were abominably ill-treated. The United Irishmen decided that they must act before it was too late, even though their plans were not completed and the second French expedition which they had been promised could not possibly arrive in time to help them. In May 1798 there were up-risings at various points throughout Ireland, but only in County Wexford, in the extreme south-east, were they at all formidable. Even here, the rebellion was over by the end of June, when the rebel camp at Vinegar Hill was stormed and captured by government troops. A small French force landed in August at Killala in

County Mayo—two months too late and nearly two hundred miles too far away. Its commander, General Humbert, had less than 1,000 men; but he carried out a short but dashing campaign before surrendering on 9 September.

The new Lord-Lieutenant who received Humbert's surrender was Lord Cornwallis, who had been Warren Hastings's successor as Governor-General of India. He had already learnt in India that government was more than grandiose liberal gestures and he agreed with Pitt in seeing Ireland's problems in terms of the techniques of government, the patient reconciliation of conflicting interests, rather than as an exercise in rhetoric. He saw that peace in Ireland depended on the conciliation of the Catholics, but he also saw that the Protestant magnates at Dublin Castle would never be persuaded to accept Catholic domination of the Irish Parliament. Catholic emancipation was only possible if a Union with the rest of Britain was negotiated, so that the Catholic element among the Irish members at Westminster was diluted by the Protestant majority among the members for England and Scotland. On the other hand, a Union with the rest of Britain would only be accepted by the Catholics in Ireland if they were promised emancipation as a result of it. Neither emancipation without Union, nor Union without emancipation, made any sense. The two things stood or fell together as one single integrated solution to the Irish question.

Throughout 1799 Pitt and Cornwallis, helped by Viscount Castlereagh, the Chief Secretary for Ireland, worked to implement this double policy. None of them accepted Fox's radical notion that the right to govern was not a form of property, and therefore they recognized that the patronage-mongers at Dublin Castle would have to be bought out: they would require compensation for the political influence they were relinquishing, just as twentieth-century shareholders were later to expect compensation for stock that was taken over by the government. It was an expensive business—eighty-four borough seats had to be bought at the current market price of £15,000 apiece, making a total of £1,260,000, and on top of this there was compensation for lost sinecures—but it was eventually managed and the Irish Parliament voted for the Union in the spring of 1800. It was approved by the British Parliament later in the year and in January 1801 a hundred Irish members joined the House of Commons in Westminster, while twenty-eight Irish peers and four Irish bishops came to sit in the Lords. A new flag and a new seal were designed for the United Kingdom of Great Britain and Ireland, which came into being on 1 January 1801.

While the heralds were designing new flags, Pitt was trying to get the Cabinet to agree to Catholic emancipation. He failed. Several of its members opposed his scheme and at least one—Lord Loughborough, Thurlow's successor as Lord Chancellor—helped to turn the King against it. George did not need much turning. In 1793 he had consented to partial concessions to the Irish Catholics, but the thought of giving every Catholic throughout his dominions the right to sit in Parliament and to hold high office in the State was too much for him. He resented, also, the way in which the thing had been done: he did not expect his principal minister to cabal behind his back in order to get Cabinet support for a measure which was known to be unacceptable to him. He said angrily that anybody who supported emancipation would be reckoned as his 'personal enemy'—a phrase which was dangerously reminiscent of the language he had used when breaking the Fox–North ministry in December 1783. Pitt must remember that he was still, first and foremost, a King's Friend: no amount of efficient government and Cabinet support would enable him to force upon his sovereign measures which neither King nor Country would accept.

Pitt did his best to change the King's mind, but it soon became apparent that if he persisted George's sanity would give way again, with disastrous results for Britain, for the war, for Ireland—and, of course, for Pitt himself as well. On the other hand, he had committed himself too deeply to Catholic emancipation to stay in office if it was not to be passed. By the beginning of February 1801 he had decided that he must resign, but before he could do so the King succumbed to another fit of insanity. Pitt prepared to pass again the Regency Bill of 1789, but fortunately George recovered early in March. Appalled by what he had done, Pitt gave a formal assurance that he would never again trouble the King on the question of Catholic emancipation. He also pledged himself not to oppose the King's new ministers. Then, on 14 March 1801, he resigned his offices.

16

The Workshop of the World
1801–1815

1 From Toryism to Conservatism

When George III first became involved in his argument with Pitt over Catholic emancipation, he turned to the Speaker of the House of Commons, Henry Addington, for help. Addington was not a brilliant man but he had, like Robert Harley a century earlier, an instinctive understanding of the independent country gentlemen. He knew that they were deeply suspicious of 'clever' politicians and particularly of those politicians whose clever ideas were at all advanced or radical. Their fears of revolution had overcome to some extent their distrust of strong executive government, but they still expected that government to be sensible and not sensational. Like the King himself, they could not stomach the idea of enfranchising papists. Pitt's arguments about the need for an integrated and contented Ireland they regarded as a lot of over-sophisticated intellectual nonsense. All they knew was that they were fighting for the British constitution and that an essential part of that constitution was the supremacy of the Established Church. They would not believe that it was necessary to destroy the constitution in order to defend it. And, in any case, Bonaparte's rule in France since he had seized power in November 1799 seemed to suggest that the worst excesses of the French Revolution were over. He was a braggart and an upstart and they distrusted him, but at least he had shown that he could govern. They still had many of the insular prejudices of their grandfathers and the war, as far as they were concerned, was a war against revolution and not a war for the balance of power in Europe. Let Europe take care of itself: they had paid high taxes for nearly eight years in order to halt the spread of anarchy and insubordination and now, when these things seemed to have been checked, it was time to relax. What they wanted now was a minister who would make a reasonably satisfactory peace, bring down the level of taxation, and then govern quietly and unambitiously. They had had enough of 'those confounded men of genius'.

Thus Speaker Addington, like Speaker Harley a hundred years before him, was the symbol of an alliance between King and Country against the professional politicians. But whereas in 1701 the alliance had been directed against the greed and factiousness of the party magnates, their apparently incurable addiction to patronage politics, in 1801 it was aimed against the men of programmes and the men of business. Those who went out—Pitt himself, Grenville, Castlereagh and several others—had all made themselves suspect at one time or another by supporting radical ideas: Catholic emancipation, the abolition of the slave trade, even the reform of Parliament. With them went men like George Rose, Pitt's Secretary of the Treasury who had played an essential part in the reform of administration and the paring down of sinecures. Addington himself, the man who had never been known to support any kind of change, became First Lord of the Treasury and Chancellor of the Exchequer. Portland, the living embodiment of Old Whiggery, stayed on as Home Secretary. There was a sharp contrast not only with 1701 but even with 1783: then the King had reacted against the East India Bill in order to get rid of Fox, but now he parted reluctantly with Pitt in order to prevent Catholic emancipation. He was objecting not to men but to measures. This was a defeat not for the politics of patronage but for the politics of programmes.

The men who came in with Addington were not an impressive collection. His brother, his cousin and two brothers-in-law were given minor offices and after a few months Hardwicke's grandson and Newcastle's second cousin were brought in to give the administration an air of Old Whig respectability. But for the most part it was made up of men who could almost be described as hereditary King's Friends. Lord Hawkesbury, the Foreign Secretary, was the son of that Charles Jenkinson who had been recognized in the 1760s as Bute's successor as leader of the King's Friends. Charles Jenkinson himself, now Lord Liverpool, was Chancellor of the Duchy of Lancaster and President of the Board of Trade. The second Earl of Chatham, who had avoided his younger brother's interest in radical measures, was made Lord President of the Council and Spencer Perceval, second son of that Earl of Egmont who had dominated Leicester House in the 1740s, was Solicitor-General and the ministry's ablest spokesman in the House of Commons. Even

Addington himself came of a family which had rendered important service to the Crown: his father, Dr Anthony Addington, had been the man who had rescued the King from the Whig physicians in 1788 and put him in the care of Dr Willis. The sons of the men who had once saved George III from the Old Whigs now came forward, in alliance with the Old Whigs themselves, to save him from the New Whigs and the New Tories, from all those who threatened him and his kingdom with radical change.

Addington's first two years in office were quite successful. He was attacked by Grenville for his peace policy, by Fox for his conservatism and by the young men like Canning, talented followers of Pitt, for his sheer mediocrity; but none of them had any chance of success as long as Pitt himself kept his promise not to oppose him. By the end of June 1802, when the King dissolved Parliament, the new ministry had made itself accepted throughout the country. Nobody could pretend that the Peace of Amiens was a great diplomatic triumph, and Sheridan's famous description of it, as a peace which all men were glad of but no man could be proud of, summed up neatly the reservations which most people felt about it. But at least it brought down taxation and boosted trade. Before the dissolution Addington announced the repeal of Pitt's income tax, together with proposals for drastic reduction of government expenditure and for the eventual repayment of the National Debt; and the election of July 1802 strengthened his hold on the House of Commons. But by the spring of 1803 not only the professional politicians but the King and the Country as well were beginning to have their doubts about Addington. There was no doubt that he was an efficient administrator and that he had done much to further Pitt's work of financial and departmental reform, but he did not seem to be the man to face up to the increasingly aggressive policy of the French. In May 1803, when she took his courage in both hand and declared war on France, most people applauded his action, but few people thought that he was really capable of waging total war against the extensive power of France and the military genius of Napoleon Bonaparte. In the previous year Canning, whose hatred of Addington's 'conspiracy against all talents of all sides and sorts' had reached an almost hysterical level, had arranged a public tribute to Pitt in the City of London as 'the pilot that weathered the storm'. Now, when the storm was raging again, all eyes were turned, as Canning had intended they should be, not to Addington but to Pitt.

Pitt's position was difficult. He had been dismayed by the new ministry's drastic naval reductions and he could not believe that Addington was the best man to wage the war. On the other hand, he was still pledged not to oppose him and he certainly would not force himself upon the King, as some of his more impetuous followers urged. When Addington suggested some kind of 'broad-bottomed administration', the sort of coalition of equals which had been common in the previous century, Pitt replied that his experience of government had taught him 'that there should be an avowed and real minister possessing the chief weight in council and the principal place in the confidence of the King . . . and that minister ought to be the person at the head of the finances'. The new and positive kind of government, which Pitt had created and Addington, for all his faults, had carried on, required a prime minister, not a federation of easy-going politicians. And if Pitt could not be that prime minister he did not propose to be a minister at all.

His former colleagues were entirely in sympathy with his desire to be the undisputed head of a new ministry, but they were not in sympathy with his scruples about distressing the King. They became increasingly impatient with his non-committal attitude in the Commons and by the beginning of 1804 many of them had deserted him. Some, like Castlereagh, had come to terms with Addington, while others, like Grenville, had thrown their lot in with the New Whigs and Fox. From February to April another bout of insanity prevented the King from taking any part in politics and so stopped the crisis from coming to a head. But once the King had recovered Pitt could not put off his decision any longer: he would either have to acquiesce in the Addingtonian system of second rate government in the interests of the King's peace of mind, or he would have to unite with the men of real ability to build a strong and efficient government. He decided to do the latter. By the end of April he was voting with Fox and with William Windham, Grenville's supporter in the Commons, against the ministry; and early in May he sent a message to the King via the Lord Chancellor saying that the critical situation of Britain and of all Europe made Addington's resignation imperative. There must be a ministry, he said, based upon 'as large a proportion as possible of the weight of talents and connections, drawn without exception from parties of all descriptions'. He promised that the King would not be 'disquieted' by any revival of the proposal for Catholic emancipation, but he could no longer promise not to oppose Addington. George III rebuked Pitt for his distrust of Addington, who had, he reminded him, rallied to the support of the Crown 'when the most ill-digested and dangerous proposition was brought forward by the enemies of the Established Church'. He gave his grudging consent to the idea of a widely based ministry, but absolutely forbade Pitt to include Fox in it. If Pitt's proposed ministry should fail, he added, he would 'call for the assistance of such men as are truly attached to our happy Constitution, and not seekers of improvements'.

This letter from George III to Pitt, dated 5 May 1804, is one of the most important documents in the history of the Tory party. At a moment of extreme crisis, when the country was in imminent danger of invasion, British politics still centred around the personal prejudices of the monarch rather than the real interests of the nation. Pitt had held office for more than eighteen years and had transformed the whole nature of the King's government. Moreover, he was proposing a government of national unity in which party differences would be transcended and individual talents pooled for the sake of the country. Addington, on the other hand, had held office for three years and stood for nothing except a mood of war-weariness which had been very real in 1801 but meant nothing in 1804. Yet to the King Addington was 'a gentleman who has the greatest claim to approbation from his King and country', while Pitt was gravely suspect as a man who associated himself with 'seekers of improvements'. The men who had gathered around the Patriot King and his Patriot Minister in 1766 had certainly been 'seekers of improvements', and some of the improvements they had sought— the reduction of corruption, the emphasis on measures rather than on men, the search for good government rather than safe sinecures— were beginning to be achieved. The Patriots, the King's Friends, the men of business and the King's Servants, under the leadership of the two Pitts, had produced something which looked like developing into a positive and progressive alternative to Whiggery. It was not as yet a properly formed party and men still hesitated to talk about 'New Tories'; but it was at any rate a tradition of government. Now all this would have to be thrown away: the King insisted that his Friends, the men who had devoted themselves to saving him and the country from the Whigs, should look backwards and not forwards. If they refused to do this, then they were not his Friends any longer.

For a man who had been brought up as Pitt had been brought up, to fear and detest the irresponsibility of Whig 'faction', it was quite unthinkable to join with Fox and Grenville in coercing the King. All his instincts revolted against such a course, which would in any case be exceedingly unpopular in the country. Not only the conservative country gentlemen but even the radically minded new classes, even some of the turbulent artisans who shouted for 'Fox and Liberty', had a deep affection for George III. He might be obstinate and dull and simple-minded and hopelessly out of date, but he was at least honest and godly. The politicians who surrounded him, on the other hand, were regarded by many people as extremely dishonest and ungodly. His convictions about Catholic emancipation and the implications of his coronation oath might be deplorable, but they were his convictions and they could not be changed. To blame a harassed old man for holding fast to that which he thought was good was uncharitable and unrealistic. The only thing that could possibly be blamed was the institution of hereditary monarchy, which had made such a situation possible; and in Pitt's eyes the monarchy as an institution was even more sacrosanct than the monarch as an individual. After his death, his monument in Guildhall was to proclaim: 'In an age when the contagion of ideals threatened to dissolve the forms of civil society, he rallied the loyal, the sober-minded and the good around the venerable structure of the English monarchy.' In 1804 the venerable structure of the English monarchy needed to be defended, he thought, against the ambitions of Fox as well as against the ambitions of Napoleon Bonaparte. He therefore obeyed the King's commands, turned his back for ever on the New Toryism he might have created and constructed the first Conservative government of the nineteenth century.

For the most part it was a continuation of Addington's ministry. Portland remained as Lord President of the Council,[1] Westmorland as Lord Privy Seal, Eldon as Lord Chancellor, Castlereagh as President of the Board of Control, Chatham as Master General of the Ordnance. Lord Hawkesbury was transferred from the Foreign Office to the Home Office. Pitt himself, of course, became First Lord of the Treasury and Chancellor of the Exchequer, while two of his most efficient and hard-working 'men of business' came in to strengthen his Cabinet: Henry Dundas, now Viscount Melville, was made First Lord of the Admiralty and Dudley Ryder, now Lord Harrowby, became Foreign Secretary. By the beginning of 1805 Addington

[1] He had been moved from the Home Office to the Lord Presidency in July 1801.

himself was back in the ministry, replacing Portland as Lord President of the Council; but he and his followers quarrelled continually with Pitt and he resigned again after a few months.

While Pitt gathered around him all those who put their loyalty to the King before their loyalty to their own ideas, the opposition could count on the support of many of the most formidable debaters in the House of Commons. Not for many years had the Whig party looked more like the vigorous and progressive party which it had always claimed to be. Throughout the parliamentary session of 1805, from January to July, it harried Pitt; and the report of the Committee of Naval Enquiry, which appeared in February, provided it with an ideal basis for its attack. The committee had been set up during Addington's ministry and its report made serious charges against Dundas, who had been Treasurer of the Navy at the end of Pitt's previous ministry. The opposition was thus presented with a perfect opportunity not only to pose once again as the champions of purity against corruption but also to split Addington and Pitt. Addington had been vehemently attacked by Pitt in the previous year for his naval incompetence and his followers were anxious to support the findings of their own committee and to prove that any short-comings in the navy were Pitt's responsibility and not theirs. Samuel Whitbread, one of the most radical of the New Whigs, moved the impeachment of Dundas in April 1805 and when a division was taken 216 appeared for the motion and 216 against. The Speaker gave his casting vote in favour of the motion. Although Dundas was in due course acquitted by the House of Lords, the voting of the impeachment was a serious blow for Pitt. It weakened him gravely in the House of Commons, losing him the support both of the Addingtonians and of those radicals who had so far sympathized with him. Even Wilberforce, the indefatigable opponent of the slave trade and Pitt's closest personal friend, voted against him on this issue. For the next three months the ministry struggled with a hostile House of Commons and with a King who became daily more querulous and more unpredictable. By the time the session ended on 12 July, George was too ill to read the closing speech.

Pitt's own illness, though less incapacitating than the King's, was more virulent. The autumn was a time of terrible strain, spent negotiating a new European alliance, organizing precautions against invasion and arguing with the King down at Weymouth, in the forlorn hope of getting him to agree to a more widely based ministry.

At the Lord Mayor's banquet in November Pitt was toasted as 'the saviour of Europe'. His reply was the last, the shortest and the most famous of all his speeches: 'I return you many thanks for the honour you have done me; but Europe is not to be saved by any single man. England has saved herself by her exertions, and will, as I trust, save Europe by her example.' The news of Napoleon's tremendous victory at Austerlitz dashed his hopes of Europe's salvation and he was broken in spirits as well as in health when he set off for London on 9 January 1806 in order to attend the opening of Parliament. He was never to sit in the Commons again: he died at his house in Putney on 23 January.

He was mourned by many people as the man who had brought the country through the dark days of 1804 and 1805, the pilot who had once again weathered the storm; but he was not mourned as the young radical, the bright hope for the future, that he had once been. Even his most devoted followers felt, for all their personal sense of loss, a political sense of relief. Now was their chance to sweep away the tired old conservatism to which Pitt had surrendered. Now at last the long-promised ministry of all the talents could be built.

But things were not to be so easy. The events of the last few years had left a heritage of bitterness and it proved impossible for Foxites, Grenvillites, radical Pittites, conservative Pittites, Addingtonians and King's Friends to agree among themselves on a really comprehensive ministry. In the end the old King, driven into a corner by the refusal of the existing Cabinet to carry on without Pitt, found himself with a ministry which was almost entirely Foxite. He had asked Grenville to form an administration, 'putting no exclusion upon anybody, but reserving to himself to judge of the whole'; and when the whole was assembled it turned out to be a collection of Fox's friends, laced with the grasping relatives of Lord Grenville.[1] Fox himself became Foreign Secretary and his even more radical lieutenant, Charles Grey, took over as First Lord of the Admiralty. Lord Moira, who had for several years been regarded as the chief link between the Prince of Wales and the New Whigs, was made Master General of the Ordnance. Erskine, the radical lawyer who had made himself a popular hero by defending those who had been prosecuted for sedition and treason in the 1790s, was the new Lord Chancellor. The presence of Grenville himself as First Lord of

[1] It was later reckoned that the Grenville family were getting £55,000 a year from public funds in 1806. See J. Steven Watson: *The Reign of George III* (1960), p. 439.

the Treasury[1] and of Addington (now Viscount Sidmouth) as Lord Privy Seal could not disguise the fact that this was a Whig ministry. By preventing Pitt from constructing a genuinely comprehensive ministry in 1804, George III had produced a situation in which one could no longer be constructed in 1806. He decided to make the best of a bad job and accept the ministry. The Duke of Portland, who twenty-three years before had forced the King to accept a Cabinet he hated and sign warrants for appointments over which he had no control, was now scandalized by the way in which the Whigs had 'stormed the Closet'. He spoke of the King's 'thralldom' and hoped that in due course he would be able to rescue him from it.

Although Fox and Grenville had conquered the King, they were far from conquering the Commons. They called their administration 'the Ministry of all the Talents', but their rigorous exclusion of all those who had supported Pitt meant that many of the most talented men in the House were now on the opposition benches. Castlereagh, Canning, Spencer Perceval and many others were only too ready to exploit every failure of ministerial policy. The first failure was in foreign policy. For years Fox had been proclaiming that the continuation of the war was the fault of reactionary ministers in Britain and that once he came to power he would end it; but now that he was in power he soon found that his peace feelers met with little genuine response. By the summer of 1806 Fox's promises of peace had come to nothing and Fox himself was seriously ill with dropsy. On 13 September he died.

If the death of Pitt had removed the steadying force in British politics, the death of Fox removed its motive force. Nobody who knew him could help liking him—even George III warmed to him during the spring and summer of 1806—and nobody who heard him could doubt his sincerity. He did not devise a programme of radical measures merely to get himself back into power, but because he believed passionately in liberty and justice and humanity. With Fox to lead it the ministry might have brought forward reforming measures which would have gained it the support of progressive men and justified its claim to be a 'Ministry of all the Talents'. But without Fox it was difficult to see how the ministry, or the New Whigs who made up the major part of it, could maintain their impetus. In October Grenville persuaded the King to dissolve

[1] For the first time since 1783 the Treasury and the Chancellorship of the Exchequer were separated. Lord Henry Petty, Shelburne's son, became Chancellor of the Exchequer.

Parliament, in the hopes of improving his majority in the House of Commons; but he had nothing to put before the electors, neither men nor measures, neither a convincing team nor a rousing programme. The traditional techniques of patronage and management won some forty borough seats for the ministry, but in the open constituencies it was a different story. In Westminster, Fox's own constituency, his successor Sheridan made common cause with the Tory candidate in order to squash James Paull, an unknown radical candidate put in at the last moment; even so, Paull got only 277 less votes than Sheridan himself. In 1784 it had been Fox, the 'man of the people', who had attacked the unconstitutional device of a premature dissolution and who had subsequently triumphed in radical Westminster; now it was the Whigs who dissolved a Parliament that was only four years old and who found themselves opposed by the radicals.

The ministry's efforts to produce an impressive programme of legislation for the new Parliament were not very successful. The Bill for the abolition of the slave trade, which had been initiated by Fox himself in the early summer of 1806, was passed in March 1807 by an overwhelming majority; but it proved impossible to agree on any other reforms. The only measure which could be called at all progressive was a Bill introduced in March 1807 with the aim of allowing Catholics to enlist in the army. At first the King gave his reluctant consent to its introduction, but later he complained that he had been misled about its scope and he asked his ministers to give him a formal promise never to raise the question of Catholic emancipation again, either directly or indirectly. He told them that 'his mind cannot be at ease, unless he shall receive a positive assurance from them, which shall effectually relieve him from all future apprehension'. He was by now almost totally blind and among the shadows in which he lived there always lurked the darker and more terrible shadow of permanent insanity. Grenville and his colleagues felt that their consciences would not allow them to desert their principles, even to avert that shadow's descent. The Duke of Portland, on the other hand, was only too ready to rescue the King from his thralldom. He gave the required assurance and at the end of March 1807 he became First Lord of the Treasury for the second time in his life. On the first occasion he had been the symbol of the Whig victory over the King; now he was the symbol of the King's victory over what was left of the Whigs.

As in 1783, Portland presided over a coalition. Pittites, Old

Whigs and King's Friends came together to save the King and the country from the dangerous innovations threatened by Grenville and his friends. There were several men of real ability in the new ministry —Spencer Perceval as Chancellor of the Exchequer, Canning as Foreign Secretary, Castlereagh as Secretary for War—but they were in no sense a team and their abilities divided them instead of uniting them. A few years before, Canning had mocked the slogan of 'measures, not men', as 'the idle supposition that it is the harness and not the horses that draw the chariot along'; but now he and his colleagues were to discover the disadvantages of having powerful horses and no harness. Apart from their readiness to shelve Catholic emancipation the new ministers had nothing in common. Within a month of taking office they advised the King to dissolve Parliament, even though it was only a few months old; and at the ensuing election, fought on the slogan of 'No Popery', they increased their majority considerably. They had shown that they were united in their defence of the existing establishment, but subsequent events were to show that they were united in hardly anything else. Perceval's policy of all-out commercial warfare against Napoleon produced a trade depression and a good deal of popular discontent, whereupon his colleagues showed themselves only too ready to use him as a scape-goat. At the Foreign Office, Canning convinced himself that his great diplomatic offensives against the French were being sabotaged by Castlereagh's inefficiency at the War Office. By the spring of 1809 things were so bad that Canning was threatening to resign if Castle-reagh was not ousted. Portland tried to hush things up, but the only result of his efforts was a duel between Castlereagh and Canning and the resignation of both men. The whole affair taxed Portland's failing health to the limit and by October 1809 he insisted on resigning. A few weeks later he was dead.

Spencer Perceval came to the King's aid in this desperate situation. He took over as First Lord of the Treasury, thus reviving Pitt's tradition of combining this office with the Chancellorship of the Exchequer, and he stiffened the drooping Portland Cabinet with a few second generation Pittites. Dudley Ryder's nephew became Home Secretary and Henry Dundas's son took over the Board of Control. For the rest, his ministry was a continuation of Portland's mixture of Old Whigs and King's Friends. Approaches were made to Grey, Fox's accepted successor as leader of the New Whigs, and also to Grenville; but neither of them would have anything to do with a ministry which they regarded as a mere continuation of Portland's conspiracy of silence on the Catholic emancipation issue.

In December 1810 it seemed that this conspiracy, which had dominated British politics for nearly a decade, was no longer to be necessary. George III relapsed once more into insanity and this time his condition was to prove permanent. The ministry passed a Regency Act based on Pitt's Bill of 1789 and in February 1811 the Prince of Wales became Prince Regent for a year with limited powers. Many of the Whigs hoped that he would bring them to power forthwith, but he was very distrustful of some of their more radical elements and he had inherited his father's prejudices as well as his father's powers. He wanted a broad-based administration which would agree to shelve Catholic emancipation, turn its back on all kinds of parliamentary reform and prosecute the war as vigorously as possible. He did not want an unpredictable New Whig ministry dedicated to the idea of change and laced with wild 'seekers of improvements' like Samuel Whitbread and his friends. At first he could avoid an open breach with the Whigs by arguing that his power was only temporary and that he did not want to construct a ministry which would be unacceptable and distressing to his father in the event of the latter's recovery. But by the spring of 1812, when the doctors despaired of the King's recovery and the Prince's powers were made permanent, he could put off the decision no longer. He offered the Whigs a fixed number of places in an administration which was to remain basically Tory. The Whigs refused angrily and a quarrel ensued which ended the Prince's long connection with the New Whigs, with the party of programmes and progress. With a sense of relief he turned back to the faithful Perceval and in May, when Perceval was assassinated in the lobby of the House of Commons by a madman, his first thought was to ask the younger Jenkinson, now Lord Liverpool, to take over. Liverpool had been a reasonably efficient Secretary for War since the resignation of Castlereagh, but many members of the Commons saw his promotion as the replacing of one second-rate King's Friend by another. The House sent a deputation to the Regent asking him to form an efficient and broadly based administration of men of talent, but this proved impossible. After attempts by Canning to woo the Whigs and by Moira to woo the Tories had both broken down, the Regent turned back to Liverpool. Liverpool's ministry, a mixture of King's Friends, Old Whigs and some Pittite Tories, was to last for fifteen years, until he became seriously ill in the spring of 1827. During those fifteen years the classes who wielded political power in Britain closed their ranks around Lord Liverpool and the Prince Regent, to ensure that Old Whiggery, Patriotism, Pittism and King's Friendism all merged into the great Conservative tradition of the nineteenth century. Only a small group of men led by Grey clung to some form of New Whiggery, while an even smaller group led by Canning tried to prove that Toryism need not necessarily be equated with Conservatism.

2 *The War against Napoleon*

For the first fifteen years of the nineteenth century the history of Europe was the history of one man: Napoleon Bonaparte. Having made himself First Consul of the French Republic in 1799 and humbled Austria at the Peace of Lunéville in 1801, he set out to build a new order which was to have far-reaching effects on Europe and on Britain. He came, he said 'to substitute an age of work for an age of talk'. Instead of intoxicating themselves with slogans about abstract rights and ideal constitutions, Frenchmen were persuaded to settle to the laborious and unromantic task of construction and conciliation. The achievements of the Revolution—the abolition of privilege, the redistribution of land, the equality of opportunity and of legal status—were preserved, but they were built into a framework of stability and continuity. The quarrel with the Catholic Church was brought to an end and a Concordat was signed with the Papacy in 1802. New and far-reaching codes of law were drawn up and a hierarchy of talent, the Legion of Honour, was created to replace the old hierarchy of privilege and birth. In May 1804 Napoleon Bonaparte created himself Emperor Napoleon I of the French and in the following December the Pope himself was brought from Rome to Paris to grace the new Emperor's coronation. The extension of the new order from France to the rest of Europe, an ambition which Napoleon had inherited from the Revolution, now took the form of satellite kingdoms ruled by Napoleon's brothers instead of satellite republics. Austrian and Prussian claims to control the balance in Germany and Italy and the Low Countries crumbled before the new kingdoms of Westphalia and Naples and Holland. As early as 1805 he himself took the title of King of Italy and was crowned with the Iron Crown of the Lombards which had once symbolized, nearly a thousand years earlier, the power of the French Emperor

Charlemagne over Italy. Within a few years he was forcing the Pope to be an obedient chaplain to his new Empire of all Europe and in 1810 he married the daughter of the Habsburg Emperor of Austria.[1] The son of that marriage, born in March 1811, would rule over an empire which would rival those of Charlemagne, of the Caesars, perhaps even of Alexander. The House of Bonaparte would do what the House of Bourbon and the House of Habsburg had failed to do: it would unite Europe.

This threatened union of all Europe was unwelcome to Britain for several reasons. Ever since the Peace of Paris in 1763 it had been clear that most European states resented British maritime supremacy and felt that Britain intervened in the wars of Europe only for the sake of feathering her own nest. If they could be persuaded to see Napoleon as their protector against the greed of British merchants and the bullying of the British navy, they might stand together to deprive Britain of commercial advantages and of diplomatic freedom of action. Furthermore, the very nature of Napoleon's new order was hostile to Britain. It combined the old expansionism of the Bourbons with the new expansionism of the Revolution; and the gentlemen of England, who hated papists and bureaucrats and militarists above all things, were horrified by a régime which brought together Catholicism, strong central government and the open glorification of an enormous standing army.

The full extent of Napoleon's European ambitions had not been revealed in 1802, but in the months which followed the Peace of Amiens British suspicions about his intentions grew steadily stronger. As well as extending his control over the satellite republics along France's northern and eastern frontiers, he initiated sweeping changes in the balance of power in Germany and Italy; and when Britain claimed that these actions were contrary to the spirit of the Treaty of Amiens he pointed out that they did not offend against the letter of the treaty. In fact, Addington had obtained no proper guarantees for the European balance of power at Amiens: he had relied on the treaties which France had already signed with the powers of Europe themselves. Now that Napoleon was strong enough to impose his will on Europe, there was nothing that Britain could legally do about it. She was not prepared, however, to accept Napoleon's new position without protest and she refused to surrender Malta—which,

---

[1] In August 1806 the Holy Roman Empire was abolished and the Habsburgs became Emperors of Austria only.

by the Treaty of Amiens, was to have been restored to the Knights of St John—until Napoleon had given proper guarantees for the balance of power in Europe. In London and in Paris the newspapers carried on a reciprocal campaign of jingoism and abuse, which was intensified in February 1803 after the official French journal, the *Moniteur*, had published a report by Colonel Sébastiani advocating a renewal of the Egyptian campaign. In April the British government presented two successive ultimatums to Napoleon, insisting on French withdrawals in Holland, Switzerland and Italy and on British retention of Malta. They were refused and after a final attempt to negotiate a satisfactory settlement had broken down Britain declared war on France on 17 May 1803.

If the peace of Amiens had been an impossible peace, a peace by which Britain had relied on non-existent guarantees of a non-existent European balance, the war of 1803 was an even more impossible war. Far away in India General Wellesley defeated the Mahrattas at Assaye and Argaum in the autumn of 1803, thus preventing French interference in India, but nearer home there was nothing but an uneasy stalemate. While the French army prevented the British from getting a foothold in Europe, the British navy prevented the French from invading Britain. The traditional levers which the two countries had always used against each other had little effect: Napoleon was not particularly worried by British conquests in the West Indies, while the French entry into Hanover, which took place as soon as the war was reopened, did not disturb George III as much as it would have disturbed his grandfather or his great-grandfather. British merchants were alarmed at the prospect of the French controlling the trade of the Elbe and the Weser, but even this turned out to be less serious than had been feared, owing to the unchallenged supremacy of the British navy in the North Sea. In 1803 British exports to northern Europe dropped from £15,015,000 to £11,372,000, but by 1805 they had risen again to £13,026,000. Napoleon's control of the ports of the Mediterranean, and particularly those of Italy, was much more effective: the export trade to southern Europe fell from £7,752,000 to £3,968,000 and by 1805 it had fallen still further, to £2,440,000.

It was clear that Napoleon's supremacy in Europe, although it could perhaps hamper British trade, could not ruin it. If he could control the whole coastline of Europe he might perhaps be able to bring Britain to her knees by robbing her of export markets; but even then his plans might be upset by Europe's need for British goods and by Britain's ability to open up for herself new export markets in America and Africa and Asia. By the beginning of 1804 he had decided that the only way to break the deadlock was to carry out an invasion of Britain. He had already been considering it in a desultory fashion, assembling bodies of troops along the coast from Boulogne to Ostend and commanding that special songs should be written for the soldiers to sing while they were conquering Britain. He had also given his blessing, though nothing else, to Robert Emmet's abortive Irish rising in the summer of 1803. But now his plans became more serious and more practicable. Instead of hoping to slip across the Channel while the British were not looking, he began to devise ways of getting proper naval cover for his attempt. During the summer of 1804, though the 'Army of England' at Boulogne was increased to 100,000 men and some 700 invasion barges had been built to carry it, the naval cover was still not forthcoming. The Brest and Toulon fleets were bottled up in harbour by the British blockading squadrons and the Spaniards had not as yet been persuaded to declare war against Britain. The newly created Emperor reviewed his invasion flotillas, but the only result was the loss of some 200 men who were drowned in a storm. During the winter of 1804–5, however, the chances of a successful invasion were improved by the entry of Spain into the war. Fresh plans were made for an invasion in the summer of 1805, supported by the combined naval strength of France and Spain, and several millions of francs were spent in improving the roads from Paris to the Channel ports.

In Britain the government's plans were largely concerned with the raising of an effective militia to resist the French if they succeeded in landing. An Act of 1802 had ordered the raising of a force of some 50,000 men by ballot, but it had allowed those upon whom the lot fell to purchase a substitute if they could afford it. This meant that many of those who would otherwise have enlisted in the regular army found it more profitable to enter the militia as substitutes; and with the raising of the Volunteers in 1803 the situation became even worse and both the army and the militia found themselves drained of manpower. Instead of one coherent, properly trained and disciplined force, there were plentiful supplies of enthusiastic but untrained volunteers and a scarcity of properly trained and disciplined men. The King, however, was only too ready to meet the enemy and plans were made for him to go with the First Lord of the

Treasury and the Home Secretary to either Chelmsford or Dartford, according to whether the French landed north or south of the Thames.

By the spring of 1805 there were eleven French ships of the line in Toulon, two in Rochefort and twenty-one in Brest. Together with eight Spanish ships in Cadiz and four in Ferrol, this would make a combined fleet of forty-six ships to cover the invasion. The only problem was how to combine them. Villeneuve took the Toulon fleet out into the Atlantic early in April and scattered the British squadron which had been blockading Cadiz, but when the French admiral in Brest asked for permission to join him Napoleon was so concerned to keep the Brest fleet intact that he refused to let it leave harbour unless it could do so without risking a fight with the British blockading squadron. Since this was clearly impossible the Brest fleet stayed where it was and Villeneuve sailed off to the West Indies in order to draw off Nelson and the British Mediterranean fleet from European waters. Once he was sure that Nelson had in fact followed him to the Caribbean, Villeneuve recrossed the Atlantic and appeared off Ferrol towards the end of July. Nelson, however, had sent on ahead of him a brig which sighted the French fleet, ascertained that it was returning to Europe and got word to the Admiralty in London. Villeneuve found a British fleet of fifteen ships of the line waiting for him off Ferrol and after an indecisive action he gave up the idea of joining the Brest fleet and put in instead into Ferrol. Another opportunity for the junction of the two fleets came in the middle of August, when Admiral Cornwallis, in command of the British Channel fleet of thirty-four ships of the line, made the mistake of dividing it into two smaller forces; but Villeneuve failed to take advantage of this slip and by the end of August it was too late. Napoleon had received news of an imminent attack from Austria and he had dispersed the camp at Boulogne and led his men back across France to the eastern frontier.

Though the Army of England had been dispersed, the danger of a combined French and Spanish fleet gaining control of the Channel still remained. Napoleon's immediate concerns were now with Europe and he ordered Villeneuve to leave Cadiz, where he had gone in August to refit, and to sail into the Mediterranean in order to provide a diversion in Italy while Napoleon himself advanced upon Vienna. Nelson, who arrived off Cadiz late in September to take command of the British fleets there, determined to attack Villeneuve and annihilate his fleet. When he sailed into action off Cape Trafalgar in the morning of 21 October 1805 he had twenty-seven ships under his command, as against the eighteen French and fifteen Spanish ships which made up Villeneuve's fleet. The gradual abandonment of the old tactics of the Fighting Instructions, with their rooted fear of 'breaking the line', was brought to a triumphant conclusion by Nelson at Trafalgar. He bore down on the enemy in two parallel lines nearly a mile apart and broke the enemy line in two places. As the leading ships in the two lines broke through the French and the Spaniards those behind them wore away to north and to south and made further breaches, until the whole enemy fleet was in disarray. Eighteen ships were taken or destroyed in the battle itself and four more were captured later. The remaining eleven limped back into Cadiz, never to emerge again for the rest of the war. But Nelson's greatest victory was also his last: a French sniper from the mizzen of the *Redoubtable* had shot him through the spine early in the battle. He was mourned by his whole fleet, by his whole country, even by his enemies. As the Spanish admiral Gravina lay dying of his wounds he told his attendants: 'I am going, I hope and trust, to join Nelson.'

Trafalgar shattered once and for all Napoleon's hopes of commanding the sea, but his grasp of Europe strengthened relentlessly. A week before Trafalgar he had surrounded an Austrian army of 27,000 men at Ulm and forced it to surrender; and on 2 December 1805 he won an overwhelming victory over the Austrians and the Russians at Austerlitz. Pitt's coalition with Austria and Russia, which had cost him much hard bargaining and many millions of pounds in subsidies, was smashed at one blow and Europe was transformed from a collection of independent states into a French sphere of influence. Lovers of anecdotes aver that the dying Pitt, when he arrived at Putney, told his niece to roll up her map of Europe since it would not be needed for ten years. The prophecy, if it was uttered, was a good one: from Austerlitz to Waterloo was to be nine years and six months.

In the autumn of 1806 Prussia, fortified with promises of British and Russian help, declared war on Napoleon. He marched into Germany and by the time he returned to Paris in July 1807 he had smashed the Prussian army, conquered the whole of eastern Germany and Poland, rolled back the Russian armies as far as the river Niemen and signed with the Czar of Russia the Treaty of Tilsit, whereby the Emperors of the West and of the East, the lords of Europe and Asia, agreed to divide the world between them. They also agreed to cooperate in closing all the ports of Europe against British trade. Russian commercial preponderance in the Baltic would enable Napoleon to make effective the blockade of Britain which he had already proclaimed in a decree issued from Berlin in November 1806. Strictly speaking, his much-vaunted blockade was not a blockade at all. Only a nation which had command of the sea could impose a blockade, in the sense of stopping ships from coming into its enemy's ports. All that Napoleon could do, as ruler of the land but not of the sea, was to stop ships from coming into his own ports. It was, in fact, a blockade in reverse, a deliberate act of commercial self-denial. He was convinced that Europe was still self-sufficient, whereas Britain had developed an unnatural and unbalanced economy which made her rely on exporting manufactured goods and importing in exchange raw materials, foodstuffs and gold. If her export markets were sealed to her, her whole economic life would be disrupted and the result would be revolution and bankruptcy. For the next four years Napoleon strove desperately to turn the whole of Europe into an embattled and self-sufficient fortress.

In reply the British Chancellor of the Exchequer, Spencer Perceval, waged unremitting commercial warfare on Napoleon's Europe. A series of Orders in Council, beginning in January 1807, declared all European ports from which British ships were excluded to be in a state of blockade. Apart from an increase in 1809, when there was a temporary loosening of Napoleon's grip on the German ports, British exports to northern Europe fell dramatically from £13,026,000 in 1805 to £2,358,000 in 1811. Even more disastrous was the boycott of British trade by the United States, where there was strong resentment of the British navy's high-handed attitude to neutral shipping. In 1805 Britain sent £7,147,000 of goods to the the United States and by 1811 the figure had dropped to £1,432,000. It was some time before the full effects were felt in the industrial areas of Britain, where 1807 and 1808 were years of relatively high employment. There was serious rioting in Manchester, Rochdale, Oldham and other towns in 1807, but it was caused by long hours and low wages rather than by unemployment. By 1809 the soaring prices of raw materials from Europe were causing concern: tar and pine from the Baltic and silk from Italy cost half as much again as they had cost in 1807. Many merchants and industrialists were caught out by the temporary improvement of 1809 and found themselves with large stocks which they could not sell except at a loss. The number of bankruptcies, which was 347 in 1809, had risen to 696 by 1811. In that year the Chancellor of the Exchequer himself told the Commons that a recent report suggested 'that there was scarcely a cotton manufacturer in the kingdom who had not diminished by one half the number of persons employed in his mills and that many of the smaller manufacturers had discharged their people altogether'. An outbreak of machine-breaking in Nottingham spread to other parts of the midlands and the north, providing the propertied classes with a sharp reminder of the dangers produced by mass unemployment among the new industrial workers. 1812, too, was a year of riots and starvation. One experienced and humane mill-owner declared that there had never been a time when English labourers had known such misery. Meanwhile, with industrial depression threatening social and financial chaos, British commitments abroad continued to mount steadily. British armies in Europe, which had cost £700,000 in 1806, were accounting for £11,600,000 in 1811; and subsidies to continental allies accounted for another £2,367,000.

Two things saved Britain from the ugly consequences of Napoleon's embargo. The first, and more important, was the fact that Napoleon needed British goods even more than Britain needed continental markets. From 1810 onwards he found increasingly that a Europe starved of British manufactures, and especially of British textiles, could support neither his armies nor his ambitions. From January 1810 onwards a new series of decrees imposed high customs duties on British goods instead of banning them altogether; and this policy produced a steady relaxation of the embargo until by the end of 1812 it had almost ceased to exist. In December 1812 Napoleon told his Minister of Commerce that he must raise another 150,000,000 francs in customs revenue and added: 'Undoubtedly it is necessary to harm our foes, but above all we must live.' Ten years before he had seen Britain as an unnatural and leech-like parasite, sucking the blood of Europe; but now he knew that without the leech the patient himself would die.

The second thing which enabled Britain to survive the embargo was Napoleon's invasion of Portugal and Spain. In the winter of 1807, after delivering an ultimatum requiring Portugal to break off all commercial connections with Britain, he invaded and occupied the country. In order to do so he had to persuade the Spanish King and his minister Godoy to allow the French army to march through northern Spain. This produced a nationalist uprising, of which the

Crown Prince Ferdinand was the figurehead, against the King and his French masters. Napoleon got both King and Prince to abdicate their claims to the Spanish throne and put his brother Joseph on it instead. Britain saw the advantage of having a foothold in the Iberian Peninsula; and a force of some 9,000 men intended for South America was diverted to Portugal and defeated the French at Vimiero in August 1808. Then, instead of pushing on into Spain, the British commander signed a Convention allowing the French to evacuate Portugal. By the time a new commander, Sir John Moore, had taken over in Portugal and decided to advance into Spain, the French had already established themselves in Madrid and had inflicted heavy casualties on the Spanish nationalist guerillas. Moore's march to Salamanca and his subsequent retreat to Corunna in December 1808 and January 1809 were masterpieces of organization and discipline, but they did little to help the Spaniards. It looked as though the Peninsula would prove a slippery foothold and in the summer of 1809 the War Office turned its principal attention to the Netherlands, where a force of 40,000 men was landed on the island of Walcheren in the Scheldt estuary. It failed to advance upon Antwerp and in December, after it had lost thousands of men from disease, it was taken off again. It seemed that Napoleon's military and commercial control of Europe remained unshaken.

But if Napoleon could invade Portugal and Spain, he could not invade their extensive colonial possessions in Central and South America. The Portuguese fleet and the Portuguese royal family withdrew to Brazil and the Spanish colonies refused to recognize Joseph Bonaparte as King of Spain. British exports to Central and South America, which had been worth £1,326,000 in 1807, had shot up to £6,382,000 by 1809. Some British manufacturers became so intoxicated with the boom in the South American trade that they hopefully exported pairs of ice-skates to Rio de Janeiro. Britain's newly acquired trade with South America continued to flourish after the defeat of Napoleon and by 1823 Canning, as British Foreign Secretary, was prepared to seek the support of the United States in asserting the independence of the former Spanish American colonies. 'I have called a new world into existence', he declared, 'to redress the balance of the old.' He was claiming too much for himself: it was Napoleon who first gave British merchants new worlds to conquer across the Atlantic by trying to limit their activities in the Iberian Peninsula.

Back in the Peninsula itself the situation was transformed in April 1809 by the arrival of General Wellesley as Commander-in-Chief. He had already proved himself an able soldier in India and in an expedition to Denmark in 1807; but in the Peninsula he was to demonstrate unmistakably that he was the greatest commander Britain had produced since Marlborough. Unlike many of his political superiors at the War Office, he believed in the war and disbelieved in the myth of Napoleonic invincibility. He saw that the French strength lay in their ability to move quickly, living off the country and imposing rapid defeats on their enemies before their lines of communication could be strained. The much-vaunted military genius of Napoleon was simply an extension of hit-and-run techniques. Wellesley therefore determined to tie the French down so that they could neither hit nor run. He established an extensive network of supply depots and he initiated a proper system of surveying and mapping. His campaigns of 1809, 1810, 1811 and 1812 were not spectacular and in each of those years he had to return to his bases in Portugal at the end of the season. But he inflicted heavy casualties on the French, by hemming them in, limiting their movements and then concentrating superior forces against them when their need to forage for food forced them to disperse. Napoleon himself never appeared in the Peninsula again after he left for the Austrian front in January 1809, but the war there was a terrible drain on his resources and the Marshals whom he put in command there were steadily worn down by Wellesley's tactics. They longed to make a dramatic move in the Napoleonic manner, but somehow it was never possible. Like chess players who spend their time dreaming of a superb winning combination, they failed to notice that their opponent's moves were steadily limiting their own freedom of action. When that opponent made his decisive move, in the spring of 1813, he carried all before him. By the end of the summer he was already hammering at the border forts of the Pyrenees and at the end of the year he was in France. Bordeaux fell to him in February 1814 and Toulouse in April. After joining the leaders of the other victorious powers in Paris he returned to England to receive a welcome such as no general had received since the days of Marlborough. He was already Marquis of Wellington and now he was made a Duke. He had done much more than win the war in the Peninsula: he had brought the prestige and self-respect of the British army to a point it had never reached before. A country which for generations had regarded standing armies as instruments of tyranny was at last persuaded to take a pride in its tradition of military greatness.

Wellington's advance across Spain had been only one jaw of the trap which had closed upon Napoleon. In 1812 the breakdown of the Treaty of Tilsit had provoked him into invading Russia and by the time he fell back into Germany, after spending five weeks in the deserted and gutted city of Moscow, he had lost the greater part of an army of half a million men. In 1813 his Russian pursuers pushed on into Germany, where they were joined by the Prussians and the Austrians. After a shattering defeat at Leipzig in October 1813 Napoleon fell back into France and in April 1814, with the Czar of Russia and the King of Prussia in triumphant occupation of Paris, he at last agreed to abdicate. The victorious powers agreed to make him Prince of Elba in his own right; but in the summer of 1815, after his attempt to return to power in France had been crushed at the battle of Waterloo, he was banished to the remote island of St Helena, to live out the rest of his life under the embarrassed surveillance of the British governor there. Since he had made himself Emperor in 1804 much of his earlier popularity as the Man of the Revolution had gone: in Spain, in Germany and in Russia he had come to be regarded as a tyrant of the old type, trampling on national and liberal aspirations. But now, on St Helena, he set to work to remake the image of himself as the defender of liberty and progress, a man of peace who had been forced to spend his life on the battlefield because the kings of Europe would not allow their peoples to embrace his new order. Britain, in particular, had opposed him with her peculiarly noxious mixture of the old and the new, of aristocratic misrule and bourgeois commercialism. Europe, instead of helping him against the British, had become their dupe, had accepted their gold and had allowed them at the end to chain him to a rock in the ocean.

This Napoleonic legend was to prove one of the most enduring products of the Napoleonic wars. The figure of Napoleon, both the legend and the reality, was to brood over Britain's relations with Europe from that time forward. In 1688 Britain had welcomed William III, the man who had invited her to become part of Europe; in 1815 she had destroyed Napoleon, the man who had warned Europe against her. In the meantime five generations of insular and suspicious Britons had done much to reject the invitation and justify the warning.

3 Conclusion

While Napoleon on St Helena was meditating on the dual nature of Britain, on the pride of her rulers and the greed of her merchants, men of substance in Britain were congratulating themselves on having preserved the best of the old and merged it with the best of the new. The balanced constitution of 1689 had been safeguarded against despotic courtiers and irresponsible magnates, against the superstition of the papists and the enthusiasm of the Dissenters. The 'circulation and increase of capital' of which Pitt had spoken in 1792 had been allowed to enrich old families and new families alike, but the respect due to birth and breeding could still be exacted. Landlords could still instruct their bailiffs to evict tenants who dared to 'interrupt gentlemen's diversion' by destroying foxes; and the laws against poaching were being suitably stiffened. As recently as 1803 a new Act had been passed enabling poachers who offered armed resistance to be hanged as felons. The labouring poor had been unsettled by the recent agrarian and industrial changes, but laws passed in 1815 to prevent the import of cheap foreign corn should bring back stability and contentment to the land. By 1813 the cost of cultivating a hundred acres of arable land had risen to well over £700, nearly twice what it had been in 1790; yet wheat prices had fallen in the course of the year from 122s a quarter to 75s a quarter. By preventing further falls the Corn Laws should enable landlords to pay adequate wages and to keep their labourers contented. What was a little disturbing, however, was the spread of education among the poor. Thanks to the charity and enthusiasm which the evangelical movement had generated, something like a million children throughout the land were receiving some kind of education. The Health and Morals Act of 1802 had provided that factory apprentices should be taught reading, writing and arithmetic, as well as being excused night work and limited to only twelve hours' work a day. In 1807 the radical Samuel Whitbread had wanted to set up parish schools on the Scottish model, but the bishops had secured the rejection of his Bill in the House of Lords. In the Commons Davies Giddy, member for Bodmin and a future president of the Royal Society, had declared indignantly that education of the poor 'would teach them to despise their lot in life, instead of making them good servants in agriculture and other laborious employments to which their rank in society had destined them'.

While the conservatively minded thought with satisfaction of the past which had been preserved, the radicals nursed in grim secrecy their hopes for the future. A generation of war against the Revolution and against Napoleon's new order had turned almost all the old radicals into pillars of the establishment: even Jeremy Bentham had turned from plans for a new heaven and a new earth to plans for an improved and more efficient kind of prison. A handful of men like Frances Burdett, the radical elected for Westminster in 1807, or Samuel Romilly, the ardent supporter of penal reform, could be said to link the new radicalism and the old. But Burdett became increasingly conservative in his views after 1815, while Romilly committed suicide in 1818. Three years earlier, Whitbread had died in the same manner: respectable Anglicans could hardly help reflecting that this was perhaps the inevitable fate of men who forsook God and the establishment for abstract philosophy and ideas of change.

While the old radicalism shrivelled and died, a new radicalism of secret societies and revolutionary violence took its place. As yet its ideas were uncertain and unformed, but it was more concerned with the revolution that had been averted in the 1790s than with the revolution that had been worshipped since the 1680s. Gentlemen of England might regard the British monarchy as the living symbol of a divinely ordained order and balance, but the new radicals saw only the pitiful degradation at Windsor and the senseless extravagance at Brighton. Men of wealth and substance might still cherish their ancient right to occupy the richest offices of Church and State, but the idea was already circulating that office should go to those who deserved it and wealth to those whose labour produced it. In spite of all that the reformers and the evangelicals had sought to do, the British Constitution and the Anglican Church still meant little or nothing to the labouring classes and to their increasingly militant leaders. More and more, those leaders were to feel with Shelley that the old institutions must die if something better was to be born:

> An old, mad, blind, despised and dying king,—
> Princes, the dregs of their dull race, who flow
> Through public scorn, mud from a muddy spring,—
> Rulers who neither see nor feel nor know,
> But leech-like to their fainting country cling,
> Till they drop, blind in blood, without a blow,—
> A people starved and stabbed in the untilled field,—

An army which liberticide and prey
Make as a two-edged sword to all who wield,—
Golden and sanguine laws which tempt and slay,—
Religion Christless, Godless, a book sealed,—
A Senate—time's worst statute unrepealed,—
Are graves from which a glorious Phantom may
Burst to illumine our tempestuous day.

APPENDIX I: RULERS, PARLIAMENTS AND PRINCIPAL MINISTERS, 1689–1815

Rulers	Parliaments	First Lords of the Treasury	Other ministers
William III, 1689–1702 Mary II, 1689–94	Jan. 1689–Feb. 1690 Mar. 1690–Oct. 1695 Nov. 1695–Jul. 1698 Aug. 1698–Dec. 1700 Feb. 1701–Nov. 1701 Dec. 1701–Jul. 1702	*Commissioners, 1689–1702, inc.: Lowther, 90–91; Godolphin, 89–97, 00–01; Montagu, 91–99.*	Danby (LPC, 89–99) Nottingham (SSN, 89–90; SSS, 90–93) Shrewsbury (SSN, 93–95; SSS, 95–98) Somers (LC, 97–00)
Anne, 1702–14	Aug. 1702–Apr. 1705 Jun. 1705–Apr. 1708 Jul. 1708–Sep. 1710 Nov. 1710–Aug. 1713 Nov. 1713–Jan. 1715	Godolphin, Mar. 1702.[1] Harley, Aug. 1710.[2] Shrewsbury, Aug. 1714.[1]	Nottingham (SSS, 02–04) Harley (SSN, 04–08) Sunderland (SSS, 06–10) St John (SSN, 10–13; SSS, 13–14)
George I, 1714–27	Mar. 1715–Mar. 1722 May 1722–Aug. 1727	Halifax, Oct. 1714. Carlisle, May 1715. Walpole, Oct. 1715 Stanhope, Apr. 1717. Sunderland, Mar. 1718. Walpole, Apr. 1721.	Townshend (SSN, 14–16; 21–30) Stanhope (SSS, 14–16) Carteret (SSS, 21–24) Newcastle (SSS, 24–46)
George II, 1727–60	Nov. 1727–Apr. 1734 Jun. 1734–Apr. 1741 Jun. 1741–Jun.1747 Aug. 1747–Apr. 1754 May 1754–Mar. 1761	Wilmington, Feb. 1742. Pelham, Aug. 1743. Pulteney, Feb. 1746. Pelham, Feb. 1746. Newcastle, Mar. 1754. Devonshire, Nov. 1756. Waldegrave, Jun. 1757. Newcastle, Jun. 1757.	Hardwicke (LC, 37–56) Carteret (SSN, 42–44; SSS & SSN, Feb. 1746) Newcastle (SSS, 46–48; SSN, 48–54) Pitt (PG, 46–55; SSS, 56–57; 57–61) Fox (SSS, 55–56)

LPC: *Lord President of the Council.* SSN: *Secretary of State for the North.* SSS: *Secretary of State for the South.* LC: *Lord Chancellor.* PG: *Paymaster General.* CE: *Chancellor of the Exchequer.* LPS: *Lord Privy Seal.* FS: *Foreign Secretary.* HS: *Home Secretary.* SW: *Secretary of War.*

[1] Lord High Treasurer.
[2] Commissioner of the Treasury, 1710; Lord High Treasurer 1711.

APPENDIX I: RULERS, PARLIAMENTS AND PRINCIPAL MINISTERS, 1689–1815

Rulers	Parliaments	First Lords of the Treasury	Other ministers
George III, 1760–1820	May 1761–Mar. 1768 May 1768–Sep. 1774 Nov. 1774–Sep. 1780 Oct. 1780–Mar. 1784 May 1784–Jun. 1790 Aug. 1790–May 1796 Jul. 1796–Jun. 1802 Aug. 1802–Oct. 1806 Dec. 1806–Apr. 1807 Jun. 1807–Sep. 1812 Nov. 1812–Jun. 1818	Bute, May, 1762. Grenville, May 1763. Rockingham, Jul. 1765. Grafton, Aug. 1766. North, Feb. 1770. Rockingham, Mar. 1782. Shelburne, Jul. 1782. Portland, Apr. 1783. Pitt,[1] Dec. 1783. Addington, Mar. 1801. Pitt,[1] May 1804. W. Grenville, Jan. 1806. Portland, Mar. 1807. Perceval, Sep. 1809. Liverpool, Jun. 1812.	Grenville (SSN, 62–63) C. Townshend (CE, 66–67) Pitt (Chatham) (LPS, 66–68) Thurlow (LC, 78–83; 83–92) C. Fox (FS, 82; 83; 06) Pitt[1] (CE, 82–83) North (HS, 83) Portland (HS, 94–01; LPC, 04–05) Canning (FS, 07–09) Castlereagh (SW, 07–09; FS, 12–22)

LPC: *Lord President of the Council.* SSN: *Secretary of State for the North.* SSS: *Secretary of State for the South.* LC: *Lord Chancellor.* PG: *Paymaster General.* CE: *Chancellor of the Exchequer.* LPS: *Lord Privy Seal.* FS: *Foreign Secretary.* HS: *Home Secretary.* SW: *Secretary of War.*

[1] William Pitt the younger.

(Based on the appendices to *The Oxford History of England*, vols. 9, 10 and 11 and to Betty Kemp: *King and Commons, 1660–1832*, Macmillan, 1959.)

APPENDIX II: GOVERNMENT FINANCE, 1695[1]-1815

	Revenue	Expenditure	Debt
1695	£4,134,000	£6,220,000	£8,400,000
1700	£4,344,000	£3,201,000	£14,200,000
1705	£5,292,000	£5,873,000	£13,000,000
1710	£5,248,000	£9,772,000	£21,400,000
1715	£5,547,000	£6,228,000	£37,400,000
1720	£6,323,000	£6,002,000	£54,000,000
1725	£5,960,000	£5,516,000	£52,700,000
1730	£6,265,000	£5,574,000	£51,400,000
1735	£5,625,000	£5,852,000	£49,300,000
1740	£5,745,000	£6,161,000	£47,400,000
1745	£6,451,000	£8,920,000	£60,100,000
1750	£7,467,000	£7,185,000	£78,000,000
1755	£6,938,000	£7,119,000	£72,500,000
1760	£9,207,000	£17,993,000	£101,700,000
1765	£10,928,000	£10,649,000	£133,600,000
1770	£11,373,000	£10,524,000	£130,600,000
1775	£11,112,000	£10,365,000	£127,300,000
1780	£12,524,000	£22,605,000	£167,200,000
1785	£15,527,000	£15,966,000	£245,500,000
1790	£17,014,000	£16,798,000	£244,000,000
1795	£19,053,000	£37,505,000	£267,400,000
1800	£31,585,000	£50,991,000	£456,100,000
1805	£55,000,000	£71,400,000	£564,400,000
1810	£73,000,000	£81,600,000	£609,600,000
1815	£79,100,000	£99,500,000	£778,300,000

[1] It was not until the mid 1690s that Montague brought some order into the Treasury's affairs; and reliable annual figures are not available before that time. This table begins, therefore, in 1695 and not in 1689.

(Based on Mitchell, B. R. and Deane, Phyllis: *Abstract of British Historical Statistics.*, C.U.P., 1962.)

APPENDIX III: THE HOUSES OF STUART AND HANOVER

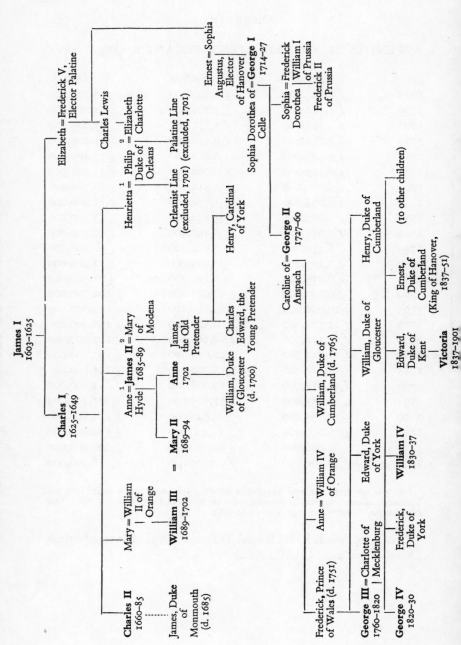

Bibliography

Like most of its kind, this list is the product of drastic compression. Selection has been based on the following principles:

Part One, being intended for the general reader rather than the professional historian, lists only those works which may reasonably be sought in any good library. Considerations of accessibility have taken precedence over those of historical importance.

Poems, plays, novels, pamphlets, philosophical treatises, etc., are not listed. For details of these—and of the paintings and buildings which are equally important for an understanding of the period— see the secondary works listed in section 7 of Part Two.

Part Two is mainly confined to recent works which have added to our knowledge of the period. Earlier works have only been listed if they contain material which cannot easily be found elsewhere; but this does not mean that classical authors like Lord Macaulay, W. E. H. Lecky, Sir John Fortescue or Captain Mahan are no longer worth reading. They have been outmoded, rather than outclassed, by the advance of modern historical research.

Memoirs and general and political histories are listed chronologically; other sections are arranged in alphabetical order of authors' names.

The following abbreviations are used:

C.U.P.	Cambridge University Press
E.H.	*Economic History*
E.H.R.	*English Historical Review*
Ec.H.R.	*Economic History Review*
H.	*History*
H.T.	*History Today*
H.U.P.	Harvard University Press
J.E.H.	*Journal of Economic History*
M.U.P.	Manchester University Press
O.U.P.	Oxford University Press
T.R.H.S.	*Transactions of the Royal Historical Society*
Y.U.P.	Yale University Press

Part One: Primary Sources

1 Collections of documents and statistics

ASPINALL, A. and SMITH, E. A., *English Historical Documents, vol. 11: 1783–1832.* Eyre and Spottiswoode, 1959.

BROWNING, A., *English Historical Documents, vol. 8: 1660–1714.* Eyre and Spottiswoode, 1953.

COSTIN, W. C. and WATSON, J. S., *The Law and Working of the Constitution: Documents, 1660–1914,* 2 vols. (vol. 1: 1660–1783; vol. 2: 1784–1914). Black, 1952.

HORN, B. D. and RANSOME, M., *English Historical Documents, vol. 10: 1714–83.* Eyre and Spottiswoode, 1959.

JENSEN, M., *English Historical Documents, vol. 9: American Colonial Documents to 1776.* Eyre and Spottiswoode, 1955.

KENYON, J. P., *The Stuart Constitution, 1603–1688: Documents and a Commentary.* C.U.P., 1966.

MITCHELL, B. R. and DEANE, PHYLLIS. *Abstract of British Historical Statistics.* C.U.P., 1962.

WILLIAMS, E. N. *The Eighteenth Century Constitution, 1688–1815: Documents and a Commentary.* C.U.P., 1960.

2 Memoirs, diaries, letters, speeches, etc.

FIENNES, CELIA, *The Journeys of Celia Fiennes (c. 1685–1703),* ed. C. Morris. Cresset Press, 1947.

BURNET, GILBERT, *History of My Own Time,* abr. edn. Dent, 1906. *Everyman's Library.*

DEFOE, DANIEL. *Tour Through the Whole Island of Great Britain,* ed. G. D. H. Cole. Enlarged edn. 2 vols. Dent, 1962. *Everyman's Library.*

JEFFERSON, D. W., ed, *Eighteenth Century Prose, 1700–1780.* Penguin, 1956. *Pelican Book of English Prose,* vol. 3.

AITKEN, JAMES, ed., *English Letters of the Eighteenth Century.* Pelican Books, 1946.

YORKE, P. C. (Earl of Hardwicke), *Life and Correspondence,* ed. P. Yorke. 3 vols. C.U.P., 1913.

HERVEY, JOHN (Lord Hervey), *Lord Hervey's Memoirs,* ed. R. R. Sedgwick. Kimber, 1952.

DODINGTON, GEORGE BUBB, VISCOUNT MELCOMBE, *The Political Journal of George Bubb Dodington,* ed. J. Carswell and L. A. Dralle. O.U.P., 1965.

BOSWELL, JAMES, *Life of Samuel Johnson*. New edn. 2 vols. Dents 1949. *Everyman's Library*.

PITT, WILLIAM (Earl of Chatham), *Correspondence*, ed.W. J. Taylor and J. H. Pringle. 4 vols. Murray,1838–40.

— *Correspondence of William Pitt with Colonial Governors*, ed. G. S. Kimball. 2 vols. Macmillan, 1906.

WOODFORDE, JAMES, *The Diary of a Country Parson, 1758–1802*, ed. J. Beresford. 5 vols. O.U.P., 1924–1931.

GEORGE III, *Letters from George III to Lord Bute, 1756–1766*, ed. R. R. Sedgwick. Macmillan, 1939.

JENKINSON, CHARLES (Earl of Liverpool), *The Jenkinson Papers, 1760–1766*, ed. N. S. Jucker. Macmillan, 1949.

WALPOLE, HORACE, *Selected Letters*. Dent, 1959. *Everyman's Library*.

WESLEY, JOHN, *Journal*, abr. edn. Epworth Press, 1903.

ROBINSON, JOHN, *The Parliamentary Papers of John Robinson*, ed. W. T. Laprade. Camden Third Series, vol. 33, 1922.

BURNEY, FANNY (Madame d'Arblay), *Diary and Letters*, ed. C. Barrett and A. Dobson. 6 vols. Macmillan, 1904.

FOX, CHARLES JAMES, *Speeches during the Revolutionary War period*, ed. I. C. Willis. Dent, 1924. *Everyman's Library*.

CREEVEY, THOMAS, *Creevey Papers and Creevey's Life and Times*, ed. J. Gore. Murray, 1948; abr. edn. Batsford, 1963.

WELLESLEY, ARTHUR (Duke of Wellington), *Wellington at War, 1794–1815: a Selection of his Wartime Letters*, ed. A. Brett-James. Macmillan, 1961.

3 *Newspapers and Periodicals*. It is unusual to find sets of eighteenth-century newspapers in ordinary libraries. The only exceptions are the *Gentlemen's Magazine* (1731 onwards) and the *Annual Register* (1758 onwards). Good accounts of the Press and its importance are, however, given in L. W. HANSON: *Government and the Press, 1695–1763*, O.U.P., 1936, and A. ASPINALL: *Politics and the Press, c. 1780–1850*, Home and Van Thal, 1949. Until the very end of the century editors did not have access to proper reports of debates in Parliament, so that newspapers accounts of these should be treated with caution. The most reliable reports of debates are in W. COBBETT, ed.: *Parliamentary History of England to the year 1803*, London, 1809–1820; continued 1803–12 as *Cobbett's Parliamentary Debates* and from 1812 as *Hansard's Parliamentary Debates*.

Part Two: Secondary Sources

1 *General*

HILL, CHRISTOPHER, *The Century of Revolution, 1603–1714.* Nelson, 1961.

ASHLEY, MAURICE, *England in the Seventeenth Century.* 2nd edn. Penguin, 1960. *Pelican History of England.*

CLARK, G. N., *The Later Stuarts, 1660–1714.* 2nd edn. O.U.P., 1961. *Oxford History of England.*

OGG, DAVID, *England in the Reigns of James II and William III.* O.U.P., 1957.

TREVELYAN, G. M., *England under Queen Anne.* 3 vols. Longmans, 1930–34.

PLUMB, J. H., *England in the Eighteenth Century.* Rev. reprint. Penguin, 1963. *Pelican History of England.*

MARSHALL, DOROTHY, *England in the Eighteenth Century (1714–1784).* Longmans, 1962.

GREEN, V. H. H., *The Hanoverians* [1714–1815]. Arnold, 1948.

WILLIAMS, BASIL, *The Whig Supremacy, 1714–1760.* 2nd. edn. revised. C. H. Stuart. O.U.P., 1962. *Oxford History of England.*

MICHAEL, W., *England under George I,* vols. 1 and 2, trans. MacGregor. Macmillan, 1936, 1939.

WATSON, J. S., *The Reign of George III, 1760–1815.* O.U.P., 1960. *Oxford History of England.*

BRIGGS, ASA, *The Age of Improvement* (1783–1867). Longmans, 1959.

THOMSON, DAVID, *England in the Nineteenth Century.* Penguin, 1950. *Pelican History of England.*

HALÉVY, E., *England in 1815.* (Vol. 1 of *A History of the English People in the Nineteenth Century,* trans. Watkins and Barker.) Paperback edn. Benn, 1961.

Note: Ireland, Scotland and Wales. Most of the works listed above give due weight to Irish, Scottish and Welsh affairs; and certain works on particular aspects of the history of these countries will be found in subsequent sections. The following general histories should, however, be mentioned:

BECKETT, J. C., *A Short History of Ireland.* 2nd edn. Hutchinson, 1958.
—— *The Making of Modern Ireland, 1603–1923.* Faber, 1966

CURTIS, E., *A History of Ireland.* Paperback edn. Methuen, 1961.

PRYDE, G. S., *Scotland from 1603 to the Present Day.* Nelson, 1962. Vol. 2 of *A New History of Scotland.*

WILLIAMS, D. *A History of Modern Wales*. Murray, 1950.

2   *Political*

ASHLEY, M., *The Glorious Revolution of 1688*. Hodder and Stoughton, 1966.

STRAKA, G. M., *The Revolution of 1688—Whig Triumph or Palace Revolution?* Harrap, 1963. *Problems in European Civilization.*

PLUMB, J. H., *The Growth of Political Stability in England, 1675–1725.* Macmillan, 1967.

FEILING, K. G., *History of the Tory Party, 1640–1714.* Re-issue. O.U.P., 1950.

— *The Second Tory Party, 1714–1832.* Macmillan, 1938.

MITCHELL, D., 'Politics without Party: the Marquis of Halifax's dream', *H.T.*, Jan. 1964.

FOXCROFT, H. C., *A Character of the Trimmer* [Halifax]. C.U.P., 1946.

HORWITZ, H., *Revolution Politicks: The Career of Daniel Finch.* C.U.P., 1968.

BROWNING, A., *Thomas Osborne, Earl of Danby and Duke of Leeds, 1632–1712.* 3 vols. Jackson (Glasgow), 1944–51.

KENYON, J. P., *Robert Spencer, Earl of Sunderland, 1641–1702.* Longmans, 1958.

BAXTER, S. B., *William III.* Longmans, 1966.

ROBB, N. A., *William of Orange, a personal portrait: the later years, 1674–1702.* Heinemann, 1966.

SOMERVILLE, D. H., *The King of Hearts: Charles Talbot, the Duke of Shrewsbury.* Allen and Unwin, 1962.

WALCOTT, R., 'British Party Politics, 1688–1714', in *Essays presented to W. C. Abbott.* H.U.P., 1941.

— *English Politics in the Early Eighteenth Century.* O.U.P., 1956.

FOOT, M., *The Pen and the Sword* [Swift and Marlborough]. Macgibbon and Kee, 1957.

HOLMES, G., *British Politics in the Age of Anne.* Macmillan, 1967.

HAMILTON, E., *Backstairs Dragon: the Life of Robert Harley.* Hamish Hamilton, 1969.

CARSWELL, J. P., *The Old Cause. Three biographical studies in Whiggism* [Thomas Wharton, George Bubb Dodington and Charles James Fox]. Cresset Press, 1954.

— *The South Sea Bubble.* Cresset Press, 1960.

PLUMB, J. H., *Sir Robert Walpole.* vols. 1 and 2. Cresset Press, 1956, 1960.

WILLIAMS, BASIL, *Life of Stanhope.* O.U.P., 1932.

WILLIAMS, BASIL, *Carteret and Newcastle.* C.U.P., 1943.

FOORD, A. S., *His Majesty's Opposition, 1714-1830.* O.U.P., 1964.

SUTHERLAND, L. S., 'The City of London in Eighteenth-Century Politics' in R. Pares and A. J. P. Taylor eds.: *Essays presented to Sir Lewis Namier.* Macmillan, 1956.

REALEY, C. B., *Early Opposition to Sir Robert Walpole.* University of Kansas Humanistic Studies, vol. 4, 1931.

HENDERSON, A. J., *London and the National Government, 1721-1742.* Duke University Publications, 1945.

JUDD, G. P., *Members of Parliament, 1734-1832.* Y.U.P., 1955.

OWEN, J. B., *The Rise of the Pelhams.* Methuen, 1957.

— *The Pattern of Politics in Eighteenth-Century England.* Routledge, 1962. *Historical Association Aids for Teachers,* no. 10.

KEMP, BETTY, 'Frederick, Prince of Wales', in A. Natan ed.: *Silver Renaissance: Essays in Eighteenth-Century History.* Macmillan, 1961.

SEDGWICK, R., 'Frederick, Prince of Wales', *H.T.,* June, 1961.

WIGGIN, L. M., *The Faction of Cousins. A Political Account of the Grenvilles, 1733-1763.* Y.U.P., 1958.

SHERRARD, O. A., *Lord Chatham.* 3 vols. Bodley Head, 1952-58.

TUNSTALL, B., *Life of Pitt.* Hodder, 1938.

EYCK, E., *Pitt versus Fox, Father and Son, 1735-1806,* trans. Northcott. Bell, 1950.

NAMIER, L. B., *The Structure of Politics at the Accession of George III.* Rev. edn. Macmillan, 1957.

— *England in the Age of the American Revolution.* 2 vols. Rev. edn. Macmillan, 1961.

— *Personalities and Powers.* Hamish Hamilton, 1955.

— and BROOKE, J. *The History of Parliament: the House of Commons, 1754-1790.* 3 vols. H.M.S.O., 1964.

DONOUGHUE, B., *British Politics and the American Revolution: the path to war, 1773-1775.* Macmillan, 1964.

PARES, R., *George III and the Politicians.* O.U.P., 1953.

— *Limited Monarchy in Great Britain in the Eighteenth Century.* Routledge, 1957. *Historical Association Pamphlets,* no. 35.

BUTTERFIELD, H., *George III and the Historians.* Collins, 1957.

RUDÉ, G., *Wilkes and Liberty.* O.U.P., 1962.

SUTHERLAND, L. S., 'Edmund Burke and the first Rockingahm Ministry', *E.H.R.* 37, 1932.

BROOKE, J., *The Chatham Administration, 1766-1768.* Macmillan, 1956.

BROOKE, J., 'Party in the Eighteenth Century', in A. Natan: *Silver Renaissance: Essays in Eighteenth-Century History*. Macmillan, 1961.

BUTTERFIELD, H., *George III, Lord North and the People, 1779–1780*. Bell, 1949.

CHRISTIE, I. R., *The End of North's Ministry, 1780–1782*. Macmillan, 1958.

— *Wilkes, Wyvill and Reform*. Macmillan, 1962.

MAGNUS, P., *Edmund Burke*. Murray, 1939.

NORRIS, J., *Shelburne and Reform*. Macmillan, 1963.

GEORGE, M. D., 'Fox's Martyrs, 1784', *T.R.H.S.* 4th series, 21, 1993.

DERRY, J. W., *The Regency Crisis and the Whigs, 1788–89*. C.U.P., 1963.

— *William Pitt*. Batsford, 1962.

REID, L., *Charles James Fox*. Longmans, 1969.

O'GORMAN, F., *The Whig Party and the French Revolution*. Macmillan, 1967.

BARNES, D. G., *George III and William Pitt, 1783–1806*. Stanford University Press, 1939.

ROBERTS, M., *The Whig Party, 1807–1812*. Macmillan, 1939.

3 Constitutional, administrative and financial

ASPINALL, A., 'The Cabinet Council, 1783–1835', *Proceedings of the British Academy*, 38, 1952.

BEATTIE, J. M., *The English Court in the Reign of George I*. C.U.P., 1967.

BINNEY, J. E. D., *British Public Finance and Administration, 1774–1792*. O.U.P., 1958.

COHEN, E. W., *The Growth of the British Civil Serivice, 1780–1939*. Allen and Unwin, 1941.

CONE, C. B., 'Richard Price and Pitt's Sinking Fund of 1786', *Ec.H.R.* 2nd series, 4, 1951.

CLAPHAM, J. H., *The Bank of England. A History*. 2 vols. C.U.P., 1944.

DICKSON, P. G. M., *The Financial Revolution in England*. Macmillan, 1967.

FEAVERYEAR, A. E., *The Pound Sterling*. 2nd edn. O.U.P., 1963.

FOORD, A. S., 'The Waning of the Influence of the Crown', *E.H.R.*, 62, 1947.

JOHNSTON, E. M., *Great Britain and Ireland 1760–1800; a study in political administration*. Oliver and Boyd (Edinburgh), 1963.

KEIR, D. L., *The Constitutional History of Modern Britain*. 6th edn. Black, 1961.

KEMP, BETTY, *King and Commons, 1660–1832*. Macmillan, 1959.

PLUMB, J. H., 'The Organisation of the Cabinet in the reign of Queen Anne, *T.R.H.S.* 5th series, 7, 1957.

PORRITT, E. and A. G., *The Unreformed House of Commons*. 2 vols. C.U.P., 1903.

PRESSNELL, L. S., *Country Banking in the Industrial Revolution*. O.U.P., 1956.

— 'Public Monies and the Development of English Banking', *Ec.H.R.* 2nd series, 5, 1953.

PRINGLE, P., *Hue and Cry*. Museum Press, 1955

— *The Thief Takers*. Museum Press, 1958.

TATE, W. E., *The Parish Chest: a Study of the Records of Parochial Administration in England*. 3rd imp., with additions and corrections. C.U.P., 1960.

THOMSON, M. A., *The Secretaries of State*. O.U.P., 1932.

TURNER, E. R. and MEGARO, G., 'The King's Closet in the Eighteenth Century', *American Historical Review* 45, 1940.

WARD, W. R., *The English Land Tax in the Eighteenth Century*. O.U.P., 1953.

WEBB, S. and B., *English Local Government*. New edn. 11 vols. Frank Cass, 1963.

WILLIAMS, E. T., 'The Cabinet in the Eighteenth Century', *H.* 22, 1937–38.

WILLIAMS, N., *Contraband Cargoes: Seven Centuries of Smuggling*. Longmans, 1959.

4 *Social and economic*

ASHTON, T. S., *The Industrial Revolution, 1760–1830*. O.U.P., 1948.

— 'The Standard of Life of the Workers in England, 1790–1830', *J.E.H.* 9 (supp.), 1949.

— *Iron and Steel in the Industrial Revolution*. M.U.P., 1951.

— *Economic Fluctuations, 1700–1800*. O.U.P., 1959.

— *An Economic History of England: the Eighteenth Century*. Corrected reprint, Methuen, 1961.

BAYNE-POWELL, R., *Travellers in Eighteenth-Century England*. Murray, 1951.

— *Housekeeping in the Eighteenth Century*. Murray, 1956.

BOVILL, E. W., *English Country Life, 1780–1830*. O.U.P., 1962.

BOWDEN, W., *Industrial Society in England towards the end of the eighteenth century*. Cass (reprint), 1965.

CAMPBELL, R. H., *Scotland since 1707: the rise of an industrial society*. Blackwell, 1965.

CLARK, G. N., *The Wealth of England from 1496 to 1760*. O.U.P., 1946.
— *The Idea of the Industrial Revolution*. Jackson (Glasgow), 1953.

COLE, G. D. H. and POSTGATE, R., *The Common People, 1746–1946*. 2nd edn. Methuen, 1956.

*DAVIES, K. G., 'Joint Stock Investment in the late Seventeenth Century', *Ec.H.R.* 2nd series, 4, 1952.

*DAVIS, R., 'English Foreign Trade, 1660–1700', *Ec.H.R.* 2nd series, 7, 1954.

DEANE, PHYLLIS, 'The Output of the British Woollen Industry in the Eighteenth Century', *J.E.H.* 17, 1957.
— *The First Industrial Revolution*. C.U.P., 1965.

DOWNES, R. L., 'The Stour Partnership, 1726–1736', *Ec.H.R.* 2nd series, 3, 1950.

FLINN, M. W., 'The Industrialists', in A. Natan ed.: *Silver Renaissance: Essays in Eighteenth-Century History*. Macmillan, 1961.
— *An Economic and Social History of Britain since 1700*. Macmillan, 1963.

GAYER, A. D., ROSTOW, W. W. and SCHWARZ, A. J., *The Growth and Fluctuation of the British Economy, 1790–1850*. 2 vols. O.U.P., 1953.

GEORGE, M. D., *London Life in the Eighteenth Century*. 3rd edn. London School of Economics reprints, 1951.
— *England in Transition*. Penguin, 1953.

GILLBOY, E. W., *Wages in Eighteenth-Century England*. H.U.P., 1934.

GRAHAM, HENRY GREY, *Social Life of Scotland in the Eighteenth Century*. Black, 1950.

HABAKKUK, H. J., 'English Landownership, 1680–1740', *Ec.H.R.* 1st series, 10, 1940.

HAMILTON, H., *Economic History of Scotland in the eighteenth century*. O.U.P., 1963.

HARRIS, J. R., 'The employment of steam power in the eighteenth century', *H*, lii, no. 175, 1967.

HECHT, J. J., *The Domestic Servant Class in Eighteenth-Century England*. Routledge, 1956.

HOBSBAWM, E. J., 'The British Standard of Living, 1790–1850', *Ec.H.R.* 2nd series, 10, 1957.

JOHNSON, B. L. C., 'The Foley Partnership: the Iron Industry at the end of the Charcoal era', *Ec.H.R.* 2nd series, 4, 1952.

KERRIDGE, E., 'Turnip Husbandry in High Suffolk', *Ec.H.R.* 2nd series, 8, 1956.

KING, GREGORY, *Two Tracts*, ed. G. E. Barnett. Johns Hopkins Press, 1936.

LASLETT, P., *The World We Have Lost*. Methuen, 1965.

*MCKENDRICK, N., 'Josiah Wedgwood', *Ec.H.R.* 2nd series, 12, 1960.

MARSHALL, DOROTHY, *English Poor in the Eighteenth Century.* Routledge, 1926.

— *English People in the Eighteenth Century.* Longmans, 1956.

*MARSHALL, T. H., 'The Population Problem during the Industrial Revolution', *E.H.* 1, 1929.

MATHIAS, PETER, *The Brewing Industry in England, 1700–1830.* C.U.P., 1959.

— *The First Industrial Nation.* Methuen, 1969.

MAXWELL, C., *Country and Town Life in Ireland under the Georges.* Harrap, 1940; rev. edn. Dundalk, Tempest, 1946.

*MINGAY, G. E., 'The Agricultural Depression, 1730–1750', *Ec.H.R.* 2nd series, 8, 1956.

— *English Landed Society in the Eighteenth Century.* Routledge, 1963.

MOFFIT, L. W., *England on the Eve of the Industrial Revolution.* Frank Cass, 1963.

MUSSON, A. E. and ROBINSON, E., 'Science and Industry in the late Eighteenth Century', *Ec.H.R.* 2nd series, 13, 1960.

NEF, J. U., 'The Industrial Revolution reconsidered', *J.E.H.* 3, 1943.

*PARKER, R. A. C., 'Coke of Norfolk and the Agararian Revolution', *Ec.H.R.* 2nd series, 8, 1955.

PLUMB, J. H., 'Sir Robert Walpole and Norfolk Husbandry' *Ec.H.R.* 2nd series, 5, 1952.

POLLARD, S., *The Genesis of Modern Management.* Arnold, 1965.

PRESSNELL, L. S., ed. *Studies in the Industrial Revolution presented to T. S. Ashton.* University of London Press, 1960.

TATE, W. E., 'The Cost of Parliamentary Enclosures in England', *Ec.H.R.* 2nd series, 5, 1952.

*TAYLOR, A. J., 'Progress and Poverty in Britain, 1780–1850', *H.* 45, 1960.

TAYLOR, P. A. M., *The Industrial Revolution in Britain: Triumph or Disaster?* Harrap, 1958. *Problems in European Civilisation.*

THOMSON, GLADYS SCOTT, *The Russells in Bloomsbury, 1669–1771.* Cape, 1940.

THOMPSON, E. P., *The Making of the English Working Class.* Gollancz, 1963.

TURBERVILLE, A. S., ed., *Johnson's England.* 2 vols. O.U.P., 1933.

USHER, A. P., *History of Mechanical Inventions.* Rev. ed. H.U.P., 1954.

WILSON, C. H., 'Treasure and Trade Balances', *Ec.H.R.* 2nd series, 2, 1950.

WILSON, C. H., *Anglo-Dutch Commerce and Finance in the Eighteenth Century*. C.U.P., 1941.

WILLIAMS, E. N., *Life in Georgian England*. Batsford, 1962.

* These articles are reprinted in E. M. CARUS-WILSON, ed.: *Essays in Economic History*. 3 vols. Arnold, 1954–62.

5 *Colonial*

ARMYTAGE, FRANCES, *The Free Port System in the British West Indies, 1766–1832*. Longmans, 1953.

CHRISTIE, I. R., *Crisis of Empire: Great Britain and the American Colonies, 1754–1783*. Arnold, 1966.

DICKERSON, O. M., *The Navigation Acts and the American Revolution*, Pennsylvania University Press, 1951.

FEILING, K. G., *Warren Hastings*. Macmillan, 1954.

FURBER, H., *John Company at Work*. H.U.P., 1948.

GIPSON, L. H., *The British Empire before the American Revolution*. 2nd edn. Knopf, 1958–.

HARLOW, V., *The Founding of the Second British Empire, 1763–1793*. Longmans, vol. 1, 1952, vol. 2, 1964.

HOSKINS, H. L., *British Routes to India*. Longmans, 1928.

KNORR, K. E., *British Colonial Theories, 1750–1850*. University of Toronto Press, 1944.

MACLACHAN, J. O., *Trade and Peace with Old Spain, 1667–1750*. C.U.P., 1940.

MARSHALL, P. J., *The Impeachment of Warren Hastings*. O.U.P., 1965.

— *Problems of Empire: Britain and India 1757–1813*. Allen and Unwin, 1969.

MILLER, J. C., *The Origins of the American Revolution*. Rev. edn. Stanford University Press, 1959.

PARES, R., *War and Trade in the West Indies, 1739–1763*. O.U.P., 1936.

PHILIPS, C. H., *The East India Company, 1784–1834*. M.U.P., 1940.

RAMSAY, G. D., *English Overseas Trade during the Centuries of Emergence*. Macmillan, 1957.

STEELE, I. K., *Politics of Colonial Policy 1696–1720*. O.U.P., 1968.

SUTHERLAND, L. S., *The East India Company in Eighteenth Century Politics*. O.U.P., 1952.

6 *Foreign Policy and War*

BAUGH, D. A., *British Naval Administration in the Age of Walpole*. O.U.P., 1966.

CLARK, G. N., *The Dutch Alliance and the War against French Trade.* M.U.P., 1923.

CHURCHILL, W. S., *Marlborough: his Life and Times.* 4 vols. Harrap, 1933–38.

COBBAN, A., *Ambassadors and Secret Agents.* Cape, 1954.

DAVIES, G., *Wellington and his Army.* O.U.P., 1954.

EHRMAN, J. P. W., *The Navy in the War of William III, 1688–1697.* C.U.P., 1953.

— *The British Government and Commercial Negotiations with Europe, 1783–1793.* C.U.P., 1962.

HATTON, R., and BROMLEY, J. S., eds., *William III and Louis XIV: Essays, 1680–1720.* Liverpool University Press, 1968.

HORN, D. B., *The British Diplomatic Service, 1689–1789.* O.U.P., 1961,

— *Great Britain and Europe in the eighteenth century.*

JOLL, JAMES, *Britain and Europe: Pitt to Churchill, 1793–1940.* 2nd edn., Black, 1961.

JONES, J. R., *Britain and Europe in the Seventeenth Century.* Arnold, 1966.

LEWIS, MICHAEL, *The Navy of Britain.* Allen and Unwin, 1948.

LLOYD, CHRISTOPHER, *The Capture of Quebec.* Batsford, 1959.

MCGUFFIE, T. H., *The Siege of Gibraltar.* Batsford, 1965.

MACKESY, P., *The War in the Mediterranean, 1803–1810.* Longmans. 1957.

— *The War for America 1775–1783.* Longmans, 1964.

MARCUS, G. J., *Quiberon Bay.* Hollis and Carter, 1960.

— *A Naval History of England: vol. I, The Formative Centuries.* Longmans, 1961.

MITCHELL, H., *The Underground War against Revolutionary France: the missions of William Wickham, 1794–1800.* O.U.P., 1965.

OMAN, CAROLA, *Nelson.* Hodder, 1947.

PARES, R., 'American versus Continental Warfare', *E.H.R.* 51, 1936.

PETRIE, C., *The Jacobite Movement.* 3rd edn. Eyre and Spottiswoode, 1959.

POPE, DUDLEY, *At 12 Mr. Byng was shot . . .* Weidenfeld and Nicolson, 1962.

PREBBLE, JOHN, *Culloden.* Secker and Warburg, 1961.

SCOULLER, R. E., *The Armies of Queen Anne.* O.U.P., 1965.

RODGER, A. B., *The War of the Second Coalition, 1798 to 1801: a strategic commentary.* O.U.P., 1964.

TAYLOR, A. J. P., *The Troublemakers. Dissent over Foreign Policy.* Hamish Hamilton, 1957.

TOMASSON, KATHERINE and BUIST, FRANCIS, *Battles of the '45.* Batsford, 1962.

WARD, A. W. and GOOCH, G. P., eds., *The Cambridge History of British Foreign Policy, vol. 1, 1783–1815.* C.U.P., 1922.

WARNER, OLIVER, *Trafalgar.* Batsford, 1959.

— *The Battle of the Nile.* Batsford, 1960.

— *The Glorious First of June.* Batford, 1961.

WEBSTER, C.K., *The Foreign Policy of Castlereagh, 1812–1815.* Bell, 1931.

WILLIAMSON, J. A., *The Ocean in English History.* O.U.P., 1941.

7 *Religion and the history of ideas*

ARMYTAGE, W. H. G., *Heavens Below: Utopian Experiments in England, 1560–1960.* Routledge, 1961.

BAHLMAN, D. W. R., *The Moral Revolution of 1688.* Y.U.P., 1957.

BECKER, C., *The Heavenly City of the Eighteenth-Century Philosophers.* Reissue, Y.U.P., 1959.

BELOFF, M., *The Debate on the American Revolution.* 2nd edn., Black, 1960.

BRAILSFORD, H. N., *Shelley, Godwin and their Circle.* 2nd edn. O.U.P., 1951.

BROWN, P. A., *The French Revolution in English History.* 3rd imp., Cass, 1965.

BUTTERFIELD, H., *The Origins of Modern Science, 1300–1800.* Bell, 1949.

CARPENTER, S. C., *Eighteenth-Century Church and People.* Murray, 1959.

CLIFFORD, DEREK, *A History of Garden Design.* Faber, 1962.

COBBAN, A., *The Debate on the French Revolution.* 2nd edn., Black, 1960.

— *Edmund Burke and the Revolt against the Eighteenth Century.* 2nd edn. Allen and Unwin, 1960.

COUPLAND, R., *Wilberforce: a Narrative.* O.U.P., 1923.

DOBRÉE, BONAMY, *English Literature in the Early Eighteenth Century, 1700–1740.* O.U.P., 1959. *Oxford History of English Literature.*

HALÉVY, E., *The Growth of Philosophic Radicalism*, trans. Morris. 2nd edn. Faber, 1934.

HARTNOLL, PHYLLIS, 'The Theatre and the Licensing Act of 1737', in A. Natan ed.: *Silver Renaissance: Essays in Eighteenth-Century History.* Macmillan, 1961.

HAZARD, PAUL, *The European Mind, 1680–1715*, trans. Lewis May. Hollis and Carter, 1953.

— *European Thought in the Eighteenth Century*, trans. Lewis May. Hollis and Carter, 1954.

HOLT, R. V., *The Unitarian Contribution to Social Progress in England.* 2nd edn. Lindsey Press, 1952.

HOWSE, E. M., *Saints in Politics* [The Clapham Sect]. University of Toronto Press, 1952.

JONES, M. G., *The Charity School Movement*. C.U.P., 1938.

KENDRICK, T. D., *The Lisbon Earthquake*. Methuen, 1956.

KNOX, RONALD, *Enthusiasm*. O.U.P., 1950.

LINCOLN, A., *Some Political and Social Ideas of English Dissent*. C.U.P., 1938.

MACCOBY, S., *The English Radical Tradition, 1763–1914*. Nicholas Kaye, 1952.

— *English Radicalism, 1762–1785*. Allen and Unwin, 1955.

— *English Radicalism, 1786–1832*. Allen and Unwin, 1955.

MACK, MARY P., *Jeremy Bentham: an Odyssey of Ideas, 1748–1792*. Heinemann, 1962.

MCLACHLAN, H., *English Education under the Test Act* [The Dissenting Academies]. M.U.P., 1931.

NICOLSON, HAROLD, *The Age of Reason*. Constable, 1960.

PURVER, M., *The Royal Society*. Routledge, 1967.

RENWICK, W. L., *English Literature, 1793–1815*. O.U.P., 1963. *Oxford History of English Literature*.

RONAN, C. A., 'Science in Eighteenth Century Britain', in A. Natan ed.: *Silver Renaissance: Essays in Eighteenth-Century History*. Macmillan, 1961.

SCHOFIELD, R. E., *The Lunar Society of Birmingham*. O.U.P., 1963.

SUMMERSON, JOHN, *Architecture in Britain, 1530–1830*. Penguin, 1953. *Pelican History of Art*.

SYKES, N., *Church and State in England in the Eighteenth Century*. University of London Press, 1934.

VEITCH, G. S., *The Genesis of Parliamentary Reform*. Re-issue, Constable, 1965.

WARNER, OLIVER, *William Wilberforce*. Batsford, 1962.

WATERHOUSE, ELLIS, *Painting in Britain, 1530–1790*. Penguin, 1953. *Pelican History of Art*.

WATSON, J. S., 'Dissent and Toleration', in A. Natan ed.: *Silver Renaissance: Essays in Eighteenth-Century History*. Macmillan, 1961.

WEARMOUTH, R. F., *Methodism and the Common People of the Eighteenth Century*. Epworth, 1945.

WHINNEY, MARGARET, *Sculpture in Britain, 1530–1830*. Penguin, 1964. *Pelican History of Art*.

WILLEY, BASIL, *Eighteenth-Century Background*. Chatto and Windus, 1940.

Index

Abercromby, General, in Canada, 264

Acts of Parliament, the Declaration of Rights and, 10–11; created by royal assent, 26; Private and Public, 43; Act of Grace, 23, 97; Act of Security (Scottish), 136; Act of Settlement, 17–18, 45, 49, 113, 134, 138, 146, 152, 155; Act of Union, 138; Aliens Act, repeal of, 137–8; Canada Act, 407n.; Catholic Relief Act, 425; Civil List Act concerning, 375–6; Combination Act, 423; Conciliatory Acts, 312; Declaratory Act, 286, 303; forbidding export of Irish wool, 81; Gin Act, 197, 237, Habeas Corpus (suspended), 421 and n.[2]; Health and Morals Act, 452; Improvement Acts, 343; India Act, 394; Licensing Act, 198; Marriage Act, 237–8, 239; Mutiny Act, 15, 104; Pensions Act (Irish), 426; Place Acts, 376; Prohibitory Act, 312; Quebec Act, 305; Regency Acts, 134, 151, 236, 440; Regulating Act, 320; Revenue Act, 287; Schism Act, 70, 146, 162; Septennial Act, 41, 154, 163, 182; Stamp Act, 280, 285–6, 302; Staple Act, 299; Test Act, 10, 416, 417; Toleration Act, 13; Tonnage Act, 101; Triennial Act, 14; Vagrant Act, 198

Adams, Samuel (1722–1803), 304

Addington, Dr Anthony (1713–90), 431

Addington, Henry, Viscount Sidmouth (1757–1844), knowledge of the country gentlemen, 429–30; his administration, 430–1, 433–8; declares war on France, 431,

442–3; his resignation, 432, 435; and Grenville's ministry, 437

Addison, Joseph (1672–1719), 35; Secretary of State, 161

Advertisements, tax on, 36

Admiralty, its First Lord, 28 and n.[1],

Africa, West, and slave trading, 300, 383

Agriculture, methods used in, 58–9; not distinguished from industry, 62–3; in Scotland, 74, 75; in Ireland, 78–9; the harvest of 1708 and, 142; and the use of capital, 328; the 'new husbandry' and, 335–6. *See also* Farming and farmers

Aislabie, John (1670–1742), and the South Sea Company, 169, 170

Albermarle, Arnold van Keppel, Earl of (1669–1718), 110

Albermarle, William Anne Keppel, Earl of (1702–54), 230

Almanza, battle of (1707), 122

America, Scottish ventures in, 75–6; English settlements in, 80; the New England colonies, 80–1, 299–300; taxation of its sugar, 196; the French war in, 244; Pitt's colonial policy and, 261–4; France's surrenders in, 275; Grenville's policy and trade with, 285–6, 302; discontent in, 290–1; becomes an expanding area, 302; taxation and, 302; denies Britain's right to levy taxes, 303; sets up Committees of Correspondence, 304; and Boston Tea Party, 304–5; and separation from Britain, 308; Congress passes the Declaration of Independence, 309, 310; repudiates royal authority, 310; signs a treaty

Brandywine, battle of (1777), 311

Braxfield, Robert Macqueen, Lord (1722–99), 421n.[1]

Bridgwater, Francis Egerton, Duke of (1736–1803), 331–2

Brihuega, battle of (1710), 125

Bristol, as a trading port, 65, 285; and slave trade, 300

British Empire, a national investment, 298; based on a framework of legislation, 298–9; exports to, 299; and parliamentary representation, 300–1; contemporary attitude to, 301

Briton, The, 282

Bunker Hill, battle of (1775), 308

Brodrick, Thomas, and the South Sea Company, 168

Bromley, William (1664–1732), 146

Brown, Lancelot ('Capability') (1715–83), 349

Burdett, Sir Frances (1770–1844), 453

Burgoyne, John (1723–92), and the American War of Independence, 311

Burke, Edmund (1729–97), 47, 300; and George III's 'double Cabinet', 272; on Grenville, 279; and 'Old' and 'New' Whigs, 281; secretary to Rockingham, 285; and the sugar islands, 298; and the American Revolution, 305, 320, 321; and the French Revolution, 316; his opposition to Court domination, 316; and a programme of economical reform, 322, 324, 374; challenges Bolingbroke's ideas, 367; and rationalism, 368, 372; reverence for the past, 368, 379; his belief in the Whigs, 374, 378–9, 389; Rockingham's party and, 374–5; his grasping of sinecures, 375; as Paymaster, 375–6, 388, 397–8; his resignation, 378; and the East India Company, 388–9, 390 and n.; relations with Fox, 390n., 419, 420; attacks Pitt's India Bill, 394, 396; and Hastings, 396–7;

and the King's insanity, 401; attitude to French Revolution, 417, 419; influence of his *Reflections*, 417–18; his death, 420; *Appeal from the New to the Old Whigs*, 419; *Philosophical Inquiry into . . . Sublime and the Beautiful*, 368–9; *Reflections on the Revolution in France*, 367, 368, 417; *Thoughts on the Cause of the Present Discontents*, 316, 374; *Vindication of Natural Society*, 367

Burney, Dr Charles (1726–1814), 365

Bute, John Stuart, Earl of (1713–92), Pitt and, 242, 249–50, 270; Groom of the Stole to George III as Prince of Wales, 245; and George's first ministry, 268–9, 271; centre of power, 271–2; his policy in Europe, 274–5; and Frederick II, 274–5; his unpopularity, 277; resignation, 277–8; and the new ministry, 279, 287; and *The Briton*, 282; and colonial interests, 300

Butler, Joseph (1692–1752), Bishop of Durham, 72

Byng, John (1704–57), admiral, and Minorca, 244, 247, 253

Cabinet Council, William III and, 19, 23; the courtiers and, 28; the main organ of government, 29–30; postition of the Secretaries of State, 31; the First Lord of the Treasury and, 31–2; the Lord Chancellor and, 45; must lead Parliament, 344

Caesar, Charles, 195

Calcutta, 320, 390; 'Black Hole' of, 260–1

Calendar, reform of, 237

Calvinism, 12; among English Dissenters, 68

Camaret Bay, attempted landing at, 92

Cambrai, Conference of (1724), 159

Camperdown, battle of (1797), 412

INDEX

France—*cont.*
alliance with the Dutch, 405;
Pitt the Younger's foreign policy
and, 405–6, 411; her weakness,
406; forms a National Assembly,
406–7; elects a National Conven-
tion, 407; plans to invade Britain,
411, 412–13; supreme in Europe,
415; her overseas Conquests, 415;
and the invasion of Ireland, 426–7;
Bonaparte's achievements for, 441;
and the Peninsula War, 450. *See
also* French Revolution
Francis I (1708–65), Holy Roman
Emperor, 223, 231, 250
Francis II (1768–1835), Holy Roman
Emperor, 408; and the Peace of
Lunéville, 414–15
Francis, Sir Philip (1740–1818), and
Warren Hastings, 394–6
Frankland, Richard (1630–98), and
Rathmell Academy, 72
Franklin, Benjamin (1706–90), and
the Hutchinson letters, 304; signs
a treaty of alliance with France,
312; and peace negotiations, 377
Frederick, Prince of Wales (1707–
1751), 182; his separate Court,
184, 200; his marriage, 199;
question of his allowance, 199–200;
a source of future advancement,
200–1, 233; his electoral influence,
206; leads a new opposition, 233,
234–5; his death, 235
Frederick Augustus, Duke of York
(1763–1827), 387, 409, 412, 414
Frederick II (1712–86), King of Prussia, 273–4, 276; invades Saxony,
244–5, 254; alliance with Britain,
252; and the Russians, 256; and
British sea-power, 257; and peace
talks, 269; distrust of Britain, 274–5
Free Briton, 198n., 199
Free Trade, and the colonies, 299;
Smith and, 399
French Revolution, 316; and Romantic Movement, 371; its influence on
English thought, 384–5, 416–17;

Shelburne and, 385; European
intervention in, 407; British involvement in, 407ff.; becomes a
war against kings, 407–8; successes
against the Netherlands, 408;
victories on land, 410; controls
the French, Dutch and Spanish
navies, 410; seen as a world threat,
413; the Dissenters and, 416;
British unrest and, 421; Bonaparte
and, 441

Gage, General Thomas (1721–87),
Governor of Massachusetts, 307–8,
309
Gardens, 349
Garrad, Sir Samuel (1650–1724), 142
Gates, Horatio (1728–1806), at Saratoga, 311–12.
Gay John (1685–1732), *Beggar's Opera*
and *Polly*, 198, 283n.
General Warrants, legality of, 283,
284, 286, 287
Gentleman, its changing meaning,
59–60; his occupations, 60
Gentleman's Magazine, 190, 247n.
George I (1660–1727), 33, 38; and
Protestantism, 70; and the War
of Spanish Succession, 146, 151;
appoints his Lord Justices, 151;
favours the Whigs, 151–2, 161;
his ministry, 1714, 152–4; visits
Hanover, 155, 163, 167; and an
alliance with France, 155–9; relations with his son, 160, 164, 166,
176n.²; his divided Court, 160;
his opening speech, 1719, 163;
and the Peerage Bill, 163–4;
Governor of the South Sea Company, 165, 168, 169; and Walpole,
170–1, 176; reorganizes his ministry, 170–1; and the 1722 elections, 171; Carteret and, 173, 175;
his mistresses, 174; his death, 180
George II (1683–1760), 35; as Prince
of Wales, 155, 166, 176n.²; Regent
for his father, 155, 158; his separate Court, 160; his accession,

484

Industry, not distinguished from
agriculture, 62; the landed gentry
and, 62; farmers and, 62–3;
communications and, 64–5; the
manufacturing centres, 66; importance of the cloth trade, 67–8;
in Scotland, 75; in Ireland, 78;
given an impetus by joint stock
principles, 103; the Board of
Trade and, 103–4; its expansion
under Walpole, 173; disturbances
in 190; Britain's increasing dependence on, 326; effect of capitalism
on, 329–30; and labour-saving
desires, 330–1; demands better
communications, 331–2; dependent on foreign markets, 333–4;
problems created by for parish
authorities, 337–40; its effect on
population, 339ff.; Pitt and, 398; the
Combination Act and, 423; effect
of Napoleonic wars on, 447–8
Informers, 189–90, 197
Insurance, Marine, 65
Ireland, her seventeenth-century
crises, 3; England's fear of her
Catholicism, 76; her internal condition, 76–7; William III and, 77,
86, 110; her continued grievances,
77–9; disbarring of Catholics in,
77–8; decline of agriculture in,
79; Wood's coinage, 174–5; dismissal of her office-holders, 175;
fear of a French invasion of, 323;
the Volunteer movement, 323, 376,
425; increase in population, 340;
obtains legislative independence,
376, 423; prosperity during Pitt's
early administration, 424; and
Pitt's free trade proposals, 424;
relief of Catholics in, 425–6;
uprisings in, 426; union with
Britain, 427–8
Italy, collapse of France's position in,
123; Spanish offensive in, 159,
188–9; Napoleon and, 410–11, 414

Jacobites and Jacobitism, 102; danger

of a restoration, 112; invasion of
Scotland, 124, 141; the City and,
142; and Bolingbroke, 146–7,
153; Ormonde's intrigues with,
153 and n.; the 1715 rising, 153–4;
the 1719 invasion from Spain,
159, 163; conspiracy of·1722, 171–
2; the 1745 landing, 220, 225, 228–
30
James I (1566–1625), and a Scottish-
English union, 72
James II (1633–1701), as Duke of
York, 4; his reign, 5–6; flies to
France, 6–7, 85, 88; stigmatized
as a revolutionary, 16; and justices,
47; supported by the Irish, 77;
his death, 112
James, Princes of Wales (1688–
1766), the 'Old Pretender', his
birth, 5, 8; disqualified as an
impostor, 8; recognized by France,
112; and the succession to the
throne, 146; intrigues with Ormonde, etc., 153 and n.; the Earl
of Mar and, 153–4
Jenkins, Captain Robert(fl. 1731–38),
his mutilation, 204 and n.[2]
Jenkinson, Charles, Earl of Liverpool
(1728–1808), 291 and n.[2], 322,
390, 430
Jervis, John, Earl of St Vincent
(1735–1823), 409, 411
Johnson, Samuel (1709–84), 36, 257,
297, 356, 360
Jones, Griffith (1683–1761), 352
Joseph of Wittelsbach, Bishop of
Liége, 118
Judges, dispense the King's justice,
26; the Monarchy and, 45; receive
a salary instead of fees, 45; and
the Privy Council, 45; their independence secured, 46; and the
magistracy, 47
Juries, Bentham and, 365; Fox and,
420
Justice, its dispensation, 26; its
principal officers, 27; and Westminster Palace, 34; and the

Lennox, Lady Caroline, Fox's marriage to, 238

Leopold I (1640–1705), Emperor, 107; and the Partition Treaty, 109; and the second Grand Alliance, 116; and the War of the Spanish Succession, 116, 118, 120

Lestock, Richard (?1679–1746), admiral, 227

Leveson-Gower, Granville, Marquis of Stafford (1721–1803), 279

Lewis, Erasmus (1670–1754), 166

Lexington, 305, 307

Licensing Bill, 198

Lisbon, Earthquake in, 350–1, 352, 356

Literature, London and, 35–6; anti-rationalism and, 368–9; the fashion for the exotic, 369–10; romanticism and, 370–1

Liverpool, as a trading port, 65, 285; the Dissenters and, 71; and slave trade, 300; its canals, 332

Liverpool, Robert Jenkinson, Earl of (1770–1828), his ministry, 440–1

Lloyd, Edward (fl. 1688–1726), founder of 'Lloyd's', 65

Local government, the Quarter Sessions and, 49; the justices and, 49–50; and Dissenters, 70–1; its need for a more professional approach, 342; widening of its scope, 343

Locke, John (1632–1704), 103, 360–1; Two Treatises of Government, 16–17; Essay concerning Human Understanding, 361

London, preservation of order in, 33; its Common Council, 33, 236; government dependence on its bankers, etc., 33–4; its great town houses, 34–5; and the arts, 35–6; its surrounding traders, 36; a lure to the countryman, 36–7; its population, 37n.; its death-rate, 37; as seen by the country gentleman, 37–8, 55n.; its coal supply, 65; a world-renowned trading centre, 65; its shipping facilities, 65

London Corresponding Society, 421

London Exchange Corporation, 34

London Journal, 198n.

Londonderry, siege of (1689), 77

Lord Chamberlain, and the theatre, 173–4, 198

Lord Chancellor, the King's deputy, 26; head of the judiciary, 27, 45; not a party office, 94

Lord High Treasurer, 31, 94; and the revenue, 27; equated with 'prime minister', 152

Lord President of the Council, 27

Lord Privy Seal, 27–8

Lord-lieutenants, 44; and the magistracy, 47; their lessening importance, 50

Loughborough, Alexander Wedderburn, Baron (1733–1805), 428

Louis XIV (1638–1715), 5, 6; William III's struggle with, 82; his Spanish marriage, 84; attacks the Elector Palatine, 84–5; and the Grand Alliance, 85; unable to invade England after Beachy Head, 87–8; his Mediterranean successes, 93; signs the Peace of Ryswick, 93, 107; and the Spanish Succession, 107ff.; and the Partition Treaties, 108, 109–11; and Carlos II's will, 110–11; provocation of the War of Spanish Succession, 112; and Blenheim, 120; makes peace overtures, 121; his Jacobite invasion of Scotland, 124; and the Allied peace Terms, 124, 125; and the Peace of Utrecht, 126; his death, 157

Louis XV (1710–74), 157

Louis XVI (1754–93), 419; summons the Estates General, 406

Louis the Dauphin (d. 1711), 84; his possible succession to the Spanish Empire, 107, 108

Lowlanders, animosity towards Highlanders, 73–5, 135

Lowther, Sir John, Viscount Lonsdale (1655–1700), supports Danby's party system, 95, 96

399–400; and the abolition of slavery, 400; and the regency, 401; his dependence on the King, 402, 434; his foreign policy, 405–7, 411; and the war of the French Revolution, 408, 409, 410; tries to negotiate a peace, 410, 411, 412; absorbs the Old Whigs, 419–20; his Treasonable Practices Bill, 422; introduces income tax, 423; and Ireland's economic problems, 424; and union with Ireland, 425, 427–8; and Catholic emancipation, 428; his resignation, 428, 430; pledged not to oppose Addington, 431, 432; re-enters office on Addington's resignation, 432–5; his services to the nation, 433–4; attacks on, 435; illness and death, 435–6

Place Bills, 43, 98–9

Placemen, 18–19; make the most of their position, 38; source of their profit, 38–9; limited vacancies among, 42; in the 1690–95 Parliament, 96, 97

Plantations, a source of wealth, 79–80; the American Settlements, 80

Plassey, battle of (1757), 261

Plumb, J. H., *Sir Robert Walpole*, 141n.[2]

Plymouth, its naval base, 88

Police Force, seen as a tyranny, 51, 189; the Fieldings and, 237

Polish Succession, War of, 201, 204

Pomfret, Earl of, 38

Poor, the, parochial obligations towards, 48–9, 55; their settlement problems, 49; regarded as a liability, 55–6; their expectation of life, 56; their subsistence allowance, 57; the administration of relief to, 57–8, 342; their rights, 58; dependence on money wages, 336

Poor Law, its more professional administration, 342

Pope, Alexander (1688–1744), 162, 362, 366, 367; and Blenheim, 349; *Essay on Man*, 350

Population, King's estimate in 1688, 54; eighteenth-century attitude to, 334; movements in, 334–5, 336, 339; increases in from 1780, 339–41; politicians and, 340; birth- and death-rates, 340–1; Malthus and, 340

Porpora, Niccolo (1686–1766), 35

Porteous, Captain John (d. 1736), 197

Portland, William Bentinck, Earl of (1649–1709), 93, 110

Portland, William Henry Cavendish, Duke of (1738–1809), 378, 385–6, 419; his ministries, 386, 438–9; Home Secretary, 420, 430; Lord President, 434 and n.; his death, 439

Porto Bello, capture of, 221

Portugal, 116n.[1]; the Methuen Treaties and, 121–2; invaded by Napoleon, 448–9

Post Office, 64, 331; and government newspapers, 198n.

Pragmatic Sanction, 223, 232

Pratt, Sir Charles, later Lord Camden (1714–1794), and Wilkes, 283

Preaching, enthusiasm and, 352–3; Methodists and, 353–4

Presbyterians, 12, 68; and church governmnt, 69; join the Dissenting Deputies, 70; and Episcopalians, 72; in Ireland, 78; and Union with England, 135, 138

Preston, Richard Graham, Viscount (1648–95), 46

Prestonpans, battle of (1745), 228

Price, Richard (1723–91), 399; and the French Revolution, 416–17; Burke and, 418; *Essay on the Population of England and Wales*, 340; *Observations on Civil Liberty*, 320, 363, 416

Prices, 142; of bread, 293n., 336, 337, 421–2

Sheriffs, the, their limited powers, 50;
dissenting, 71

Shovell, Sir Cloudesley (1650–1707),
admiral, 86, 123

Shrewsbury, Charles Talbot, Duke
of (1660–1718), Secretary of State,
94, 95; his retirement, 107; Lord
Chamberlain, 143; secures the
succession to George I, 147; and
George's Whig ministry, 151, 152

Sidgwick, William, 339

Sinking Fund, 194 and n., 303; Pitt
the Younger and, 399

Slavery and the Slave trade, English
ports and, 65; Royal Africa Company and, 80; French threat to,
115–16, and n.[1]; In the W. Indies,
299–300; abolition of, 400, 438

Smith, Adam (1723–90), 399 and
n.; *Wealth of Nations*, 364–5, 366,
381

Smith, John (1655–1723), 140

Smith, Sir Sidney (1764–1840), 413

Smith, Sydney (1771–1845), 359

Smollet, Tobias (1721–71), 47; and
The Briton, 282

Smuggling, 51, 57; the Excise and,
191–2, 397–8; the Spanish and,
204; Act to deal with, 398

Society of Friends. *See* Quakers

Somers, John Somers, Baron (1651–
1716), 98, 105, 110, 133, 151;
and the War of the Spanish
Succession, 113; at Anne's accession, 128; his Regency Bill, 134;
and the Act of Union, 139; and
the new Cabinet, 1708, 140, 141,
143

Society for Commemorating the
Revolution in Gt. Britain, 416

Society for Constitutional Information, 317

Society for the Defence of Bill of
Rights, 317, 363

Society for the Suppression of Vice,
359

Somerset, Charles Seymour, Duke of
(1662–1748), 143–4; and the succes-

sion, 147; and George I's Whig
ministry, 151; his self-importance,
164 and n.

Sophia of Hanover, Electress, 113,
146; the Tories and, 133–4

South Sea Company, 34, 80, 204;
launching of, 144–5; and the
National Debt, 165; its financial
proposals, 165–6; its political implications, 166; its temporary
success, 166, 167; crisis caused by
its failure, 167–8; Walpole and,
168–70, 171, 172; Committee's
report on, 169–70; and the Convention of the Pardo, 205; Pelham and, 236

Southey, Robert (1774–1843), 371

Spain, 75; possessions in the Netherlands, 82 and n.; controlled by the
Holy Roman Emperor, 83; Louis
XIV and, 84–5, 93; and the Grand
Alliance, 85; the Partition Treaty
and, 108–10; and the War of
Succession, 118, 121–2; her dislike
of France, 157; challenges the
Peace of Utrecht, 158; joins the
Quadruple Alliance, 159; Britain's
foreign policy and, 179, 185–6;
trading war against, 185; British
trade relations with, 202–4; the
West Indies merchants and, 204;
the Patriot war with, 204–6, 221–
2, 225, 231, 232; loss of her
colonies, 260, 274, 276; Britain
declares war on, 273; the peace
terms and, 275–6; and the American War of Independence, 313,
383; and Vancouver Island, 406–7;
makes peace with France, 410;
and Cape St Vincent, 411; and
the Napoleonic wars, 444, 445–6;
Napoleon and, 448

Spanish-American Trade, 124n., 126,
232; the South Sea Company and,
144, 145, 202

Spanish Succession, struggle for,
107–11; the Treaty of Utrecht and,
125–6

addson, p.161